The Shell Book of the British Coast

The Shell Book of the British Coast

Adrian Robinson & Roy Millward

DAVID & CHARLES
Newton Abbot London North Pomfret (Vt)

Shell U.K. Limited while sponsoring this book would point out that the authors are expressing their own views.

British Library Cataloguing in Publication Data

Robinson, Adrian
The Shell book of the British coast.
1. Coasts – Great Britain
I. Title II. Millward, Roy
551.4′5 GB457.21

ISBN 0-7153-8150-4

Photoset by Typesetters (Birmingham) Limited, and printed in Great Britain by Butler & Tanner Limited, Frome for David & Charles (Publishers) Limited Brunel House Newton Abbot Devon

Published in the United States of America by David & Charles Inc North Pomfret Vermont 05053 USA

Contents

To Joyce

Preface

For so small a country Britain has a coastline of astonishing variety and subtlety. In its length of 9,655km (6,000 miles) there are majestic cliffs which rival in splendour those of the famous Big Sur coastline of California. At the other end of the spectrum, the marshland fringe of north Norfolk or the Essex estuaries provides another type of setting to contribute to the richness of the coastal scene and in its own way is as interesting and curiously inviting as the more dramatic cliff coastlines of Highland Britain which stand poised to resist the vigour of the Atlantic storms.

In many areas, man has left behind a rich endowment of the past either in muted form as in the worn-down grassy ramparts of a once stoutly defended Iron Age promontory fort or more strikingly in the imposing castles with which Edward I ringed Snowdonia. The defence of the coastland is an oft-recurring theme over the centuries and there are many monuments which point to the resolve to resist any would-be invader.

Even an occasional visit to the coast can lead to an awareness that changes are constantly taking place. Beach levels can alter drastically from summer to winter, and for those parts which are susceptible to the continual gnawing away of the sea, like the clay cliffs of Holderness or the Isle of Sheppey, the changes are often quite spectacular as buildings tumble over the edge into the sea. On the other side of the equation, new lands can be won from the sea especially around the margins of major inlets like Morecambe Bay or the Wash which are being steadily infilled and seemingly made ready for man's reclamation. What is often overlooked is that our coastline is a precious endowment from the past which can so easily be mutilated beyond repair. The sandy beach which gives such enjoyment to thousands each summer along the east coast of England or the sand dunes of the Moray Firth coastlands represent an indirect inheritance from the Ice Age and its immediate aftermath. With the sand being moved continually by waves the beach can so easily disappear and though renewal is possible this is not always guaranteed. The events at Hallsands on the south-east coast of Devon at the beginning of the present century provide a salutary warning that man's interference with nature – in this case the removal of the beach shingle for making concrete – can have disastrous and long-lasting consequences. Even where exploitation has not taken place beach levels can fall through natural wastage as part of the general pattern of change. The success of the renewal schemes of the past decade, such as at Portobello near Edinburgh and along the shores of Bournemouth Bay, seems likely to encourage other towns whose prime asset is a fine sandy beach to keep a close check on future trends and if necessary take remedial action in good time.

In an overcrowded island such as Britain, conservation, in its broadest sense, provides the only real insurance for the future. The inter-war years saw many precious areas tainted by an uncontrolled and unsightly development. What was but a trickle of building in the 1920s and 30s could well have become a flood in the post-war era, but fortunately the National Trust and government-sponsored bodies like the Nature Conservancy Council and the Countryside Commission acted to prevent the ruination of much coastland that was still beautiful and unspoiled.

The events over the past decade, leading to the purchase and protection of many new areas of coastland, have meant that the future now looks much more hopeful than at any time this century. Problems still abound in a car-conscious age where land has to be found for parking close to some of our finest coastal walks, or cliff-top paths rested and restored after being overworked and eroded by visitors to well-known beauty spots. But the coastline of these islands, along with the upland wildlands, still provides some of the best oases of solitude and tranquillity. The freedom to walk beaches left in virgin state after a falling tide or to follow the ups and downs of a cliff-top path in the knowledge that there will be no car rounding the next bend, are pleasures that will be eagerly sought in the closing years of this century and well on into the next. These considerations were uppermost in the minds of the authors when they were visiting the coastline preparatory to writing the itinerary which forms the later chapters of the book, providing a record of the present coastal scene either in terms of nature's endowment or man's influence over the past centuries. Although maps form an integral part of the text, a full appreciation of the coastline, especially when visited on foot, can only come about with the aid of the 1:50,000 Ordnance Survey series or even the larger scale 1:25,000 maps in specific areas.

Inevitably, in a wide-ranging work of this nature we are indebted to many other researchers who have carried out detailed studies of particular stretches of coastline and whose writings we have consulted. The views expressed and the conclusions drawn are, however, those of the authors and are, in the main, derived from our own examination and knowledge of the coast over the past thirty years. Apart from a few maps which have appeared elsewhere in articles and were drawn for this purpose by Ruth Rowell and Kate Moore of the Geography Department of the University of Leicester, the majority of the cartographic illustration was undertaken by Gwyneth Robinson. Helen Millward has again taken responsibility for compiling the index while (unless otherwise stated) the photographs throughout the book are from the authors' own collections. For the reader, it is our hope that the scenic beauty, diverse character, cultural heritage and above all the distinctive qualities of the coastline of Britain, of which we were acutely aware in the preparatory fieldwork and subsequent writing of the book, will emerge from the text to give lasting pleasure and fulfilment.

1 Coastal Life and Habitats

Animals and plants living beside the sea show a surprising adaptation to their surroundings which sets them apart from their land counterparts. In adapting to the special conditions which exist on the seashore and coastlands they have developed forms, life-styles and life-cycles which make them fascinating to study. Compared with inland areas the coastline is a dynamic zone – the pounding force of breaking waves on the shore is such that animals have either to bury themselves or else develop great suctional holds to enable them to cling to bare rock faces. Gale force winds can carry sand from the foreshore well inland and bury vegetation; normal plants would die, but many coastal grasses have the ability to grow through the freshly deposited sand and indeed depend on its nutrients for continued vigour. It is, however, in their ability to cope with periodic immersions in salt water that seaside plants are so distinctive. The twice daily rise and fall of the tide around the shores of Britain means that the littoral zone is covered by salt water for varying periods of time and to varying depths. Some coasts, like parts of Norfolk and Suffolk, may only have a tidal range of a few feet but others, notably the shores of the Bristol Channel, can experience a 12m (40ft) tide. The height of the tide also varies from day to day, with the largest ranges experienced once a fortnight on spring tides and with the smaller neap tides in between. Nothing is therefore static and both coastal plants and animals have had to adapt to this ever-changing condition.

A group of salt-tolerant plants, halophytes, has developed which is able to withstand the twice daily immersion in sea water. But even within the group there are some plants which can survive being covered for several hours each tidal cycle while others can only withstand a brief wetting by the sea. Withstanding immersion is possible because these plants have a cell-sap concentration greater than that of salt water. This enables them to take in nutrients and water through their cell walls by a process known as osmosis whereas, in an ordinary land plant a reverse flow would occur and in consequence the plant would die. Some of the halophytes which endure covering by salt water for several hours have developed osmotic pressures equivalent to 100 atmospheres to ensure their survival. Other plants, higher up the beach near the high-water line, have much lower cell-sap concentrations. As different species of plant are involved there is a marked zonation from mid-tide level right up to the high-water line and beyond. Distinctive plant associations thus form bands following each other in orderly progression to make a unique patterning which reflects the close control exerted by the rise and fall of the tide. This type of zonation is best displayed in salt marshes but it can occur in other coastal habitats.

Equally important and noticeable are the rapid changes which can take place along the shore where the coastal setting changes, for example from a sandy bay to a rocky headland. Even on a cliff coastline there are variations which provide differing living conditions for plants and animals. A change of rock type, a variation in the dip of the strata, perhaps faulting leading to the development of fissures and caves, can all give rise to different habitats which will suit some plants and animals but not others. Sea birds, in particular, seek out a particular type of cliff face when it comes to building a nest for breeding. Some manage on the narrowest of ledges while others, like the gannet with its huge volcano-like nest, require a wide platform or a cliff-top site. Relationships like these provide subject matter for endless study and a reason why so many find the coastline of absorbing fascination.

Although many stretches of coastline, especially in the northern parts of Britain, retain their wild and unspoiled form, there are others under considerable pressure from man, through building, industry or simply leisure activities. Popular areas like parts of the Cornish coast at Kynance Cove or Bedruthan Steps, where there can be as many as 150,000 visitors each year, show the effect of this pressure by human erosion. The thin turf cover is quickly worn through and then rain soon turns the area into a muddy morass or cuts it up by gullying. Sand-dune areas with their incomplete vegetation cover are equally vulnerable to the tramping feet of visitors. Only strictly enforced conservation measures can hope to arrest the destruction of some of our most precious coastal sites for future generations to enjoy. Fortunately organisations like the Nature Conservancy, National Trust and the

Royal Society for the Protection of Birds have been in the forefront of conservation of what is increasingly recognised as a very fragile environment.

Pollution, through industrial discharges and crude untreated sewage, presents another problem. While it is true that the sea can act as a natural cleanser to a remarkable degree, there are undoubtedly local pockets of gross pollution. Some of the worst offenders are seaside towns which still use the sea as a cheap and effective method of sewage disposal. It is surprising how many of our major resort towns still pollute the sea on which their prosperity depends, for apart from the health hazard from raw sewage there is the aesthetic offence which it can cause on popular beaches. Some local authorities, wishing to give the right image, have no option but to employ council workers to remove the offensive material. Fortunately the problem is lessening as more coastal towns build full treatment plants like their inland neighbours who have never had access to a cheap means of disposal. Industrial pollution tends to be localised, with the Mersey and Tees the worst offenders. Chemical plants and steelworks discharge effluent noxious to the environment but in many cases it is remarkable how quickly the sea can restore the natural balance. In the Tees and Mersey excessive discharges of industrial wastes mean that sea water is unable to counter the departure from the norm, but even here a complete biotic desert is not created. What often happens is that certain species flourish in waters which have become chemically more acceptable to them and a sea 'bloom' may arise. Other species find the changed environment adverse and consequently disappear. It is this limitation of species rather than complete annihilation which is the most worrying aspect of pollution. Much has been achieved to remedy the situation in recent years and it seems only a matter of time before acceptable standards apply to our estuaries and coastal seas, and ensure that the excesses of the past are not repeated.

Sandy Beaches

Although most favoured by man – as witness the jostling crowds at resorts like Blackpool and Bournemouth – sandy beaches are perhaps the least rewarding and exciting of the coastal habitats in terms of the animal and plant life. The number of species actually living on the tide-covered beach is extremely small, because the soft mobile sand is at the mercy of every wave and easily disturbed. Ordinary flowering

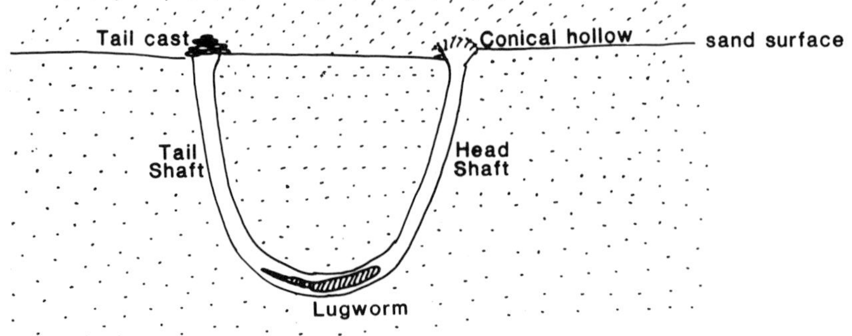

The habitat of the lugworm

plants find the situation impossible, even those with high salt-tolerance levels, and the only animals that can survive do so by burying themselves below the mobile surface layers. Small algae-like diatoms which need light for growth (the process known as photosynthesis) are present, but these will die if buried by the disturbed sand.

Of the burrowing animals the best known example is the lugworm (*Arenicola*). It prefers fine sand or a mixture of sand and mud in which to bury itself, and can range over a large part of the foreshore. Though seldom seen unless dug out from its burrow with a spade, the lugworm announces its presence by the coiled ring of sand it leaves on the surface, and which consists of material left behind after it has digested and extracted any food particles, mainly organic debris. A few inches away will be the slight depression marking the entrance to the lugworm's U-shaped home; it can live in the same burrow for a considerable time as it imports a fresh supply of sand as the tide comes in. Up to 20cm (8in) long, its fat, juicy body makes it an excellent bait for fish. The need to live in a submerged tube out of the way of wave disturbance is also the life-style of the sea potato (*Echinocardium*) which inhabits the exposed lower parts of a sandy beach. Like the lugworm it is seldom seen and has to be dug out from its 15cm (6in) deep chamber. Its presence, however, is often shown by the thin papery tests which litter the strand-line. At this highest level of the beach, along with the flotsam and jetsam brought in by the last tide, lives the sand hopper (*Talitrus*). It tends to stay in its burrow during the day (marked by a hole in the sand) but comes out at night to feed, jumping about in search of its food.

A walk along the strand-line with its collection of debris brought in

OYSTERCATCHER

by the tide can be very revealing, for it draws attention to the presence of animals which are not normally seen. There are often numerous empty shells mixed up with seaweed, decaying vegetation, wood and, increasingly, indigestible plastic. Most common is the cockle (*Cardium*) which, in certain sheltered locations like the Loughor Estuary near Swansea, is the basis of a lucrative industry. The globular bivalve shell with distinct ridges usually lies buried just below the surface and is harvested by scraping away the surface sand with a broad rake. As the density of the cockles can be as high as 3 million a hectare, they form a rich harvest for the gatherers who set out in their carts from places like Penclawdd, the cockle 'capital', on the north coast of the Gower Peninsula. The cockle is quite adept at burying itself quickly in the sand by means of a powerful muscular foot; some species can use this foot as a spring and leap about the beach, often to escape attack by predators. Apart from man's interest, the cockle forms a succulent food for gulls and oystercatchers. Both birds are skilled in getting into the tough shell, the oystercatcher watching for the cockle to open its valves when feeding and then darting its beak into the open gape. The herring gull is not so quick and therefore resorts to bringing the cockle to land and then dropping it onto a hard surface to break the tough, ridged shell.

Another bivalve shell commonly found littering the beach is the very distinctive razor shell (*Ensis*), so named from its likeness to the old fashioned cut-throat razor. In their very distinctive shape they show a remarkable adaption to their habitat, for they are able to move vertically down through the surface sand layers with great speed. It has no need to move laterally, for it feeds in a vertical position by

Common shells found around the British coasts: 1 edible mussel; 2 razor shell; 3 winkle; 4 necklace shell; 5 barnacle; 6 Iceland cyprina; 7 otter shell; 8 Venus shell; 9 rayed trough shell; 10 thin tellin; 11 Baltic tellin; 12 dog whelk; 13 edible whelk; 14 scallop; 15 prickly cockle; 16 carpet shell; 17 limpet; 18 oyster; 19 striated Venus shell

projecting a siphon which catches any food particles as they flow by on the tide. Another suspension feeder is the wedge shell (*Donax*) with its polished multi-coloured valves and slender shape which enables it to slide back under the sand should it be exposed by a passing wave. It, too, has a short siphon which filters out material from the sea water at high tide. Apart from birds, the bivalves' natural enemies are the necklace shell (*Natica*) and the sand-burrowing starfish (*Astropecten*). The latter buries itself just below the surface of the sand with its projecting arms ready to seize any passing mollusc or crustacean, often swallowing it whole.

Amongst the crustaceans on the sandy beach, the best known is the common shrimp (*Crangon*) which feeds near the low-water line and is itself a predator. It prefers to lie hidden in the sand during the day but comes out at night to feed on small worms. Should it be uncovered during the day its camouflaged body gives it some protection against its enemies. It can also bury itself by shuffling its legs to remove sand and form a hollow into which it will gradually sink. It is never buried very deeply, enabling the shrimp netter to make a considerable haul by walking along the surf zone where each passing wave will expose the shrimps.

Beyond the line reached by most high tides, the backshore zone acts as a nursery ground for plant colonisation. Piles of seaweed brought in by the powerful waves of the winter months form an obstacle around which blown sand will accumulate. These sand hummocks with an organic core form ideal sites for plant colonisation especially if they are beyond the line reached by normal high tides. Certain coastal plants like the prickly saltwort (*Salsola*), sea rocket (*Cakile*), sea sandwort (*Honckenya*) and various oraches (*Atriplex*) are able to withstand occasional wetting by salt water but would not survive periodic immersion. Thus they are ideal for establishing themselves on these raised sand hummocks and as they grow they attract more sand around them. Other plants like the sea couch grass (*Agropyron*) are now encouraged to grow, and in time a distinct belt of low fore-dunes can arise in front of the main dune belt. Provided winter storms do not completely override and destroy the new fore-dunes they will gradually form a second distinct dune belt with the ubiquitous marram grass, the best coloniser of loose sand, finally establishing itself. In this way the coastline is able to extend itself seaward, and explains why so many dune areas consist of distinct, broadly parallel features.

The most common sight on our sandy beaches are the sea birds which use the zone near the water's edge for feeding. Few species are restricted solely to this type of coastal setting. Waders are often most noticeable on a rising tide when the waves disturb the sand and uncover cockles and molluscs which form a tasty meal for the oystercatchers. Sanderlings, which breed in the cold arctic wastes and come to our shores in the winter months, run along the water's edge picking up morsels like sandhoppers and small amphipodes which are exposed as the backwash uncovers the surface sand layers. The ringed plover, named from its conspicuous black collar bordered with white, is also to be seen along the water's edge of the sandy beach.

Isolated beaches, away from well-beaten coastal tracks, may form breeding grounds for the grey and common seal, though offshore drying sandbanks like those of the Wash give a much greater sense of security and carry larger herds. Britain is fortunate in that its shores have about half the total world population of the grey seal. With their protected status they have recently increased in numbers, but as they feed on fish there have been angry protests from fishermen which has led to selective culling in certain areas like the Farne Islands off the Northumberland coast.

Sand Dunes

Where a wide sandy foreshore faces the direction of the prevailing wind, it offers a steady supply of material for building a dune belt beyond the high-water line. Some sand-dune belts extend for several miles inland and are believed to have developed over thousands rather than hundreds of years. In their natural state they provide a base for skill-testing golf courses and the seaside links of Scotland are justly famous. Dune areas need careful management for there is always the threat of blown sand, especially if the vegetation cover is ruptured; valuable farmland could then be covered and lost. To prevent this many former sand-dune areas have in the past half-century been planted with conifers, so that Newborough Warren in Anglesey and the Culbin Sands on the Moray Firth in Scotland are now vast forests.

Many natural dune areas exist around our coasts under different names – towans in Cornwall, burrows in south Wales, warrens in north Wales, meols in Lancashire, links in Scotland. In spring and summer a host of plants flourish on their well-drained soils; in winter they are relatively dry and form ideal walking country. There is always something exhilarating in crossing successive dune ridges from an inland road and then suddenly catching that first glimpse of the sea. In summer they are popular with families, their sheltered hollows making ideal picnic spots when the open beach is too windy to enjoy. Over-popularity of certain dune areas like those of Winterton on the Norfolk coast or Braunton Burrows in north Devon can bring its

The sea holly (*Eryngium*), with marram grass, colonising the dunes of Scolt Head Island, Norfolk

problems as they are very susceptible to human erosion. Many dunes which were formerly covered with marram grass are now bare hillocks of sand with great scooped-out hollows or blow-outs created by the wind. On some of the most frequented dune areas, like Holkham on the north Norfolk coast or Gibraltar Point Nature Reserve in Lincolnshire, it has been necessary to build restricted walkways of wooden sleepers through the dune belt to prevent widespread damage by visitors.

Of all the dune plants, marram grass (*Ammophila*) is the most widespread, owing to the fact that it grows with great vigour especially when supplied with fresh sand that gives it necessary nutrients. With an extensive root system and the ability to send up new shoots from buried stems, it is ideal for colonising mobile dune areas. Its deep ramifying root system allows it to find water and in addition its incurled leaves reduce water loss through transpiration to a minimum. When given fresh supplies of sand it maintains a healthy green appearance, but on inland dunes, where it has extracted nearly all the nutrients from the sand, the marram takes on a grey, withered look. Before this stage is reached many dunes have developed a more varied vegetation, all the plants having one common characteristic, namely the ability to withstand long spells without water. They achieve this in various ways; the sea holly (*Eryngium*) for example, has blue-grey waxy leaves which help to conserve water on hot summer days. Seen in clumps when in flower the sea holly makes an attractive plant with its clustered heads of light-blue flowers. Equally attractive is the sea bindweed (*Calystegia*) which has purple flowers on the ends of creeping stems.

It is on the flat links between main dune belts that the richest flora develops, for here the water table is nearer the surface and there is less likelihood of sand disturbance. In spring and early summer the links can be a blaze of yellows, purples, whites and pinks from plants like heartsease, sweetly scented thyme, hawkbit, bird's foot trefoil and others which flourish on well-drained soils. Many of the dune plants are winter annuals germinating in autumn and completing their life cycle in the spring with the shedding of seed. In this way they avoid possible desiccation in the summer months. There are differences in the vegetation found in the various dune belts, with a richer flora occurring in the wetter areas of the west, the Welsh coast for instance having a much richer flora than East Anglia. Perhaps the most exciting sandy areas are the flat lands of the west coast of the Outer Hebrides where the calcareous sand brought in by the westerly gales forms the machair. This fertile shelly sand is able to support a rich vegetation partly of grassland but with a host of flowering plants so that, seen in late June and July, the machair of western Lewis or Uist makes an unforgettable sight as its rich carpet of flowers dominates the grassland. The land is grazed but this seems to improve the wealth of flowers in the pasture.

Some dune systems have a characteristic dominant plant like the burnet rose of the Welsh dunes or the sea buckthorn of the east coast. Buckthorn bushes on the east Scottish coast can be more than 6m (20ft) high and form an impenetrable scrub with sharp thorns to deter any intruder. Their most distinctive feature is the bright orange berries which cover the bushes in autumn and early winter and provide a valuable source of food for many birds. The buckthorn is also valued as a dune stabiliser, for its vigorous growth and excellence as a wind break prevent wind erosion. Together with the buckthorn there is often a mixed dune scrub of blackberry and gorse bushes, and even elder when the dune soil is relatively moist. All this is part of a vegetation succession which is constantly evolving and thus giving variety to dune coastlines.

As successive dune belts form they often leave distinct hollows or slacks between them. If these are deep enough to reach the water table – especially in the winter months – they can become temporary lagoons, which will carry a very different vegetation pattern from the dune ridges. The most common plant of the damp slacks is the dwarf

COMMON TERN

willow (*Salix*) with its characteristic creeping stems and furry flowerheads. Although some of the lagoons may be 1.5m (5ft) deep in the winter months they will begin to dry out from March onwards, and it is then that the willow begins to grow rapidly and spread onto the adjoining lower dune slopes. Where the lagoons remain as permanent features of the dune system – for example, in the South Haven Peninsula in Dorset – rushes colonise the water margins. More common is the dried-out slack which in the summer months forms a wet pastureland with plants like the hairy hawkbit, meadow buttercup, lady's smock, purple orchid, marsh helleborine and grass of Parnassus. It is here also that the increasingly rare amphibian, the natterjack toad, lives out most of its life. During the day it mostly lies buried in the sand but emerges at night to feed on insects. Any shallow lagoon between the dune ridges will form an ideal site for breeding. In order to withstand the high temperatures of the sand surface in the summer months the natterjack secretes a mucus which helps to keep its skin moist, and it can thus survive long periods of drought. Nevertheless it is a threatened species, for the young toads in particular often fall prey to keen-eyed seabirds should they venture out during the day.

Although sand dunes are a favourite haunt of many different types of seabird, few look upon these areas as their main breeding ground. The herring gull will nest in the marram grass of the dunes, but this is only one of many sites the bird may choose in which to lay its three eggs from mid-April on. For the various species of tern (*Sterna*) sand dunes provide a habitat where they can lay their eggs in mere scrapes in the sand, often only partially hidden by the drooping leaves of the marram grass. They prefer young dunes close to the sea where they are in close proximity to their feeding grounds; the little tern, for example, choosing sites just above the high-water mark. But this backshore site carries its danger, not so much from higher than average tides but from human disturbance. With the increasing threat of falling numbers of breeding pairs the tern has been singled out for attention and there are many sites as at Spurn Point, Gibraltar Point and Blakeney, all on the east coast, where public access is restricted during the breeding season. At Blakeney they can still be seen, though only from afar – a small price to pay for colonies which now number about 1,000 pairs of common tern and about 500 pairs of sandwich tern. But the danger remains for these graceful 'sea swallows', especially for the little tern of which there are only about 2,000 breeding pairs in the whole of Britain, and for whom the increasing numbers of herring gull nesting in sand dunes in recent years pose a threat to survival. Of all the terns, the arctic tern is most interesting. As its name implies it winters in the Arctic wastes, but makes the long journey to northern Scotland each summer to breed.

Other birds which favour dunelands by the sea are the oystercatcher and ringed plover. Both have primitive nests made out of a few pebbles or shells and bits of withered grass. The black and white oystercatcher is easily recognisable because of its long orange-red beak with which it probes the sand near the water's edge in order to prise out cockles and shrimps. Ringed plovers are quite different in appearance with a black and white collar, grey back and plump body. Their primitive nest may be easily trampled as it is a mere hollow in the sand and its four eggs are well camouflaged against being stolen by herring gulls. Numbers of breeding pairs are still relatively small and the wonder is that they have survived at all.

Shingle Beaches

Because pebbles are easily rolled by the sea, shingle beaches form a rather lifeless habitat for both animals and plants. It is only beyond the normal high-tide line that vegetation is able to gain and maintain a footing amidst the stony waste. Old shingle ridges (fulls), though seemingly inhospitable, do carry a range of plants which have adapted themselves to their surroundings; for example shingle complexes like Dungeness, The Crumbles near Eastbourne or the Ayre Peninsula at the northern tip of the Isle of Man, carry a patchy vegetation. Some of the plants like the yellow horned poppy (*Glaucium*), viper's bugloss (*Echium*) and even the sea dock (*Rumex*) grow surprisingly tall and lush. The poppy and bugloss with their prominent yellow and blue flowers respectively, provide attractive colouring where the plants grow together en masse. What is remarkable is the way in which they apparently find water even in the driest summer. At a depth of a few feet, rainwater remains between the pebbles and, together with surface condensation from dew, provides enough moisture for survival. Apart from water some humus is essential, and this often comes from decaying seaweed and other vegetative matter cast up by the sea in storms, as well as from the decaying remains of the plants themselves. With their incurved leaves and waxy surface, the plants are adapted to water conservation. They also have a deep root system which enables them to seek water at depths of 1m (3ft) or more. Many have a prostrate rosette form which helps water retention, while the sea campion (*Silene*) can form large mats covering the shingle surface and this helps to prevent water evaporation.

Of the more unusual shingle plants which are found only in a few areas of the British coast, the sea pea (*Lathyrus*) is perhaps the most fascinating. With its creeping habit it can cover large areas of shingle, and in summer the mass is coloured pink and light purple with tiny flowers. The seed pods which follow in late summer are similar in appearance to the cultivated garden pea and in the past have been gathered for their sweet, succulent contents. The aptly named Shingle Street on the Suffolk coast, close to the mouth of the river Ore, is one area where the sea pea dominates over other shingle plants. Another edible plant is the sea kale from which the cultivated variety has been derived. In its natural state it is a vigorous-growing plant with fleshy leaves and a deeply penetrating root system. Although not common it is found in a number of scattered localities along the south coast of England. Once it was regarded as a delicacy, its young shoots being gathered, blanched and then cooked in much the same way as asparagus.

Not all the plants of the shingle beach are indigenous. One alien is the tamarisk, an evergreen shrub which was introduced from the Mediterranean as a protection against strong coastal winds and which can reach up to 4.6m (15ft) in height, though as a garden windbreak it is usually trimmed as a hedge. Its feathery hanging fronds are made up of hundreds of thread-like leaves which effectively reduce water loss. It can grow equally well on sandy soils, hence its popularity in many gardens along the south coast of England. In places it has spread onto open shingle and sand areas to become part of the natural vegetation.

Shingle spreads, made up of hundreds of old beach ridges as at Dungeness, can be desolate places and seemingly unattractive save on a still summer's day. The patchy cover of plants gives the whole setting an arid look which has not been improved by the haphazard use made by man. Dungeness Foreland, a shingle spread covering many square miles, now has two huge nuclear power stations, a series of gravel workings, squatter's cottages and tarred fishermen's huts with their litter of old rusting gear and abandoned cars. And yet before man found a use for such areas it must have been a haven of tranquillity with broom bushes, nesting birds, open skies and the roar of pebbles combed by the breaking waves. Now seemingly it is too late to save it. Fortunately the other great shingle feature, Chesil Bank which runs for almost 32km (20 miles) from Burton Bradstock in the west to the Isle of Portland in the east, is still unspoiled largely because it is inaccessible save at a few places. Although the crest of the ridge, said to have been formed by a great storm in 1853, is largely devoid of vegetation, the inner side overlooking the great lagoon – The Fleet – has bushes of the shrubby seablite (*Suaeda fruticosa*). This bush is an introduction from the Mediterranean and thrives on the well-aerated 'soil' of the inner margin of Chesil Bank.

Seabirds find shingle ridges attractive for breeding and both Dungeness and Chesil have their colonies. It is often the lagoons, both natural and artificial, that have the most exciting birds – the mute swan in the case of The Fleet and the great crested grebe, shelduck and common tern on Dungeness.

Rocky Shores

The most visible signs of life along our coasts often occur where there is a rocky shore composed of outcropping strata, shallow pools and boulders. To the active, this type of coastline represents the ideal setting for a holiday for it gives an opportunity to explore the glistening pools or turn over boulders in expectation of surprising a sheltering crab. Even bare rocks provide a home for the specially adapted limpets and barnacles which cling with great tenacity by means of suction. Plants too have solved this anchorage problem, particularly the seaweeds with their strong holdfasts. Bladder wrack (*Fucus vesiculosus*) is very much at home in this setting and commonly completely drapes the whole of the rock surface. It is able to withstand considerable wave activity by floating its long fronds as a wave rushes by.

Although perhaps not quite so apparent as in the saltmarsh, there is a broad zonation on a rocky shore. Seaweeds, for example, are arranged in three colour groups related to the plant's photosynthesis on which it depends for growth and survival. Green seaweed functions best in bright light and therefore is found at the highest levels of the shore. The brown seaweeds come next as they are able to function satisfactorily with less light. The red seaweeds occupy the lowest levels where the light values are least and so occur near the low-water line or offshore. Of the three groups the brown varieties are most common and therefore most familiar. The bladder wrack is the easiest to identify because of the swellings – air bladders – which occur in pairs over the surface of the frond. These bladders keep the seaweed floating when the tide is in and allow photosynthesis to continue. On the other hand the knotted wrack (*Ascophyllum*) finds difficulty in withstanding violent seas because it lacks the strengthening midrib found in the bladder wrack, though the two types are often found together.

Animals, being mobile and therefore able to seek shelter, show a much greater degree of tolerance to the varying conditions found on a rocky foreshore. At the highest level, often marked by the black film of the lichen *Verrucaria*, the periwinkle (*Littorina*) is commonly found. For protection they often crowd together in cracks and fissures in the rock surface, venturing out in calmer conditions to feed on the green algae at lower levels. Below the periwinkle zone comes the stalkless (acorn) barnacle (*Balanus*), a jelly blob commonly seen on old pier supports with a range of colours depending on the species. Even more common is the limpet (*Patella*) which needs less shelter for it can cling resolutely to the bare rock face by means of its powerful muscular sucker. Like the periwinkle the limpet lives mainly on algae and therefore, in spite of its apparent static position, has to move around the rock face in search of food. Towards the low-water line the mussel appears, often in great colonies grouped together and attached to a rock by means of horny threads. The mussel feeds on plant plankton and where the food supply is particularly rich, as around sewage outfalls, the mussel banks are most profuse.

Also near the low-water line are the solitary sea anemones which, in a vast array of colour, provide some of the most beautiful forms of the rocky shore. They are best seen in rock pools when the tide is out, for then their tentacles are often on open display. Appearance is deceptive in that the anemone can sting in an attempt to ward off predators. The sea slug however seems immune, and therefore can make a rich picking of both anemones and sponges. Also in rock pools, though often seeking shelter under a boulder, is the shore crab known to many rock explorers. More interesting is the much less common hermit crab which has developed a fascinating relationship with the anemone to the advantage of both, a process known as symbiosis. The hermit crab is quite happy to use an empty shell for a home and, once it has established itself, the anemone comes and settles on the outside. In this way it is carried around on the crab's back and so has a much greater chance of finding food as well as of feeding on the leftovers of the crab. In return it protects the crab by means of its sting cells. The ragworm is another animal which uses the hermit crab as a host, and in return for free transport and protection it keeps the shell clean and aerated.

Mud-flats and Saltings

Where sea water carries tiny particles of suspended silt which settle out at the turn of the tide, mud-flats develop. At the heads of estuaries and bays and on low, flat, shelving coasts like those of Essex, these flats are extensive. When first deposited the mud is sloppy and almost impossible to walk on; it is therefore only from the air that the appearance of such ramifying systems of creeks can be really appreciated. As there is usually more organic material available than on either sand or shingle beaches, mud-flats carry a much richer flora and fauna. Since the plants are submerged on each tide those growing between the high- and low-water marks have to be true halophytes. Once established, often with a single species covering a vast area, the plants aid the rapid upbuilding of the marsh level as they trap silt with each incoming tide. As it gains in height the salt marsh extends its outer edge seaward – a process which ultimately leads, through reclamation, to the extension of the land frontier (see Chapter 3). The rising level of the marsh means that the upper parts are covered by sea water for shorter periods, and this enables plants which are only semi-halophytes to colonise the zone near the high-water line.

At the lowest level of the flats, only the plants which can tolerate long periods of immersion in salt water can hope to survive. Typical is *Zostera*, a ribbon-leaved wrack, sometimes known as eel grass, which can be submerged for more than five hours of each tidal cycle. It is a flowering plant with partly enclosed florescences which are pollinated under water. Another coloniser of the lower mud-flats is the algae

Enteromorpha with long slimy, green, filamentous strands; though, needing sunlight, it cannot be immersed for too long a period. Both the *Zostera* and *Enteromorpha* form vast tidal meadows which provide ideal grazing grounds for winter bird migrants from the Arctic. The Brent goose, for example, finds the eel-grass meadows of the Essex coast very much to its liking, as well as also those on the south-coast marshes of Langstone and Chichester harbours. In an average year it has been estimated that no fewer than 14,000 Brent geese (about 20 per cent of the total world population) feed on our saltings.

As noted earlier a distinctive feature of salt marshes is the clear zonation of plant communities. On the landward side of the *Zostera* zone there is often a belt dominated by *Salicornia*, variously known as the glasswort or marsh samphire. This is an annual and therefore only of limited use in building up the marsh, although it traps silt during the summer and autumn months. It is an easily recognisable, fleshy plant with a short root and main stem 15–23cm (6–9in) tall from which stubby side shoots sprout out at regular intervals. In the past it was gathered in the autumn for pickling, though in this respect it is not so palatable as the rock samphire (*Crithmum*). More widespread was its former use as a source of soda for the glass-making industry.

The fleshy halophytes, glasswort (*Salicornia*) and seablite (*Suaeda maritima*), both annuals which colonise the lower mud-flats

The most successful coloniser of sloppy mud, rice grass (*Spartina*): isolated clumps can quickly extend to form a continuous sward

Often closely associated with the glasswort is the annual seablite (*Suaeda maritima*), another fleshy plant but with numerous branching leaves. It can grow up to 46cm (18in) tall, and although pale olive-green in summer it turns red in autumn to give the marshes a rosy glow of colour before the final die-back in winter.

Foremost amongst the colonisers of sloppy mud and for a rapid build-up of marsh levels is rice grass (*Spartina townsendii*). In just over a century this hybrid between a native species and one introduced into Southampton Water from America in 1875 has colonised large areas of mud-flats along the south and east coasts of Britain. Through its vigorous growth it dominates the middle marsh levels to the exclusion of many other plants, its strength lying in its tufted rhizome crown from which stout, rigid leaves and spiky flower stalks grow to heights of 0.6–1m (2–3ft). It can spread by water-dispersed seed or by an extension of its underground stem, with isolated tussocks quickly merging in a few years to form a continuous sward. Although initially other plants like the glasswort or the sea purslane (*Halimione*) may be present, the rice grass quickly snuffs them out. So far it has spread northwards as far as the Humber and Mersey, often as a result of deliberate planting by coastal protection authorities. In places it has been grazed as a *Spartina* meadow, though it is not so succulent as other grass species.

Where rice grass is not dominant, this middle zone of the marsh is occupied by a number of other interesting plants. Foremost is the sea purslane with its wiry stem and oval-shaped olive-coloured leaves. Because the purslane grows best on a well-drained, aerated soil, conditions not usually found on the salt marsh, it tends to form ribbon growths along the edge of creeks. Other plants in this zone include the sea aster with its clusters of purple flowers in late summer and the sea lavender (*Limonium*) both of which can cover large areas of marsh and make an impressive sight when in flower. More localised is the golden samphire (*Inula*) which has dark-green fleshy leaves and flower heads of deep gold.

As the marsh level rises, the grasses which are usually less tolerant of salt begin to appear. Along the west coast, in areas like the Ribble Estuary, manna-grass (*Puccinellia*) is dominant. It is tall growing and quite vigorous, and can make good quality pasture. Where there is a sandy substratum the red fescue is commonly found and may even completely replace the manna-grass. Scurvy grass (*Cochlearia*), which in spite of its name is not really a true grass, occurs quite frequently in the upper marsh. It takes its name from the fact that it contains an oil which prevents scurvy and was therefore eaten by sailors from Captain Cook's time onwards.

With a rich and plentiful supply of food at all levels, the mud-flats and saltings are the home of many different animal species. Some live solely on the plants, though many act as scavengers and predators. The *Zostera* zone is the home of big jellyfish which attach themselves to the eel grass by means of suckers. Mud snails are also common including the tiny spire shell (*Hydrobia*), only 8mm (⅓in) long. In some areas it reaches a density of over 50,000 a square metre and as it feeds on minute fragments of organic debris in the mud it can only survive where there is an assured rich supply of food. It tends to bury itself just under the mud surface as the flats uncover, but emerges at the surface when the incoming tide brings a fresh supply of food. Almost as common is the small crustacean *Corophium* which lives in a U-shaped burrow but comes to the surface in search of food. Two bivalves, the twin-shelled tellina (*Macoma*) and the furrow shell (*Scrobicularia*) burrow more deeply but connect with the surface through their feeding siphons. Another burrower is the common ragworm (*Nereis*) but it catches its food by poking out its head to catch any passing animals. Mud shrimps like *Callianassa*, a deposit feeder and *Upogebia* which strains its food from passing water, also occur on this lower mud zone.

Both plants and animals of the mud-flats provide food for the huge flocks of migrant birds in the winter months. The Brent geese have already been mentioned and while they prefer eel grass (*Zostera*), they will also eat *Enteromorpha* if present. Shelduck feed on spire shells which are found in the eel grass zone and do so by swinging their bills in the surface layers of mud and then sifting out any small organisms. Other ducks like shovellers and teal also live on spire shells. On the other hand, waders like oystercatchers, dunlin, plovers and godwits find small molluscs, gastropods and crustacea as a welcome winter food supply as they forage the mud-flats and saltings. Dunlin prefer wet mud and can often be seen in large numbers near the low water line seeking out their prey. Sometimes they drop in from flight when they see tellins and small worms to their liking.

Sea Cliffs

With a multiplicity of different rock types and formations, the cliffs of Britain provide a wide variety of habitats for both plants and animals. Hard igneous rocks such as are found in the castellated cliffs of Land's End or the broken coastline of the Lizard might seem, at first sight, to offer little. But the opening up of crevices by wave erosion, often along fault planes, gives shelter to both sea birds and specially adapted plant species. Even apparently vertical cliffs have narrow ledges where a slightly harder bed projects and this is sufficient to allow gulls, auks and birds with similar nesting habits to establish a home. Some of the most suitable cliffs are those formed of flagstone, as in Caithness, or limestone, as in south Pembrokeshire. Both these rock types are characterised by well-developed bedding planes and vertical joints, and these give rise to tabular platforms where birds requiring more space to build a nest can be accommodated.

Cliffs by their very nature tend to be isolated, inaccessible places and this undoubtedly favours bird colonisation. Ideally offshore islands give the most protected setting for breeding birds and it is on these that some of our biggest colonies are established. Some coastal cliffs can give a fair degree of protection because of the difficulty of approach. St

Abb's Head in east Scotland teems with bird life, not because the area is particularly isolated but because it is virtually impossible to reach the actual cliff face except perhaps by being let down on a rope. Even areas where visitors are constantly walking the cliff-top path seem to offer a relatively safe protected haven for most sea birds, as witness the huge colonies in what is now a Royal Society for the Protection of Birds (RSPB) reserve at Bempton on the Yorkshire coast.

At the lowest level, where the cliff is in direct contact with the sea, the rocks are often covered with the black lichen which grows in association with the orange *Xanthoria* and the green tufts of the sea ivory. Where the climate is relatively warm, as along the coasts of the Cornish peninsula, the edible rock samphire, golden samphire and sea spurrey are able to maintain a tenacious hold in tiny crevices and rock gullies. As its name implies, the rock samphire (*Crithmum*) is almost entirely confined to cliffs. Originally it came from the Mediterranean and so can only grow in the south of Britain, being found no further north than Suffolk. A plant with a long woody rootstock and a much-branched stem with bright green leaves, it was once extensively gathered and then pickled by boiling with vinegar and spice. Gathering was a dangerous pastime – a fact appreciated by Shakespeare for, in *King Lear*, Edgar in his well-known description of the white cliffs of Dover pronounces 'half way down hangs one that gathers samphire, dreadful trade!' The golden samphire (*Inula*) occurs in the spray zone at the foot of cliffs and with its large daisy-like golden flowers in July and August provides a brilliant splash of colour. More delicate is the sea spurrey (*Spergularia*) which, with its pink flowers, is confined to the south west of England and Wales because of susceptibility to frost. Most brilliant of all is the import from South Africa, the mesembryanthemum (Hottentot fig), which has been cultivated in seaside gardens and parks for many years and now forms many wild patches on the cliffs. It has thick, fleshy, pointed leaves with a triangular cross-section, and often grows in thick mats with stems trailing over the rock surface. Because of its exotic range of colours it has become increasingly popular in recent years. It grows best in Devon and Cornwall, though on the west coast it is found as far north as Galloway.

Another plant which is restricted to rocky cliffs is the wild or sea cabbage. Again it is an import from the Mediterranean but grows well in the southern part of Britain. It flourishes best where there are narrow cracks in the rock and prefers a limy soil, hence its local occurrence on the Great Ormes Head near Llandudno and in the Isle of Purbeck near Swanage. In the past its thick fleshy leaves were gathered for cooking, which is not surprising as it is the parent of the cultivated cabbage. Though seldom forming a splash of colour on the cliff face – its yellow flowers are too small even when grouped to make much of an impression – it has a long period of flowering from early summer right through to autumn.

Perhaps the most common plant of the rocky cliff is the sea thrift or sea pink (*Armeria*), though it has a much wider distribution being equally at home on the cliff top, in the salt marsh or growing on shingle ridges. Even the most casual coastal visitor cannot fail to have noticed the compact rosette form from which its long flower stalks arise. It flowers over a period of some months, with its pink or light purple flowers making an impressive show en masse and is often found with the sea campion, easily identifiable because of its 'bladder' and white flowers.

Where there is more soil on the cliff top, the typical maritime plants intermingle with their land counterparts so that on the coastal paths of Cornwall or Pembrokeshire the rich variety of the vegetation is quickly apparent. Along with the pink tufts of the sea pink and the white flowers of the sea campion there are bluebells and red campions and primroses in spring. Where the bracken has not made too many inroads and choked the flowering plants there is a wealth of colour that is perhaps only surpassed by the floral richness of the machair of western Scotland.

Apart from seeing interesting vegetation, the cliff walker has an unrivalled opportunity to study our breeding sea birds. Bird reserves such as those provided by the RSPB can provide an ideal introduction; for instance the almost vertical chalk cliffs of Bempton to the north of Flamborough Head have been opened up to the public since the war and have become justly famous for their sea-bird colonies. In the nineteenth century sea birds in many places suffered persecution through indiscriminate shooting and the fact that in early summer the nests were raided by groups of men known as 'climmers' who descended the cliff-face by rope and filled baskets with eggs for sending to confectioners and bakers. The 1954 Bird Protection Act brought this to an end and, since that time, many species have increased in numbers. For instance at Bempton there are now believed to be as many as 50,000 pairs of kittiwakes nesting, while almost as numerous are the guillemots, in spite of the fact that these suffered greatly from nineteenth-century depredation. Two new species have even become established at Bempton in the present century – the fulmar which first nested in 1922, and the gannet in 1937. The appearance of the latter was particularly notable in that it marked the first time that this bird had chosen a mainland cliff site for nesting. Previously it had been confined to islands off the coast where huge gannetries had long been established.

The gannet requires more room for nesting than many other sea birds for it builds a relatively large volcano-type nest from pieces of seaweed and other similar material. From this vantage point it can look down into the sea, spot a fish and then dive almost vertically to spear its prey. Because of the great pressure it is subjected to on entering the water it has developed a padded breast and sleek head, enabling it to plunge dive and, with its binocular vision, seek out surface-swimming fish such as mackerel. Although a breeding colony of about 200 pairs has been established at Bempton it is on isolated offshore islands that the great gannet population explosion of this century has occurred. Large numbers of birds now cover the Bass Rock in the Firth of Forth, Ailsa Craig in the Firth of Clyde and Grassholm off the Pembrokeshire coast. On Grassholm there are about 20,000 breeding pairs with their nests covering the island top, each carefully spaced out a safe pecking distance from its neighbour. The increase in gannet numbers has been particularly striking since 1950 and it is estimated that there are now over 150,000 birds nesting in Britain. One suggestion is that the general rise in temperature over southern Britain in the past fifty years has led to an increase in surface fish like mackerel and saithe which form the gannets' main source of food.

Of all the birds which live and breed on the cliff face it is the small oceanic gull, known as the kittiwake from its distinctive call, that is best adapted. It has short black legs which are most unsuitable for walking but ideal for landing on a narrow ledge. Like the gannet it seeks its food from the surface waters by plunge diving, but it builds a nest on a narrow ledge out of any flotsam and jetsam it can find cast up on the shore. This nest is a more compact structure than the loose nest of the gannet, for guano is used to cement the strands together. For birds like the fulmar and razorbill which make only primitive nests loss of eggs through rolling off the narrow ledge must be considerable, but the guillemot has partly solved the problem by laying a single pear-shaped egg which will not roll so readily while incubating.

PUFFIN
RAZORBILL
GUILLEMOT

Like the kittiwake, the fulmar too walks with difficulty, so that it spends much time floating in colonies on the sea surface; in the air, however, it is master of the uplifting air currents of the cliff face. Without a proper nest it prefers a wider ledge for laying its single egg so that there is less chance of it rolling away. If all goes well the incubation lasts about fifty days and the chick hatches covered with white down. From an early age it puts on weight rapidly and is able to defend itself by squirting an unpleasant oily liquid at any intruder – the name itself means 'foul gull'. Although occurring widely throughout Britain, the biggest colonies are in Scotland both on the coast and more especially on the offshore islands. Records of the presence of the fulmar on St Kilda go back some 900 years. Since they were first

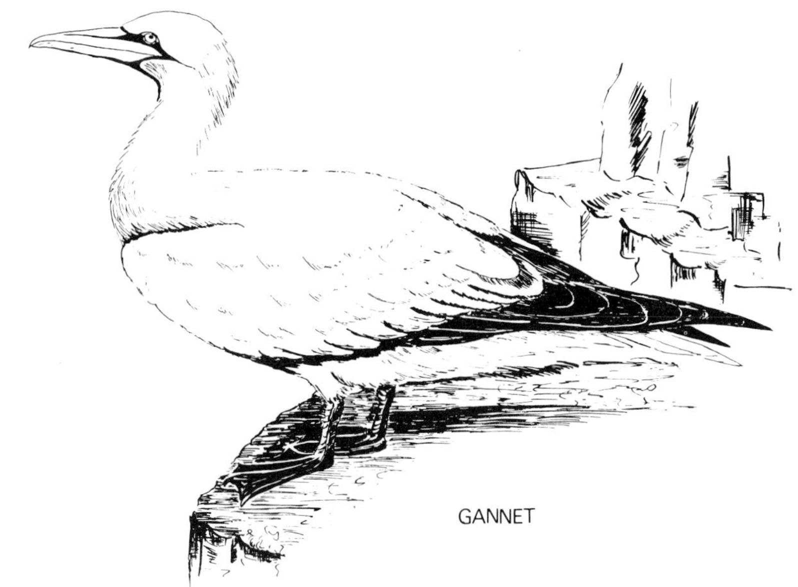
GANNET

recorded on the island of Handa off north-west Scotland – now an RSPB reserve – their numbers have increased spectacularly, especially in the Orkney Isles.

Two other auks deserve further mention because of their numbers, namely the guillemot and the razorbill. Both prefer the cliff, sometimes even hiding under a boulder if available. Unfortunately both guillemots and razorbills are probably declining in total numbers, partly as a result of attacks by gulls and partly because of the already mentioned temperature change which has altered the pattern of fish migration.

It is however the decline of the puffin, another auk, which gives greatest concern, for this comedian amongst sea birds has, for complex reasons, virtually disappeared from areas it once dominated. Puffin Island off the north-west tip of Anglesey has probably had puffins nesting on its limestone top since the time of the Celtic saint Seriol in the sixth century, but the brown rat has taken its toll over the years. The herring gull shows no mercy and can kill even adult birds let alone an unattended chick. Apart from these predators, the puffin's need for a burrow as a nesting site has led to considerable erosion and the destruction of the thin soil layer of the cliffs so that suitable areas for nesting are now more difficult to find. Fortunately, although mainland colonies have declined, there are still huge numbers of puffins nesting on St Kilda although these too in time may suffer from self-inflicted erosion created by burrowing.

Burrowing birds seem particularly prone to decrease in numbers in the face of active competitors and this applies to the Manx shearwater as well as to the puffin. Because of its clumsiness on land the shearwater can only hope to survive if it remains hidden in a burrow during the day and then emerges at night when, under cover of darkness, it scours the sea up to a hundred miles from its nesting place in order to find sufficient food to carry it and its young through the next day. Should it fail to return in darkness it may suffer attack from gulls which can make short work of a shearwater, leaving only the breastbone and wing feathers as evidence of their killing. The 'Manx shearwater' suggests a connection with the Isle of Man, and indeed this exists in the fact that the Lords of Man found the bird a delicacy at table. Formerly they nested in many parts of the Island, particularly in the offshore Calf of Man in the south, until rats completely cleared out the burrows. Now that these predators have been brought under control, the Manx shearwater is once again nesting on the Calf, although up to now in relatively small numbers. For the biggest colonies it is necessary to visit the Pembrokeshire islands of Skomer and Skokholm (managed by the West Wales Naturalists' Trust) where there is an underground 'city' of thousands of birds. The visitor sees little evidence of them because of their nocturnal habits, though should he be fortunate enough to be on Skomer on a moonlit night he will certainly be aware of their presence as they leave the safety of the burrow. Rhum in the Inner Hebrides is another island which plays host to the shearwater, and some birds are believed to nest at heights of up to 610m (2,000ft).

Coastal Conservation

With increasing demands made on the use of the coastline by man, either for housing, industry or simply leisure activities, there is an inevitable and continuous threat to the remaining unspoiled stretches where solitude can be guaranteed and unsullied vistas still remain. Even allowing access by providing a coastal footpath can be viewed as a blow against nature in that certain species of sea birds sometimes lose the sense of security and freedom which is so important to many species in the breeding season. It is to counter this that the Royal Society for the Protection of Birds has been active in establishing specific coastal reserves like those at Bempton and Minsmere. In some

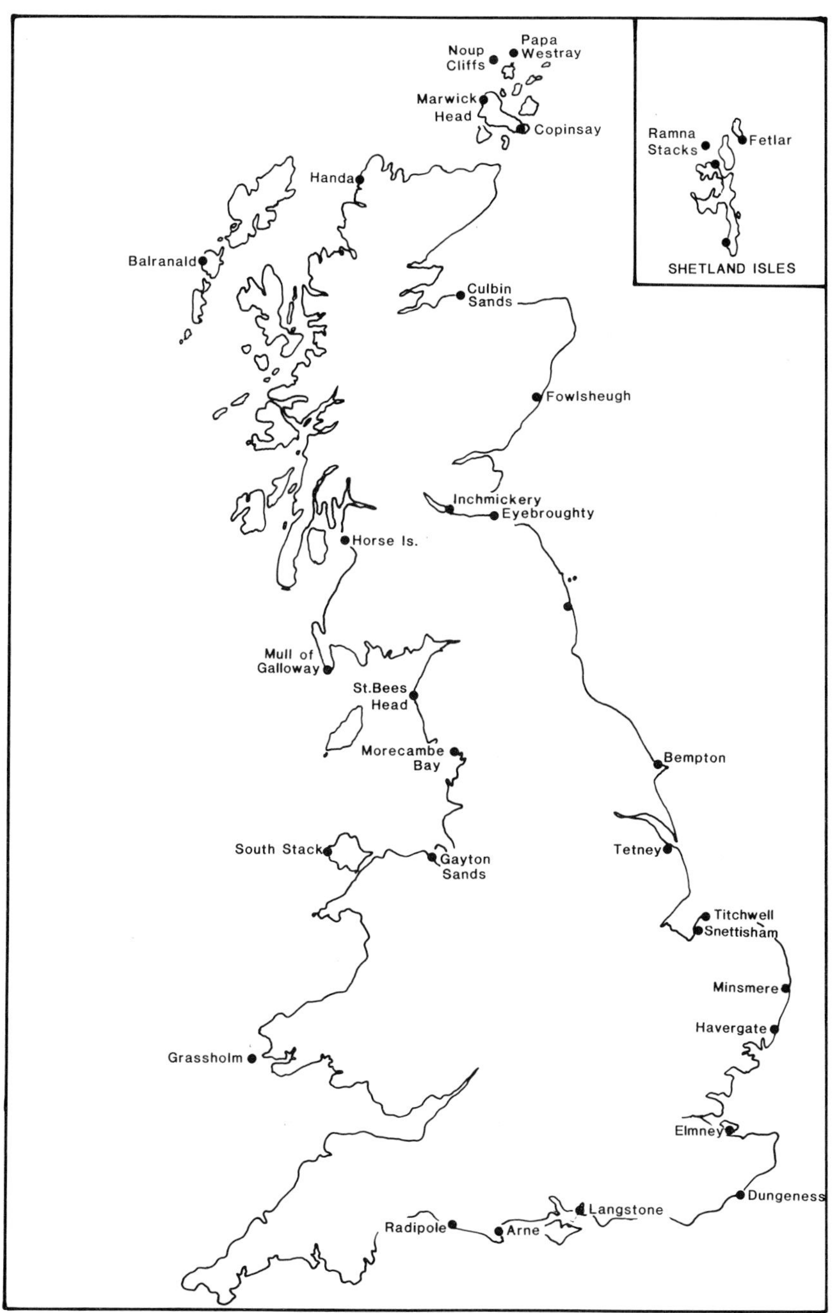

Reserves of the Royal Society for the Protection of Birds

cases the land can be bought outright or held in permanent trust, but often the provision of a reserve can only be undertaken with the active cooperation of the local landowner. Once established the RSPB has to provide facilities which on the one hand try to preserve the natural setting for the birds and yet allow the public to have a sight of their activities. There are often well-marked paths, viewing platforms and literature available for the interested layman; and at Minsmere wooden huts as hides are provided on the shore for the general public with other hides within the reserve for Society members. Minsmere has been one of the great success stories of the Society and arose from the acquisition of a stretch of low-lying land on the Suffolk coast between Southwold and Aldeburgh which had been flooded during World War II as an anti-invasion measure. The shallow lagoons, dotted with tiny islets, quickly became a bird's paradise with true sea birds, marsh birds and land birds making use of the varied habitat and protection afforded by the reserve. On a single day in summer it is possible to see more than fifty species, including the avocet which has become the badge symbol of the Society. Even outside the reserve, colonies of Sandwich terns are able to breed on the adjacent coastal dunes.

Apart from the RSPB reserves which cater specifically for those interested in bird watching, many other stretches of coastline have their protected bird colonies run by local naturalist trusts. Foremost is the Norfolk Naturalists' Trust which led the way in coastal conservation in East Anglia at a time when large areas were threatened by unsightly development. The Cley marshes, with a specially constructed bird observatory, provide excellent opportunities to study birds like the bittern, reedling, migrant waders and waterfowl. Further west the same Trust administers about 162ha (400 acres) of dune and salt marsh near Holme next the Sea. Large flocks of oystercatchers, knots and dunlins are to be seen, as well as waders and passing migrants. A similar organisation, the Lincolnshire Trust for Nature Conservation, administers the Gibraltar Point reserve south of Skegness. This area, where the coastline is being extended by the addition of foreshore ridges of sand, has its bird observatory and field station which also provides accommodation. Apart from nesting terns on the spit it is possible to see winter flocks of fieldfares, snow buntings, shorelarks and sea birds on passage. The recently built information centre provides both explanatory exhibitions and literature. Spurn Point in Yorkshire, the home of the army during

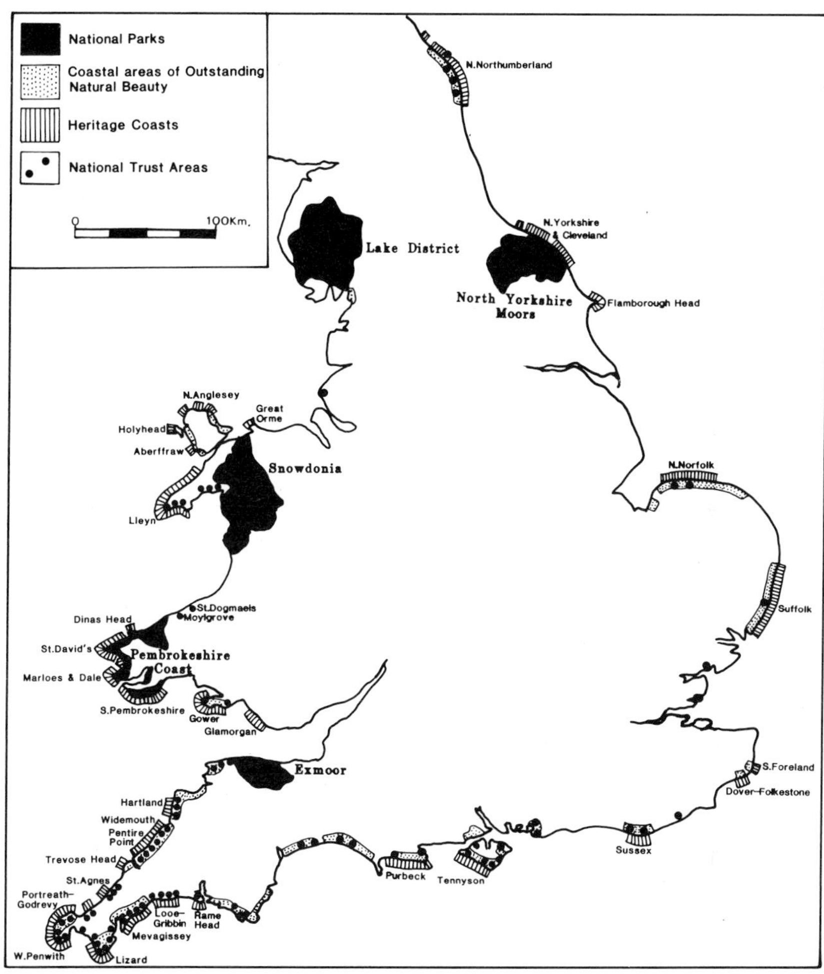

National Parks, Heritage Coasts and other protected sections of the coastline

both wars, is similarly now under the control of the Yorkshire Naturalists' Trust and, while little can be done to remove the gun emplacements and underground bunkers left behind, the Trust guarantees access and the opportunity to study birds and other coastal life on this sand spit projecting out into the waters of the Humber.

What was started by local naturalist trusts has now been copied and extended by the Nature Conservancy founded by Royal Charter in 1949. This body not only provides advice on the conservation and control of our fauna and flora but also owns property, including many sites of scientific interest, around our coastline. Scolt Head Island on the north Norfolk coast is leased to it by the National Trust, and with its varied setting of a shingle ridge, sand dunes and sheltered salt marsh, has a wealth of bird life. Its ternaries are justly famous, but in addition there are often large flocks of waders, and migrants like Brent geese as well as oystercatchers, shelduck etc to be seen. Access is by boat from Brancaster Staithe, though there is a limitation to the number of would-be visitors in the breeding months of May and June. Not far away is Holkham National Nature Reserve, also controlled by the Nature Conservancy Council, which offers a similar setting of dunes and salt marsh. These are but two of the many stretches of coastline now under the control of the Council so that, along with the National Parks Commission with its vast lengths of coastline in Pembrokeshire, Snowdonia, Exmoor and north Yorkshire moors, there is at last some provision made for preserving the remaining unspoiled sections of the coastline. Some may claim that the establishment of the National Parks from 1949 onwards came too late to save many areas, but at least it prevented the unsightly shack and caravan type of development expanding into some of the loneliest parts.

Fortunately the National Trust had been in being since 1895 and had already acquired large sections of coastline, particularly in the south-west peninsula, either outright by gift or in trust. The launching of Enterprise Neptune in 1965 was intended to strengthen its hold on vulnerable areas and merge some of its existing stretches of coastline by purchase from private individuals and bodies. The success of the scheme has meant that hundreds of miles have been added to the trust's coastal holdings, giving access for the first time to some well known beauty spots. The National Trust also manages precious areas like the Farne Islands off the Northumberland coast, now designated a Nature Reserve. Altogether there are twenty-eight islands in the group ranging in size from the largest, Inner Farne, down to the tiniest unsubmerged rock. Nearly all the Farnes consist of igneous rock known as whinstone, which weathers into a columnar mass often with deep clefts and fissures; in places there are patches of boulder clay and a light peaty soil covering.

The attraction of the Farnes is in the variety of the bird life making use of these different conditions, for no fewer than eighteen species of sea bird breed here. Shags and fulmars tend to use the higher cliffs but for the kittiwake the tiniest ledge will suffice as a nesting site. It is on the offlying stacks like the Staples that the rocks teem with bird life, particularly guillemots, razorbills and cormorants. Along the island shores there are a few shingle and sandy beaches where the oystercatcher and ringed plover can nest, but by and large it is the cliffs that have the big colonies. The Farne Islands' best known bird is the eider duck and, although it mainly occurs where there is a sufficient soil covering in which it can make its nest, it also finds a home on the bare rocky Longstone. Protected since the time of St Cuthbert who lived here from 676 to 684, there have been times when this lapsed and the eider was threatened with extinction, such as when the monastery was founded on Inner Farne in 1255 and the birds formed an accessible source of food. Subsequently the islands' other resources like seaweed, guano, eggs, fish and seals could be made to pay a handsome dividend for the owner, and again the bird population suffered. Inevitably over-exploitation led to disaster so that by 1856 only two pairs of breeding eider ducks remained. Fortunately the island came into the hands of Archdeacon Thorp who immediately introduced conservation measures, including having wardens patrolling the eider nesting areas. Later this role was taken over by the Farne Islands Association who in turn handed it over to the National Trust in 1925. The problems were not over for with perhaps 50,000 people wishing to visit the islands each year, rigid conservation had to be maintained. Certain restrictions are now placed on visitors but they have not proved too irksome, and thousands still make the boat trip across from Seahouses from April onwards.

The role of the National Trust in preserving unspoiled many hundreds of miles of coastline and giving access for the walker, is nowhere better seen than in Cornwall. At the present time the Trust owns or administers more than a third of the total length of coastline of the county, with some notable stretches having been acquired following the Enterprise Neptune appeal. As these represent some of the wildest, storm-battered coastal areas of Britain, their preservation in a natural state is essential. The National Trust has done noble work as guardian, not only by allowing access but by maintaining footpaths and repairing damaged sections where over-use by visitors has led to erosion. The Mecca of many tourists is Tintagel with its Arthurian legends. Though the Trust can take no responsibility for the monstrosity of the Castle Hotel perched high on the cliff-top of Barras Nose as a monument to insensitivity of the Great Western Railway directors who sanctioned it, even here it tries to maintain the natural beauty of the coastline. In fact Tintagel cliffs were one of the first purchases of the Trust, coming within two years of its foundation in

1895. In contrast to the starkness of the coast of north Cornwall the south coast has a milder appearance, especially around the shores of rias like Helford river and Carrick Roads. Helford river is justly famous for its unspoiled character with woods and gardens, often with sub-tropical vegetation, coming down to the water's edge. The Trust has ownership of land at both Penarvon Cove and Frenchman's Creek, while at the fishing hamlet of Durgan some of the cottages are in its possession. These areas at least seem safe from development and serve to indicate to local planning authorities what is needed for good coastal management.

Conservation often means restoration following the ill-use of the coastline by the military, and though much has been done in this respect there are still too many unsightly blockhouses, concrete hutments and former gun-battery platforms still awaiting clearance. In some of the most visited sections of the coastline conservation involves repairing the damage caused by excessive trampling by humans. The approach to Kynance Cove in Cornwall has recently been restored by the Countryside Commission as part of a national plan covering vulnerable sites. The stripped turf has been subject to re-seeding and a new path laid out to make the descent to the cove a less hazardous undertaking. But improving facilities in this way could be self-defeating in that it might encourage more visitors to Kynance and other similar beauty spots. This is the dilemma that has to be faced by bodies like the Countryside Commission, National Trust, Nature Conservancy and even private landowners who allow access to the coastline. It is a problem that is likely to grow rather than diminish, as the richness of the British coastline is appreciated by many more people in future years.

References

Barrett, J. *Life on the Seashore* (Collins, 1974)
Burton, J. and Lockley, R. M. *The Island of Skomer* (Staples, 1950)
Burton, M. (ed). *The Shell Natural History of Britain* (Michael Joseph, 1970)
McMillan, N. F. *British Shells* (Warne, 1973)
Norfolk Naturalists' Trust. *Nature in Norfolk* (Jarrold, 1976)
Pembrokeshire Coast National Park. *Birds of the Pembrokeshire Coast* (1979)
Ranwell, D. S. *Ecology of Salt Marshes and Dunes* (Chapman & Hall, 1972)
Soper, T. and S. *Beside the Sea*, (BBC Publications, 1979)
West Wales Naturalists' Trust. *Skomer Island* (nd)

2 Lost Lands

Legendary lands lost beneath an encroaching sea are part of the folklore of many parts of the coast. In Cornwall there are many stories about the vast territory called Lyonesse which formerly existed off the south-west tip of the peninsula, until a great submergence let in the sea so that today only the cluster of islands forming the Scillies projects above the waves. As usually told, the Lyonesse legend relates to a period when man was inhabiting the area and farming the land. Local fishermen can point to submerged reefs and, more remarkably, straight sunken walls of boulders which occur off islands like Samson, all evidence they claim of a once fertile country overwhelmed by the sea in which many prosperous cities and no fewer than 140 churches disappeared.

William Borlase, the famous Cornish historian writing in 1753, remarked on the extensive sand-flats which at low water connect many of the islands surrounding the shallow inland sea. On a low spring tide there was no difficulty in walking across from Tresco to Bryher and Samson. But again the best evidence of drowned lands Borlase claimed, came from the lines of stones running out from the shore on Samson Flats. The stones, which can still be seen, stand on end as uprights with small boulders forming an infilling to give a continuous wall not unlike, in appearance, many of the field boundaries of the islands today. The pioneer archaeologist O. G. S. Crawford made a visit in the 1920s and came away convinced that here was evidence of human fashioning, perhaps the work of Bronze Age man.

But, to support this theory, a rise of sea level during the past 3,000 years of more than 3.7m (12ft) would be necessary to submerge what were once tilled fields on land. This amount of recent submergence is much greater than is recognised elsewhere and here the legend of Lyonesse comes into sharp conflict with known recent sea-level changes in Britain. That the sea has risen considerably from a low point at the end of the Ice Age, about 10,000 years ago, is undisputed; but it is generally conceded that much of the rise took place before about 4000BC. The difficulty can be resolved if another interpretation is placed on the origin and purpose of the boulder walls. Instead of being land boundaries, the boulders can be looked on as forming great fish weirs, covered each tide but draining out at low water – an easy way of trapping fish. If they are simply huge fish traps then it is unlikely that they are prehistoric in date. One suggestion is that they were built in medieval times – and Crawford himself in the 1940s did not dismiss the idea – though it is curious that documentary evidence is lacking and that the method was abandoned relatively early.

Whatever the interpretation placed on the Scilly Isles' boulder walls, it is clear that there has been some loss of land through submergence in the lowland fringes to some of the islands. The evidence for this is archaeological, from cists and hut circles partially submerged on the foreshore of islands like Little Arthur, St Martin's and Tean. As these features are prehistoric in date the most likely period of submergence would have been in Romano-British times when a widespread rise of sea level occurred throughout southern Britain.

Stories about drowned lands have long been current in Welsh literature and in some cases have gained greater plausibility following offshore searches for the remains of building foundations, lost castles and churches. As early as the seventeenth century expeditions were being made to see the sunken ruins of the manorial estate of Llys Helig lying about 3km (2 miles) off the mouth of the river Conwy in Gwynedd. Traditionally this had long been regarded as the site of the sixth-century 'palace' or *llys* of a local chieftain which had been overwhelmed by the sea in the later Dark Ages. Later expeditions, some in this century, have apparently confirmed the existence of straight lines of boulders often arranged at right angles to one another. Inevitably this gave rise to the speculation that here indeed were the foundations of the large hall of the so-called palace. But, as Dr J. North has pointed out in his masterly survey of Welsh sunken sites, the stones could equally well represent the boulder trains left behind by a retreating ice front during the later stages of the Ice Age.

Welsh folklore also refers to the hundred, Cantref y Gwaelod, mentioned as early as the thirteenth century as being the vast land from Bardsey Island in the north to the mouth of the Teifi in the south and extending far out into the waters of what is now Cardigan Bay. Altogether it covered 2,072sq km (800sq miles) and had sixteen cities

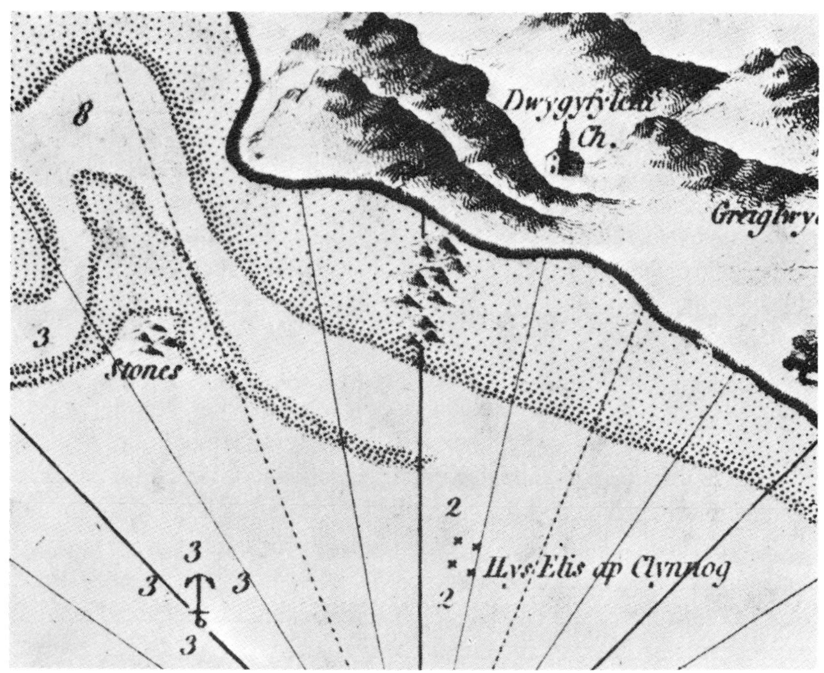

Conwy Bay, with the supposed site of Llys Helig (by Lewis Morris, 1736)

ruled over by the Lord of Gwyddno, Garanhir, the whole lowland protected by embankments with controlling sluice gates. Seithennin the keeper, according to the thirteenth-century legend, was guilty one evening of drinking too much at a banquet so that he neglected to close the sluices at the appointed time. The sea rushed in and flooded the vast area with its settlements but on a clear day it was possible to look down through the water and see the remains of the old embankments, buildings and even hear the church bells ringing!

The fact that this elaborate and fanciful story persisted over several centuries, becoming more exaggerated on re-telling and yet seemingly gaining more credence with the passing of time, is an indication of how difficult it is to debunk old legendary tales. Adherents could point to three great causeways or *sarns* of stone running out into the bay for several miles, which had defied 'scientific' explanation. At exceptionally low spring tides great lengths of these causeways are exposed; Sarn Badrig or St Patrick's Causeway, the most northerly of the three, runs for no less than 24km (15 miles) out into Cardigan Bay and at its broad seaward end there is a huge boulder 4m (13ft) across. Passing over the causeway in a boat it was easy enough to imagine seeing

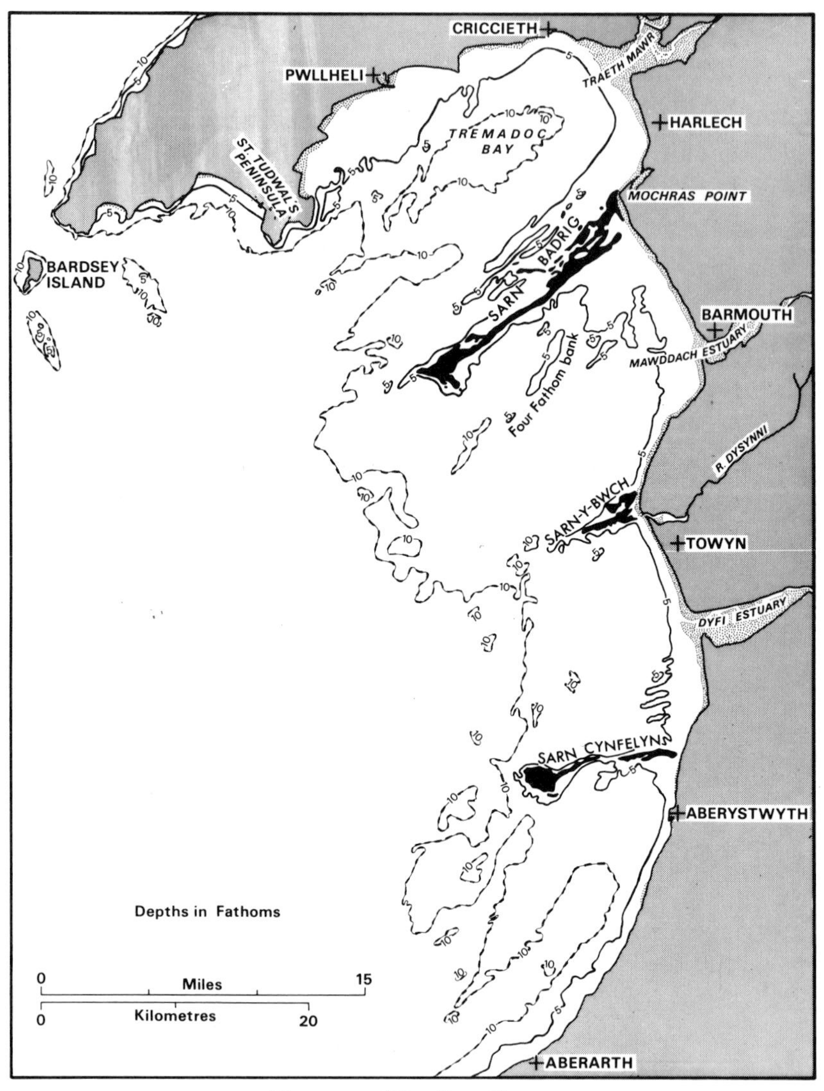

The sarns of Cardigan Bay

squared stones which could be remains of the great walled embankment which, after Seithennin's indiscretion, had been reduced to its present flattened state; the question as to how such gigantic engineering could have been undertaken never entered into the discussion. In recent years however there has been general agreement that the 'walls' are simply the remains of great boulder moraines left behind by a series of glaciers which came down the west-coast valleys

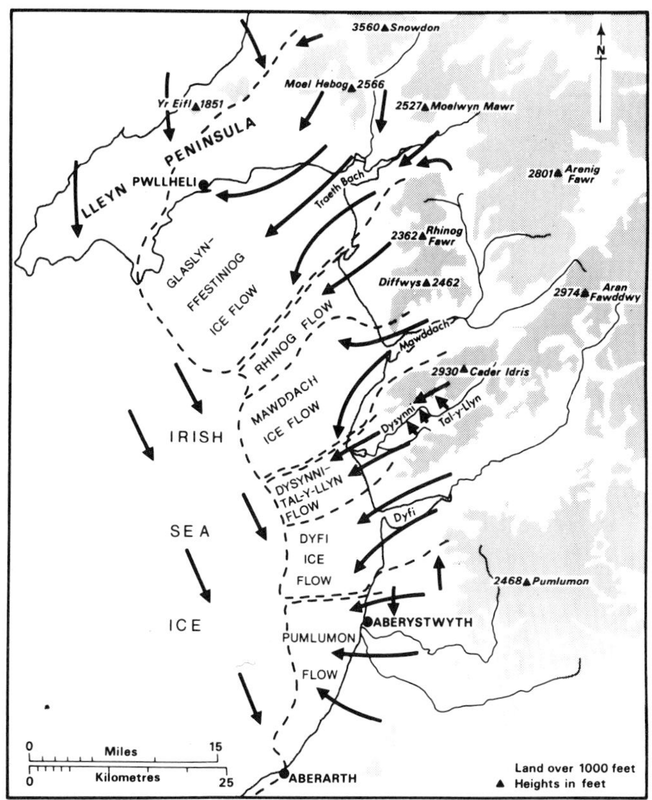

The formation of the sarn features of Cardigan Bay by glacier streams

and pushed out onto the floor of Cardigan Bay, first as separate entities but later joining together. Their lateral moraines thus fused together and left behind great ridges of glacial debris – the present-day sarns.

Any sand and clay which was part of the glacial moraine has long since been washed out of the deposit leaving only the coarse boulders. Some idea of the size of these can be gathered from the foreshore of Mochras (Shell) Island south of Harlech, the point from which Sarn Badrig takes off. The other two sarns are also approachable, Sarn y Bwch lying directly offshore of Tonfanau Camp north of Tywyn while Sarn Cynfelin runs out into the sea opposite the mouth of the Wallog valley north of Aberystwyth. It is possible to walk out for a distance of almost 1km (½ mile) from the shore on the back of Sarn Cynfelin, though care must be taken to choose a falling spring tide. While picking one's way over the large cobbles which make up the sarn and then looking back along the line of the curious feature running out at right angles from the coastline, scientific explanations tend to be forgotten and the old legend of the lost *cantref* is recaptured. Highways of the sea like the sarns, or former castles like Caer Aranrhod off the southern entrance to the Menai Strait, conjure up a glorious and prosperous past, the very antithesis of Welsh history. But perhaps that is all the legends were intended to do.

Apart from loss of land through a rising sea level, many coastal areas of Britain have been affected by blown sand which has covered former cultivated fields. The south-west facing shores of the Isles of Scilly provide one example. According to C. E. P. Brooks there were periods of sand invasion before 200 BC and for several centuries after AD 1300, both associated with stormy conditions. The storms of the thirteenth and fourteenth centuries in fact brought havoc to many parts of the coast through frequent gales which carried beach sand well inland. Kenfig Burrows, on the southern coast of Wales and now hemmed in by the great Margam steel complex in the west and the railway sidings to the north, was once the site of a sizeable settlement, commonly referred to as a city. We do not know when dune-sand first appeared along the south Wales coastline though there is evidence that prehistoric man found the area attractive. If there were sand dunes in existence then, they must therefore have been relatively stable. By the fifth century the area was sufficiently isolated for the hermitage of Theodoric to be built on a site close to the present steelworks. There was clearly little danger from moving sand at this early date; the real threat did not come until medieval times.

In the twelfth century, sometime after 1140, the Normans built their castle and small town of Kenfig. The town church of St James was built in the next decade along with houses for the burgesses who were attracted to live in this newly created settlement. By 1281 there were no fewer than 142 burgesses recorded as living there, so that by thirteenth-century standards it was a fair-sized town. Its prosperity rested on its coastal trade, as is shown in a document which records that in 1184 there were as many as twenty-four ships anchored at the estuary mouth – presumably the mouth of the Afon Kenfig. But in a few years the fortunes of Kenfig were to change dramatically. Sand dunes, once restricted to a narrow belt along the shore, now began to move inland and to encroach on farmland as well as the streets and buildings of the town. By 1485 the site had been virtually obliterated by the sand, and the townspeople had completely abandoned the place.

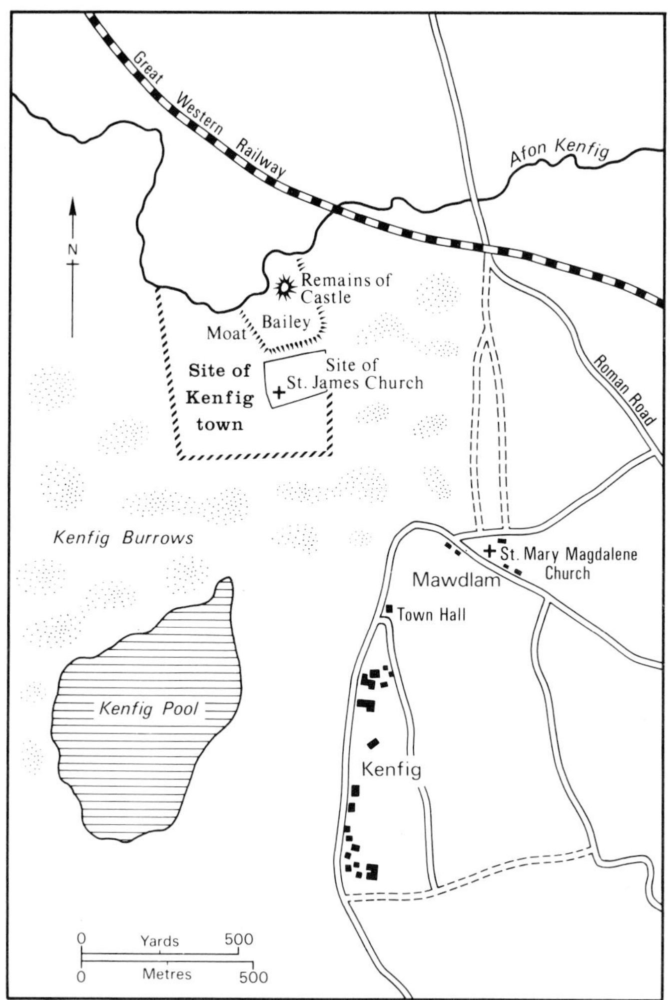

The site and features of the former 'city' of Kenfig

Many were now worshipping at the church of St Mary Magdalene at Mawdlem. When the Tudor topographer John Leland visited the area in 1538 he could only describe Kenfig as 'a little village on the east side of the Kenfig River, and a castel, booth in ruine and almost shoked and devourid with the sandes that the Severn Se there casteth up'. This single sentence sums up the fate of Kenfig.

Today even less remains in what has now become a vast sand warren. Between Kenfig Pool – a shallow expanse of water formed by the sand ponding back the drainage – and the railway, the confused array of dunes gives little hint that a town once existed on the site near the castle. Some have claimed they detect a rudimentary street plan, but this is very conjectural. Only the castle mound remains and the rough stonework of its ruined keep, now partly buried beneath the enveloping sand. The successor of the 'city' of Kenfig is no more than a collection of houses straggling along one side of the road leading to Porthcawl. The 'Town Hall', occupying the upper room of an inn, is perhaps symbolic of the diminished fortunes of the former borough which continued to have Parliamentary representation until 1832. Its original borough mace and ale-taster's cup were formerly housed here but have now passed to the National Museum of Wales in Cardiff.

Sometimes legend and history are closely intermingled as in the sand-dune areas of north Cornwall where, both at Perranporth and St Minver parish, churches suffered burial by advancing sand. Perranporth today is a seaside resort which grew up largely in the late nineteenth century, its name recalling its historical association with the Celtic saint Perran or Piran. Over the centuries the wide sandy beach to the north of the resort has supplied thousands of tons of shelly sand to feed the coastal dune belt, now unhappily occupied by a caravan and chalet holiday-complex. Fortunately this has only covered a small part of the southern dunes and there is still a tangible link with the historic past in the form of two ruined churches.

Although the exact account of events which led to the churches being buried beneath the dune sands is still partly speculative, it is certain that the lands north of Perranporth were once a valued possession of the monastery of Lamberran and were centred on an oratory, possibly founded by St Perran in the sixth or seventh centuries. After about 700, the lordship of the whole region passed to the monastery of St Petroc at Padstow and this ownership continued to the time of Domesday Book of 1085–6. Later the lands came under the control of Exeter Cathedral and it was their officers on a visitation in 1281 who first noted that the area was suffering severely from the effects of advancing sand so that it was only worth a paltry 10 shillings.

Although this is the earliest documentary evidence of the advancing sand dunes it is clear that the problem had existed for some time previously. The original oratory was abandoned in the twelfth century in favour of a new building about ½km (¼ mile) further inland. This was the furthest migration possible since the new site marked the extreme boundary of the monastic lands. The fact that the early oratory was allowed to remain virtually intact hints that the move to the new site was brought about by the threat of burial by sand dunes.

Although only a short distance away, the new church seems to have been safe, at least for some time. On its seaward side there was a substantial brook which formed a good barrier against the advancing sand, but in the seventeenth century tinners were allowed to drain this brook and almost immediately sand encroachment began again. By 1804 the threat of burial by sand was so great that the parishioners decided to remove the greater part of the church, stone by stone, and to use the material for the church of Perranzabuloe, 5km (3 miles) further inland. The remains of the partly dismantled church, like the early oratory, were completely covered by sand until re-excavated in 1918.

Amazingly, in the early nineteenth century, the early oratory was fully uncovered again, almost intact. The indication of a building appeared through the sand in the 1790s and it was certainly visible in 1805 for it was noted by the Cornish historian Lysons on his visit to the area at that time. Throughout the rest of the nineteenth century the church was visible but a further threat of burial, coupled with vandalism, led to the whole building being encased in a hideous concrete shell in 1910. Until quite recently it remained in this state with the hollow often flooded during the winter months making it impossible to reach the church marooned in its curious location. Now it has been decided to completely bury the church once more and perhaps save it for future generations to re-excavate.

In the accounts of the Perranporth dunes we have no suggestion that farmland or village sites were lost as a result of the sand incursion. Further north in the parish of St Minver on the east side of the Camel Estuary opposite Padstow, there is a hint of the sudden abandonment of a village which once lay between the church of St Enodoc and the estuary shore. It is even claimed that remains of houses with furniture still in place were found under the sandhills, indicating a sudden and violent storm. Stone querns which were recovered now line the church approach, but whether they originally came from the buried village is not known. The church of St Enodoc, parts of which date back to Norman times, was partially buried right up to the mid-nineteenth century. Today it lies isolated within its protective hedge amidst the dunes which now have been turned into a golf course. But for the action of the vicar in 1863 who was finding it increasingly difficult to enter the church – he had to climb down through a gap in the roof – to maintain the ecclesiastical link, the church would have become defunct. For a sum of £650 the fabric was repaired and the enveloping

The church of St Enodoc by the side of the Camel Estuary opposite Padstow

sand cleared away, the hedged enclosure was built and once again church services could be held in this remote but romantic setting.

Scotland, too, has its legendary stories of lands lost through sand burial, and as elsewhere each contains a germ of truth. The best known, largely because of the large area involved and the scale of the sand invasion, relates to the lands of the Culbin Estate on the south shore of the Moray Firth. The estate was first mentioned in a document of 1240 when it was the property of the de Moravia family, and this link continued until the fifteenth century when it passed to the Kinnairds. The estate covered 3,600 acres and incorporated 16 farms, mainly engaged in mixed farming. Picturesque and over-dramatised stories tell of a major sandstorm in the winter of 1694–5 when the whole estate was engulfed. This is most likely an exaggeration for the storm probably represented the culmination of a series of sand incursions which had been going on slowly over the centuries. Since the 1695 storm the bare sandhills have made little further progress inland. From time to time there have been reports of the upper parts of farm buildings appearing through the sand, and occasionally when a hollow has developed in the dunes the rigs of old ploughland have been uncovered. But there is little evidence of this today for the huge sandhills, some of the largest in Britain, have now been covered with conifers as part of an extensive afforestation scheme carried out by the Forestry Commission after World War I. Looking at this man-made landscape it is difficult to see how the towering sand dunes could possibly have developed as a result of a single storm in the late seventeenth century.

When we come to the east coast of England we are on surer ground for it can be amply demonstrated that land is, at the present time, being lost to the sea. We also know from historic documents and even past eye-witness accounts that erosion has been taking place over several centuries, certainly since about AD 1200. Losses have been considerable along certain vulnerable stretches of Yorkshire and East Anglia, and other east-coast counties like Essex and Kent have not escaped. Southwards from Bridlington to the neck of Spurn Spit, a distance of over thirty miles, the clay cliffs of Holderness have a history of almost continuous retreat during the past 750 years. During this time, if present rates of erosion are any guide, land almost a mile in width has disappeared into the sea. This is much less than the estimate given by the geologist Thomas Sheppard in 1912 in his book *The Lost Towns of the Yorkshire Coast*, but he took the view that erosion had been continuous since Roman times. This is now regarded as highly unlikely, which helps to explain why so many settlements mentioned in Domesday and sited on the coast were ultimately to disappear during the succeeding centuries. Altogether more than thirty places listed in the Domesday record no longer appear in the Holderness landscape and even larger places like Hornsea and Withernsea have predecessors which now lie, figuratively speaking, beneath the waters of the North Sea.

In assessing the scale of past erosion, it is to nineteenth-century records that we must turn for a more accurate picture of past losses. Local publications and even local artists provide graphic pictures of churches balanced precariously on the cliff top with huge waves about to demolish them. That churches did find themselves in this position and were ultimately consumed by the sea is not disputed. At Kilnsea in the extreme south of Yorkshire, where the clay cliffs give way to the narrow neck of sand forming Spurn Spit, the parish church was on the cliff top in 1826. Just inland a widening of the village street served as a market place with its fine cross said to date back to the time of Edward IV. The last burial in the churchyard took place in 1823 and, with the threat of destruction ever present, the last church service was held late

Kilnsea church as it must have appeared prior to its destruction by natural forces in the 1820s

in 1824 before the onset of the winter storms. Within a decade the whole church had gone, the market cross had been dismantled and re-erected much further inland at Hedon, and the whole community scattered as the sea devoured the cottages of the village. The tower of the church fell with a tremendous crash in the autumn of 1830 and thereafter the two hundred people who lived in the parish had to worship elsewhere. Today Kilnsea consists only of a few houses strung along the main road to Spurn, an abandoned chapel and a shop – the former Bell Inn. A plaque on the wall of the latter indicates that it was once 488m (534yd) from the sea, but because of subsequent erosion it is now considerably less.

Kilnsea was not the first village to disappear at the southern end of the Holderness coast for the Cartulary of the Abbey of Meaux speaks of another village, Sunthorpe, which once lay between Kilnsea and the sea. It apparently was destroyed some time in the sixteenth century. Sheppard was able to name no fewer than twenty-five other places which have suffered a similar fate.

Erosion continues almost unabated at the present time. After the 1953 floods a limited stretch of shoreline at Kilnsea was given sea defences in the form of a concrete promenade, groynes and a stone facing to the clay cliffs. Twenty years later the whole structure had been reduced to a mass of rubble. The problem is not simply one of withstanding the direct attack of the sea; alternate wetting and drying out of the clay soon induces weathering and leads to mud slides and slumps developing under the concrete facing. While mud-flows spew out onto the beach the upper cliff face fritters away; high tides are able to reach the cliff foot and direct wave attack steadily undermines the clay face. Any material which falls onto the beach is quickly removed so that there is virtually no additional sediment as a result of the erosion. Throughout the whole length of this coast the sandy beaches remain low and therefore do not form a first valuable line of defence against the onslaught of the waves. Only at Barmston in the north are there beds of sand exposed in the cliff face but they appear to contribute little to the adjacent beach. A row of bungalows built on the cliff top in the immediate post-war years has now all but disappeared, the sea having picked them off one by one in the past decade.

In the face of this unending onslaught by the sea, man's attempts to resist seem puny and ineffective. Without artificial defences like the sloping sea wall at Withernsea it would be foolhardy to build near the cliff top. This has been increasingly recognised in recent years and now much of the Holderness coast is peppered with caravan and chalet

The ruins of the coastal defences at Kilnsea: they have proved unable to withstand the ceaseless attacks of the sea

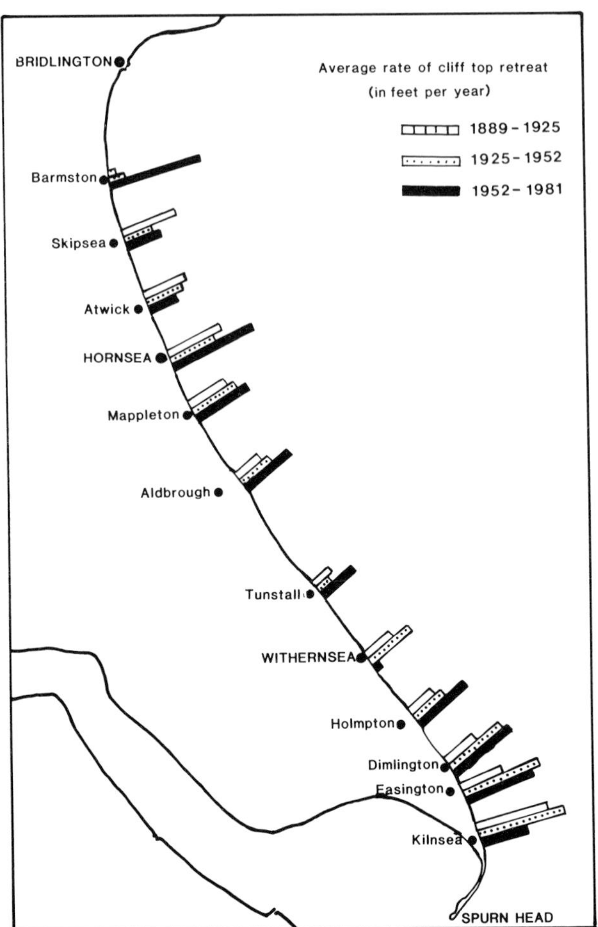

Rates of erosion for selected stations along the Holderness coast

sites rather than villages and hamlets, a picture so different from early medieval times when more than a score of settlements felt safe from the sea's destruction.

The rate of cliff-top retreat is very variable along different stretches of this same coast and there are also marked changes from year to year. In the south at Dimlington where the cliffs are over 24m (80ft) high, an average annual retreat rate of 2m (7ft) has been recorded since the middle of the last century. But average figures like this mask the real nature of the changes taking place. Just a little to the north at Holmpton, a major slip of the cliff face in 1978 led to a loss of more than 6m (20ft) overnight. Since then there has been no further retreat, presumably while adjacent sections erode as the sea attempts to maintain a straight coastline. Taking the Holderness coast as a whole about 122–152m (400–500ft) of land has been lost in the past century. The situation is not likely to change much in the future for, except at places like Withernsea and Hornsea, the two largest settlements, coastal protection costing more than £1 million a mile length cannot be justified. Faced with this apparently insuperable difficulty it seems that Holderness is destined to retain its unenviable distinction as one of the fastest eroding coastlines of the world.

This lost world beneath the waves of Bridlington Bay is not confined to the area of clay cliffs. The long spit of sand which runs in a gentle curve to end in the spatula-shaped Spurn Point at the mouth of the Humber, has also seen its fortunes change with the passing centuries. It was here that, shortly after 1240, a new town called Ravenserodd was founded. Its site was clearly described in the Meaux Abbey Cartulary as 'being in the utmost position of Holderness between the sea and the Humber. It was distant from the mainland a mile or more. For access it had a sandy road no broader than an arrow's flight yet wonderfully maintained by the tides and the ebb and flow of the Humber'. This leaves no doubt that Ravenserodd lay at the end of a sand spit similar to the present Spurn, though not in its exact geographical position. Later coastal changes here have led to a westerly migration of the spit feature, so that any thirteenth-century town would have been some distance east of Spurn Point and now covered by the Binks sandbank. It was the instability of position of the tip of the Spurn spit which led to the destruction of Ravenserodd after only a hundred years. Piecemeal erosion began to undermine the town as early as 1346 but the final, almost catastrophic phase of destruction, probably came as a result of a storm-surge similar to that which affected the east coast of England in 1953. As the relevant section of the Cartulary relates, the town was:

> . . . totally annihilated by the floods of the Humber and the inundation of the great sea . . . And so, with this terrible vision of waters seen on every side, the enclosed persons with the reliques, crosses and other ecclesiastical ornaments flocking together mournfully imploring grace, warded off at that time their destruction. And afterwards, daily removing their possessions, they left the town totally without defence, to be shortly swallowed up, which with a short intervening period of time, by those merciless tempestuous floods, was irreparably destroyed.

The whole description given in the Meaux records could well apply to events which led to the destruction of Old Winchelsea in East Sussex in 1250 after a storm destroyed 300 houses and a number of churches. Unlike Ravenserodd, Old Winchelsea was able to linger on for a time before finally being abandoned after a severe storm-surge on the eve of St Agatha in 1287. The ultimate fate of the town had been anticipated some years before, so that Edward I had built his New Winchelsea on higher ground inland and encouraged the burgesses of the original settlement to move there.

It is not surprising that both Ravenserodd and Old Winchelsea with their low exposed sites might have been expected to prove vulnerable to attack by the sea in the stormy thirteenth and fourteenth centuries. Bishop Felix could not however be accused of lack of foresight in 630 when, to promote the conversion of East Anglia, he chose to found his episcopal see of Dunwich on a cliff top some distance from the sea. That it subsequently grew into a sizeable town is shown by the fact that Domesday records 24 freemen each with 40 acres of land, 136 burgesses, 178 poor and 3 churches. During the reign of Henry II it was still a 'towne of good note, already with much riches and sundry kinds of merchandizes' with only the hint of coast erosion which was ultimately to bring about its destruction. Its borough charter was granted in 1200 and with it the right to hold a Monday market and a July fair. This must have been the high-water mark in the fortunes of the town, for by the end of the thirteenth century it was in decline, by which time it had lost much of its trade to the nearby new port of Blythburgh. But the real reason for its eclipse was an increase in the severity of coast erosion. As an early guide book put it: 'Seated high up on a hill composed of loam and sand of a loose texture, on a coast destitute of rock, it is not surprising that its buildings should have yielded to the impetuosity of the billows breaking against and easily undermining the foot of the precipices.' The continual losses taking place from medieval times can be seen in the history of its churches with St Michael's being destroyed by 1331, St Leonard's sometime after 1350, and those dedicated to St Martin and St Nicholas during the fourteenth century. The church of St John the Baptist in the Market Place was demolished in 1540, to be followed by the chapels of St Anthony, St Francis and St Catherine before 1600. Later centuries have also taken their toll for St Peter's was dismantled in 1702 while the last victim, All Saints, gradually came closer to the cliff edge in the nineteenth century until finally, in 1912, it went over the top. Huge pieces of flintwork were occasionally seen on the beach until quite

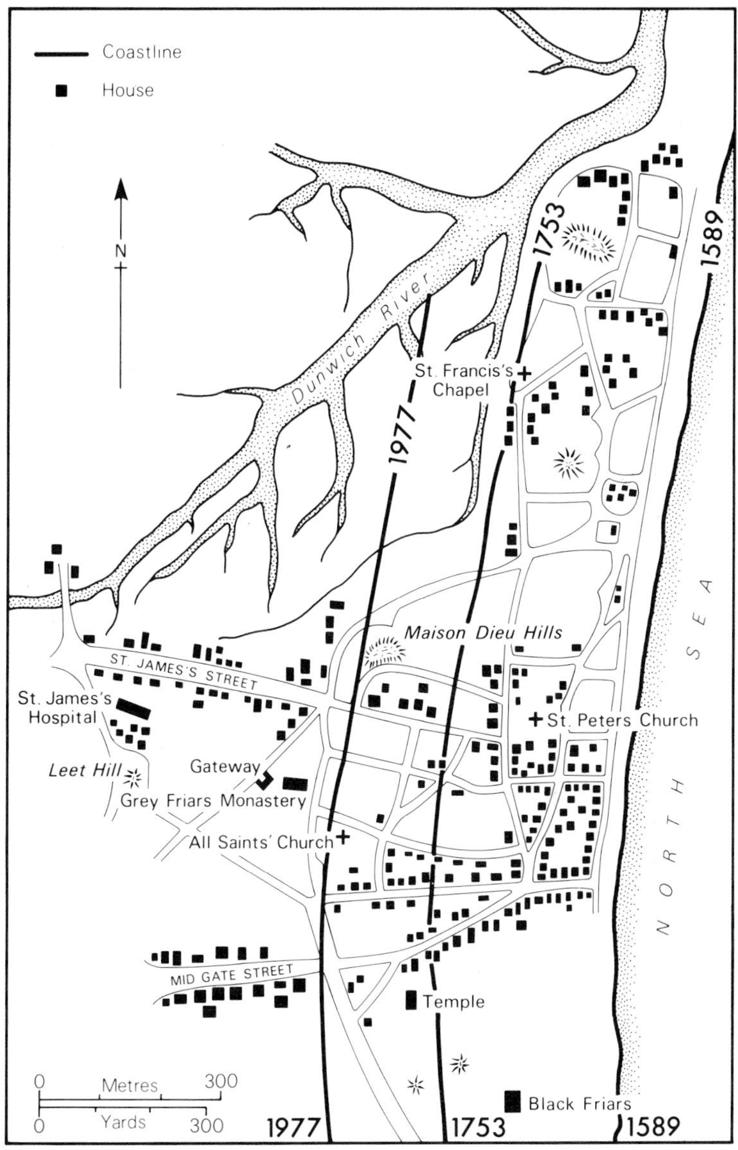

The retreat of the cliff top at Dunwich: stages since Elizabethan times

recent times. Before it finally disappeared it was recorded in water-colour by Turner (see page 150).

When Ralph Agas made his map of Dunwich in 1589 it was still a viable entity, though erosion was proceeding rapidly. A measure of this erosion can be seen on the map in the book Thomas Gardner

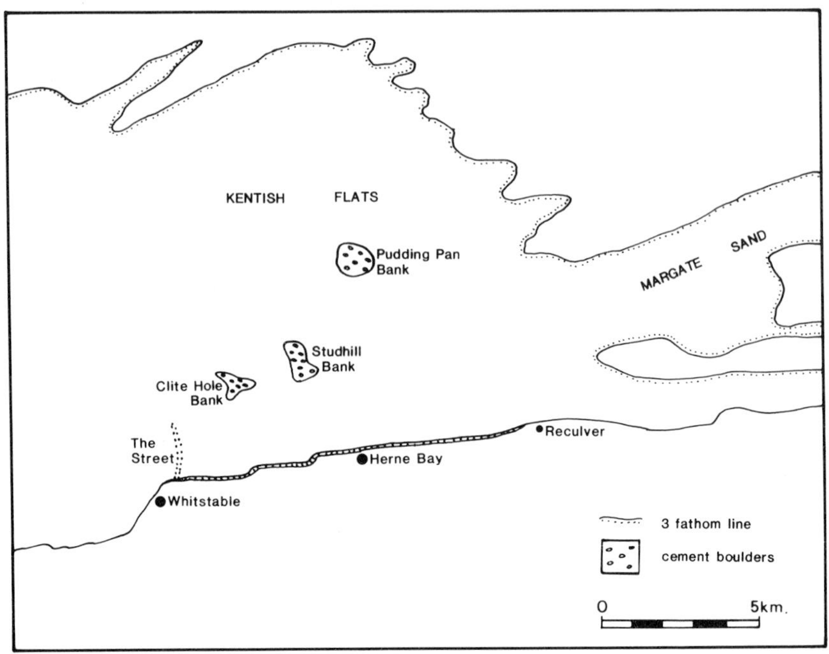

The Kentish Flats with the boulder banks once thought of as offshore islands

published in 1753 of his native town. Gardner reproduced the Agas map and on it added the coastline of his day. Between the two dates the soft clay and sandy cliff had retreated almost 244m (800ft), equivalent to an average of 1.4m (4ft 9½in) a year. Since 1753 erosion has continued, though apparently at a reduced rate of about 0.7m (2ft 6in) a year. This, however, has been sufficient to remove the greater part of the town which now, deprived of its borough status, is a mere shadow of its former glory. Sandy sunken lanes ending on the cliff top now mark the lines of the original streets which have so far survived the onslaught of the sea, and the occasional gravestone from the cemetery of All Saints comes to light amidst the thicket and scrub covering parts of the now deserted cliff top. With this type of erosion once proud buildings are totally consumed by the sea, so that it would be useless for the underwater archaeologist to search for anything substantial.

In recent years marine archaeologists have recovered many treasures of the past. What is remarkable is the way in which their ill-equipped predecessors often turned up finds whose significance is only now being fully realised. One productive area lies off the north Kent coast. Thomas Pownall, writing as early as 1777, noted that many of the fishermen's cottages strung out along this coast had samples of red earthenware of Roman date. Enquiry revealed that they nearly all came from the Pudding Pan Bank about 6km (4 miles) offshore, which at low water was covered by only about 2m (7ft) of water. With the pottery came considerable quantities of 'cement stone' septaria from the London Clay beds outcropping on the sea bed of the Kentish Flats. The red Samian ware was common enough in Roman Britain, most of it made at Lezoux in Gaul. But its association with the cement stones really attracted Pownall's attention, indicating the remains of a Roman building. He then went on to argue that here, now submerged beneath the waters of the outer Thames Estuary, was a Roman pottery manufactory which was subsequently destroyed by the rising sea level of later centuries. Today this idea seems fanciful, though in the eighteenth century many were willing to believe that a whole vast province of Roman Britain had disappeared under the waters of the southern North Sea. The speculation was given credence by the fact that considerable erosion of the cliffs was taking place along the coast and the ridge of gravel running out from the shore at Whitstable, and long known as 'The Street', pointed to the submergence of some man-made feature.

In spite of this 'evidence' put forward by Thomas Pownall, the conjecture that the Roman coastline lay at least 6km (4 miles) north of the present one is no longer tenable. The considerable quantities of Roman Samian ware dredged from the sea bed, mainly bowls with handles, point rather to a Roman galley bound for London being wrecked on the submerged shoal of the Pudding Pan. Therefore, although of great interest to the archaeologist and antiquary, the remains do not tell us anything about the position of the coastline of the time or any subsequent history of drowning.

Much the same argument can be used to dismiss the often made and colourful suggestion that the Goodwin Sands were once the core of a vast estate called Loomea lying off Deal. It was owned by Earl Godwin and consisted, so the legend relates, of thousands of acres of 'goodlie pasture'. Disaster came in a terrible flood of 1099 when 'all the lands were drowned and lost for ever'. The lost land idea persisted over the centuries and seemed to have been revived and strengthened in the nineteenth century when Trinity House engineers started to put down boreholes through the sands in the search for a firm foundation for their navigational beacons. In one borehole they found a bed of clay at a depth of 4.5m (15ft) below the surface; this was immediately seized upon as evidence to support the Loomea legend. Another boring in 1849, however, passed through 24m (78ft) of sea-sand before reaching the solid chalk base on which the Goodwins rest and this effectively destroyed the whole concept of a submerged estate.

But though it is easy to dismiss the whole idea as being imaginary, the date of the flood, given as 1099, is of interest in that it marks the beginning of a whole series of disastrous storms which affected the English coastline from the twelfth century onwards. Prior to that time it is possible that the top of the Goodwin Sands was raised above high-water level – rather like the Scroby Sands off Yarmouth today – and carried some fishermen's huts during the summer months. This temporary occupation could have been expanded in the accounts to become permanent habitation, so that when the sands were overwhelmed, it represented a major loss of land and settlement, hence the tradition of the lost estate.

References

Ashbee, P. *Ancient Scilly* (David & Charles, 1974)
Doble, G. H. *The Saints of Cornwall*, part 4 (Chatham, Parrett & Neaves, 1965)
Gardner, T. *A history of Dunwich* (1753)
Gray, T. *The Buried City of Kenfig* (1909)
Hamilton, H. (ed). *The counties of Moray and Nairn: The Third Statistical Account of Scotland* (Collins, 1965)
North, F. J. *Sunken Cities* (University of Wales, 1957)
Sheppard, T. *The Lost Towns of the Yorkshire Coast* (Brown, 1912)
Smith, R. A. 'The wreck on Pudding Pan Rock, Herne Bay, Kent', *Proceedings Society of Antiquities*, 21 (1907) pp 268–92
Steers, J. A. *The Sea Coast* (Collins, 1952)

3 New Lands

The dramatic events which often accompany coast erosion give the impression that Britain is wasting away under the relentless attack of the sea. The contribution made by the sea to the outbuilding of the land margin, especially through the deposition of sand and silt, is less obvious. On balance it seems probable that there is a net gain of land, especially where man-made reclamation works speed up the natural process. Around the margin of the Wash, in the Holbeach area for example, piecemeal enclosure has extended the land frontier by as much as 5km (3 miles) since the early seventeenth century. The extensive fertile acres of Romney Marsh in Kent were once a brackish-water swamp, liable to flooding by every high tide and therefore useless except for fishing. Now with protective sea walls along its vulnerable sections it forms one of the richest agricultural areas of the country. The same is true of the margins of the Ribble Estuary where huge embankments have transformed what were natural saltings into rich arable fields.

Compared with Holland, reclamation in Britain has been on a modest scale. Natural conditions do not allow the Wash or Morecambe Bay to be wholly reclaimed in one operation such as happened in the Zuider Zee. In the Wash, for example, the sea bed descends to more than 37m (120ft) below the sea surface in a central trench known as Lynn Well, and it would clearly be impossible to build a huge barrage across such a deep. In any case much of the reclaimed bed of the sea would be no more than sterile sand and therefore useless for agricultural purposes. Not that this deterred Victorian engineers or speculators who, in 1846, obtained Parliamentary powers to reclaim 12,140ha (30,000 acres) of the south-east corner of the Wash by building huge containing embankments out into the bay. Sir John Rennie, perhaps the most famous marine engineer at that time, was called in to prepare the scheme. Capital was no problem as Victorian

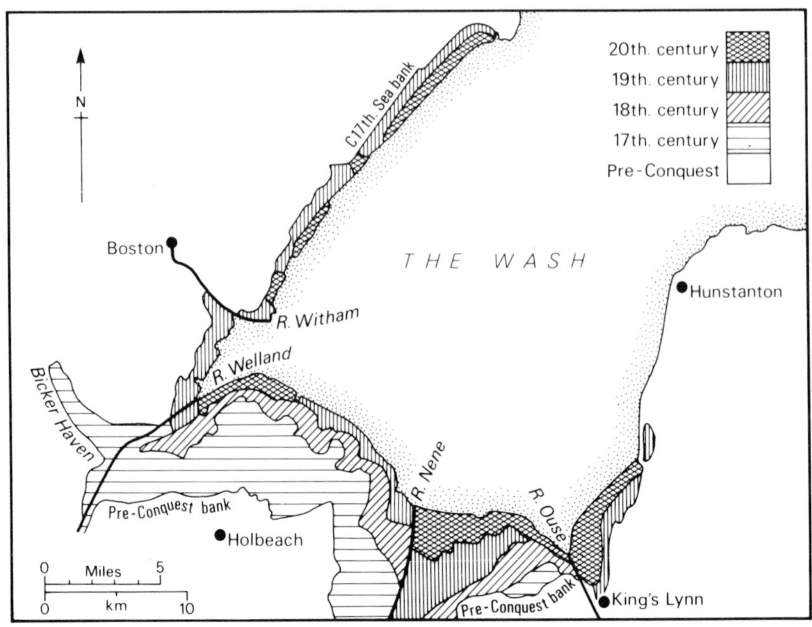

The Wash: stages in the gradual extension of the land frontier

speculators were only too willing to invest in such a grand project, especially one designed by the respected Rennie. They were however sadly misled and disappointed for by 1876, when an amending bill was presented to Parliament, £325,000 had been spent but only 728ha (1,800 acres) reclaimed, half of which was natural salting. The rest was barren sand flats and therefore of no economic value. With such little return the Norfolk Estuary Company soon ran out of funds, leaving virtually nothing to show for thirty years of endeavour.

Since this abortive attempt to win land from the sea, reclamation in the Wash has reverted to the time-honoured method of enclosing the margin of the bay strip by strip. The saltmarsh must be 'ripe' for enclosure with a thickness of about 0.6m (2ft) of silt overlying the sea sand. The natural process of accretion, with vegetation playing a key role, has to be artificially speeded up by cutting trenches or 'grips' across the marsh parallel to the shore. Huge earthen embankments are then thrown out into the saltings with their vulnerable sections faced with stone to withstand wave attack. Once an area is sealed off in this way it is drained and the salt gradually removed either by natural leaching or by liberal dressings of gypsum, so that within a few years the former salt marsh is converted into a man-made pasture. Perhaps after about seven years the land can be ploughed and used for arable crops, which give a much better economic return for capital outlay. Strip reclamation by this method has been going on around the Wash shores for centuries and still takes place once land is ripe for inning. The head of the bay between the Welland and Ouse rivers, including the estuary of the Nene, has seen the greatest strip of land added in the past 350 years.

Canalisation of the lower courses of the rivers to aid drainage of the Fens has contributed greatly in making land available for reclamation, and altogether it has been estimated that some 48,562ha (120,000 acres) have been added through the successive reclamation schemes. In the past decade a large enclosure of 243ha (600 acres) has been made in the area of the Wingland marshes between the Nene and Ouse river mouths. A further large area is at present being taken in at Freiston north of the mouth of the river Witham and further schemes will come into operation as soon as the saltings have acquired the necessary thickness of silt.

Apart from reclaimed land for agricultural purposes the Wash seems likely to be used in the future for water storage, involving the building of huge circular containers on the sand flats to act as fresh-water reservoirs. Preliminary work has already led to the construction of an artificial island out in the Wash to see whether such a structure is able to withstand battering by waves. Much will be learnt from this experiment that will be of value for future land-reclamation schemes.

The history of reclamation around the Wash is reflected in the settlement pattern of the area between the mouths of the Welland and Nene rivers, where a number of parishes have been elongated as the coastline has pushed forward over the centuries. One of the parishes, Holbeach, contains no less than 9,173ha (22,666 acres) and is 27km (17 miles) long, surely one of the biggest in the country. A detailed study of this area, known as the wapentake of Elloe, has been made by H. E. Hallam. He has shown that each parish contains a mother village where there was a nucleus of settlement as early as Saxon times, but in addition there are later hamlets founded on new lands won from the sea in succeeding centuries. This pushing forward of the frontier of colonisation is typical of many of our marshland areas once adequate sea walls have been built and drainage works established. A pre-Conquest sea bank, long known as the Roman Bank but almost certainly of later date, meant that the mother villages of Holbeach, Moulton, Whaplode, Fleet, Gedney, Lutton and Tydd St Mary were able to establish a number of daughter hamlets by the time of the

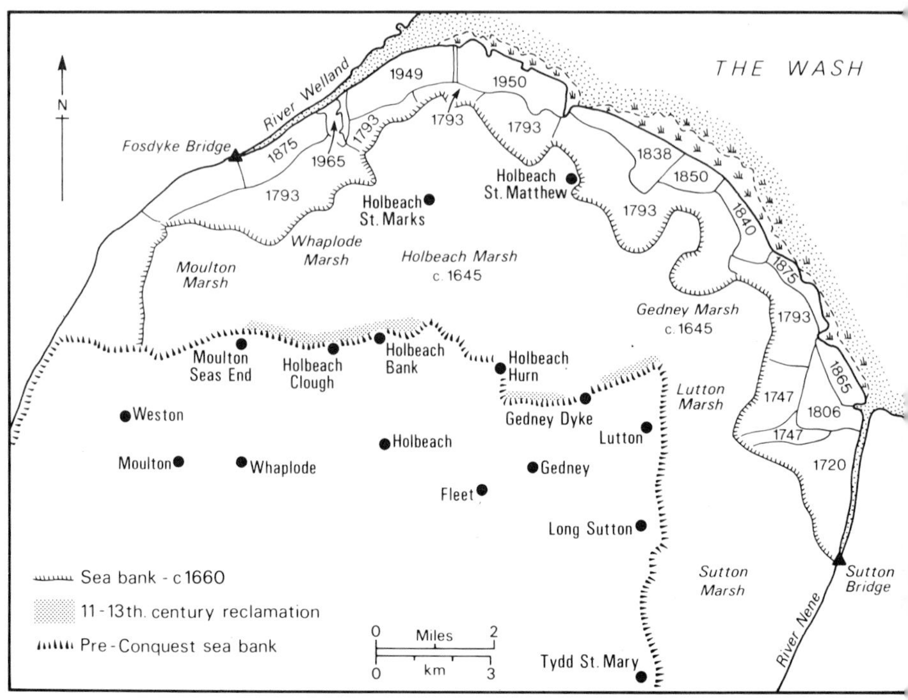

Between the Welland and Nene rivers: stages in the reclamation of the Fens

Domesday Survey. Most were sited on or close to the sea bank, with their settlers farming the new lands and extracting salt. Holbeach Bank, Holbeach Hurn, Gedney Dyke and Long Sutton came into being in this way. Some of the new land was given to inland abbeys like Thorney or Crowland, who were responsible for building fine twelfth-century churches like that at Whaplode. A document of 1220 shows that a further sea wall outside the main Roman Bank had been built at Gedney by that date, all part of the on-going process of reclamation. Gedney Dyke most probably began life as a salter's hamlet and extensive low mounds, the 'waste' of the former salterns, are still to be seen in the present landscape. In the parish of Moulton further new lands appear in the latter half of the thirteenth century with names like Westneuland, Crosneuland, Northneuland, Litilneuland and even New Neuland. Each new enclosure was carefully subdivided and farmed by a large number of tenants.

A stream meanders into the Torridge estuary at Instow. The shipbuilding town of Appledore may be seen on the opposite shore (*Anthony J. Lambert*)

Expanding population encouraged the search for and development of rich arable lands in later medieval times so that by about 1660, when a major drainage scheme for the Fenland was promoted, large areas of Holbeach Marsh, Gedney Marsh and Sutton Marsh had already been reclaimed from the sea. Further strips were added in the eighteenth and nineteenth centuries as more and more of the saltings were enclosed on a piecemeal basis. The straightening of the lower part of the Nene also made further land available, and converted what had been a bell-mouth shaped estuary into a narrow river-mouth exit. After further large enclosure in Victorian times, the saltings outside the sea bank were allowed to mature for a period of about seventy-five years, but since World War II further large strips have been enclosed and there are prospects for even more reclamation in the near future. Nature cannot be unduly rushed, but the steady, unspectacular movement forward of the coastline which has been taking place over the past thousand years seems likely to continue.

Another area which has seen large-scale natural and artificial reclamation is Romney Marsh. At the time the Romans invaded north-east Kent in AD 43, almost certainly the great shingle foreland of Dungeness did not exist nor was there a Romney Marsh on its inner side. In their place there was a shallow bay backed by a line of cliffs which ran in a gentle curve from near Fairlight in the south-west to Hythe in the north-east. Within the bay there were sandbanks which were not covered at high water, and these provided dry points for early settlement. The predecessors of places like New Romney, Lydd and Dymchurch were in existence in Roman times, for pottery fragments dating from the second and third centuries have been found, as well as evidence of Roman saltworks. Between these island sites and the cliff-line of the mainland there was a shallow flat, covered at spring tides, but with navigable channels which allowed boats to reach the Roman fort of *Portus Lemanis* (now Stutfall Castle) near Hythe, and possibly as far inland as Appledore. Not surprisingly no evidence of settlement has been found in this wetland of sand-flats and marshes.

The change from this early watery landscape to the present green fields of Romney Marsh took place over several centuries. A general lowering of the sea level from about the eighth century onwards meant that there was land fit for settlement and farming. We know from

The spit running northwards at the entrance to the harbour at Christchurch, Dorset

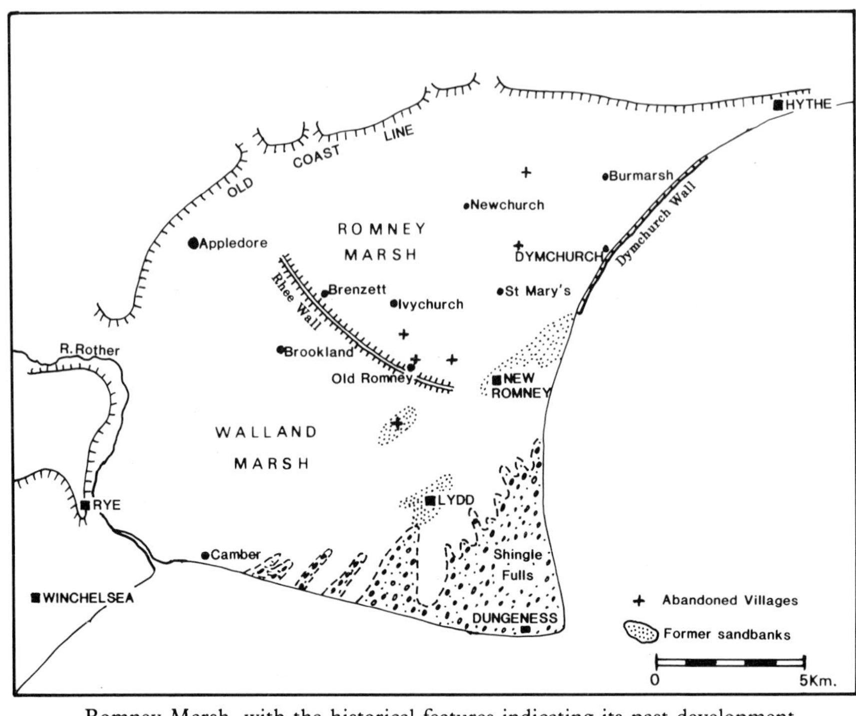

Romney Marsh, with the historical features indicating its past development

documents that parts of the marsh around Burmarsh in the north-east corner were reclaimed as early as AD 850. By the time of the Domesday Survey in the late eleventh century further large tracts had been enclosed, largely through the efforts of religious houses like Christ Church and St Augustine's Abbey in Canterbury. Villages like Newchurch and Ivychurch were also founded and these too point to religious colonisation. Between 1162 and 1170 a large area of Fairfield parish, still known as Becket's Innings (after the Archbishop of Canterbury) was taken in. Thomas Becket's successor, Archbishop Baldwin, also reclaimed a large area of land around Brenzett and Brookland between 1184 and 1190 by establishing a network of straight drainage ditches which are still to be seen in the present landscape. By the thirteenth century nearly all the land in Romney Marsh was in the hands of the Church. Other religious houses active in reclamation included Robertsbridge and Battle Abbeys.

Occasional storms still led to flooding, and in 1287 the river Rother changed its outlet from near New Romney to its present mouth south of Rye. The old bed of the river forming a great loop across Walland

Marsh gradually silted up, and was finally reclaimed by the Guldeford family in the fifteenth and sixteenth centuries. (The same family was also responsible for enclosing a large area near East Guldeford in 1562.) The 1287 storm made it clear that no reclamation work was likely to be successful unless accompanied by protective sea banks sufficiently high to prevent overtopping by the highest tides. Help both on this and on drainage works to keep the land free from surface water was sought from Dutch engineers, and names like Watering (a Flemish name for a drainage district) and Sperringbrooke (reedy hollow) begin to appear. Even the Rhee Wall, a great thirteenth-century engineering project designed to carry water from the upland fringe right across the Marsh to flush out the rapidly silting New Romney harbour, could be Dutch in origin, for the name in Flemish means boundary. The line of this straight watercourse with its central hollow and raised banks can still be traced, and in part is followed by the B class road across the Marsh. The most substantial of the sea walls the Dutch built to keep out the high tides ran north-eastwards from Dymchurch and, because of its importance to the whole Marsh, has been rebuilt several times, the last after the 1953 storm-surge. Hopefully the fertile acres of Romney Marsh, now carrying arable and market gardening crops as well as providing the traditional sheep pastures, are safe from future inundation and will remain as a permanent feature of the map of south-east England.

For north-west England there is a different time scale of reclamation with Victorian enterprise and expertise well displayed in the new lands bordering the south side of the Ribble Estuary from Southport as far as the outskirts of Preston. Man has played a dual role here, for not only has he built sea banks to keep the tide at bay, he has also kept the Ribble in a straight-jacket which has aided accretion in the estuary. Although the Ribble training-wall scheme was begun near Preston in the 1850s, the major extension to the works in the lower part of the estuary occurred later. This ultimately had a marked effect on siltation so that between 1918 and 1948 the rate of accretion increased by as much as 50 per cent. As more silt was laid down to cover the formerly bare sand-flats, the salt-loving vegetation was able to colonise more and more of the estuary margins and thus pave the way for further extensive reclamation projects.

The plant succession of the sea saltings has been studied by W. G. Berry. Just below the high-water mark of the neap tide, filamentous algae such as *Enteromorpha* and *Rhizoclonium* are the only forms

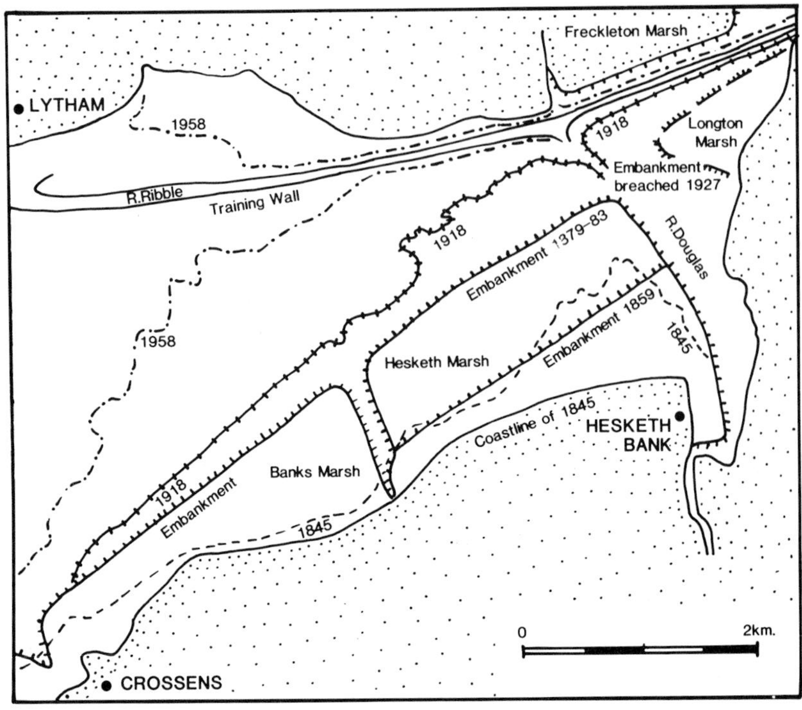

The reclamation of the marshes bordering the river Ribble (*after Berry*)

which can survive long periods of submersion in salt water. Where they cover the mud surface they are able to build up its level by about 8cm (3in), not a great amount but sufficient for other plants like the marsh samphire (*Salicornia*) to take root. These help with the accretion to some extent, but it is only with the colonisation of rice grass (*Spartina*) that mud is filtered out of the rising water of the tide. *Spartina* was artificially introduced into the Ribble Estuary in 1936 as part of a planned planting policy; so successful was the experiment that in a matter of twenty years it had become completely dominant and covered almost half the total area of the lower marsh. As the level of the marsh was raised so the sea manna grass (*Puccinellia*) was able to take hold, and it is this plant more than any other which gives the Ribble marshes their distinctive character. Around the high-water mark it becomes a continuous sward which provides pasture for grazing animals. As the saltings belong to the Duchy of Lancaster and are a valuable asset, their extension during the past century has been carefully mapped. Berry has shown how they have crept out into the estuary so that today they extend almost to the training walls lining the Ribble. Their greatest advance seems to have taken place since the building of the river walls, though the exact relationship is not clear.

Although some of the earliest innings were in the parishes of

The saltings (as yet untamed) bordering the Ribble Estuary, and the huge sea bank which protects the reclaimed lands behind

Penwortham and Freckleton, the largest and most successful of the nineteenth-century schemes were further seaward along the southern shore close to Hesketh where a large area of salting was 'captured' from the sea in 1859 by building a 5km (3 mile) long embankment. Success follows success and a further extension of the saltings, no doubt aided by the presence of the new sea bank, made another strip ripe for reclamation. The new area, much larger than the first, became Hesketh Marsh and was enclosed by 1883. Much of the drive for land reclamation came from the Hesketh family of Rufford who benefited considerably from their efforts; lower down the estuary nearer Southport this incentive seems to have been lacking, but with the completion of Hesketh Marsh a straightening of the coastline was inevitable. This took the form of another large enclosure of over 4,047ha (10,000 acres) with the building of an embankment between 1890 and 1895. The new area, forming the Banks and Bonny Banks Marshes, provided first-class arable land and, with a 9m (28½ft) high embankment to protect it, is still producing cereal and root crops almost a hundred years later.

Not so fortunate has been the history of enclosure of Longton Marsh farther up the estuary beyond the gap formed by the river Douglas. The building of a sea bank here began in 1898 but with only a limited amount of capital available the work was skimped, the bank top being raised to only 7m (24ft) above mean-tide level. The inevitable happened in March 1907 when a very high tide led to overtopping and breaching in several places. Repairs were put in hand and the gaps once more sealed, but no improvement was made to the height of the bank as a whole. A further exceptionally high tide in October 1927 did even more damage, and this time there was no reprieve. The marsh was abandoned to the sea and the former reclaimed land quickly returned to a natural salting, and this is how it remains today.

While reclamation for agricultural purposes provides a valuable addition to the ever dwindling reserve of first-class farm land and partly compensates for land lost through erosion by the sea, in money terms the most valuable reclamations are those undertaken in urban areas. A number of our coastal towns have benefited by extending their frontage seaward; Southport in particular, since blossoming into a planned resort town in the 1820s, has taken advantage of new land added to the coastline. An early map of the area dated 1736 shows that at that time there was an extensive belt of sand dunes along the shore fringed by a salt marsh. This 'New Marsh' became the site of the main street of the town, Lord Street, when development began about 1824; the sand-dune belt was also built over and today underlies the streets running inland from Lord Street. On the seaward side a further belt of sand dunes began to develop early in the nineteenth century and, as the town grew, they too were built over with hotels and boarding houses facing a wide promenade. With the sea continuing to retreat, more land became available for development in this century. Prince's Park, a marine lake, pleasure grounds and a pier have now been added to the growing resort, while to the north near Crossens other reclaimed land has been used for a golf course. So much has been added by reclamation in the past 150 years that it is now difficult to appreciate how much Southport owes to its good fortune in being developed on an accretive coastline.

Although Southport is perhaps the best example of urban development on land formerly covered by the sea, the pattern has been repeated elsewhere on a more limited scale. Industrial sites near the water's edge often lie on reclaimed land. In the Tees Estuary, part of the area known as Seal Sands has been embanked and filled with power-station ash and other man-made debris so that today it forms an impressive industrial site. The Welsh side of the Dee Estuary has also seen reclamation for industrial purposes in the area from Flint to Point of Air. The recent development of the Brighton Marina where, in addition to a harbour, land has been artificially added to house the

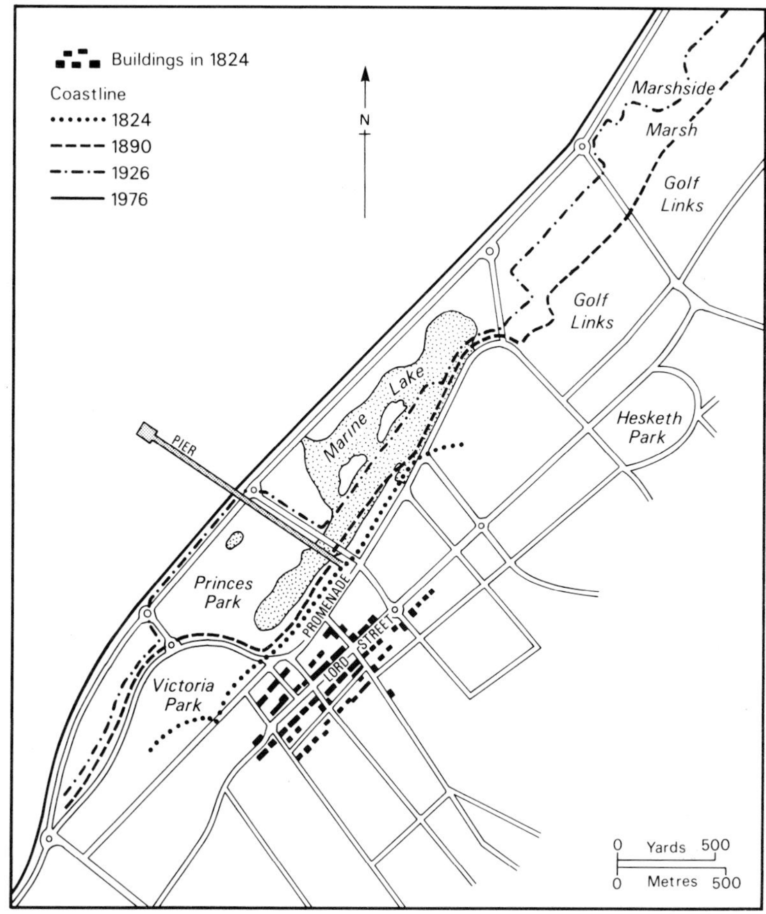

Southport and the stages in its growth since the early nineteenth century

ancillary services necessary for such a vast new complex, is an example of a leisure activity which has benefited from taking 'land' from the sea.

Wrestling with nature in this way has always been an entrepreneurial dream. In north Wales one man, William Madocks, can claim to have altered the natural coastline by his own single-handed efforts and to have left behind as his memorial a large area of reclaimed land at the mouth of the Glaslyn Estuary as well as the miniature town of Tremadog. Madocks was a member of parliament for Boston in Lincolnshire and probably had seen reclamation in action in the Fenlands. From an early age he had a vision, perhaps somewhat tinged with romanticism, of turning the bare tide-covered flats of the Glaslyn

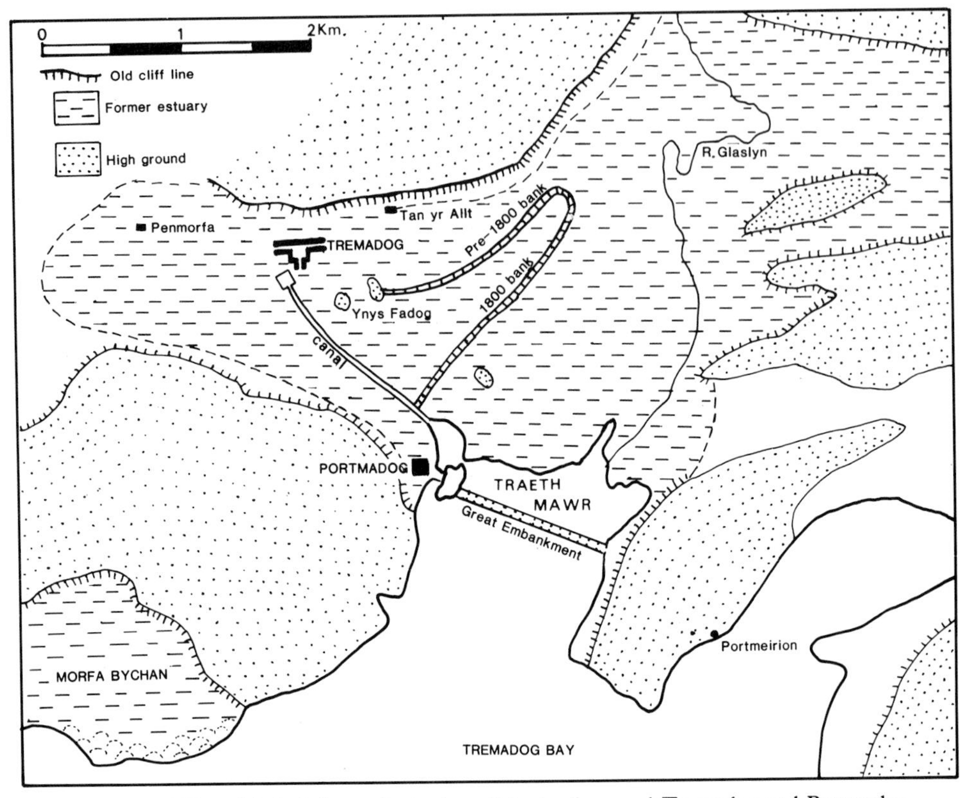

William Madocks' transformation of the land around Tremadog and Portmadog

Estuary into a profitable pastureland and granary for the local people whose standard of living was little above subsistence level. The natural setting of the area in itself was magnificent, with the penetrating arms of Traeth Mawr and Traeth Bach running back into the Snowdonian foothills. It was the larger of the two inlets, Traeth Mawr, that Madocks sought to reclaim. His opportunity came in 1798 when he was able to purchase the small farm and surrounding lands of Penmorfa where some reclamation had already been attempted on a piecemeal basis. Madocks' plan was on an altogether larger scale and involved the complete sealing off of the seaward end of the Glaslyn by constructing a huge embankment, 1.6km (1 mile) long, and diverting the river itself through an artificial channel cut in solid rock at the western end.

To further his purpose, Madocks brought in the engineer James Creasey from Lincolnshire, who already had experience of drainage and reclamation works in the Fens. A trial earthen bank was built in

1800, but it was not until 1808 that work began on the more substantial Great Embankment, and after three years of effort the gap was finally sealed in July 1811. Although the storms of the succeeding winter did breach the embankment, the necessary repairs were made and so the Glaslyn was now under Madocks' control. Unhappily the cost of the venture and especially the unexpected cost of repairs absorbed nearly all his capital. He was left virtually bankrupt and thus never really able to exploit the gains made in sealing off such a huge area of land from the sea. For the reclaimed land to be fully effective it needed much better drainage than Madocks could now afford and so most of it was left in permanent pasture, useful in summer but tending to be waterlogged in winter. Arable land was restricted, and this is still the pattern almost two hundred years later.

It would be wrong to belittle the achievement of Madocks; for not only did he reshape the map of this corner of north Wales, he was responsible also for founding his own town of Tremadog and played a major role in the development of nearby Portmadog. Shortly after arriving in the area in 1798 Madocks purchased a cottage which he later extended and this became his home – Tan yr Allt. Close by he laid out his town of Tremadog on reclaimed land. A T-shaped plan was adopted with the top of the T forming part of the main road which ran through to Port Dinllaen from whence one could embark for Ireland, hence the name Dublin Street. It was on this turnpike road that Madocks built his coaching inn, town hall and market house which looked onto the market place, with the houses and shops of the town arranged in neat terraces around. Running southwards lay London Street, the present road to Portmadog, which did not then exist. On the southern outskirts of the town a church and chapel were built, the whole making a compact but extremely simple layout. Most of the layout has survived to the present time as an outstanding example of early nineteenth-century town planning. Commerce and trade were vital, as Madocks realised, and so he built a water-powered woollen mill, a fulling mill and a corn mill. To improve communication there was also a canal link to the coast at Portmadog. The line of this is still traceable through the fields, though the basin at its head where goods were loaded and unloaded, and where Madocks kept a boat to entertain his guests, has now been filled in.

The building of the Great Embankment and the diversion of the Glaslyn through an artificial exit led to the creation of a scoured-out harbour, and in 1824 this became Portmadog. Although Madocks died

William Madocks' Great Embankment across the Glaslyn Estuary at Portmadog. It is now used by the narrow-gauge Ffestiniog Railway

before the port and town were fully developed, based on a growing slate-export trade in the mid-nineteenth century, without his initial efforts nothing would have happened. The Great Embankment was used as early as 1836 by the narrow-gauge Ffestiniog Railway to bring down slate from the inland hills to be shipped from Portmadog. This source of wealth enabled Portmadog to grow much more rapidly, though with less planning, than its near-neighbour Tremadog. Its relatively greater growth was accentuated when the main-line railway reached this corner of Wales in 1865 and ran through Portmadog rather than taking the inland route. Today the slate trade is finished and Portmadog relies on tourism, with holiday flatlets built on its former slate quays and yachtsmen tying up along the wharves where slate was once shipped in great quantities. The slate railway has survived though it, too, is completely geared to the holiday industry, each summer carrying thousands of visitors along the Great Embankment before starting the climb into the hills to Blaenau Ffestiniog.

References

Bailey, F. A. *A History of Southport* (Downie, 1955)

Barron, J. *A history of the Ribble Navigation from Preston to the Sea* (Preston Corporation, 1938)

Beazley, E. *Madocks and the Wonder of Wales* (Faber & Faber, 1967)

Berry, W. G. 'Salt Marsh development in the Ribble Estuary', *Liverpool Essays in Geography*, pp 121–35 (Methuen, 1967)

Hallam, H. E. *Settlement and Society: Study of Early Agrarian History of South Lincolnshire* (Cambridge University Press, 1965)

Millward, R. and Robinson, A. *South East England – The Channel Coastlands* (Macmillan, 1974)

Norfolk Naturalists' Trust, *Nature in Norfolk* (Jarrold, 1977)

Wheeler, W. H. *A history of the Fens of South Lincolnshire* (Newcombe, 1897)

4 Coastal Curiosities

One of the attractions of coastal scenery, not only in Britain but throughout the world, is that it exhibits unexpected, unusual and often inexplicable forms. The great dynamic forces unleashed by the sea can carve rocks into fantastic shapes and create features which lend themselves to legend and myth. Man, too, seems to have gone out of his way to add to the diversity of the coastal scene, sometimes furthering nature's workmanship but often simply creating follies for his own amusement. Names associated with many coastal features are inviting in themselves – Lot's Wife, Devil's Frying Pan or Three Chimneys inevitably rivet the attention, excite the imagination and provide a breeding ground for local folklore.

The exposed cliffs of our western seaboard are especially rich in features which have been variously labelled as curios, wonders or simply works of nature. Many have been looked upon as the work of the Devil and were to be avoided lest Satan should be lurking there. Fanciful stories surrounded them, and as soon as they appeared in the guide books were eagerly lapped up by Victorian tourists. Huntsman's Leap in South Pembrokeshire is a case in point. The 'leap' is a narrow cleft cut into the 60m (200ft) limestone cliffs of the Castlemartin Peninsula and was formed as the sea exploited rocks which had been shattered by faulting. The name is supposed to have arisen after a huntsman in the chase across the bare featureless plateau-top suddenly came upon the wide gash and had no alternative but to jump it, which he did successfully. One story relates that when he returned to the scene of his triumph he was so astounded by his feat that he slipped to his death in the sea below. Another version is that when he arrived home he took fright at his achievement and died. The 'leap' is in fact unleapable, as is the similarly named feature cut in the deep-red Old Red Sandstone rocks near the village of St Brides, also in Dyfed.

Repetition of names for broadly similar features is of common

The 'Parson' off the Devon coast, south of Dawlish, where the red sandstone beds have acquired a white collar of guano

occurrence. Isolated columns or stacks have a number of names depending on their appearance, the most common being Lot's Wife with obvious biblical association. One of the chalk stacks which make up the Needles at the western end of the Isle of Wight was so named, but unfortunately the sea claimed it during the last century. Other 'Lots' exist on the wild Galloway shore south of Dumfries. In this same area of south-west Scotland there is the Barrel of Beef stack near the entrance to Loch Ryan – a prominent landmark for ferry passengers from Ireland bound for Stranraer. Perhaps the most descriptive designation is that of the Parson and Clerk for a pair of red-sandstone stacks lying in front of the cliff face south of Dawlish in south Devon. After Brunel had opened this fine scenic stretch of his broad-gauge railway in the 1840s the stacks could be seen by every excursionist, and were quick to attract fulsome descriptions in the guide books of the time. Passengers were even advised to disembark at Dawlish station and then make their way to the promontory 2km (1½ miles) to the south. There they could obtain close-hand views of the Parson and check the comment that 'the sea seems to have little respect for the sanctity of his person' – a reference to the rapid erosion going on at the time. The Clerk was looked upon as a 'whimsical figure, his head silvered with guano and with bristles like a hedgehog, while his raiment was of many colours'.

For scenic grandeur the bay south of Duncansby Head in Caithness, with its succession of offshore stacks, is probably unrivalled. The reds, yellows and greens of the cliffs are repeated in the stacks which, on a fine day, have an enhanced beauty as they rise out of a deep ultramarine sea with a white ruff of foam around their base. But what gives the Duncansby stacks an edge over their rivals is their tapering shape, so that 'spires' seems the appropriate description. While the hard flagstone base of the cliffs is able to withstand wave attacks, the upper sandstone readily succumbs to weathering, hence the tapering shape. Seen in the crisp early morning light of a fine summer's day there is a harmony of colour shades which only nature seems able to conjure up. The interplay between the erosional efforts of the sea and the various rock types has led to such a rich variation of form that Duncansby Bay can lay claim to be one of the most exciting stretches of coastline in Britain.

In the same area there is the partly broken stack known as Thirle Door. The name, oddly enough for this corner of north-east Scotland, is of Anglo-Saxon origin (*thirl* meaning 'to pierce') and clearly refers to the hole in the centre of the stack. Eight hundred miles away on the Dorset coast is the better known Durdle Door which has the same Saxon derivation. The hole (or door) has been carved out of a tough

Duncansby Spires, Caithness

limestone ridge which lurches into the sea at the end of a short peninsula. Now attacked on three sides by the sea it is questionable how long the feature can survive in its present form, yet it must have retained its basic form for over a thousand years since it was named from its unusual shape. Clear proof of antiquity and unchanging shape is also provided by the isolated conglomerate stack of Thurlestone Rock which stands as a lonely sentinel in Bigbury Bay in south Devon. The name is once again taken from the pierced (thirled) stone which rises out of a low platform of upturned slates covered with slippery bladder wrack. At low tide it is possible to walk out to the stack and pass under its arch. It must have retained its holed shape for hundreds of years, certainly since it was first mentioned in a Saxon charter of AD 845 as a boundary mark. This permanence is remarkable in that the stack lies in the direct path of the raging storm-waves which sweep unimpeded into Bigbury Bay from the Atlantic when backed by the full force of a south-westerly gale.

The relentless pressure of the sea has given rise to another exotic feature of our western coasts – the blow-hole. In its usual form it consists of a large funnel-shaped head in the cliff top which leads down to a narrow chimney that connects with a sea-cave below. During heavy seas and at high tide waves sweep in and are then ejected with great force through the chimney as a water spout, often accompanied by a roar or bellow caused by the escape of compressed air. Not surprisingly the blow-hole and its activity has been looked upon as supernatural and the work of the Devil and many of the names associated with the feature bear this out. Near Flimston in the Castlemartin Peninsula, not far from the already mentioned Huntsman's Leap, is the Devil's Cauldron. From the flat downland top it is so hidden as to be passed by almost unnoticed, but by walking out onto the small projecting peninsula it is possible to peer down into the steep-sided hole to the sea below. The feature has been etched out as waves gradually consumed shattered beds of limestone coinciding with a fault system. On its western side the cauldron is in direct communication with the open sea through a narrow gash and there is also a natural arch to the south. It is possible, when the military authorities allow access (see page 217), to descend to sea level at the foot of the limestone cliff and see the cauldron entrance from below.

The Lizard Peninsula of south Cornwall is particularly rich in blow-holes because the sea has carved out the softer, shattered beds of parts of the peninsula, but has had less effect on the much tougher

Durdle Door, on the Dorset coast, is a pierced spine of resistant limestone beds

serpentinious rocks. Close to Cadgwith on the east coast there is the Devil's Frying Pan. A crater-like form when seen from above, there is a drop of almost 60m (200ft) to the surging and spitting waters in the cave below so that on a stormy winter's day the name is apt. Across on the western side of the Lizard is the much visited Kynance Cove with a whole range of coastal forms carved out of the dark serpentine rock. Between the obelisk-like rocks known as The Steeple and Asparagus Island, there is the narrow fissure called the Devil's Bellows which occasionally obliges with a violent water spout and an accompanying rumbling sound of thunder. The first Victorian travellers who visited the spot were encouraged to carry a letter and hold it over the mouth of another orifice, the Devil's Post Office, where the indraught of air would snatch it from their hands and carry it to the mystical recipient waiting below. If it did not quite reach the bottom before the 'blow' had begun again, it would be hurled skywards once more, though seldom returned to the sender. Yet another blow-hole occurs just east of the Lizard lighthouse and can be reached by following the coastal path. The circular chasm, known as the Lion's Den, came into being as a result of the collapse of a cave roof one night in February 1847.

The Bullers of Buchan is yet another collapsed cave feature in which the sea surges and boils, hence the name. It lies on the coast of Buchan in north-east Scotland about 3km (2 miles) north of Cruden Bay, and can be approached from the main Peterhead road. Dr Johnson on visiting the area insisted on being rowed into the Pot and spoke of the 60m (200ft) deep hole with some awe: he found difficulty however in explaining how the 'rock perpendicularly tubulated' came into being.

Some rocks, limestone for instance, have joints which are particularly susceptible to widening by the sea. Worm's Head – a detached portion of the Gower Peninsula which has often been likened to a partly submerged worm or sea monster – is one example. The 'head' is accessible for a few hours on either side of low water, the inner and outer sections linked by a natural arch of limestone, the Devil's Bridge, while on the north face of the 'worm' there is a very well known blow-hole which on stormy days booms and occasionally spouts.

At the other end of the kingdom in north-west Scotland, there is a narrow band of ancient limestone which ultimately reaches the north coast at Durness Associated with it is another of nature's impressive coastal forms, the Smoo Cave. Here at the head of a narrow inlet just east of the village a great chasm opens into the limestone wall, 37m (120ft) across and some 12m (40ft) high. It is possible to walk down steps and enter the sand-strewn floor of the sea-cave. Although Sir Walter Scott painted a somewhat exaggerated picture, the cave is nevertheless impressive, certainly when one stands against the back wall and looks out to sea. The name is almost certainly Norse and derived from *smuga* meaning 'cleft'. There are really three caves, for behind a rocky barrier is an inner rock passage with a deep pool which leads to the waterfall by which the Allt Smoo stream enters the cave from above. Potholers have explored beyond and have found a third cave with many stalagmites. The inner cave with the pool was first entered in 1833, and in the heyday of the Victorian traveller a local entrepreneur had visitors lifted over the barrier in a boat and then rowed into the inner cave, all for the cost of 10s. The complex of Smoo caves can hardly have been formed by the sea in their present rather protected position, so at some time in the distant past waves must have finally broken through the limestone wall of the cliff and entered an earlier-formed subterranean cave system etched out by rivers. All that was left for the sea to do was to add the finishing touches to the grand design.

Anyone in search of the unusual would do well to explore the coasts of north Devon and Cornwall on foot, especially the tracts well away from the main roads where there are cliff features found nowhere else in Britain. At Millook, a few miles south of Bude, the sea has cut a clean face across a tightly packed succession of sandstone and shales of the Culm Measures which have been compressed into a herring-bone or zigzag patterning. At Hartland Quay the same rock formations have been carved into fantastic shapes by the continuous pounding they receive from the Atlantic rollers. In the same area, for good measure, there are coastal waterfalls where modest streams tumble out of their over-large valleys onto the foreshore 18m (60ft) below. The most impressive is at Speke's Mill Mouth where the sharply folded and upturned beds of sandstone and shale form a tight downfold clearly seen in the cliff face close to the fall. Past pressures and earth movements have clearly played their part in the development of the Three Chimneys on the south Wales coast close to Tenby. Here three thick beds of sandstone have been turned vertically to run down the whole height of the cliff face. Further round the coast, in the west-facing St Bride's Bay, similar sandstone beds have been rolled over to reveal the smooth back of the Sleek Stone as it gently falls away into the sea.

In the archipelago of the Inner Hebrides, geological history has left an indelible imprint on the present coastal scenery. About 60 million years ago vast outpourings of lava from a number of volcanic centres in Mull, Skye and the Ardnamurchan Peninsula covered hundreds of square miles. Fairly rapid cooling led to contraction cracks and the creation of broadly hexagonal columns, and where these occur in the cliff face they form a wall of organ pipes which can run for many miles, as along the east coast of Skye. On the island of Staffa the sea has broken into the wall and etched out the well known Fingal's Cave. It was visited in 1829 by the young Mendelssohn, who later caught the atmosphere of the setting in the 'Hebridean' Overture. Much earlier the palisade wall must have been a well known sea-mark for the Norse seamen, who likened the basalt columns to their own stave houses built of vertical timbers. It was the great naturalist and traveller, Sir Joseph Banks (see also page 85), who first brought Staffa into prominence and that by sheer accident. On a journey to Iceland in 1772 his ship was blown off course and forced to seek the more sheltered waters of the Sound of Mull. When calmer weather came the ship was able to continue her voyage and passed close to the mysterious isle. The notes Sir Joseph made on the fantastic shaping of the basalt columns led Thomas Pennant to this lonely spot two years later on his famous tour of Scotland. Then followed a succession of visitors willing to risk the choppy seas in the hope of a brief landing at Fingal's Cave. Both Wordsworth and Scott made the pilgrimage, and have left us their impressions in poetry and prose.

The same lava beds on nearby Mull are also responsible for another geological curiosity, the fossil tree, 12m (40ft) high, found in the cliffs south of Rubha na h-Uamha in the west of the island. The tree-trunk was discovered by J. MacCulloch early in the nineteenth century and the event recorded in his *Description of the Western Islands of Scotland* published in 1819. The approach for any would-be observer is through the difficult boulder-strewn country known as the Wilderness, and arrival must be timed for low water. What you see is not the actual tree-trunk except for a little charred wood, but rather a cast infilling of bleached basalt – white trap – surrounded by the ordinary columnar basalt. Almost equally difficult of approach is another of Mull's coastal wonders, the Carsaig Arches. These lie on the south coast of the Ross of Mull and can only be seen after a 5km (3 mile) walk from the hamlet of Carsaig to reach Malcolm's Point where the lava cliffs are over 213m (700ft) high and, on a rocky platform at their base, an isolated stack is pierced by an arch. Beyond is the cauldron with its spire rising 37m (120ft) and pierced by a lancet 'window'. The columnar basalt adds a dramatic quality to the setting, with the castellated cliffs and spire-like columns hinting of human shaping. The whole scene, however, is the work of nature.

Volcanic activity has long ceased in this western seaboard region of Scotland, though when Dr Johnson made his visit to the Hebrides in 1775 he was convinced that Dun Caan on the island of Raasay was a volcanic cone which occasionally emitted puffs of smoke from vents (caves) on its southern flanks. After looking at the top of the 518m (1,700ft) flat-topped mountain he came away without seeing any emissions, but still remained convinced that here was a volcano. Part of the Dorset coast however did at one time offer some semblance of subterranean activity. In Ringstead Bay, between Weymouth and Lulworth Cove, the high cliffs are formed of a variable sequence including beds of bituminous earth and slaty shale with iron pyrites. After prolonged rainfall the beds are subject to spontaneous combustion producing dense clouds of acrid smoke from an underground fire, although the event is a very rare occurrence and the last time it was seen was in 1825. Then, after a particularly wet spell, Holworth

A contemporary print of the Great Chasm which opened up in the Undercliff west of Lyme Regis as a result of a major landslip in 1839

Cliff began to slide bodily down, carrying with it a fisherman's cottage and garden. Two years later the cottage, still upright and habitable, was 152m (500ft) lower. While the slow slide was in progress occasional puffs of smoke were seen rising from fissures in the unstable cliff face, and in the exaggerated writing of the period the event was described as a 'scene wasteful and wild as chaos, where stillness reigns and Great Nature dwells in aweful [*sic*] solitude'. The phenomenon of a smoking cliff soon attracted more than local attention and it was not long before visitors were probing the surface to find the source of the fire. On 15 May 1827, local fishermen dug into a cavern of hot combustible material and immediately the whole ground burst into flames. The fire continued throughout the summer of 1827 and for a short time visitors came to Weymouth Bay to see the miniature Vesuvius and were asked, somewhat hopefully, to compare the setting with the Bay of Naples. Gradually the flames and smoke subsided and since that time Holworth Cliff has not produced another spectacular display. The events of 1825–7 are sufficiently remembered for the current 1:25,000 OS map to feature 'Burning Cliff'.

Unstable cliffs are also a feature of the east Devon coast and it was in the section near Lyme Regis that one of the most spectacular coastal landslips of all time took place at Christmas 1839. Altogether about 8ha (20 acres) of the cliff top subsided and opened up a wide ravine, known as the Great Chasm, between what became known as Goat's Island and a new inland cliff. What was remarkable was the way in which Goat's Island remained perfectly horizontal so that afterwards cultivation and animal husbandry went on as before.

Goat's Island still exists though natural vegetation has made deep inroads into its cultivated fields during the past 140 years. The whole area in fact has returned to its wild state so that the thicket of trees, shrubs and ground vegetation is all-encroaching save along the solitary coastal path. Since 1955 the coastal strip has become a Nature Reserve and it is possible to enter it either at Lyme Regis or close to Seaton at its western end. It is worthwhile walking through the whole length of the reserve, though three hours should be allowed to complete the journey. The geology of the area explains the development of the landslip, for the permeable upper chalk and greensand beds allow water to pass through until they meet the underlying Gault Clay. This leads to weakening of the strata at the junction and ultimately brings about complete collapse such as happened in 1839.

Because the area has remained relatively undisturbed over the past 140 years, it provides a fascinating field laboratory for both naturalist and biologist. The ash wood in the Great Chasm is the only known example we have of natural development and succession on virgin soil, while the way in which hawthorn and more recently sycamore have taken over is quite alarming, and gives a realistic picture of recolonisation once man ceases to interfere. Because of the relative isolation of the area there are many uncommon and even rare shrubs and plants, including the spindle and wayfaring tree as well as orchids and rock roses. The path winds its way steadily through the jumbled terrain of disturbed chalk and is easy to follow except after heavy rain. Once off the track the hawthorn and sloe, together with their entanglements of bramble, honeysuckle, ivy and everlasting pea, make penetration virtually impossible. It is not surprising, therefore, that some 120 species of birds have been recorded in the reserve, though this number includes some sea-bird migrants.

Another example of past landslipping, though this time in much harder and older rocks, occurs in the southern part of the Isle of Man in the area known as The Chasms, where the 90m (300ft) cliffs are made

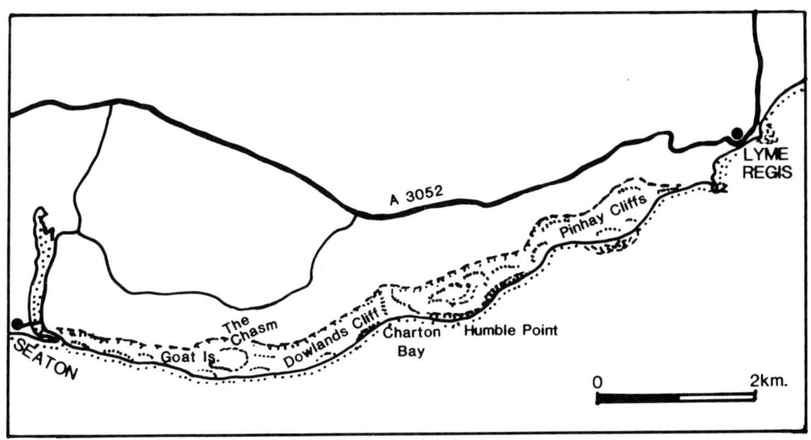

Landslip coastland between Seaton and Lyme Regis, now a protected area

up of hard flaggy grits overlying a bed of slates. In the distant past the grits have slipped forward over the slates and in doing so have opened a succession of fissures, often arranged at right angles, coinciding with the jointing of the strata. The fissures can drop right down to sea level, and those near the cliff face form narrow inlets of the sea. The deep gashes cover an area of several acres and, though access is unrestricted, care must be taken in following the tracks through the scrub of gorse bushes. When precisely The Chasms came into being is not known. Certainly they were here in prehistoric time when man selected a low platform nearby on which to build a stone circle. What seems most likely is that the joint planes were opened up during the extreme climatic conditions of the Ice Age when there would be much more water about than at present, and when alternate periods of thaw and freeze were taking place with great rapidity.

Compared with the majestic cliff coastlines of the upland west, the lowland coasts of south and east Britain provide far fewer examples of the unique and unusual. At Tetney in Lincolnshire, close to the Humber entrance and a little distance inland behind the protective sea wall, lies a succession of small circular ponds which have long been known locally as 'blow wells'. Some are quite small and even occur in the back gardens of houses, but the largest measures some 90m (300ft) across. In the eighteenth century they attracted Lincolnshire's most famous son, the naturalist Sir Joseph Banks. He found it difficult to find their true bed by sounding, hence the tradition arose that they were bottomless or even went right through to the antipodes. They certainly have steep sides which give the holes a cone-like shape, but their origin lies in the fact that rainfall falling on the inland chalk wolds seeps underground and is forced through to the surface of the marshland at places like Tetney under artesian pressure. The ponds never freeze over and, with their reedy margins, have become haunts of wild fowl. They seldom bubble or blow, though after a period of heavy rainfall the water pressure builds up considerably from below.

Not far from the Tetney 'blow wells' is another puzzling feature of this Lincolnshire coastland. Between the main coastal road and the sea bank running along the south Humber shore is an area of rolling ground, made up of low rounded hills and shallow hollows. Some of the farms there have the name 'fitties'. In spite of first appearances which might suggest the contrary, the landscape is basically man-made for this was an area of salt extraction in medieval times, 'fitties' meaning reclaimed salterns. The irregular mounds represent discarded mud debris from which the salt was extracted by evaporation and burning. There are concentrations of abandoned salterns north east of the villages of Tetney, Marsh Chapel, North Coates and Grainthorpe. The process came to an end early in the seventeenth century, but the fossilised landscape still tells the story. Another area of former salt-workings, this time dating back to Roman times, can be seen by the side of the main road linking Skegness with Boston near the village of Wainfleet St Peter.

In a similar lowland situation amidst the salt marshes of the Dengie Peninsula in Essex there is a succession of low ridges which rise perhaps 2.4m (8ft) above the general level of the green saltings. What makes the ridges remarkable is that they are formed almost entirely of shells, some whole but many in fragments. Cockle shells predominate but there is a fair sprinkling of oyster, whelk, mussel and gastropod contributing to the composition of the ridge. Although these shell ridges occur throughout the Dengie salt marshes the most accessible group lies near the ancient church of St Peter's-at-the-Wall at Bradwell. Beyond the church the path leads along the sea wall to Sales Point and here there is a shell ridge, the Cockle Spit, joined to the shore. Although almost covered at high tide, with waves breaking high up on its outer side, the feature seems stable, for it has remained basically with its present shape and in its present position since the storm-surge which caused the East Coast floods in 1953.

Oddities created by nature have caused greater excitement than those fashioned by man because of the difficulty in explaining their origin. For coastal curiosities where the hand of man is apparent, historical evidence can often be called in support. In the case of the Physgyll Cave on the lonely Galloway shore 5km (3 miles) south of Whithorn, what was once a natural cleft in the sea cliffs was turned into a hermit's cell or retreat. Tradition associates it with St Ninian who was active in this area as a missionary in the second quarter of the fifth century; but whether the association is real, or the cave only inhabited at a later date, there is no doubt of its Christian significance. Clear confirmation of this came in 1871 when an incised cross of early form was found cut in the rock face near the entrance. Subsequent examination and excavation revealed other crosses, so that the cave may have become the Mecca for pilgrims wishing to venerate St Ninian. All the crosses have now been removed from the cave walls in case of vandalism, but some are seen in the attractive tiny museum at Whithorn. The cave is still worth visiting for its own sake and its associations, and there is a pleasant walk down to the shore through bluebell woods alive with colour in early May.

Another cave with human associations, this time going back perhaps 10,000 years, occurs at Paviland in the Gower Peninsula. It was to this rather inaccessible spot on the shore that the archaeologist and geologist William Buckland came in 1823 and uncovered the remains of a skeleton covered with red ochre. Ever since, the find has been known as the Red Lady of Paviland, though later studies showed that the bones were those of a young man in his twenties who lived in the late Pleistocene and was given a ceremonial burial. The cave can be approached from the east at extreme low water, though care must be taken in climbing down from the headland.

A short distance east, nearer Port Eynon, lies yet another cleft in the limestone, but this one claims distinction because of the way in which it has been sealed off by a towering wall of masonry pierced by 'windows'. No one really knows the purpose of this eerie structure – the Culver Hole. Inside the thick wall there is a honeycomb of rectangular holes, but for what function? The name 'Culver' perhaps gives the best clue, being Anglo Saxon for pigeon, suggesting that this curious structure set into the cliff is most probably a pigeon loft like the columbarium of nearby Penrice Castle. Presumably it was built to provide food during the winter months, and could date from medieval times.

Considerable pains were taken by our ancestors to maintain a fresh food supply, especially of meat and fish during the winter months, and at Port Logan in Galloway we have a fishpool that is still functioning.

The pond is basically a natural feature – a cauldron – by the cliff edge about 1km (½ mile) west of Logan village. It has vertical sides festooned with ivy and mesembryanthemum with the hollowed-out pool at the bottom, and on its outer side is in contact with the sea through a grille which allows water to enter at high tide. The unique Logan fishpool began life in 1800 when it was decided to take advantage of the natural hollow and turn it into a fish larder for nearby Logan House. In its time it has been stocked with cod, pollack, coalfish, perch, wrasse and plaice. What was once the lord's private larder is now a tourist attraction where the visitor can see the fish (mainly large cod) being fed with morsels of limpet by the keeper, and even be invited to participate.

Churches are commonplace around our coasts, but some attract special attention because of unusual features or functions. This is true of the tall barn-like building at Peter's-at-the-Wall in the Dengie Peninsula of Essex. Built largely of material obtained from the ruins of the third-century Roman fort in which it is built – especially the distinctive red tiles set in the walls – it was later used as a barn until the 1920s when the historic significance of the building led to its restoration as a chapel. The site is looked upon as the centre from which Bishop Cedd began his mission to the Angles in AD 654. In keeping with the time, the bishop chose a lonely spot overlooking the saltings and the wide expanse of water of the Blackwater Estuary.

Early churches were often founded in these out of the way sites, especially those associated with the Celtic saints, a coastal location often arising simply because it was the point where the saint made his landfall after a sea journey. If it lay close to a life-giving spring which could also supply a baptismal well this was an added advantage. One of the most picturesquely situated is that of the chapel of St Govan at the south-east corner of the Castlemartin Peninsula in south Wales. The tiny fifteenth-century chapel we see today, wedged in a cleft in the almost continuous wall of limestone cliffs, is on a site of much older significance; for leading out of the main chapel is a rock-cut chamber which could easily be the original hermit's cell. A well, once fed by a spring that has now run dry, lies further down the cliff-face to complete the picture of what we imagine a Celtic saint's retreat to have been. Though this section of the coast has been taken over by the Ministry of Defence it is always possible to reach the chapel. Another

The Culver Hole, Gower, where man has made use of a natural fissure in the limestone cliff, to build what some have explained as a pigeon loft

similar building, this time dedicated to St Patrick, lies in ruins on the crest of a sandstone headland at Old Heysham on the shores of Morecambe Bay in Lancashire. Estimates vary as to its exact age, though a date about 800 is not impossible. At one time the chapel and some nearby rock-hewn graves – supposedly Norse – were under the care of a custodian, but tragically the site seems to have been abandoned and left to decay.

Of great antiquity and interest is the site at Richborough, a few miles to the north of Dover where, within the former Roman fort of *Rutupiae*, a huge concrete base, in the form of a cross, has long excited the imagination. It was once tunnelled under in the hope that it was put there as a weighty capstone over a hoard of buried treasure. It has also been claimed as the base of a Roman pharos akin to that at Dover (see page 137), this time to guide shipping through the shallow Wantsum Channel. But the most likely explanation is that it was the foundation for a gigantic triumphal arch built to honour Julius Agricola who was responsible for completing the conquest of Britain in the second part of the first century. As Richborough was the probable landing-place of the Claudian invasion of AD 43, and later became a main supply point, the choice of site would have been a natural one. It would also have been symbolic in that it would remind seafarers from the continent that here was a major outpost of the Roman Empire. The arch probably did not survive more than 150 years in its original position, and after its statues had been removed the site was used as a signal station.

Roman remains on the coast always attract attention because of their antiquity, especially if they are situated in out of the way places. Ravenglass in Cumbria is one of the few natural harbours on this stretch of coastline, and so became one of the main supply bases for the Roman garrisons scattered in the Lake District. It also had a fort of its own on a 1.6ha (4 acre) site overlooking the harbour. Beyond is a bath-house which has survived to a remarkable extent through having become part of a later medieval building. Some of the walls stand 4m (12ft) high and there are niches where bathers could leave their clothes. Like so many of these small isolated monuments the bath-house is in need of careful restoration and preservation.

Industrial working, especially quarrying, has left its distinctive mark on many parts of the coastline and often contributed to the unusual. Both in the Isle of Portland and the Isle of Purbeck the quarrying of fine building stone from the local limestone beds has gone on since the seventeenth century. The choicest stone has always been the cream-coloured Upper Freestone and, in the Isle of Purbeck, the quarrymen gouged out underground galleries leaving supporting columns of stone. The weighty blocks were then lowered over the cliff edge into waiting barges by means of a simple crane or whim. The best known quarries are those near Durlston Head south of Swanage where the Tilly Whim Caves were formerly open to the public. Although completely man-made and dating largely from the time of large-scale working early in the nineteenth century, the Tilly Whim still have an air of natural mystery about them, not surprisingly since there are many stories of contraband having been stowed away in their innermost recesses. The stone from the Purbeck quarries also went to build nearby Durlston Castle, the home of the eccentric George Burt, which dates from the 1880s. Just south of the castle on a cleanly cut platform there is the 40 ton stone globe which Burt had built from fifteen carefully selected segments (now within the Country Park).

Provided suitable rock was available, coastal quarrying was always in favour because of the relative ease with which the hewn stone could be transported by sea, especially before the railways came. In Abereiddi Bay, on the coast of Dyfed between St David's and Strumble Head, the slate beds were exploited to a considerable degree in the last century. Huge coastal pits were excavated as the slaty beds were removed, and one of the more seaward quarries was later flooded by cutting a channel to the sea so that a tiny harbour came into being. Much of the slate was taken to the more substantial harbour at nearby Porth Gain where a fleet of 350 ton steamers was ready to carry the Abereiddi slates to all parts of the kingdom. Porth Gain itself is a surprise for, on what is basically an unspoilt coastline, huge hoppers of a former roadstone company completely dominate the harbour.

Abandoned quarries are commonplace along the coast of Wales and at the mouth of Nant Gwrtheyrn, which lies in the shadow of the triple peaks of Yr Eifl on the Llŷn Peninsula, the ghost town of former chapel, manager's house and the terrace rows of the quarrymen, remain as a reminder of a past era. Attempts have been made by both developers and hippy colonies to bring back life to the place, and the publicity which followed has led to Gwrtheyrn becoming a curiosity for the tourist willing to walk the dirt road down to the valley-mouth settlement. It only needed to be included in books and pamphlets extolling the virtues of such an out of the way and secluded spot for the tourists to be attracted in their thousands.

The inter-war years saw two interesting coastal developments which perhaps reflect the attitude and aspirations of the period. On the sandy coastlands of Suffolk at Thorpeness the concept of a planned resort for the upper middle classes began to take shape from 1910 onwards when Stuart Ogilvy created the artificial lake known as The Meare and allocated plots for substantial houses running down to the water's edge. Further building in a curious mock-Tudor style with an emphasis on black weatherboarding followed along the sandhill fringe of the coast and more inland around the central green dominated by a country club, almshouses and hotel. Tennis courts, swimming pool and above all a golf course, were designed to provide much needed relaxation for the moneyed classes who came from the metropolis. The branch railway line to Aldeburgh, already in being, was given a 'halt' a mile to the west. Oddities were welcome in the strange resort, so that an early windmill from Aldringham re-erected on the common was a natural acquisition and seemingly not out of place. It has now found a use as a Heritage Coast centre where the visitor can learn about the adjacent stretch of coastline. Close by is the dominating structure of The House in the Clouds, in reality a disguised water tower. Thorpeness proved attractive and the increased use of the motor car in the 1930s gave much easier access. It also brought the day visitor, so that the rather exclusive image of the place lapsed and there was even some wooden-shack development on the sand dunes to the south. After a post-war period of neglect when this type of development was not in favour, there are signs of a revival with new houses being built and a general mood of tidying up the place. But what is to be done with the monstrous concrete church built in 1936–7?

The other seaside town development is even more unusual and owes its origin to the dreams of one man, the architect Clough Williams-Ellis. Anxious to provide an outdoor museum for buildings of varying architectural styles, he bought up an estate on the back of the peninsula which runs between the Glaslyn and Dwyryd estuaries in north-west Wales. Here, from 1926 onwards, he erected buildings which were completely at variance with the local vernacular style but which somehow seemed to form an acceptable grouping in their hill-side setting which many have likened to the Italian resort of Portofino. With gardens, workshops, restaurant and hotel the whole development was unique for this country and, while not to everyone's

The House in the Clouds – a water tower at Thorpeness on the Suffolk coast liking, commanded respect. As with Thorpeness it had an exclusive image at the outset, but economic hard truths have now led to the day visitor being encouraged to pay his entrance dues.

References

Arber, E. A. N. *The coast scenery of North Devon* (Dent, 1911)
Ellis-Gruffyd, D. *Coastal scenery of the Pembrokeshire Coast National Park* (Greencroft, 1977)
Hoskins, W. G. *Devon* (Collins, 1954)
MacCulloch, J. *Description of the Western Islands of Scotland* (1819)
McLaren, M. *The Shell Guide to Scotland* (Ebury, 1978)
Millward, R. and Robinson, A. *The Lake District* (Eyre & Spottiswoode, 1970)
—— *South East England: The Channel Coastlands* (Macmillan, 1973)
Omand, D. *The Caithness Book* (Highland Printers, 1973)
Scarfe, N. *Essex: A Shell Guide* (Faber, 1975)
Vaughan-Thomas, W. and Llewellyn, A. *The Shell Guide to Wales* (Michael Joseph, 1969)

5 Pavilions, Parades, Piers and Promenades

The Growth of Resort Towns

Seaside resorts, perhaps more than any other type of town, highlight a history of development which, if not unique, is certainly distinctive. Although some have grown up as appendages to earlier fishing villages, many were newly laid out on virgin sites, often reflecting the vision of a single landowner or group of individuals who left behind a very personal embodiment of their ideas. The result is that even today, in spite of all the trappings which have been added in this century, the original basic plan shows through giving the resort a freshness and frankness of architectural expression, no mean achievement in an age when uniformity tends to be the norm.

At the outset the pioneers responsible for the creation of the seaside town leaned heavily on experience gained from the inland spa. The relationship is so close that our earliest resort, Scarborough, began life as a spa by the sea, though as a town its history, based on its castle and harbour, goes back at least to the tenth century. It was the chance discovery by a Mrs Farrow in 1626, of a medicinal spring coming out of the cliff to the south of the harbour which was to add a new dimension to the then small port and enable Scarborough to become a 'spaw' and a rival to inland Harrogate and Bath. When in 1667 a Dr Robert Wittie pronounced on the curative properties of the spring water which he claimed could cure at least thirty diseases as well as being a 'Soveraign remedy against Hypochondria, Melancholly and Windiness', the future of Scarborough as a spa was assured. This emphasis on the spa rather than the seaside resort was natural in that in the seventeenth century neither the sea nor the coastline had proved attractive for visitors.

It was only when the cult of sea bathing and imbibing sea water had been established that Scarborough's history as a seaside resort began. Proof that this had happened by the first decades of the eighteenth

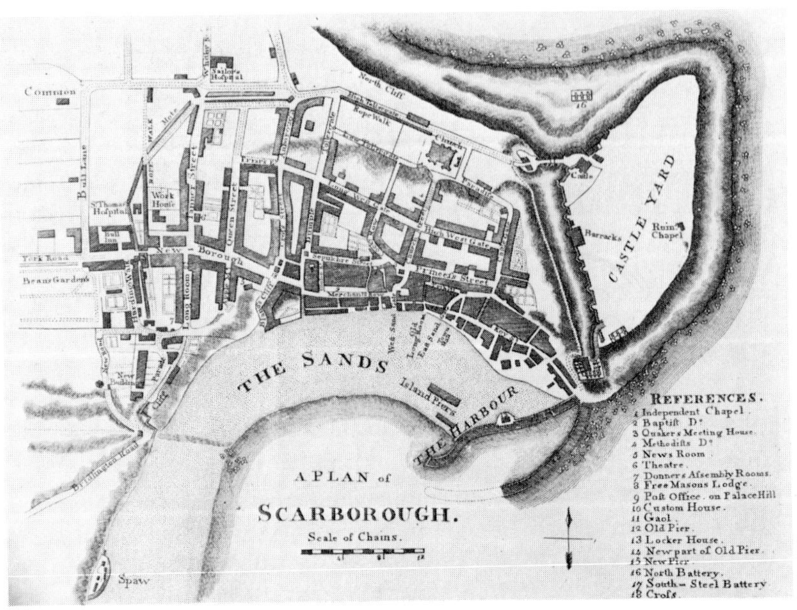

Scarborough in the eighteenth century, when it was beginning to emerge as a resort

century is provided by the famous drawing by John Settrington of 1735, which shows not only the spa pavilion but also bathing machines by the water's edge (their first recorded use in England) and a scattering of bathers disporting in the sea. But the influence of the inland spa continued to be felt in the growing seaside resort. Places like Bath and Tunbridge Wells had their masters of ceremony who conducted the whole enterprise – men like Beau Nash – so it was natural that Scarborough should appoint a similar personality, Dicky Dickens, to perform the same role. During the day the visitor could participate in sprightly exercises on the sands or even horse racing along the beach, but the evenings were reserved for more serious business. In the Long Room of the Pavilion on the cliff top Dicky Dickens saw that there was dancing, the playing of cards and billiards and a hazard table. The Pavilion was run by a Mr Vipont who had migrated from Hampstead Spa to the now rapidly growing and increasingly fashionable resort. Meanwhile the irrepressible Dicky Dickens had a new Pump Room built at the spa after the original building had been swept away in a cliff fall. In Victorian times Sir Joseph Paxton, architect of the Great Exhibition of 1851, was

The marina in the inner harbour at Ramsgate, Isle of Thanet

TORTUS

John Settrington's drawing of the developing seaside resort of Scarborough in 1735

commissioned to build a splendid new Pavilion along with terraced gardens and balconies to give an uninterrupted view of the beach. The latter have survived to the present though Paxton's pavilion was unfortunately destroyed by fire in 1876. In its place the present spa building was erected, the work of Thomas Verity. Scarborough even today reflects a great building surge in late Victorian times for, in addition to Verity's pavilion, there is the imposing pile of the Grand Hotel built of yellow and red brick. Rising as it does thirteen storeys from the beach it stands symbolic of the great confidence of the Victorian Age. Alongside is another relic of a century ago, the inclined cliff railway which still carries visitors from the town to the foreshore.

If Scarborough can lay claim to the title of 'Queen of the Northern Watering Places', then Brighton is its obvious parallel for the south coast. Although the two resorts show marked differences in present-day appearance, there are certain similarities in their early growth. Brighton, for so long a small fishing town on the Channel coast, suddenly took off as a watering place after Dr Richard Russell of Lewes settled there in 1753. The doctor, with his dissertation on 'The

The chalk cliffs at Flamborough Head are 500ft high and are capped by glacial deposits (*R. L. White*)

Brighton Pavilion, John Nash's excursion into the eccentric and fantastic

use of Sea Water in the Diseases of the Glands', advocated a treatment which immediately brought in visitors. Instead of the ghastly sulphureous waters purveyed at the inland spas, Brighton could offer pure sea water, perhaps diluted with milk for the delicate! So that the more conservative might also be attracted to the Sussex coast, Dr Russell also developed a chalybeate spring at what is now known as St Ann's Well Gardens in Hove.

The spa resort was only a beginning for, after the Prince Regent discovered Brighton at a mere 80km (50 miles) journey from London, the town was destined to become the most fashionable place in England. George, Prince of Wales, as he was then, first came to Brighton in 1783 for the first of many visits he was to make in subsequent years. His attachment to the town became more firmly rooted after he secretly married Mrs Fitzherbert in 1785. With his love for horses equalling that of women it is not surprising that the first building he commissioned in Brighton was the Royal Stables, a great glass dome decorated in Indian style and more fitting as a palace than as a home for horses. But it was the Royal Pavilion, transformed

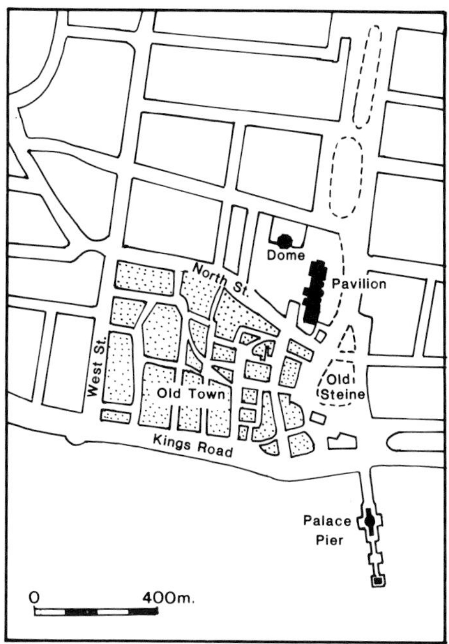

Brighton: the original core around which the fashionable resort developed

by John Nash between 1815 and 1822, that gave the town its most distinctive appearance and air of fantasy. With its onion domes, minarets, tracery, columns and parapets, it owes much to the romanticism aroused by poets and artists who were discovering the wonders of India in the early nineteenth century. Inside, however, there is much that is Chinese: hand-painted wallpapers of birds, butterflies, flowers and shrubs adorn the Saloon, while the Music Room has wall-paintings of Chinese landscapes. Perhaps most impressive of all is the Banqueting Room with its great murals of Chinese figures and a domed ceiling painted like a palm tree. Here was a dream palace that established Brighton as the premier resort of the country, and whose eccentricities were soon copied in more muted tones by other places anxious to acquire similar follies to attract the visitor. Not everybody was suitably impressed, and the Pavilion in particular came in for criticism. As one contemporary commentator put it 'one would think that St Paul's Cathedral had come to Brighton and pupped'. But in spite of this and similar strictures, Brighton Pavilion survived to outlive its critics and today forms the centrepiece of this still remarkable and unique seaside resort.

Although Brighton is usually looked upon as a basically Regency town, its greatest period of development came slightly later with the

Brunswick Square, another of Brighton's architectural masterpieces

building of Kemp Town in the east and Brunswick Town in the west in the 1820s. Two young Sussex architects, Busby and Wilds, were given the opportunity to show their skills in laying out the crescents, squares and terraces on land owned by Thomas Kemp, Lord of the Manor. The whole setting recalls the improvement scheme of John Nash in Regent's Park in London which had only just been completed. Miraculously Kemp Town survives almost in its original form today, to provide yet another facet to Brighton's architectural heritage. Busby also played a part in the development of the western suburb, Brunswick Town. With these two great layouts the stage was now set to give Brighton the finest seafront in the whole country, some would argue in the world. The great lawns which front Brunswick Terrace and Brunswick Square give the resort a spaciousness sadly lacking in modern planning, and altogether there are almost 11km (7 miles) of promenades facing the waters of the English Channel in the combined townships of Brighton and Hove.

What was happening in Brighton in the 1820s had its parallel elsewhere, though on a smaller scale. At Teignmouth in Devon a wide expanse of sandy foreshore covered with wild thyme was laid out as a green and promenade known as the Dẹn. On the inner side the gently sweeping curve of terraced houses was dominated by the Royal Hotel in the centre and the Public Assembly Rooms at one end. The Esplanade followed later when Brunel brought his railway along the coast and then had to build a huge sea wall to protect it from the sea.

There is still very much of an early nineteenth-century flavour to Teignmouth for, although later growth has occurred, the older resort centre has remained quite small, hemmed in by the red sandstone cliffs to the north and the river mouth to the south. This limitation probably explains why Teignmouth never experienced the explosive development that occurred nearby at Torquay. Instead it has seemed content to remain a small resort – it acquired a pier in 1865 – while continuing to function as a port exporting the ball clay from the inland Bovey Basin. Other Devon resorts like Dawlish, Seaton and Sidmouth have remained similarly undeveloped so that much early nineteenth-century building still remains, and therein lies their charm.

In terms of site and situation Torquay had so much in its favour that it was inevitable that a seaside resort would grow up in the sheltered northern corner of Tor Bay. More importantly, land was available for growth when the Palk family decided to invest in a well-planned layout of roads following the contours of the hill overlooking the sea. Splendid villas, each set in its own grounds, marked the beginning of development, though the true beginning of the resort dates from the 1830s when the Parade was laid out on tidal flats reclaimed near the harbour. Praise from Macaulay who noted the Italian softness of the air, and later Ruskin who termed it 'the Italy of England', helped to publicise the resort. But to succeed, Torquay needed more than soft air or a fine marine aspect. A spa on Beacon Hill was opened in 1857 but it never paid its way and unlike at Hove or Scarborough it was not instrumental in bringing in visitors. Only slightly more successful was the Winter Garden where the architect used glass and ironwork in the manner of Crystal Palace. For a time it was well patronised but gradually, as fashion changed, it was left derelict and finally transported to Great Yarmouth in 1903. One reason for the failure of the Winter Garden was competition from the Assembly Rooms in Abbey Road where, at Christmas 1879, the Gilbert and Sullivan opera HMS *Pinafore* was performed with great success. Up to this time the town council had remained aloof and insensitive to the needs of the growing resort. Their chance came after 1892 when the town received its borough charter. More land was reclaimed from the foreshore and later used to lay out Princess Gardens, still one of the delights of the town, especially since it has been recently extended and re-landscaped. Today as part of the bigger urban complex of Torbay, Torquay has a liveliness which proves attractive not only in the summer months but also for early- and late-season holidays. In spite of recent developments

Llandudno as it appeared in the 1850s, following a period of very rapid development

its nineteenth-century beginnings still show through, though they are perhaps less obvious than in Brighton or Scarborough.

Torquay, like other resorts, benefited from early railway development, with the inland line being extended to the coast in 1848. But for a decade earlier railways had begun to spread their tentacles across the country, a process which was to acquire great momentum after 1850 so that in time they reached even the most isolated parts of the kingdom. Of the score of new seaside towns which the railways helped to develop, Llandudno in Wales and Skegness on the Lincolnshire coast can be used in illustration, for both preserve in their layout, architecture and general appearance some of the features created by their sponsors over a century ago. Of the two resorts, Llandudno can claim precedence. In the 1840s this corner of north Wales was virtually empty except for small inland market towns, but into this region the Chester to Holyhead Railway began to make inroads and immediately the outlook changed. Hugging the coastline for much of its length the railway brought into being a clutch of small resorts, in the brief span of about twenty years, from Prestatyn in the east to Llanfairfechan in the west. In order to cross the Conwy Estuary the railway had to move inland after leaving Colwyn so that Llandudno was, as it still is, served by a short branch line. This, surprisingly, had little effect on the town's development, for the site on a low warren set between two imposing limestone headlands was itself enough to ensure success.

Llandudno as it was intended to be. The railway which was to run out to the pier was stopped on the outskirts, so that Llandudno gave up its aspiration to be a packet station serving Ireland

It was the agent of Lord Mostyn, John Williams, who first saw the potential for a new resort and under his influence an auction was held at Conwy in August 1848 that led to the selling off of part of the Mostyn estate in small plots. Stringent restrictions were placed on the developers and this, above all else, determined the character of Llandudno. In certain areas only substantial villas, each with a wide frontage, were permitted. Along the gentle curve of the bay a promenade was laid out with a parade of terraces together with the Queen's and St George's Hotels. One of these, Gloddaeth Terrace, was described in a contemporary account as having been 'built after the design of Mr Chater of Birmingham, in the Italianate style of architecture. The Crescent is beautifully situated, each row will be replete with every accommodation required by the most fastidious as a well-arranged marine residence; and in front of the entire range there will be a private esplanade which will be turfed and laid out in ornamental parterres with a broad gravel walk in the centre of the promenade'.

Behind the sea front the remainder of the resort was laid out to a formal gridiron plan. Streets were wide and often tree-lined and this still shows even though Mostyn Street and Gloddaeth Street suffered as they became the main shopping area of the town. Early iron arcades survive in places, but one has to look above street level to see the

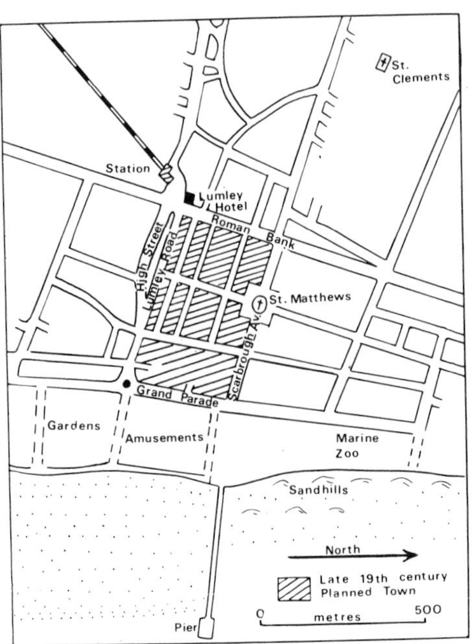

Skegness, a planned resort of the 1870s, with its regular layout of streets

character of the original buildings. As a result of a fairly rapid phase of development, perhaps lasting no more than about thirty years, Llandudno stands as one of the finest of the Victorian resorts, as much a product of planning as the better known and oft cited town of Saltaire near Bradford.

An overall plan of development was not, in itself, a recipe for assured success as Skegness was to discover some twenty years later. The potentialities of this small fishing hamlet which had existed for centuries attracted both the local landowner and the railway authorities who were pushing into this rural corner of the country in the 1870s. Wainfleet was intended to be the original terminus of this branch line of the Great Northern Railway but Vivian Tippet, estate agent of the Earl of Scarborough who owned the land on the coast, persuaded the railway authorities to extend it for a few miles to the fishing hamlet of Skegness. Immediately plans were made to lay out a new resort on the low sandy coast, with a simple plan using Lumley Road, Roman Bank, Castletown Boulevard and Grand Parade to form the sides of a rectangle within which the development was to take place. As events turned out the northern part was not built, so that the intended central position of the parish church never materialised until a much later date. Yet in spite of its stunted growth and later additions this century, Skegness has the appearance of the planned town with its wide tree-lined streets, broad grass verges and above all its simple gridiron plan. The Grand Parade, now sadly mutilated by the need to keep abreast of changing fashions and tastes, still retains something of the original design. It cannot however be compared with the Crescent at Llandudno nor the Esplanade at Eastbourne, the creation of the Duke of Devonshire. The explanation, at least in part, is that Skegness came about thirty years too late to cater for the genteel. Instead it found itself having to adapt to the mass invasion of thousands of trippers who poured off the excursion trains run from the East Midlands industrial towns and even London. It was to attract the excursionist that the most famous of all seaside posters – the Jolly Fisherman prancing on the sands of Skegness with the caption 'Skegness is so bracing' – was commissioned in 1908. The artist John Hassall was paid only £12 for his sketch, little knowing what the impact would be on future generations.

Piers

For a seaside resort to be in the top league, a pier was an absolute necessity. Although the concept dates from the early years of the nineteenth century when piers were used for embarking and disembarking passengers on an open coast, it is the Victorian era that is associated with their main development. Statistics prove the point, for in the decade 1860–70 the 'pier mania' led to no fewer than twenty-five being built around the coasts of Britain. Some resorts like Brighton were able to support two, one serving as a port of call for passing steamers and the other simply for promenading and recreation. Both uses were important, for no one would wish to begin their holiday at Brighton by being ferried ashore in a small boat and then unceremoniously dumped on the open beach. At Ryde the visitor had to endure a piggyback ride on a porter or alternatively face a 1km (½ mile) walk across wet sand when the tide was out. This not very encouraging prospect for the visitor was remedied in 1813 when the town fathers of Ryde decided to build a pier over 365m (400yd) long running out from the promenade. Later it was doubled in length so that passengers bound for the Isle of Wight could disembark safely at all states of the tide.

In a few years Ryde pier proved itself and encouraged Brighton to follow suit. In keeping with the 1820's fashion for suspension structures (Telford's bridges across the Conwy and Menai Strait were built in this decade), the Chain Pier was built; and at its opening in 1823 its praises were sung in song:

> That elegant structure, light airy and free,
> Like the work of enchantment hangs over the sea.

Thackeray summed up the feelings of many when he wrote, 'Here for a sum of twopence you can go out to sea and pace the vast deck without need of a basin.' J. M. W. Turner visited and painted it – the first of many artists who recorded it, in watercolour or oil, before it was finally swept away in a storm in 1896. From the outset the Chain Pier was designed for strollers as well as packet-boat passengers and it was not long before the promenade deck was occupied with booths and souvenir shops, a weighing machine and even a band when the boat left for Dieppe.

Later piers had added attractions so that gradually they became associated with leisure and pleasure. The pavilion, often mimicking the Royal extravaganza at Brighton with minarets and domes, was sited on the broadened toe, as far out to sea as possible. Often piers were huge structures and therefore liable to be battered mercilessly by winter storms. Even if they survived wave attack they were very easily burnt down. This dual fate does not, however, seem to have deterred the Victorian entrepreneurs who designed even bigger and more monstrous Pavilions, so that these great pleasure domes for the visitor soon became part of the Victorian seaside holiday, with perhaps a summer show or concert. Larger resorts vied with each other in providing the best in pier entertainment, Blackpool like Brighton having more than one pier for the purpose. The penny slot machine made its appearance about the turn of the century to compete with fortune tellers, performing fleas and all manner of unusual diversions. Clacton went one better and in the 1930s, when piers were still in fashion, erected a big dipper in order to bring a fairground atmosphere to the seaside.

Because of their situation, as well as their size, piers have proved extremely vulnerable to damage by storms and collisions from passing ships. If damage by fire is also taken into account, it is clear that few piers have managed to survive in the form they originally enjoyed in the middle of the nineteenth century. Even where damage has been minimal, there has been need for constant repair and replacement either of rusting ironwork or of rotten timbers which may have

The Chain Pier at Brighton as seen in a contemporary print. It was finally destroyed by a storm in the closing decade of the nineteenth century

suffered from the attentions of the boring teredo worm. In the past when piers were popular and able to show a profit from their leisure and entertainment facilities, repairs formed part of the annual running costs. In recent years, with the decline of the traditional British seaside holiday and the escalating costs of repairing these ageing structures, more and more piers have been closed and abandoned. Perhaps the most famous is the Brighton West Pier, built in 1863 but with its Pavilion added in 1893 and Concert Hall in 1916 to make it a multi-purpose structure. Sadly, at present it lies rusting while discussions go on to try to save it from demolition, each passing year bringing further deterioration and adding to the final bill of restoration, if indeed that should be the outcome. A local society, with Sir John Betjeman as president, has been formed to preserve this Victorian inheritance. Finance is the great stumbling block to survival and one suggestion is that the pier should be turned into one large funfare, a role claimed to be in keeping with the pier's original function as a place of entertainment.

Hopefully there is recognition that new thinking is needed before more of the country's piers are lost forever. At Weston-super-Mare the Birnbeck Pier, which connects an islet to the coastline and has subsidiary branches from the island itself, has become a liability in recent years with no steamers now calling and the walk along the promenade deck no longer exciting in a car-conscious age. For many a view of the sea can now only be enjoyed from the comfort of a car and insulated from the elements. With this in mind it has been suggested that a stone causeway be built as a link with the island, and cars accommodated in a huge new car park with an almost all-round view of the sea. The causeway would provide a sheltering arm for a new marina, the other need of a present-day resort. Conservationists, including the local Victorian Society, do not find the scheme attractive and some claim that the whole proposed development is not viable. Doubts have for instance been expressed about the value of a marina on a coastline with a 12m (40ft) tide. The controversy is a measure of the dilemma now facing many local authorities who have inherited a pier from a past age.

Loss of its pier completely alters the character of the English seaside resort (few piers, as opposed to jetties, were built in Scotland). But where actual damage has taken place, the prospect of retention is even more precarious. Southend Pier, the longest in Britain, had its seaward end destroyed by fire a few years ago, and now seems unlikely to return to its former glory with a railway along its 2,102m (6,600ft) length into the Thames Estuary. Skegness Pier, actually severed as a result of a storm during the winter of 1978, would be very costly to repair even if its future financial stability was more assured.

Not every pier can be saved and many hardly deserve to be for they are top-heavy, cumbersome structures whose loss would not be severely felt by future generations. What is needed is a national plan to save the best examples of this unique form of Victorian architecture, and in this connection a stronger case could be made out for Clevedon Pier in Avon than for many similar in need of repair. The pier was built in 1869 largely from railway metals salvaged from the South Wales Railway, and this gave it a wispy form of great delicacy and a lightness of structure which may have helped it to survive the high tides of the Bristol Channel. Listed as a Grade II building the pier was test-loaded in the early 1970s for safety purposes, but unfortunately one section collapsed under the strain. Since that time the pier has become an albatross around the neck of the local authority who owns it. Conservationists naturally would like to see it preserved after being restored to its original form. As Sir John Betjeman has remarked, its unique method of construction has given it an appearance 'as delicate as a Japanese print as it was seen striding out into the calm sea'. One can only hope that these words from the great upholder of Victorian architecture will be sufficient to save it.

Clevedon Pier, a light feathery structure running out into the Bristol Channel but now severed near its extremity

With now less than fifty piers remaining in Britain, this 'Victorian anachronism', as one commentator put it, is in danger of becoming a rarity if not totally extinct by the twenty-first century. It seems unlikely that any new structure will be built, although materials and engineering expertise have increased considerably since the first piers were thrust out defiantly into the sea. Much more likely, new development will be concentrated on terra firma, preferably on the sea front if land is available. In many resorts land has been reclaimed from the sea by the local authority and laid out in boating pools, pitch and putt courses and sunken or terraced gardens. Some of this newly won land will undoubtedly be sacrificed for the huge covered-in leisure centres which are springing up in many seaside towns as they seek to entice the holidaymaker indoors when the weather is indifferent outside. Imagination and faith will be needed if uniformity, with every British seaside town being made to look alike, is to be avoided.

A case could be made for the revival of the Victorian Winter Garden or Floral Hall in an up-to-date form. After the Great Exhibition of 1851 scores of miniature glass palaces grew up in the resorts and, apart from the exotic vegetation, there was the delight of tea taken to the melodies of the string trio – the forerunner of the Palm Court orchestra. Such rendezvous became the haunt of the genteel in the afternoon, providing a necessary retreat after the walk along the promenade and infinitely preferable to outdoors where one might have to endure the raucous strains of the local brass band. Special attractions will undoubtedly play a part in the survival of many resorts, especially those which artificially prolong the season. Blackpool is fortunate to have its well-established illuminations in the autumn, first introduced after World War I, although as early as 1880 electric lighting had been introduced on the piers and promenade. A century later the dazzling lighting displays still attract, perhaps symbolising the last embers of a dying summer when the days have shortened and the onset of winter cannot be long delayed.

References

Anderson, S. H. *Seaside Piers* (Batsford, 1977)
Griffiths, G. D. and E. G. C. *History of Teignmouth* (Brunswick Press, 1965)
Howell, S. *The Seaside* (Studio Vista, 1974)
Musgrave, C. *Life in Brighton* (Faber & Faber, 1970)
Russell, P. *A history of Torquay* (Torquay Natural History Society, 1960)
Young, D. S. *The story of Bournemouth* (Hale, 1957)

6 Climate: Where to Holiday and Retire

Like lemmings, the British still make an annual dash to their native coast in spite of the increasing popularity of package holidays to sunnier climes in recent years. Four times as many people choose to spend their annual holiday by the sea rather than in the countryside; some make a pilgrimage year after year to the same resort and, after retirement, it becomes their choice for a permanent home. Bungalow suburbs have grown up around many resorts, especially those of the south coast, as a response to this increasing demand for a place by the sea. Towns like Eastbourne, Worthing, Bognor, Brighton and Bournemouth have such a high proportion of senior citizens that the area has been disdainfully dismissed as the geriatric coastline.

The choice of a particular area for a holiday or as a place of retirement is largely an expression of personal tastes; but often weather and climate play an important part in the decision making, if only expressed in simplest terms such as the desire for milder winters or sunny, dry summers. This in itself is an acknowledgement that the weather experienced along the coast is different from that inland. How far this intuitive feeling stands up to scientific analysis can be tested by looking at the statistics for temperature, rainfall, wind and fog, which together are responsible both for the daily weather and the longer-term climatic pattern.

The climatic distinctiveness of the coastland zone, perhaps extending inland for a distance of 8 to 12km (5 to 8 miles), arises from the way in which land and water surfaces react to incoming solar radiation. For a land surface the heat transfer to the soil and bedrock is by conduction which means a fairly rapid warming up during the day, though to a limited depth. At night the reverse is true, so that once the sun has set there is a rapid cooling off effect. Over a 24-hour period one can therefore expect marked fluctuations of temperature – in other words a large diurnal (daily) range. On the other hand, in the sea the

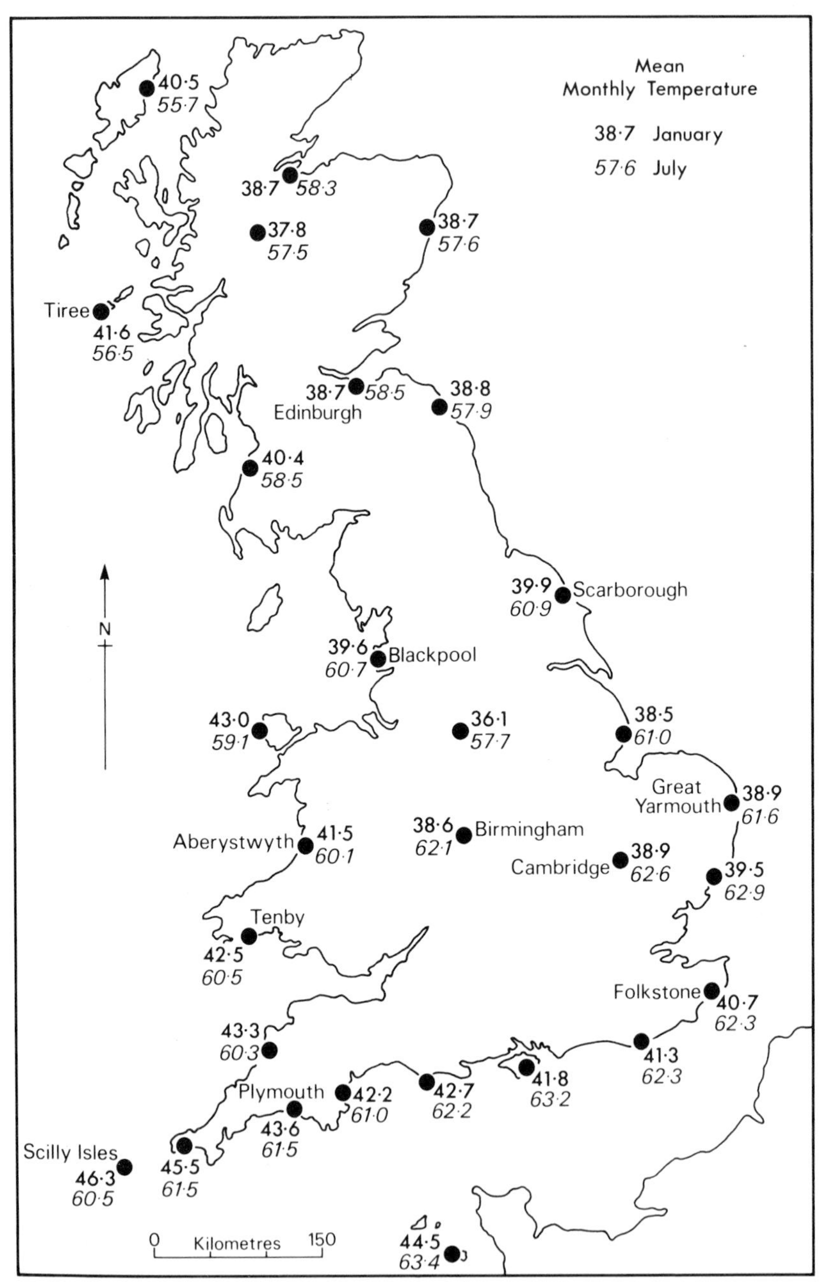

Monthly mean temperatures for selected coastal and inland stations

heat transfer is much less though it extends to a much greater depth (water is a better conductor of heat than soil). There is also a very pronounced heat loss due to evaporation during the daylight hours, so that actual water-surface temperature does not change greatly between day and night. Another noticeable difference is in the higher radiation values found along the coast compared with inland. At Aberporth, on the shores of Cardigan Bay, the radiation values are 25 per cent higher than for a nearby inland station, while along much of the south coast of England this radiation differential has been found to be about 15 per cent, possibly due to the clearer maritime air. On the other hand, what is known as the Albedo effect (reflected radiation which takes into account different types of receptive surface) varies between sea and land surfaces – values over water are about 10 per cent compared with 3.5–4 per cent for a dry, sandy surface. These dissimilarities may appear academic, but they do contribute to the distinctive local climate which seems to prevail at the coast.

Temperature

One of the most noticeable aspects of living by the sea is the smaller annual temperature range brought about by cooler summers and milder winters. Gorleston near Yarmouth has a January mean temperature of 4.4°C (39.9°F) and a July mean of 16.4°C (61.5°F). The corresponding figures for the neighbouring inland station of Cambridge are 3.8°C (38.9°F) and 17°C (62.6°F). Thus the annual range at Gorleston is 1.2°C (2°F) less than at Cambridge. Though not a large difference it is a significant one, especially as these figures are mean values, and hide the fact that a coastal site seldom experiences night frosts. When daily temperature figures are analysed the advantage of a coastal site, particularly in the winter months, becomes even more apparent. Night minimum temperatures for inland Cullompton in Devon average 2 degrees C (4 F) lower than for nearby Sidmouth on the coast, where the diurnal range is 2.5 degrees C (4.5 F) less. Much of this is due to the warmer daytime maximum values for Cullompton which can be 2 degrees C (4 F) higher in mid-afternoon. Sidmouth, like many coastal stations, tends to be affected by local sea breezes in the summer months and these tend to keep the afternoon temperatures down (see page 123).

Even for coastal stations there is a marked variation in annual temperature range, which is not surprising considering that from the

Channel Islands in the south to the Shetlands in the north there is a latitude difference of over 20 degrees. What is perhaps not fully realised is that there is a decrease of annual temperature range as one goes north. At St Helier in the Channel Islands, for example, the difference between the January and July mean temperatures is 10.5 degrees C (18.9 F), whereas the comparable figure for Lerwick in the Shetlands is only 8.5 degrees C (15.3 F). In practical terms this means that the Shetlander can expect much less by way of extreme conditions than his more southerly Channel Island counterpart. Expressed another way, he has to endure 'top coat' weather for much of the year though little by way of actual freezing conditions. The highest annual ranges of temperature occur along the east coast where the continental influences are most keenly felt, especially in the winter months. Along the coast of East Anglia, for example, there is an annual range of almost 14 degrees C (25 F) due to high summer, and low winter, temperatures. Coastal stations in the west like Tenby, on the other hand, have an annual range of only 11 degrees C (20 F), largely due to higher winter temperatures. In view of this it is not surprising that the South West has proved so attractive as a retirement area, though it has to be borne in mind that although there is less likelihood of freezing temperatures here in winter, the summers are cool.

For the summer visitor, with perhaps a fortnight to while away by the sea, figures for annual mean ranges of temperature are of little interest. He is much more likely to be concerned with the temperatures to be experienced in the holiday months of July and August. In statistical terms there is little to choose between the two months, for although August is slightly warmer, the days are correspondingly shorter. Sea temperatures are also slightly higher in August due to the time-lag in temperature build-up, though the difference is hardly noticeable. If expected highest temperature was the sole criterion in choosing a holiday area, the shores of the Thames Estuary, taking in the resorts of Southend, Herne Bay and Margate would top the list, followed by the Channel Coast resorts stretching from Lyme Regis in the west to Folkestone in the east. Less favoured as regards temperature are the coasts of Wales though there is a recovery further north along the Lancashire coast, probably reflecting the higher August sea-water temperatures immediately offshore. By the same token the north-east coast of England and the east coast of Scotland are less favoured due to a wedge of cold water running close inshore. The south shore of the Moray Firth has a surprisingly high

August mean temperature for its latitude – comparable with the north-east coast of England which lies much further south.

For those seeking congenial conditions in retirement, it is the winter temperatures, particularly those of January and February, that are critical. The west coast benefits in full from the warm waters of the North Atlantic currents and it is here, often irrespective of latitude, that some of the highest winter mean temperatures are found. The island of Tiree, off the south-west coast of Scotland, has a January mean temperature higher than that of Eastbourne on the favoured Sussex coast. Where the full benefit of the warm Atlantic current is combined with a southerly latitude, the mildest winters of all can be expected. Not surprisingly therefore the South-west Peninsula and especially the Scilly Isles come out best in the January mean temperature figures which can be as high as 7.9°C (46.3°F). Even within the Peninsula there are favoured coastal situations like the coast of Mount's Bay, the so-called Cornish Riviera which figured prominently on pre-war railway posters, where the January mean temperature reaches 7.5°C (45.5°F). By way of contrast, Folkestone can only expect to average 3.8°C (38.9°F) for the same month.

While it is true that as regards summer temperature the south-east coast has the edge, taking the year as a whole the Penwith Peninsula in the extreme west of Cornwall probably comes out best in most people's reckoning. To some extent this is confirmed by actual climatic statistics. If 15°C (60°F) is taken as an acceptable temperature for comfortable outdoor activity, the Penwith Peninsula has the lowest number of degree days – the number of days when the temperature is below this figure multiplied by the deficiency in degrees – in the whole country, with 3,000. By comparison the Northumberland coast has over 4,500, while an inland upland area like the Grampians of Scotland can exceed 6,000. On the whole degree-day values relate to latitude, though the west coast seems more favourable than the east coast. The north Wales coast resorts like Rhyl fare better than Cromer or Sheringham in East Anglia although they are in approximately the same latitude.

Sunshine

Temperature alone, especially mean values, can only be a crude way of measuring the suitability of a particular area for holidays or retirement. For the holidaymaker, sunshine values, whether daily,

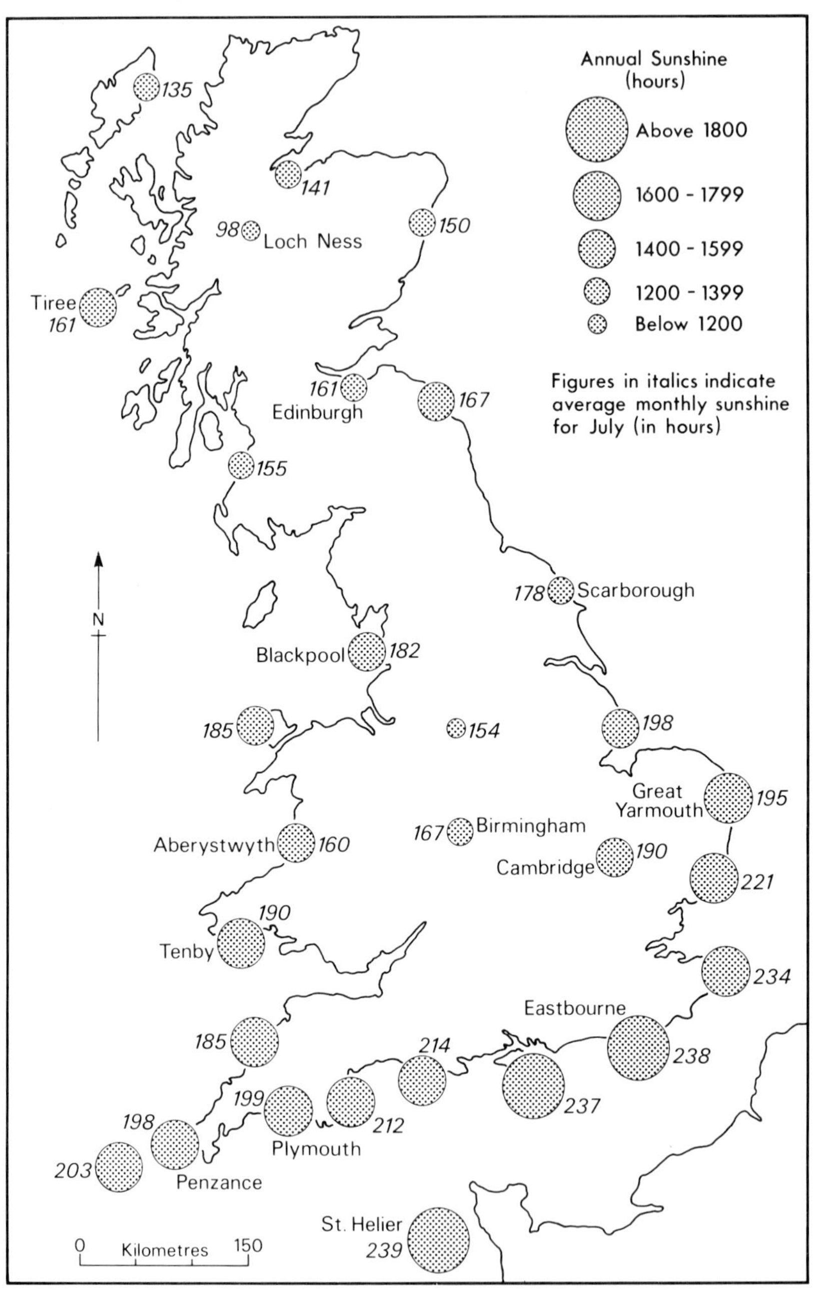

Annual sunshine totals for selected coastal and inland stations, with the July totals

monthly or annual totals, can often be a better guide, consequently many resorts take pride in displaying their sunshine figures prominently in their brochures. Because of local climate characteristics coastal resorts are invariably better placed than their inland counterparts, assuming uniformity of elevation and latitude. Cambridge, for example, can only muster 1,488 hours of sunshine a year compared with the 1,720 hours recorded at Felixstowe. The most favoured coastal resorts are those on the sheltered eastern side of the Isle of Wight (Sandown and Shanklin) and the Sussex coast (Eastbourne and Hastings). In both these areas the yearly total of bright sunshine exceeds 1,800 hours; only St Helier in Jersey can claim to do better than this. Local topography can be important, especially shelter afforded by high ground. Eastbourne (1,828 hours) undoubtedly benefits from the Chalk Downs to the west, and Torquay (1,733 hours) in the shadow of Dartmoor, and Penzance (1,672 hours) in the lee of the granite upland of Penwith, are similarly favoured. The east coast of England has a slight advantage when it comes to sunshine and can expect about 50 extra hours compared with the west-coast resorts in the same latitude.

Because of its longer days, June usually records the highest monthly sunshine totals and so is a more favourable month than September for those able to take holidays outside the normal summer season of July and August. The advantage of a southerly situation is clearly seen by comparing the sunshine figures for Worthing and Blackpool for the month of June; whereas Worthing's monthly total can be around 223 hours, Blackpool can expect only 183. In winter the percentage difference is much greater, for the comparable figures for the month of January are 67 hours and 44 hours. But even these relatively low figures for coastal resorts are vastly superior, both in summer and winter, when compared with the sunshine expected for inland situations. In July Loch Ness in the Great Glen can only expect 98 hours, compared with 161 hours for the island of Tiree in only a slightly more southerly latitude. Even Inverness, only 80km (50 miles) away from the Loch Ness station but on the coast, can total 141 hours for the same month.

Although the monthly differences between inland and coastal situations vary from month to month, there is no doubt of the advantages enjoyed all the year round by the latter. Inland sites, especially upland ones, suffer from the build-up of cloud clusters around the peaks, especially in the afternoon when convective air currents develop. In contrast cloud cover can often disperse over the sea when an offshore wind is blowing. Even in favoured situations like the south east of England where inland altitude differences are not unduly pronounced, it is not uncommon to be basking in the sun on the beaches of Brighton only too aware of the dark thundery clouds hanging over the downs a few miles inland. Similarly, while rain-laden skies cover the mountains of Snowdonia, Llandudno can be enjoying a sunny day, its peninsula site being sufficiently far removed from mountain influences. The string of south-coast resorts along the Sussex and south Kent coasts from Bognor to Folkestone enjoy another advantage in that the sun is over the sea for the greater part of the day. The holidaymaker content to lounge in a deck-chair for hours on end can stare blankly at the sea and still acquire that very desirable tan.

Precipitation

Rainfall and snow amounts are usually less along the coast than for inland sites. In part this is due to lack of height, so that most of the rain is frontal in character. As the depressions come into the British Isles from the Atlantic, their frontal systems are usually active in the west but tend to weaken before the east coast is reached. Combined with the effect of relief, the result is that the west coast has on average about 50 per cent more annual rainfall than corresponding places on the eastern seaboard. The lowest annual totals are therefore found around the shores of the Thames Estuary at places like Canvey Island and Southend. For the whole of the east coast, from Margate as far north as Holderness, there is less than 63.5cm (25in) rainfall in an average year. This is in contrast to the west coast where totals of between 76 and 101cm (30 and 40in) are recorded. Newquay in Cornwall is typical of a west-coast resort in having 87cm (34.2in) a year, yet inland the total quickly rises to almost 127cm (50in) on Bodmin Moor 16km (10 miles) away. Lee coastal situations also tend to give lower rainfall totals as witnessed at Torquay and Teignmouth with totals in the middle thirties and undoubtedly benefiting from the protection afforded by Dartmoor. Dartmoor itself has almost 254cm (100in) a year in its highest parts, so that the coast is dry in comparison. A similar relationship prevails in north-west Wales for, whereas the Snowdonia peaks can expect almost 508cm (200in) a year, low-lying coastal Anglesey has less than 100cm (40in).

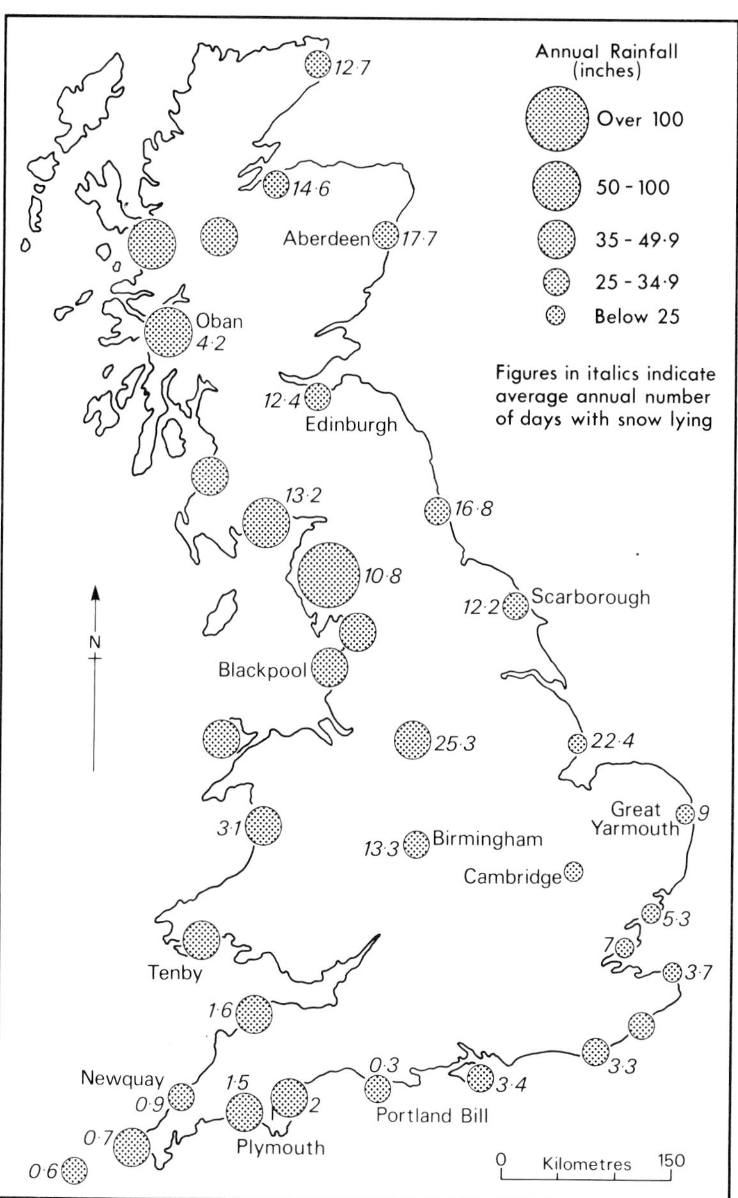

Annual rainfall figures for selected stations, with the days of lying snow

Not only does the coastal zone receive much lower annual totals, but the frequency and length of duration of the rainfall is considerably reduced. Often on a cloudy day it is dry on the beach while steady rain is falling in the mountains. Anglesey clearly benefits from the fact that it projects out into the Irish Sea. A peninsular situation often escapes the worst excesses of a rainy day and therefore it is not surprising that, along the English Channel coast, places like Portland Bill and the tip of Dungeness have only about 63.5cm (25in), about 13cm (5in) less than resorts like Brighton and Eastbourne. Conversely coastlines at the head of bays often receive relatively high rainfall, especially if they lie facing the direction of prevailing rain-bearing winds and are backed by mountains. Morecambe Bay, a favourite retirement area for Lancastrians, has an annual total in excess of 100cm (40in) in consequence of the upward lift given by the nearby foothills of the Lake District mountains. In contrast, the shores of the Solway Firth, in a rain-shadow zone, have only about 89cm (35in).

Some of the highest precipitation totals for coastal stations occur in north-west Scotland. Western Mull, for example, often has 152cm (60in) a year, while part of south-west Skye, with the nearby Cuillin hills dominating the skyline, can expect over 178cm (70in). But actual figures such as these give little more than a hint of what to expect for there are many variations even for places only a few miles apart. The intricacies of topography play a considerable part in determining the actual rainfall recorded, especially where the coastline has prominent headlands and deeply inset fjord embayments. Unfortunately statistics are not available from a close network of stations in this area, but what is known hints at a fascinating picture of how local settings affect the actual rainfall amounts.

The Scottish mountains, reaching to heights of over 1,219m (4,000ft) in the west and in the central Cairngorms, create an effective rain shadow for much of the east coast. As a result Aberdeen, with 84cm (33in) a year has only 5cm (2in) more than Eastbourne. Even lower totals occur around the Moray and Cromarty Firth coastlines where towns like Elgin and Nairn record 66–69cm (26–27in) a year. Most surprising of all is the average of 61cm (24in) measured at Tarbat Ness lying at the end of the long peninsula separating the Dornoch and Moray Firths. If rainfall total was the sole criteria this isolated and unspoiled corner could claim superiority over all the Channel coast resorts, but unfortunately it lacks their high summer temperatures or large sunshine totals. Nevertheless the peninsular coastline of north-east Scotland has much to commend it especially as the mountains are not far away and provide a rich variation of landscape which is lacking in south-east England. In June the days are long, and in periods of settled weather such as occurred in 1976 it is one of the pleasantest places in Britain in which to spend a holiday by the sea.

Very little coastal precipitation especially along western shores, falls in the form of snow – a reflection of mild winter conditions which result from the effects of a relatively warm sea. In the South-west Peninsula snow only lies on one day a year on average, and even as far north as Oban the comparable figure is only four days. In contrast the influence of the European continent makes itself felt along the east coast so that there is a much greater possibility of snowfall. Lowestoft, for example, has an average of 9 days a year when lying snow can be expected, while further north at Whitby this rises to 12 days. More northerly latitudes seem to affect the total little for Wick, too, has a figure of 12 days of lying snow. But these coastal figures are much less than for inland stations in the same latitude. The inland spa town of Buxton, situated high in the Peak District of Derbyshire, might have between 20 and 30 days a year when there is snow lying in the streets. Sometimes the fall is so heavy that the town is completely cut off as the approach roads, including the main A6, become blocked. Balmoral, wisely used only as a summer retreat by the royal family has, in an average year, as many as 55 days when snow lies on the ground.

Fog

The way in which the weather experienced along the coast differs from that inland is further shown by the incidence of fog. Along the west and south coasts of England this varies from 6 to 10 days a year, while for the east coast the figure increases to between 10 and 20 days. There is a marked fall-off in Scotland, where most coastal towns can expect only a few days fog a year – perhaps an indication of the more turbulent air conditions found there. Inland the fog figures are much higher not only, as one would expect, in industrial areas, but also in country towns. Birmingham with 39 days a year of foggy conditions and Harrogate with 41, are typical. Taking the country as a whole fog is about 2½ times more frequent inland than along the coast.

There is, however, one special type of fog which only affects the coast, the sea mist or 'haar' as it is sometimes known locally, and which can be troublesome for holidaymaker and inshore boatman alike. Although limited to a narrow strip of coastland up to about 8km (5 miles) wide, it can persist for several days in periods of settled anticyclonic weather. It is most likely to develop in early summer when onshore winds blowing across a cold sea meet the warmer land, and although developing in early morning can persist for several hours and occasionally all day. Similar still conditions in the autumn months can also lead to sea mists forming along the coast of the South-west Peninsula, yet one has only to travel a few miles inland to be in brilliant sunshine. Such sea mists can persist for several days with perhaps a clearance occurring in the evening. A starry night gives hope for better things, but all too often the mist has returned by morning to herald yet another grey, chilly day.

Wind Conditions

One night in 1961 at Lerwick in the Shetlands a gust of wind of 173mph was recorded, the highest-ever wind speed in the British Isles. While this was clearly exceptional, there are many records of gusts exceeding 100mph and nearly all relate to coastal situations. It would be rare indeed for wind speeds of this magnitude to occur inland nor are they as frequent. This is shown by figures for gales (wind speeds exceeding 34 knots) at coastal and inland stations. In an average year Wick can have 38 gales, Tynemouth 34, Dungeness 27, Plymouth Hoe 31, the Scilly Isles 53, Aberporth 30 and Tiree in the Inner Hebrides 55. These totals stand in complete contrast to those recorded at inland stations, Kew in London perhaps having only 1 gale a year.

The great difference is largely an expression of the varying degrees of exposure experienced at coastal and inland sites. Islands like Scilly and Tiree seem particularly vulnerable as they lie in the direct path of the south-westerly winds which reach them over large expanses of open sea. Along the eastern coast these winds are offshore and therefore less likely to produce gale-force conditions. Where gales do occur here they are most likely to be associated with onshore north-east winds. North-westerly gales, coming as they do on the back of a deep depression moving into the North Sea, can have serious consequences on the East Coast, not so much from wind damage but because they are liable to raise the sea level by several feet. This is what happened in February 1953 and led to the flooding of vast tracts of low-lying coastland and considerable loss of life and damage to property. Fortunately storm-surges caused in this way are comparatively rare, perhaps only occurring with great severity once every fifty years. But as the events of 1953 showed, a low-lying coastal situation, even though it might have a fine view of the sea, carries considerable risks. Undue reliance on sea banks and other man-made protective works can be misplaced, for the pounding waves so easily reduce them to rubble and consequent breaching.

Along the east and south coasts of England, areas which experience the highest summer temperatures, there is often a marked local wind blowing inland from the sea from about midday onwards. This sea breeze is most marked during high summer when the inland temperatures are much higher than those over the sea, but it can occur, though in a muted form, any time between about March and October. The first indication is often a gentle breeze which begins to blow about four hours after sunrise and, over the next few hours, gradually strengthens so that by mid-afternoon it can be quite strong. Being onshore and having come over a relatively cool sea surface, it can cause the sunbather to shiver or perhaps seek a more sheltered spot. It can be dangerous in that it lowers the temperature felt without affecting the real power of the sun, so that sunburn can result quite unknowingly. Such a sea breeze can develop when the temperature difference between land and sea exceeds about 5 degrees C (9 F). Often the temperature difference is much larger than this, and it is on these occasions that the strongest breeze sets in. Along the Channel coast there is often an opposite local breeze at night when the temperature figures are reversed. A warm wind now flows out from the land to the sea aided by the downslope air movement from the South Downs. The land breeze usually starts about three hours after sunset and is strongest on clear nights.

Climate and Choice

Faced with a mass of climatic and weather data, how is the layman to decide which coast best suits his needs when it comes to choosing a holiday area or, more critically, a place by the sea for retirement? For the holidaymaker with perhaps a week or two in the year to spend by the sea, usually in the months of June to September, temperature and sunshine are probably the main considerations. The coast of south-east England certainly comes out best in the statistics, particularly the section from the Isle of Wight to Yarmouth. Sea-water temperatures for bathing, especially in the early part of the summer, favour the Channel coastline rather than East Anglia, though later in the year the difference is much less.

For those seeking a more active holiday, the highest summer temperatures assume less importance and amount of rainfall and number of rainy days come into the reckoning. Also the quality of the coastal scenery, its natural unspoiled beauty and its accessibility for walking, are factors to be considered. Other parts of the coastline, away from the rather urbanised south-east coast, might prove more attractive. South Devon and north Cornwall immediately come to mind, while in Wales the Pembrokeshire National Park area has similar virtues. For a drier holiday the neglected Northumberland coast north of the coalfield, and the equally little known coastline of south-east Scotland from Berwick round to Dunbar, are probably unrivalled. Their accessibility, however, is inferior to that of the South-west Peninsula where a long coastal path follows the cliff top for over a hundred miles. The shores of the Moray and other nearby firths are remarkably dry for such a northern latitude and, with fine unspoiled beaches and small resorts, have much to offer the holiday-maker with less sophisticated tastes. Sunshine figures are reasonable and there is the added bonus of long hours of daylight in June and July.

Inevitably the choice of an area for retirement merits much closer scrutiny as regards climate and a longer-term assessment of its potential. As already mentioned, the south coast of England has proved attractive as is shown by the high percentage of retired people in resorts like Eastbourne, Worthing, Bognor and others of smaller size. Their relatively high sunshine figures for the year include better than average figures for the winter months. The coasts of the South-west Peninsula do not lag far behind in the winter season and as they have much milder conditions, especially in the extreme tip of Cornwall, this area could reasonably claim an overall advantage. Certainly the chance of snow is much less in Cornwall than in Sussex or Kent and this applies to other western areas as well, such as Pembrokeshire and even the Llŷn Peninsula in north-west Wales. Peninsular situations experience a marked maritime climate and therefore benefit most of all from mild winter conditions. Coastal climates however, do suffer from extreme windiness and therefore sheltered sites should be sought. The shores of Tor Bay in south Devon, including the resorts of Torquay, Paignton and Brixham, derive shelter from westerly winds due to the nearness of Dartmoor; but they are open to easterly winds and therefore can experience bitterly cold snaps when the wind is in that quarter.

For those seeking a southerly situation, greater solitude and no large summer invasion of holidaymakers, the Dorset and east-Devon coasts are attractive. Combined with fine coastal scenery and a varied countryside inland, small places like Budleigh Salterton, Sidmouth, Seaton and Lyme Regis have much to commend them. Because of their southerly aspect they do not suffer from the full force of easterly winds blowing directly onshore. For many, a more urban environment seems attractive, and an argument could be advanced in favour of bigger towns like Bournemouth and its neighbours which now take up nearly the whole of the coastline of Poole Bay.

In stark contrast to south-facing coasts, places with a northerly aspect can be subject to biting cold winds in the winter months even though these winds are coming off the sea. The north-Kent coast, with its resorts like Margate, Broadstairs and Herne Bay, is unfavourably placed in this respect as is also north Norfolk around Cromer and Sheringham. To some the bracing climate of these places is an attraction rather than a disadvantage, emphasising that personal choice rather than cold scientific argument can be the main deciding factor. There is no doubt that many are attracted to a particular spot from past associations, often from having spent many pleasant summer holidays there in the past. This can be dangerous in that a mere glimpse from a few weeks in the summer can be totally misleading as to what it is like in an all the year round context. An attachment to a particular holiday resort can also unduly influence the ultimate choice of a retirement area.

The shores of Morecambe Bay illustrate this tendency to retire to a long-loved resort. Many Lancastrians, wishing to escape the pressures of crowded resorts like Blackpool and Southport, choose places like Arnside, Silverdale or Grange-over-Sands which, though not far away in distance, are poles apart in the life-style they provide. With a reasonable climate stemming from a southerly aspect, sheltered by the Lake District from the cold northerly winds and with maritime advantages from being sited on low projecting peninsulas, these former Victorian resorts have become increasingly popular for those seeking a place by the sea. They offer both solitude and the contrasting scenery of Morecambe Bay and the nearby southern Lake District. Grange-over-Sands, rather surprisingly, has reputedly the highest percentage of retired people for any coastal resort, though in actual numbers it obviously falls far short of the totals reached by south-coast towns like Eastbourne and Bournemouth. Whether others coming from different parts of the country would find these small Morecambe Bay resorts equally attractive is open to doubt because of the considerable amount of adjustment and adaptation necessary in moving into new territory – considerations which should not be overlooked when such an important decision has to be made. Inevitably personal circumstances and temperament can sometimes play a major part when the final choice has to be made.

Coastal Holiday Areas in Terms of Weather and Climate

COAST	CLIMATIC ADVANTAGES	TYPE OF HOLIDAY
South-east England (Sussex and Kent)	Best summer temperatures, highest sunshine figures, south-facing shores along the Channel coast. Warm sea 16°C (61°F) in August.	Beach; bathing and leisure activities provided by numerous resorts.
South-central England (Hampshire, Dorset and east Devon)	High summer temperatures, above average sunshine figures, warm sea, south aspect, shelter from northerly winds.	Quiet, uncrowded atmosphere once west of Bournemouth. Coastal walks, pleasant inland scenery. Small, rather genteel resorts, some still retaining a Victorian atmosphere.
South-west Peninsula (south Devon and Cornwall)	Mild winters with little snow on the coast. Early spring and summer. Low annual temperature range. Relatively low rainfall in lee of Dartmoor.	Beach; sheltered coves and rocky shorelines to explore. Fine inland scenery. Boating and surfing.
South-west Wales	Early spring on Pembrokeshire Peninsula, sheltered south-facing coves. Relatively low rainfall in spring and early summer.	Coastal walks in Pembrokeshire National Park. Caravan and chalet sites.
West Wales	Good weather in late spring when easterly influence prevails. Lee situation then gives high sunshine.	Self-catering in chalet and caravan sites. Yachting, especially from harbours of Llŷn Peninsula.
North Wales	Relatively low rainfall for coastal resorts in lee of Snowdonia; good sunshine figures.	Leisure parks and holiday camps. Good walking inland.

Lancashire	Seas much warmer than for corresponding parts of the east coast.	Varied range of indoor pleasure activities, beach; extended autumn season.
Cumbria	Shores of Morecambe Bay have mild climate and low rainfall totals on tips of peninsulas. West coast more exposed.	Walking, bird watching, inland excursions to Lake District. Boating from west-coast ports.
Galloway	Similar climate to Morecambe Bay with climatic advantages derived from long, projecting peninsulas.	Quiet, isolated peninsulas give solitude. Boating and fishing from old harbours.
West of Scotland	Late spring and autumn offer best chance of relatively dry conditions. Easterly winds in May and early June can give high sunshine figures in the North West and adjacent Hebridean islands.	Walking and touring by car. Sea trips to offshore islands. Choice of coast and country, both unspoiled.
North of Scotland	Element of luck in missing spells of heavy rain and cold northerly winds; late spring or autumn offers best chance. Long days in June and July.	Touring; sandy inlets with empty beaches.
North-east Scotland	Better weather as regards sunshine, summer temperatures and low rainfall than many would expect for Scotland and the northerly situation. Peninsulas between the major firths have a maritime climate of their own.	Some resorts, but relatively untarnished by artificial trappings.
South-east Scotland	Best when offshore wind is blowing giving fine, dry weather. Worst in spring with a north-easter.	Scenic beauty based on coastal castles, small fishing harbours and majestic cliff scenery around St Abb's Head.
North-east England	A continuation of the above though with slightly warmer summers.	Fine sandy beaches attract, but can be dismal on cloudy days. Only hardy bathers, as water offshore is cold except at height of summer. More and more resorts are going in for indoor leisure centres.

East Anglia	Warmest and driest part of coast in summer, especially when south-westerlies are affecting other parts of the country. Can suffer from sea mists, and north-facing coasts are prone to biting winds early and late in the season.	Pleasant if not wildly exciting coastal scenery. Good cliff-top walks between the resorts. Suffolk coast still largely unspoiled and offers good bathing and boating once the estuary section is reached at Bawdsey.
Thames Estuary	Lowest rainfall totals and high sunshine values, though cannot outshine Channel coast.	Resort coast with all that means in terms of wet-day entertainment. Caravan sites are taking over low coasts where land is cheap and not needed by industry.

Climatic Assessment of Retirement Areas

COAST	AREA AND RESORTS COVERED	CLIMATIC CHARACTERISTICS
Eastern Channel	Dover to the Solent: Folkestone, Hastings, Eastbourne, Brighton, Worthing, Bognor Regis.	High sunshine and summer temperatures. Rainfall can be heavier than expected both in winter, brought by the south-westerlies off the sea, and in summer from thunderstorms which develop over France. Cold snaps are rare and most parts do not feel the full force of the biting northerlies or north-easters.
Western Channel	Solent to Start Point: Bournemouth, Swanage, Lyme Regis, Seaton, Sidmouth, Teignmouth, Torquay, Dartmouth.	A little less sunshine and slightly more rainfall than further east. South Devon benefits from shelter of Dartmoor. Easterly winds can be troublesome in winter in places around Tor Bay. Mild weather can have a soporific effect.

South-west Peninsula	Start Point to Burnham-on-Sea: Plymouth, Penzance, Newquay, Bude, Ilfracombe, Minehead.	Mild winter climate and early spring. Winds can be a problem, especially westerly gales along north coast of Cornwall, but sheltered coves and valley sites avoid exposure of the plateau top. Lack of snow another good point. North coast more bracing than south.
Wales	Gower Peninsula to Dee Estuary: Tenby, Milford Haven, St David's, New Quay, Aberystwyth, Barmouth, Pwllheli, Anglesey, Llandudno, Colwyn Bay, Rhyl.	Surprising amount of sunshine for parts of coastland well away from the mountains. West coast often benefits from spells of easterly weather in spring when it can be very dry and sunny. But northerly winds in winter can make the north Wales coast resorts very draughty.
North-west England	Formby Point to Solway: Southport, Blackpool, Morecambe Bay, Silverdale, Arnside, Grange-over-Sands, Silloth.	All rather open to the prevailing south-westerlies so that relatively mild conditions have to compensate for higher than average rainfall. The peninsula-girt northern shore of Morecambe Bay has best all the year round climate.
South-west Scotland	Solway Firth, Galloway round to Clyde.	Similar climatically to north-west England though slightly colder both summer and winter. Long peninsulas of Galloway, Kintyre have low rainfall but are exposed to winter winds. Frost not common and number of days of lying snow is low.

Northern Scotland	Clyde and north-west coast to Cape Wrath including the Hebridean islands and resort-packet ports like Oban, Mallaig, Ullapool; along north coast to Duncansby Head.	Not everyone's choice climatically but if low annual temperatures, windiness and spells of prolonged rainfall can be borne, the dramatic conditions present a challenge to those seeking escape.
Eastern Scotland	Duncansby Head to Berwick including the penetrating firths.	Colder than the west coast but remarkably dry, especially near tips of peninsulas. North-easterly winds in winter and spring mean a late start to warmer weather, but this is often balanced by a pleasant autumn.
North-east England	Berwick to the Wash: Whitley Bay, Saltburn, Whitby, Scarborough, Bridlington, Cleethorpes, Mablethorpe, Skegness.	Bracing climate, healthy for those active in body and mind. Not very wet, but spells of sea mist especially in spring when water offshore is still cold. Continental air blowing across the North Sea brings occasional heavy snow.
East Anglia and Thames Estuary	Wash to North Foreland: Hunstanton, Cromer, Great Yarmouth, Clacton, Southend, Herne Bay, Margate.	Driest part of the British coast with high sunshine figures in summer, though in spring North Sea cloud may drift in over coast. Range of temperature much greater than for west coast due to low winter means. Easterly and northerly weather can bring very chilly conditions and north-east Kent can have heavy snowfalls, even in late spring. Settled summer anticyclonic weather can bring heat-wave conditions, usually tempered by a sea-breeze.

References

Bodin, S. *Weather and Climate* (Blandford, 1978)
Chandler, T. and Gregory, S. *The climate of the British Isles* (Longman, 1976)
Finch, C. R. 'Some heavy rainfalls in Great Britain' *Weather* 27 (1972) pp 364–77
Kidson, C. 'The Exmoor storms and Lyn floods' *Geography* 38 (1953) pp 1–9
Manley, G. *Climate and the British scene* (Collins, 1952)
— 'Topographic features and the climate of Britain' *Geographical Journal* 103 (1944) pp 241–58
Taylor, G. A. (ed) *Climatic resources and Economic activity* (David & Charles, 1974)

7 Coastwise Sailing

Because of the present-day dominance of road and rail as means of travel and transport, it is difficult to think back to the time when goods and people were mainly moved by sea round the coast from port to port. A London directory of 1768 listed no fewer than 580 places in England and Wales where water transport was available and, although a few were newly emergent canal towns, the vast majority were small seaports. The reason why coastal trade enjoyed such an important position was explained by Adam Smith in his *Wealth of Nations* (1776) when he wrote: 'it requires only six to eight men to bring by water to London the same quantity of goods which would otherwise require fifty broad wheeled waggons, attended by a hundred men'. Bulky goods like coal and corn figured largely in the coastwise trade, but the movement of people was not unimportant. There was, for example, a flourishing passenger service in the eighteenth century between London and the Kentish resorts with perhaps up to 20,000 making the sea journey in the Margate hoys each summer. Longer trips were also possible, like the regular passenger service which operated between Leith and London in the summer months. If the winds were unfavourable the sailing vessels might take up to three weeks to pass along the east coast, but at least the voyage was much cheaper than the corresponding journey by coach.

Travel time was considerably reduced in the early decades of the nineteenth century when steamboats replaced the old sailing packets and soon this led to a great increase in coastal traffic. By 1842, for example, there were no fewer than sixteen steamboats plying the Thames between London and Gravesend and carrying more than a million passengers. In other parts of Britain a similar picture of ever-growing sea traffic continues up to the mid-nineteenth century. By then, however, the railways were beginning to pose a threat, largely because they could provide a much speedier, though more costly, service. The demise of the coastal passenger service was a very gradual process, but it meant that many former small harbours underwent decline and even suffered complete extinction in a few cases.

In recent years this decline has been to a certain extent reversed, largely through the mass interest in sailing and messing about in boats, so that many former harbours have experienced a new lease of life. While to many outsiders the weekend sailor seems to spend a disproportionate amount of time in painting and refurbishing his craft, there is no doubt that in many cases he has breathed new life into formerly dying communities. The deeply set harbour of Solva in Dyfed, where emigrant ships once sailed for America, is now a hive of activity on summer weekends, and scores of boats lie at anchor in the sheltered waters of the inlet. Mooring charges, the hire of cranes for lifting yachts in and out of the water, ship chandlering, trade in the local shop and especially the inn, have all contributed to a fresh injection of capital, even though the effect is not to everyone's liking.

With better facilities and changing economic conditions, local fishing is also on the increase in some places, and the visitor can experience all the thrill of waiting for the return of the fishing fleet with the chance to buy from their catch or watch the packing of lobster and crab for a distant market. At Ravenglass on the Cumbrian coast the time of return of the fishing boats is announced on a board by the slipway, creating an air of expectancy. On the Northumberland coast at places like Craster, the wives of the fishermen are once again busy in their sheds dressing the locally-caught crabs, yet another sign of increasing prosperity for the many small harbours and coves around our coasts.

All this renewed activity serves as a reminder that Britain is an offshore island with the sea still playing an important role in the life-pattern of coastal communities, as it has done over past centuries. The same dangers of working in inshore waters are also still present, and the need for local knowledge and experience has not diminished even with the introduction of modern aids to navigation. Skill in seamanship and a familiarity with the coastline and the hidden dangers offshore are just as necessary today as they have been in the past. From time immemorial, a good visual memory of the coastline as seen from the seaward has been recognised as an essential aid to fixing position, especially under conditions of poor visibility. At an early date, distinctive coastal features acquired descriptive names like The Naze (nose), Golden Cap, White Nothe, Barrel of Beef (stack), Cape Wrath etc, which soon became part of the everyday language of the seafarer. When, from the thirteenth century onwards, sailing directions for the east coast of England came into use, they relied heavily on visual observations of natural features of the coastline as well as on specially erected beacons and other sea-marks. Many of the sailing directions in fact contained sketched profiles taken from on board ship. When sea charts came into general use in the sixteenth century these coastal views were incorporated on them, and a realistic attempt made to portray the actual shape of the coastline.

Sea Charts

In spite of interest shown by Tudor monarchs, especially Henry VIII and his daughter Elizabeth I, in maritime affairs, it was a Dutchman who produced the first set of charts of the coastline and coastal waters around Britain. The cartographer was a remarkable man, Lucas Waghenaer, a pilot of Enkhuisen, whose *De Sphiegel der Zeevaert* appeared in 1584 and consisted of twenty-three charts covering the waters from the Baltic to Cadiz. At that time war between England and Spain seemed inevitable, so it was decided to produce an English copy of the sea atlas together with a translation of the sailing directions. It appeared four years later in 1588 as *The Mariner's Mirrour*. History does not relate whether it was used by the English fleet in their tussle with the Spanish Armada, but it is not unlikely as the person responsible for its production was Howard of Effingham, Lord High Admiral of England.

Once the threat from Spain had receded, *The Mariner's Mirrour* became widely used amongst English seamen for navigating the waters around our coasts. Soon a Dutch collection of charts, suitably anglicised, became known as a 'waggoner', and such charts dominated the market for the next hundred years. It is easy to see why they were so popular, for not only did they give a clear indication of the coastline and harbour approaches, they also marked off-lying rocks and other dangers and gave soundings of the depth of available water. Suitably hand-coloured sets of sea charts were to be found in every gentleman's library, and those which survive in good condition are collectors' pieces and fetch high prices at auction. This is understandable for, apart from their practical value, they were objects of cartographic beauty with elaborate cartouche work around the title and set of scales, and delightful sketches of fishes and sea monsters to fill in the ocean.

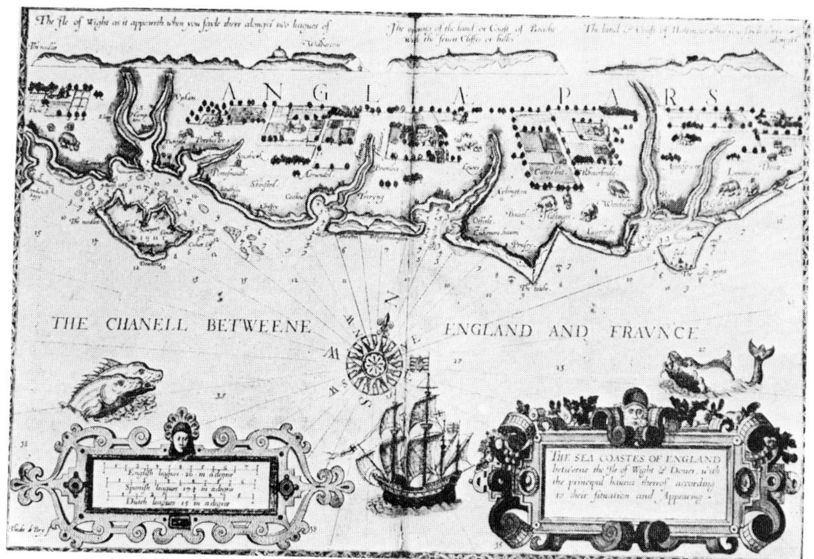

Waghenaer's *Mariner's Mirrour* gave the first real help to the navigator sailing the coasts of Britain. The original was Dutch, but was quickly adapted for English seamen

For a seafaring nation it took Britain a long time to enter the chart-producing business, and it was not until Charles II came to the throne in 1660 that the situation was resolved. Even so *The English Pilot* produced by John Seller in 1670 was based on old Dutch copper plates which had been bought for scrap and then refurbished. This practice quickly earned the condemnation of the Secretary to the Admiralty, Samuel Pepys, who sought the help of the king to initiate an entirely new survey of the British coasts. This was undertaken by Captain Greenvile Collins who, from 1681 to 1688, made a complete circuit of the British Isles including the Orkneys and Shetlands. The end-product was an atlas of forty-eight charts bound together to form *Great Britain's Coasting Pilot*, issued in 1693. Although the individual charts left much to be desired in terms of accuracy, Collins had been given an impossible task in the seven years he spent at sea. Critics there were, but no one could produce a better alternative so it is not surprising that his atlas went through no fewer than fifteen editions between 1693 and 1792.

Soon after this the private chartmaker had to compete with officially produced Admiralty charts, for the Hydrographic Office was founded in 1795 and quickly established itself as the foremost producer of accurate charts covering the world. A great surge forward in the charting of the coasts of Britain occurred in the first half of the nineteenth century, so that by 1850 most of the coastal waters had been surveyed. In place of the earlier highly decorative, but none too correct, charts, the Admiralty product was sober and restrained, relying on accuracy rather than beauty for its reputation. 'Faith in God and the Admiralty chart' had some justification, for as well as being based on good sea surveys the charts were constantly kept up to date, especially in waters liable to change. The notorious Goodwin Sands and the shoal banks in the approaches to the Thames were given special attention, and this remains so today. Although initially the Admiralty surveyors mapped the coastline as well as the sea bed, this is no longer the case, and charts now rely on Ordnance Survey maps for land detail.

Alongside official charts used by larger vessels there are specialist productions, still in the hands of private firms, catering for the needs of fishermen, yachtsmen and amateur sailors in general. Stanfords and Imray, Laurie, Norie & Wilson, for instance, can trace their beginnings as chartmakers right back to the seventeenth century. Many of the fishing charts which are heavily used, often under cramped conditions, have been given a special toughened backing paper so that they are often referred to as 'bluebacks'. Information about sea-bed deposits which might be useful for trawling or fish breeding are a feature of these. Yachtsmen have large-scale charts of harbour approaches and even photographs of the channels available to them. Charts, whether official Hydrographic Department or private publications, emphasise hazards like rocks and shoals, as well as the appropriate type of marker buoy.

Lighthouses

The provision of charts is but one aspect of the quest for safe navigation of our coastal waters and from earliest times a wide range of sea-marks have been built for the same purpose. Dangerous headlands, where an unsuspecting vessel could easily run ashore at night or under conditions of poor visibility, were obvious places to erect towers, perhaps with a brazier or fire basket. In the Mediterranean, fire beacons, the precursors of the modern lighthouse, were in use at least 2,000 years ago. The earliest lighthouse known in Britain is the former Roman pharos at Dover, on the eastern heights above the town. Dover was one of the major ports of Roman entry into this

The Roman pharos next to the church of St Mary within the walls of Dover Castle

country and this lighthouse tower, which could have been built as early as AD 100, is one of the finest and most substantial buildings of the period to survive in Britain. It once saw service as the bell-tower of the adjacent church of St Mary de Castro. Both church and pharos,

St Catherine's Oratory, set high above the coast of the Isle of Wight

enclosed in a huge earthen bank, lie within the walls of Dover Castle. The pharos is built of flint to a height of 19m (62ft), but the top part is medieval. The lower 12m (40ft) however is the original construction of Roman brickwork and local greensand blocks interspersed with bands of red Roman tiles. Formerly there was a tower of similar construction on the western heights as well. Although no other Roman lighthouse is known in Britain, along the coast of Yorkshire and north Devon there are the remains of signal stations which could have provided help to the sailor.

Following the building of the pharos at Dover there was little further activity in this field for the next thousand years. If lighthouses were built at all during the so-called Dark Ages they have left no tangible remains. Only in the twelfth and thirteenth centuries when the medieval church seems to have become involved, largely on humanitarian grounds, do we find a resumption of lighthouse building. Some of these ecclesiastical lights have survived and nearly all are substantial buildings of architectural merit. Perhaps the best example is the prominent, octagonal tower on top of St Catherine's Down in the southern part of the Isle of Wight. The provision of this light arose from a lawsuit about a vessel which was wrecked on the offshore reefs in the winter of 1314. The vessel was owned by a monastery in Picardy and the monks sought redress from the local squire, Walter de Godoton (Godeton, Godyton), who had managed to rescue much of the cargo of wine and sell it for his own profit. After a court hearing and a threat of excommunication from the pope, Godoton was ordered to make amends by building an oratory and lighthouse on the nearby hill-top to prevent any future strandings. This was duly done, as a record of 1328 shows, and today the tower with the fragmentary remains of the oratory alongside stand as tangible proof of the lawsuit 650 years ago. The light was probably an open fire which burned from the top of the tower and would have been lit as a warning to sailors during stormy weather. At the time of the Dissolution, the arrangement seems to have lapsed. Trinity House later stepped in and in 1780 began building a new lighthouse close to the former oratory, but the work was never completed once it was realised that a much better position lay nearer the cliff edge. The remains of the partially completed lighthouse are still standing on the downland crest, and look down on the new light which Trinity House built in 1840. It is worthwhile making the walk up to the former oratory from the car park on the main coastal road, if only for the tempting views on a fine day.

Many of the ecclesiastical lights were not purpose built but simply adaptations of existing buildings. The chapel on St Aldhelm's Head in the Isle of Purbeck in Dorset served as a place of worship and also incorporated a guiding beacon for seamen when the need arose. A

The squat chapel built at St Aldhelm's Head in the Isle of Purbeck with what is reputedly a fire beacon rising from its roof

walk of about 3km (2 miles) along a stony track from the farm at the road-end beyond Worth Matravers brings you to this squat building with its fine Norman door and vaulted interior, dedicated to the saint who was first Bishop of Sherborne. In the centre of the roof is a curious cylindrical structure which is reputed to have been a receptacle for a fire lit to warn mariners of the projecting headland and its off-lying limestone reefs.

Many other chapels situated in similar positions near the cliff top have had claims made for them that they served as beacons to warn the sailor of dangerous headlands. Undoubtedly some were attended by hermits who, as part of their religious life, kept lonely vigil to provide a service of benefit to passing shipping. The service was not necessarily free for, where circumstances permitted, dues were collected to maintain the fire beacon. One hermit, Richard Reedbarrow, has passed into the records, for his name appears in the Meaux Abbey Cartulary as 'being responsible for the light at Ravensporne near the end of Spurn Spit at the entrance to the Humber'. Because of coastal changes nothing remains of the light nor of the former port of Ravenserodd which is believed to have stood nearby, but Spurn Spit has a long history of lighthouse building with numerous attempts made to provide shipping bound for the Humber ports with a guiding beacon. After Reedbarrow's light had perished through coast erosion, Angell's lighthouse was built in 1674 but this suffered the same fate. In 1760 the engineer John Smeaton provided yet another light, but because of further coastal erosion and an alteration in the navigable channels six further lights were provided between 1778 and 1851. The present light, now under the control of Trinity House, is again under threat, and it has been necessary to build a concrete apron to prevent the washing away of the sand dunes which front it.

Trinity House, the authority responsible for providing and maintaining lighthouses and other sea-marks around the coast of England and Wales, can claim a long and distinguished history of service in the quest for safer navigation in coastal waters. The Brotherhood of Trinity House of Deptford Strand in London were granted their charter as early as 1514. This was reinforced by an Act of Parliament in 1566 which gave them virtual monopoly in erecting lights, beacons and 'other signes for the sea'. Though later challenged by the Crown to whom the granting of rights to private individuals to build lighthouses was a profitable source of income, Trinity House clung tenaciously to this privilege. Even so they seem to have been rather tardy in building lighthouses. Possibly the first was erected at Lowestoft in 1609, though two years earlier they had taken over two towers at Caister near Yarmouth for use as light beacons. Further building took place at intervals, so that by 1801 the Brethren had twenty-three lighthouses under their control. At that time there were still a number of private lights at various points on the coast, but an Act of Parliament in 1836 transferred them all to Trinity House on payment of suitable compensation. Today all the lighthouses on the coast of England and Wales are under their jurisdiction, along with some 30 lightships at sea and almost 700 buoys (see page 145) which have to be maintained and re-positioned should the need arise. The most recently built lighthouse stands near the tip of the great shingle promontory of Dungeness in Kent – a slender pencil of interlocking concrete blocks pointing skywards, with the old lighthouse standing forlorn alongside.

Scotland, as in so many things, has taken an independent approach in the building of lighthouses. Although some private ones were built during the seventeenth and eighteenth centuries, the main task of lighting the intricate Scottish coastline fell to the Commission of Northern Lighthouses, a body akin to Trinity House. The story of this Scottish institution largely revolves round the unique contribution made by one family, the Stevensons (which included the author, Robert Louis). Successive generations of the family were closely involved with lighthouse-building over a period of two hundred years, so that nearly every light and beacon in these northern waters bears evidence of their workmanship.

A start was made in 1786 when a body of nineteen trustees was founded to promote a scheme for lighting the Scottish coasts. Their first task was to find a suitable engineer and their choice was an Edinburgh lampmaker, Thomas Smith, who had been experimenting for some years with various forms of reflector. Kinnairds Head on the north-east coast near Fraserburgh, North Ronaldsay in the Orkneys, Eilean Glas on the island of Scalpay in the Outer Hebrides and the Mull of Kintyre, were the four initial sites chosen. In spite of tremendous difficulties in design and construction, all were functioning by the winter of 1789. Shortly afterwards Smith took on Robert Stevenson as assistant and this initiated a period of tremendous activity and enterprise. Robert Stevenson has been named as the greatest of all lighthouse engineers and amongst his triumphs was the lighting of the infamous Bell Rock, a sunken ledge of red sandstone lying well offshore but in the navigable approaches to the Firths of Tay and Forth. His son Alan clearly benefited from his teaching so that in time he was given responsibility for the difficult construction of the Skerryvore light, set on a pinnacle rock west of the island of Tiree.

After the retirement of Robert Stevenson in 1843, Alan took over. A decade later the Crimean War had started and in a curious way led to the building of a group of lighthouses in the Shetlands. The reason was that the British fleet returning from blockading Russian vessels in the White Sea were in danger of stranding on the unmarked islands of the Shetland group. Amongst the lights commissioned at this time was the famous Muckle Flugga rock. This isolated mini-Matterhorn rising 60m (200ft) out of the sea in a pyramid tested the ingenuity of Stevenson, but it was duly completed and so became, as it still is today, the most northerly lighthouse in the British Isles.

Apart from their interest in lighthouse construction, the Stevenson family left their mark on the coastline in other ways, notably in the design and construction of a score of tiny fishing harbours. Many of these were given breakwaters and quays when the Fisheries Board was anxious to provide alternative means of employment to farming.

Sea-marks

In his quest for safer navigation in the shoal-beset waters around our coast man has often made use of a variety of sea-marks other than lighthouses and light beacons – church towers, windmills, masts and chimneys have all been pressed into service as day-marks for fixing position at sea. The ancient church of Reculver, on the north coast of Kent, is one example. In AD 669 a priest, Bassa, was given the ruins of the former Roman fort of *Regulbium* in order to build a minster. His church was simple in design, but was added to later in Norman times, the principal addition being the distinctive twin towers with steeples at the western end. In 1809 when the church was pulled down, largely to satisfy the whim of the vicar's mother, Trinity House stepped in to preserve the towers, the Twin Sisters, which had for so long provided navigators with a clearly visible sea-mark. The Brethren also ordered the building of a great concrete bastion on the seaward side of the church to prevent further erosion, and had two pyramidal beacons erected on top of the towers to make them even more visible from the sea. Now, almost two hundred years later, the towers remain, though no longer of value to navigation but of great interest because of the site's archaeological importance.

Another example of a church used as a marker is in the Isle of Wight at St Helens, where any visitor to Bembridge harbour must notice the church tower standing naked on the beach. The original chancel was lost through erosion, and the tower would have suffered a similar fate but for Trinity House preventing its collapse and then painting its seaward side white to be used as a sea-mark for vessels entering the eastern Solent or seeking anchorage off the Nab.

An example of a windmill used as a sea-mark is the one which formerly stood at Shottenden in Kent which, although 16km (10 miles) inland, sat high on the Downs and was in consequence easily visible from the sea. Even clumps of trees became familiar to seamen, who would use them as a sighting mark when making their way through intricate waters in approaching harbour. Samuel Pepys in his Naval Minutes refers to one such clump near Harwich, while the famous Chanctonbury Ring on the South Downs once fulfilled the same function.

Other day-marks include unlit beacons which originally were simple piles of stones, rather like cairns, set on prominent points along the coast to make them clearly visible from the sea. Many are now elaborate structures of concrete, often given a distinctive shape to aid

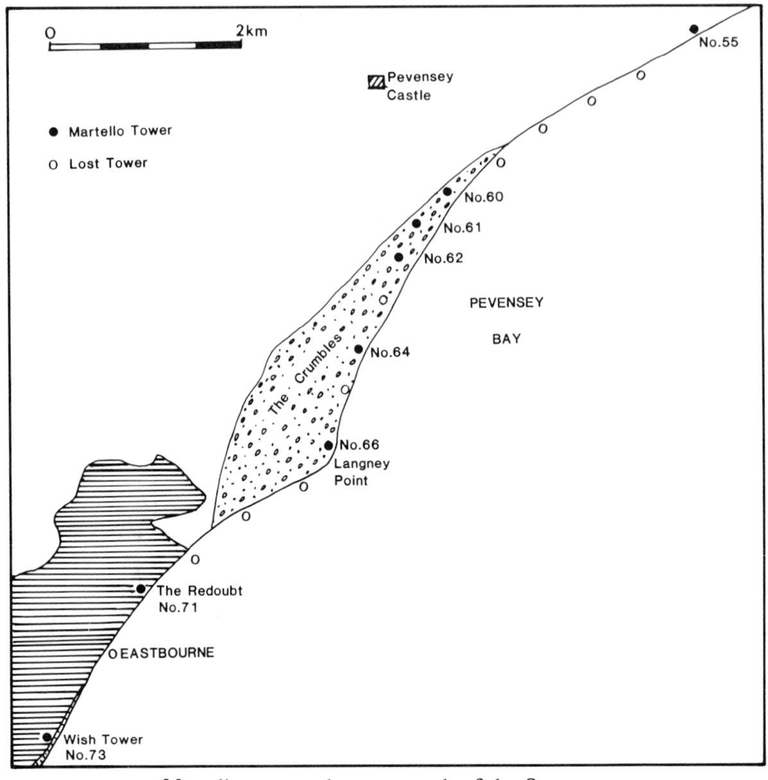

Martello towers along a stretch of the Sussex coast

identification. In Anglesey there are twin Coal Rock Beacons, triangular in elevation but T-shaped in plan. They were built in the early years of the nineteenth century on Carmel Head as sighting-marks for vessels rounding the north-west corner of the island, bound for Liverpool. On the other side of Anglesey on the projecting Llanddwyn Island, really a peninsula only cut off from the mainland at high spring tides, there is a 6m (20ft) high beacon which was built to aid the sailor making his way towards the southern entrance to the Menai Strait and the port of Caernarfon. Some beacons on isolated reefs or rocks were provided with platforms or even a primitive shelter, so that they could be used as a refuge following shipwreck. Attempts to provide similar refuge beacons on sandbanks have not been very successful, for the lack of a suitable foundation has invariably meant that the beacon has been destroyed after a few years. The most famous, Bullock's Beacon, was erected on the Goodwin Sands in the middle of the last century and was even provided with a store of food and water, but it was doomed to failure from the outset, in spite of the novel pile-structure used in its construction.

Martello towers form a gratuitous kind of sea-mark dating back to the threat of invasion during the Napoleonic Wars at the beginning of the nineteenth century. Massive, squat, circular structures of stone or brick – altogether 105 – were built around the coasts of south-east England from Aldeburgh in the north to Seaford in Sussex in the west in the space of only three years from 1805–8. Strangely other such towers were built in more remote places like Ireland, Jersey and, most surprisingly, the Orkneys. Basically Italian in design and named after Cape Mortella in Italy where a similar circular defensive tower proved its worth during an English invasion of 1794, they presented individual strongpoints able to withstand prolonged attack from an invading force. Many no longer exist, for coast erosion has taken its toll. Those which survive have been put to a number of uses for, in addition to providing good sea-marks, many have been turned into water-towers, cafés, museums, or even private homes. Their sheer bulk has made it difficult to alter them drastically, so that the martello tower still remains very much part of the coastal scene.

Buoys

The inshore leisure sailor, especially the one who only puts to sea at weekends or during the summer-holiday period, is likely to be less knowledgeable about the intricacies and pitfalls of local navigation than the fisherman who has learned through years of experience. Fortunately tangible help is available in that inshore sailing guides relating to each section of the coast and large-scale charts give information on the system of buoyage and beacons which exists in British coastal waters. For centuries Trinity House has assumed responsibility for providing and maintaining the main buoys, about 700 in all, marking the shipping lanes and dangerous reefs and sandbanks. Local harbour authorities also maintain floating sea-marks in areas under their control, and adopt the same method of designation as Trinity House. On entering a channel in the direction of the flood (ingoing) current, buoys on the port (left-hand) side are coloured red, or red and white check, and are can-shaped. On the starboard (right-hand) side black, or black and white, conical buoys mark the edge of the channel. To mark shoals in the centre of the channel middle-ground buoys with distinctive topmarks are used, their colour and shape

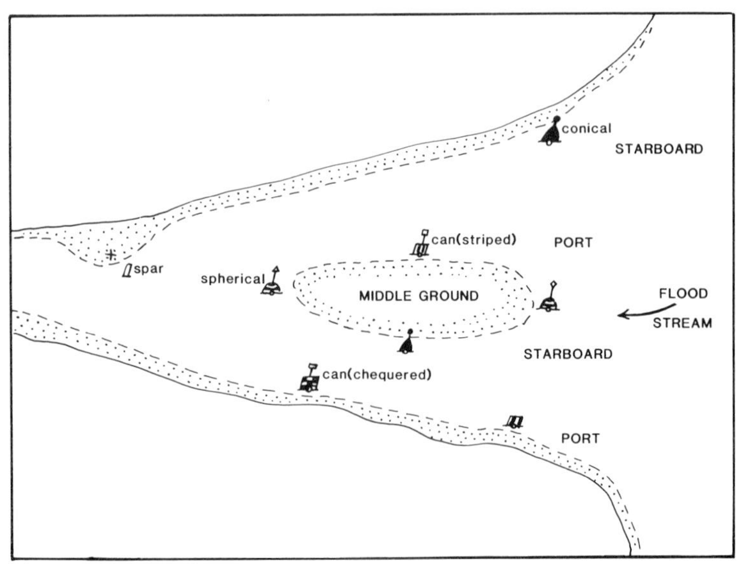

The buoyage system used in British coastal waters

reflecting the best navigable channel to follow either to the right or left of the sandbank. In busy shipping lanes the buoys have a flashing light, but in most of the smaller harbours they remain unlit and the local boatman has to 'feel' his way in carefully after dark. Sometimes a simple spar buoy suffices to mark the tip of a shoal, especially one which is liable to change position from time to time.

Rescue Services

In recent years even small craft have equipped themselves with sophisticated navigational aids like Decca, inertial systems and satellite fixing devices; but in spite of this the well-tried methods of seamanship still hold good. Traverse sailing and plotting the course by dead reckoning, with occasional three-point fixes on land objects as a check, still serve the majority of small-boat enthusiasts, including the yachtsmen who by sail alone still challenge the natural forces. In facing the elements, accidents to craft inshore inevitably occur, some unforeseen but in many cases as a result of ignoring warning signs of deteriorating weather. In either case, assistance is at hand, and the coast is ringed with lifeboat stations, the characteristic shed and the steeply sloping ramp running down into the sea to allow quick launching. The coastal distribution of the lifeboat stations is interesting in that it reflects both the intensity of the shipping traffic and the danger which the natural elements present. For the north-east coast of England there are no fewer than fourteen full stations between Amble and Bridlington maintained by the Royal National Lifeboat Institution. Further south the number decreases with only one station, Skegness on the Lincolnshire coast, a reflection of the fact that the main shipping channels are now much further offshore. For some areas the RNLI maintains fast inshore rescue boats and increasingly they are proving useful in holiday areas, for the growth of sailing as a hobby has meant that the lifeboat is now often needed just as much in the summer months when a small craft has got into difficulty as in the severe storms of winter. Inshore waters and the 'inland' seas around Britain need respecting just as much as our mountain tops and the foolhardy and ill-equipped are liable to suffer the same fate in both situations.

References

Beaver, P. *A history of lighthouses* (Peter Davies, 1971)
Hague, D. B. and Christie, R. *Lighthouses, their architecture, history and archaeology* (Gomer Press, 1975)
Mair, C. *A star for seamen* (John Murray, 1978)
Mead, H. P. *Trinity House* (Low (Sampson), Marston, 1947)
Sutcliffe, S. *Martello Towers* (David & Charles, 1972)

8 The Coast and the Artist

It would be surprising, in view of the length and variety of the coastline of Britain, if seascapes did not form part of the output of established artists. That having been said, landscape artists have shown a much greater willingness to portray countryside scenes, only occasionally making excursions to the coast. Constable is the outstanding example for, although he was born and lived much of his life close to the tideway, his coastal pictures are something of a rarity and little known, certainly when compared with his rural scenes in Dedham Vale and the Stour Valley. For many marine artists the coastline was simply the backcloth for their portrayal of ships in full sail, often battling against mountainous seas.

Amongst artists who captured the wildness, hazards and dynamic atmosphere of the coastal scene, J. M. W. Turner stands pre-eminent, not only in terms of output but also because of the new dimension he brought to art. In the watercolour drawings he made for a set of line-engravings published as *Picturesque Views in England and Wales* in 1825, Turner included a large number of coastal and estuary scenes. His fascination with water as a moving force is shown in his painting 'The Fall of the Tees' and in the many castle subjects which include a river in the foreground. But it is in the truly coastal settings that his gifts of capturing the turbulent atmosphere and ever-changing pattern of sea and sky really come to the fore. Stormy seas, surmounted by equally stormy skies, characterise his portrayal of 'The Entrance to Fowey Harbour' and also dominate the equally dramatic seascape of Holy Island (Lindisfarne) off the Northumberland coast.

Nature has always been a force to be reckoned with so that in many of his paintings Turner portrays man struggling against hostile elements. Even under quieter conditions, as in his painting of the Kent cliffs between Folkestone and Dover, conflict is the theme; not this time man struggling against natural forces but rather pitting his wits against the authorities. Smuggling of contraband goods across the narrow waters of the Straits of Dover was commonplace in the early years of the nineteenth century and formed the subject matter of a number of Turner's coastal paintings. He must have been very familiar with the illicit trade and in his Kent coast painting portrays a coastguard official supervising the location of brandy casks buried below the sandy beach. A mule stands by ready to whisk away the captured booty.

The contrast between the natural and the man-made is a recurring theme in Turner's coastal pictures, especially his sequence of coastal castles. The huge lofty battlements seem to have had a peculiar fascination for the artist, as though they were the one human object that was on a parity with the splendour and scale of nature. Flint Castle, one of the late thirteenth-century castles built by Edward I on the north Wales coast, figures as the backcloth for two paintings depicting shrimpers working their nets through the shallow waters of the Dee shore in the early morning, just as the rising sun is beginning to bathe the scene in a warm glow. To John Ruskin writing in 1878, almost fifty years after the picture had been completed, this was 'the loveliest piece of pure water colour painting in my whole collection'.

Turner's interest in depicting various forms of human activity taking place along the shoreline is further exemplified in the paintings of Caernarfon and Beaumaris Castles, set by Edward I at each end of the Menai Strait. Pure seascapes form only a very small part of Turner's considerable output of coastal pictures. It was his view, now widely accepted, that landscapes and, to a lesser extent seascapes, owe as much to man as to nature. Only the wildest and remotest stretches of coastline can be considered truly natural and these were areas which Turner never visited nor seemingly wished to depict. For Caernarfon the view is of the castle battlements from a boat, but Turner also includes a coracle fisherman on the beach. At Beaumaris the castle occupies the middle distance, but the foreground is dominated by longshore fishermen digging for lugworms. All three castle paintings were derived from the journey Turner made to north Wales in 1792, his first-ever sketching tour. It was on this visit as a young man that he probably first became aware of the splendours of mountain and sea, 'the two great voices' of Wordsworth. He himself describes in his diary the impact of Snowdon when 'seen to be impregnated with gold and silver from the rays of the setting sun', an impression faithfully recorded in the background to the Beaumaris Castle painting.

The cliffs and hill-top town of Dunwich as seen by Turner. The ruined church of All Saints and other buildings speak of decline under the constant threat of erosion

In a completely different mood is the watercolour of Dunstanburgh Castle on the bleak low shores of the Northumberland coast. This was one of a number of fortifications in the border region built to repel the Scots but, unlike the Edwardian castles of north Wales, had been allowed to fall into ruin. Its great circular gatehouse towers (still in existence when Turner visited it), along with the jagged outlines of the crumbling castle walls, proved ideal material for Turner; and in the painting he captures a mood of isolated splendour on the rocky headland formed of the columnar rocks of the Whin Sill. Turner had probably seen Dunstanburgh in his youth and later refreshed his memories of the scene from an illustration in Boswell's *Antiquities.* It obviously made a life-long impression on him, for the castle was used in no fewer than five of his paintings. However, in order to bring out the dramatic qualities of the exposed site Turner indulged in a little artistic licence and allowed himself to raise the headland much higher than reality. This was a wrecker's coast, and in some of his Dunstanburgh paintings a dismasted and stranded vessel is being looked over by locals in search of salvage. Although the storm has abated the sea is still angry, and dark-coloured waves break on the

St Michael's Mount, off the Cornish coast, a dramatic coastal scene which Turner found very much to his liking

beach with all the ferocity that this coastline knows when a stiff nor'-easter is blowing.

More placid waters fill the canvas of a number of Turner paintings of the East Anglian coast. His watercolours of Aldeburgh and Orford in Suffolk encapsulate the bustle of small ports in the early nineteenth century. Both are river and harbour scenes, which allow more detail to be incorporated than in many of his open coastline settings. For Aldeburgh the central theme is the River Alde as it sweeps past the southern fringes of a town made famous in the poems of George Crabbe and subsequently in the music of Benjamin Britten. Part of the long strand of shingle running for several miles to Orfordness is shown together with its martello tower which at that time must have been very fresh in the memory, having been built in 1807 to counter the threat of a Napoleonic invasion. As with his Dunstanburgh paintings, Turner found it necessary to indulge in a little artistic licence to give more prominence to the town and its parish church. At the time Aldeburgh was beginning to emerge as a fashionable resort but the main activity was still fishing, the focal point of interest of the painting. As the fishermen toil, wearily dragging in their nets, a sense of tranquillity and peace is provided by the boat gliding by in full sail, and the brilliant white light of summer which characterises the Suffolk coastline obviously caught the mood and imagination of Turner. His painting of Orford, a few miles down-river, forms a companion piece, as it represents a summer scene of stillness in the early morning air with the mists having just risen from the neighbouring marshes. The town, with its huge castle-keep alongside the parish church, shows off its past glory as a contrast to the present humble activities of the crab fishermen in the foreground.

Turner's use of coastal themes to portray hardship and danger is exemplified in his watercolour of Morecambe Bay. With its expansive flats drying out at low water, there had been a passage across the sands from time immemorial in order to avoid the long detour around the head of the bay. It was a dangerous crossing for there were channels to be forded, quicksands to be avoided and, above all, the perils of being stranded by the rapidly advancing tide. Guides were essential to lead the long caravans of carts, pack-trains and travellers but even so each year claimed its toll of drownings. A sense of urgency and anxiety prevailed and this atmosphere is captured by Turner in the faces of his hurrying travellers, some on foot but others dependent on the skill of the coachman using his whip to drive the horses forward. Already the tide is flooding up the channels and one group dragging their hand-cart seems in danger of being cut off. The majestic setting of the painting, with the Lake District in the background, has to take second place in the mind of the artist whose main task is to convey the perils of the road across the sands. To Ruskin the painting represented an evening in spring when the breaking waves were catching the last light of sunset before the dark-blue tones of night advanced over the sea. The theme has been repeated many times since Turner's day, but no one has succeeded to the same extent in combining the atmosphere of the natural setting and the fear of the travellers.

An equally hazardous journey in the late eighteenth and early nineteenth centuries was that along the north coast of Wales around the headland of Penmaenmawr. Again this was a subject that fascinated Turner who could always see the eternal battle raging between man and nature. For centuries the route around the headland had been fraught with danger and had even deterred the Romans who chose instead to drive their road through the inland hills. The building of a massive sea-wall in 1772 did little to lessen the danger for at high tide the sea could still pour over the road when lashed by northerly gales and, as the intrepid Dr Johnson found on his tour of north

Wales, it was best to get round the headland by taking to the sands at low tide. Turner naturally chose the more dramatic way with a stage-coach battling round the headland road in danger of being swamped by the waves on one side or buried by a rock fall from above. It was from observations on his visit to north Wales in 1792 that the painting was conceived. In his diary of the time Turner records 'that tremendous mountain running by the sea side with the Puffin or Preston's shore . . . a fine scene'. His painting is a faithful recording of this much earlier impression, much of it being in shadow with the sombre theme shown up in varying tones of brown and with the coach's anxious passengers looking at the dual hazards of sea and landslide.

Apart from Turner the other well known English painters of the early nineteenth century made only rare excursions into the coastal scene and then not always successfully. Most of their paintings lack the delicate lighting effects of sun on water, or the contrasts of colour and tone when the sun is low in the sky at morning or dusk, which are so apparent in the Turner watercolours. Artistic licence was very much the order of the day as an aid to composition, and in some cases complete misplacement is apparent. One of Gainsborough's rare sea-scapes – labelled Mettingham Castle and now on view at Anglesey Abbey, a National Trust property near Cambridge – is of a seaside scene, and yet in reality Mettingham Castle lies more than ten miles inland close to the banks of the River Waveney.

Gainsborough is rightly thought of as a portrait painter and therefore his neglect of his native coastline is not surprising. For his fellow Suffolk artist, John Constable, the omission is less understandable, bearing in mind his great love of landscape scenes. Born in the village of East Bergholt in 1776, a year after his great contemporary Turner, he matured slowly and it was not until after 1800 that he began to paint the pictures on which his reputation mainly rests. He never had to live in penury like the youthful Turner for he was able to depend on the small allowance given to him by his well-to-do miller father. This saved him from the pressure of having to paint or perish, but it may also have delayed his maturity.

Although today Constable is rightly regarded as an artist of the countryside with his many paintings of scenes around his home in the Stour valley of Suffolk, he did produce a number of fine and largely underestimated seascapes, nearly all the result of rare excursions he made to the coast. The earliest to be exhibited at the Royal Academy,

Although not usually looked upon as a marine artist, Constable did produce a number of fine coastal scenes, such as this one of Weymouth Bay

and dated 1820, was of Harwich lighthouse and the low shore on which it stands. It was painted probably in the hope that his patron, General Rebow, would purchase the work. More dramatic is the sketch he made of Weymouth Bay in 1816, when he spent part of his honeymoon at Osmington. With a darkened sky sending a shaft of light to illuminate the beach below the crumbling cliffs, it has an atmosphere that is not usually associated with Constable. More typical perhaps is the National Gallery oil painting of the same scene which he completed in 1817. This has a more usual Constable sky with scurrying clouds casting fleeting shadows on the distant hillside.

But though the Weymouth Bay paintings were from a very happy period in his life, they still convey the impression that Constable felt more at home with inland scenes. He never fully came to grips with the inherent problems posed by coastal settings – the dominance of sea and sky. By the time he visited Brighton in 1824 with his ailing wife Maria, his distaste was given full expression in a letter written to his friend Archdeacon Fisher. Seashore scenes he considered trite and 'are so hackneyed in the Exhibition and are in fact so little capable of beautiful sentiment that landscape is capable of . . . that they have done a great deal of harm to the art'. In spite of this stricture his Brighton sketches, which he ultimately used in his paintings 'Brighton

Beach' (1824) and 'Chain Pier' (1827), served him well. When his Chain Pier oil painting was hung at the Royal Academy Exhibition in 1827, the art critic of *The Times* pronounced Constable as being 'unquestionably the finest landscape painter of the day', much to the discomfiture of his rival Turner. Perhaps the review proved an encouragement that had previously been lacking for even in his sadness following his wife's death in 1828 he painted Hadleigh Castle, set high on the Essex shore overlooking the wide expanses of marsh and sea at the entrance to the Thames Estuary. By now he was able to write, 'I was always delighted with the melancholy grandeur of a sea shore. At Hadleigh there is the ruin which from its situation is a really fine place – it commands a view of the Kent Hills, the Nore and North Foreland and looking many miles to sea.' Perhaps the painting, following the bereavement, expressed his feelings of emptiness in terms of the vastness of sea and marshland. Certainly by using oil Constable achieved a heaviness which in his other coastal works had seemed inappropriate. It is significant that when he returned to painting coastal scenes, as in his portrayal of Littlehampton Harbour in 1835, he preferred watercolour. The painting is also notable in that it shows how the artist had developed and varied his technique in the intervening years. Instead of solid colour he was able to give the subject extra vibrance through a process of scraping out.

Of all the regions of the country East Anglia stands out in the late eighteenth and early nineteenth centuries as having the most gifted landscape artists, especially those associated with the Norwich School. Two of their number, John Crome (born 1768) and John Sell Cotman (born 1782), are important for they achieved national rather than local fame. Although both are thought of as artists of the Norfolk countryside, Crome in particular produced some noteworthy coastal views. His 'Yarmouth Water Frolics', 'Yarmouth Beach' and 'Yarmouth Jetty' were all painted following a visit to the port and resort in 1808. Slightly later came his 'Cromer Beach' showing the crumbling yellow cliffs under a threatening grey sky. John Cotman also made periodic visits to the Norfolk coastline and has left us a number of coastal settings which form the backcloth to his representation of ships at anchor. Later he was to travel abroad and it was a stormy return passage from Le Havre to Southampton in 1817 that gave him 'a new sense of grandeur and sublimity'. It was on this voyage that he made the drawing for his most famous marine work, the view of the Needles stacks at the western extremity of the Isle of

Wight, a painting now in the Norwich Museum.

Another East Anglian painter with a limited though important set of seascapes is Philip Wilson Steer (1860–1912). As a young man he came every summer between 1884 and 1891 to the thriving artist's colony at Walberswick on the south side of Southwold Harbour entrance. Nearly all the pictures which resulted include groups of colourfully dressed girls, and they are noteworthy for the way in which Steer used the rather elusive highlighting effects which characterise this coastline in summer. In the painting of the open sea off Walberswick his effects have been compared with Whistler's marine studies.

The impact which a group of artists choosing to live together can have on the local region is perhaps best seen in Cornwall where both the Newlyn and St Ives Schools have had periods of great fulfilment and served as a magnet drawing others from different parts of the country. They developed in the late nineteenth century when earlier schools like those of Bath, Bristol and Norwich had declined. Newlyn can trace its beginnings to the early 1880s following an invasion of artists who found the old fishing town to their liking. One of the earliest arrivals was Stanhope Forbes who found 'every corner was a picture' and, more important for a figure painter, people who seemed to fall naturally into place and harmonise with their surroundings. Many of his local scenes, like his 'A Fish Sale on a Cornish Beach' owe much more to the groups of people rather than to the place. Whereas Turner generally included human figures as secondary elements in a larger setting, in the paintings of Stanhope Forbes the role was usually reversed. As a result the distinctive atmosphere of his paintings derives from the stern, uncompromising expression on the faces of the fisherfolk rather than the wildness of the Cornish cliffs or the loneliness of the shoreline.

Across the other side of the Penwith Peninsula the art colony of St Ives can trace its beginnings to the years 1883–4 when both Whistler and Sickert came in search of pastures new. Along the sea front of Porthmeor a group of old sail lofts was converted into studios which, over the years, have been used by artists who have come to be regarded as belonging to the St Ives School. Whistler's stay in 1883 was short but it resulted in a brilliant series of seascapes, mostly small oil sketches painted out of doors. He was able to write to a friend, 'The country you know never lasts me long and if it had not been for the sea I should have been back before now'; a sentiment with which many

John Cotman's impression of the Needles stacks as he entered the Western Solent on his return voyage from France

visitors to Cornwall would agree, contrasting the superb quality of the coastal scenery with the comparatively dull inland areas. Many of Whistler's sea sketches like his 'Green and Gold: the Great Sea' have a sparkling brilliance which only the clear maritime air can give. To some they recall the effects achieved by Constable with his 'Brighton Beach'.

Of the modern St Ives painters, Ben Nicholson has an established reputation based on a wide range of subjects. He lived in St Ives from 1939 to 1958 and included a number of seascapes amongst his many paintings. His introduction to the coastal scene came much earlier than his arrival at St Ives, for it dates from 1923 when he visited Paul Nash at Dymchurch in Kent. His 'Dymchurch Wall', painted in bold straight lines, shows the influence of Nash's watercolours. By 1940, when he was firmly settled in St Ives, he had developed his own distinctive style and attained maturity of expression. This continued during his stay in Cornwall and in his picture of Mousehole painted in 1947 there is a combination of contrasting elements, the crystalline crispness of still-life being used alongside the spaciousness of natural form and a generally open layout. Another coastal view, this time of St Ives Harbour and painted in 1957 from the terrace of his home, is notable for the way in which he chose to highlight three red-painted boats from the wealth of subject matter within his compass.

When we consider Wales there are few artists, either national or local apart from Turner, who seem to have proved equal to the task of recording on paper or canvas the unrivalled beauty and sheer magnificence of coastlines like those of the Gower Peninsula, Pembrokeshire, Cardigan Bay or the Llŷn. Often the Welsh coastline was simply included in a mammoth collection of sketches or prints covering the whole of Britain. This is the case with William Daniell's series of 304 aquatints entitled *A voyage round Great Britain*, based on visiting nearly every headland, beach and seaside town in the years 1813 to 1825. Most of Daniell's work was done from land though occasionally, as at South Stack on Holy Island in Anglesey, he went out to sea to sketch the cliffs and the islet with the famous lighthouse perched on top.

Apart from great compendia like that of Daniell, other seascapes of the Welsh coast tend to be single commissions, sometimes by an established artist though more commonly by a lesser known painter. In a neglected field the work of the Birmingham artist David Cox (1783–1859) stands out. Every summer in the forties and fifties of last century, Cox took up residence in the cosy village of Betws-y-Coed in Snowdonia and painted many local scenes which became well known and encouraged other Victorian landscape painters to visit the area. Less familiar are his works relating to the Welsh coast. His 'Rhyl Sands', a light and breezy effort, shows the resort just as it was beginning a period of rapid development in mid-Victorian days but before it had acquired a brashness that made it very different from resorts like Llandudno or Colwyn Bay. Of the same period is the painting which Cox made of Beaumaris and the adjacent Anglesey coast. The principal theme is a turbulent sea thundering against the sea wall which protects the southern flank of the town, while in the background are the town's main buildings of note, including the fine tower of the parish church. Also prominent is the fine sweep of Bulkeley Terrace, built of local limestone and sited to take full advantage of the open view across the waters of the Menai Strait to the mountains of Snowdonia. As in many of Cox's drawings the storm clouds are passing and the eastern skies are lightening as if to herald a more peaceful end to the day.

Victorian painters like Cox were masters of the dramatic, and in their coastal pictures they were able to give full expression to the

An aquatint by William Daniell, showing the lighthouse at South Stack in Anglesey, from his series *A voyage round Great Britain*

dynamic qualities of a stormy sea. In this century the emphasis has changed and, for an artist like Graham Sutherland, attention to detail and a search for unexpected and unusual twists of nature has been very much to the fore. Sutherland first visited Pembrokeshire in 1934 and immediately his art was affected by facets in the landscape which had not occurred to him previously. He later wrote: 'It was in this area that I learned that landscape was not necessarily scenic but that its parts have an individual figurative detachment.' The headwater creeks leading down to Milford Haven gave him the ideas which, after a period of gestation, were to become the basis of his expressionist paintings. His other love was the estuary shores near the Picton Castle estate and Sandy Haven, where gnarled tree roots exposed in the bankside and the multiplicity of curious rock forms became subjects of his fertile imagination. Lighting effects could completely alter an ordinary scene, and in Pembrokeshire Sutherland found the clear air both magical and transforming. Subject matter which he found in Porth Clais, south of St Davids, on the shores of the Cleddau estuary or in the drowned valley of Solva – his 'hidden places' – were used by him as the basis of a group of Pembrokeshire paintings. Their attraction lies not only in the fine line-work but also in the richness and subtlety of colour hidden in familiar objects.

After a gap of more than twenty years, most of which was spent in France, Sutherland returned to south-west Wales in 1967 in connection with the making of a television film devoted to his work. He soon discovered that the Pembrokeshire countryside and coastline, which he thought he had exhausted, had still much to offer. More paintings followed, and these have become the core of a collection which is now housed in a specially built annexe at Picton Castle, east of Haverfordwest and open to public view. In a sense the collection at Picton is a memorial to Sutherland, and stemmed from his wish that paintings done in a particular area are best seen in that area. With this in mind, a visit to the art gallery should be followed by a journey to the shores of the nearby creek where the artist found so much of his inspiration.

Considering the richness of the Scottish scenery, especially along its western seaboard, it is surprising that few artists of national renown ever made their way north. By and large the Scottish coastline has been left mainly to homebred artists who have produced some noteworthy pictures. None has specialised in coastal settings though a surprisingly large number from about 1850 onwards have made occasional forays into the field of seascapes. One of the better known of the Scottish Victorian artists was William McTaggart (1835–1910) who first made his mark in the 1860s. Basically he was a landscape artist in the purest sense though, like so many of his predecessors including the great Turner, his portrayal of natural scenery was nearly always accompanied by a human element, usually a group of people. Only 'The Wave', painted in 1880, deals purely with nature.

Many of McTaggart's seascapes record events in Scottish history. Perhaps in this he showed his provincialism but being away from the mainstream of artistic development it did offer the chance of developing his own form of impressionism. McTaggart, however, was not unaware of events in the art world outside his native Scotland, for each year he made the journey to the National Library of Scotland in Edinburgh to see a display of Turner watercolours which formed the centrepiece of the exhibition. Indeed some of his paintings, like the one depicting sunset over water, show the influence of the great master of watercolour. Most of his coastal painting however was done in oil and some like 'The Storm', painted in 1883, achieve considerable atmospheric effect and stress the constant dangers to be faced by those earning a living from the sea. Anxiety is also shown in 'Daybreak, Kilbrannan Sound', also dating from 1883, where three children wait patiently for their father to return from a night's fishing. The love which McTaggart had for specific themes in his paintings is best shown in 'The Coming of St. Columba' and 'The Sailing of the Emigrant Ship', both recording on canvas two of the major events of Scottish history – the founding of Christianity in the late sixth century and the mass exodus from the impoverished Highlands in the nineteenth.

McTaggart spent much of the summer at Tarbert on Loch Fyne each year and latterly was joined by two other Scottish painters of seascapes who came under his spell, Colin Hunter and Hamilton Macallum. An early work of Hunter was his 'On the West Coast of Scotland' dating from 1879, which shows a much freer use of colour than McTaggart ever adopted. Macallum, perhaps less gifted, tended to produce pictures which have come to be regarded as examples of social history rather than pure art. The gathering of sea wrack (seaweed), one of his themes, was and still is an important industry along the west coast and in some of the Outer Hebridean islands. From it soda, potash and iodine can be extracted, and seaweed factories play an important part in the economy of islands like South Uist. Another local artist and contemporary of Macallum, Joseph Henderson, took up the same theme in his 'Kelp Burning'.

Much of Scottish landscape painting in the last century reflected the renewed interest in the Highlands following Queen Victoria's purchase of Balmoral, but it was mostly stereotyped and formal. In the present century it has become less stylised, and in the hands of pioneers like William Gillies (1898–1973) a new breadth of vision and experience has been exploited. Although tending towards the abstract Gillies chose real landscapes for his subject matter, and it is said that he would often pour over a map to find the exact location to give his picture a meaningful title. He often employed a decorative idiom which has been likened to later Braque, a real possibility for he spent much time training in Paris. His watercolours have always proved more acceptable than his oils with the public, especially those of the Fife fishing villages and West Highland scenes painted during the inter-war years. Some of his paintings were done with a hog brush with little or no drawing involved, while others used ink lines as a lynch pin to tie together a loose structure of full-bodied colour. Many of his watercolours are atmospheric and intense, for example his 'Morar' (1928). Now, over half a century later, the painting continues to convey the sense of relative remoteness of this place which still miraculously exists. A later work, 'The Cliff, Dalbeattie' which he painted in 1953, shows further developed skill in portraying the essence of a coastal scene for he was always experimenting and searching for new ground. Although teaching and administrative duties curtailed his painting latterly, he did have the satisfaction of being largely instrumental in the emergence of the Edinburgh School.

John Miller, who succeeded Gillies as President of the Royal Scottish Water Colourists in 1967, has tended to concentrate on the harsher realities of the west coast in preference to the softer contours of the eastern seaboard. His knowledge of the shores of the Clyde gave him a sense of belonging which he portrayed in a forceful manner, often using dark tones to express the bleakness and exposure of a coastline battered by Atlantic storms. There was now a new feeling of liberation which found expression not only in his own paintings but in the work of others like John Fleming, David Mclure and John Houston, all of whom sought membership of the RSW. Even more recent is the work of Bet Low, perhaps heralding a new era of minimal art. Subjects like her 'After Sunset Northern Isles' and 'Cliffs and Beach' are very expressive, yet accompanied with an apparent simplicity of colour wash. But behind the simplicity lies a great deal of thought and appraisal of the distinctive moods and lighting effects found in these northerly latitudes.

For a more formal exposition amongst contemporary artists it is necessary to return to England and in particular to the work of Nicholas Bradley-Carter. After his early training in southern Germany he now works in Dorset, very much in the tradition of Cox, Cotman and especially Turner. His watercolour seascapes include such subjects as 'The Cobb at Lyme Regis', 'Herring Boats at Rye' and 'Off-shore Dover'. All are done in freely flowing colours and many take advantage of the unique qualities of early morning light. Like the Turner watercolours there is an emphasis on human activity, whether it be fishing or in the ever-continuing work of the coastguard. In this approach he is very much in tune with one of Turner's admirers, Samuel Palmer, who pronounced, 'Landscape is of little value but as it hints or expresses the haunts and doings of man'.

References

Baldry, A. L. *British Marine Painting* (The Studio Limited, 1919)
Cordingly, D. *Marine Painting in England 1700–1900* (Studio Vista, 1974)
Firth, J. *Scottish Watercolour Painting* (Ramsay Head, 1979)

Hardie, M. *Water Colour Painting in Britain*, Vol 3 The Victorian Period (Batsford, 1968)
Hardie, W. *Scottish Painting, 1837–1939* (Studio Vista, 1976)
Hayes, J. *The Art of Graham Sutherland* (Phaidon, 1980)
Irwin, D. and F. *Scottish Painters at home and abroad 1700–1900* (Faber & Faber, 1975)
Shanes, E. *Turner's Rivers, Harbours and Coasts* (Chatto & Windus, 1981)
Shaw, E. *Turner's Picturesque Views in England and Wales, 1825–38* (1979)
Sutherland in Wales: A catalogue of the collection at the Graham Sutherland Gallery (The Picton Castle Trust and the National Museum of Wales, 1976)

9 North-west England

Cumbria

From the marshy strand of the Solway to the ravaged shore around Millom, the Cumbrian coast is a legacy of the Ice Age. In the south the ice deposited great quantities of boulder clay, which forms low, rather drab cliffs. Only at certain places, like St Bees Head, does the solid rock show through and immediately transforms the whole coastal scene. In the north towards the Solway Firth the influence of the Ice Age is less obvious; bays and estuaries, like Moricambe, represent former low-lying lands and river mouths drowned in the general rise of sea level which followed the melting of the ice from about 12000 BC onwards.

Port Carlisle has fragmentary remains of an ill-fated attempt to give Carlisle access to the sea. In 1819 the Earl of Lonsdale built a harbour here at the end of a canal from Carlisle, but the unpredictable channels of the Solway changed course and left only a shallow-water approach to the port. The final blow came in 1856 when the railway replaced the canal. Now the former break-water of the harbour lies isolated in the waters of the Solway, the canal is no more than a muddy ditch flanked with hawthorn bushes. A fine row of terraced cottages with Solway House as the centrepiece is the only real evidence of a planned canal port. Hereabouts the road along the Solway shore is lapped by high spring tides bringing in silt which promotes the growth of the fine, springy Cumberland turf.

Bowness-on-Solway, so named to distinguish it from the other Bowness on the shores of Lake Windermere, lies at the 'official' end of Hadrian's Wall though it is now believed that the Roman defence system extended much further round the coast (see Silloth). There is little to be seen of the Roman fort for it has been built over and much of its stone 'quarried' for later buildings. The coastal road continues around the end of the Cardurnock Peninsula, mainly on a raised beach above the saltings which run out to a wide sandy strand. Scars, formed of boulders which have come out of the clay, are a feature of the fore-shore, and there are fine views across the Solway to the purple hills of Galloway. The remains of the embankment of the former Solway Junction Railway are a reminder of the great iron bridge, 1,792m (1,960yd) long, which spanned the firth until it perished through ice damage in 1910, never to be rebuilt. Its approach from the south lay across the raised bog of Bowness Moss, in parts a veritable sponge up to 15m (50ft) deep; extensive drainage was needed and then the rails were laid on a platform of brushwood faggots. Today the old railway track provides one of the few safe routes across the moss, alive in early summer with the waving white heads of cotton grass.

Anthorn, on the shores of Moricambe Bay is no more than a collection of farms and cottages by the roadside, with a greensward of turf and thrift in the foreground and a distant view of the Lake District mountains. Accretion is still going on at the head of the bay and 150ha (260 acres) were added between 1860 and 1900, according to J. A. Steers in his *Coastline of England and Wales*. Curiously at the outer end of the bay in the

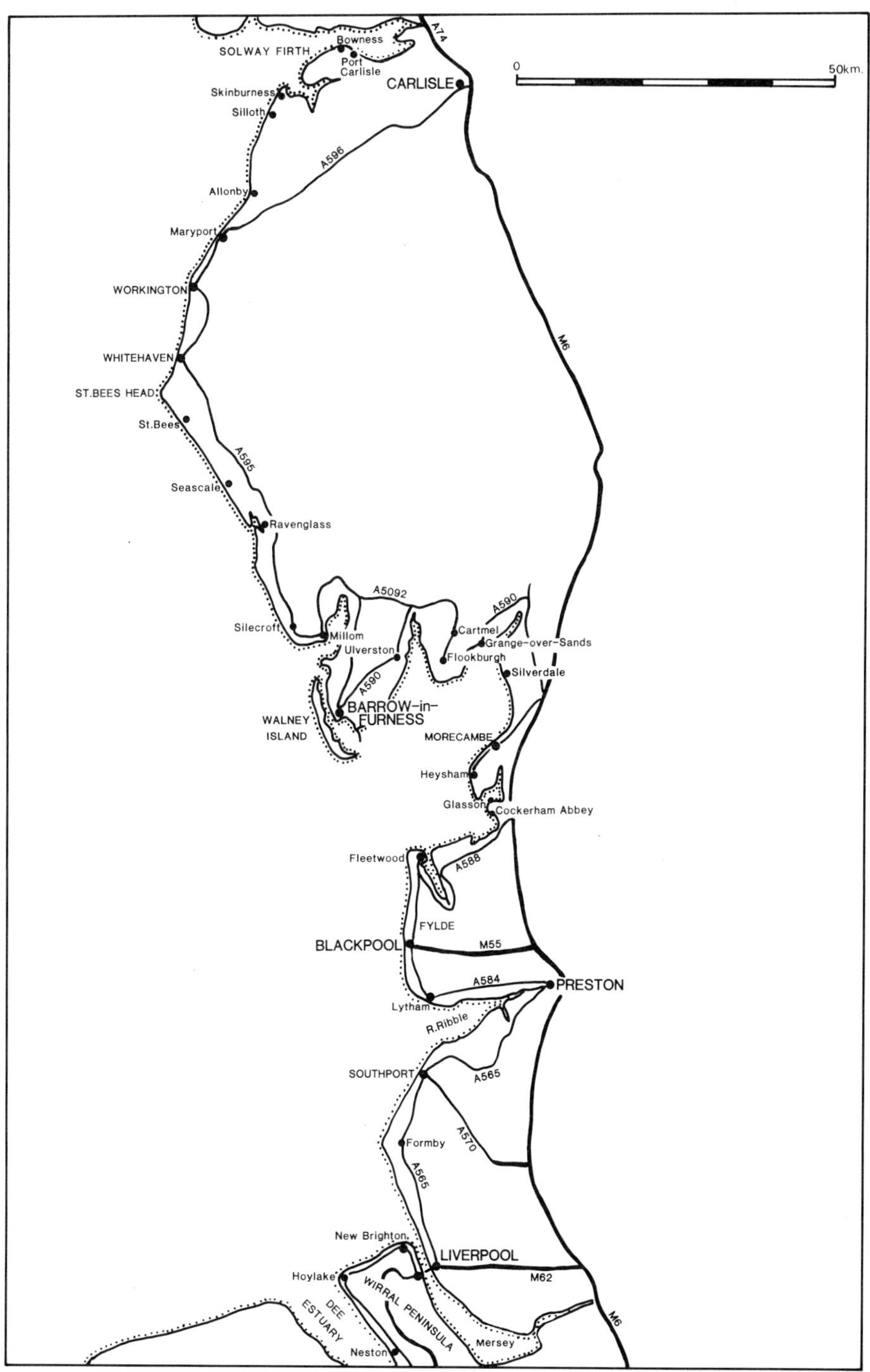

The coast of north-west England

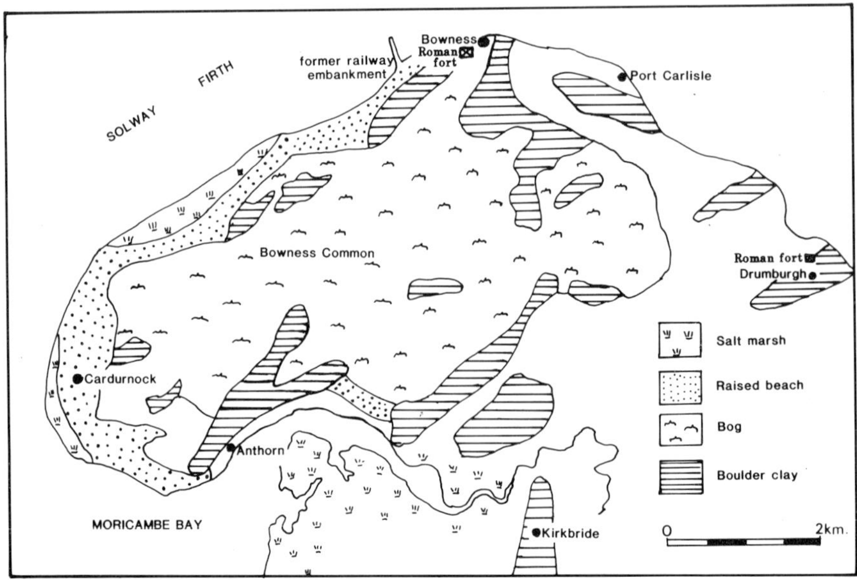

The Cardurnock Peninsula, with its salt marsh and raised beach

lee of Grune shingle spit, the saltings lost 38ha (95 acres) in the same period.

Skinburness, now a small resort and outpost of Silloth, has little to suggest that Edward I tried to found a town here in 1301, largely to provide a base for his forays into southern Scotland. Erosion quickly put an end to the plan (though the town was given market rights). Instead a safer site inland at Newton Arlosh was chosen in 1305 and a rudimentary town was established under the guidance of the monks of Holm Cultram Abbey.

Silloth The formal rectangular plan of cobbled streets, the church and other mid nineteenth-century buildings leave no doubt that here was an attempt to create a Victorian town (both port and resort) rather like West Hartlepool (see page 369). It began life in 1854, with the formation of the Carlisle & Silloth Bay Railway & Dock Company as part of yet another attempt to provide Carlisle with an outport. The railway was opened two years later with its terminus at a deep-water dock which could accommodate vessels up to 6m (20ft) draught at high water. In addition to cargo ships – they still tie up at the Carr's flour mill wharf – there was a twice-weekly service to Liverpool and once a week to Dublin, Belfast and the Isle of Man, but in spite of this attempt to become a packet station, Silloth failed as a port. Now the railway is closed and the station gradually disintegrating. Silloth, the resort, fared better and still finds favour as a quiet place to relax; with its wide green and line of pines along the dunes it has a spaciousness unique for north-west holiday towns. While trying to attract visitors in the nineteenth century it made the unusual claim that its mean annual temperature of 49°F (10°C) was 1 degree higher than that of Hastings. Comparable sunshine figures were not given however!

The whole length of the coastline from Skinburness southwards formed part of a Roman defence system built at the same time as Hadrian's Wall. In addition to major forts like Beckfoot and Maryport, detailed fieldwork by R. L. Bellhouse has shown that there were intervening mile fortlets and watchtowers as on the Wall, and these coastal fortifications are now thought to have been linked by a system of roads and embankments. What is even more remarkable is the suggestion that there was

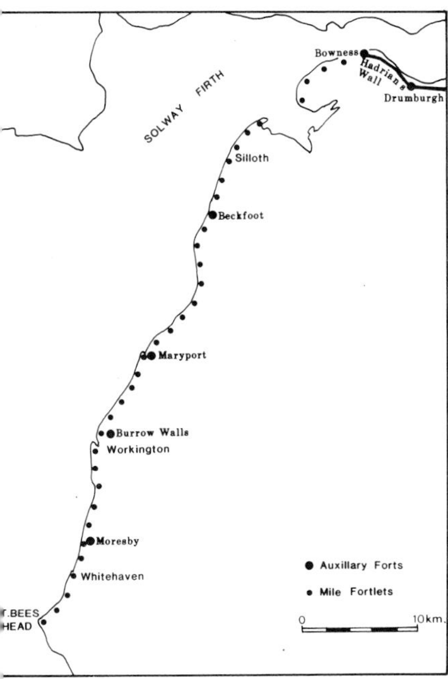

The Roman defence system between Bowness and St Bees Head (*after Bellhouse*)

once a wooden palisade as part of the defence work, a feature unknown elsewhere.

Allonby grew up as an inviting eighteenth-century resort, but soon fossilised because it was left out of the railway network – the nearest station was 6km (4 miles) away at Aspatria. Its attraction today lies in its fine greensward of thrift and trefoil, with golden gorse bushes crowning the dunes. The only real hint of its eighteenth-century birth lies in the terrace of cottages at North End. The coast road running southwards to Maryport is attractive because of its nearness to the shoreline, here consisting of brown sand and pebbles. There are extensive views across to Criffel and the Cairnsmore of Fleet. For the most part the road follows a raised beach behind which rises a grass-covered bluff of boulder clay – the old coastline.

Maryport Before 1749, only the small fishing hamlet of Ellenfoot existed at the mouth of the river Ellen together with a house built by Humphrey Senhouse (senior) and named 'Velantum' after the supposed Roman station on the site. His son (also Humphrey), anxious to provide an outlet for the northern part of the Cumberland coalfield, laid out a new town with a regular pattern of streets, possibly with the earlier planned Whitehaven in mind, and named it after his wife Mary. While the coal trade flourished, Maryport grew, but by the 1930s decay had set in and the town had one of the highest rates of unemployment in the country. The harbour was officially closed in 1961 and this seemed the final blow. In the past decade things have begun to pick up as a genuine attempt has been made to tidy up the town and port. The sandstone quays and old coal basins are a distinct asset for recreational reasons in this leisure-conscious age. Because car owners can travel further afield for employment, many of the older houses with a fine situation have been renovated and occupied. One employer is the Thames Board Mill Company a short way along the coast at Siddick, and there are other newer industries nearby.

Workington The developing town has been forced to turn its back on the sea because the coastal strip is occupied by the land-hungry steelworks. The first ironworks were started some distance inland at Seaton in 1763, but later there was a move to the coast. Unlike for its neighbours, Maryport and Whitehaven, there was no formal town plan and the untidy growth has not been helped by periods of depression. The town had an interested local family, the Curwens of Workington Hall who owned local mines, but they never ventured into town planning like the Lowther or Senhouse families. However, with one of the best artificial harbours on the Cumbrian coast, Workington can look forward to a more assured future than some of its rivals.

Harrington, on Workington's outskirts, represents a brave attempt at rehabilitation of a former derelict coal port. The old tips around the small harbour have been removed and the whole area landscaped. A marina has been created out of the old harbour but, though pleasant, is not buzzing with activity.

Whitehaven, once proud of its coal trade with Ireland

Whitehaven is perhaps the best example we have in the country of a seventeenth-century planned town – the efforts of the local Lowther family. Their interest in the area began in 1634 when Christopher Lowther built a small pier to serve a tiny fishing hamlet located on the southern edge of the present town. His son, Sir John Lowther, was responsible for laying out the regular gridiron plan of the new town, and in 1675 he built himself a mansion, The Flatt, as part of the urban development. This was later rebuilt by his son, Sir James, who completed Whitehaven's development. The church formed the centrepiece, rather as it did in a medieval planned town, and was given a spacious plot off the main street. Later development has modified Lowther's original concept, for many of the early mansions have been pulled down to give way first to terrace rows and, more recently, to blocks of flats. Few of the original buildings now remain, though the National Westminster Bank in Lowther Street has part of one of the town houses built in 1705 behind it. What was once the Assembly Rooms, with Tuscan columns and bays, stands in Howgill Street. The harbour took shape concurrently with the growth of the town and over the past two hundred years has been gradually expanded, the last major development being the Queen's Dock of 1872–6. Compared with the volume of shipping using the port when the coal trade was at its height, the present traffic is not great for a harbour of this size.

South of Whitehaven the coastal scene changes as high rocky cliffs appear for the first time towards St Bees Head. On the plateau top overlooking Whitehaven the chemical firm of Marchon and its associated subsidiary companies have built large works since they first moved here in 1943. Once established, the works found themselves sitting on top of valuable anhydrite deposits and this furthered their development. Close to Whitehaven the cliffs are of brown sandstone belonging to the Coal Measure formation, but as St Bees Head is approached the deep-red sandstones make their appearance and dominate the whole coastal setting as far round as St Bees village. The only break in the line of cliffs is at Fleswick Bay where a small stream has cut a deep valley.

St Bees can claim to be one of the oldest settlements on this coastline, for it was here

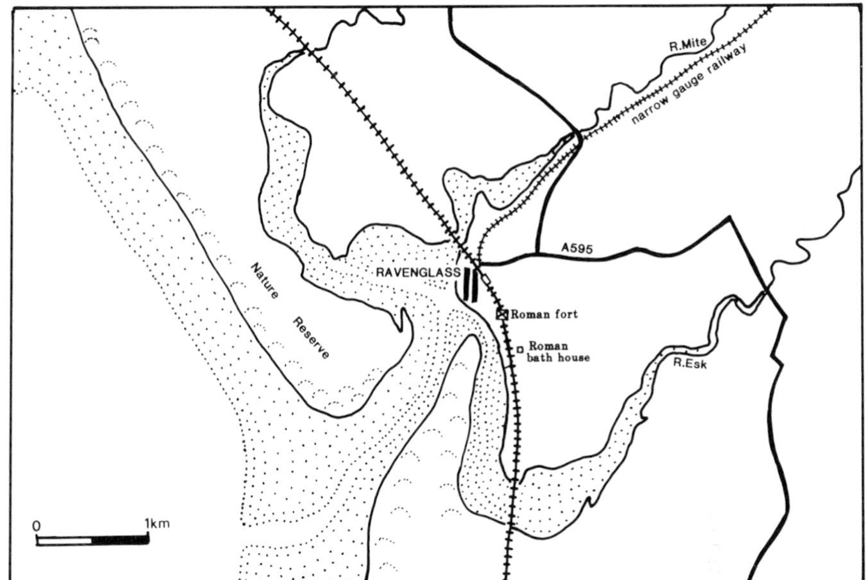

Ravenglass, one of the few natural breaks in the coastline of Cumbria

in this lonely, isolated valley-mouth that a Benedictine nunnery was founded about AD 650. Later destroyed by the Danes, it was refounded again early in the twelfth century, and it is to this latter period that the present buildings belong. Local stone was used, and although the red sandstone is rather soft when first quarried it hardens on exposure to air. The history of settlement can, in fact, be taken back several thousand years more, for on the slopes of the Rottington Valley as well as on the site of the new car park near the beach, recent excavations have shown that Mesolithic man lived and worked. Artefacts, including many microliths, probably fashioned from beach pebbles of igneous rocks first brought here by the ice, have been dug up at these sites.

The coast from St Bees south-eastwards is largely formed of cliffs cut out of the boulder clay coastal shelf. Easily eroded by weathering and frontal attack by the sea, the coastline has steadily retreated over the years; however the problem is not as great as for similar cliffs on the Holderness coast of Yorkshire, one reason being that the Cumbrian glacial beds also contain sand and gravel which help to build up and maintain a wide beach which in turn reduces wave attack. The railway hugs the cliff edge for many miles making it impossible to reach the beach except at a limited number of places. Near the mouth of the river Calder the Windscale Atomic Power Station occupies a considerable area, the choice of site being determined by the relative isolation of the area and its proximity to the coast.

Seascale Nikolaus Pevsner tersely comments, 'On the sea front there is nothing to report'. But it could all have been very different if the plans of the directors of the Whitehaven & Furness Junction Railway had materialised. In 1870 they accepted proposals for the creation of a genteel seaside resort complete with boulevards, crescents and promenades. With a formal centre focussed on a short pier, the rest of the resort was to have a spacious layout with curved streets full of villa residences. In some ways the plan recalls Torquay where the hillsides overlooking Tor Bay were given contour planning. Unfortunately the flat boulder clay shelf at Seascale offered no natural basis for such landscaping so that although plans were drawn up by Edward Kemp, they got no further than the drawing board. Only minor development took place, to the extent that there are now three small hotels. At the car park plastic-covered mesh cages full of pebbles are necessary to provide protection for the boulder clay cliffs, so susceptible to erosion. A golf course now takes up much of the land that was once earmarked for the resort.

Ravenglass lies at the point where the rivers Irt, Mite and Esk join to form a spacious estuary, now partially enclosed by a pair of sand spits across the entrance. At low water the small fishing boats lie keeled over on the bare flats, but when the tide is in the scene is very different for there is still an active fishery here and a notice board on the sloping ramp at the end of the main street announces when the returning boats are expected. As the area is the only natural harbour on this stretch of coastline, the Romans found it convenient as a supply base and built a fort, *Glannaventa*, overlooking the estuary. Victorian vandalism allowed the Furness Railway to cut straight through the fort, but fortunately a nearby bath-house with walls still standing up to 4m (12ft) high was spared and is worth a walk through the woods from the railway station. The other attraction of Ravenglass, apart from the cottages in the main street, is the narrow-gauge railway – Old Ratty – which starts here for Eskdale. Although on the coast itself the dunes are part of a Nature Reserve (with a Romano-British bloomery site), the area nevertheless comes within the missile-testing station located at Eskmeals to the south. From this point the boulder clay cliffs resume and the coast is largely unspoiled. At Gutterby a local spring gave hope that a spa resort might develop but nothing came of it, although the name survives.

Silecroft lies off the main coastal road at one of the few routes down to the shoreline. Being on the railway it must have had hopes of becoming a resort especially after its hotel was built. But there has been little progressive development since, so that the coast now only carries a caravan site and golf course overlooking a shingle beach backed by low clay cliffs. The best feature is the towering lump of Black Combe which forms an ever-present backcloth.

Millom There was little here until a century ago, for the medieval Millom Castle lay on the slopes of the hills to the north and a well-farmed plain lay towards the coast at Hodbarrow Point. But on this plain in 1856 the Hodbarrow Mining Company discovered a vast deposit of haematite. The ore body extended south under the Duddon Estuary and in order to mine it the waters of the estuary had to be drained. Therefore in 1888 a great sea wall, the Inner Barrier, was built to prevent flooding by high tides. But later subsidence caused problems and this prompted the building of another wall, the Outer Barrier, between 1900 and 1905. The winning of ore went on through the present century right up to 1968, though in later years at a decreasing rate. Millom's fortunes have been closely linked with the mine. When mining prospered at the turn of the century the town with its parallel streets of red-brick houses and grey slate roofs developed apace, with an ironworks as well as the mine providing employment. But once the ore had gone by the late 1960s the life-blood of the community drained away, and the town suffered deep depression. Light industry has provided a partial answer though the relative isolation of the area has limited enquiries from industrialists. Fortunately as one of Millom's favoured sons, Norman Nicholson, has proclaimed, there are compensations in living with Black Combe as a backcloth and the fine spread of dunes at Haverigg Point to the west.

Barrow-in-Furness Across the Duddon Estuary, with its extensive areas of drying sand, fringing marshlands and bare limestone outcrops as at Foxfield, is the broad Furness Peninsula. Askam is a mining village based on haematite, as is Hodbarrow on the opposite side of the water. The presence of this mineral here and at Dalton was a factor of great importance in the creation of the industrial complex of Barrow from the mid-nineteenth century onwards. The census of 1851 showed a mere handful of people living beside the banks of the Walney Channel but by 1873 there was a port of over 40,000 inhabitants with ship-building and iron and steel industries. The opening of part of the Furness Railway in 1846, connecting the iron mines of Dalton with the shipping wharves on the Walney

Ravenglass – houses by the harbour

Channel, proved the starting point of this industrial development and accompanying urban growth. James Ramsden, managing director of the Furness Railway, was in fact the main driving force behind the development of the town and he was largely instrumental in starting other projects that would give employment to a growing workforce. With the co-operation of one of the local landowners, the Earl of Burlington (later the Duke of Devonshire), a great urban mesh of wide streets was laid out with squares at the main intersections.

The opening of the Schneider blast-furnace at Hindpool in 1859 and the Barrow Haematite Steel Company in 1866 provided the necessary base for large-scale industrial growth. In 1869 Ramsden started the Barrow Shipbuilding Company with the object of capturing the market for iron-built vessels; later this company became Vickers and is still one of the biggest employers in what has now become a depressed town. Individual buildings naturally reflect the period during which the town grew and include the parish church of St. George built in 1859 and the Town Hall in a gothic style which recalls similar buildings in Manchester and Rochdale. Three of the town's founders are commemorated in monuments – Ramsden, Jacques Schneider and Lord Cavendish, who represents the interests of the Devonshire family.

Walney Island acts as a great shield to Barrow on its seaward side. It is largely formed of glacial deposits, clays, gravels and sands though at each end wave-processes have built up spits. Parts of the coastal strip are taken up with marram-covered sandhills, which form a valuable natural asset for the laying out of golf courses. At the eastern entrance to the Walney Channel, Piel Island may well have been an early Norse site though the castle we see today was built by the monks of Furness Abbey. Roa Island – a misnomer in the sense that it is joined to the mainland by an artificial causeway – has its fishermen's cottages and inn while the straggly spindly ridge of fine shingle running out to nearby Foulney Island seems to be an Ice Age relic modified by the wave action which is very pronounced on this exposed outer bastion. Walney Island has been inundated on a number of occasions, and as early as the fourteenth century the monks of

Furness were erecting dykes to prevent flooding. Today the island is both a playground and a suburb of Barrow, and includes Vickerstown estate, very much a company-planned affair, begun in 1901 with ideals similar to those of Port Sunlight.

The coastal road round the peninsula from Barrow towards Ulverston is always close to the sea and has fine views across Morecambe Bay with the Heysham Nuclear Power Station very prominent. Close to Bardsea is a small country park principally for bird watchers. Morecambe Bay has the largest number of wading birds in Britain including oyster-catchers, lapwings and dunlins. A mile to the north is the Gothic Conishead Priory, conceived in 1808 as a 'tolerable Gentleman's House' though it was 1836 before finally completed. The name is taken from the twelfth-century priory on the site – a far cry from its use by a Buddhist community today.

Ulverston, formerly a manor of the monks of Furness Abbey, is a town with ancient market rights and a sixteenth-century church. Like other centres in Furness it grew rapidly in the nineteenth century following the discovery of rich iron-ore deposits nearby. The construction of a canal in 1795 under Sir John Rennie considerably improved the commercial fortunes of the town for it gave it access to the sea and encouraged industrial growth along its banks. On top of Hoad Hill there is an imitation of the Eddystone lighthouse erected in 1855 in memory of Sir John Barrow, a long-serving secretary of the Admiralty who was born close by at Dargley Beck on the southern outskirts of the town.

Cartmel is the name given to the more easterly peninsula projecting southwards into Morecambe Bay and in its centre is the attractive market town of the same name. It is much visited because of its fine priory church, founded in 1188 and which is virtually complete although, apart from the gatehouse, nothing remains of the other monastic buildings. At the height of its power the priory exercised as much control over the Cartmel Peninsula as Furness Abbey did on its surrounding countryside.

Flookburgh is further south than Cartmel, on the main road running through the peninsula. It was an ideal place for a market centre to grow up and indeed was given a market charter. That it did not blossom into an important town is difficult to understand for even in the eighteenth century it was an important coaching centre lying on the 'sands' route across the drying banks of the head of Morecambe Bay. Today, although the elements of a small country town are there, little development has taken place. The name is supposedly taken from *fluke* (a plaice) and *burgh* (a settlement), and refers to the former very important fisheries for flukes, shrimps and cockles off the nearby coast. Because of its former charter the village possesses ancient market regalia and two halberd heads, one in the shape of a fluke. Formerly the settlement lay much closer to the sea but what was once salt-marsh was enclosed in 1807 with the building of a 5km (3 mile) embankment between Cowpren Point and the sharp limestone promontory of Humphrey Head. About 243ha (600 acres) of land was reclaimed and the two farms of West Plain and East Plain came into being. In October 1828 the embankment was undercut in the west through a change of course of the river Leven with the result that West Plain lost most of its reclaimed land; only the rapid building of a new north-south embankment across Low Moor prevented a similar fate overtaking East Plain. For the past century and a half West Plain has remained a natural salting, mainly of grass and, though extensively used for grazing, open to the high spring tides. Much of East Plain became a World War II airfield, and the buildings left behind are now a holiday site.

Grange-over-Sands only began to develop as a resort following the arrival of the Furness Railway in 1857. The site is a good one, sheltered by the Cartmel hills to the north and west and with unimpeded views across the sands of Morecambe Bay. The earliest houses were on elevated sites and mostly mock-Tudor in style; hotels quickly followed once the Victorians discovered that here was an exclusive resort, well served by a railway hugging the shore with the station almost on the beach, and with the Lake District mountains close at hand. The layout of the resort itself is attractive in that the large stone houses have extensive gardens planted with exotic shrubs which only survive because of the mild maritime climate. The name, Grange-over-Sands, denotes that long before the resort developed the nearby shoreline was the landfall for the route across the sands of Morecambe Bay. Until the coming of the railway this sand-crossing was favoured because it avoided the long detour around the heads of the many estuaries. It can be walked today from Hest Bank, but it is advisable to seek advice about the tides or better still join an organised party with an experienced guide. Grange still attracts as a quiet resort though in recent years it has become more popular as a retirement centre. It now has the dubious distinction of having the highest percentage of retired people in the whole country.

Arnside is on the east side of the Kent Estuary, and, like Grange-over-Sands on the opposite side, it can trace its main growth to the link-up established by the Furness Railway and the building of the viaduct in 1857. Up to that time there had been only limited settlement although an inn, the Fighting Cock (later renamed the Crown Hotel), was in existence as early as 1660. It was a favoured spot for Victorians interested in yachting, and annual regattas were held. Boat building gave employment and the industry survives lower down the estuary at Ashmeadow, originally just an inn. The building of the promenade in 1897 gave Arnside the semblance of a resort with a short terrace of boarding houses providing accommodation. As in so many of the smaller coastal settlements, new buildings have crept in and the area is now favoured for retirement. Great flocks of greylags as well as the other common sea birds of Morecambe Bay – avocets, spoonbills, knot, dunlin and oystercatchers – settle on nearby Meathop Marsh and provide an ideal way for the bird watcher to while away the hours.

Lancashire

Silverdale is yet another favoured retirement centre though it has less contact with the sea than its near neighbour, Arnside. The old line of limestone cliffs, perhaps dating from the high sea level of about 4000 BC, is now out of reach of the waves and a grassy sward of fine turf extends outwards for a considerable distance before the sands of the bay are reached. It is possible to take a car onto the marsh edge close to the village, or alternatively to follow the narrow road to the south towards Jenny Brown's Point where there is a fine vantage point for looking across the whole of Morecambe Bay.

Morecambe A combination of circumstances dictated that what was once a small resort – Poulton by the Sands – should blossom into the largest of the towns

The reclamation of East and West Plains at the head of Morecambe Bay (*after Rollinson*)

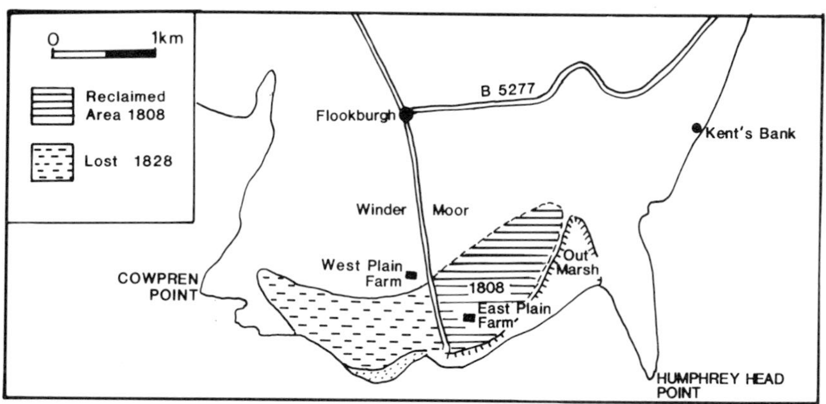

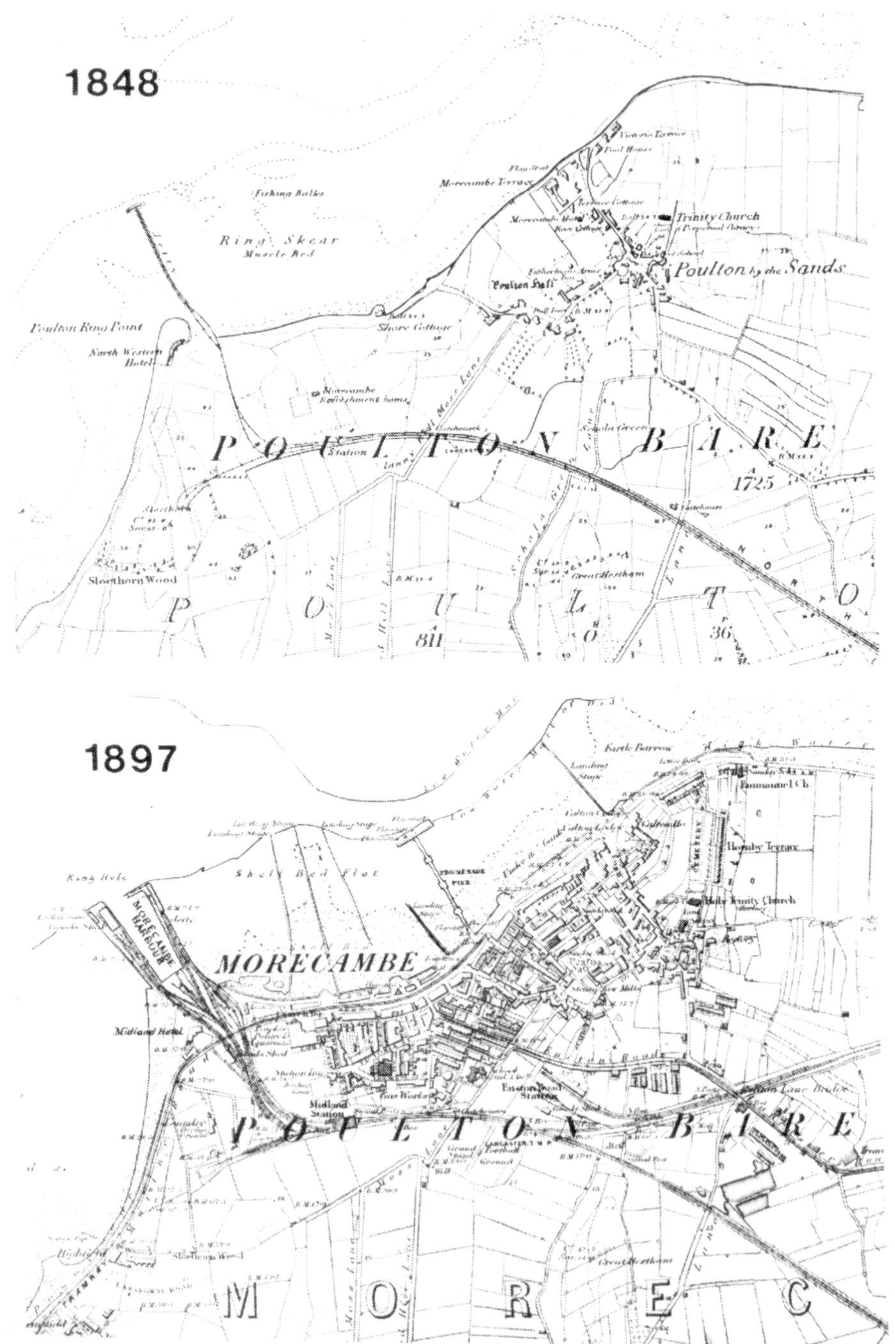

Two stages in the growth of Morecambe

bordering on Morecambe Bay. From the outset both port and resort development were contemplated, though the initial moves centred on providing Lancaster with a link to the sea. A proposed railway connection involved two rival companies, the North Western and the Lancaster & Carlisle. The former won the day and opened its line from Lancaster to Poulton Pier on Whit Monday 1848. Two years later there was a connection across the Pennines to the Yorkshire industrial towns, so giving increased possibilities for trade.

The rail link with both the Lancashire and Yorkshire industrial towns also gave the rail company the opportunity to develop what was then Poulton as a seaside town. There had already been moves in this direction, and as early as 1829 regattas were being held off the shore in what a contemporary guide book called 'our English Bay of Naples'. The new Morecambe developed alongside the original village but closer to the point where the railway company built its pier, and today the core of the old Poulton still survives on the north-west outskirts, especially in the network of narrow streets around Trinity church. Once the railway was built there was no holding back development, with the North Western Hotel on the seafront the first to appear. When a local landowner, Robert Taylor, died in 1850 nearly all the land in the vicinity of Poulton village came up for sale and was quickly snapped up in small lots.

The railway company appear to have exerted a considerable overall influence in the development of the town for they were anxious that the resort should flourish even if their port venture failed. Initially, the latter was a great success for as well as commercial cargoes from the Baltic, Spain and farther afield, a thrice-weekly passenger-boat service to Belfast was inaugurated in 1851. There was even talk of building a large dock, but in the end a second pier was built alongside the first and a sheltered harbour formed between the two. By 1860 prospects for both port and resort looked rosy but then nature took a hand. The channel off the pier began to silt up rapidly making it impossible for boats to call except near the time of high water, and the railway company found it impossible to maintain the necessary regular timetable of a packet service. By the turn of the century the port of Morecambe was operating under great difficulties and this forced the Midland Railway Company (who had taken over the old North Western) to develop Heysham, which lay much closer to the deep-water channels of Morecambe Bay. Morecambe was therefore left to develop almost solely as a resort, a role which it took on with zest. New hotels were built and a succession of amenities added, including new piers, baths, indoor amusement centres and conference halls. In the season Morecambe now attracts a wide range of visitors and is in no sense a miniature Blackpool, for it has tried to avoid the brashness of Lancashire's premier resort.

Heysham, now in urban continuity with Morecambe, is very much centred on the harbour built in 1904 for the Irish packet service. On its southern flank is the massive ungainly pile of the Heysham Nuclear Power Station while farther down the coast is the much older chemical works bordering on Middleton Sands. It is to Little Heysham that we must turn for a glimpse of the original Saxon settlement on this coastline for here there are two pre-Domesday churches. The oldest, St Patrick's Chapel, only 7m (24ft) by 2m (8ft) and now in ruins, stands perched on the cliff edge. There is no sure indication of its age but it could date from the eighth century. Equally fascinating are the rock-hewn graves in the form of shallow trenches cut into the sandstone bedrock; again their age is uncertain but they could belong to the era of the Celtic saints. The approach to the chapel is through the churchyard of St Peter's, the other pre-Norman church with a fine Saxon west doorway. Both churches lie at the end of the narrow village street which, despite its tourist additions, still retains an old-world atmosphere.

Sunderland lies close to the mouth of the river Lune and seemed to the Quaker merchant, Robert Lawson, the answer to Lancaster's need for a trading port on the coast. At the end of the seventeenth century he began building a quay and a string of

The sparse remains of Cockersand Abbey

warehouses which still stand and one of which has the date 1707 carved on it. Shortage of building material forced him to use erratics from the local boulder clay as well as some fine carved sandstone blocks which could only have come from the ruins of Cockersand Abbey across the estuary. Under Lawson's guidance Sunderland flourished for a time, but after he became bankrupt in 1728 the port languished and no further development took place. In its present fossilised form it has much to attract and fascinate.

Glasson was the successor to Sunderland as the outport for Lancaster. In 1783 a harbour basin was built with fine sandstone quays lined with warehouses, two inns and rows of terraced cottages. Much of this setting has survived to the present time, though pleasure boats now take up most of the harbour berths. It seems a far cry back to the end of the eighteenth century when Glasson had a flourishing trade with the West Indies importing sugar, rum, cotton and hardwoods while exporting cargoes of furniture, woollens and cotton goods. It is strange that although the Preston to Lancaster Canal had been built by 1797, it was not until 1826 that the short link to Glasson dock was made, even though this was an obvious step and of great importance to the Lancaster merchants.

Cockersand Abbey Though only the chapter house and some other fragments remain of this twelfth-century foundation, the site is dramatic for it lies within a stone's throw of the sea and on an unspoiled coast-line. The buildings were of red sandstone quarried close by, for this is one of the few parts of this coast where there is a solid rock foundation. The same rock also gave the abbey a raised site above the surrounding marshes and kept it relatively free from flooding before the present sea defences were built. The best approach is from the main A588 road in the direction of a building on the shore near Crook Cottage. Nearby, the old lighthouse at the mouth of the Lune has been replaced by an unsightly iron lattice construction next to the house at the lane end. The walk southwards along the coast to the abbey ruins is mainly along a sea wall built to protect the boulder clay cliffs from erosion. Below are the saltings, mainly of spartina (rice grass) which has successfully colonised large areas of the flats, while the views across the Lune estuary are memorable in the low light of a summer's evening.

The coast of Fylde is very much of this

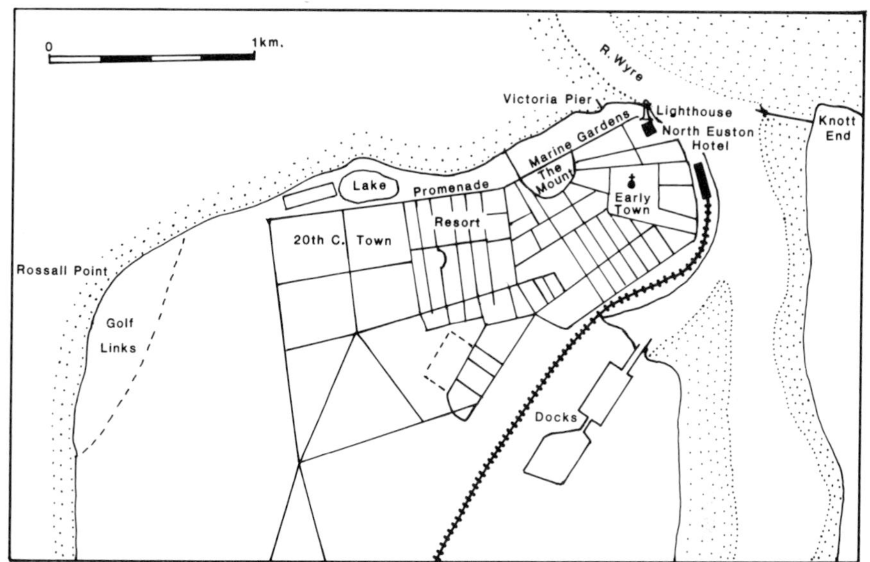

Elements in the street plan of Fleetwood reflecting the stages of its development

marshland fringe character, especially the Pilling and Cockerham Marshes, and the coast road can be flooded at high water as the tide surges up the intricate pattern of marsh creeks. Salt-tolerant grasses, samphire, sea aster and sea pink are the most commonly occurring plants and, as it is a favourite area for shooting, there are hotels like Fluke Hall on this windswept coast. Towards the mouth of the Wyre at Knott End sand increasingly takes over from the mud-flats on the foreshore, giving conditions suitable for the resort development that characterises the coastline to the south.

Fleetwood A new spirit was abroad in the 1830s, perhaps fired by the great opportunities brought about by the railways which were beginning to spread across the length and breadth of the country. Here on a flat site near the mouth of the river Wyre the new age took the form of an experiment in town planning under the guiding hand of Sir Peter Hesketh-Fleetwood, owner of a number of large estates in the Fylde. The new town was to be both port and resort, with the railway serving the needs of both. Sir Peter employed one of the foremost architects of the day, Decimus Burton, pupil of John Nash and one who had already made his mark at south-coast resorts like Hove and St Leonards. Work began in 1837 to the grand design of a radiating network of wide streets converging on a central space, the Mount. No expense was spared as can be seen from the buildings which have survived from the Burton era – the North Euston Hotel with its Doric columns, the former Customs House, St Peter's Church, Queen's Terrace and two unusual lighthouses.

For a time all appeared to go well, with Sir Peter laying down strict regulations over the management of what was virtually his own town. The arrival of the railway in 1840 meant that Fleetwood now became the terminus of the line from London. From here it was possible to board ship and sail to Ardrossan in Scotland, and even Queen Victoria gave the route her blessing in 1847, though in the reverse direction. That same year, however, saw the completion of the main line to Scotland across Shap and immediately Fleetwood lost importance. Sir Peter had also over-reached himself financially and was forced to sell part of his estate to carry on, but this proved insufficient and the new town stood half complete. Building regulations were now relaxed, so that the later town was hardly comparable with the Burton development of the 1830s. After Sir Peter's death in 1866 the Fleetwood Estate Company took over but only terrace rows and modest villas found a place in their plans, the emphasis now was on attracting trade to ensure survival. The railway company opened a new dock in 1878 and in the closing years of the century a Grimsby firm established a trawler fleet here to fish Icelandic waters. Resort development also took place to the west of the original town, Fleetwood concentrating on the things nearby Blackpool ignored, namely quietness and unorganised entertainment. Recently the port has had a new lease of life with the development of container traffic with Ireland, and to stand on the headland near Burton's low light and watch the broad-beamed container ships hug the shore as they come into their berths is a show that few resorts can lay on for their visitors.

Blackpool It is ironical that Sir Peter Hesketh-Fleetwood, in having to sell off part of his estate to finance his own new town, should release the land on which this premier west-coast resort would soon rise. No real development took place until after 1850 though the fine stretch of sands had attracted bathers previously. As early as 1789 there is an account by William Hutton of Blackpool as a sea-bathing resort, in which he describes the etiquette to be followed by both ladies and gentlemen anxious to try the new pastime. Although a branch railway into Blackpool from Poulton-le-Fylde had been built by 1846, it did not immediately bring about the rapid growth which usually occurred. It was not until the 1860s that real progress was made following the building of the North and Central Piers. Later the promenade was extended and the Winter Gardens Pavilion built. The 1880s saw the first electric tramway and in the following decade the Tower was erected, modelled on the Eiffel Tower but only half the height. Though it is still Blackpool's most distinctive landmark the impact it makes is lessened through the buildings which crowd around its base.

The growth of the town went on rapidly throughout this period but not to any overall plan because the land was sold in small plots and developed by speculative builders. More recently expansive residential estates have appeared, so that the town is now continuous with many former village centres of the Fylde. The only real break occurs in the south where the airport intervenes between the southern suburbs and St Anne's. Although many of the former visitors who once came to Blackpool for their one and only holiday of the year now go off in search of the sun, there seems to be little waning of interest and activity. The season is exceptionally long due to the attraction of the illuminations in the autumn and the increasingly popular winter weekend breaks at many of the hotels. Whereas many resorts seem to be settling into hibernation from mid-September onwards, Blackpool remains busy for much of the year.

Lytham St Anne's The threat of being swallowed up by Blackpool led to the two separate entities of Lytham and St Anne's joining as a borough in 1922. Of the two, Lytham is by far the older, for it can trace its history back to pre-Norman times and was listed in Domesday Book as *Lidum*. Its main attraction today is Lytham Hall, a former monastic site which once was a farming cell of Durham. The association with Durham is further shown in the dedication of the parish church to St Cuthbert – a church originally of thirteenth-century date but rebuilt in 1770 and again in 1834 to take account of the increasing size of the settlement. St Anne's, the other partner, took its name from a chapel-of-ease built in 1873. Being nearer the open sea it has developed more as a resort, though it is considerably quieter than Blackpool, its near neighbour to the north.

Ribble Marshes The banks of the lower part of the Ribble Estuary are formed of fine sand with a certain amount of mud on their inner margins which have been steadily colonised by vegetation and form extensive saltings. At the lowest level the vegetation consists mainly of filamentous algae like *Enteromorpha* (eel grass) which can withstand long periods of immersion in salt water. As the green strands colonise the mud-flats they build up sediment around them and in time can raise the marsh level by as much as 76mm (3in). At a slightly higher level other salt-loving plants like the marsh samphire come in and these too can help to trap silt and so raise the level even more. A plant which is even more effective is *Spartina* or rice grass. Since it was artificially introduced into the estuary in 1936 it has colonised huge areas and in many places has become the dominant vegetation. It grows in clumps which in time merge to form a more continuous cover. On its inner side and at a slightly higher level the rice grass gives way to sea manna grass which is less tolerant of salt-water immersion. At the highest levels the sea manna grass forms a complete sward and is extensively grazed by animals. Other plants found in this zone include sea aster and sea purslane. The gradual upward growth of the saltings has meant that since the middle of the nineteenth century large areas have been enclosed and reclaimed (see page 67).

Merseyside

Southport The history of the resort is very much bound up with reclamation of land similar to that which occurred in the nearby Ribble Marshes. A map of 1736 shows the area in its natural form before extensions of the shoreline took place and allowed the town to develop (see page 71). Although it is still an attractive resort, Southport's character has changed with the years; its nearness to Liverpool has meant that it has become a favoured residential area with the department stores of Lord Street serving both a resident population as well as the summer influx of visitors. This tree-lined street, started in 1825 and subsequently extended to the west in 1854, still has the most rewarding buildings of the town including the principal hotels, banks and Town Hall. The other notable thoroughfare is the Promenade, laid out about 1830 by Sir Peter Hesketh-Fleetwood, again with a succession of hotels dating from the mid-nineteenth century (see F. A. Bailey, *A history of Southport*, 1955).

Formby, though now very much a commuter town for those working in Liverpool, was once a fishing village with a tortuous approach up the Alt river, but silting here and the gradual growth of sand dunes to seaward sounded the death knell for the small port. The sandhills at Formby Point form a belt more than 1.6km (1 mile) wide with individual dunes more than 15m (50ft) high. Although the recent planting of conifer belts has helped, as the upper

An early print of Lord Street, the main thoroughfare of the early-nineteenth-century resort of Southport

Formby sand dunes. Conservation attempts have been initiated by the National Trust

sandy beach dries out completely the prevalent onshore winds pick up the finer sand and carry it inland. There is some doubt as to when the dunes first formed, some authorities suggesting that there were none at Formby prior to 1600. This seems unlikely though it is possible that from the seventeenth century onwards the blown sand became troublesome. The church, for example, seems to have been moved to its present inland site in 1746, and records of the same period speak of farmlands becoming buried by advancing sand. It is possible that renewed dune activity at the time coincided with a gradual silting up of the main Formby Channel offshore which, from medieval times to the eighteenth century, was the main approach route into the Mersey from the north. A gradual silting up and its replacement by the present Crosby Channel could well have initiated such shoreline changes. Beyond Blundellsands and Crosby, both residential suburbs of Liverpool, the waterfront is dominated by docks, including the new container port at Seaforth.

New Brighton The Wirral Peninsula, bounded by the Dee and Mersey estuaries on two sides and the open coast facing Liverpool Bay on the other, consists of a foundation of red sandstone rocks with an overlay of boulder clay and sands. At its north-west corner, where there is an outcrop of red sandstone, a Liverpool merchant, James Atherton, bought 69ha (170 acres) in 1830 with the intention of developing an exclusive watering place. Prior to that time there had been only a few fishermen's cottages set amidst sand dunes on a rocky heathland. Atherton established a steam ferry across to Liverpool and gradually persuaded many of the wealthy Liverpool citizens to purchase plots for villas, but unfortunately no sooner had he formulated his plan than there was a major disagreement with his son-in-law partner which brought development to an abrupt halt. When it was resolved and building resumed, it was on a much more modest scale so New Brighton tended to become the preserve of the day-tripper from Liverpool rather than a rather exclusive residential area for the well-to-do – inevitably the promenade soon became known as Ham and Egg Parade. With the building of the Grand Palace and Pavilion in 1880 New Brighton now set out to cater for the masses. The railway link under the Mersey, however, still makes it a residential suburb of Liverpool though it prides itself in having much to offer the visitor including an indoor amusement park, a large boating lake and a bathing pool that can accommodate 4,000 bathers. The promenade has been considerably extended and, with good views over the Mersey and Liverpool Bay, finds favour with the car owner happy to sit and watch the shipping.

Further to the west at Leasowe there has been considerable erosion of the shoreline during the past 200 years. Leasowe Castle (now the Railwaymen's Convalescent Home), built in 1593 as a sporting lodge or stand for the Derby family, was once in the centre of a huge racecourse where horse racing took place from the seventeenth century onwards. It has many features of interest including the fitments from the Star Chamber of Westminster which the owner purchased in 1634. Now almost the whole of the former racecourse (racing was abandoned and transferred to Newmarket in 1732) lies under the sands of Liverpool Bay with a great embankment known as Mockbeggar Wharf facing the sea. There used to be lighthouses on the shore at Leasowe dating from the early eighteenth century, but the outer one has long since perished through erosion while the inner light no longer functions as shipping is unable to use the former inshore passage into the Mersey.

Hoylake has become a favoured residential area with the famous golf links of the Royal Liverpool Club on its doorstep. The name refers to a former anchorage or channel offshore called High Lake or Hoyle Lake shown on all early charts of the Dee approaches, but this has now completely silted up. Development at Hoylake began earlier than at New Brighton for Lord Stanley, the local landowner, built the first hotel here in 1793 and by 1816 it was noted as a place for sea bathing. Building leases were granted by the Stanley family for villa residences amongst the sandhills, and development was such that a new church was built in 1833. The golf course started as a racecourse and it was only in 1869 that it was converted to its present use. A daily omnibus service to the Liverpool ferry was started in 1861 but after only five years was replaced by a narrow-gauge railway. By 1878 this was converted into a normal-gauge line, and in less than a decade the Mersey Tunnel gave a direct route to Liverpool. The line was soon extended as far as West Kirby and this too became increasingly favoured as a residential area.

Off Hoylake the Bunter Pebble Beds appear and these have helped to stave off erosion with the red sandstones forming a natural breakwater. Offshore lies Hilbre Island, once a cell or chapel of the monks of Chester. Leland, the antiquary of Henry VIII, wrote of its importance in 1540 when it acted as a station for customs officials because of its position at the mouth of the Dee.

Neston, one of the more ancient settlements of the Wirral, was at one time on the shore of the Dee Estuary and had a quay where boats tied up rather than attempt the difficult passage to Chester. From the mid-sixteenth century Neston's Old Quay suffered badly and so a 'New Quay' was established about 2km (1 mile) further down the estuary at **Parkgate**. With a relatively deep-water channel lying close inshore, this lower quay attracted the Irish packet service and there were four boats a week sailing to Belfast. Inclement weather or unfavourable winds however often meant a long delay for intending passengers and soon a settlement grew up on this section of the Dee shore. The Irish packet service lasted until about 1820 when further silting of the Dee prevented vessels from using the quay. Parkgate, with its inns, then turned into a quiet resort offering fine views across the estuary. It still has its old world character but now attracts the day visitor who, from the promenade, can enjoy the view across the Dee marshes.

The Isle of Man

Set like a jewel in the midst of the Irish Sea between Lancashire and Ulster, the Isle of Man can claim links with both sides. Geologically and physically, it is not unlike the Lake District without its lakes, for its principal rock formation – the Manx Slates – is comparable with the rocks of the southern Lake District and of much the same age. Historically and culturally Man leans towards the Celtic west, but with an overlay of Norse which is reflected in its parliamentary system and many of its ancient customs.

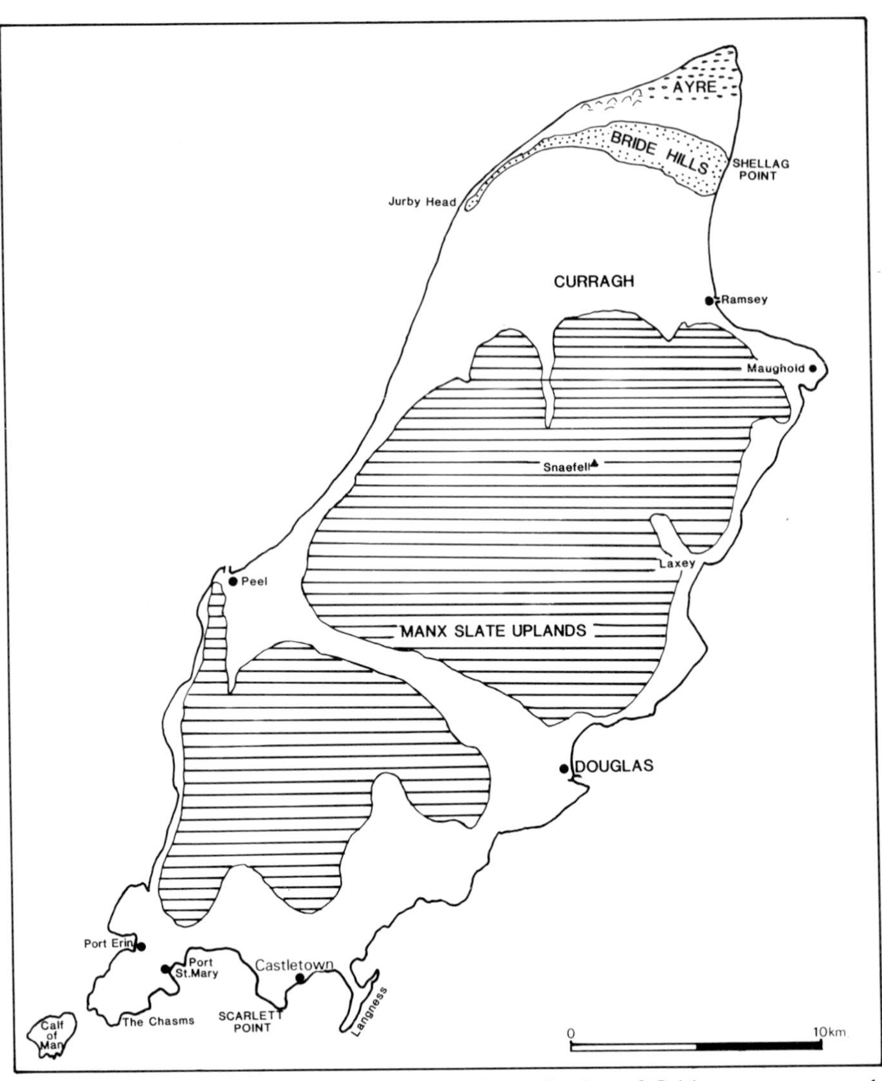

The Isle of Man

Having been ignored by the Romans, the island was won over to Christianity in the late fifth century when missionaries from Ireland landed on its shores. Evidence of this early conversion is still found in the present landscape – there are about 200 tiny rectangular churches or cells (keills), now with only the foundations remaining. Examples occur in Maughold churchyard – Maughold was formerly a monastery founded in the seventh century – along with a fine collection of Celtic crosses, grouped together under cover.

The other great event of historic significance was the arrival of the Norse invaders in the ninth century and their subsequent settlement. In time the Isle of Man became the southern bastion of a great Norse kingdom which included the Orkneys and Shetlands. Peel Castle, with fortifications dating back to the tenth and eleventh centuries and including a round tower which was once used as refuge against the early Viking invaders, is the most imposing present-day monument to this important period in the history of the island.

With a coastline over 150km (90 miles) in length, there is rich variety in its setting, various rock types giving rise to distinctive features. The Manx Slates, which occupy three-quarters of the island, are such a variable formation that they can give rise to jagged cliffs, narrow inlets, long sweeping bays set between imposing headlands, and a wealth of unspoiled coastal scenery, especially along the west coast south of Peel. This part of the coast is inaccessible by road and therefore has to be enjoyed at leisure on a day's walk to Port Erin. Around Peel itself there is a tiny enclave of red sandstone, which not only gives a distinctive colouring to the nearby cliffs but also determines the appearance of the town. In the south east, around Castletown, there is also a different rock type present - Carboniferous Limestone, together with an underlying bed of conglomerate. In the Langness Peninsula this basement conglomerate sits on top of the Manx Slate series which, being softer and more easily eroded by the sea, has been carved into numerous fissures and chasms, with the conglomerate forming a capstone over a succession of natural arches. In the nearby peninsula, a bed of igneous rocks has also proved difficult for the sea to remove - consequently it projects to form Scarlett Point. Because of the interesting geology and natural history of this short stretch of coastline near Castletown, a nature trail has been established for visitors.

Perhaps the most striking feature of the Isle of Man coastline occurs in the extreme south-west corner of the island, close to the tiny port and resort of **Port St Mary**. Here the Manx Slate formation consists of seaward-dipping beds of grit overlying slaty beds. As the slates have slipped forward, possibly as a result of movement under the extremely arctic conditions of the last Ice Age, so the grits have been prised apart to form narrow fissures at the surface. The area, known as the Chasms, occupies several hectares of heathland on the cliff top, and because of its deeply-set network of clefts, some of which run down to sea level, it is much visited. Care must be taken, however, as the ground is covered with gorse and heather which tends to mask the narrow fissures.

In contrast to the cliffed coastline described above, the northern part of the island is made of softer and younger formations, which give rise to a gentler and more destructible landscape. Towards the end of the Ice Age, the ice sheet covering the present Irish Sea remained stationary for a time across what is now the Ayre Peninsula, and when it finally retreated northwards it left behind a huge morainic dump of contorted sands, gravels and clays, which today form the arcuate Bride Hills. The moraine runs right across the width of the island from coast to coast, forming Jurby Head in the west and the more spectacular Shellag Point in the east. Everywhere the soft glacial beds are subject to slumping and slipping as well as undermining by constant wave attack.

Beyond the Bride Hills there is the low flat plain of shingle ridges - a former raised beach - which run out to the Point of Ayre (Norse *eyrr* - pebble beach). Seen on a fine summer's day, the Ayre has much to offer, but in winter it can look inhospitable.

Nearly all the settlement in the island is concentrated on the coast. **Douglas**, the capital and largest town, still retains the air of a Victorian resort, with its parade of colour-washed boarding houses overlooking the promenade. It is the principal tourist centre as well as the starting point for numerous excursions - one can go, for example, by steam train to Port Erin or by electric tramway to Ramsey. It also retains its horse-drawn trams, which run the whole length of the promenade. Before 1860, the capital of the island was at **Castletown**, which still retains its old Parliament House. The finest building in the town is Castle Rushen, which dominates the small harbour. As for many of the older buildings, the local limestone has been used in its construction. At **Peel**, on the western coast, it is the warm red sandstone which gives a distinctive character to the town. It has been used for many of the Victorian boarding houses, and also forms the impressive ruins of Peel Castle and St German's Cathedral, set on a small islet near the harbour mouth but connected to the mainland by a short causeway.

The Chasms, near Port St Mary on the Isle of Man

Peel's other claim to fame is its sizeable fishing fleet, which brings in the herrings for the kipper-curing sheds around the harbour.

North of Douglas, and set near the mouth of one of the many narrow glens which run down to the coast from the upland interior, is **Laxey**, once the centre of a flourishing lead mining industry but now with only the gigantic water wheel – Lady Isabella – to give a hint of former prosperity. Further to the north is **Ramsey**, with its long sweeping beaches on either side of the harbour and the terminus of the Manx Electric Railway. Of the other small coastal towns only **Port Erin** and **Port St Mary**, both in the extreme south west of the island, reach any size. Both are now small resorts catering for those who prefer solitude rather than the bustle and activity of Douglas.

10 Wales

The North Coast

The Welsh shore of the Dee Estuary is not scenically different from the Wirral, for there are natural features common to both. Each is fringed by saltings and a low flat which give way to cliffs. On the Flintshire (Clwyd) side the cliffs are about 1km (½ mile) inland and represent an ancient shoreline. The main road and railway hug the coast by keeping to the flats, and it is here that the principal settlements and industries are located. As around Parkgate in the Wirral, the saltings are gradually taking over from the bare sands of the Dee though here, in addition, man has extended the land frontier by dumping colliery and industrial waste. The Dee coastal flats have long been used for industrial purposes with giant steelworks like those at Shotton (now only a shadow of its former self), metal-smelting works, paper mills and rayon factories all located to take advantage of the good communications. The picture is however now rapidly changing as old industries close down and the search goes on for new light industries to replace them. The best way to see this coastal strip is by train, for the Chester to Holyhead line hugs the shore for considerable distances, especially in the Dee estuary section.

Flint The campaigns of Edward I in the late-thirteenth century to subdue the Welsh and establish English trading boroughs in north Wales led to an array of castle towns. One of the first was Flint, with its castle on the shore and its regular-patterned town running inland. Both castle and town were begun in July 1277 and completed in four years, the castle being sited on a low bluff of yellow sandstone close to the water's edge, for it was intended that it should be supplied by sea. The same local sandstone was used in its building, though a harder red sandstone was brought in from either the Wirral or the Chester area for lintels, quoins etc. Originally the town lay at the castle gate, but today it is separated from it by the Victorian railway engineers who chose to drive their line between the two. Flint, in spite of some industrialisation, has remained quite small, so that it is still possible to appreciate the inner core of the town with its gridiron pattern of streets that Edward decreed should be laid out 700 years ago. The former Castle Mills (closed in 1977) were architecturally completely out of character with the town though they provided much-needed employment. Textile working first came to the area in 1908 when a German firm introduced silk making, but the works were later taken over by Courtaulds who manufactured viscose rayon products. A further mill lies along the coast at Greenfield. Between the two lies Bagillt, once the site of a colliery and lead smelter using ore from the inland Halkyn Mountain. There is a suggestion that the Romans had a lead-smelting site on the Dee shore at nearby Pentre Ffwrdfan from where the concentrated pigs were sent to various parts of the Empire. They had the distinctive marking *Ascani* which points to a Flintshire source.

Amidst this industrial setting is the oasis of solitude provided by the ruins of Basingwerk Abbey, founded in 1131 and later belonging to the Cistercian Order. Although lying within a short distance of the coast the ruins, consisting of the walls of the church, cloisters, dormitories and refectory, are

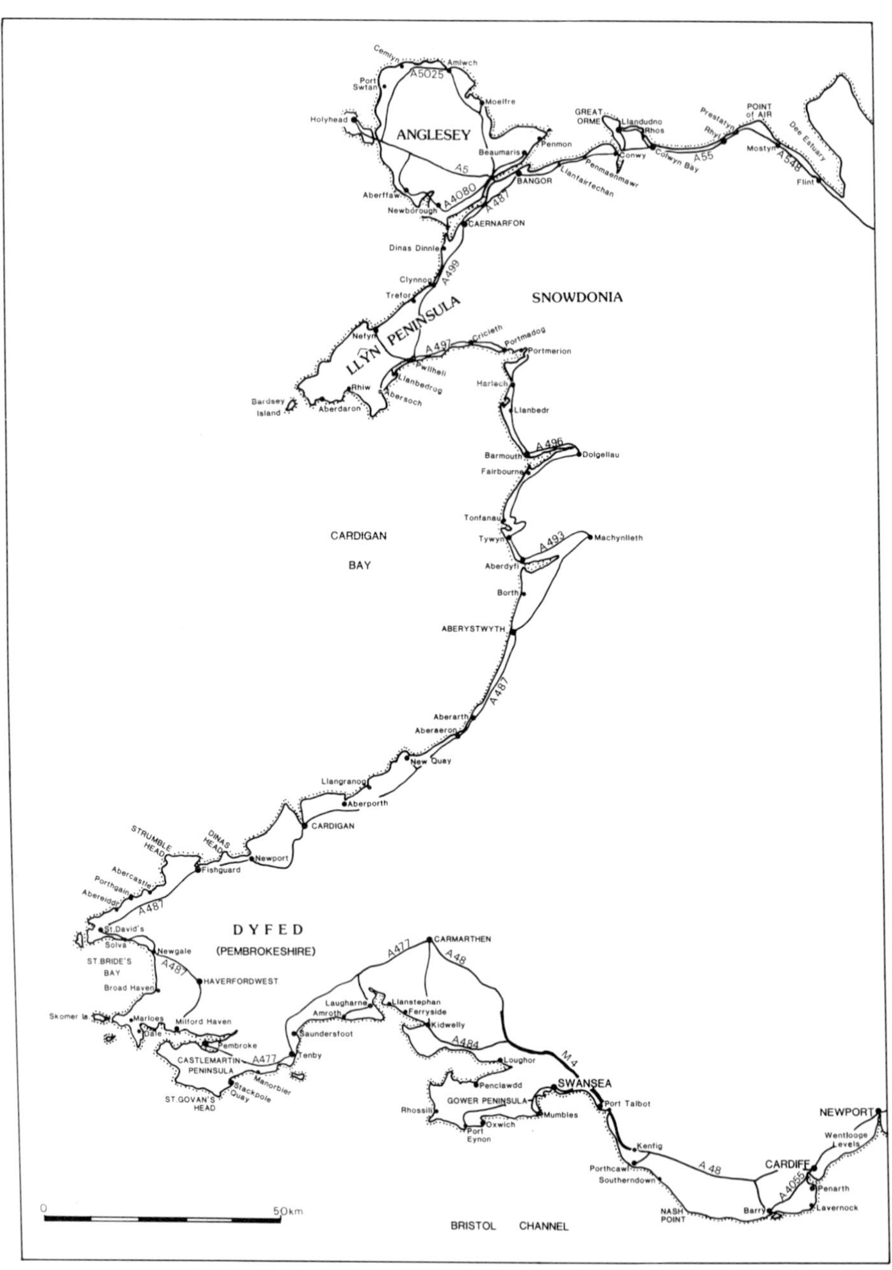

The coast of Wales

The port quarter of Rhyl, a part of the town neglected by visitors

hidden in the trees at the entrance to the Holywell Valley. Records show that the abbey had its own corn mill as early as the thirteenth century using the water power of the stream coming down the valley from St Winifred's well, with huge ponds built to give a constant supply and necessary head of water. Later, in the water-power phase of the Industrial Revolution, the original monastic sites were taken over and further developed to be used for a whole suite of new industries which crowded into the lower end of the valley.

Mostyn Quay is the best of a number of poor harbours on the Dee shore. Formerly noted for importing copper ore from Anglesey for a nearby smelter and exporting coal from collieries around Bagillt, it still retains some coastwise trade and has a small ship-repair yard. Pit props for the nearby colliery are stacked in adjacent yards.

Point of Air is a prominent ness of shingle and sand at the north-west corner of the entrance to the Dee Estuary. Its name is probably derived from the Norse *eyrr* meaning 'pebbles' (like Ayre, in the north of the Isle of Man). The natural setting has been ruined by indiscriminate building of wooden shacks and large areas given over to caravan sites (the ever-present complaint for much of the north Wales coast). The Point of Air colliery, its workings running out under the Dee, is the one remaining mine of the north Wales coalfield and takes up the eastern part of the promontory. Fortunately along the shoreline itself the natural setting is retained with high dune ridges capped with marram grass and scattered clumps of sea holly and yellow-horned poppy. In some of the muddier hollows, and on the beach itself, salt-tolerant vegetation forms part of the coastal scene. Towering above all is the eighteenth-century lighthouse, no longer in use but perhaps the only acceptable man-made addition to the landscape.

Prestatyn, although the first resort along the north Wales coast to be reached by the railway, was not the first to be developed. Prior to this, it had a long history, for on its southern outskirts lies the site of Roman baths, while in later centuries Offa's Dyke, the great political boundary of Mercia, ended here. Throughout medieval times Prestatyn was a castle site of the princes of Powys, the most powerful of the Welsh kingdoms. The area later turned to industry, first lead mining in the mid-eighteenth century and then limestone quarrying. But

Llandudno promenade, with its fine terraces, as laid out in the 1850s

even in 1811 there were only 178 people recorded at the census. Little growth occurred throughout the first half of the nineteenth century and even the coming of the railway in 1840 had minimal effect, leading to the growth of an inland village rather than a coastal resort. It was not until the early years of the present century that the selling of the Pendre estate triggered off a phase of expansion. Later the Penrhwlfa estate also came onto the market and with Lord Abercrombie, the town and country planner, masterminding the whole project, was developed as superior villas. The inter-war years saw the first real hint of resort development in the form of a holiday camp on the coast developed jointly by the LMS Railway Company and Thomas Cook, the travel firm. More recently another camp has been added together with a leisure centre and swimming pool, and only now can Prestatyn claim to rival its other neighbours further along the coast.

Rhyl, only a short distance to the west, has had a completely different history. Although often looked upon as the creation of the Chester to Holyhead Railway of 1840, the area had acquired a reputation as a centre for sea bathing as early as 1807, when it formed the seaward part of the parish of Rhuddlan, an old Edward I castle town dating from the thirteenth century and 3km (2 miles) inland. The introduction of cold- and hot-water baths in 1835, together with the building of a new Anglican church, acted as a spur to growth; but it was the Rhyl Improvement Act of 1852 that led to sustained development by creating a rough grid pattern of streets between the railway and the shore. The houses were modest, but the building of St Thomas's church by Sir Gilbert Scott in 1861 was perhaps more symbolic of the faith the town's fathers placed in future development. At the other end of the town, near the mouth of the river Clwyd, the rather marshy ground and belt of sand dunes limited housing development. Instead it proved an ideal site for the Rhyl Palace and Summer Gardens. This late-Victorian funfair is still very much the core of the present-day amusement centre and boating pool and has kept pace with changing tastes. In a curious way this area at the mouth of the river Clywd has the most attractive setting in the whole of Rhyl, with fishing boats and the occasional small coaster tied up at the wharf. Recently 'resort' Rhyl has come to grips with the present by building a huge glass leisure centre on the seafront.

The lower part of the Vale of Clwyd is flat

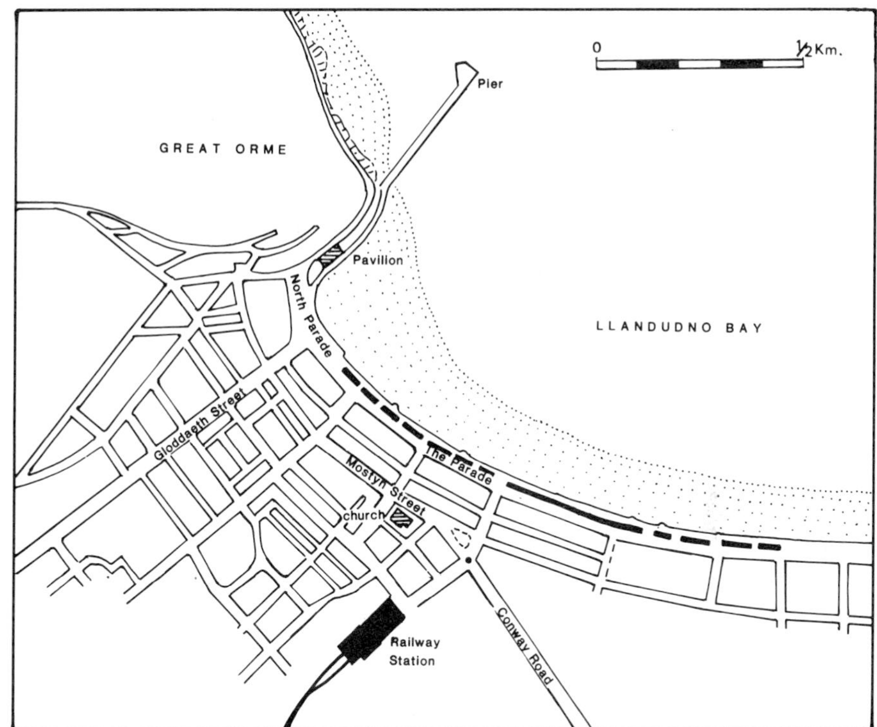

The planned basis of Llandudno can still be seen in its street pattern

and featureless, as is the coastline itself with its caravan sites and their shops and other facilities strung out along the main coastal road. Pensarn, the resort of Abergele, made an attempt early this century to develop, but did not get beyond a single terrace. The difficulty with resort development was the barrier created by the railway which hugs the shoreline. Beyond Pensarn the coastal scene changes completely as a broad belt of limestone reaches the coast to give prominent cliffs and headlands like Tan Penmaen. There has been considerable quarrying of limestone around Llanddulas, and there are loading jetties running out to the low-water line.

Colwyn Bay can trace its beginning as a resort to the carving-out of a new parish from the original Llandrillo in 1844, but growth was slow even when the railway came a few years later and was not helped by the building of a huge coastal embankment from material scooped out of a ballast-pit alongside (now occupied by the funfair). Growth only came when the Pwllycrochan estate came up for sale in 1865 and was sold off in small lots 'to meet the great and increasing demand for marine residences on the coast'. Fortunately, though development was piecemeal and largely unplanned, the layout was spacious and the villas solidly built in the local limestone. This part of the town south of the main coastal road still retains its open character and contrasts markedly with the rather cramped setting of the older quarter of the resort near the station. The original Pwllycrochan House still stands and is now the Rydal Preparatory School.

On the shore itself the promenade known as The Parade was laid out and extended to the Colwyn Bay Hotel. This building, completely dominating the coastline, is symbolic of the Victorian atmosphere which still pervades much of the town. The great growth which took place during the last quarter of the nineteenth century led to the granting of local government status and a

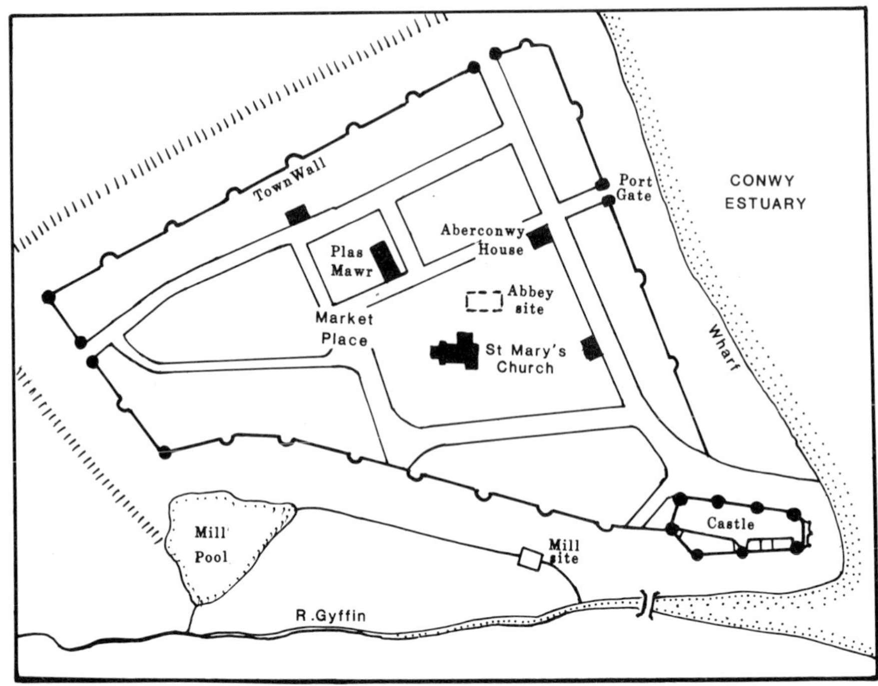

Historic features of the Edwardian castle town of Conwy

change of name to the present name Colwyn Bay dates from this time. Previously it had been New Colwyn to distinguish it from the village of Old Colwyn farther east along the coast.

Rhos-on-Sea is now in urban continuity with the western end of Colwyn Bay and to many is simply a more modern and pleasant suburb of that resort. It has one outstanding feature, the tiny chapel dedicated to the Celtic saint Trillo and nestling almost hidden under the modern promenade. Although doubts have been expressed as to the age of the present vaulted structure built of limestone blocks – the Royal Commission on Ancient Monuments regards it as comparatively modern – its setting on the coast, and the presence of a spring coming out of the limestone, is in keeping with a possible Celtic foundation.

Llandudno is a town laid out on a tombolo – a connecting strip of sand linking a former offshore island, in this case the Great Orme, to the mainland. The original settlement lay high up on the top of the Orme around the ancient church of Saint Tudno, but on this windswept site little development was likely. Instead a more sheltered spot was found in the lee of the great limestone wall, and it was here that in 1840 a new parish church of St George was built. The real development came a decade later when the local Mostyn family sold their land for development (see page 103). Llandudno soon reached its optimum size. Any hope of development as a packet station for Ireland was quickly snuffed out, because of the continued growth of Holyhead. During the last century it never extended much beyond the original planned network of wide streets close to the promenade. Even today some land has not been fully taken up towards the Little Orme. In retrospect *Murray's Guide* of 1858 was a trifle optimistic when it declared that Llandudno was likely to become the Welsh Brighton. Perhaps this lack of development is now an advantage for the town is small enough to retain an individuality which makes it pleasing to many visitors. There is plenty on offer, including a cable tramway and aerial ropeway to the top of the Great

The many circular towers of Conwy Castle dominate the fishing quays and traffic-congested streets of this fine late-thirteenth-century walled town

Orme, or an exciting journey around its edge along the Marine Drive built in the 1870s. For the more adventurous there is the opportunity for a sail along the coast to Anglesey or a more distant trip to the Isle of Man.

Conwy can claim to be the most perfectly preserved of the fortified towns which Edward I strategically placed in this corner of north-west Wales in order to contain the Welsh; its foundation in 1283 leading to the moving of the monks of Aberconwy Abbey to a new settlement at Maenan. The attraction of Conwy as a site was the fine natural defence provided by a long spine of hard grit which ran out into the estuary at this point, and which was used as the base for the castle and as a quarry for the town walls, although the quay wall was built of a local lava. Red sandstone was imported for the castle masons to shape into window casings and mouldings as well as springers for the arches. In the space of only five years between 1283 and 1287 the basic elements of the town took shape, consisting of the castle, town walls, quayside and regular street pattern which Conwy retains today. None of the original buildings remains intact, though there is a suggestion that the stone basement of the house known as Aberconwy (now under the care of the National Trust) may date from the fourteenth century. The large house in High Street named Plas Mawr dates from 1583, and may be the site of Otto's Hall which occupied one of the original burgage plots of the planned town. The parish church incorporates parts of the former monastic buildings of Aberconwy Abbey, and can therefore claim undisputed continuity of site over seven centuries. Once the strategic importance of the castle town declined following the Act of Union between England and Wales in 1536, it had little to support it save its fisheries. Thomas Pennant, the eighteenth-century writer and traveller, commented that 'a more ragged town is scarcely to be seen, within', though he did add 'or a more beautiful, without'.

Apart from sea fishing which continues today, the Conwy Estuary once had a flourishing mussel industry, with anything up to 800 bags a week being sent to markets all over the country in the mid-nineteenth century. Many of the mussels contained small 'pearls' which, though of small value, attracted comment from writers and poets like Drayton and Spenser. Today, in spite of traffic jams which seem to be part of the way of life of the town in summer, the castle is once more the focus of attention. Its bastion-like appearance set on a rock projecting out into the Conwy has suffered from successive river bridgings - Telford's in 1825, Robert Stephenson's railway bridge in 1848, and finally FitzSimon's span of 1958. Now, hopefully, there is talk of a tunnel under the estuary that will take away much of the coastal through-traffic and allow Conwy once again to become a pleasant place to live in and visit.

Penmaenmawr is very much overshadowed by the great stone quarries of the 'mountain' which give it an industrialised look. In spite of this it attempts to maintain its resort character based on its fine stretch of sand. There is also the covered-in ironwork arcade of the central parade of shops as a reminder of its Victorian origin. For long the coastal route from Conwy round the Penmaen headland was fraught with difficulty and, because of rock falls, many early travellers had to take to the beach. In 1772 an engineered road was made for the first time and this was reconstructed by Telford in 1827. The present tunnels, the only satisfactory answer, date from the 1930s. So much of Penmaenmawr mountain has been removed by quarrying that its great archaeological interest is in danger of being overlooked. In Neolithic times it was the centre of an axe 'factory', for the igneous rock outcrop was ideal for shaping into implements. Nearby, at Graig Llwyd, the slopes are still strewn with the waste from the prehistoric workshops, and from here axe-heads, adzes, chisels and hammerstones found their way to various parts of the country. On the eastern side of the mountain a feature dating back to the Bronze Age, with an even older trackway, has long been known as the Druid's Circle. Before quarrying did so much damage to the mountain top Dinas Penmaen had, according to *Murray's Guide* of 1874, enclosures of loose stone walls, some as much as 4m (12ft) high and 4m (12ft) thick, with hut circles within.

Llanfairfechan is also still very much dominated by Penmaenmawr 'mountain' though now its north face is beginning to retreat inland as a coastal plain develops towards Bangor. This flatter land enabled the laying out of the small Victorian resort down by the water's edge, while the earlier 'llan' village lies inland up a side valley; between the two, runs the main coastal road (A55) dominated by Christ Church, dating from 1864. Much of the original village was destroyed by a severe flood coming down the valley of the Afon Ddu in 1673. In the present century Llanfairfechan shared in the development of villa estates which was commonplace in Edwardian times, the main architect being Herbert Luck North, a pupil of Sir Edwin Lutyens. His roughcast houses, with small heavy slates on their roofs, are pleasing examples of a domestic architecture now freeing itself from the uniformity imposed by Victorian red-brick styles.

The road from Llanfairfechan westwards which runs along the edge of the flat coastal strip, is one of the few sections of the north Wales coast to be free from caravan sites, and the aesthetic benefit is enormous.

Aber, possibly of Roman origin on the road across from Caerhun (Canovium) in the Conwy Valley and later a palace of the princes of Gwynedd, was the starting point for the route across the Lavan Sands to the Anglesey shore near Beaumaris in the days before Telford built his Menai Bridge.

Llandygai, lying on a shelf above the Ogwen Valley, has the unmistakable appearance of a planned estate village with cottages clustered around the sixteenth-century church. Close by is the entrance to Penrhyn Castle, now under the care of the National Trust though the estate is still under the control of the Penrhyn family. The castle as we see it today dates from 1827–47, but it incorporates earlier buildings, including parts of a medieval house. On the edge of the estate close to Bangor is Port Penrhyn, built in 1790 to

Portmeirion, creation of Clough Williams-Ellis, on the Llŷn peninsula

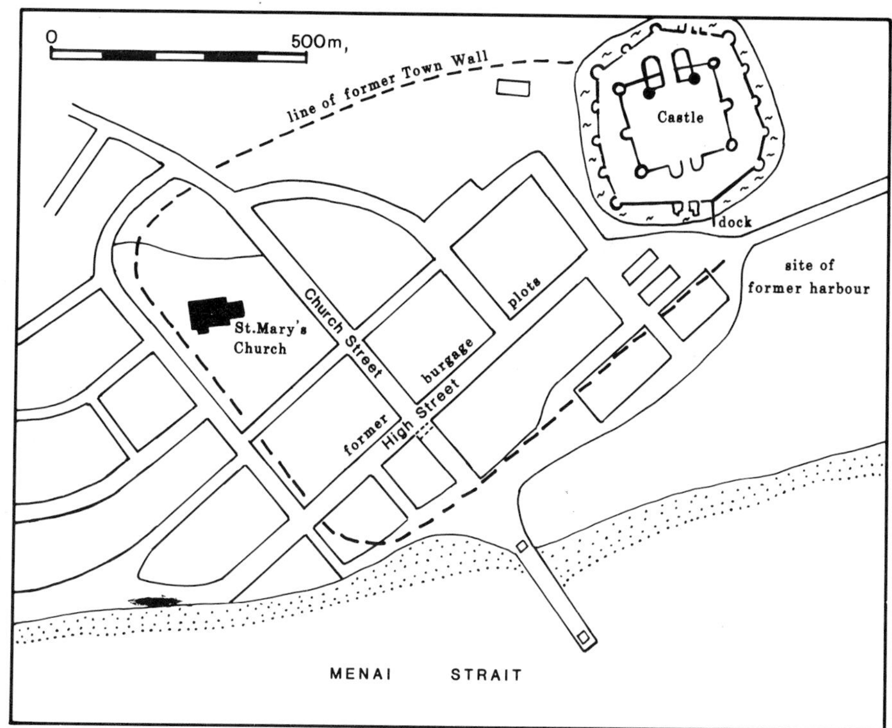

Beaumaris still has the regular street pattern that it was given in the fourteenth century

export slate from the inland quarries near Bethesda. After this trade almost ceased the quays became derelict but the port, including the harbourmaster's house, has recently been restored. Now once again trade has returned in the form of dredged sea-sand and local fisheries.

Bangor has a curious site, occupying a long valley hemmed in by steep ridges on either side. The cathedral, dedicated to St Deiniol, occupies part of the valley floor and is not unlike St David's in this respect. The reason, in both cases, is probably historical, for both are early foundations of Celtic saints who often chose sites where spring-water was available. Although the present cathedral is mostly thirteenth to sixteenth century and heavily restored by Sir Gilbert Scott in the nineteenth, its foundation as a monastery in AD 546 makes it one of the oldest religious sites in Britain. The former bishop's palace was divided when the present A5 road was driven through to relieve traffic from the High Street but part of it, a sixteenth-century house, remains as the Town Hall. Dominating the ridge which separates the town from the Menai Strait are the imposing buildings of the University College dating from early this century although the college had been founded (using the old Penrhyn Arms Hotel as its centre) in 1884. In spite of being close to the Menai Strait, Bangor has made little of its waterfront. The old Garth Pier is closed and awaiting restoration while Beach Road, which runs alongside Penrhyn harbour, has only recently been tidied up.

The coast of Cardigan Bay, at Aberporth

The Menai Strait, formed as ice over-deepened what were once two opposing river valleys, is narrowest about 3km (2 miles) from Bangor and it is here that the nineteenth-century engineers, first Telford in 1826 with his suspension bridge and Stephenson in 1849 with his tubular railway bridge, chose to leap the gap into Anglesey. Both bridges have been partially rebuilt (particularly the railway bridge which had a road opened on top in 1980) but even today they remain as symbols of great engineering skill and enterprise – ventures into the unknown which put Britain in the forefront for this type of construction. Before Telford bridged the Strait as part of his London to Holyhead road link, the crossing had to be made by ferry near the present railway bridge. This was so dangerous that no fewer than 180 passengers were drowned between 1664 and 1842. The siting of the original railway bridge by Robert Stephenson was influenced by a rock in the middle of the strait which could be used as a foundation for a central pier. Stephenson's original design also included two cast-iron arches, but this was rejected by the Admiralty as they might impede navigation of tall-masted sailing vessels. Happily these have now been added to the rebuilt bridge, with pleasing visual effects. Between the Britannia railway bridge and Telford's suspension bridge are a number of islets; on one of these the small church dedicated to Saint Tysilio stands amidst gravestones on an almost bare rock. It can be approached across a causeway at all states of the tide.

Anglesey

The building of the nineteenth-century bridges ended centuries of isolation during which Anglesey's sole contact with the mainland was by some half-dozen ferries across the dangerous waters of the Menai Strait. Telford's bridge in particular altered the situation and led to the growth, not only of the settlement of Menai Bridge itself but of numerous other small towns on the island and to the development of a tourist trade taking advantage of the many fine beaches and rocky coves of the varied coastal scenery.

Beaumaris The approach from Menai Bridge along the edge of the strait is one of the most pleasant coastal drives in Wales. The road, often cut out of solid rock, is now somewhat overgrown with trees with the result that the original fine views across to the mainland can only be glimpsed infrequently. When the route was first made in

The grouping of historic features at Penmon and the related religious site on Puffin Island

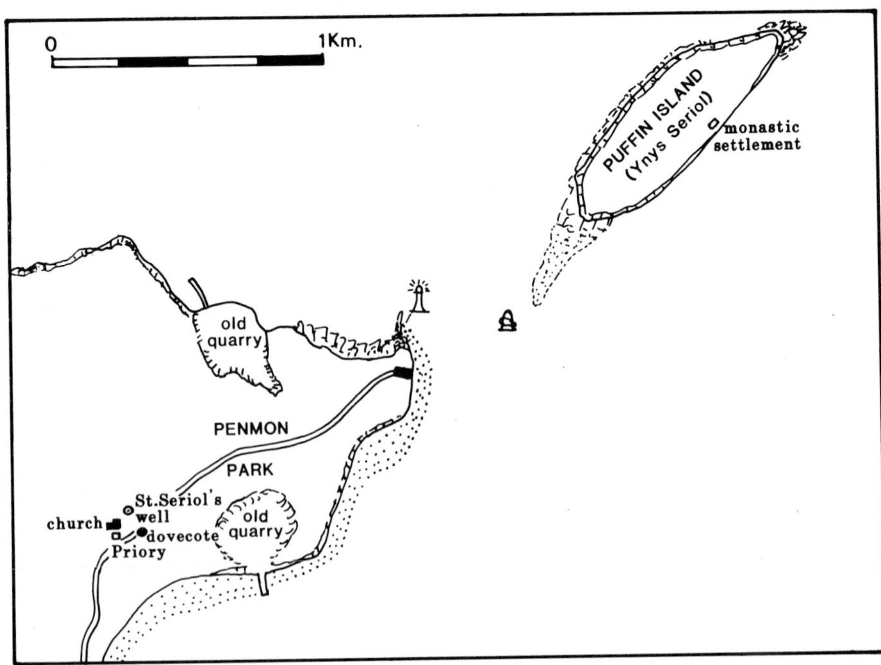

Penmon Priory, the church and well of St Seriol and the early-seventeenth-century dovecote form an interesting complex

the 1820s it led to the building of large villa residences along the edge of the Strait, but unfortunately a more recent tower block represents an unwelcome and out-of-character intrusion. Happily Beaumaris itself still retains its nineteenth-century appearance though the layout of the town, some of its buildings, and above all the castle, betray its medieval origin. Here was yet another of Edward I's plantations, the only one not on the mainland and presumably controlling the northern approaches to the Strait in the same way as Caernarfon protected the southern access. It was sited on low marshland – the *beau marais* – with the castle being completed by 1295. That summer, no fewer than 3,000 men were employed, perhaps a sign of urgency in case of a Welsh revolt. Like nearly all Edward I's castles it was supplied from the sea, from a dock built close to the southern entrance and connected to the Menai Strait by a short canal. Nothing remains of this, as the site has been filled in and used as a carpark. The castle is of perfect design with an inner ward contained by a high wall with turrets, then an outer concentric wall and, finally, a deep moat. It was built mainly of local limestone, but with some sandstone which must have come in by sea. The squat form of the castle comes as something of a surprise, particularly because of its low-lying site, and it clearly had to rely on its own impregnability to resist attack instead of natural defences.

The town, laid out alongside the castle, followed the traditional grid network of streets. Burgage plots were allotted to would-be settlers from England, who were granted free rent for the first ten years by way of encouragement. The town wall, which came later, only survives in fragments; but the town church of St Mary, although partly restored in later centuries, still occupies its central position. For the building of Beaumaris, Edward had to displace the Welsh inhabitants of nearby Llanfaes. This he did by founding the town of Newborough on the other side of the island and giving it a charter in 1303. Medieval Beaumaris hardly expanded at all and even in the seventeenth century, although a number of merchants lived in the town and there was a flourishing leather trade, little growth occurred outside the original walls. The main phase of growth came in the first half of the nineteenth century after the building of the Menai Bridge, when Beaumaris sought to become a fashionable resort. In 1835 the Bulkeley Arms in the main street and the Victoria Terrace overlooking the greensward were built, both designed by J. A. Hansom (of cab fame).

Penmon The road beyond Beaumaris to the south-east corner of the island leads past the limestone quarries, now idle, where much of the stone for Beaumaris Castle was originally quarried. Originally Penmon must have been a typical Celtic cell dating from the sixth century when St Seriol first came here and settled beside the cool clear waters of a limestone spring. The holy well still survives behind the church, though the present covering is much later in date. This church of St Seriol, rebuilt between 1120 and 1170 as a cruciform building, contains a fine Celtic cross of about AD 1000 in the south transept. Penmon Priory, under the care of the Department of the Environment, dates from the twelfth century, and consists of refectory and dormitory, with the much-altered prior's house adjoining. The whole setting is enhanced by the nearby dovecote, one of the finest examples remaining in the country. It dates from about 1600 and was probably built by the Bulkeley family who lived close by at Barton Hill. Inside is a massive domed roof leading to an open cupola, and walls which have nesting-boxes for perhaps a thousand birds.

By the dovecote is the entrance to Penmon Park and its toll road which leads to the point opposite Puffin Island, also known as Priestholm or Ynys Seriol; the last name is perhaps the truest, for the Celtic saint established himself here as well as at Penmon. The ruins of the church date from the twelfth century. Although birds flock to the island in great numbers, only the occasional puffin is seen, for their nest burrows fall easy prey to the island's rats; it is the cormorant, shag and fulmar that populate the limestone cliffs. This limestone – blue-grey in colour – dominates the coastline to the west, and has been extensively quarried and shipped to places like Liverpool Bay for maintaining the training walls of the Mersey entrance. There is no coastal road round to Red Wharf Bay so an inland route has to be followed beneath the ramparts of the Iron Age hill fort of Bwrd Arthur. Red Wharf Bay is a fine stretch of sand, famed for its cockle gathering and, although there is an inn and carpark on its western margin, development has been slight. Not so at nearby Benllech which has become a bungalow retirement area in recent years. With its fine stretch of sands it is the best known resort of the east coast – though not the most attractive or quietest.

Moelfre, a few miles to the north where the limestone cliffs have given way to more rugged grits and flags, has a pleasanter appearance with some old cottages round the tiny harbour and an easy cliff-top walk towards the lifeboat station and the offshore island of Ynys Moelfre. A mile inland lies Din Lligwy, a native village of rude limestone huts huddled together for defence, and dating from the fourth century. The approach through the field passes close to the twelfth-century chapel of Capel Lligwy in its fine site overlooking the sandy bay to the north. Further along the coast and overlooking Traeth Dulas Bay is the farmstead of Pentre Eirianell, the birthplace of one of Wales' most famous sons, Lewis Morris. He was the eldest of four brothers and in a varied career in the first half of the eighteenth century was in turn estate surveyor, custom's officer, chartmaker and mining engineer, in short a gifted man of many parts. His manuscript estate-plan of Bodorgan on the other side of the island still survives, while his chart of the coast of Wales and an atlas of harbour plans, both dating from 1747, are becoming increasingly sought after as antiquarian maps. A fine obelisk to the family was erected in 1910 by the Cymmrodorion Society, which was largely founded by Lewis and one of his brothers. It stands on a rocky knoll overlooking the farm and gives fine views over the bay and the coastline to the north.

Amlwch is now only a small town with a care-worn appearance, having a tiny cleft of a

South Stack, an islet just off the most westerly point of Holy Island

harbour. There is only the slightest hint of its former importance when the nearby Parys Mountain was being gutted for its valuable copper-ore deposits. Although the presence of copper had been known for a long time, it was not until 1764 that the valuable lodes were discovered, to be followed by decades of feverish activity when thousands of tons were brought to the smelters at Amlwch for partial concentration before being shipped round the coast to Swansea. Amlwch felt the full effects of the mining bonanza: the harbour was enlarged to take coasters of 100 tons, a new church was built in 1800, a school in 1820, and there were no fewer than 60 alehouses. All this came to an end before the century was out, once the richer lodes had been exhausted. The harbour became almost unvisited and derelict and it is only with the recent interest in sailing that its old ore-quays are being used again. The offshore oil-terminal buoy has also helped to revive the port as a servicing centre. On the outskirts of the town, on the eastern edge of Bull Bay, is the bromide extraction plant of ICI. Inevitably it looks out of place in the low-cliff surroundings but in this case the siting is unavoidable and it has brought employment to hard-pressed Amlwch. This whole stretch of coast was once more industrialised, for at Porth Wen there are former brickworks which used the local boulder clay, and a mile to the west at Porth Llanlleina there are remains, in the form of a boiler-house and chimney, which suggest an ill-fated mining venture for copper.

Cemaes Quiet except for a few weeks in the summer when visitors throng the main shopping street and the harbour wall, this former small port, with its massive breakwater, has scanty remains of former fishermen's cottages. There is still some part-time fishing, but the boats in the harbour are mainly for pleasure. Old prints show a very different place in the nineteenth century when the harbour, filled with sailing vessels, was the life-blood of Cemaes where essentials were brought in and the products of its hinterland carried away. The surrounding cliffs provide pleasant walks. That to the east leads to the quaint fourteenth-century church of Llanbadrig, a name which more than one writer has linked with St Patrick. Outside the church looks ordinary, but inside the remarkable restoration of 1884 by Lord Stanley who

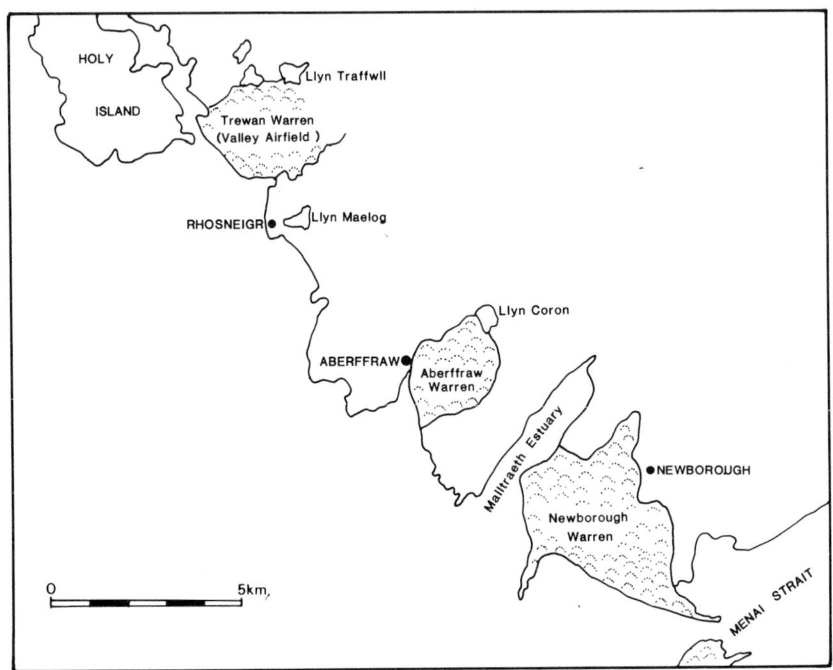

The sand-dune areas of the south-west coast of Anglesey

became a Moslem, speaks volumes. To the west the cliff walk, in early summer bright with sea thrift, brings the Wylfa Nuclear Power Station, destined to become an industrial archaeological monument in the twenty-first century, quickly into view.

Cemlyn provides a variation in the coastal scene for here the cliff-line breaks down and its place is taken by a bay-bar of pebbles with a lagoon behind. The area, famous as a bird sanctuary, is now under the protection of the National Trust who have provided a carpark at its eastern end. The lagoon was originally natural, but there is now a controlled outlet, and small islets have been built up for nesting birds amidst clumps of sea aster. On top of the pebble ridge itself are patches of sea cabbage and the spreading orache. Towards the lagoon margin sea pink, sea aster and fleshy sorrel flourish.

Port Swtan is the next bay with road access, for the extremity of Carmel Head can only be approached on foot. West-facing, it has recently become popular on account of its sandy beach backed by yellow cliffs. A car-park, café, restaurant and sea-food factory come as something of a surprise in a corner of Anglesey which has for long remained undeveloped. Other coves along this coast have fine sandy beaches and all give good views across to Holyhead harbour and the off-lying Skerries. The lighthouse on the Skerries was the last privately owned one in the country and was finally sold for £½ million. It still has an important role to play warning shipping making for Liverpool and the giant oil-tankers which moor and unload off Amlwch.

Holyhead, although known superficially by travellers to Ireland, is seldom visited in its own right; yet it is a town not without historic interest and Holy Island, on which it lies, has prehistoric features. The Welsh name for the town, Caer Gybi, is instructive in that it suggests an original fortress site. In fact one was built by the Romans, probably at the end of the third century, as part of a defensive system against Irish raiders –

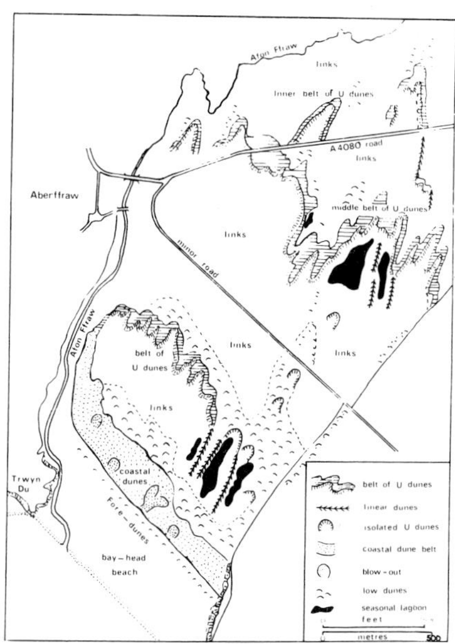

The sand-dune complexes making up Aberffraw Warren

rather like the Saxon Shore forts of south-east England. Part of the walls of the fort remain to a height of over 3m (10ft) and they now enclose the parish church, dedicated to the Celtic saint Cybi. Both lie just behind the High Street on a raised site overlooking the harbour. The inner harbour, from which the car ferry sails for Ireland, was designed by John Rennie and completed in 1821. The arrival of the railway from Chester in 1849 confirmed Holyhead as the Irish packet station, for up to that time it had many rivals, including Llandudno. The much larger 'New' harbour, with its 2km (1½ mile) long stone breakwater, was not completed until 1873 and was designed as a harbour of refuge. Another breakwater has been recently added to serve the aluminium works lying to the east of the town.

Holyhead Mountain, which provided the stone for the breakwaters, rises to over 213m (700ft) and is worth climbing for the view over the town. On its southern flanks are some well-preserved groups of hut circles now under the care of the Department of the Environment – the remains of a settlement dating from the second to fourth centuries AD. Further on, the road comes to an end overlooking the islet of South Stack with its lighthouse. The cliff scenery here is particularly impressive as the rocks have been contorted into tight folds. Swooping guillemots, razorbills and kittiwakes accompany the visitor willing to make the descent and bridge-crossing to the lighthouse promontory. The less visited southern part of Holy Island has bays like Trearddur, a well-established resort, and the lesser known and in many ways more attractive Rhoscolyn.

On the east side of the narrow strait which separates Holy Island from Anglesey lies the first of the sand-dune areas which figure prominently in the scenery of the south-west coast – Tywyn Trewan – used by the RAF as the Valley air station. It was during the building of the airfield in 1943 that the remarkable Iron Age treasure of Llyn Cerrig Bach, now in the National Museum of Wales, was found. Another small dune-area occurs east of the small resort of Rhosneigr, while standing prominently on the headland to the south is the mound of Barcloddiad-y-Gawres, a Neolithic burial chamber within which are five standing stones ornamented with spirals, chevrons and zigzags. There is nothing quite like it elsewhere in the United Kingdom, the nearest parallel being that of New Grange in Ireland.

Aberffraw Although only a village, it has the form of a small town with a central market square and nearby church. It was once of much greater importance in that it was the seat of the Princes of Gwynedd, but there are no surface remains of their former 'palace' although air photographs suggest excavation would be worthwhile in the field west of the village. Across the river lies another great dune complex with three main dune belts. Some of the parabolic dunes are still active and migrating inland. To the west of Aberffraw and approached by a narrow lane which ends blindly at the coast, is the church of Llangwfan, situated on an island of boulder clay which, until the building of an encircling wall, was being rapidly eroded. Although the tiny building probably only dates from the fourteenth century, the isolated site hints at a much earlier Celtic foundation.

Newborough When Edward I decided to build Beaumaris as a fortified town he removed the Welsh inhabitants of nearby Llanfaes to this isolated corner of Anglesey where they were to form a Welsh town – Newborough. Although given a charter and market rights it never really established itself, and this is the appearance it gives even today. The marram grass of the nearby dunes of the warren was the basis of a local industry – the making of mats, nets and ropes – but because of dune erosion attempts were made to limit the cutting of the grass. The industry was still active in the nineteenth century with the mats being sold in Caernarfon market. From the main village street there is a road through the dune belt (now owned by the Forestry Commission and planted with conifers during the past thirty years) to a large carpark on the coast near Llanddwyn Island. Altogether there are about 13sq km (5sq miles) of dune landscape and, prior to the planting of the conifers, blowing sand posed great problems. The dune belt has probably existed since early prehistoric time for flints dating from about 6000 BC have been found around some of the projecting rock ridges. At various times the migrating sand has moved inland, the stormy thirteenth century in particular leading to the burial of many acres of good farmland, and it is recorded that in December 1331 no fewer than 75ha (186 acres) were lost. In the past some agriculture must have taken place on Llanddwyn island for there are traces of old fields near the sixteenth-century church of St Dwynwen, another of the fifth-century Celtic saints. From the island – a seaward projection made of tough, uncompromising igneous rocks – there is a fine sweep of beach running for over 5km (3 miles) to the end of the sand spit at Abermenai Point. In earlier centuries there was a ferry-crossing at this southern entrance to the Menai Strait, but this was later replaced by one directly opposite Caernarfon.

The Llŷn Peninsula

Caernarfon, as well as commanding the southern entrance to the Menai Strait, lies at the gateway to the long peninsula running out from the mountains of Snowdonia into the turbulent waters of the Irish Sea. Although it is easy to think of Caernarfon solely as yet another castle town of Edward I, the history of settlement here goes far back to before the time when the Romans es-

Newborough Warren and adjacent coastline

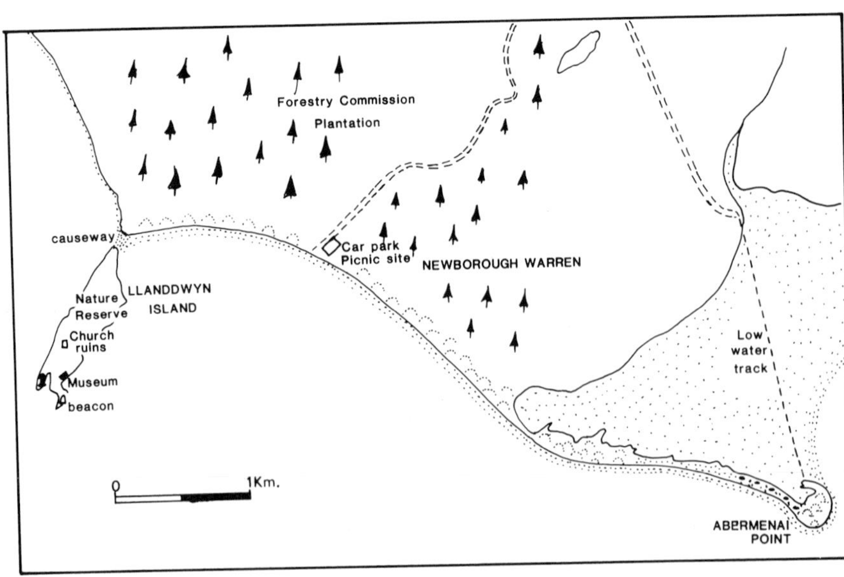

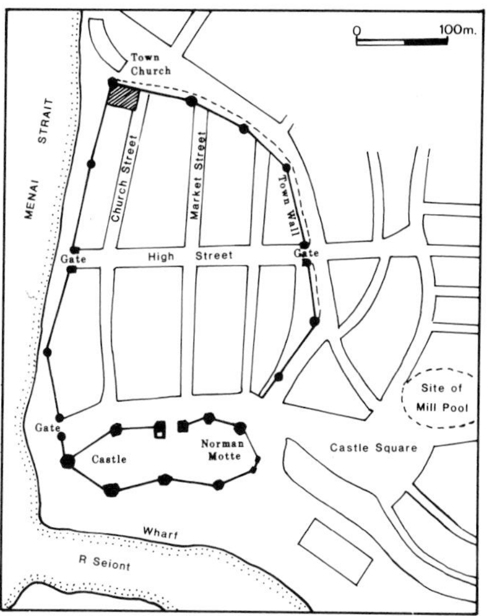

Caernarfon: from Welsh settlement to Norman castle and thirteenth-century town

tablished their fortress of *Segontium* on a bluff overlooking the present town. After they left there was probably a Welsh settlement on the same site for the parish church, dedicated to Saint Peblig, lies next to the Roman remains. The present site of the town at the point where the Afon Seiont enters the Menai Strait was chosen by the Norman earl, Hugh d'Arranches, and it was his castle that was incorporated in the Edward I defences built shortly after 1283. The town, surrounded by massive walls and a moat, followed the simple gridiron plan with the area split up into regular parcels of land for the burgage plots. As in other castle towns in north Wales, English settlers were brought in, and by 1298 it was recorded that there were fifty-six burgage plots occupied. A town chapel was built into the north-west corner of the walls with St Peblig's retaining its status as parish church. Since 1301 successive Princes of Wales have been crowned here, so that the royal borough has some claim to be considered the capital of Wales. Now it lives partly on its historic past, but also functions as the market town for a large area around. The buses in the market square, on a Saturday, look somewhat ramshackle, but their presence tells of services to outlying villages in Snowdonia and the northern Llŷn. The market square by the castle lies outside the original town walls, for there has been considerable expansion since medieval times. In the nineteenth century there was a large export trade in slate from the quays bordering on the river Seiont, now the castle carpark. Today only yachts and launches tie up in the lower part of the river, for the commercial activity of the port now centres on the small dock on the north side of the town with its direct access into the Menai Strait.

Dinas Dinlle on the open coast beyond the village of Llandwrog with its pseudo-Gothic buildings erected by Lord Newborough, has the remains of an Iron Age hillfort now being ravaged by the sea which is tearing into the soft boulder-clay cliffs on its seaward side. A few bungalows and a hotel border the road which runs along the coast behind the protection of a shingle bank towards Fort Belan, built by Lord Newborough in the late-eighteenth century and used by him as a bathing place reached from his nearby country house, Glynllifon Park. It is now a tourist attraction with cannons fired for visitors in the summer months.

Clynnog The low shelving coast to the south of Dinas Dinlle offers little by way of exciting scenery and there are few tracks down to it from the main road. Clynnog provides some compensation because of its historic past, suggested by the large church for what is now a small roadside settlement. The building we see today is largely sixteenth-century in design, but leading from it by a short passage is the detached chapel of St Beuno, founded in AD 616. It was the cult of St Beuno and the nearby holy well which made Clynnog one of the stopping places on the pilgrims' road to Bardsey.

Trefor was once a quarrying settlement which depended on the fine stone obtained from the nearby Yr Eifl. Much of it was exported by sea and the jetty remains, though now idle. There is a fine sandy beach and caves in the cliffs to the west. The inner of the three peaks which make up Yr Eifl, has an Iron Age hillfort, Tre'r Ceiri, on its summit – in size and state of preservation one of the finest in Britain. Inside its reasonably complete boundary wall there are foundations of about 150 hut circles. The igneous rocks responsible for the triple heads of Yr Eifl also form the impressive cliffs falling steeply to the sea. At the mouth of the Gwrtheyrn Valley a former quarrying settlement with chapel and substantial terrace rows lies abandoned and rapidly falling into decay, though recently a programme of restoration has been started. The approach is down a steep unmetalled track from the village of Llithfaen, and is a pleasant walk on a summer's day. It is hard to believe that the whole settlement was not finally abandoned until the 1950s, but nature is quick to reclaim. Until the seventeenth century a huge tumulus, Bedd Gwrtheyr, existed in the valley, reputedly the burial site of the British king, Vortigern.

Nefyn The road which has been forced inland around the Yr Eifl mass approaches the coast once again near Pistyll, with its tiny church dedicated to St Beuno. Some 3km (2 miles) further on is Nefyn which, although of village size, has the appearance of a town. At the time of Edward I it was already in existence, for the king held court here and it was shortly afterwards made a Welsh borough. Today, with caravan parks around and guest houses in the town and at **Morfa Nefyn** close by, it is a favourite holiday centre particularly for Midlanders. The beach at Morfa Nefyn is a fine stretch of sand running in an arc round to the headland of Porth Dinllaen. At the beginning of the nineteenth century this apparently out of the way place was seriously considered as a rival to Holyhead as the packet station for Ireland, the attraction being the shelter afforded by the headland (formed of volcanic beds) and the deep-water bay in its lee. Although a long straight road from Pwllheli was built as part of the great projected highway from London, nothing came of the harbour scheme, although it was revived again during the railway mania when the Great Western proposed a broad-gauge line from Worcester. The Chester to Holyhead line won the day and Porth Dinllaen was simply allowed to remain as a tiny settlement with a pub and a handful of cottages.

From Nefyn to the tip of the Llŷn Peninsula the coast is formed of cliffs of Pre-Cambrian rocks, some of the earliest beds in Britain. Though not particularly high except near the end of the peninsula, the scenery is varied because the sea has exploited weaknesses in the rocks and carved out clefts, caves and off-lying stacks. Access is limited, but at Porth Oer there is a carpark with a path to the beach. Here are the 'whistling' sands which at certain states of the tide make a squeaky noise when walked over, supposedly through the tiny sand-grains rubbing together.

Bardsey Island lies only 3km (2 miles) off the end of the Llŷn Peninsula but the waters around can be so treacherous as to make the passage difficult if not impossible. In summer, boats leave Aberdaron for the island following the route taken by the pilgrims and saints (believers) who once made the journey to this holy isle. The earliest record of any religious foundation dates from AD 615 with the founding of St Mary's Abbey, of which little remains except the much later tower. Both abbey and six farmhouses shelter under the high ridge which forms the eastern backbone of the island. One of the farms is used by the Bardsey Bird and Field Observatory, founded in 1953, which attracts hundreds of naturalists each year. Apart from birds there is much to interest the geologist, botanist or historian. The island, formerly owned by Lord Newborough, is now run by the Bardsey Island Trust formed in 1977. Not only will its wildlife and natural beauty be preserved, there is now for the first time public right of access. For those unable to visit the island itself, its main features can be seen from the top of Mynydd Mawr, approached along narrow country lanes westwards from Aberdaron.

Aberdaron, now a quiet resort with a fine sandy beach, was once the land terminus of the pilgrims' way to Bardsey. The church by the beach leaves no doubt as to the religious importance of the place, and the first building on the site could well be seventh century in date. For a time in the nineteenth century the church was in danger of being destroyed

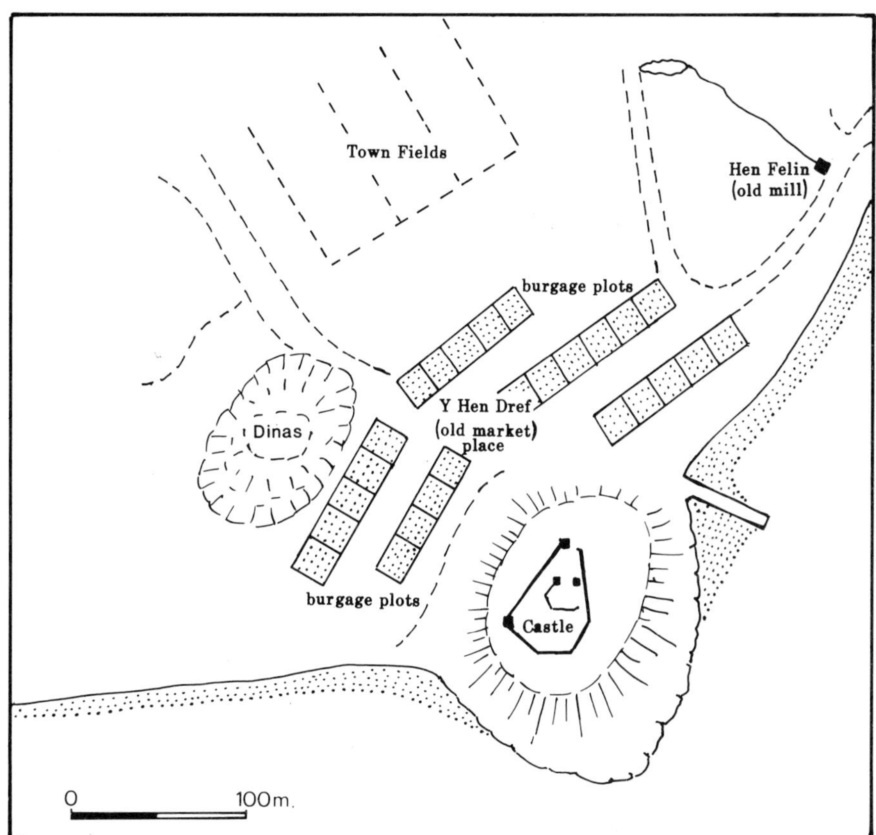

Cricieth

by the sea and was even abandoned at one stage. Happily it was restored in 1860 and is in character with the tightly packed cluster of cottages which form the heart of the village by the brook.

Rhiw, perched on a hill top, enjoys magnificent views across the fine sweep of Hell's Mouth Bay below. The bay, with its 5km (3 miles) of sandy beach, has been cut out of softer boulder-clay deposits and is only easily accessible at its western end. St Tudwal's Peninsula to the east stands out prominently and has fine cliffs of sandstones and flags. Although there are lanes and tracks, this is an isolated corner which is seldom visited.

Abersoch is in complete contrast to Rhiw, for in summer it has hordes of tourists, especially those interested in boats, for its small harbour is very sheltered from the west. Before it was 'discovered' it must have been a sleepy fishing village in the Dylan Thomas mould. The 'harbour' is the river mouth of the Afon Soch which has a curious course, rising near Hell's Mouth Bay and then making a great loop to the north and passing through a gorge before reaching Abersoch. The explanation is that a glacial lake formed to the west during the Ice Age, and the gorge marked its overflow channel. Afterwards the ice melted and the lake drained away, with the Afon Soch using the line of the overflow to reach the sea.

Llanbedrog is even more sheltered than Abersoch, for it nestles under the hill of Mynydd Tirycwmwd, formed of a tough granite porphery which resists wave attack. The restored church lies close to the good sandy beach but somewhat separate from the main part of the village. The headland and lee-beach relationship found at Llanbedrog is repeated, with variations, along the remainder of the south coast of the Llŷn Peninsula. Each headland consists of hard igneous rock, while the beach to the east consists of either sand or shingle, sometimes backed with dunes or, more usually, low cliffs of boulder clay.

Pwllheli can claim to be the 'capital' of the Llŷn for it is the largest town, the shopping and market centre, as well as being the terminus of the Cambrian Coast railway. The town itself is unpretentious and without apparent design. Like Nefyn it was probably a medieval Welsh borough and therefore completely different from the planned castle towns of Edward I. It was formerly an important port, with the long spit ending in the jagged Gimlet Rock (formed of dolerite) forming its southern flank. This is now the resort part of the town with its hotel, guest houses and seaside bungalows. Much of the main holiday activity is centred on Butlin's Camp, 5km (3 miles) away to the east beyond the next headland of Pen-y-chain. The low coast is scenically dull until hard rock once again appears in the cliff-line, this time providing the headland setting for Cricieth Castle.

Cricieth There was a Welsh castle sited on top of the prominent rock of red felsite long before Edward I made his excursions into this part of Wales. He simply took it over, rebuilt it in part, and then added a small settlement with market place on its inner side. All this took place in the 1280s following the defeat of the Welsh prince Llewelyn. Though modern Cricieth is very much centred on the main road the old town around the castle, known in Welsh as Yr Hen Dref, can still be made out; and although the buildings have inevitably changed over the centuries many still occupy the original 23 × 18m (75 × 60ft) burgage plots. Down by the harbour, in the lee of the castle rock, in what was the Victorian resort quarter, is a cottage named Hen Felin, which occupies the site of the town's former corn mill. Unlike many other Welsh resorts Cricieth has retained an exclusive air, favouring the visitor who is quite content to make his own amusement or simply enjoy the fine coastal scenery. Thus it is in complete contrast to Morfa Bychan to the east with its caravans, camping sites and cars on the beach at Black Rock Sands.

Portmadog at the head of the Glaslyn Estuary developed in the nineteenth century as a slate-exporting port. With its inland twin Tremadog the settlement was closely associated with William Madocks, MP for Boston. It was Madocks who put in hand the great reclamation of the upper part of the Glaslyn by building a great embankment and, when Samuel Holland, one of the great slate kings with quarries up in the hills was anxious to export his material, built a huge quay and storage sheds (see page 71). Portmadog town has now become a shopping area for this corner of Snowdonia as well as a centre for tourists visiting the fine sandy beaches around Borth y Gest and Black Rock Sands. Purpose-built flats now occupy the peninsula by the Ffestiniog Railway terminus to serve the many yachtsmen now using the port.

Portmeirion is impressively set on the south-facing slopes of a low peninsula running out into the Glaslyn Estuary almost opposite Borth y Gest. It is unique not only in Wales but in the whole of Britain, and the dream of the architect Clough Williams-Ellis (see page 93). An existing nineteenth-century house by the water's edge was adapted as a hotel at which many notabilities stayed in the 1930s – Noel Coward is said to have written *Blithe Spirit* while here. Gradually the seaside village took shape as Clough Williams-Ellis assembled a collection of buildings which he brought from various parts of the country. His gatehouse, campanile, villas, lighthouse and town hall, set on the steep slopes of the wooded peninsula, are not to everyone's taste. Nevertheless, he succeeded in adding something which was not totally destructive of the natural coastal scene, a quiet resort of distinctive character unsullied by the dull uniformity of the twentieth century. Now an annual antiques fair and twice-weekly firework displays in the summer months seek to attract visitors.

Llandanwg was the parish out of which the Edwardian castle town of Harlech was created, but its church is now in grave danger of being overwhelmed by sand

Barmouth Bridge carries the Cambrian Coast railway across the Mawddach Estuary

Cardigan Bay

Harlech is yet another of the Welsh coastal castle towns associated with Edward I's ring of defence around Snowdonia. As with Cricieth, visible across the waters of Tremadog Bay, a coastal rock provided an ideal natural defence site. It has been suggested that at the time of the building of the castle in 1283 the great sand-flat of Morfa Harlech did not exist and ships were able to sail right up to the castle base. This seems unlikely, and for supply purposes use was probably made of the inlet at Llandanwg, some distance down the coast. The town which grew up by the castle walls has always been small for there is a limited area of flat land on which to build. From the castle ramparts the views across the sand dunes to the coast or northwards to the mountains of Snowdonia would be difficult to surpass. The fine sandy beach, wide dune belt, golf course and indoor swimming pool now attract as many visitors as does the castle.

Llandanwg is the original parish from which the planted town of Harlech was carved out in the thirteenth century. Today the settlement consists of a handful of cottages, a shop and the church which is steadily being covered by blown sand, making it impossible to enter and view an early inscribed stone inside.

Llanbedr, a little distance inland but on the main coast road, is one of the more attractive villages of this coastal strip known as Dyffryn Ardudwy. It is the starting point for an inland excursion into the Rhinogs via the Roman Steps as well as the road out to Mochras (Shell) Island. Part of the approach to Mochras, formed of boulder clay with sand dunes at its southern end, is tidal and impassable around high water. It is privately owned and used as a holiday camp for caravans and tents. The beach consists of sand and huge boulders that have come out of the clay cliffs which are slowly retreating under sea attack. Running out at an angle to the coast in a south-westerly direction is the boulder ridge known as Sarn Badrig – the causeway of St Patrick. Much of it dries out at low spring tides and it is possible to land on it under calm conditions. With rough seas running it presents a considerable danger to shipping and one variant of its name is Shipwreck Reef. Although associated with the legendary story of the flooding of the lost lands of Cantref y Gwaelod (Bottom Hundreds), it is a natural feature, like the two other similar features further south (see page 42).

The coastal sand-dune belt to the south of Shell Island is a favourite site for caravan parks which somehow seem less offensive here than do the larger sites along the north coast. In compensation there is always the fine skyline of the rugged inland Rhinogs. As Barmouth is approached the outer bastions of this fine mountainous area of the Harlech Dome come closer to the coast and gradually snuff out the low-lying coastal strip.

Barmouth (Abermaw) was for long a small fishing hamlet isolated by lack of a road along the north shore of the Mawddach Estuary. While their husbands fished in Cardigan Bay, the wives carried on a small cottage woollen industry. Groups of terraced cottages hung precariously on the steep slopes behind the present town. With the development of sea-bathing the atmosphere of the place changed, and Barmouth became almost a typical English seaside town in a Welsh setting. The arrival of the railway in 1866 acted as a spur to further development and three-storey blocks of apartments sprang up on the shore. They never formed a continuous frontage so that the full effect was lost. The church of 1889 found space on the steep backslope above the town and, symbolic of the railway age, was built partly of red sandstone imported from Chester. With its railway still functioning and increasing numbers of visitors coming in each year by car, Barmouth still attracts as it did in Victorian times. The pleasantest quarter of the town is around the harbour where there is also a foot-ferry across the Mawddach to the end of Fairbourne spit. Fishing boats still tie up by the harbour-master's office and lobster pots are piled high on the quayside. All this is in contrast to the funfairs and stalls found near the station, which seem to attract the majority of the visitors.

Fairbourne is a modern resort with holiday bungalows, best known for its narrow-gauge railway which runs along the length of the Ro Wen spit projecting out into the southern part of the Mawddach Estuary. The railway, which only runs in the summer season, was originally built to carry building materials but was converted into a narrow-gauge steam line in 1916. The spit consists of a storm beach of pebbles brought in by the huge breakers which pound the shore when westerly gales are blowing. Its northern end is formed of sand dunes, while salt marsh provides good grazing land for sheep. All the west-coast salt marshes tend to be broadly similar, only differing in the types of plant which are dominant in particular situations.

Immediately to the south the coast changes in appearance as the coastal strip is gradually pinched out and cliffs run down to the water's edge. Both road and railway have to negotiate this stretch, and rock falls from above are common. There is a slight broadening at Llwyngwril where a great spread of shingle has formed – probably debris originally dumped by ice.

Llangelynin is a tiny church hamlet hemmed in between the road and railway. The low squat church is interesting, but the railway prevents access to the beach.

Tonfanau is dismal in that the coastal strip is dominated by the remains of an old war-time camp, used at various times in the past to provide temporary accommodation for refugees. The sandy beach, with its scatter of large boulders, marks the beginning of yet another causeway – Sarn y Bwlch – which runs out at an angle to the coast. It is not as long as St Patrick's causeway farther north, but is similar in appearance and origin.

Tywyn The road is forced to make a long detour inland around the drowned lower part of the Dysynni Estuary before heading back to the coast at Tywyn. Although its Victorian seaside quarter, consisting of a single short terrace, is close to the beach, the centre of the town is almost 1.6km (1 mile) inland near the church. It is this church which gives the clue to the antiquity of Tywyn. Cruciform in plan, it is much larger

Sarn Cynfelin, which runs out at right angles from the coast of Cardigan Bay for several miles

than one would expect, the reason being that it has monastic associations going back to the time of St Cadfan in the sixth century. Although the present building is of much later date, it contains a stone with inscriptions in Welsh and dating from about AD 750 – possibly the earliest example we have of the use of the language. Many of the summer visitors who come to Tywyn do so for one purpose – a journey on the Talyllyn Railway which runs inland up the Fathew Valley as far as Abergynolwyn. Built in 1866, it originally carried slate from the inland quarries. Its present use as a tourist attraction dates from 1951 when it became one of the first 'Little Trains of Wales'.

Aberdyfi has an individuality which sets it apart from other small Welsh resorts, and none is more attractive. Like Barmouth in a similar situation on the north side of an estuary mouth, Aberdyfi remained a small port until after the arrival of the railway. Even then it did not develop to any great extent so that it remains a rather fashionable resort for the golfer and yachtsman. Although still served by the Cambrian Coast Railway it is in something of a backwater, and this could well save its present pleasant aspect of brightly coloured houses strung out along the main road.

The Dyfi Estuary is the last of the great submerged valleys which make such major indentations into the coast of Cardigan Bay. Like the others it owes its present form to complex events in the Ice Age when the sea level moved up and down as warm phases succeeded cold. During periods of low sea level, provided the area was ice-free, the rivers cut a valley floor well below that of the present. During the subsequent rise of the sea this valley would be drowned to form an estuary and, in time, as both river and sea brought in sediment, the estuary gradually choked with sand – the condition we see it in today.

Borth consists of a straggling collection of hotels, chalets and bungalows by the side of the road which runs the length of the spit on the south side of the Dyfi Estuary. Its popularity stems from its accessibility – first by rail and now by car – and the excellent sands exposed at low water. There is also a submerged forest which is sometimes uncovered from beneath the sand, with the stumps of trees like alder, birch and pine which flourished when sea level was lower. Inland the scene, though dreary, is of great interest for the great bog of Cors Fochno, which is likely to have begun to form at the same time as the submerged forest, has peat beds which have yielded pollen grains giving an insight into past vegetation. Although attempts have been made to drain parts of it by driving an artificial channel along its western margin, much of it remains in its natural state and is now likely to be preserved because of its scientific value.

From Borth southwards to Aberystwyth, cliffs return once again with rocks like grits, sandstones and flags resisting wave attack to give quite impressive features. Accessibility is difficult except on foot, but it is worthwhile taking the track down to Wallog to visit yet another of the sarns of Cardigan Bay – Sarn Cynfelin. Again this natural ridge of boulders which runs out to sea for several miles is believed to be the remains of a glacial morainic dump left behind during the Ice Age more than 12,000 years ago. The sarn once acted as a natural breakwater for small coasters unloading limestone for the kiln that stands on the shore.

Aberystwyth is now thought of as a nineteenth-century university town where the Welsh heritage and tradition is kept alive. This is true, but it is much more, for Aberystwyth had an interesting foundation, followed by a period when it was an important port, and later acquired a reputation as a lively resort. The latter might seem surprising in view of the stony beach but the truncated pier, now very much an eyesore, gives a clue. Although some development on resort lines was taking place in the early nineteenth century, for instance South Marine Terrace and Laura Place, it was the arrival of the railway in 1864 which gave wider contact with the outside world. The journey on the Cambrian Coast Express from Birmingham or Shrewsbury was long and tedious, but for those not in a hurry the magnificent countryside passed through en route was all part of the holiday. Fine hotels were built by Thomas Savin as part of his railway plan, but unfortunately he went bankrupt shortly afterwards and his Aberystwyth Hotel came up for sale when still incomplete. It was bought by the committee of the University of Wales who were in process of starting a college at that time, and explains why the rather curious Gothic building on the southern end of the seafront became the nucleus of the Victorian university which opened its doors to its first students in 1872. Later expansion made the seafront site hopelessly inadequate, so that new development took place on Penglais; here also is the National Library of Wales, started in 1911. If academics dominate the town in term time, the student boarding houses become the preserve of visitors for two brief months in the summer – a useful deployment of resources since copied elsewhere.

Settlement history at Aberystwyth began with a planted town created in the reign of Edward I at the end of the thirteenth century. It was carved out of the parish of Llanbadarn in 1277 with a new castle of which the mound and fragmentary stonework still remain at the southern end of the promenade. An earlier Norman castle lay a short distance up the Ystwyth valley at Rhydyfelin where there is a motte and bailey today. With the new castle on the coast, this earlier defensive work fell into disuse but the name of *Aberystwyth* was transferred to the new town though, in reality, it lies at the mouth of the Rheidol river. The town charter was granted in December 1277 with the right to wall the new town, and by the end of the century there were over 140 resident burgesses. Apart from the castle the only hint of Edward I foundation is in the gridiron pattern of streets which is immediately apparent to any visitor arriving at the railway station.

The rocky coast southwards of the Ystwyth Valley is not easily accessible but there are some tracks down from the main coastal road. Where the grits and sandstones outcrop the effect is often striking, especially as landslips have added variety. But south of the caravan camp at Morfa Bychan boulder clay takes over so that at Cwm Ceirw farm the 30m (100ft) high cliffs are formed entirely in glacial beds. Undercut by the sea and gullied by weathering they are reminiscent of the clay cliffs of Filey Brigg on the Yorkshire coast. Settlements are few though Llansantffraid is not without interest. The church is set in a circular churchyard indicating an ancient site, while on the south side of the stream there are groups of former fishermen's cottages, now very desirable residences set in a higgledy-piggledy confusion of tight lanes. The coast itself is dull with a pebble beach of flat stones and a clay cliff. The former tiny harbour must have taxed the skill of the local fisherman bringing in his boat after a day's fishing. Aberarth is similar though larger and at the mouth of a bigger river.

Aberayron can claim to be the most charming of the coastal towns of Cardigan Bay with its fine groupings of houses and cottages around the large harbour dating from the early years of the nineteenth century. It is a planned town with a gridiron pattern of streets optimistically named Victoria Street, Oxford Street etc. The houses, many of late Georgian style, have been colour-washed in various pastel shades. Market Street with its open space close to the inner harbour has a solid-looking Town Hall with clock and cupola while at the other end of the scale there are the single-storey fishermen's cottages in Drury Lane. With grassy slopes running down to the harbour walls and chestnut trees set around the quay, the whole effect is stunning on a fine summer's day.

New Quay An abrupt turn in the coastline provides a sheltered harbour and advantage of this was taken in 1833 when the Harbour Company was formed. John Rennie suggested a design for a pier. The town quickly established a reputation for shipbuilding but this has all gone and lobster fishing has taken over, with the pots piled high on the quayside next to the old warehouse. With its narrow, steep streets New Quay is not a place for cars except out of season. In summer the retired population – it is a favoured spot for old sea captains – is swelled by visitors staying in the guest-houses, hotels and huge caravan park along the coast to the north. Rows of cottages and houses ranged in tiers above the harbour give a Cornish or even continental flavour to the place. Dylan Thomas, who lived here in 1944, thought of it being very Welsh and some think it provided part of the setting, if not some of the characters, for his word-play *Under Milk Wood.*

Once round New Quay Head the coast resumes its original line but is largely inaccessible except on foot. At Coybal Bay the sea is gradually stripping off the layers of gritstone from the seaward dipping cliffs leaving almost unnaturally smooth, rounded surfaces to plunge under the water. Here and elsewhere in the vicinity the beach is formed of huge rounded grey boulders, although sand is sometimes found near the low-water line. Cwmtudu, a deeply set bay, is accessible by car, for there is a temporary break in the line of the hog's back cliffs. Anyone expecting solitude and seclusion could be in for a surprise for a curious junk shop which has assembled a huge collection of oddities, often brings in visitors.

Llangranog A wider gap in the cliff-line, formed by the valley of the Afon Hawen, has allowed a larger settlement to grow up. Quiet for three-quarters of the year, it comes alive in the three summer months with families taking advantage of the fine sandy beach. There is a walk to Ynys Lochtyn past the Iron Age hillfort of Pen-dinas-lochtyn – both National Trust – for the more energetic. Llangranog must have been a quiet spot with its own community life before the car and summer cottagers took hold; even the intrepid Victorian tourist found it too far from the nearest railway and tended to bypass it.

Cardigan or, more correctly, Aberteifi, lies 3km (2 miles) inland from the coast and until the administrative reorganisation of the 1970s was the county town. Much earlier *Murray's Guide* of 1877 spoke of much of its business having recently been transferred to Aberayron, but with its Norman castle overlooking the fine bridge over the Teifi and its long High Street with church, chapels and market, Cardigan continued in its county town status. It was formerly an important port in spite of silting of the lower estuary causing a decline in its seaborne traffic, and a number of sizeable warehouses

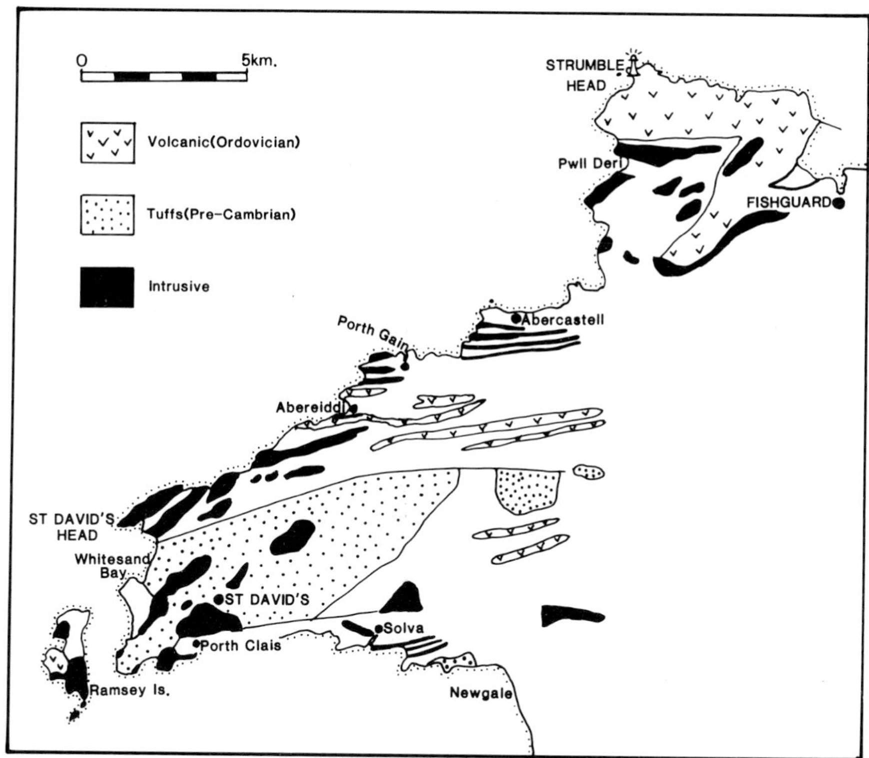

Map of the geology of the western extremity of the Pembrokeshire Peninsula

stand by the bridge. The castle dates from 1091 and must therefore be contemporary with the first Norman incursion into Wales. It was subsequently rebuilt but only parts remain today. To appreciate the present role of Cardigan it should be visited on market day when the town is alive with countryfolk, especially in the arcaded market hall which lies under the Guildhall and dates from early Victorian times. Resort Cardigan flanks both sides of the lower estuary, once famous for its salmon fishing. On the east bank is Gwbert with its golf course and hotel, while opposite lies the huge expanse of Poppit Sands, its natural setting somewhat marred by caravans.

The Pembrokeshire Peninsula

Once across the Teifi, the Pembrokeshire National Park is soon entered. Founded in 1952 it is a coastal park par excellence, for nearly all that is worth preserving is on or close to the coastline, and although one has to walk the coastal path to appreciate its full beauty and variation, the car user can make the occasional sally down to even the remotest parts. One such point is Ceibwr Bay, a narrow cleft or ria cut in shales and sandstones and one of the few breaks in the cliff-line between Cemaes Head and Newport Bay. For the most part the coastal lane through Moylgrove runs too far inland to give more than the occasional glimpse of the jagged cliffs.

Newport The name hints at a planted town and this is what it is – castle, church and street pattern all forming the classic arrangement of such settlements. Market Street runs down from the castle and the stream, with steps down to it, must have provided the original water supply. The town was founded by the Norman lord, Robert Martin, between 1190 and 1195, almost a century before the Edward I castle towns of the north. The church of St Mary probably was of the same date. **Parrog**, now giving access to the fine sands of Newport Bay, was the site of the original port. The old stone breakwater and cottages remain but there is little else to remind one of its former importance.

Dinas Head, forming the western boundary of Newport Bay, owes its continued existence to Silurian rocks which offer considerable resistance to wave attack. It can be approached from Parrog by the Pembrokeshire Coast Path or more easily by taking the main road to Dinas Cross and then turning down the narrow lane to Cwm-yr-Eglwys. From there the whole coastline of Dinas Island can be walked, ending up at the inn at Pwllgwaelod. The designation 'Island' is appropriate in many ways for what is really a peninsula is severed from coast to coast by a deep flat-floored channel which would only require a rise of sea level of about 8m (25ft) to turn it into a strait. The channel originated in the Ice Age, when ice over Cardigan Bay impounded a series of glacial lakes against this coast; the Dinas Valley is considered to be the overflow channel from one of these lakes to the next. **Cwm-yr-Eglwys** itself is not without interest for together with a small caravan and yacht park at the entrance to the valley there is a sheltered sandy beach, the delight of small children. The name is a reminder of the church of St Brynach which stands by the shore, now a ruin after being badly mauled in a storm of 1859. Further damage occurred during the winter of 1978 when the protective sea wall was breached.

Fishguard inhabitants, disappointed at not finding their town the initial terminus of the South Wales Railway which went to Milford Haven instead, never lost hope, and in 1913 a huge new breakwater was built at Goodwick to create a deep-water harbour. It was intended for Atlantic passenger liners but this traffic never materialised and they had to be content with the Irish packet service to Rosslare. Much earlier the natural harbour inlet around which Old Fishguard grew had shipbuilding and fishing interests, and today is still the most pleasant quarter of the town with its colour-washed cottages, now much in demand by the boating fraternity who use the old harbour. The newer part of the town, with its small square and market hall, occupies a higher site, whence there are good cliff walks through gardens towards Goodwick. The views are most impressive with Old Fishguard below and Dinas Head thrusting out to the north-east, while inland the green coastal shelf rises in steps to the Presceli Hills. Beyond Goodwick, in the direction of Strumble Head, is Carregwastad, the spot where the French invasion force landed in February 1797, the last to do so on British soil.

The coastal scenery and countryside changes abruptly as Strumble Head is approached, due to the presence of volcanic rocks which form jagged ridges and tors, the relatively poor farmland compensated for by the majestic cliff scenery with each prominent headland formed of tough igneous rock. The lighthouse at Strumble Head dates from 1908 when Fishguard hoped to attract the transatlantic liners. It is squat and depends on the height of the cliff to beam its rays over a wide area. The approach is along gorsy lanes with high hedgebanks and past ancient farmhouses. At the coast itself bare cliffs alternate with grassy slopes, the latter a blaze of colour from squill, sea pink and bladder campion in early May. Another accessible point by car is Pwllderi with its fine views towards St David's Head.

Abercastle is approached through the charming hill-top village of Mathry which had a large fair in medieval times. Although quiet today, its natural harbour was once active in the coastal trade with places as far away as Bristol. Its main warehouse is now a boat shed, and there are other former commercial buildings on the east side of the harbour. Small terrace fields climb the valley side and fields of early potatoes crown the headland top. The fine cromlech at Longhouse Farm, known as Carreg Samson, is worth the short walk from the road which climbs up out of the valley for it is one of the finest in Wales with a huge capstone resting precariously on only some of the uprights. The cromlech once was incorporated into a stone wall but now stands isolated in the

Carreg Samson cromlech, with its huge capstone supported by stocky pillars, looking out towards the coast near Abercastle

field near the farm. Dating from about 3000 BC it was formerly covered with an earth mound but this has long since disappeared. This part of the coastal plateau provides much richer farmland than around Strumble Head for the volcanic rocks have given place to softer shales and the coast, though still rugged, lacks some of the boldness further north and east. Some rocks were once of commercial value so that the stretch of coastline towards St David's Head bears traces of past quarrying and industry.

Porthgain comes as a complete surprise in that the unsuspecting visitor seeking a sheltered cove finds himself confronted with massive harbour works, huge stone hoppers and former brickworks, all now abandoned but seemingly destined to stay as a monument of industrial archaeology. The first port here was built in the 1860s but it was remodelled in 1903 when trade in exporting stone was at its height. Up to 1931 small coasters still visited the port to pick up cargoes of stone. Now all is quiet and, although suggestions have been made for redeveloping the harbour, Porthgain Village Industries Limited is firmly in control. The Sloop Inn, dating from 1743, and a café cater for the summer visitors in search of the unusual. A fine single-storey terrace of cottages has been recently restored and is partly occupied as an art gallery.

Abereiddi was also once alive with industrial activity, for the slates of its cliffs were quarried in the last century. At first they were taken to Porthgain for loading into waiting sailing vessels but later 'the blue lagoon quarry' on the headland north of the bay was connected by a narrow channel with the open sea to enable vessels to enter and load at high tide. Today all is derelict as at Porthgain but sufficient remains, including the track of the old tramway, to conjure up a picture of past activity at this remote place. The problem now is to prevent erosion in the bay, and a new sea wall has been built to protect the cottages where the quarry workers once lived.

St David's This most westerly of the Welsh peninsulas attracts attention on two counts – the variety of its coastal scenery and the historic importance of 'Dewisland' as the region is called. After the slaty beds of Abereiddi, igneous rocks become increasingly prominent, associated immediately with much bolder cliffs. The same beds also form prominent rocky hills like Carnllidi, Penberry etc, which lie only a short distance in from the northern coast. Although volcanic beds outcrop around Whitesand Bay they have been eroded below sea level so that the lower valley has been infilled with glacial material and blown sand. The fine beach, one of the few sandy strands on this coastline, provides a steady supply of material for the sand-dune area known as the Burrows. Now the whole natural setting has been somewhat spoiled by the huge caravan camp, car park and golf course. The white sand of the beach which stretches unbroken for almost 1.6km (1 mile) between rocky headlands has fortunately escaped the hand of man though in summer the area teems with holidaymakers. In spring when the early potatoes are just showing through or the fields of daffodils are in bud – both indicative of the mild maritime climate – the beauty of the place is unrivalled. The next bay to the south, Porthstinian, is rocky, with an outlook across Ramsey Sound to Ramsey Island – simply a detached part of the mainland plateau, both in geology and topography.

The south coast of Dewisland undergoes a marked change in scenery for the igneous rocks give way to Cambrian sandstones and flags renowned for their variegated colours. At Caerfai the cliff top has been quarried in the past to provide the purple stone for St David's Cathedral. Confronted with a whole range of rock types of varying degrees of resistance the sea has fashioned a multitude of different coastal features ranging from stacks, islets, caves and gashes to larger inlets like that of Porth-Clais, once the port for St David's. Now under the care of the National Trust the quays and lime kilns of this tiny port were restored in 1976.

The historical interest of Dewisland naturally centres on St David, the patron saint of Wales. Not only was he born in this part of Dyfed in the sixth century, he was the founder about AD 520 of the monastic *llan* out of which the present cathedral grew. It is at least the third building on this site and was begun about 1180, though what we see today represents the work of many different periods, including the west front rebuilt by John Nash in 1789. Unfortunately he was allowed to use St Mary's College alongside as a quarry, so that in restoring one building he ruined another. Fortunately the Bishop's Palace, though a ruin, still exists as witness to the power and wealth of the church in medieval times, its splendour owing much to the influence of Bishop Gower who held office 1327–47. All the religious buildings of St David's lie rather hidden along the broad valley floor below the town and are best seen from The Pobbles, a continuation of the High Street. Apart from the cathedral, the coastal landscape of Dewisland has other associations with Dewi Sant. South of the 'city' is the cliff-top chapel dedicated to his mother St Non and rebuilt in 1934. The well, typical of the Celtic saints, lies close by, but its enclosure is modern. St Justinian's Chapel, close to the lifeboat station opposite Ramsey Island, is a sixteenth-century rebuilding of the earlier cell on the same site dedicated to a friend of St David. Again the saint's well is to be seen. At Whitesand Bay, a place of landing for pilgrims making for St David's, there was the chapel of St Patrick. There is now little to see but, when it was excavated in 1924, the skeleton of a young man was unearthed beneath the chapel floor.

Solva, at the head of a drowned valley inlet, is the Welsh equivalent of Boscastle in Cornwall and in every way as attractive. Solva was once an important port to the extent that passenger vessels sailed from here to America, though by the nineteenth century only the occasional coaster, bringing in limestone or coal, tied up at the wharf. Now a large car park takes up part of the upper harbour, with the old lime kilns lying on the opposite bank. The National Trust has control over much of the coast to the east with its two thrusting peninsulas of Dinas-fawr and Dinas-fach, which may have been used by prehistoric man as promontory forts. Solva in recent years has become a tourist attraction with its inns and restaurants providing a variety of fare from the deep freeze. It is also a boating paradise, its sheltered harbour providing safe anchorage for the weekend sailor.

St Bride's Bay is shaped out of softer Carboniferous beds which offer less resistance to the sea than the older rocks to north and south. Newgale Sand at the northern end is something of a misnomer,

The Sleek Stone north of Broadhaven, where a sharp fold of sandstone runs out from the foreshore

for although sand is exposed when the tide is out the main feature is the great pebble ridge – a miniature Chesil Bank – formed of flat stones piled high above the coastal road which runs behind. The coastline is an intricate one, for the harder sandstone bands tend to form headlands while the shale beds have been cut back to form small bays or inlets. From the sixteenth century onwards this corner of Pembrokeshire had a flourishing coalmining industry. So little now remains except for a colliery chimney at Trefran, the last mine to close in 1905, that it is difficult to think of the area in these terms today. In the absence of harbours small vessels were beached at high water, loaded with coal from carts as the tide fell and then floated out to sea again when the tide rose. The only loading quay was at Nolton Haven, where there are remains of a feeder tramway.

Broad Haven and **Little Haven** have taken advantage of their fine sandy beaches and become small resorts. Little Haven is the more attractive of the two, its narrow streets having a compactness and attractiveness reminiscent of Cornish villages. To the north of Broad Haven is the feature known as the Sleek Stone, where a sharp upfold in the sandstone has been smoothed by the sea along the curved bedding plane. There has been considerable slipping of the cliffs of friable shale here. The village of **St Bride's** lies tucked away in the south-west corner of the bay. The church, restored in 1883, is obviously on an old site; certainly the head of a small inlet is just the place a Celtic saint would seek out. With the long line of cottages on the low cliff, it is a fitting introduction to the Old Red Sandstone coastland. Apart from the red cliffs themselves faulting has led to the formation of geos (deep steep-sided inlets) including the great gash of Huntsman's Leap. The cliff top around is a wealth of colour in late spring when red campion, sea pink, bluebell, yellow vetch and primrose are all in bloom. The haven has its old lime kilns set into the walls of the former Kensington estate – which gave its name to the well known area in London. At low water there is a wide expanse of wet sand set between the red rocks thrusting seawards as reefs.

Huntsman's Leap, Castlemartin – the most famous of the geos of the Pembrokeshire coast

Marloes Peninsula The road through the village of Marloes ends in a huge car park laid out by the National Trust, the first indication of the number of visitors who now seek out this once quiet area that the naturalist R. M. Lockley made famous by his bird studies in the 1930s. His book on the island of Skomer, now run by the West Wales Naturalists' Trust, first drew attention to what is one of the finest sea-bird islands around our shores (see page 34). During the summer months boats make the trip to the island from St Martin's Haven and Dale if the weather is suitable. The island is formed almost entirely of volcanic rocks and faulting has created the two inlets of North and South Haven at its eastern end. The island of Skokholm to the south, another bird sanctuary, is formed of sandstone. Gateholm, attached at low water to the Marloes Peninsula, is also of sandstone, and though now uninhabited like the other islands, once had a sizeable prehistoric population. The approach to the fine sweep of Marloes Sands and Gateholm is by the lane which leads down to the coast from the National Trust car park beyond Marloes Court Farm. With its fine yellow strips of sand broken by rocky ribs and cliffs with huge supporting buttresses of sandstone pierced by caves, this is one of the most picturesque of the Pembrokeshire beaches. At the eastern end are three vertical columns of sandstone, the Three Chimneys. The best way to see the coastline is to take the Pembrokeshire Coast Path around both the Marloes and Dale Peninsulas; only then does the great variation in the coastal scenery really emerge, enhanced by a carpet of flowers on the cliff top, especially in late spring and early summer. The path runs for a distance of 269km (167 miles) and was opened in 1970.

Dale, a peninsula running out to St Ann's Head at the entrance to Milford Haven is almost an island, for there is a cross-valley following a major fault in which the settlement itself lies. Now quite small it was important in medieval times when it had a weekly market and an annual fair. There was also an early chapel on the site of the present St Ann's lighthouse. Near the latter the coastal cliffs of red sandstone are particularly spectacular. Dale Point, thrusting out into Milford Haven, has a nineteenth-century fort now used as a Field Study Centre – one of the first to be established and known to many generations of students. From Dale there are boat trips to Skokholm and Skomer.

Milford Haven has now 'arrived' as a major port after a long and chequered history of hope and failure. That its natural deep-water ria is one of the finest in western Britain is undisputed; the great surprise is that not until the last decade did it really establish itself and then only through oil. Even with virtually no settlement around the north shore in Elizabethan times Shakespeare could write, 'and, by the way, tell me how Wales was made so happy as t'inherit such a haven'. It was not until 1793 that the present town of Milford began to take shape after Sir William Hamilton obtained an Act of Parliament to build quays and docks. A

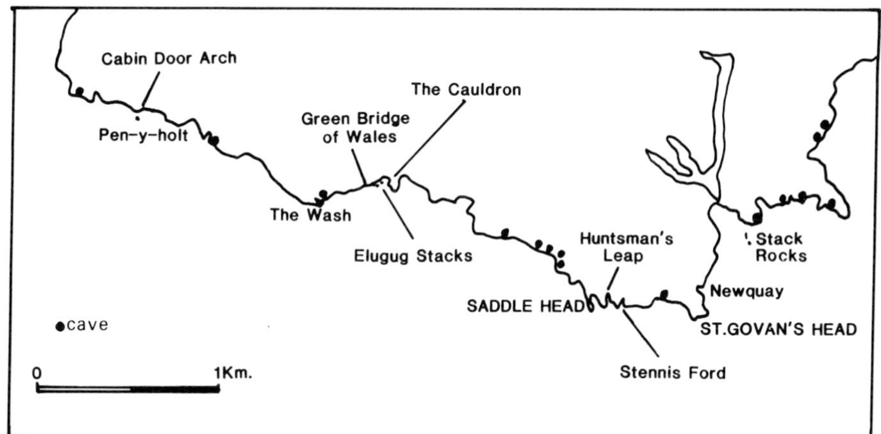

The south coast of the Castlemartin Peninsula with its varied cliff features

group of Quaker whaling families from North America were the first to settle, and they are commemorated in street names like Starbuch Road and Nantucket Avenue. The plan of the town was simple with three parallel streets running along the sloping ground overlooking the water. The best houses were built along the lower terrace, the middle street tended to become the shopping centre, while the uppermost street contained the most ordinary terraces without a view of the great haven. With the shores now dominated by four major oil refineries, the setting of the original planned town has been radically altered. For Milford oil has been a saviour, especially after the gradual decline of the fishing industry in recent years, but it has brought problems as pollution is an ever-present danger.

Pembroke is also a planned town but of a much earlier date. It was laid out with its great castle set on a limestone bluff overlooking the haven in 1110 after Henry I made Gilbert of Clare the first Earl of Pembroke. The narrow peninsula only allowed one major axial street with burgage plots running down to the water's edge on either side. The castle was rebuilt about 1190 when the great donjon arose. In complete contrast is Pembroke Dock which grew from 1814 onwards after the Admiralty established a dockyard here in preference to Milford Haven. Although the dockyard closed in 1926 the town is still an important residential centre, especially now that new industries have come to the haven and the recently built bridge at Neyland has linked the north and south shores.

Castlemartin Peninsula It is a tragedy that part of the coastline of this peninsula lying south of Pembroke town is inaccessible because it forms part of a military training area. The coastline totally excluded runs from Linney Head in the west to the Stack (Elugug) Rocks in the east, and even the section from this point to St Govan's chapel is not always open to visitors, especially on weekdays. What is disturbing is that for a time after World War II it was possible to walk the whole length of this magnificent stretch without restriction, but even the designation of the National Park and the creation of the Pembrokeshire Coastal Path has not been able to force the hand of the military authorities.

The fine scenery begins at Freshwater West, a bay which is fortunately still accessible and has been hollowed out of the softer Old Red Sandstone formation though the harder ribs form rocks on the foreshore. Wide expanses of sand have been blown inland by the westerly wind so that there is an extensive sand-dune area. It was a favoured site for prehistoric man and contained several Bronze Age burials which were subsequently covered by blown sand. An even earlier Mesolithic site excavated at Little Furzenip has yielded over 7,000 flints. The most impressive feature is the Devil's

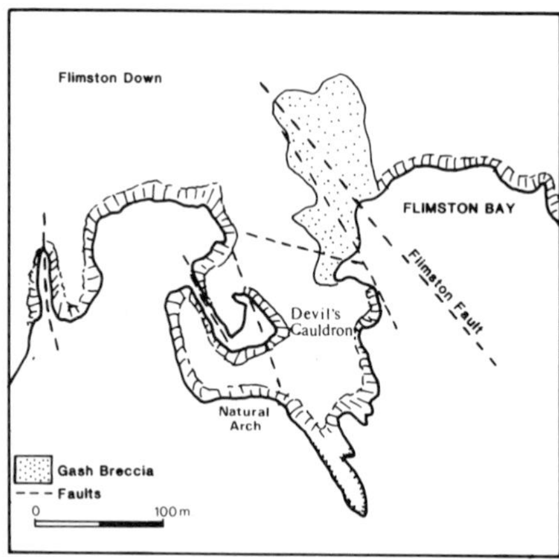

Faulting and the formation of the Devil's Cauldron near Flimston (*after Thomas*)

Quoit, which is a Neolithic burial chamber.

Linney Head marks the beginning of the limestone cliffs which run along the entire southern coast of the Castlemartin Peninsula as far as St Govan's Head. Although the inland plateau, used as a military training area, is dull and featureless, the sea has fashioned a plethora of fantastic shapes along the cliff-line. Off Pen y holt Bay there is a fallen stack of limestone while, further along, the flat surface of The Wash - coinciding with a prominent bedding plane - is separated from the main line of cliffs by a major rift. It is at the Stack Rocks, where access into the military area is possible at certain times, that the fantastic shaping of the rocks reaches its height. These isolated stacks (the alternative name Elugug is Welsh for guillemot) are crowded with sea birds in summer including the guillemot, razorbill, and kittiwake which nest amongst the thick cover of the tree mallow. Close by is the Green Bridge of Wales, a natural arch shaped like a great buttress 'supporting' the cliff face. Given time the arch will collapse and a stack similar to the present Elugug will be formed. The Devil's Cauldron on the east side of Flimston Bay is perhaps the most exciting single feature of the whole coastline, consisting of a steep-sided hole, once a blow-hole, which is now in contact with the sea through a natural arch on its southern side. A major fault has led to the sea also cutting a gash on its north-western side.

Further east towards St Govan's Head faulting has led to the formation of the Huntsman's Leap, a very narrow fissure cut out by the sea but still retaining a rock link between its opposing walls (see page 78). It is one of several similar 'geos' on this coastline and lies about 1km (½ mile) west of St Govan's chapel, another access point. The chapel, nestling halfway down the cliff face in a wider cleft, dates from the thirteenth century, but it may represent a much earlier Celtic site, possibly a hermit's cell of the fifth century. A rough rock-cut cell and stone altar, with a well just below, are possibly remains of the earliest Celtic foundations. Formerly a place of pilgrimage because the healing waters of the well were of help to cripples, the chapel and the great limestone cliffs which run out to St Govan's Head are always accessible. For the coast controlled by the military to the west one must enquire at Bosherston Post Office for times of access. **Bosherston** is a tiny village, perhaps most visited for its pools and water lilies, and for access to the bathing beach at Broadhaven.

Stackpole Quay is the next point on the coast accessible by car. The old estate with its fine breakwater enclosing the small harbour was taken over by the National Trust in 1976 and is in process of renovation. The harbour once exported cargoes of stone from the quarry just behind and imported coal, but now all is quiet, though much visited. From the Trust car park there is a fine walk over the cliffs to Barafundle Bay to the south. In the opposite direction the Coast Path soon encounters the red sandstone cliffs with the promontory fort at Greenala Point. Freshwater East, with its fine sandy beach, has been ruined by the shack development that was allowed here in pre-war days and which still casts a blight. Inland a new holiday village stands as the present-day answer.

Manorbier The approach along the country lane from the west is the best way to yet another sandy bay with its backing of dunes. For a while the glory of the place, the twelfth-century castle, is temporarily hidden from view for it is tucked away up the valley. It was the birthplace of the traveller, writer and scholar Giraldus Cambrensis in 1146. Opposite it on the slope across the valley is a church of about the same date. The eastern headland of the bay, known as Priest's Nose, has caves as well as a notable cromlech, with a 5m (15ft) capstone, known as the King's Quoit. Shrinkle Haven has fine vertical cliffs of sandstone bands, while at Lydstep Point the limestone returns again. The headland is now National Trust property and from the car park there are fine views across to Caldey Island. The original house at Lydstep, built by Viscount St David's, is now a caravan park, but there is access to the fine caverns of the headland at low water. Between Giltar Point and the outskirts of Tenby there is yet another sandy bay backed by dunes – the Burrows. They have blocked the entrance to a former estuary of the Ritec which was open to shipping as far inland as St Florence in the eleventh century. Subsequent reclamation, including a sea bank built by Sir John Owen in 1811 and later strengthened by the railway embankment of 1865, has greatly altered the former setting.

Tenby has a coastal setting in the lee of yet another limestone headland that gives it a slightly Italian air in spite of its predominantly Georgian appearance. A settlement has nestled under the cliff since at least the ninth century and probably early on had a castle for protection. The present ruin dates largely from the thirteenth century and the town walls, including the famous five-arched gateway, are of slightly later date. It was always an important fishing port, even after becoming a resort in the early nineteenth century, and the Victorian visitor was encouraged to taste the delights of the locally caught sole, turbot, brill, sewin and mullet. In medieval times it was a prosperous place as shown by the size and grandeur of its parish church of St Mary. The tall tower is thirteenth century, probably contemporary with the laying out of the medieval town, though the nave represents fifteenth-century rebuilding. It has been suggested that the town benefited in the twelfth century from Flemish weavers who settled here in the reign of Henry I.

Much of what we see today represents the development of the resort town from the end of the eighteenth century onwards. In this Sir William Paxton was the leading figure and he built the Public Bath House at his own expense in 1805. Three and four-storey houses followed around the edge of the bay, and soon became favoured as boarding houses. Not only did the Victorians come for the summer season which lasted from June to early October, but the mild climate began to attract an increasing number of winter visitors. Today it is still very much a resort town which has retained cherished links with the past. One of the most notable of these is the Tudor Merchant's House (National Trust) dating from about 1500 which has survived with adjoining buildings of much the same age.

Saundersfoot has a completely different history of development from Tenby and though not as ancient nor occupying such a fine natural site, it is not without interest. With its harbour now filled with yachts and boats the impression is of a modern leisure-conscious resort and to some extent this is true. The harbour was built in 1829 for sound commercial reasons – the export of coal from the nearby Pembrokeshire coalfield; the main collieries producing valuable anthracite lay a little distance inland at places like Bonneville, Stepaside, Begelly and Thomas Chapel. Tramways were built to the coast – one with tunnels hugs the cliff face north of Saundersfoot to Wiseman's Bridge – and by 1864 over 30,000 tons of coal a year were being shipped. All came to an end in the 1930s when the collieries closed one after the other, so that today caravans and camping have come in to replace coal. Nearby **Stepaside** also had its ironworks, opened in 1849 based on local ore and anthracite, and there are still substantial remains in spite of production having ended over a hundred years ago. At both Wiseman's Bridge and Amroth pebble beaches block the lower parts of the valleys, but the problem here is erosion and sea defences are needed to prevent flooding. A submerged forest was formerly seen on the foreshore off Amroth at low water, but a better example occurs at nearby Marros Sands where prostrate tree-trunks lie on the clay surface. **Pendine**, which once had hopes of becoming a small resort and was famous in the 1930s for car racing on its fine stretch of hard sands, is now very much controlled by the Ministry of Defence who have taken over large areas of the dune belt and adjacent marshland, though access is still possible at certain times to the restricted areas. From Pendine the main road runs inland at the foot of the old cliff-line until it reaches the Taf Estuary.

Laugharne was once a borough and still retains the atmosphere of one though now just a small country town with much to offer the visitor willing to spend several hours exploring its main street and back alleys. It began life in the early thirteenth century at a time when the English were beginning to push the Welsh into more remote parts of their own country. To further this the inevitable castle was built, sited on a rocky bluff overlooking the lower estuary with a planned town alongside, the principal street running northwards for about 1km (½ mile) up a short valley to the church, again in an imposing position. This is still the basic pattern of the town though side streets and cobbled alleys have now filled out the original plan. The town was given its charter in the fourteenth century and today there is a Town Hall, a compact white building with a clock tower. Laugharne also became an important port both for coastal trade and for vessels going farther afield to Europe, though this is hard to believe today when only a muddy creek winds into the shore through the saltings. It is from these saltings that one can best savour the whole atmosphere of the place with the rose-coloured walls of the castle in the foreground and a distant glimpse of the former boathouse home of the town's adopted poet son, Dylan Thomas. It was while living in Laugharne at various periods between 1936 and 1953 that Thomas wrote many of his poems and also the radio play *Under Milk Wood* which finally established his reputation, though occasionally it has been claimed that New Quay (see page 210) and not Laugharne was the setting. A rough map drawn by Thomas himself of the layout of his 'Llangerub' shows a distinct resemblance to that of Laugharne but the reference in the play to the steep street dipping down to the harbour recalls the topography of New Quay. As Thomas lived in the two places it is likely that he used both to conjure up the life of a small Welsh country town with its intrigue and gossip which prompted his assemblage of finely drawn characters. The writing was certainly done at Laugharne, mainly in the small shed by the cliff path above the boathouse home. This gave him the seclusion he needed in what he once described as 'this timeless, mild, beguiling island of a town'. Once the Thomas pilgrims have departed, having visited his simple grave in the churchyard and the museum to his memory in the old boathouse, the sleepy character of Laugharne is still there to be savoured.

Llanstephan occupies an even more secluded site in the south-eastern corner of the isolated peninsula between the estuaries of the Taf and Tywi, south of the main A40 road. The approach can be made either direct from Carmarthen or through an intricate network of lanes with high hedgebanks from St Clears. The original traveller into the peninsula used neither, but forded the estuaries at low water or crossed by ferry when the tide was in. This was also the 'Pilgrim's' route and at Llandeilo-Abercywyn the pilgrim's church and hospice survive as part of a farmhouse. Across the small stream to the west there is another ruined church, now roofless and buried amongst the trees and undergrowth overlooking the Taf marshes. The village of Llanstephan was never a chartered borough like Laugharne though it, too, has a castle and thirteenth-century church. The castle lies isolated, set high on a rocky bluff away to the south, but the climb to the thirteenth-century ruins is worthwhile for the view it gives. Below, lies the sandy strand fronting the cottages which make up the quarter known as The Green, while the main street of the village lies a little way inland around the church. Across the estuary the view takes in the elongated waterfront of Ferryside and the sand dunes of Pembrey Burrows beyond. In the far distance is the distinctive outline of Worm's Head, at the end of the Gower Peninsula.

Ferryside, as its name implies, grew up as a

crossing point of the Tywi Estuary. The coming of the railway – the main line to Fishguard and Pembroke – added a new dimension, for it was not long before seaside villas and boarding houses were springing up to cater for visitors wishing to take advantage of the sandy strand. Now it has its commuters to Carmarthen as well as a rash of retirement bungalows.

Kidwelly is a town of two parts facing each other across the Gwendraeth Valley. On the right bank is the Norman castle built between 1106 and 1115 when the English hold on the region was being strengthened by Henry I. The old Norman town only covered 3ha (8 acres) and was enclosed with an earthen bank, part of which still remains. Apart from the imposing castle the only other medieval feature is the fourteenth-century gatehouse. The town was given two weekly markets and a fair in 1283, a measure of its importance at the time. In view of this it is strange that a later town should be built across the river, centred on the parish church of St Mary. Little remains of the medieval setting here or the port which once gave it trade and commerce.

To the south of the Gwendraeth Valley lies the extensive area of Pembrey sand dunes, partly afforested and partly used as an airfield. A country park at the southern end, approached from Pembrey village, gives access to the entrance to Burry inlet. During both world wars the area was used for making munitions.

Burry, along with adjacent **Llanelli**, formerly flourished as a coal exporting town served by mineral lines which linked it with collieries inland. Docks were built but they no longer serve the coal trade which has died out. Dominating all is the huge power station built to use the locally produced coal. Llanelli still has its steel and tinplate industries on which the prosperity of the town was originally built, but here as elsewhere they are under threat. Being the largest town of the area its central shopping core shows inevitable redevelopment, though the Victorian Town Hall still dominates. The lasting impression is of street after street of terraced houses each with plaster rendering and brightly painted.

Loughor is the crossing point of the estuary and once was an important Roman site (*Leucarum*). A Roman altar stone with ogham characters was found during excavations but there is little to see on the ground. Within the site of the Roman town a later Norman castle was built about 1100 to control the estuary's ferry crossing. The bridge came much later when the turnpike road was built.

The Gower Peninsula

Across the wide flats of the Lougher Estuary lies the hilly peninsula of Gower. In many ways it is a unique coastal area, partly because of the rich variation of scenery within such a small compass, but largely because it has retained a natural setting even though it is on the fringe of the south Wales industrial belt. Only in the east, close to Swansea, has suburban development taken place and even this is now largely contained. Much of the credit for the conservation must go to the Gower Society which was active in pre-war days when little planning legislation existed to protect areas such as this against unwholesome and unworthy development.

Much of the beauty of the Gower coastline is a reflection of the geology of the peninsula. Three basic rock types are present: the tough and solid Old Red Sandstone which tends to form the backbone of hills, the grey-white Carboniferous Limestone which resists the onslaught of the sea and forms the major headlands of the south coast, and finally the much softer Millstone Grit which has been etched out into bays, as at Port Eynon and Oxwich. All the rock strata have been folded and faulted to some extent and this again leads to a rich diversity of coastal form, especially as the sea can exploit weaknesses in the limestone to form caves, blow-holes and narrow fissures. Past changes of sea level have left behind raised beach platforms around much of the south coast, while on the north side of the peninsula the old cliff-line is now well inland, fronted by marshland which extends over the former estuary flats.

Penclawdd was one of the few places in Gower served by the railway and, though the line has long closed, the station survives in mutilated form. It is for its cockle industry that the place is best known and for centuries women have gone out across the marsh in their flat donkey carts to gather cockles brought in on the rising tide. The industry has declined recently and birds like the oystercatcher do great harm to the shellfish. The whole of the south shore of the Burry inlet once participated in the cockle-gathering industry and there are ancient tracks across the marsh towards the low-water line. Most of the gatherers now come from Crofty and nearby Llanmorlais.

The lower road westwards from Penclawdd to Llanrhidian runs along the inner edge of the marshland fringe just below the old cliff-line, and at high tide it is often covered as water surges up the creeks. The marsh is typical of the west coast with samphire and glasswort the dominant plants at the lower levels while sea lavender, plantain and rushes cover large parts near the high-water line. The whole of the Burry inlet is steadily filling up, aided by artificial reclamation on the north side where land at Burry Port and Llanelli has been taken in for industry. At its outer end there is the long projecting spit of Whitford Burrows, formed of limestone pebbles with sand dunes. It is now under the control of the National Trust and therefore safe from the caravan development which has crept into this far corner of the Gower. Another area of sand dunes occurs on the approach to the islet of Burry Holms from the village of Llangennith. The islet, which forms the northern end of the fine sweep of sands bordering Rhossili Bay, is of limestone and had its Iron Age coastal fort and later Dark Age cell of St Cenydd. There are also medieval chapel remains on this ancient site.

Rhossili, at the southern end of the bay, consists of a cluster of houses around the church, a hotel and a group of coastguard cottages, but the view over the wide sweep of sand of the bay to the north is its chief glory. The bay is backed by grassy cliffs which lead to a well-marked platform at about 30m (100ft) and then the steep rise to Rhossili Downs with its backbone of hard Old Red Sandstone. In a southerly direction there is a pleasant cliff-top walk towards Worms Head, another projecting limestone islet like Burry Holms but on a much larger scale. Worms Head (OE *wurm* = dragon), really a detached remnant of the coastal plateau, is in two parts with a narrow neck between and can only be approached at low water (see page 80). The

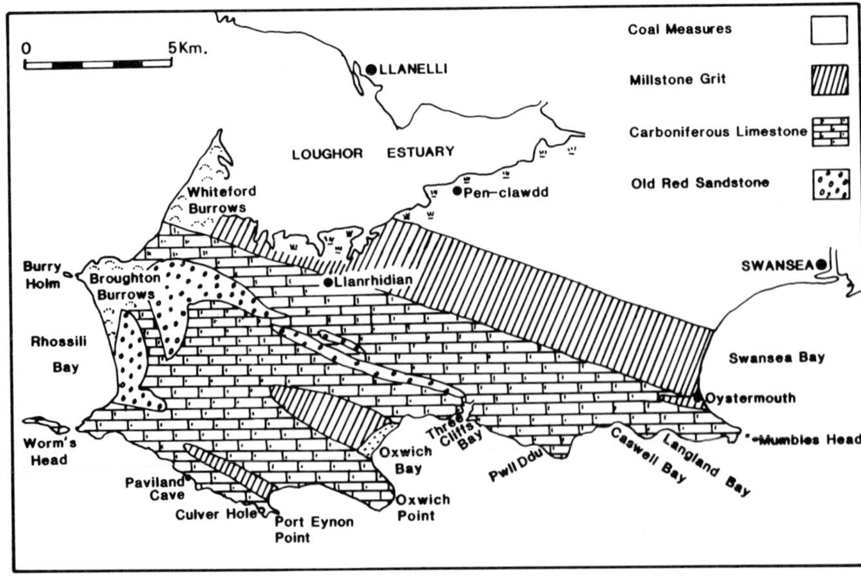

The geology of the Gower Peninsula

The dipping limestone beds forming so much of the coastline of southern Gower

well-worn track out to the headland is across National Trust land left in rough pasture and gorse. Further inland the land is well farmed and there is a survival of the old medieval open field system with its individual strips. Early crops like broccoli and potatoes do well in this maritime setting.

The coast round to Port Eynon is for walkers only, though there are various tracks down from the inland road. One leads to Paviland Cave, made famous following the discovery in 1823 of a skeleton known as the Red Lady of Paviland, but in fact the bones of a young man (see page 87). The cave can only be entered at low water and access can be difficult. The limestone cliff scenery hereabouts is impressive with the individual beds dipping inland.

Port Eynon, the largest of the south Gower villages, has its share of commuters, retired and those with a holiday home. The wide sandy bay has been etched out of a downfold of Millstone Grit beds and is backed by a fringing belt of dunes. Heavy human traffic has led to restricted access with duck-board tracks down to the beach. The view eastwards along the coast is spectacular, with the white-washed cottages of Horton standing out in the middle distance. A walk southwards towards the limestone headland leads to Culver Hole (see page 87), a curious mixture of the natural and the man-made.

Oxwich Bay is a larger-scale replica of Port Eynon in that it has been carved from a soft outcrop of Millstone Grit with limestone headlands at either end. On the western fringe the limestone runs out for 1.6km (1 mile) to Oxwich Point and is worth the walk through the woods past the medieval church, possibly on the site of a much earlier Celtic cell. To the east the sharp point of Great Tor cliff forms the other end of the bay. Weekend traffic is now so heavy that huge car parks dominate the western end of the beach, but a short walk onto the dunes of Oxwich Burrows will soon bring relative solitude. The dune belt has ponded back streams coming down from Penrice and formed a huge area of wetland with extensive reedbeds and willow groves. In spite of the summer invasion the village with its dispersed cottages and houses still retains some charm, especially around Oxwich Green and the seventeenth-century farmhouse of Pitt. There is also Oxwich Castle, really a sixteenth-century fortified manor house, on the site of an earlier Norman castle.

The tiny Bishopston creek enters the sea, through a break in the limestone wall, to form the picturesque Three Cliffs Bay

Three Cliffs, though small in comparison with either Port Eynon or Oxwich, is perhaps the most picturesque of the Gower bays. Hemmed in by towering limestone cliffs the river makes its way in a gigantic loop around a ridge of sandhills across the entrance. The whole setting, with its rich variation of landscape features and colour tones, is an ideal subject for the artist. Unfortunately although the bay is partly owned by the National Trust some pre-war shacks remain, and in spite of the fact that many have been smartened up they still tend to mar the natural beauty. What is more, they jealously guard their preserve with 'private' and 'keep out' notices. The approach to the bay must be made on foot from the main road and even here there is a lack of adequate parking facilities.

With Swansea only a short distance away, the south Gower coastland becomes much more developed beyond Three Cliffs, with original tiny hamlets swelled by successive additions of scattered bungalows or larger estates. Fortunately the coastline itself has been largely spared so that the limestone cliffs around Caswell Bay retain their natural splendour. Faulting, leading to crush zones in the limestone, has been exploited by the sea to give cave developments like Minchin Hole and Bacon Hole, both of which have yielded remains of long extinct animals like the mammoth and woolly rhinoceras. Human cave dwellers are also in evidence from remains of their pottery and worked bone implements. **Pwll Du Bay** is a larger feature but again owes its origin to shattered limestone beds worn away by the sea. Across its mouth there is a succession of shingle bars which push the tiny Bishopston stream well to the east. Caswell Bay itself has more sand, is easier of access and, considering its situation, remarkably unspoiled with its grey cliffs, bright yellow sands and pine-clad slopes giving it an almost Mediterranean appearance. **Langland** is more developed for there are now large estates covering the cliff top.

Mumbles Head sees the return of the undeveloped cliff-line though there are large car parks, cafés and a lifeboat station. On the outer of the two islets beyond the limestone headland is the lighthouse built in 1793 to warn shipping as it approaches Swansea. The famous Mumbles Railway – really a

Old Fishguard, Pembrokeshire

horse-drawn tramway – which began life in 1802 and was therefore one of the first passenger-carrying lines in the world, ran along the shores of Swansea Bay to Mumbles village. In 1893 it was extended to Mumbles Head, once famous for its oyster fisheries. The smacks brought the oysters in from deeper water and they were allowed to 'fatten' in the nearshore zone before being harvested. The trade has long since gone but is commemorated in the name of nearby Oystermouth, 1.6km (1 mile) along the coast, now better known for the extensive ruins of its Norman castle, once the key to English control of the Gower Peninsula. The coastal road around the shores of Swansea Bay carries such heavy traffic that it is almost impossible to go slowly enough to take in the view which Walter Savage Landor once described as being superior to that of the Bay of Naples. With hindsight it seems tragic that the old Mumbles Railway was allowed to close in the early 1960s.

South Wales

Swansea, the name meaning Sweyn's Isle, evokes the time when the Norse sailed this coast in the ninth and tenth centuries. To the Welsh it is the equally expressive Abertawe, the mouth of the river Tawe. The settlement only really began to grow when the Norman lord, the Earl of Warwick, built the castle in 1116 and laid out a town around it. With a reasonable port and fertile coastlands it grew quickly, and obtained its charter in 1165. This early development continued throughout late medieval times but the town was completely transformed by subsequent industrialisation based on local coal and imported copper and tin. Docks were now essential and these were gradually built out into Swansea Bay from 1859 onwards. Post-war rebuilding has made the city the major shopping centre for west Wales; unexpectedly it still lingers on as a resort with terraces of boarding houses lining the coast road running towards the Mumbles. On the eastern side the new marine road passes the latest of Swansea's industries, the Ford Motor works, built partly on the dunes and partly on reclaimed marshland. Further inland is Llandarcy oil refinery, a mixture of contorted piping and huge storage tanks; another refinery lies across the river Neath on the outskirts of Port Talbot.

Rhossili Bay, Gower (*Wales Tourist Board*)

Port Talbot cannot claim the antiquity of Swansea but it shared in its industrial growth. The name arose through the interest of the Talbot family who lived in nearby Margam. Today the town is heavily dependent on the Abbey steelworks, a great complex of rolling mills, strip mills and blast furnaces occupying a long stretch of coastline south-east of the town with its ever-lengthening waste tips sterilising more land of the Morfa Mawr dune belt. A new purpose-built harbour to take the big ore ships was opened in the early 1970s with its great pier arms extending well out into the bay. As a result the original dock, dating from 1835, now has only a limited coasting trade.

Kenfig is associated with many legendary tales, but hard facts are difficult to come by concerning this area which is now a vast complex of dunes covered with tussocky grass, spindly marram and dwarf willow (see page 47). The one tangible feature is the original castle, with its disintegrating masonry set high on an artificial mound amidst a sea of sand dunes. Old prints of the last century show a much more substantial building. It was founded in the twelfth century by Robert, Earl of Gloucester, during the Norman advance into south Wales. A town grew up under its protection, possibly on the seaward side, but there is now nothing to see for this area forms part of Kenfig Burrows. The town was important enough to be granted a charter and even as late as 1886, long after any semblance of a town remained, there was a borough portreeve, recorder and aldermen. The dune belt covers a considerable area and extends along the coast as far as Sker Point where a tough resistant conglomerate forms the headland. Just inland is Sker House, once a grange of Margam Abbey which owned all the land hereabouts including the foreshore.

The well-bedded limestone cliffs of Southerndown, as seen from the grounds of the now-demolished Dunraven Castle

Porthcawl is now chiefly a day resort centre for the thousands who come from the industrial valleys to sit on the beach, scramble amongst the rocky pools or visit the pleasure grounds of Coney Beach. But it began life as a bay called Pwll Cawl, part of the parish of Newtown Nottage, and had possibilities as a port for the export of coal from the inland Maesteg Valley. A tramway was built shortly after 1825, and in 1866 a small dock with huge walls of limestone blocks gave hope that a considerable coal trade would develop. It was not to be, for the dock entrance proved difficult to enter in rough weather and the coal trade sought other outlets. Only a small tidal basin now remains as a refuge for pleasure craft. The best part of the town is to the west towards Rest Bay with its dune belt and more spacious layout. The house known as The Rest was built over a century ago as a retreat for miners. Further on is the old village centre around the mother church at Newton Nottage, and in its narrow twisting streets it still preserves some of its original character.

Merthyr Mawr is another great expanse of sand dunes like that at Kenfig, and here too the south-westerly gales carry the sand inland. Planted pines have suffered from the advancing sand though some degree of stabilisation has been achieved in recent years. On the opposite side of the Ogmore river is the small resort of Ogmore-by-Sea which straggles along the coast before merging into Southerndown. The white limestone cliffs gradually increase in height and impressiveness, and Witches Nose promontory, with its more compact basal limestones, has its caverns and spouting blow-holes. Promontory forts like the one with multiple ramparts close to Witches Nose, and more simple enclosures, point to considerable prehistoric settlement; but today the coastal belt consists of rich farmland with scattered hamlets. Dunraven Castle, a Victorian building, has been demolished, but its parkland setting remains and forms a valuable local amenity. At Dunraven the older Carboniferous Limestone beds are overlain with the younger Liassic Limestone in almost perfect fashion though millions of years separate their deposition; unfortunately the whole of the limestone coast of South Glamorgan can only be approached at a few points where lanes lead down to the sea. One approach leads to Nash Point with its imposing cliff of horizontally bedded limestone and rocky platform swept clean of sediment at its foot. A large car park on the cliff top allows a steep descent to the foreshore or a walk eastwards along the top past the lighthouses, one abandoned but the other still warning shipping of the dangerous Nash Sands close offshore. Though it is possible to navigate through the narrow gap between the sands and the land, the currents are swift and have brought many a small coaster to its doom on the rocky foreshore.

A short distance to the east brings one to St Donat's Castle (now a college) whose earliest features go back to 1300. The church nearby is Norman though with later additions. From Llantwit Major, one of the more pleasant villages of the Vale of Glamorgan with its fine church founded about AD 500, it is possible to take a lane down to the coast again following the edge of the valley of the Col-hugh. At low water there is a fine expanse of sand below the upper beach of huge rounded boulders and there is yet another Iron Age defensive structure known as Castle Ditches. The unspoiled and almost untenanted coastline comes to an abrupt end at Aberthaw where huge cement works and power stations completely dominate the coastal setting. By now the valley of the Thaw and the neighbouring hamlets are so overwhelmed by these man-made works that it is difficult to imagine a time when the mouth of this small valley, one of the few really large breaks in the wall of limestone cliffs, was the site of a small port with trade across the Bristol Channel and even to the West Indies. It was from here that the great engineer John Smeaton obtained the limestone for building his Eddystone lighthouse, largely because the stone had properties which made mortar able to resist sea-water attack. Today the only tangible remains of the former port is the empty shell of a warehouse. The valley has been blocked off by a concrete wall and there are extensive saltings where ships once anchored.

Font-y-Gary, now a caravan park, is another place with access to a cove on the beach. There are layered cliffs of Liassic Limestone with a shelf just above the beach where a harder bed outcrops. The nearby village of **Rhoose** has benefited, economically at least, from the employment offered by the power stations and cement works, while the flat land on its doorstep is now the site of Cardiff's municipal airport.

Porthkerry is approached down a lane close to the park of Porthkerry House, once the home of the Romilly family who were looked on as model landlords because of the care they lavished on their tenants and workers. They built cottages and introduced new methods of farming. The church, with its stout limestone tower, has only a cottage and farm beside it, perhaps typical of many Celtic hamlets in times past. A deep valley separates it from a much older structure – the ramparts of an Iron Age promontory fort known as the Bulwarks.

Barry is known for two achievements: its rapid growth following the building of its docks in the 1880s, and the more recent development of Barry Island as a leisure centre and holiday-camp complex. Yet it has a much earlier history in that the offshore island of limestone was for centuries occupied by a single farm and famed for its large rabbit population. Earlier still it had been the cell of the Celtic saint Baruch, and the ruins of a chapel named after him are preserved in a wired off enclosure overlooking the harbour entrance and alongside the huge spread of tarmac of the holiday-camp car park. It was the creation of the harbour by sealing off the two ends of the strait between the island and the mainland and then digging out dock basins, that completely transformed Barry. It is remarkable that a harbour was necessary in view of the nearness of Cardiff docks, but the lack of enterprise on the part of the owners, the Bute family, encouraged David Davies to create Barry as a port to handle the Rhondda coal shipments. The digging out of the first docks in 1884 and the building of a railway network with the hinterland had an immediate impact, and by 1913 the port was exporting up to 11 million tons a year. This was to decline dramatically in the 1950s and today Barry, like Cardiff, has virtually no coal trade. Instead it is specialised imports like bananas and timber as well as general container traffic which keep the port alive. In contrast the leisure industry has seen almost uninterrupted growth this century though its character has changed with the years. Barry Island caters for the thousands of day visitors – now coming by car instead of by train – as well as the longer-stay holiday-makers. Being so close to Cardiff, many commute daily from Barry into the city, while the recent development of industries, like the petro-chemical complex at Cadoxton, have done much to cushion the effects of the depression which followed the decline of the coal trade.

Sully Island, though much smaller than Barry Island, is similar in that it is also a detached block of limestone. It is best approached from Barry but there is no through route around the coast as a section of the former road has been severed by coast erosion. A shingle causeway connects the island with the mainland making it possible to cross at low water. On the other approach road there is a huge caravan site overlooking St Mary's Well Bay which, though smart in itself, detracts from the natural beauty of this stretch of coastline.

Lavernock has a rebuilt nineteenth-century church very close to the cliff edge which at this point makes a sharp turn to the north. The somewhat overgrown footpath to the point is worth taking for the superb view it affords of the fine line of striped cliffs running towards Penarth. At the base there is a bed of red marls, followed by green marls, black shales and layers of the white lias limestone; gentle folding has led to a synclinal (downfold) structure in the beds. There is continual erosion taking place, largely through weathering, leading to cliff falls rather than direct wave attack of the cliff base. Rocky reefs and broad expanses of shingle and boulders on the beach gradually give way to a sandy strand as Penarth Pier is approached. Lavernock Point also provides good views across the Bristol Channel to the limestone (Carboniferous) islands of Flatholm and Steepholm, and it was from here in 1897 that Marconi sent the first wireless telegraphic message across 6km (3½ miles) of water to be picked up on Flatholm.

Penarth The cliffs increase in height northwards until they end in the fine Penarth Head, in the lee of which Penarth Dock was built in 1859, quickly followed by the development of the town on the plateau top above. Both were the creation of the Windsor family, lords of the manor of Penarth. Although a pier (1894) and promenade, with Italian style gardens, gave a resort-like atmosphere, it was as a residential centre in late Victorian times that Penarth was to blossom, palatial grey stone houses being built for those who had made their money in coal and commerce in Cardiff. Once the railway link was built, commuters sought to buy less substantial red-brick villas and Penarth quickly became a 'desirable suburb' of Cardiff, a role which has been reinforced in recent years.

Cardiff, the *caer* or fort by the Taff, is of Roman origin, possibly as early as the first century AD. As the importance of the site grew, a new and larger fort was built some distance away about AD 300 and it was this later fort that became part of the Norman castle. With its massive walls and motte in one corner of the enclosure, the castle is still a dominating feature of Cardiff's townscape. It was under a Norman lord, Robert fitz Hamon, that the present town was begun in 1081 with the laying out of a network of streets south of the castle, broadly rectilinear in plan and soon it became the largest medieval borough in Wales. Real prosperity for the town had to wait however until the mid-nineteenth century with the development of the South Wales Coalfield. Not only did the city become the hub of commercial transactions – the recently restored Coal Exchange near the docks is a measure of its importance – but it also became the principal port. The first dock was excavated from the soft tidal silts by the second Marquis of Bute in 1839, and others followed as the coal traffic expanded. The last was the Alexandra Dock in 1907 with its coal hoist and cranes to cope with the shipping which at that time was still considerable. Today the docks are strangely quiet, with the coal trade having virtually disappeared and the authorities anxiously searching for other traffic. Cardiff still wears the air of a Victorian town, though the laying out of Cathays Park with its assemblage of twentieth-century neo-classical civic buildings gave it the necessary edge over its rivals for the role of capital of Wales.

The coast to the north east of Cardiff is entirely marshland and this continues beyond the mouth of the Usk at Newport. Between the Taff and Usk the Wentlooge Levels area of reclamation is protected from the huge tides of the Bristol Channel by a great bank known as Peterstone Great Wharf. Straightened drainage ditches (reens) cover the area, with reeds flourishing in the damp watercourses. In the past the marshland has suffered from flooding as high spring tides, fanned by south-westerly gales, have overtopped the protective bank. One of the most famous of the floods was in January 1607, an event commemorated by a plaque showing the level the flood water reached on the wall of St Bride's church at Wentlooge. East of the Usk the Caldecot Levels tell the same story. Peat beds, dating from about 1000 BC, underlie the present marshland silts and, as they have shrunk, so buildings have tilted as, for example, Whitson Church. Nearer the mouth of the Usk, Nash church has a tablet similar to that of St Bride's recording the level reached during the same 1607 floods.

Almost the entire area is vulnerable to drowning, the exception being at **Goldcliff** where there is a solid rock outcrop by the sea wall, the name Goldcliff coming from the mica of the Keuper and Rhaetic beds which glistens in the sun. The place is also noteworthy in that a Roman stone was discovered here in 1882; although its exact purpose is unknown it may represent a boundary mark. How much use the Romans made of the marshland is open to doubt, but they did have a large fort and settlement a few miles to the north at Caerwent on the inner edge of the level. Much of the drainage of this wetland dates from medieval times for there is a record of 1245 giving permission for the Cistercian monks of Moor Grange Farm to dig ditches and drain the damp pastures. Today the marshland has the great Llanwern steelworks on its doorstep and villages have expanded to meet the housing needs of steelworkers.

Wentlooge Levels: the disastrous flood of 1607, depicted here by a contemporary artist

11 England: The South-west Peninsula

Avon, Somerset and North Devon

The southern shore of the Bristol Channel may be taken to begin at Avonmouth. As far as the river Parrett the coast runs approximately north to south and therefore completely cuts across the grain of the country, with the result that a series of headlands are formed of hard rock while intervening softer beds make up embayments in the coastline. At Clevedon two converging ridges of limestone meet to form an attractive cliff section north of the resort. Beyond the Yeo marshes rises the prominent limestone ridge of Middle Hope; it was once an island which became tied to the mainland as the intervening ground silted up. Weston-super-Mare nestles under another limestone headland, Worlebury Hill, while to the south the projecting Brean Down, rising to over 98m (320ft) and an excellent viewpoint, forms the southern shore of Weston Bay. In the broad sandy bays between the limestone promontories the tide can retreat for more than a mile from the shore. The flats widen even more towards the mouth of the Parrett, but there is an ever increasing percentage of mud.

Once across the sluggish Parrett the coastline takes on an east-west alignment and also begins to change in character. As one journeys west, progressively older and harder rocks are encountered and with them the cliff-line rises in increasing splendour, especially on reaching the north Devon border. This is classic coastal scenery, first examined in all its complexities by Newell Arber who in 1911 published his *Coast Scenery of North Devon*, the first real scientific description of a cliff coastline in Britain.

Clevedon Although now claimed by the Bristol commuter belt, it has retained its Victorian air to a remarkable extent. The best viewpoint over the town and the wide sweep of the Bristol Channel coast is from Dial Hill (88m, 290ft), a short distance inland. It was under this hill that the original village, a collection of farms and cottages, blossomed into a Regency bathing place in the early nineteenth century. The *Clevedon Guide* of 1829 by John Rutter spoke of it as 'a picturesque place well calculated for the residence of invalids who require a pure air'. Already forty substantial villas had been built but this was only the beginning of a development which reached its peak in mid-Victorian times, especially after the building of the pier in 1869. A curious mixture of Gothic, Jacobean and pseudo-Italianate styles were used for the villas as can be seen in Princes Road. In addition there were robust terraces in, for example, Herbert Road, and together they make Clevedon an important Victorian survival with a distinctive architectural heritage. The local Civic Society is anxious that the best of the last century should not be swept away under present pressures to meet the needs of the retired and the commuter. Already tasteless infilling has had a disastrous effect, and the Victorian pier has been severed and in need of repair. It seems a far cry from the time when steamers called to take holidaymakers on trips to exotic places like Chepstow and Tintern, Swansea and Tenby, Lynmouth

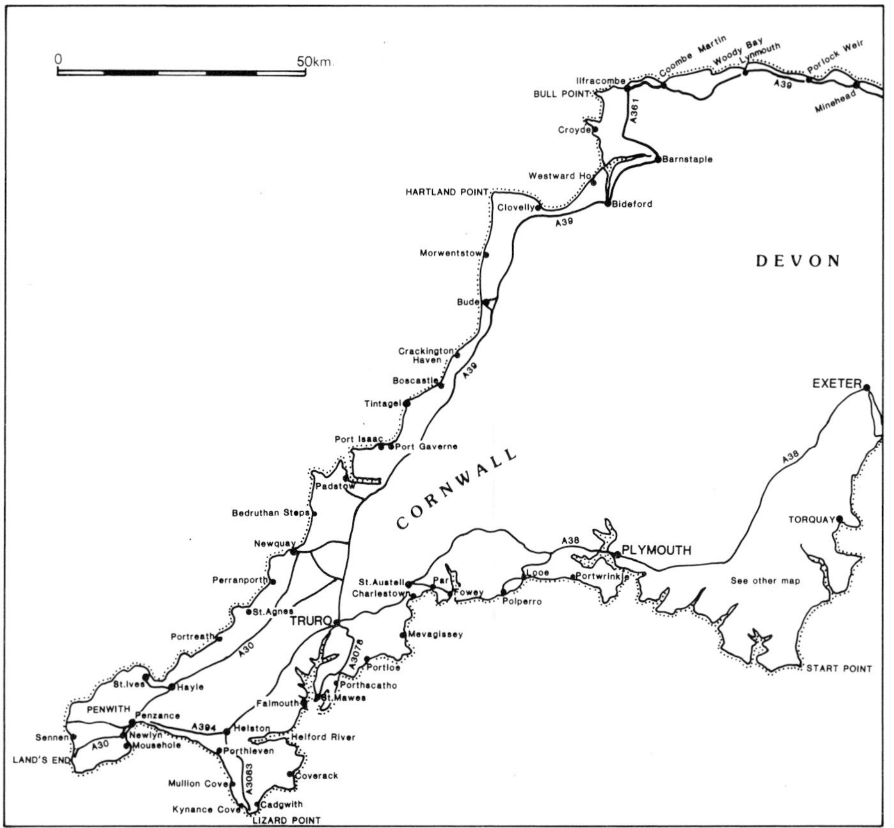

The coast of the South-west Peninsula

and Ilfracombe. Standing curiously aloof a short distance down the coast, is the parish church of St Andrew with its late Norman tower. In the churchyard is the grave of Arthur Hallam, friend of Tennyson, and immortalised in the poet's 'In Memoriam'.

The coastline around the mouth of the river Yeo is typical of the Somerset Levels. Hedge-banked fields with willows lining the drainage ditches (rhines) and brick farmhouses with cattle sheds huddled around, dominate the landscape. Natural salting has been reclaimed with new fields taken in north of the Yeo. In Woodspring Bay coastal defence works have proved necessary to prevent flooding for storms in the past have occasionally caused considerable damage. In the famous flood of January 1606 which also inundated the Wentlooge Levels on the other side of the Bristol Channel, water reached a level of 1.5m (5ft) inside Kingston Seymour church, although it is 3.2km (2 miles) inland from the coast. The long ridge of Middle Hope hill forms an essential bastion against attacks by the sea and its raised site found favour with early man for on its limestone top there are traces of early field systems. At its foot stand the remains of Woodspring Priory, dating from 1226 when it was founded by the Augustinian canons.

Weston-super-Mare developed in a similar fashion to Clevedon but has grown much more rapidly in the present century into a resort with a countrywide reputation. Although it began as early as 1810 with the building of the Royal Hotel, the core of the resort is very much Victorian in appearance. The Royal Crescent dates from 1847 and the

Town Hall from 1856, while Claremont Terrace forms another fine nineteenth-century sweep. Birnbeck Island was joined by a bridge and at its outer end, a pier was used for steamer trips. From the middle of October to Christmas the island was the scene of intense sprat-fishing with nets stretched across to the mainland. It was not unusual for £10,000 to be earned in a season. All this has gone and Weston relies on summer visitors, retired residents and a range of light industries on the outskirts for its livelihood. One of its joys is the limestone ridge of Worlebury Hill, at the western end of which is a 4ha (10 acre) Iron Age camp with four ramparts following the contours of the hill. It must have been a place of settlement for there are scant remains of hut circles and circular pits which contained human skeletons. Brean Down, on the other side of the Axe estuary, also has its prehistoric camp as well as ancient field systems. Both limestone ridges give fine views across the Channel to the aptly named islands of Flatholm (with lighthouse) and Steepholm, both outliers of the Mendip limestone.

South of Brean Down there is a wild expanse of foreshore very exposed to the westerly winds, which have carried sand inland to form a narrow belt of sandhills running north from Burnham-on-Sea for 6km (4 miles). In places the belt is 1km (½ mile) wide but narrows towards the north. Individual dunes can be up to 9m (30ft) high and are colonised by marram grass and sea buckthorn. Bungalows, shacks and caravans cover the coastal strip and there is much 'human' erosion of the dune belt, so it is a surprise to find the eleventh-century church of St Mary in the dunes at Berrow on what is now a golf course. There is another small church at Brean dedicated to the Celtic saint Bridget. Both must at some time have been partially buried in the sand.

Burnham-on-Sea, the third and smallest of the resorts on this west-facing section of the Somerset coast, is perhaps the most pleasant. It has an early core around its fifteenth-century church, the tower of which leans because the foundations, quite unbiblically, were on sand. Inside is a seventeenth-century marble altarpiece, designed for Whitehall Chapel by Inigo Jones but out of scale in this village church. Burnham made a bid as a canal port after the completion of the Glastonbury Canal in 1832, but the enterprise was a failure and the route was used for the railway in 1852. Even that has now gone. There are two lighthouses, one on the beach and the other amidst the houses, which once served as a leading line for vessels entering the Parrett Estuary.

Stert As with the other Somerset rivers there is no crossing near the mouth of the Parrett, so Stert Peninsula opposite Burnham can only be approached by a long detour through Bridgwater and a journey through country lanes. After Weston and Burnham this is a lonely landscape of marshland, shingle ridges and mud-flats. From Wall Common to Stert Point there is a prolific growth of rice grass which has now formed a complete sward after being introduced from Poole Harbour in 1928. On the peninsula there are as many as twenty shingle ridges formed mainly of flat stones of Liassic Limestone carried by wave action from the west. They make an overlapping sequence which helps to protect the marshland behind (reclaimed in medieval times) from being periodically flooded. Fenning Island, once quite separate, is now joined to the peninsula by a shingle bar. It is not until Stolford is reached that solid rock appears on the foreshore as a succession of blue-grey limestone reefs. Further west the huge concrete mass of Hinkley Point Nuclear Power Station rests on a similar foundation.

Lilstock, approached down a lane from the tiny village with its ruined church, was once a small port with a tiny harbour that is now choked and neglected. The sea can also be approached from the main coastal road (A39) at Kilve where the church, with a Saxon font, lies within 1km (½ mile) of the coast. Nearby are the remains of a chantry. It was a remote area when visited by Southey and Wordsworth; the 'Kilve by the green sea' and Kilve's 'delightful shore' of their writings fortunately still survive. Near the shore there is a curious red-brick building with a chimney, all that remains of an attempt to

The building at Kilve in which oil was extracted from local shale

The large Victorian house is now a boarding school, and holiday chalets cover the eastern cliff.

extract oil from local shale. The coastal road continues inland around the northern end of the Quantocks, where St Audrie's Bay has fine vertical cliffs of red Keuper Marl with a sandy beach and limestone reefs at their feet.

Watchet typifies the re-birth of many of our small coastal ports during the past decade as a result of labour troubles in the major docks. The harbour is buzzing with activity with vessels up to 2,500 tons unloading a variety of cargoes from the Mediterranean and Baltic countries. Although the ships have to sit on the mud bed at low water, the large tidal rise takes them out without difficulty. Watchet has a long history for there has been a settlement nestling in this break in the wall of red marl cliffs since Saxon times when the town, though small, was important enough to have its own mint. It may even have its origins in the sixth to seventh centuries for the parish church is dedicated to the Celtic saint Decuman. After the Conquest the manor of Watchet passed to the Mohun family who built nearby Dunster Castle. The first real evidence of a harbour dates from the time of Henry VIII when a contemporary plan shows a harbour arm, probably built of timber piles with a stone core, rather like the Cobb at Lyme Regis (see page 276). The present harbour dates from 1861 when a much larger basin was enclosed. A railway link to Taunton came the following year and this gave Watchet a much larger hinterland for its trade, including iron ore from the Brendon Hills brought down to the port by a railway laid along the Washford Valley. A major disaster occurred in 1901 when the harbour was largely destroyed during a storm but it was rebuilt with greater solidity and has lasted to the present day. Esparto grass for the local paper mills, established about 1750, was once an important import, but today it is wines, wood pulp, cork, glassware and timber. Exports include crated motor-car and tractor parts.

To the west of Watchet the cliffs rise steadily to reach almost 76m (250ft). Formed of red marl and capped by the more solid Liassic Limestone, they drop in height as Blue Anchor Bay is approached with its holiday camp dominating the low coastline. The recently re-opened railway hugs the coast in this section and on a fine summer's day there are extensive views to the east. Around Blue Anchor the cliffs are exciting, with the dull-green rock of the headland interlaced with bands of white gypsum and contorted strata dipping towards the sea where it overlies a harder sandstone bed. In places the action of the sea has hollowed out small caverns.

Minehead Many look upon the town simply as a modern resort of hotels, guest houses and wide streets, but these are simply nineteenth-century additions to the original settlement situated on the hill above around the parish church of St Michael. Narrow, curving cobbled streets and colour-washed cottages provide a welcome change for the visitor willing to climb to the upper town. Another old part of the town exists around the harbour, built in the lee of the headland and approached by the promenade road. Its stumpy harbour arm and scattering of fishermen's cottages give little indication of its former importance as an exporter of woollen goods and barrels of herrings to the Mediterranean. It was as early as the fifteenth century that the first jetty was built by the Luttrell family of nearby Dunster Castle, an association which lasted until 1951 when the family sold their rights to the local council.

The coast to the west of Minehead is accessible only on foot and the first part, as far as Greenaleigh Point, is well known to visitors to the resort. The cliffs are formed mainly of hard Devonian slates but the slopes are unstable in places where they give rise to the broken ground known as the Brockholes. Hurlstone Point, which overlooks Porlock Bay to the east, is formed of sandstone. There is a fine storm beach running around the edge of the bay and this gives a natural protection to the lowland embayment where barley is a favoured crop. A harbour is tucked under the cliff at the western end of the bay, where a natural bank of shingle together with an enclosing stone wall give shelter. A cutting through the shingle bank forms the entrance channel and is marked by broom beacons. Occasionally storms sweep the shingle into the channel and a bulldozer is called in to clear a new route. The whole setting of **Porlock Weir**, as the harbour area is known, is made attractive by the old thatched cottages, the inn and shops and the ceaseless activity of the boating fraternity. The harbour is still owned by the Porlock Manor Estate and there is a pleasant drive through its coastal woods by way of the toll road from Porlock Weir which ultimately rejoins the main coastal road at the top of Culbone Hill.

Beds of limestone set in shales and marls form harder 'teeth' in this north Somerset cliffline between Watchet and Minehead

Closer to the coast and approached on foot by a branch path is tiny Culbone church, largely twelfth-century but with a Celtic cross close by which hints of a much earlier foundation. Certainly in its out-of-the-way situation set in a deep combe with a water supply at hand, Culbone has a Celtic air about it. The other approach is by the Somerset and North Devon Coast Path, though landslips mean that the path has to be repaired periodically. This section of the coast consists mainly of hog's back cliffs with a pronounced rounded upper shoulder and a steep cliffed base wherever the sea has been able to attack. Tough grits are responsible for the cliff scenery and a particularly resistant bed is responsible for the promontory known as The Foreland. Short steeply falling valleys have their small streams which often end in waterfalls, to the west of which, as at Coscombe Water, there was a Roman signal station – Old Burrow Fort. The coastal slopes are everywhere steep and at Countisbury Hill reach 302m (991ft) within .5km (¼ mile) of the shoreline. From the lonely church on top there are fine views westwards across Lynmouth Bay and beyond.

Lynmouth has so completely changed in appearance over the past quarter of a century that a visitor who last saw it in the late 1940s might find the present setting very strange. The alteration was the result of devastation caused by the floods of 15 August 1952, when over 23cm (9in) of rain fell in twenty-four hours on the higher parts of Exmoor and unleashed a torrent of water in the East and West Lyn rivers that swept 40,000 tons of boulders into Lynmouth. Rebuilding has taken place and the river is now confined to a deeply set walled channel so that never again can it wreak so much damage. Although buildings have been tastefully restored in the shopping centre, the huge boulders which litter the river bed and extend as a fan out to sea serve as a reminder of that grim night when thirty-one people were drowned. For some the event has been turned into a tourist attraction for, after paying an entrance fee, it is possible to walk up the Lyn Valley to see some of the changes wrought by the flood. A cliff railway still runs in the season from the shore to the larger settlement of **Lynton** 274m (900ft) above – the Lynton Lift Railway built in 1890 when Victorians were beginning to discover the delights of the north Devon coast. Lynton was never part of the national railway network, but it did have a link with Barnstaple in a spectacular 2ft gauge line, opened in 1898 but closed in 1936 when charabancs and cars began to come in increasing numbers.

From Lynmouth there is direct road access to the eastern end of the **Valley of the Rocks**, one of the more spectacular features of the coastline. It is a curious, twisting, steep-sided valley which wends its way almost parallel to the coast for a distance of about 1.6km (1 mile) west of Lynton. At its farther end there is a spectacular view of the sea. What is remarkable about this valley apart from the absence of a stream, is the bare, often castellated rock piles which give it its name. Those which form part of the broken cliff are reminiscent of the tors of Dartmoor, though formed of coarse gritstone and not granite. The most probable explanation of this unusual coastal feature is that it was formed during the Ice Age when ice in the Bristol Channel pressed against the north Devon coast and meltwater drainage cut a deep, flat-floored valley with great speed parallel to its margin. Once the ice melted there was no permanent drainage left to carry on the work of valley formation and so the Valley of the Rocks was left high and dry, stranded well above the sea. The curious rock formations were most likely formed at the same time as a result of a freeze-thaw process under the prevailing arctic conditions. In this we have a true link with the Dartmoor tors which are believed, by many, to have been formed in the same way and at the same time. Occupying the western end of the valley is Lee Abbey, a nineteenth-century house built by Charles Bailey on the site of a former small manor house. It was never a true abbey, though it is now an Anglican retreat.

Woody Bay is well-named, for the rather unstable slopes are richly wooded. There is a scenic drive through the woods by a private toll road which gradually makes for the plateau top at Martinhoe. The surprise here is to find a Roman signal station, dating from AD 60-75, with a double rampart and ditches. Until the conquest of south Wales the local tribe there, the Silures, posed a threat to the tenuous hold which the Romans had on the north Devon area. Unlike the short-lived station at Old Burrow Fort (see page 235), at the Martinhoe station there were barracks for about eighty men and a furnace attached to the armoury. The station lay close to one of the major breaks in the coastline where the Heddon stream forms a deep, scree-filled ravine cut right down to sea level. Between here and the next major break at Combe Martin the cliffs have the same typical hog's back form but, with the grit beds sloping inland, erosion has created distinctive shapes in the Great and Little Hangman cliffs.

Combe Martin is best described as a long straggling village which occupies the valley floor as it wends its way for more than 3km (2 miles) inland. The size of the village is deceptive and puzzling for it is not really a resort, and although there is market gardening on the rich valley sides this is not the full explanation. From the thirteenth century right up to 1875 there were lead and silver mines in the valley – workings exist under the present village – and rich seams of iron ore below the Little Hangman. The thirteenth-century church of St Peter, one of the best along this coastline, reflects the past wealth of the place.

At Combe Martin there is a pronounced change in the appearance of the coastline for the grits to the east now give way to a series of bluish-grey or silvery slates and shales. Small coves and rocky promontories abound, but at Watermouth there is a much deeper inlet which runs almost parallel to the coast at its outer end, possibly ice-formed like the Valley of the Rocks. Its sheltered harbour is now fully developed with moorings for yachts and pleasure craft, and is even used by the occasional 'working' boat belonging to local lobster fishermen.

Lundy, a granite island lying about 17km (10 miles) off the nearest point of the North Devon coast, has a name derived from the Old Norse meaning 'puffin island'. Puffins still nest but are increasingly rare compared

The distinctive hog's back profiles of the cliffs known as the Great and Little Hangman, near Combe Martin

with other seabirds like the kittiwake, fulmar and Manx shearwater which breed on the island. Most visitors arrive by boat from Ilfracombe on a day trip which allows two hours ashore though with only a sheltered cove in the south-east corner of the island to act as a landing place, strong easterly winds might make landing impossible. In the short time available on a day trip it is not possible to see more than a glimpse of the island. Although only 5km (3 miles) long and seldom more than a kilometre wide, Lundy has a wealth of natural and historic features, making it worthwhile to stay at the island hotel or in a self-catering cottage.

Starting at the landing beach in the south there is a steep walk up to the plateau top with its settlement of hotel, inn, shop and cottages clustered around the church. To the south is the ruin of Marisco Castle, a reminder of the family who owned the island in the twelfth century. A short walk to the south-west corner brings the Devil's Limekiln, a 100m (300ft) deep chimney cut into the granite cliffs, into view. The 120m (400ft) high cliffs of the west coast are constantly battered by the Atlantic waves and a wealth of detail, including isolated stacks, natural arches, narrow clefts and steep-sided coves, contribute to the best coastal scenery of the island. The coastal path runs the whole length of this western seaboard, first past the old lighthouse erected by Trinity House in 1815 on the highest point of the island, Beacon Hill 150m (500ft), and then on past hut circles to the northern lighthouse.

Apart from the cliff scenery, Lundy can offer many features of historic interest: Bronze Age tumuli, the foundation of a fourth-century Celtic chapel dedicated to St Elen and the ruins of the medieval Marisco Castle, as well as the nineteenth-century buildings of the main settlement. After the Heaven family acquired the island in 1830, they built the manor house (now Millcombe House), developed the manor farm and erected the present early Victorian church. Subsequently Lundy passed to the Harman family who introduced Soay sheep and Sika deer and bred a Lundy pony. Since 1969 Lundy has been under the guardianship of the National Trust though administered through the Landmark Trust.

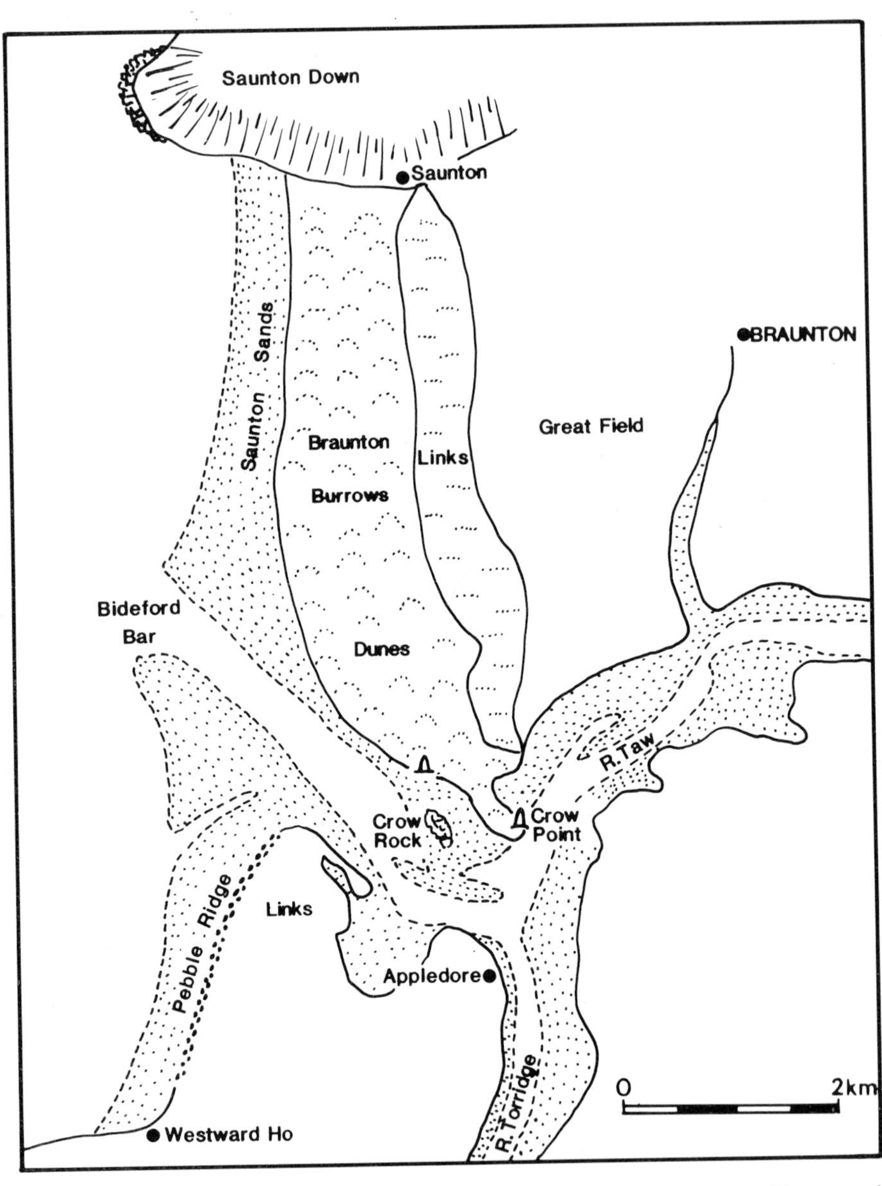

Braunton Burrows and the estuary mouth of the combined Taw and Torridge rivers

Ilfracombe developed from an inland nucleus around its thirteenth-century parish church by spreading down the valley to the rock-girt harbour under Hillsborough. The harbour, which faces east, is protected by a ridge on its northern side named Lantern Hill, from the chapel and light which in the past guided vessels into port. The natural setting of the lower part of the town and harbour is reminiscent of the Valley of the Rocks, and it is possible that it has a similar origin – ice pressing against the coast. Up to the end of the eighteenth century the town and port depended on the herring fishery, and it remained quite small. Its reputation as 'a bathing place and agreeable summer residence' seems to have been established after 1830 and the Bath House, with its Greek Doric entrance, dates from this time. Montpelier Place, Hillsborough Terrace and Bath Place all belong to this early period of growth. A further spurt came after the arrival of the railway from Barnstaple in 1874. Previously many visitors had arrived by sea, for there were regular packet services with Bristol, Swansea and even Hayle in Cornwall. This later Victorian development added yet another dimension to the town. Surprisingly Ilfracombe has not grown as much in the present century so we still have a resort of Georgian and Victorian appearance. The railway is now closed but this has had little effect on the holiday traffic. Ilfracombe still has a link with its past sea traffic, for there are services across the Bristol Channel to the south Wales ports during the summer as well as trips to Lundy Island.

From Ilfracombe it is a pleasant walk of 5km (3 miles) along the Somerset and North Devon Coast Path to Lee Bay, which has developed into a small resort with hotels and boarding houses taking advantage of the sandy beach. The path continues to Bull Point with its lighthouse erected in 1879 after a series of disasters on the nearby Morte Stone reef. This reef is a detached part of the long spine of up-ended slates which runs out to form the peninsula at Mortehoe. It is now under the care of the National Trust and makes a pleasant walk with Lundy ever present on the distant skyline. Barricane Beach, also National Trust, adjoins it on the south and was a favourite spot for the early Victorian tourist searching for shells filling the gaps between the rocks. Some were of rare species like the wentle trap, elephant's tusk, cylindrical dipper and bearded nerite. The whole setting of Morte Bay is completed by the fine strand of Woolacombe Sands, over 3km (2 miles) long and facing the full force of the mighty Atlantic rollers. Westerly winds not only bring in the huge breakers but also carry the sand inland and pile it against the edge of Woolacombe Down. Benefiting from its fine natural setting Woolacombe has become a favoured holiday spot in recent years.

Croyde has its old village with a number of thatched cottages, but there has been considerable recent growth towards the coast to take advantage of the fine sandy beach tucked in between the Baggy Peninsula and the more stumpy Saunton Down. Hard sandstones are responsible for Baggy Point, while an outcrop of less resistant slates forms Saunton Down. Both tend to have rounded landforms and contrast strongly with the jagged Morte Peninsula to the north. A fine raised beach – formed during a period of higher sea level during the Ice Age – exists along the southern shore of both peninsulas. Another feature is the large boulder of red granite about 1km (½ mile) west of the Saunton Hotel. It measures 2m (7ft) by 1.5m (5ft) and most probably came from Scotland as a result of ice transport. Another boulder of white granite exists on the south side of Croyde Bay, and most likely has a similar history.

Braunton Burrows is a vast expanse of sand dunes extending from the cliffs at Saunton southwards to the mouth of the Taw-Torridge Estuary. The dunes reach a height of almost 30m (100ft) in places and are highly mobile, especially where the natural vegetation of marram grass has gone and blow-outs have formed. On the inner side bracken has taken over and in many ways is more effective as a dune stabiliser than the marram grass. In turn the bracken gives way to dune pasture and then to the fertile alluvial soils which make up Braunton Great Field, one of the few survivals in the country of the ancient strip-field form of land-holding and farming.

Westward Ho! on the south side of the Taw-Torridge Estuary provides a complete contrast to the sand-dune belt to the north by reason of the famous pebble or 'popple' ridge – a straight bank of shingle which runs for over 1.6km (1 mile) and is raised well above the sands and marsh on either side. In the past century it has suffered erosion in the south near Westward Ho! village, but new ridges have formed further north close to the estuary mouth. However, it seems to be losing more material than it is gaining, so that it is gradually wasting away. In spite of

twentieth-century development the whole area is still attractive, for behind the ridge there are sand dunes and meres with part of the area laid out as a golf course. The development of Westward Ho! followed the publication in 1855 of Charles Kingsley's book of that title, which was set in this out of the way corner of north Devon. A development company took over and during the next thirty years produced a tasteless settlement completely out of keeping with the natural setting. Only the nearby and older **Appledore** can offer the visitor a combination of old-world charm and thriving industry. Formerly called Tawmouth, the settlement goes back at least to the eleventh century, its network of narrow streets giving a hint of this antiquity. Some of the cottages may be Elizabethan in date though the church is nineteenth century. There is still a flourishing shipbuilding industry where local craftsmen still display their skills in specialist construction.

Buck's Mills The southern shore of Barnstaple (Bideford) Bay as far as Hartland Point has been carved out of the contorted beds of the Culm Measures, a variable assemblage of sandstones, shales, slates, limestones and the occasional band of sooty coal – the culm which gives the whole formation its name. The cliffs are very broken for the beds are subject to slipping, and along the base there is a prominent raised bench cut in the solid rock. Access is difficult except at Buck's Mills where a narrow road runs down the steep valley floor to the settlement huddled near the shore. There is a broad similarity with the better known Clovelly, but Buck's Mills is less pretty-pretty and commercialised, though not without its visitors in the summer months. As with many of the streams on this coast the final drop to the beach is over a hanging lip, and at Buck's Mills the fall passes through what looks like a huge lime kiln. The shale cliffs near the slipway are very liable to erosion, and there was a considerable fall in 1979.

The steeply dropping cobbled street of Clovelly. In summer it is crowded with visitors making their way down to the tiny harbour at its foot

Clovelly The huge car park at the top of this single-street hamlet, with restaurant and gift shops, betrays what Clovelly has now become – a tourist Mecca besieged by visitors in the summer. Out of season, especially when the late afternoon sun casts its long shadows over the deep notch in which the settlement lies, the real charm and uniqueness of the place where Charles Kingsley's father was once rector emerges once more. The steep, cobbled and stepped street leads down past cottages, inn and small chapel to the harbour with its great breakwater which gives protection against the north. Clovelly was once an important fishing port on this otherwise harbourless stretch of coastline and herrings and mackerel were once netted in their thousands. The harbour was created when George Cary built the first breakwater in the sixteenth century, and the Cary family figured prominently in Kingsley's *Westward Ho!*, shortly after which Clovelly was discovered by the Victorians. It was saved from complete development by being the

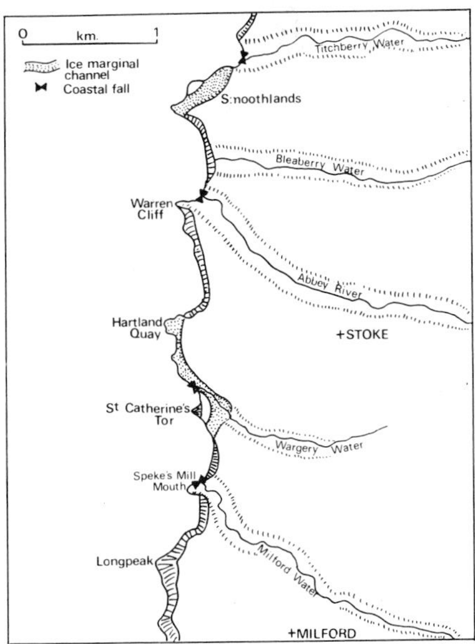

The hanging valley coastline south of Hartland

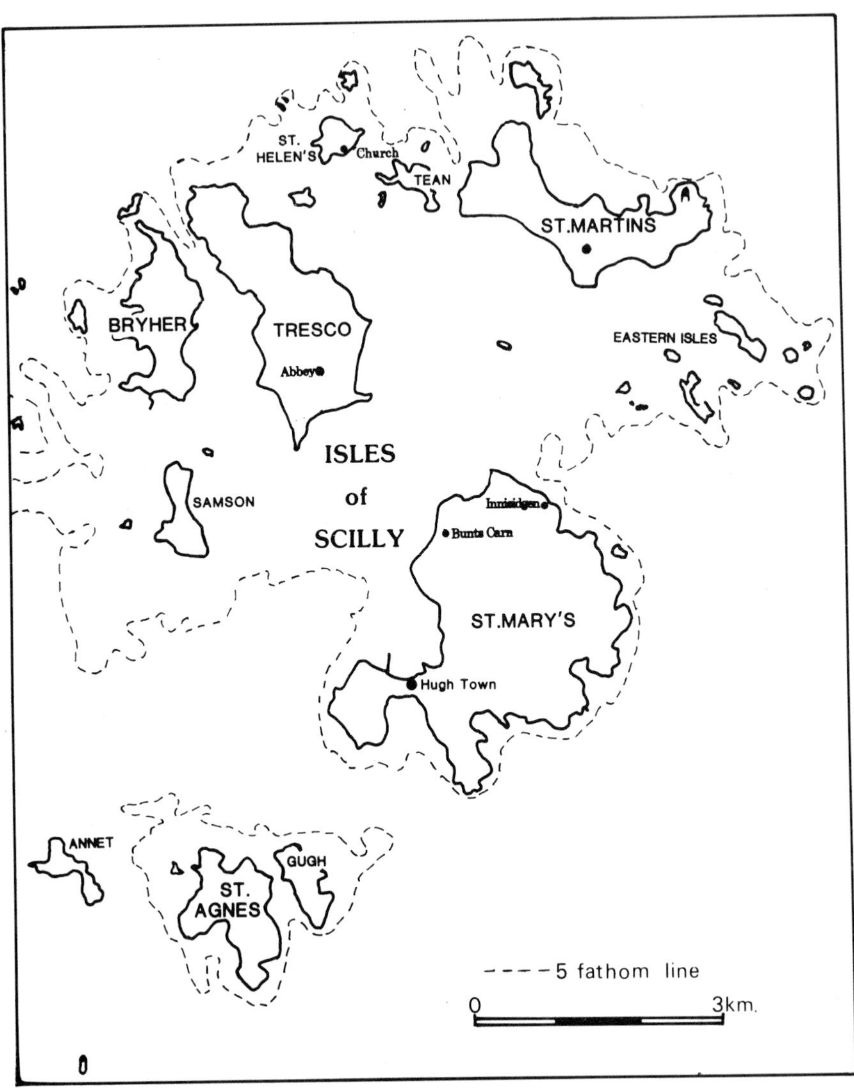

The Scilly Isles

estate village of nearby Clovelly Court and it still retains this appearance. To the east the wooded cliff drive, known as The Hobby, was a favourite excursion of almost 5km (3 miles) in Victorian times and can still be followed today.

Hartland is the name of the huge parish in the extreme north west of Devon that includes some of the finest cliff scenery in Britain. The best lies on the north to south section running southwards from Hartland Point, for here the culm rocks run out at right angles to the shore. It is as though the huge seas which roll in from the Atlantic have drawn out the hard sandstone fangs of the formation and left them as jagged offshore reefs, the graveyard of many a vessel. At the point itself there is a lighthouse which can be approached by a narrow road. Close by is a smoothed-out concave rock resembling the interior of a vessel, with a chink through which the sea penetrates in rough weather and a chasm that forms an open chimney to the sky. All this detail in the cliff results from the pounding of the sea which has removed the weaker strata. Further south at Hartland Quay, where there is another road down to the coast, there is the remains of a former harbour built in 1566 in the lee of one of the many rocky promontories. It was once important enough to have its own harbour master's office, now the hotel. Small coasters called with their cargoes of lime and coal and took off barley and wheat. All this came to an end when the breakwater was destroyed at the end of the last century. By then too the railway had reached Barnstaple, and though Hartland acquired the reputation of being the farthest parish in England from a railway, the latter gradually took away the coastal trade. Hartland is the subject of a delightful book by the local vicar, the Reverend Pearse Chope, with the informative title *Farthest from Railways*.

The other distinctive feature of this coastline is the large number of coastal waterfalls from valley mouths which 'hang' over the cliff edge. At Speke's Mill, the stream drops 49m (160ft) in a series of falls. The same is true of the Abbey river a little farther north where a mill once harnessed the water power. The falls are associated with a dismembered valley system which is best seen in the flat-floored section that winds around the conical peak of St Catherine's Tor, a short distance south of Hartland Quay. For long these hanging coastal valleys presented something of a mystery but it is now generally recognised that they were formed by meltwater streams from an ice front which pressed in on this coast as in the case with the Valley of the Rocks (see page 236). The result is a richly varied coastal setting, but it has to be walked for there are few access points by car.

The Isles of Scilly

Although only about 45km (28 miles) from the mainland and a twenty-minute helicopter flight from Penzance, the Isles of Scilly are a world apart, with an array of islands ranging in size from mere pinnacles of rock thrusting out of the sea to the largest, St Mary's, which is still less than 10km^2 (4sq miles) in area. The other larger islands in the group are St Martin's, Tresco, Bryher, Samson, St Agnes and St Helen's, and together they have almost 160km (100 miles) of coastline. Formed almost entirely of granite the islands rise to over 60m (200ft) in several places, though good inland vantage points are few. It is the coastline which offers the best views, especially to other islands of the archipelago, as well as the best scenery. Although granite predominates there is rich variety in the coastal setting, ranging from castellated cliffs to wide sandy strands. Most of the coastline is accessible by footpath, and because of their small size each of the islands can be comfortably walked in one day. Another feature of the Isles of Scilly is the variation from island to island, so that a week spent exploring each in turn can be scenically rewarding, with natural and man-made features contributing to the wealth of interest, whether it be in the flowers and shrubs, the sea birds and seals, or evidence of past settlement.

St Mary's forms the ideal base from which to launch excursions to the other islands and from the quayside of Hugh Town (the 'capital') there are boat excursions each day of the week during the season. Hugh Town, with its network of narrow streets and colour-washed cottages, sits astride an isthmus which connects the Garrison with the main part of St Mary's and is able to offer two sandy beaches with favoured sheltered spots. Northwards from Hugh Town there is a coastal path leading alongside bay-head beaches like Porth Mellon and Porthloo to Halangy Down, with its fine prehistoric Bants Carn and an adjacent ancient village site with hut foundations of granite on a sward running down to the sea. There are other prehistoric burial chambers, dating back to about 2000 BC, further round the north coast at Innisidgen (See *The Ancient Monuments of the Isles of Scilly*, B. H. St J. O'Neill, HMSO). In spring and early summer this coastal walk is a blaze of colour from plants like cineraria, arum lilies, gladioli (Whistling Jacks) and agapanthus,

New Grimsby harbour, the port of entry for Tresco Abbey Gardens

many of which were once cultivated but have now become garden escapes. In addition, there are endless hedgerows of fuchsia, escallonia and other evergreen shrubs that enjoy the mild climate and are able to withstand the salt-laden winds. The hedges round the tiny enclosed fields that are such a feature on most of the larger islands were planted almost a century ago and give the necessary protection to the early bulb crops of narcissi and daffodil and, more recently, potatoes and broccoli.

The eastern side of St Mary's is more rugged, with granite cliffs eroded to give striking forms such as those of Deep Point, Porth Hellick Point and Newfoundland Point, all with their upstanding 'tors', not unlike those of Dartmoor but now in a coastal setting. But there are also sheltered bays and coves, particularly Pelistry Bay with its fine sandy shore, and the deep inlet of Porth Hellick where a carpet of wild yellow mesembryanthemum covers the low sand dunes fringing the head of the bay. More striking cliff scenery occurs around Peninnis Head, the last promontory to be rounded on the circuit of the island before the return to Hugh Town.

Tresco owes its popularity to the Abbey Gardens, with their wealth of exotic plants brought from all parts of the world and encouraged to grow in this sheltered maritime setting. The idea of a sub-tropical garden paradise belongs to Augustus Smith, who in 1834 obtained a lease of the island from the Duchy of Cornwall. What was originally a rather barren windswept area on the eastern side of the island was gradually transformed – first by the planting of a shelter-belt of trees such as the Monterey Pine, sycamore, elm and holly. The slopes facing south east were then landscaped, and hundreds of different plants, brought by seamen from places as far away as South Africa and New Zealand, were planted in pockets of soil between carefully planned walls of granite boulders.

The Tresco Abbey Gardens are probably at their peak in May. The island has much else to offer along its short coastline of about 10km (6 miles). From the nineteenth-century Tresco Abbey (built by Augustus Smith, though on the site of a much earlier Benedictine foundation), it is but a short walk to the eastern shore-line across a dune assemblage dominated by mesembryanthemum. These eastern beaches, like that of Pentle Bay, are well sheltered and look out across the shallow inland sea to the islands of St Martin's and St Mary's. Fine white granite sand makes up the shore and at intervals there are rocky headlands and granite boulders to break the continuity. Particularly self-contained is the bay of Old Grimsby, the original landing place for Tresco, but the quay lacks water at low tide and most boats now discharge their passengers at New Grimsby on the other side of the island. Near the quay and set in its own sub-tropical garden is the Island Hotel, while beyond it the footpath continues around an embayment fringed by a huge sweep of rhododendron bushes which give a blaze of purple in the spring.

The north coast of Tresco is barren, with a low plateau covered with stunted heath plants interspersed with bleached boulders of granite. The cliff-top views compensate, particularly across to St Helen's, Tean and the upstanding sentinel of Round Island with its lighthouse. Further on stands King Charles' Castle, set high on the cliff top and built between 1550 and 1554 but unfortunately wrongly sited to protect the narrow strait separating Tresco from Bryher. It soon became a 'white elephant' and led to the building, in 1651, of another castle, Cromwell's Castle, whose remains still stand, though closer to the shore. After the north-west coast of Tresco has been rounded, the settlement and harbour of New Grimsby soon come into view and are approached through narrow lanes set between hedged fields, with their crops, in spring, of bulbs and new potatoes. It is at New Grimsby that passengers from the other islands land en route for the Abbey gardens, a walk that takes the visitor across the waist of the island past the Abbey farm and then alongside the waters of the Great Pool.

St Martin's appears bleaker than the other islands, largely because its northern half is almost entirely taken up with open maritime heath. But St Martin's has its devotees and on a fine summer's day there is no finer walk than around its coastal fringe. After landing at the island's only quay, there is an uphill walk to Higher Town and thence the footpath continues eastward to Chapel Down with its prominent red and white Day Mark, dating back to 1683. Close by, in Bread and Butter Cove, the low cliffs just above the cobbled beach are formed partly of a true boulder clay left behind as the great ice sheet that once covered the British Isles reached its southernmost limit. The walk to the western end of the island with its views across to Tean can be made either along the heathy top overlooking the northern bays and short stubby granite promontories, or by taking the more sheltered southerly route which leads through Middle Town and then on to Lower Town. These southerly slopes are more favoured, and the landscape of hedged fields of escallonia, veronica, fuchsia and pittosporum (the last named a native of New Zealand and the most effective of all the windbreak shrubs) stands out in contrast to the bleakness of the northern heathland.

To the south east of St Martin's lie the **Eastern Isles**, made up of a number of uninhabited islands and myriads of tiny rocks where seals bask in the sun. The islands have not always been without habitation – in 1962 an exceptionally severe storm exposed a prehistoric site on Nornour. Although probably originally Late Bronze Age, it subsequently became a Roman trading post, as is apparent from the finds of enamelled brooches, rings, bracelets, glassware and figurines imported in the mid-second century from Gaul.

At the other end of St Martin's, the island of **Tean** lies only a short distance away and it also has its prehistoric features, notably burial chambers and a stone row. Beyond lies yet another uninhabited island, St Helen's, with the ruins of a tiny granite church where, each August, services are still held.

Bryher, while only separated from Tresco by a narrow strait, is completely different in character. Small hedged fields greet the visitor who has landed at the quay overlooking the New Grimsby Channel. Three hillocks – Samson, Gweal and Watch Hill –

dominate the island's relief, while to the north lies the windswept Shipman's Head downland. Elsewhere the tiny enclosures of hedged fields cover much of the waist of the island. Bryher has always been a popular destination for excursionists from St Mary's, and now that there is an hotel it is possible to make a longer stay and enjoy the solitude once the day-visitors have taken the last boat back to Hugh Town.

Samson, in contrast to many of the bigger islands in the Scilly group, is bare and windswept and now uninhabited. Two rounded knolls of granite give it an easily recognisable profile. Though not on everyone's list for visiting, boats do disembark passengers on the wide sandy strands which border the eastern side of the island. Apart from guaranteed solitude, another attraction is the lines of granite boulders which run out from the low cliffs across the wide sandy beaches. Their regularity seems to indicate that they have been placed there deliberately by man, though there have been various suggestions as to the reason for such massive works. Formerly they were looked upon simply as field boundaries which had become submerged following a rise of sea level – this would imply a prehistoric date. Recently a more favoured explanation is that they are fish weirs, possibly constructed as late as the sixteenth century.

St Agnes is the most distinct of the inhabited islands, and though far from the cultural and geographic centre of St Mary's, it is favoured by many visitors to Scilly. Its charm lies in its compactness, with its settlement concentrated around the prominent lighthouse, which is no longer used, but is the second oldest in Britain, dating from 1680. Because it is such a prominent sea mark for those sailing the shallow waters between the islands, the light tower is still kept a gleaming white by Trinity House.

Close to the eastern side of St Agnes is the detached island of **Gugh**, which can be reached, except towards the time of high water, by a sand causeway. Beyond St Agnes, stretching away westwards to the notorious reef of the Bishops, with the lighthouse which replaced that of St Agnes, is the only other sizeable island of the Scillies, **Annet**. Because it is uninhabited, it is now a bird sanctuary, being the principal nesting place in Britain of the Manx Shearwater and the Storm Petrel. Both are nocturnal birds and therefore evening trips are often arranged from St Mary's to see them return after a day spent roving the ocean in seach of food. Annet also has the last remaining colony in the Scillies of the Puffin, for elsewhere this bird has suffered in recent years from attacks by the Great Black-backed Gulls and a lack of suitable burrows for nesting. The best time to visit Annet is probably May, when a large part of the island is a blaze of purple and deep pink from the blooming of the Sea Thrift.

Cornwall

Morwenstow village is near the coast, and visited because of its fine Norman church and its associations with the Reverend Stephen Hawker. Much has been written about the eccentricities, and less about the undoubtedly humane character, of this man. From a hut on the nearby Vicarage cliffs he saw the Atlantic and this dangerous coast in all its moods, and during his long period as vicar (1834–75) was responsible for saving many lives from shipwrecks. It was in this hut that Hawker wrote many of his books and poems. The whole coastline as far as Bude and even beyond is rugged, with the highly contorted succession of sandstones and shales responding to erosion by the sea. Where streams reach the coast they normally cascade to the beach, as the valleys are seldom adjusted to the present-day sea level. Strawberry Water at Welcome Mouth and Marsland Water close by are but two examples.

Bude is situated at one of the few large gaps in the rocky wall of north Cornwall and for this reason was chosen as the starting point for a 48km (30 mile) canal running inland to Holsworthy. It was built in 1819–26 to carry shelly lime sand to sweeten the acid soils of the interior. Most of the canal has now gone, but its impressive last 1km (½ mile) with its huge lock at the seaward end is still very much part of present-day Bude as is the adjacent small canal quarter with warehouses lining the basin. Resort growth came much later and was largely due to a local landowner, Sir Thomas Acland, who saw the potential of the wide sandy beach and built a row of small lodging houses, two hotels and some villas to attract both visitor and permanent resident. The scheme might have come to nothing but for the fact that Bude was chosen in 1898 as the west-coast terminus of the railway. This has now gone but the resort, though not exciting, still attracts through its fine sandy beach and impressive cliff scenery close at hand. A walk along the beach either to north or south brings into view the contorted strata which has been shaped into a succession of upfolds and downfolds. In the centre of the town, close to the canal entrance lock, is the low castellated mansion known as The Castle – a folly of about 1850, once a private house but now used by the council. Large hotels occupy prominent sites on Summerleaze Downs while the parish church (a daughter church of Stratton out of whose parish Bude was created) occupies a central position.

The coast road to the south of Bude runs close to the cliff top and gives fine views of the rugged cliffs carved out of the intensely folded Culm Measures. Widemouth Bay has sand and a typical modern resort type of development, crowded in the season but looking careworn at other times of the year. Reefs on the foreshore both to north and south make even a modest sea angry. At Upton the cliff face has one of the finest features which even this spectacular coast-line has to offer – a huge anticlinal sharp fold with four thick beds of sandstone separated by thin beds of shale. Farther south at Millook (approached down a 1 in 3 hill) the cliff to the north of the stream mouth has an intricate pattern of tight folding with a zigzag formed by a sequence of alternate sandstone and shale layers. Further along the coast towards Dizzard Point there is a huge area of landslipping, and with cliffs well over 152m (500ft) high the effect is spectacular.

Crackington Haven, once a sleepy, out of the way hamlet with the Manor House taking in guests and generating its own electricity from a pond in the garden, has been discovered in the car age. It could well have been developed much earlier, for in 1836 there was a proposal to build a huge harbour of refuge extending well out into the bay flanked by the long promontory of Cambeak. It was to be called the Duke of Cornwall's Harbour and be served by a railway from Launceston. Although the plans were drawn up and are still to be seen in the Hydrographic Department at Taunton, the whole project got no further than the drawing board.

The coastal track which runs along the cliff top for 8km (5 miles) to Boscastle is one of superb views which change as each promontory or rise is passed. The stack of Samphire Rock (named after the golden samphire and not the glasswort of saltmarshes) is all that remains of a promontory which has been cut off from the main cliff-line. Just to the north is a feature called the Northern Door, where the sea has cut right through a narrow peninsula at sea level but left a roof to form a natural arch. Now the deep inlet of Pentargon, where the stream falls over the cliff edge in a series of falls, has to be rounded. Shales predominate throughout and give rise to classic rounded hog's back cliffs.

Boscastle, with its ria type harbour formed from the drowned lower part of the Valency Valley, is quite unique in north Cornwall. After many years of neglect the harbour area has been tidied up now that it is largely under the control of the National Trust. The main part of the village, which it is easy to miss because of the one-way street system, consists of rows of cottages descending steeply on both sides of Fore Street. The remains of the site of Botreaux's Castle, which gave its name to the settlement after its founding by a Norman overlord, lie at one end of the street. Boscastle never had a borough charter nor market rights, and yet acquired the appearance of a medieval town. The port is of the same medieval date though the first reference we have to a pier to protect the inner harbour is in 1587. During the eighteenth and nineteenth centuries it rose to prominence importing coal and fertilisers while exporting slate, china-clay and corn. Even under relatively calm conditions entry and exit was not easy, and vessels had to be warped through the twisting entrance by means of ropes fixed to both sides. On the southern side of the harbour one can walk from Forrabury Church, across an open field which still retains its ancient strips, to the Iron Age promontory fort of Willapark.

Tintagel is perhaps the best known place on this coastline, but for the wrong reason. The old village – a single street off the main road – is without character and has only one building, the Old Post Office (National Trust), of interest. This low stone cottage, with its heavy slates weighting down the roof timbers, was probably a manor house dating back to the fourteenth century. Parts have been restored, including the stepped chimney by the front porch. The church of St Materiana stands quite aloof from the village on the cliff top; its situation and dedication suggest a Celtic foundation and the present building has Saxon and early Norman features. An inscribed stone, possibly a Roman milestone, adds yet more history to this isolated site. From the village street there is a track to Tintagel Island, the Mecca for most visitors, but in spite of romantic associations with King Arthur – and the legends go back at least to the time of Geoffrey of Monmouth in the twelfth century – there is no supporting archaeological evidence. What we have on the island are the remains of small rectangular huts of a Celtic monastery, the oldest dating perhaps to about AD 500. Nearby stood the twelfth-century chapel of St Juliot, built by the Earl of Cornwall who also began the castle, now under the care of the Department of the Environment and forming the most substantial remains for the visitor to see. The coast is magnificent, for the Culm Measures have now given place to Devonian rocks which include volcanic beds. These have been subject to both thrusting and faulting, and the result is dark black cliffs riddled with caves and inlets. It is a harbourless coast so that, in the last century, slates from the Trebarwith valley had to be loaded into vessels beached on the sandy foreshore of Trebarwith Strand. This is very much a slate coastline and not very accessible except on foot, for the main coastal road is now running well inland.

Port Gaverne, a natural inlet, was once a place of export for the local Delabole slate, and the road down to it was built for that trade. It also had a flourishing pilchard fishery of which the cellar and kippering kiln remain. Now all is silent and the old rock-cut quay, where ships were once loaded with slates, is given over to leisure craft.

Port Isaac is only just over the headland but is a much larger settlement with narrow streets tightly packed around the head of the harbour. It also exported Delabole slate before the railways took away the traffic. A fishery still remains, largely through the co-operative Port Isaac Fishermen Limited who maintain lobster storage tanks and a cold store. Formerly it was the pilchard fishery that gave employment but, as elsewhere, this has died and the former cellars are now idle or derelict. When both the pilchard and slate trades were flourishing Port Isaac (the Isaac is probably a corruption of the Welsh *isaf* = lower) was a prosperous place which could afford to build the huge Methodist Chapel which now dominates the port. The parish church is well inland at St Endellion.

Port Quin is another small port situated at the head of a narrow fault-guided ria, and seems likely to survive unaltered now that it is largely owned by the National Trust who let out their cottages during the season. Its former prosperity rested on pilchards rather than slate exports and there is a huge shed – a pilchard palace – where the fish caught in their thousands were pressed into barrels, salted and smoked so that the large catches could be fully used. One can imagine the buzz of activity after a pilchard shoal had been sighted offshore before being cornered by the seine netters and brought into port.

The coastline around Port Quin is more exciting in that there is a much greater variety of rock types present as well as a series of major faults. Kellan Head, the

---

Padstow

Stephanie Anne

headlands enclosing Port Quin, and Trevan Point all have lava beds, many of which show a pronounced 'pillow' form through having been deposited under water. Cliff Castle and Rumps Point, forming the outermost points of the Pentire Peninsula, owe their existence to a resistant greenstone rock. The Rumps has an Iron Age promontory fort, perhaps the finest of the forty or more situated along the Cornish coastline. There are three lines of ramparts, the middle one being most impressive in that it is built of weathered slate faced with a continuous kerb of boulders. Pottery finds and wine amphorae suggest occupation from the first century BC to the first century AD, with the inhabitants having close continental links.

Padstow Estuary is the only major ria feature on the north coast which can compare in size with those of the south like Falmouth, Fowey or Plymouth. It lacks their deep water however, for it is largely choked with sand, not as some have supposed through inland china-clay activities but largely through the presence of glacially deposited outwash material when ice came very close to this coast. The Doom Bar (formerly dune-bar) across the estuary mouth has seriously limited the size of vessels able to use the port of Padstow. Considerable quantities of lime-rich sand have been removed from the bar in the past – as much as 100,000 tons a year with a carbonate of lime content as high as 80 per cent – but this has done little to diminish the shoal or make it less of a navigational hazard. The tremendous amount of sand on the estuary margins has also led to serious problems inland, involving the burial of the medieval church of St Enodoc (see page 49). Prior to it being dug out of the sand in 1863 only the spire was showing. Today it lies in the centre of a golf course surrounded by a wall and tamarisk hedge, the approach being through the Daymer Estate with its substantial houses in a pinewood setting.

On the other side of the estuary is the older and more substantial centre of **Padstow**, once an important coastal and fishing port which merited a rail link with Wadebridge, Bodmin and the main line to the south-west peninsula. It remains a town of character with the atmosphere of a medieval fishing port in its narrow streets close to the harbour where slate-hung cottages cluster around the quayside overlooking the waters of the Camel Estuary. The original settlement probably dates from the founding in the sixth century of the cell of St Petroc on the site of the present church of thirteenth-century date. The fact that Padstow was a sizeable port even in medieval times meant that the much prized Caen stone could be imported from Normandy for use in church building. As a town Padstow has been very much influenced throughout history by the local Prideaux family who since the sixteenth century have lived in Place House above the town. The house is believed to be on the site of the monastery founded by St Petroc but later destroyed by the Danes in AD 981. Throughout history the town has relied on the sea for its prosperity, first to export the products of the hinterland like lead-ore, antimony, slates, grain, cheese and then the inevitable pilchard fishery. There is still a huge fish market, though the emphasis is on shell fish, crabs and lobsters. Boat building, once a very big employer of labour, still continues on a limited scale. The railway came late (1899) and finished early, so it had a minimal effect on the growth and character of the town unlike at nearby Newquay. Compared with some of the larger Cornish resorts Padstow comes as a pleasant relief, for it has managed to preserve much from its past.

The rock type and its response to wave attack have made the coastline between the Padstow Estuary and Newquay one of great variation. Softer rocks like slates readily succumb, and form shallow bays often with fine sandy beaches which now inevitably attract caravan and camping sites if not chalet development. Harder rocks include greenstone or the much sought after Cataclews stone which was formerly quarried on the north-west side of Harlyn Bay and extensively used for church building throughout north Cornwall. It is a basic igneous rock of finer grain than granite but not as hard, dark grey in colour and speckled with brown mica. Harlyn Bay has another claim to fame, for workmen digging foundations for a house in 1900 uncovered an

Iron Age cemetery of about 130 graves which had been buried by blown sand. Jewellery found with the burials indicates that it was in use in the fourth and third centuries BC. A small private museum with five of the original graves covered with glass roofs, exists on the site. Blown sand also caused the abandonment of the church of St Constantine, 1km (½ mile) inland from the coast.

One of the features of the coast is the large number of caves, some of which can be entered at low water though many can only be seen from a boat. The largest and most famous is at Trevelgue Head close to Newquay where the natural cave known as the Banqueting Hall is 183m (600ft) long and which, because of its fine acoustics, has been used for concerts. Other caves exist at Bedruthan Steps, with its fine coastal scenery of isolated stacks set amidst golden sands. This National Trust area is much visited and the resulting erosion has led to the laying of plastic matting along the cliff path. This is a problem that will have to be increasingly faced as the more popular sections of the coast attract large numbers of visitors during the summer season. Natural erosion by the sea has taken its toll of the Iron Age coastal fortress of Redcliffe just north of Bedruthan Steps. There are three defending ramparts but the area they formerly enclosed has been much reduced, a reminder that even on a 'hard' rock coast the ceaseless attack of the sea can be effective over a 2,000 year period.

Newquay is a holiday resort whose large hotels and boarding houses overshadow its long history as a port. It is one of the few harbours on the north Cornish coast sheltered from south-westerly gales, and therefore it is not surprising that as early as 1440 Bishop Lacy of Exeter persuaded the local people to build a harbour wall within which ships could lie at anchor. Inevitably this soon attracted a fishing fleet, especially as shoals of pilchards seemed to frequent the bay to the north. The Huer's House on Towan Head – the only really old building in Newquay – is a vantage point where a watcher would scan the bay for the tell-tale dark patch in the water before signalling to the waiting fishermen below. The harbour was very much improved by J. T. Austen, the builder of Par harbour, in 1838, and could now house a large fleet of fishing vessels. With the coming of the railway Newquay became a china-clay port for the pits lay only 16km (10 miles) to the east. Originally the railway ran right down to the harbour – the cutting in solid rock can still be seen – but now the terminus is well short of the coast. The railway brought the tourist, as well as Welsh slate and yellow brick, so that much in Newquay today is late Victorian, like the Headland Hotel, the Methodist church and substantial villa residences near the station. With so many holiday camps and caravan sites in the vicinity, Newquay is very much the local shopping centre, and its streets are likely to be crowded with visitors especially when rain drives them from the fine sandy beaches for which the resort is justly famous.

The town has grown considerably in recent years and now extends southwards to the head of the Gannel Estuary. This is a deeply penetrating inlet, but it is choked with sand and has long ceased to have any commercial value though a medieval port did exist near its mouth. Villages like Crantock and Cubert have a quiet charm, but they lie inland from the coast by reason of the encroaching nature of Penhale Sands – a great area of sand dunes 5km (3 miles) north of Perranporth which reach a height of over 60m (200ft) though they rest on a solid rock-base at depth. Perran Beach is a vast bay of sand exposed at low water and, facing due west, it acts as a continuous supply of blown shell sand which has been so banked up against the old cliff-line that the latter only shows through at one point. Legends abound about the lost town of Langarrow which once stretched from Crantock to Perranporth, and an act of divine retribution which caused the town to be buried overnight along with its inhabitants. Archaeological work has perhaps provided an explanation for this ancient legend for there is evidence of late Bronze Age settlements buried in the sand. Whatever took place in prehistoric times, there was certainly sand movement in the medieval period, as evidenced by the story of St Piran's oratory, dating perhaps from the sixth or seventh century (see page 48).

St Agnes Beyond Perranporth the isolated hill of St Agnes Beacon dominates the coastland. In the past the area around has been ripped apart in the search for metals, mainly tin and copper, and even the coast shows it, for apart from the mines and associated ruined buildings on the cliff-face there are the tiny ports which at one time occupied every available cove. St Agnes is very much a nineteenth-century mining settlement though it has some sixteenth-century cottages around the church. Now the whole district has its old Cornish engine houses dominating the skyline in all directions, fenced off mine shafts, and scattered cottages with their smallholdings carved out of the waste, as the sole remains. John Opie, one of the most famous of Cornish artists, was born close by at Harmony Cot near Trevellas Cove. Opie would hardly recognise the place today with its night spot, restaurant, and gliding club headquarters on the coastland behind. Trevaunance Cove, where the steep valley from St Agnes drops down to the sea, was the scene of many attempts by the Tonkin family to provide a harbour where ores could be loaded and shipped. All their efforts came to nothing, the last in the 1920s, with now only a heap of rubble to show for past endeavours.

Portreath achieved more success in terms of harbour development though it was always a difficult port to enter during the winter months and tons of ore would accumulate on the quayside as vessels rode out the storms before negotiating the narrow entrance. The dock was built by Lord de Dunstanville with the dual purpose of importing coal to work the pumping engines at his Camborne and Redruth mines and of exporting their tin and copper ores. He was also responsible for building a tramway, which included a steep incline worked by a stationary engine, from the plateau top down to the harbour. Although the track has gone its line up the hillside can still be discerned. The harbour, too, survives though the port has now been bought up by a development company and houses erected where the ore dumps once lay.

Reskajeage Cliffs provide a short break in the mining landscape and, as they are now under the care of the National Trust, will remain inviolate. The road runs close to the edge so that even for the motorist it is but a short walk across springy turf and heath to enjoy the view. Broken and continually battered by the sea, the cliffs now have a multiplicity of shapes, with angular promonotories projecting between cavernous inlets. All this diversity stands out in marked contrast to the billiard-top flatness of the coastland behind, itself the product of marine abrasion in the distant past.

Once across Red River there is an immediate change of coastal scene for the cliffs quickly give way to the vast area of sand dunes which extends all the way to Hayle. At Gwithian blown sand has covered a former Bronze Age settlement which has been dated to between 1400 and 1200 BC, and careful excavation has shown that there were once square cultivated fields enclosed by thorn hedges, and even revealed the scratch marks left by the wooden ploughs used at the time. There is nothing to see now but the site is interesting for it proves that the present dunes must have formed since that time. They could even be considerably later, for nearby on the same dunes there was once the oratory of St Gothian (a corruption of Gwithian) dating from the seventh century. The foundations of the tiny building were found in 1828 by a local farmer who used the remains as a cowshed for a while before they became totally ruinous. There was an adjacent cemetery as well as baptistry, and many believe there was once a village as well. All have now gone.

Hayle St Ives Bay, with its inlet to Hayle, was a favoured entry point for prehistoric invaders and, being one of the few natural harbours on the coast, continued to prove useful in later centuries. During the height of the Cornish mining revolution, Hayle became both an important port and an industrial town. Today it is dominated by the huge coal-burning power station, but this is only the successor of a large number of

Botallack tin mine, north of Cape Cornwall, with its ruined engine houses which once held machinery to haul the tin ores from the undersea workings

former industrial enterprises. The huge ironworks of Messrs Harvey with their furnaces, foundries and tall chimneys once dominated the town, for the firm was the foremost builder of steam engines, not only for draining the Cornish mines but also for land reclamation in Holland. The early eighteenth-century smelting works are remembered in the name of a suburb, Copperhouse, and there were tin smelters nearby. A rail link with the Camborne-Redruth area was built in 1837, though it was another twenty years before Hayle was joined to the main-line system at Penzance. Coal, timber, sulphur and oil are still brought into the port, though the shallow approach limits the size of vessels. Across the harbour is Phillack with its fifteenth-century parish church and some older cottages, many using the black scoriae of the old copper slag as building stone. On the other arm of the estuary and en route for St Ives is Lelant, once an important medieval seaport and housing the mother church of St Ives. It has little to show of its antiquity for it is largely a villa suburb of Hayle. Carbis Bay, a little further on along the St Ives road, is a modern resort with a holiday camp atmosphere.

St Ives It is surprising that this town with its fine natural sheltered harbour should not have become a parish of its own until 1826. Its fine fifteenth-century church dominates the waterfront and is one of the finest buildings of its type in Cornwall having been a chapel-of-ease to Lelant. Whatever the reason for its tardy ecclesiastical recognition, the town flourished from medieval times onwards, first on account of its fisheries and later because of its artistic associations and tourist invasion. John Smeaton built the pier in 1767, though this was subsequently lengthened in the nineteenth century when the fishermen's chapel of St Leonard at the pier's inner end was extensively restored. Although the waterfront now has its restaurants, gift shops, ships chandlers and amusement centres, it was once dominated by pilchard cellars and curing houses which can still be seen though now adapted to other uses. Once the branch railway arrived tourists flocked in, attracted by the narrow, steep curving, cobbled streets and alleys, typically 'Cornish' though not in the same sense as those of Mevagissey or Polperro. Artists had arrived before the tourist invasion, with Whistler, Sickert, Brangwyn and others working here (see page 156). More recently Dame Barbara Hepworth, the sculptor, and Bernard Leach, the potter, found sanctuary here. Two artists' societies have grown up, the Penwith Society and the St Ives Society. There are a number of excellent exhibition galleries including the former house and studio of Barbara Hepworth following her death in 1975.

With the greenstone forming St Ives Head and the metamorphosed rocks formed by contact with the hot granite magmas, the coast towards Land's End takes on a grander character. At Cape Cornwall granite itself forms the entire cliff-face and, with its vertical jointing and false horizontal bedding planes, the characteristic castellated appearance becomes more common. Greenstone forms the prominent peninsula of Gurnard's Head while the many coves and zawns (the local name for narrow clefts in the cliff-face) often result from the removal of the softer tin or copper lodes by the sea. Between Pendeen and Cape Cornwall there has been much past mining along the cliff face, including the famous Botallack mine where the former mine buildings perch precariously on a ledge just above the sea. Above are the remains of the storage sheds, flues and the former substantial manager's residence – now a museum and restaurant. Botallack closed in 1912 but other coastal mines continued to work in the Cape Cornwall area. The Geevor mine near Pendeen, with its huge unsightly sheds, continues in being, having taken over some of the workings of the original and highly productive Levant mine.

Apart from mining this coastland of Penwith, with its flat shelf nestling under the granite hills of the interior, has long been favoured for settlement. There are many prehistoric sites at places like Zennor, Porthmeor and Lower Boscaswell, each with its small irregular fields of Iron Age date surrounded by thick granite walls, dotting the landscape. Both the coast and the coastal shelf are worthy of a day's exploration on foot, for to simply drive along the narrow, twisting road is to miss the true character of this unique coastal landscape.

Land's End After the primitive and unspoiled setting of the Penwith hamlets and farms, the furthermost point of the English mainland comes as something of a shock, although it is not really very different from that other terminal point, John o'Groats, in its commercialism. The huge car park and dominating hotel proclaim its chief function and the bare granite, now stripped of its thin turf cover shows how many take advantage of standing on the very edge of England. All must have been different when the artist J. M. W. Turner came here and painted the scene with its intricate cliff patterning and the views out to the Longships light, only some 3km (2 miles) distant. The Scillies are much more difficult to pick out for it requires a day of clear polar air to bring out their low outlines on the distant horizon. A little to the north lies Sennen Cove, once an important fishing port but now largely dependent on tourism and so rather lifeless in winter.

Although the whole of the south coast of Penwith from Land's End round to Mousehole is formed of granite, such is the nature of the rock and the way it has been carved out by the sea that there is no lack of variety in the coastal scene. The cliff walk from Land's End south-eastwards to Gwennap Head is one of the finest in the South West. Offshore are the islets of the Armed Knight (named from its appearance) and Enys Dodman, a huge archway of stone. At Pordenack Point the granite cliffs are over 60m (200ft) high and seem to have been built with huge blocks of stone carefully set one on top of another, while beyond lies the first of the logan (rocking) stones. Gwennap Head is reached after a further 3km (2 miles) and in many ways it is a much more exciting land's end to the peninsula. The Cornish name of Tol-Pend-Penwith (the holed headland) is more descriptive, for here a deep funnel formed by the collapse of a cave roof descends to the sea. From the shore the fine columns of weather-beaten granite, sometimes likened to Gothic spires, look most impressive.

On the lee side of Gwennap Head lies the hamlet of **Porthgwarra** where the boats (once pursuing lucrative lobster-fishing around the Runnel Stone offshore) are hauled up the granite ramp. The next valley has the fifteenth-century church of St Leven (which can also be reached by road) with its ancient cross, well and ruined baptistry nearby, all pointing to an original Celtic foundation. A little further east, on National Trust land, stands the famous Logan Stone weighing over 60 tons which Lieutenant Goldsmith overturned in 1824 simply to prove what the Cornish historian William Borlase had claimed to be impossible. For his pains he had to replace the stone in its original position. Those who visit the stone should also include in their walk nearby Treryn Castle, an Iron Age promontory fort with three impressive defensive ramparts. Much more modern is the Minack Theatre set in a natural amphitheatre halfway down the cliff-face where, during summer evenings, open-air plays are performed. The approach is through Porthcurno, past the Cable and Wireless Training Centre. The last of the major coves before Mousehole is reached at **Lamorna**, now well known for its hotel, but once one of the principal exporting ports for granite even though there was no true harbour. Prior to the quarrying which scarred its sides the valley was a well known beauty spot of the Victorians, who admired the setting of watermills amongst the hazel and alder copses lining the small stream.

Mousehole has acquired a reputation amongst visitors that is difficult to understand. Perhaps it is the name which attracts or the hope of quaintness which every visitor to nearby Penzance expects of Cornwall. The original name, Port Enys, is more descriptive in that it speaks of the offshore isle of St Clement which afforded protection for the harbour in easterly gales. The settlement was almost completely destroyed by the Spanish in 1595, only the manor house in Keigwen Street escaping and even this has been more recently restored, though its fine porch, supported on granite columns, is probably original. For the rest the town consists of narrow streets huddled round the harbour which was much improved in 1861. The parochial centre is 1km (½ mile) up the valley at Paul.

Newlyn In spite of its declining fishing industry and the rashness of the local authority in pre-war days when it razed the old fishing quarter to the ground, there is still a hint of past glory. The fishing fleet now goes farther afield than formerly with mackerel one of their principal catches. On a smaller scale, lobster and crab fishing provide a living for a few. It was the attractiveness of the fishing community which led to the founding of the Newlyn School of artists in 1883 and the building of the large art gallery in 1895. Many of the young founding artists had been trained in France and favoured local outdoor studies as subjects rather than more formal studio painting. Although a few contemporary artists still live in Newlyn in recent years the school has been overshadowed by that of St Ives (see page 156). Newlyn's other claim to fame rests on its choice as the station for establishing the datum plane for measuring heights in the British Isles, following observations of mean-tide level here by the Ordnance Survey between 1915 and 1921.

Penzance Old railway posters used to promote Penzance and the sweep of shore around Mount's Bay as the English Riviera. Although of ancient origin and a stannary town right up to 1838, it was the coming of the railway in 1859 that brought it fame. Victorians flocked to this distant resort in search of milder winters and many eventually took up residence, introducing exotic plants and shrubs which were more at home in the Mediterranean than in Britain. The town always had a small harbour and shared the fishing with Newlyn, and today it is the transit port for the **Scilly Isles** (see pages 243–6) and a base-station for Trinity House who maintain the buoys and light-vessels around these dangerous coasts. The town is mainly early nineteenth-century in character with Market Jew Street having notable buildings, particularly the Market House of 1837. The parish church of St Mary lies on the headland which gives the town its name (*Pen*, headland; *sans*, holy).

Mount's Bay The road from Penzance around the edge of the bay towards Marazion lacks good views for the railway has appropriated the actual shoreline. Early in its life the railway had to pay the penalty for its exposed situation, for in 1869 about 152m (500ft) of the viaduct carrying the line was destroyed in a storm. As Marazion is approached and the railway has finally turned inland, views of St Michael's Mount open up, a gigantic rocky tor rising out of the sea. It was once part of the mainland – a nearby submerged forest shows how sea level has risen – but now can only be approached across a low-water stone causeway or by boat when the tide is in. Crowning the 70m (230ft) high summit of the rock are monastic remains which date back to the reign of Edward the Confessor who granted the site to the Abbey of Mont St Michel on the Normandy coast, to which it bears a striking resemblance. Now under the care of the National Trust it can be visited during the summer months. It is in part a fortress as well as a monastery, and during the 1870s a new wing of residential buildings was added. On a clear spring day the sight of the abbey seen against the light is of a jewel set in a sparkling sea.

Marazion itself is disappointing and has been ruined by the constant through traffic making its way along its narrow main street. Its cottages are spattered with dust and grime from the heavy lorries and there is little to suggest that it was once an important borough. After Marazion the main road leaves the coast, but it is still possible to reach the cliff edge down narrow lanes or by the Coast Path. The walk is rewarding for, though the cliffs are not high, there is a rich variety of colour and intricate detail, reflecting rock differences. The long point of the Greeb, really detached from the mainland except at low water, is formed of greenstone as is Cudden Point, 3km (2 miles) further along the coast. Between rocky headlands there are fine bay-head beaches like Praa Sands which inevitably has attracted the caravanners. The cliff path continues around Rinsey and Trewavas Heads, both formed of granite, and within a further 3km (2 miles) Porthleven comes into view.

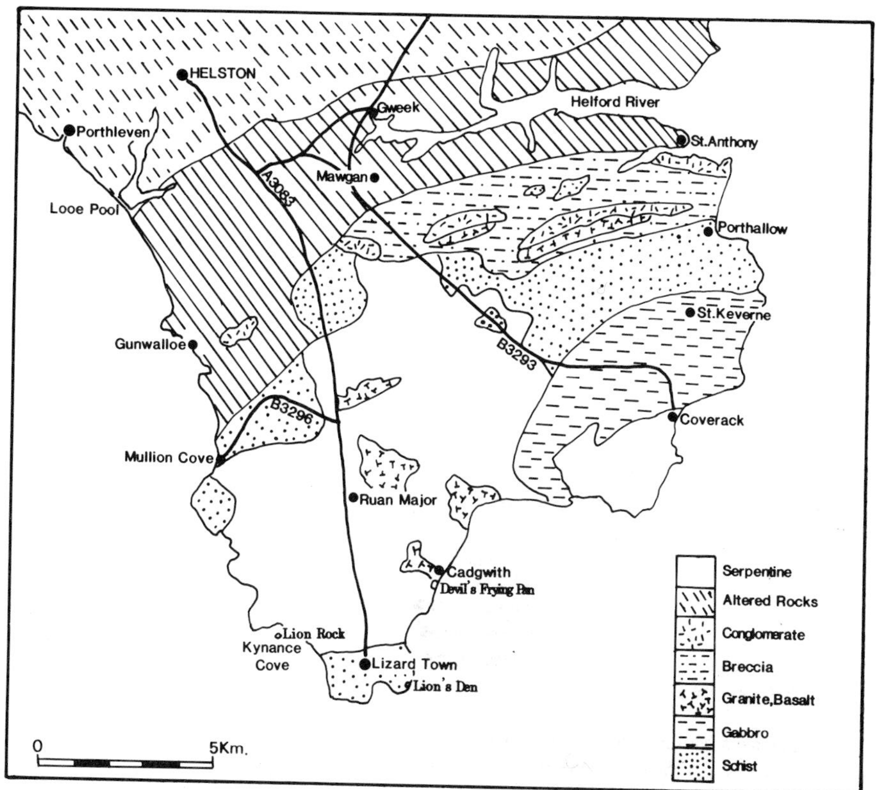

The complex geology of the Lizard

Porthleven, the port for Helston just over 3km (2 miles) inland, has a harbour facing directly south west, so that there has always been a tussle with the sea. In the early nineteenth century, trade in stone and copper ore necessitated the building of a commercial harbour but in 1824, within six years of completion, it was almost completely destroyed by a severe storm. Although quickly rebuilt, further storms inflicted damage and it was decided to fit lock gates to the inner harbour. Today it is still a working port with a boat-building yard and fish-canning works. The massive granite quays are lined with old fish cellars and salthouses along with the imposing Harbour House and Harbour Hotel, both of eighteenth-century date. Close to the harbour there is a geological curiosity – a huge boulder of microgranite standing isolated on the beach. Though something of an enigma it seems most likely to have been brought to its present position by ice and, if so, this represents the most southerly point of ice advance on the British mainland.

A walk southwards along the cliff edge from Porthleven brings one to Loe Bar, a 1km (½ mile) long ridge of fine shingle which has trapped the waters of Loe Pool in the valleys behind it. The fresh water of the pool formerly seeped through the shingle quite naturally, but now a culvert has been built through the shingle to drain off the surplus. In the past there have been dramatic happenings here after heavy rain when, as the level of water of the Pool rose by as much as 3m (10ft), the mills in the tributary valleys could not work. It was then that gangs of workmen would be brought in from Helston to cut a trench through the bar to release the pent up waters; once the lake level had fallen the sea would rapidly restore the breached bar. Much of the area around is owned by the National Trust which has provided visitors with a car park within a short distance of the northern end of the Pool.

Gunwalloe is an unexpectedly romantic spot for in the corner of the sandy cove a fourteenth-century church is tucked away under a promontory. The tower of an even older church was actually built into the rock and now stands isolated close by. It is best approached from the south via Poldhu Cove with the car park on the cliff top giving a fine view over the whole bay. The only jarring note to the fine coastal setting is the huge corrugated barn of the local farm. Poldhu is dominated by its huge hotel set conspicuously on the skyline. This too seems out of character with the natural setting.

Mullion Cove, the next accessible spot on the coast and now a National Trust harbour, shows a sense of care and good taste. The road up to Mullion village, sited on the exposed plateau top of the Lizard, was once used by fishermen to bring their catches inland. The tiny but well protected harbour now has only a few boats drawn up on the concrete ramp, but the old fish cellars survive along with the former mill-race. The Cornish name, Porth Mellin or Mill Cove tells the original purpose of the settlement long before it became yet another of the small Cornish ports engaged in the pilchard fishery. The harbour dries out at low water and is not easy to enter in storms because of the dangers of the offshore islet. The cliffs around are dark and foreboding but they give us the first taste of the rock serpentine for which the Lizard Peninsula is famous.

Kynance, though well known and rightly so because of its magnificent coastal scenery, can only be approached by car along a toll road which turns to the west about 1.6km (1 mile) north of Lizard Town. The cove itself and adjacent cliff top are owned by the National Trust and therefore saved from any possible commercialisation. To fully appreciate the setting it is best to approach near the time of low water when the bright yellow sandy beach is bared and stands out in marked contrast to the sombre tones of the cliff-face. Once described as the finest cove in the kingdom its beauty stems largely from the group of isolated stacks standing with their feet in the white foaming surf surging around them. The Victorian tourist gave them names like Asparagus Island (from the plant that grows on its top), Gull Rock and Bishop's Rock; caves with names like the Kitchen Parlour and the Devil's Mouth, and the blow-hole known as the Devil's Letter Box, complete the picture. The rock is almost entirely serpentine, black in its normal weathered appearance but often variegated with stains of red, green and white steatites. To the north, towards Vellan Head, there is an outcrop of soapstone, first discovered in 1755 by a Mr Chaffers and then much sought after for the manufacture of porcelain. Chaffers later went on to found the Worcester Porcelain Company and the quarry was much used until a better and more accessible supply was found. For the ordinary visitor Kynance has an entrancing beauty and variety which it would be hard to equal even on this fine unspoiled coastline. For the geologist the interest lies in the serpentine and the way in which the sea has removed crushed beds of the rock along fault planes or opened up former dykes of gneiss, a softer rock and therefore more easily removed, to create the succession of stacks, caves, penetrating fissures and blow-holes.

Lizard Town is straggling and somewhat depressing in that one expects more from the main settlement of this fine unspoilt peninsula. It is best to make straight for Lizard Point, 1km (¾ mile) to the south. From the car park there is a pleasant cliff-top walk both to the east and west. That to the east skirts the lighthouse (built in 1753 but modernised this century) and then leads on to the Lion's Den, a great blow-hole formed through the collapse of the roof of a former cave. Just east of the lighthouse there is the isolated stack known as the Bumble. The point itself is scenically grand though most visitors have their attention diverted by the serpentine sheds where the green stone is highly polished and then made into a great variety of ornaments and objects, not all of the highest artistic taste. The cliff path to the west soon leaves all this behind as it makes for Polpeor Cove with its fine cave accessible at low water.

Bedruthan Steps, on the north Cornish coast, with its succession of stacks reminiscent of Kynance Cove on the western coast of the Lizard Peninsula

The east side of the Lizard Peninsula is more sheltered than the side facing Mount's Bay and offers more natural and safer harbours. Landewednack has a tiny harbour at Church Cove where the lifeboat was once stationed. **Cadgwith,** a little to the north, is more enticing to the visitor with its thatched cottages huddled together at the mouth of the deeply cut valley. Boats still take out visitors in search of bass and pollack, though lobster fishing is more profitable. Pilchards were once the main catch and the old 'palaces' still remain near the head of the beach. Everywhere is a general air of contentment as the older people congregate around the boat-repair sheds. In spring the farmers come down to the cove to gather the seaweed cast up by the winter storms and lay it in the early potato trenches. A short walk to the south of Cadgwith brings one to the Devil's Frying Pan, another of the blow-holes caused by the collapse of a former cave roof. This one is particularly impressive and interesting in that it was formed only just over a hundred years ago in 1868.

The coast to the north and east of Cadgwith is inaccessible except on foot. Stumpy promontories like Carrick and Chynhalls Point have their Iron Age promontory forts taking advantage of the natural defensive qualities of the site. **Coverack** is a larger port than Cadgwith for it has none of the topographic restrictions of the latter, but this makes it less appealing to the tourist though more favoured for retirement. **Porthoustock** is yet another former small fishing port, but now taken over by a quarrying company for the export of stone (gabbro). Abandoned quarries lie to the north on the way round to Porthallow which has retained a part-time interest in fishing.

Helford River, a ria (drowned river valley) par excellence, has reasonably deep water near its entrance and so became an ideal sheltered anchorage for shipping and was much used during World War II. The many branching creeks, former tributary valleys, break the continuity of the steep wooded slopes running down to the water's edge. Towards its head the ria becomes very shallow and large flats appear at low water. Gweek was once a small port where colliers could tie up and unload their cargoes once a fortnight on a spring tide, but oyster culture and yachts dominate present-day activity. Helford village, much nearer the sea, once had aspirations as a port but now relies on its collection of thatched cottages to arrest the visitor's attention. In this quiet backwater there is none of the bustle of Polperro or Mevagissey, and the fact that no sizeable settlement has ever grown up on the banks of Helford river is perhaps a reflection of the nearness of Falmouth.

Falmouth With its much larger, deeper and more branching ria than Helford it was inevitable that the Fal Estuary should become much more important commercially. Earlier settlements and ports like Penrhyn and Truro tended to lie some distance inland, partly for reasons of safety, but once this danger of sea attack had passed, Falmouth was able to grow rapidly as a port and make increasing use of its deep-water berths. When Henry VIII built the nearby Pendennis Castle late in his reign there was no settlement at Falmouth save a single cottage and this was still the picture at the end of the sixteenth century. Just over a decade later in 1613 Sir John Killigrew founded a town, much against the wishes of the residents of Penrhyn and Truro. Yet in spite of its late artificial plantation there is little in Falmouth to suggest a planned layout. The main centre of the town is an axial street, known in its various parts as High Street, Market Street, Church Street and Arwenack Street, lying close to the estuary shore. It is here that the oldest buildings of the town have survived, including the church dedicated to King Charles the Martyr (1662), the Customs House (*c*1820) and the Royal Cornwall Polytechnic (1833). The town received its charter in 1661 and this was followed in 1670 by Sir Peter Killigrew building the quay which was to determine the fortunes of the place over the next two hundred years. Almost immediately Falmouth was chosen as a mail packet station, a situation that lasted until 1852 when Southampton took over. But all was not lost for within a decade docks had been built and the town quickly established a reputation for ship repairing. Recently, in spite of the building of a huge dry dock to accommodate 90,000 ton tankers, there has been a threat of closure and there is much anxiety about future prospects.

Falmouth the resort seems more secure in this respect for it has much to offer the visitor with its fine sandy beaches, spectacular cliff scenery close at hand and town of character. The resort quarter lies mainly on the seaward side of the peninsula, and here the hotels and guest houses are strung out along the sea front. Overlooking the bay is Pendennis Castle with an approach road up to it from the marine drive (one-way traffic) which encircles the headland. Sub-tropical plants abound as a reminder of Falmouth's warm winter climate, adding a sense of dignity as well as setting the tone for the resort in an age where the brash and vulgar seem all too commonplace.

St Mawes looks across the mouth of the Fal to its larger neighbour though at one time it was the more important of the two. Its name commemorates the Welsh prince who turned monk in the sixth century and founded a cell close to a spring by the shore; the original well survives just above the Victory Inn. The present settlement is dominated by a string of houses, cottages and hotels which line the waterfront to take full advantage of the view over the estuary. At the end of the promenade lies the clover-leaf castle built by Henry VIII in 1542 to repel any French attack. St Mawes became a borough twenty years later and had two MPs until the Reform Bill of 1832. The parish church is curiously sited at St Just in Roseland (from *rhos* meaning heath). It lies almost at the water's edge on a side creek of the Fal and is one of the traditional landfalls of Joseph of Arimathea. More likely it was a secluded site favoured by a Celtic saint.

Between the Fal Estuary and St Austell

Bay, the coastline is a walker's delight though the going may be difficult in places. Using the South Cornwall Coast Path it is possible to explore much of this unspoiled cliff-line, with the tiny coastal hamlets and ports providing acceptable breaks. For those with less time to spare it is possible to make the occasional sally from the inland road down a deeply cut lane to the coast and then undertake a more limited exploration on foot.

Mevagissey is the only one of a group of former fishing ports on this stretch of coast-line to have survived to any extent from the days when the pilchard fishery was at its height and vast numbers were salted and packed for export to the Catholic countries of Europe. The three-storied buildings overlooking the quays give just a hint of this former flourishing trade, and although not on its former scale, fishing is still important and visitors can congregate around the harbour to watch the activities of the fleet. Tourism has been a saviour to the town though it creates problems, not the least being the car traffic using the narrow streets. Any visitor in summer would do well to park well outside the town. Better still would be a visit in early spring or late autumn when the full character of the slate-hung cottages can be appreciated.

The inner harbour dates originally from the sixteenth century but the outer works were only built in 1866 and in effect trebled the capacity of the port. When fishing was prosperous in Victorian times Mevagissey was dismissed as a place of dirt and smells; tourism has changed that as well as the character of the fishing to some extent, with boats to be hired for line fishing though crabbing is still very much the preserve of the locals.

Pentewan, 1.6km (1 mile) to the north, is in complete contrast for there is a vast sandy bay-head beach and an equally vast caravan park as part of the setting. Its present appearance however is deceptive for it was once a flourishing china-clay port, the harbour having been built in the 1820s by a local landowner, Sir Charles Hawkins, as a rival to nearby Charlestown. Dock gates were fitted so that vessels could load at all times, and a tramway ran down from the pits around St Austell, at first horse-drawn but later converted to steam traction. For a time the port flourished but with easterly gales liable to pile up sand and block the harbour entrance, Pentewan lost favour. In this century trade slackened off and the last vessel loaded its cargo here in 1940. The old tramway link is virtually unrecognisable, but Hawkins's church and cottage rows still remain.

Charlestown is a gem with its colour-washed cottages overlooking the deeply set lock basin. Only small vessels can pass through the narrow entrance and then tie up waiting to be loaded from lorries which tip their dusty cargoes down chutes into the ships' holds. The whole is a man-made creation, the idea of Sir Charles Rashleigh (hence the name) who in 1790 called on Sir John Smeaton to design a port. Initially horse-drawn waggons trundled down from the inland clay pits but, unlike at Pentewan, no railway link was ever built. Over the years the small harbour has lost ground to neighbouring Par, but the settlement still remains a good example of late eighteenth-century planning.

Par Harbour, 5km (3 miles) to the east and at the side of a sand-filled bay, is later and more commodious than both Pentewan and Charlestown. It was developed through the enterprise of Joseph Treffry who in 1837 became sole owner of the rich Fowey Consols copper mine and within five years had built Par Harbour to export the copper ore as well as having erected a lead and silver smelter nearby. Once the copper veins ran out Par turned to china clay as its principal export, and Treffry was again to the fore in forging railway links with the inland pits. The trade still flourishes today and vessels usually jostle for the limited quayside space. Huge sheds where the china clay is processed before export surround the harbour, and everywhere there is a coating of white dust from the works. Even Par Sands are white, but this does not seem to deter the thousands who caravan nearby.

Lobster pots at Polperro, where Cornish 'quaintness' attracts hordes of summer visitors who crowd the narrow streets

Fowey on a ria like Falmouth has an equally fine natural harbour. There is greater evidence of a former sunken river valley here for the slopes are steep and the town has to cling to the hillside. Most of the older part is around the waterfront near the church of St Nicholas (originally St Finnbarr). Above is the house, known as Place, which the Treffry family created as a battlemented mansion surrounded by high walls out of an earlier fifteenth-century building. It was in the late medieval period that Fowey achieved its greatest glory as a port when, from a base on the penetrating creek, sailed the 'Fowey Gallants' – nothing more than pirates who pounced on any shipping they could find in the western Channel. This brought inevitable reprisals, first from the Spanish and later from the French who burned down the town in 1456. The oldest buildings therefore date from shortly after this time and include the Ship Hotel, basically fifteenth-century but renovated in 1570, and once the town house of the Rashleigh family. The Town Hall of 1792 also embodies a much earlier building, and the modern façades of houses in many of the streets bordering the waterfront conceal much earlier interiors. The nineteenth century saw a spurt in building once the Victorians had found the place. New substantial houses were built towards St Catherine's Point castle ruins including The Haven, once the home of Sir Arthur Quiller-Couch who used Fowey in his Troy Town novels. Further south, towards Gribbin Head, is Menabilly, once the country house of the Rashleigh family and later the home of the novelist Daphne du Maurier who also used the vicinity for the setting of some of her books.

Fowey is not the port it once was but still has a considerable china-clay trade. It was this that led to the building of the railway from Lostwithiel in 1864, although fortunately the railway never penetrated the centre of the town but instead led to the formation of a small industrial suburb around the quays which lie upstream. Although taking second place to Par in terms of tonnage of china-clay shipped Fowey's future is quite bright as the fine natural harbour is now proving its worth for leisure craft while nearby beaches like Readymoney Cove provide excellent bathing.

The coast to the east of the Fowey Estuary is quite unspoiled with cliffs of slate, in their variegated colours of green, red and grey, giving rise to a jagged and spectacular outline. It is difficult of access except on foot, but this is all the more attractive in that it counteracts the crowded places like Fowey and Polperro.

Polperro has been so overcooked commercially that much of its original charm has disappeared under the overlay of gift shops, pisky parlours and the like. This is a pity, for the harbour area, at the end of a long winding valley approach, still epitomises the Cornish fishing town of the past. Its name possibly derives from St Peter's Chapel which once stood on Chapel Hill (*Pol Peyre*, Peter's Pool). Although the port is of some antiquity it never had a parish church of its own for it lies in Lansallos parish and has only the chapel-of-ease of St John the Baptist built in 1838. When the fishing industry was at its height, the harbour was full of boats and the area around was the scene of great activity. The lower part of each harbour cottage was generally used as a fish cellar, the second or dwelling floor being reached by steps and often with a porch (orrel) covering the entrance to keep out the winds. The harbour walls have been damaged on numerous occasions, even though they look sturdy enough to withstand any storm, and during bad weather the narrow entrance is usually closed to fully protect the boats lying at anchor within the small 1ha (3 acre) harbour. The Victorian tourist who ventured here came not only in search of the picturesque but also to view the submerged forest on the beach just inside the old quay or to scour the nearby cliffs for the 'Polperro fossil' (a species of Pteraspis), which has left a sizeable imprint on the slate rocks.

Looe, East and West, are twin boroughs which date back to as early as 1201 when they were artificially created as towns on opposite banks of the river estuary. East Looe, the larger and more exciting of the two, was cut out of St Martin's parish, whose church lies 3km (2 miles) away to the north east. West Looe had its mother church at Talland, an even more remote and distant spot than St Martin's. Both required a chapel-of-ease, that at West Looe being used as a church again after a period when it functioned as a Guildhall. Unlike at Fowey there is a bridge connection across the harbour, and this gives a fine view of the two settlements. The first bridge, downstream from the present, was built as early as 1436 but was replaced by the present granite structure in 1853.

East Looe, with its Old Guildhall fitted with exterior stone stairs and wooden balustrade, has the greater appeal; and though its narrow twisting streets are crowded in summer, there is much to attract with houses going back to the sixteenth and seventeenth centuries. At one end lies the parish church, the former chapel-of-ease of St Mary dating from 1259. Beyond there is the promenade and the fine sandy beach which makes East Looe a resort. Fishing is still carried on, and the waterfront is not without interest for the port has become a centre for the sport of shark fishing. Over the past 150 years many attempts have been made to make fuller commercial use of the Looe Estuary. In 1828 a canal link was forged with inland Liskeard but such was the nature of the terrain that it had to climb 198m (650ft) in 10km (6 miles) using no fewer than 24 locks. The railway of 1869 ultimately took over, but had to face the same problems so that loaded trucks running downhill hauled the empties up the incline. Granite was the main export and it was from the quays of East Looe (now the car park) that stone was shipped to build Westminster Bridge and the Thames Embankment.

West Looe has less to commend it for it is more Victorian in character, much of it being rebuilt after the arrival of the railway. One kilometre (½ mile) out to sea lies Looe Island which, in spite of legends associating it with Joseph of Arimathea, has little by way of tangible remains save a group of monastic cells which were once linked to Glastonbury Abbey, hence the Joseph legend.

From Looe round to Rame Head, including the open Whitesand Bay, the coast is largely formed of slate strata and subject to a surprising amount of erosion in places. In the past there has been slipping and mass movement of the cliffs especially at the western end of Downderry. Nearness to Plymouth has led to a certain amount of

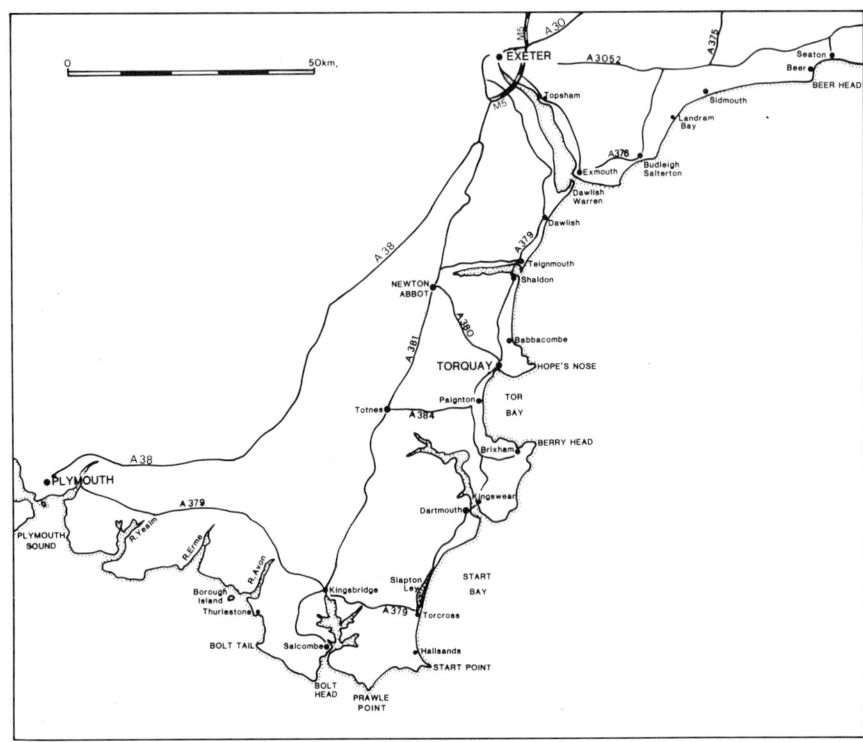

The coast of south-east Devon

development of variable quality. That at Downderry takes the form of elaborate Mediterranean-style houses set at intervals along the cliff-face with palms and maritime pines planted haphazardly to give an apparently natural setting. A raised beach forms an undercliff and is occupied by less substantial chalets.

Portwrinkle, a few miles further to the east has more character, though it is somewhat dominated by its large hotel and adjacent golf course. It has the only harbour on this stretch of coastline but even this is primitive. A recently built jetty inspires a little more confidence than the old breakwater of piled boulders, but it would need an expert seaman to bring even a small boat into the harbour when rough seas are running. Yet fishermen once used the tiny port to set out for pilchard fishing in the Channel and then make their return before nightfall. At the western end of the village near the harbour there is a fifteenth-century pilchard cellar.

Whitesand Bay (named from its light-coloured sand) stretches away to the east to end in the peninsula of Rame Head. It is worthwhile making for this southerly point both for its fine views and for the tiny chapel, measuring only 6m (20ft) by 3m (10ft), dating back at least to 1397 and dedicated to St Michael. Like so many similar buildings in prominent cliff-top positions it could well have functioned as a lighthouse or navigational beacon in medieval times (see page 139).

South Devon

Plymouth Sound is the largest of the rias which typify much of the coastline of the South-west Peninsula. Although a large settlement developed on land between two of the main branches, Plymouth Sound was too wide and open to give natural shelter so that between 1812 and 1840 a 3km (2 mile) long breakwater was built with a lighthouse at its western end. Over 4 million tons of limestone blocks were dumped into the waters of the Sound to form this breakwater, and immediately led to the creation of a large safe anchorage, of use mainly to naval vessels. Between the breakwater and the Hoe lies Drake's Island, formerly St Nicholas's Island and named after the chapel which once stood on it. On a clear day it is possible to see the Eddystone lighthouse, 24km (15 miles) away to the south. The present lighthouse, the fourth, was built of granite blocks and completed in 1882.

As far as the entrance to Salcombe Harbour the south Devon coast is remarkable for the number of rias which, although small in themselves, do form barriers to communication and therefore give rise to a number of isolated peninsulas. The coastline of each has to be explored separately down narrow, sunken lanes which lead off from the main A379 road. The South Devon Coast Path similarly has to make inland diversions to cross many of the inlets, though in the summer foot-ferries operate across some. The rias, like the much larger Plymouth Sound, were formed by the drowning of the former river valleys during the post-glacial rise of sea level. This reached its peak about 4000 BC, and since that time the drowned valleys have become choked with sand to a considerable depth. At the mouth of the Erme, for example, the true rock bed and former valley floor lies almost 24m (80ft) below the present sand flats.

The coastline is cliffed throughout, and formed of rocks belonging to the Dartmouth Slate formation. Though rugged, the cliffs are seldom vertical; much more typical is the profile which slopes gradually down from the 91m (300ft) high plateau surface. Narrow inlets often serrate the lower cliff especially in the section south of Noss Mayo, and offshore reefs and small islets are common. Apart from one or two small sections it is a lonely shore with the cliff-top a blaze of colour from the spring flowers, or bathed in deep russet tones from the dying bracken of autumn.

Wembury village lies just inland but its church, dedicated to St Werburgh, is on the coast, its fourteenth-century tower a well known landmark for mariners making for Plymouth. It was described by Galsworthy in *Swan Song* when Soames Forsyte made his return to the ancestral home.

Newton and Noss Mayo lie on either bank of a side creek of the Yealm. The former has

Coastal features of south Devon from Bigbury to Start Bay

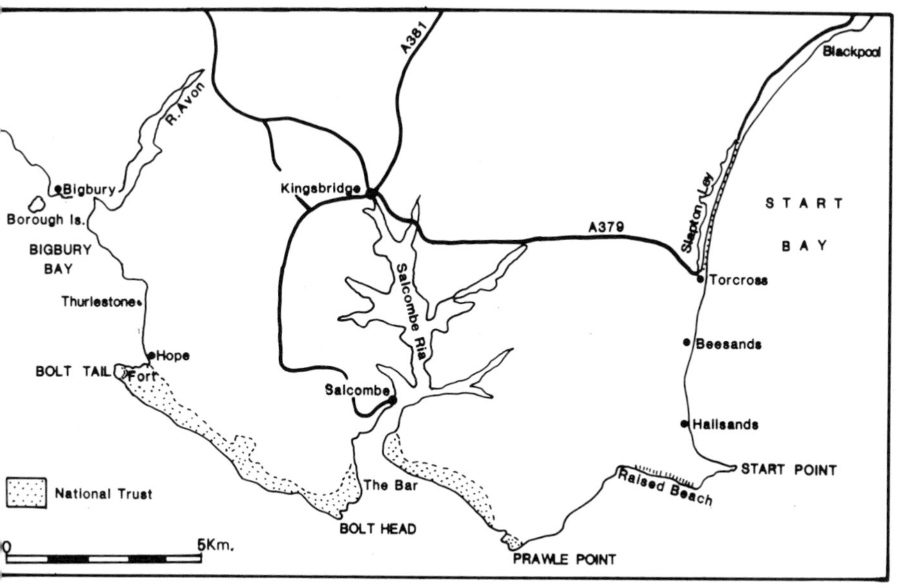

Salcombe Harbour, a shallow but deeply penetrating ria whose upper reaches are navigable as far as Kingsbridge

its hotels and villas, while the latter owes much of its character to the local squire, Lord Revelstoke, who built the church in 1882. The original parish church of St Peter is on the cliff top near Stoke Point and was once used as a navigational beacon. It is now an overgrown ruin following its abandonment in the 1870s, but the area is well worth visiting if only for the superb coastal scenery brought about by the massive slates of Stoke Point.

Bigbury has been developed as a minor resort and retirement area with villas and bungalows ranged along the gently sloping cliffs overlooking Borough Island. The latter was formerly known as La Burgh and once had a chapel dedicated to St Michael (no remains) and its inhabitants participated in the pilchard fisheries. Now it has an enormous hotel on its inner side which can be reached by a curious elevated tractor even when the tide covers the sand-flat linking Borough Island with the mainland. At low water it is possible to walk across the sand-link and if the visit is made in spring there is a carpet of blue on the island from the abundant wild squill.

Thurlestone is another place which has been developed in recent years for those who wish to retire and spend long hours on the golf course. Its name is much older and derives from the distinctive holed stack (Anglo Saxon *thirl* = hole) which lies on the coastal platform to the south. Apart from its shape it is unusual in that it is formed of a red conglomerate in contrast to the slates of the nearby cliffs and the offshore reef by which it is approached.

Hope consists of two parts, Inner and Outer, though both are on the coast and only separated by a narrow pointed peninsula. Inner Hope, with its rock-girt harbour was once the centre of a flourishing pilchard fishery, but is now given over to lobster fishing, artists and tourists. Outer Hope has its thatched cottages, hotel and boarding houses. Both settlements lie in the lee of Bolt Tail, which owes its prominence to beds of

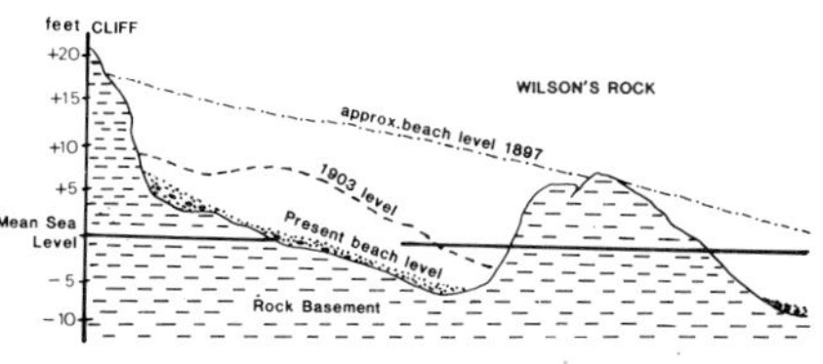

Beach profiles of Hallsands showing the great loss of shingle

green hornblende-schist, a tenacious and much altered rock which resists the attack of the sea much better than slate or sandstone. Along with the closely comparable mica-schist it outcrops along the entire coast to the east as far as Start Point, broken only by the gap formed by the entrance to Salcombe harbour. The first section from Bolt Tail to Bolt Head is entirely owned by the National Trust and makes a magnificent walk. Everywhere there is a gradual slope from the path which hugs the plateau edge down to the rock foreshore. Tiny sandy coves like Soar Mill punctuate the grey rock-skirt of the cliff base. In places the schist is overlain with a considerable thickness of a light-brown clay known as 'head' which was formed during the Ice Age. Unlike the schist it is liable to mass movement down the cliff face, especially in the section below Bolberry Down. At Bolt Tail, where the mica-schist is replaced by the much greener hornblende-schist, there is a promontory fort dating back to the Iron Age with ramparts protecting the landward side of this natural defensive site.

Salcombe, 1.6km (1 mile) up the ria and on its western slopes, has made use of its sheltered harbour since earliest times. On this inlet it was inevitable that a small port would develop, for above this point the numerous branching creeks become shallow and dry out into extensive mud-flats at low water. Today the lower part of the estuary is filled with moored craft of all types, and the water's edge lined with boatyards, ship's chandlers etc. There was a time when merchant ships would tie up alongside the short quay and unload their delicacies from the West Indies and Mediterranean countries. The town first came into prominence in the mid-eighteenth century when its situation, mild climate and fine scenery began to attract residents who built substantial villas. One of these was later occupied by the famous historian, J. A. Froude, a Devon man. It is said that while staying here Tennyson went out yachting, an experience which influenced him when writing his famous poem 'Crossing the Bar',

Hallsands in 1897, before the removal of the beach shingle led to the gradual destruction of the fishing hamlet but other places make the same claim. There is certainly a rocky bar which severely restricts the entrance and undoubtedly has prevented Salcombe from becoming a larger port. Today it is content to live off tourism and its associated spin-off. Since it was 'discovered' in the post-war years its narrow streets have become overcrowded and uncomfortable with summer visitors. Fortunately a foot ferry connects with the other shore at East Portlemouth and gives access to another unspoiled stretch of coastline running eastwards to Start Point. Towards Bolt Head there are the exotic gardens of Sharpitor (National Trust) where palms and other trees and shrubs from warmer climates flourish in the terraced garden. The house is now the Overbecks Museum of great local interest.

The coastal setting eastwards is largely a repetition of the stretch between Bolt Head and Bolt Tail, with the schists again giving rise to a rocky cliff-line, largely draped with 'head'. To the east of Prawle Point (Anglo Saxon for look-out), in Lannacombe Bay and beyond, the head forms a prominent coastal bench which because of its sheltered, south-facing slopes is ideal for growing early vegetables. Start Point lies in the distance – a rugged spine of grey, contorted rock with the lighthouse near its extremity.

Start Bay The coastline to the north is in complete contrast to what has gone before. There are new rock types to diversify the coastal setting, and a different 'grain' to the shoreline. With the various outcrops of rock running west to east, there is a succession of ridges and valleys. The sea has been able to wear back the ridge ends and infill the lower valleys by throwing a shingle bar across them, resulting in a remarkably straight coastline running northwards for several miles to the village of Strete.

Hallsands, formerly a fishing hamlet but now only a collection of ruined cottages set on a rocky shelf at the cliff foot, finally succumbed in 1917 after being wrecked by a storm. The disaster really began in 1897 when a contractor was given permission to take away shingle from the beach for use at Devonport. In a few years ½ million tons was removed and the beach lowered up to 3.7m (12ft) in places. Piecemeal erosion began shortly afterwards and although concrete sea walls were built, they proved much less effective than the natural shingle beach in giving protection to the village. Now its ruins, often quoted as a supreme example of man's folly in interfering with nature, act as a magnet for those tourists who know the story.

Beesands has been more fortunate and has survived, though not without occasional storm damage. Some of its cottages still house local fishermen while others are used by weekenders. Boats have to be drawn high up the shingle beach out of reach of storm waves – a difficult haul after a day out crab-fishing or wrestling with a shoal of mullet.

Torcross, at the southern end of Slapton Sands (a misnomer for the 'sand' is formed of fine shingle), has some pretence as a roadside resort with a hotel, café and shops as well as a row of cottages almost on the beach. This nearly proved their undoing during a storm in January 1979 when many were damaged. The result of bad initial siting has proved costly in terms of new sea defences.

Slapton village is sited a little inland high on the old cliff-line which formed before the present shingle bar led to the development of the freshwater lagoon of Slapton Ley. It has a Field Study Centre for students interested in natural history. There were formerly two lagoons but the upper (northern) one is now largely infilled and reed covered. Open water persists in the lower lagoon and provides sport-fishing as well as a haven for wintering birds. In the last century the osprey was to be seen. The bay bar, which has led to the development of the lagoon, is of some antiquity, though the present coastal road is only just over a hundred years old. In the past the shingle bar has occasionally been breached by storms, though the last time this occurred on a large scale was 1824. Seakale grew wild on the shingle bank and was subsequently cultivated as a culinary vegetable, first at Bath in 1775, after which it was introduced to Covent Garden in 1792.

Blackpool attracts because it is a quiet cove, quite unlike its better known namesake, though now it has a car park and ice-cream stalls in summer. Its sands hide a submerged forest, but this is only uncovered after a severe storm has combed down the beach. From this point the road bends inland as it approaches Dartmouth.

Dartmouth is Devon's equivalent of Fowey, for it is sited a little way up a deep-water ria which has long provided a good harbour. Originally there were two waterside settlements, one near the upstream ferry and the other about 1km (½ mile) nearer the sea. Between the two lay the Mill Pool, a side-creek which, when reclaimed, provided much-needed land for further settlement. Dartmouth was a flourishing medieval port with its harbour entrance guarded by two fifteenth-century forts. After reaching its zenith during the time of the Newfoundland fisheries and the cloth trade, Dartmouth's fortunes declined considerably. In the nineteenth century attempts to revive it as a packet station and passenger port proved futile due to competition from Plymouth and later, Southampton. Railway extension in 1864 did not help for a local landowner prevented the Dart being bridged and so it had to end on the east bank at Kingswear. This last section of the line is no longer operated by British Rail but steam trains of the Dart Valley Railway Company still run from Paignton.

Although scarred by bombing in 1943, the damage has been tastefully rebuilt including the restoration of some of the town's finest buildings like the colonnaded Butterwalk with its fine carving and plasterwork. There are many other old buildings, including a house called The Cherub in Higher Street dating from 1380, and Agincourt House of 1413 in Lower Street. Bayard's Cove near the castle built by Henry VIII has a quay where ships tied up in the Middle Ages, a row of old houses and the Customs House of 1739. After a period of decline there has been a recent change of fortune largely because Dartmouth's old-world atmosphere has become a tourist attraction while its fine harbour has a large number of moorings for leisure craft. The naval link with the past – it provided Drake with ships to attack the Armada – is retained by the Royal Naval College established in 1905 high up above the town.

Beyond the entrance to the Dart the coastline of steep cliffs and sandy coves is largely inaccessible and difficult to walk even on foot. The rocks of grit and hard shales form prominent bays, while sharp-nosed points like Froward and Sharkham owe their origin to hard igneous beds.

Berry Head, though much ruined by the quarrying of limestone, is worth visiting because of the fine views it gives over Tor Bay. It has a long history of fortification going back to Iron Age times when there was a promontory fort. Later the Saxons, who gave it the name (Anglo Saxon *byrig* = 'fort'), used it as a look-out station; and there were further fortifications built during the sixteenth and seventeenth centuries. It is the Napoleonic fort, built during the invasion scare of 1802, that now claims most attention.

Brixham has long been recognised as one of the premier fishing ports of the South West, and although it has shared in the ups and downs of the industry it still has a working fleet. The original harbour was formed by a small break in the wall of limestone cliffs and it was here that part of the Newfoundland fishing fleet was based in the sixteenth century. Cod brought back from these fishing grounds was re-exported to the Mediterranean countries from whence ships returned with fruit. As the English Channel fisheries also expanded in the nineteenth century a need was felt for a much bigger harbour and so the great outer breakwater was begun in 1843. The town is in two parts – Lower Brixham with its houses clustered around the quays, and Higher Brixham on the plateau top. Although fishing is still important the town has now become a favourite of the boating fraternity, and more recently a place of retirement.

Paignton, now in urban continuity with Torquay, is the older of the two settlements. It began as a tiny nucleated village of pre-Conquest date around the church about 1km (½ mile) inland and was known in medieval times as Paignton Well. The area around the parish church still has an air of antiquity and there is a late-medieval house surviving in Coverdale Tower, the sole remains of what was once a medieval palace of the Bishops of Exeter. The church can trace its origin back to Saxon times from remains of paving stones; but its chief glory is its Norman west door, font and part of the chancel dating from about 1100. The whole setting of old Paignton stands out in contrast to the much newer resort with its laid out gardens, aquarium and host of hotels and boarding houses, all there to take advantage of the fine sands on either side of the promontory of Roundham Head. A tiny harbour lies in the lee of the headland and is the starting-place for trips around the bay as well as being a base for the crab and lobster fisheries.

Torquay is the largest of the resorts which seem to occur every few miles along this favoured coastline. Although the present town shows unmistakable evidence of nineteenth-century development, the earliest settlement here dates back to the founding of Torre Abbey in 1196 and the subsequent building of a small quay on the north side of Tor Bay. At this time the main settlement lay about 1.6km (1 mile) inland at Tormohun, under the tor which gave it its name. Subsequent growth tended to be nearer the coast so that in the great expansion which took place in the early decades of the nineteenth century, it was the south-facing slopes overlooking Tor Bay that were developed for housing. Such building was possible following the decision of the local Palk family to lay out their estate with roads following the contours of the hillside overlooking Tor Bay. Here, splendid villas, each set in its own spacious grounds were built. The port meanwhile hardly developed, for although Tor Bay had long been a sheltered anchorage, the harbour of Torquay was too tiny to accommodate large vessels. The fact that the railway which reached Torre from Newton Abbot in 1848 met with considerable opposition from landowners when a link-up with the harbour was suggested, did not help Torquay to become a port of any consequence. Major works which led to the creation of the outer harbour in 1870 came too late for commercial interests, but soon proved of great value for regattas, and the growth of pleasure craft since World War II means that the harbour is now a considerable asset to the resort town.

It is easy to see why Torquay, now part of the bigger urban entity of Torbay, is the premier resort of the area with fine hotels, shops and amusement centres. But like so many of the Devon resorts it is fast becoming the retreat of the elderly, either as residents or as out of season visitors. But Torquay and the surrounding area have much to offer for all age groups. The coastline is particularly fine, with a multiplicity of form brought about through a complex succession of rock types varying between limestone, shales, grits and igneous dolerite. For example, London Bridge is a natural arch of rock where the sea has attacked along cleavage planes. Hope's Nose is a remnant of limestone while 1km (½ mile) along the coast to the north, Black Head is dolerite. Much closer to Torquay is the great cleft in the cliff known as the Daddyhole, formed as the sea has worked along a great thrust plane with its shattered rock. To the student of past history, Torquay can offer the well known Kent's Cavern which lies a little inland from Anstey's Cove. Although the existence of the fine labyrinth of caves had been known for many centuries, it was not until 1865 when William Pengelly began his systematic scientific examination that the full significance of the site was recognised. In a series of excavations over a fifteen-year period, Pengelly found evidence of human occupation along with extinct animal remains including mammoth, cave bear, sabre-toothed tiger, woolly rhinoceros etc. The cave is now artificially lit and as a tourist attraction has the advantage that it is open all year.

Babbacombe Bay, between the Torquay headland and the entrance to the Teign, is hardly a true bay and would provide little shelter for shipping save when the wind is from the west. At its southern end the influence of Torquay is greatly felt in the 'suburbia' atmosphere of places like Babbacombe and Oddicombe. The coastline, almost entirely cliffed, becomes increasingly rugged towards the north where the red Permian sandstone, conglomerate and

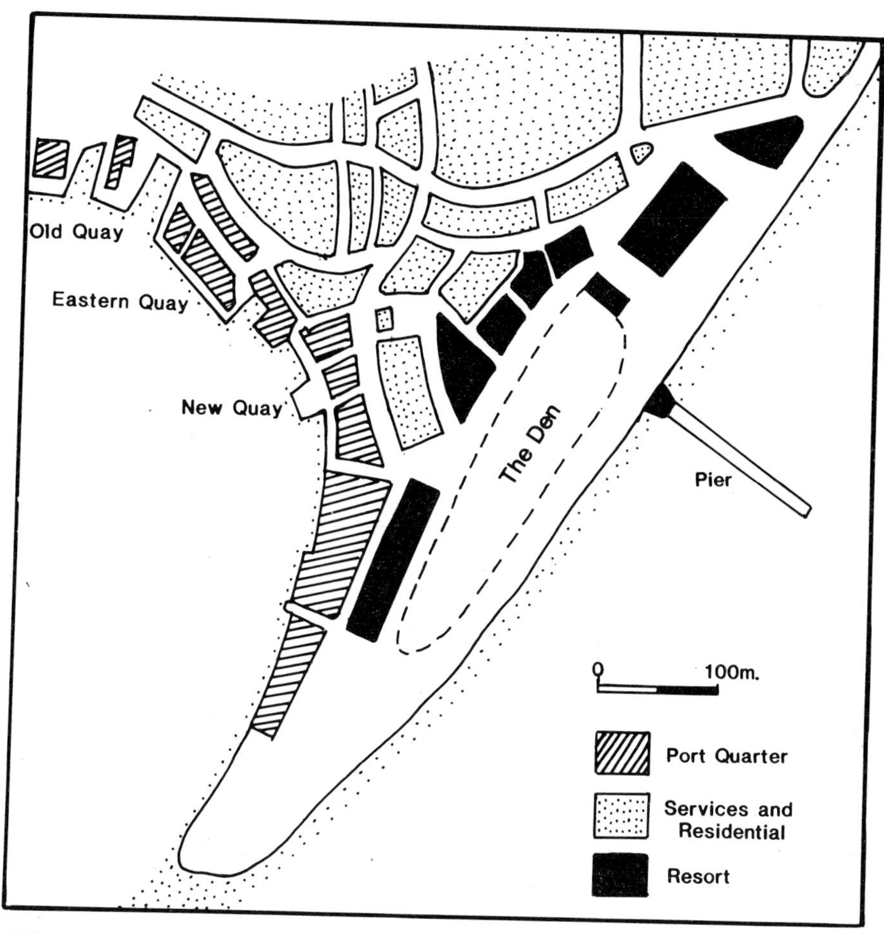

Teignmouth with its 'quarters' reflecting the various interests of this small coastal town

breccia come in. Between the numerous short blunt headlands are fine sandy coves, the best and most accessible (by cliff railway) being at Oddicombe.

Teignmouth Approaching by the main coastal road from the south, it is possible to obtain a fine bird's eye view of town and estuary mouth from the prominent Ness Head which stands sentinel over the harbour entrance. The route is through the engaging village of Shaldon where there are some fine Georgian houses around the triangular green and older thatched fishermen's cottages in the narrow backstreets, and then along the shore to the carpark near Ness House. From here it is a short climb through woods of evergreen oak to Ness Head. For the beach south of the headland there is access by a stone-lined tunnel. From the high vantage point of Ness Head the whole setting of the estuary can be appreciated, especially at low water when the sandbanks have dried out. These create certain difficulties for the coasters who regularly use the port to load ball clay brought down from the inland Bovey Valley by lorry. Another problem is that the sandbanks are constantly changing shape and position, and seem to follow a cyclical pattern of development. Local pilots, whose job it is to bring in the coasters, have to keep constant watch and be ready to move the spar buoy marking the main navigable channel. On occasion a large narrow sandbank can grow out from the Ness

Brunel's broad-gauge railway ran along the coast at Dawlish. The tower used for the atmospheric system is seen in the distance

towards the pier and so restrict the entrance channel that the pilots have to go out at low water to cut an artificial channel across the offending bar of sand and then allow nature to do the rest.

Teignmouth owes its early development as a port to both the Newfoundland cod fisheries and the more local Channel fishing grounds. It still has a few local fishermen including seine fishers who drag the estuary entrance in season. But today it is the ball-clay trade on which the port depends for its prosperity. The loading wharves lie to the west of the town in the curve of the river. As might be expected, the resort quarter lies facing the open sea. A fine crescent, with the Royal Hotel as centrepiece, was built in the 1820s together with an Assembly Hall (now a cinema and bingo hall). All overlook the open space of the Den which was once a sandy warren but is now a much prized asset. Between resort and port quarter there is the main shopping centre and, with Teignmouth now a favoured retirement area, there is plenty of activity here all the year round.

To the north the shore is dominated by Brunel's railway which he built in 1846. Originally designed as broad-gauge and operated on his own atmospheric principle, the line was run close to the sea to give it easy gradients though subject to storm damage on a number of occasions. There is a pleasant walk along the sea wall as far as the sandstone headland where the railway tunnels and the path goes inland. Off the headland lies the prominent stack of the Parson with its white 'collar' formed of bird droppings. At low water it is possible to scramble out to the stack across the sand-stone boulders slippery with seaweed, though inadvisable to attempt to round the headland.

Dawlish, the next resort, began, like Paignton, in pre-Domesday times as a hamlet set around a church about 1km (½ mile) inland. Its present growth dates largely from the early decades of the nineteenth century when settlement spread down the valley to the seashore. The small stream was straight-ened and the valley floor landscaped, with villas lining the gentle slopes on either side. The arrival of the railway in 1845 brought a surge of settlement, but also disadvantages. It was an age of progress which swept aside all thoughts of harmonising new invention with existing landscape. Thus Brunel was allowed to build his line right along the shore, crossing the valley mouth in a low viaduct which comes between the town and the sea. Even amid the excesses of the twentieth century, this example of Victorian vandalism is unforgivable.

The railway continues to hug the shore to the north until Dawlish Warren is reached. This is very much a product of the postwar years, during which the former sand-spit has been developed with chalets, amusement centres, a short promenade, caravans, carpark and golf course. In its original setting at the beginning of the century the Warren consisted of two parallel sand spits with an open body of water, the Greenland Lake, in between. During this century erosion of the outer spit, mainly sandhills covered with marram grass, has led to the draining of the lake and its later use as a carpark. The warren seems very susceptible to erosion and strenuous efforts have been made by the coastal protection authority – using plastic cages filled with pebbles – to arrest the relentless attack of the sea. It is best at its lonely outer end where there are fine views across the mouth of the Exe to Exmouth, and where solitude can be found even in the height of summer amidst the yellow of sea lupin. It is not possible to cross from the far end of the spit to Exmouth, but a foot ferry runs from a point a little to the north at Starcross. Also at Starcross is the red-brick pumping station which Brunel built to create the necessary vacuum for his ill-fated atmospheric railway. With a coal yard next door, the building is in danger; but it seems worthy of preservation, if only as one of the few tangible remains of Brunel's costly failure.

Exmouth looks most impressive and inviting from the end of Dawlish Warren. Nearness to Exeter helped it to establish an early lead as a coastal resort, but it was later left behind as Brunel's railway of the 1840s opened up the west side of the Exe Estuary and fostered the development of Dawlish, Teignmouth and Torquay. Its own railway link did not materialise until 1861, and then it was only a short branch-line. Although now very much a commuting centre for Exeter, the older part of the town near the waterfront still shows traces of its development as a watering place from the 1790s and also of its late-Victorian expansion, for example in Bicton Place and The Beacon. As a fishing port its history goes back many centuries earlier, but silting of the mouth of the Exe hampered later development. Even the construction of the present small dock in 1871 did little to arrest the town's decline as a port, though it still has fishing and boating industries. The promenade begun by Lord Rolle and later extended towards Orcombe Point, today forms a pleasant marine drive. Orcombe Rocks are ideal for scrambling about on as the eroded red sandstone forms a natural playground. The National Trust

Dawlish Warren: the spit was in danger of disappearing (*after Kidson*)

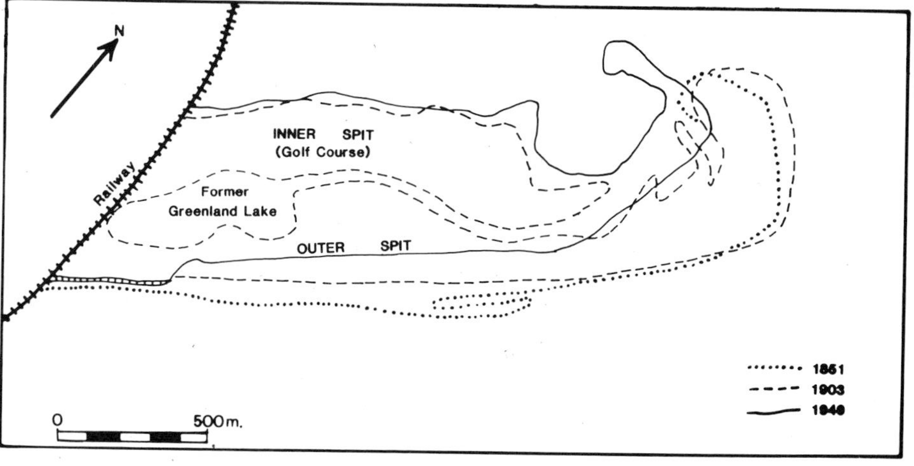

owns the coastline here but unfortunately has no control over the next promontory, Straight Point.

Budleigh Salterton grew up relatively late in a narrow valley which runs obliquely to the shore at the mouth of the wide Otter Valley. In medieval times there were salt-pans here, hence the 'Salterton' of the mid nineteenth-century resort. The cliffs of red sandstone to the west of the town contain the well-known pebble bed with its multi-coloured stones formed of a number of rock types. Both the author Anthony Trollope and the painter John Millais lived in the town, the latter in a house called The Octagon. The beach was the setting for the famous painting 'The Boyhood of Raleigh' – the famous Elizabethan explorer had been born a short distance away at Hayes Barton Farm. A cliff-top walk to the west of the town around the edge of the golf course on West Down gives particularly fine seascapes, taking in the whole sweep of coastline from Portland Bill to Berry Head on a clear day. Although favoured by the retired, Budleigh has not developed to the same extent as the other resorts along this section of the east Devon coast and the railway, which came as late as 1903, was one of the first branch-lines to be closed.

East of the mouth of the Otter, there is the South Devon Coast Path which for 8km (5 miles) to Sidmouth runs along an unspoiled cliff-line. Only at Ladram Bay, with its caravan site, is there road access. The cliffs at Ladram are low but the whole setting – a sandy beach broken by numerous stacks – is attractive.

Sidmouth occupies a valley gap made by the river Sid through the red marl which forms the cliff-face extending eastwards from High Peak. This prominent viewpoint, rising to over 152m (500ft), has a capping of sandstone and was the site of an Iron Age camp, now partially destroyed. Erosion has been continuous over the centuries for the red marl of the lower cliff is readily worn away by the sea. Comparison of a map of Sidmouth Manor dated 1789 with one of the present time indicates that some 19m (62ft) of the cliff have been lost over the past two centuries. Erosion has also been a problem at Sidmouth itself and must have been a factor in preventing the building of a harbour. Periodical flooding of the town in the early nineteenth century led to the building of the first sea wall in 1835.

The original village probably grew up a little way inland around the parish church of St Nicholas which, though rebuilt in 1859, is of much earlier foundation. Resort development started about 1780, and at the turn of the century it was fashionable for the nobility to build themselves 'cottages' – really substantial residences – close to the sea. Many like The Knowle, Woodlands and Royal Glen later became hotels. After the visit of the Duke and Duchess of Kent in 1819 there was further development, and the town can today boast of fine rows like Fortfield Terrace, York Terrace and Elysian Fields. On the esplanade the terraces are particularly striking and with their wrought-iron balconies the houses are much in demand. Because of its shingle beach, which includes small pebbles of semi-precious stones to be searched for, Sidmouth has never been a family resort. It grew only slowly in the latter half of the nineteenth century, for the railway branch-line only arrived in 1874 and even then stopped far short of the shore. Today it has become the preserve of the retired with over 35 per cent of the residents of pensionable age.

To the east the coastline is the seaward edge of greensand plateau country. The lower part of the cliff is again formed of red marl which has been deeply furrowed by weathering. At Salcombe Hill the upper cliff consists of a great slab of sandstone rock which is more resistant to erosion. With the rocks dipping gently to the east, chalk begins as a cap-rock on the cliff top at Dunscombe Bottom. From here to Beer Head chalk occupies more of the cliff face and with it an increasing tendency for landslipping to occur. Certain sections of this coastline, even beyond the Dorset border, have been subject to great landslips in the past centuries, many of which have been accurately documented.

From Branscombe Mouth (carpark and café) it is possible to walk through a tangle of the landslip country towards Beer Head. Alternatively an approach can be made from the village of Beer by walking southwards to the headland. Whichever route is chosen the landslip country, known as Under Hooken, provides dramatic scenery with its tormented topography clothed in a dense cover of deep undergrowth.

The last major landslip at Under Hooken took place in March 1790. It happened because the chalk of the cliff top allows water to pass through to the underlying greensand. Here it accumulates because its further downward passage is prevented by the impervious red marl, and when in time the sands are washed away this brings down the chalk from above. During the 1790 landslip a great fissure opened on the cliff top and a mass of chalk, 228m (250yd) wide and 549m (600yd) long, slid gently down towards the sea. Offshore, where the previous day fishermen had placed their lobster pots in 5m (18ft) of water, the sea bed rose bodily to form dry land. After almost two hundred years of further slipping and weathering, the features of the old 1790 landslip are still there in a modified form - great slender pinnacles of chalk separated from the main inner cliff by a narrow valley.

Beer, nestling in the lee of the chalk cliffs running out to the headland, has a history going back to Roman times for there is evidence that they worked the famous underground quarries of a hardened chalk as building stone. Also Beer stone has come to light in buildings of Roman Exeter. The cream-coloured blocks can be cut easily *in situ* for it is relatively soft, but it hardens on contact with the air and so makes a reasonable building material. With age it turns a grey colour, as can be seen in many of the older cottages in Beer. From the valley mouth in which the village lies, it is but a short walk over the headland to Seaton. Along the top the views are striking, with the long sweep of chalk cliffs running out to Beer Head and boats drawn up on the shingle beach below.

Seaton lacks the lustre of Sidmouth for it began to develop in the mid nineteenth century when Georgian delicacy had given place to Victorian solidity. Although there was a settlement around the fourteenth-century church, sited inland from the coastline, it was not until after 1868 when the branch railway arrived that Seaton became a resort. The railway link is now closed though the last section to Colyton has been reopened as an electric tramway. There is still a small fishing industry around the harbour mouth and a flourishing yacht club. The river Axe has been forced against the red cliffs by a huge bank of shingle. The growth of this spit from the west sealed the fate of the inland port of Axmouth but the latter is still worth visiting with its thatched cottages giving it a picturesque appearance lacking in Seaton. Recent coast protection works along the sea front should make the town less vulnerable to winter storms.

The 11km (7 mile) stretch of coastline between Seaton and Lyme Regis is taken up almost entirely with landslips - a replica on a larger scale of the Under Hooken cliff west of Beer Head, and of similar cause. The whole area has been designated a Nature Reserve (see page 84).

12 South and Central England

Dorset

Lyme Regis acquired its royal title from Edward I when it became a free borough in 1284; formerly it had only been a small fishing hamlet at the mouth of the tiny river Lym, and part of the manor of Glastonbury Abbey. The valley was too small to contain the developing town and it soon spread up the adjacent valley side so that today the main street is quite steep with its houses occupying the original burgage plots in Broad Gate. The early fishing harbour was quite inadequate for the developing borough so the Cobb, 1km (½ mile) to the west, was built consisting of a breakwater made of rows of tree trunks driven into the sea bed and filled with rocks and stones. Today a more substantial structure replaces the medieval 'La Cobbe', as it was named in a document of 1295. During the next century the artificial harbour proved its worth, largely as it was the only sizeable haven between Exmouth and Weymouth, and the town became the home of rich merchants who owned fifteen large vessels trading principally with the Mediterranean countries. Storms seriously damaged the Cobb and, with periodic raids from the French in the fifteenth century, the town failed to retain its former medieval importance. In the late eighteenth and early nineteenth century Lyme became favoured as a watering place, particularly after a local innkeeper persuaded Lord Chatham to make a visit and give it his stamp of approval. Fashionable society accustomed to Bath then took an interest and this led to the building of the Assembly Rooms in 1775. Among the many visitors was Jane Austen who described the town in her last novel *Persuasion.* Town houses were built facing Broad Street though in many cases new fronts were simply added to existing buildings. Away from the centre, on the flatter land at the top of the main street, fine Regency houses were set in spacious grounds, their iron balconies looking out to sea. Strangely the town has never established a complete link up with its harbour at the Cobb, which has tended to become trippery in recent years.

Lyme Bay, as far east as the beginning of the great shingle ridge of Chesil, is a cliffed coastline broken at intervals by small valleys which often form the only way down to the shore from the main inland road (A35). For the most part the cliffs are composite, consisting of a lower section, mainly Jurassic clays and shales and an upper portion formed of Cretaceous sandstone. Both Stonebarrow and the better known Golden Cap display this composite structure, the latter being best seen from the shore at **Seatown** where there is an inn and carpark, with a footpath leading to the top along the cliff edge. The 'cap' is of greensand which sits on top of softer and more erosive clays, and much of its distinctive character is due to the different colouring of the two formations. Seatown is one of the places along this coast where pebbles are collected from the beach, stacked in plastic sacks and then sent away to The Potteries for the flint to be used in the making of porcelain. On the western side of the Golden Cap headland is the ruined chapel of St Gabriel, amidst a tangle of vegetation. It dates from the thirteenth century when it was built as a chapel-of-ease to the mother church of Whitchurch Canonicorum.

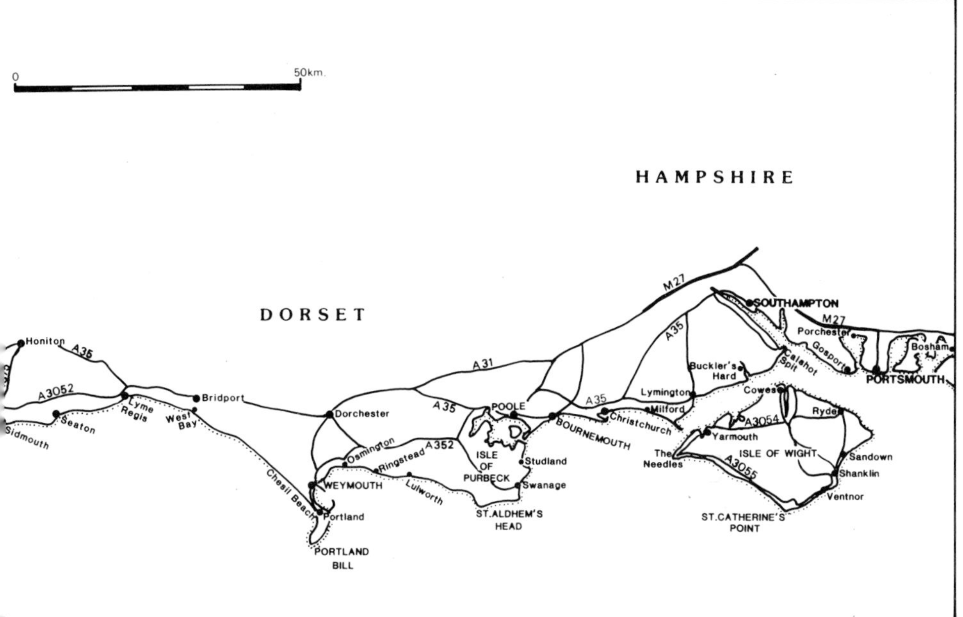

The south coast of England from the Devon border to the Isle of Wight

A little to the east of Lyme Regis is the aptly named Black Ven formed of black and dark-grey marls. It was a major slip of these beds in 1908 that triggered off the burning of a band of bituminous shale so that dense smoke poured from the cliff-face and the 'Lyme volcano' was born. The dark shales and marls of the Charmouth area have long been a fossil collector's paradise. It was here that in 1811 a young schoolgirl uncovered the almost complete skeleton of an ichthyosaurus which she sold to the Lord of the Manor for £23. Some years later she found an almost complete specimen of a plesiosaurus and then the first pterodactyl skeleton to be discovered in Britain. Such was her fame that she set up a fossil shop in Lyme and on her death in 1847 the Geological Society of London had a memorial window placed in the parish church.

Bridport is a pleasant town but 3km (2 miles) inland so that it developed its port at West Bay where the river Brit breaks through the ribbed cliffs of calcareous sandstone. The harbour is entirely artificial with a basin first built in 1740 and rebuilt in 1824. The entrance is narrow between two projecting piers which have been repaired after damage during World War II. There is still some commercial trading and a few fishing boats are based here, but the place is now a resort rather than a working port. On the east side is a substantial terrace built in 1885 which, with steeply pitched roofs at varying angles and tile-hung walls has a whimsical and out-of-place appearance in this harbour setting. But compared with the more recent buildings on the west shore it stands out as yet another example of Victorian solidity. Both pale into insignificance compared with the sheer bulk of the East Cliff which, though less than 30m (100ft) high, rises vertically from the beach and in the deep ochre colouring of the Bridport Sandstone, completely dominates the shoreline.

Chesil Beach, without parallel in Britain, extends for 29km (18 miles) from near Burton Bradstock in the west to the Isle of Portland in the east. As the coastal road runs a little distance inland and there is also the large body of water known as **The Fleet** impounded between the shingle ridge and the old inland coastline, access is only possible at a few points. The pebbles of the barrier are graded in size with the largest cobbles at the Portland end, and so gradual is the change that it is said that smugglers landing on the beach at night with their contraband were sure of their exact position from the size of the pebble at a particular spot. Landing even under the best conditions was never easy because of the undertow created by the steep shelving foreshore; during storms, conditions were made impossible and Chesil has a long record of wrecks. During one severe storm in November 1824 an ordnance sloop was carried bodily onto the crest of the ridge and the crew simply disembarked and walked into Portland. Theories abound about the origin of this unique geological feature but none is entirely satisfactory. The pebbles have come partly from flint beds in the chalk on the floor of the English Channel and partly from the varied succession of rocks in the cliffs as far west as Devon. One suggested origin is that as sea level rose after the end of the Ice Age so this great bank of shingle was rolled forward until it established a tenuous join with the mainland in the west and the Isle of Portland in the east. What is unexplained is the remarkable grading of the pebbles and why such an accumulation should occur over a limited stretch of the Dorset coast. On a clear day the best view of the shingle bank and enclosed Fleet is obtained from Weare Hill just before the coastal road drops down into Abbotsbury. This last-named village, taking its name from its former owner the Abbey of Glastonbury, consists mainly of one long main street of honey-coloured cottages. Some bare remains of the Benedictine monastery, founded in 1044, have survived to the south of the village, though the only outstanding building is the abbot's tithe barn dating from about 1400. The nearby hilltop has a small chapel built by the monastery in the late 1300s. Below it runs the track leading to the swannery which has existed since the thirteenth century. Some 500 swans now nest amongst the reedy pools on the edge of the Fleet. When the abbots were in occupation, decoys were used to lure duck as a source of fresh meat during the winter months but now the decoys are used for

One of the many small quarries on the Isle of Portland. Limestone was extracted from the prized beds and then loaded directly into small boats moored nearby

research purposes and any birds which enter are ringed for further study. To the west of the village a road down to Chesil Beach passes sub-tropical gardens where magnolias, camellias and other plants and shrubs which would normally succumb to frosts flourish in the equable maritime climate.

The Isle of Portland, projecting well out into the Channel, is an example of the resistance offered by limestone beds to the constant forces of marine erosion. Because of its prominent situation it has a number of defensive fortifications dating from past centuries. The biggest is the Verne Fortress built by convict labour in the early nineteenth century and now a prison training-centre. Set high at the northern end of the isle it overlooks the much earlier and less substantial Portland Castle on the strand below, built by Henry VIII in 1520 as part of a system of strategic defences around our vulnerable shores. Two other 'castles' deserve mention – the Pennsylvania, now a hotel, built about 1800 by the then governor of the island, John Penn, grandson of the Quaker William Penn; and the nearby Rufus Castle perched overlooking Church Ope Bay.

Apart from its defensive potential Portland achieved fame because of its great quarries. It is said that the fine qualities of Portland Stone were first recognised by Inigo Jones when he built the Banqueting Hall in Whitehall (1619–22) and it was subsequently used for other London buildings including St Paul's (1675–1710). There are six beds in all which provide suitable stone for working and shaping and all have been quarried at various times. Today most of the quarries are abandoned and give the island an unkempt appearance. Defence needs have also taken their toll and at Portland Bill itself there is a huge car park and refreshment huts which completely destroy what must have been a fine natural setting. However it is still possible to find solitude within a short distance by following the cliff-edge path to the north east past tiny quarries where stone was once loaded into waiting vessels below. Now there are tarred fishermen's huts and winspits to lift the boats out of the water when storm waves threaten.

Weymouth has a name disguising the fact that the settlement originated as two distinct centres on either side of the mouth of the river Wey. Only the one to the south, planted in the parish of Wyke Regis, was originally so called. That to the north was Melcombe Regis, an artificial plantation of the thirteenth century, this time in the parish of Radipole. Of the two, Melcombe had the best site for subsequent growth, and so has virtually become present-day Weymouth. Its early history and development was closely connected with its role as a wool-staple port in the reign of Edward III, although what we see today had its origin in the craze for sea bathing in the mid eighteenth century. The first machines were placed on Melcombe beach in 1748; but it was after the visit in 1780 of the Duke of Gloucester, who built a house, Gloucester Court (now a hotel to the north of the town) that the resort became fashionable. Further interest shown by George III led to the erection of several splendid terraces: Royal Terrace (1816), Brunswick Terrace (1823), Waterloo Place (1834) and Victoria Terrace (1850). The result is that present-

Osmington – the site of the mudflow

day Weymouth is very much a Georgian resort and the statue of George III which faces up the Esplanade commemorates the real founder of the town. A walk along the seafront is an exercise in appreciation of changing architectural fashion, beginning with Georgian red brick and ending with the stucco-rendered walls and bow window frames of a later period. The original Weymouth did not have room for spacious growth in the first half of the nineteenth century and had to be content with a long terrace fronting the sea. To the south is the harbour with its ferry terminal for the Channel Isles, a route now under threat with the development of a sea link from Portsmouth which is more conveniently placed in relation to the urban areas of the South East.

Osmington Mills, with its dark tumbled cliffs of shale and mudstone, represents a return to the cliff scenery found west of Bridport. The cliffs of Black Head to the west of the straggling one-street village were the scene of a great glacier-like mudflow early this century. The reason for the spectacular mass movement of the outer cliff face was the existence of a fault running parallel to the coast; this fault wall, formed of impervious Kimmeridge Clay, held up water which was draining seawards, but ultimately the pressure became too great and a great rupture occurred. According to one observer, the pent-up and super-saturated beds poured through the gap like a bursting out of lava from the side of a shattered volcano. Although the intervening years have brought a mellowing of the original feature, it is still possible to imagine the impact which the event must have had on the inhabitants of the sleepy village when they woke up one morning to find what has been claimed to be the largest and most remarkable mudflow in Britain on their doorstep.

Mud slide at Osmington, caused by pent-up waters (*after Arkell*)

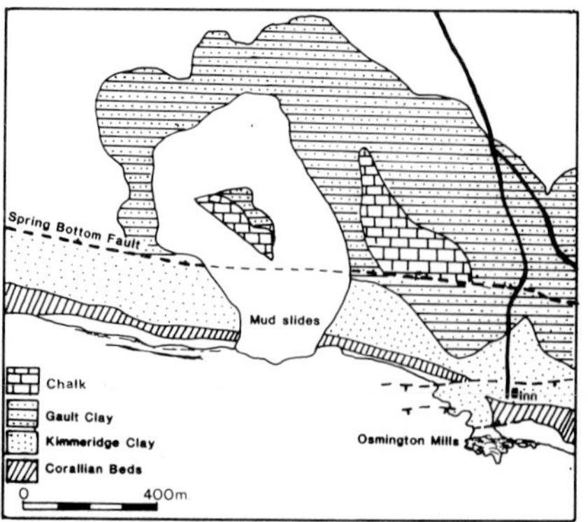

Ringstead is shown on the current Ordnance Survey 1:50,000 map in Old English lettering and thus immediately attracts attention. It is clearly a deserted village – one of several in Dorset – for there are the remains of house platforms and hollow ways in a grassy field a little distance along the coastal footpath towards Osmington. At the adjacent Glebe Cottage there is also the blocked up chancel arch of the former village church. Various suggestions have been made for the reason and time of the desertion but there are few hard facts. Some would claim that the Black Death of 1348 took its toll while others suggest a French raid of 1420 led to the destruction of the village. More likely is the abandonment of the village over a period of time as new methods of farming, involving the creation of huge sheep runs on the neighbouring chalk downs, required fewer people and provided less chance of a livelihood. Certainly it had been abandoned before 1480 when burials were transferred to Osmington. Another curiosity lies close by on the slopes of Ringstead Bay to the east. Between 1824 and 1827 the cliff face suddenly began to emit great clouds of heated vapour as though from the vent of a volcano because of the decomposition of iron pyrites and the adjacent bituminous shale of the Kimmeridge Beds after prolonged rains. The name Burning Cliff persists to the present day, though it is many years since it last sent up its smoke signals (see page 83).

At White Nothe the chalk reappears and immediately it is associated with landslip topography. The next 32km (20 miles), part of the **Isle of Purbeck**, contains some of the finest coastal scenery to be found in Britain. It is true that caravan and camping sites, the military and even the ordinary day visitor

Stair Hole, a miniature Lulworth Cove. The limestone wall has been breached to reveal the intense folding of the rock formations

pose a constant threat, but luckily there are long stretches which remain in a natural state. Access points are few, so only by walking the Dorset Coast Path can one see the details of coastal form. The downland landscape ends abruptly in vertical chalk cliffs at Bat's Hole and Swyre Head, the former with caves at its base which can be entered at low tide after a walk along the shingle beach from Durdle Door. Access to the latter is along a toll road and through a caravan site to a carpark sited a little way back from the cliff edge. A short walk brings the 'Door', a natural arch cut in Portland limestone, into view. To the east the line of the limestone continues in the partly submerged Man-of-War rocks before the chalk once again forms the cliff-face.

Lulworth Cove is quite remarkable and even though now much visited and over-commercialised its natural beauty remains, with the chalk cliffs forming a backcloth to the blue waters of the cove. The entrance is through a narrow gap in the sharply folded Portland limestone strata. Once this wall was breached the sea was able to attack the softer clay beds behind until it reached the chalk, which is now being slowly eroded. At Stair Hole, just west of Lulworth, the outer limestone wall has been partially broken and the sea is beginning its work on the less resistant Purbeck Beds, which are intensely folded and stand vertical in places. Once these give way the sea will have full play on the softer Wealden Beds and another Lulworth will be created.

Worbarrow Bay The military still retain control of a large area, including the coastline to the east of Lulworth, and the track from Tyneham village down to Worbarrow Tout is only accessible during August. The Tout is a limestone peninsula which the sea is nipping into from both sides, so that in time the headland will be severed to form an islet. From the end of the headland there is a fine view westwards over Worbarrow Bay which, like Lulworth Cove, is carved out of softer Wealden strata. Dominating the cliff top is the Iron Age hill fort of Flowers Barrow, though this is now inaccessible because of the danger of unexploded shells. The fort is already half destroyed by the erosion which has taken place during the past two thousand years.

Kimmeridge Bay has dark cliffs of shaly clay with a limestone strip running through it. Another limestone band outcrops on the foreshore where it forms a wave-cut platform known as The Flats. Although popular in summer the bay still has character, with small fishing boats lying at anchor and locally caught lobsters and crabs available from the tarred sheds on the beach. Across the bay stands the nodding donkey of an oil-pumping unit, for this is one of the few places on the mainland where there is oil to be found from a bed in the Cornbrash formation, 457m (1,500ft) underground. The output is small and taken away from the storage tanks by road tanker. The Kimmeridge shale contains a bed of 'coal' which was once quarried and burnt as fuel though its sulphurous smell must have been offensive. This same bed was also worked to make discs – coal money – for armlets and from time to time these are found locally. It is an industry that dates back almost 2,000 years, and bracelets made from Kimmeridge 'coal money' have turned up at Romano-British sites near Dorchester. There is also an oil-shale bed which was once used in the manufacture of alum as well as for glass-making. Altogether the Kimmeridge Bay rocks have yielded a surprising variety of commercial products.

The inherent natural beauty of much of the Dorset coast, especially Purbeck, has demanded special treatment and fortunately this need has been met by the Countryside Commission. In 1974 a 113km (70 mile) length of the Dorset Coast Path was opened, and as most of it comes within the Nature Conservancy's definition of an Area of Outstanding Natural Beauty, its future as a walker's paradise is now assured.

Chapman's Pool, approached through Worth Matravers village, is a small-scale replica of Kimmeridge Bay, having been eroded out of the same softer shale and clay beds. The bay once housed a lifeboat station, but when this was given up it became the preserve of a group of lobster fishermen. The visitor will find the cliffs around a happy hunting ground for white ammonites with their spiral casts, sometimes several feet across. Care must be taken for landslips are common on the unstable cliff-face. Cliff recession is quite rapid and the former driveway to Encombe House which once ran over the top of Houns Tout, the cliff to the west, has largely disappeared.

St Aldhelm's Head, the most southerly part of the Isle of Purbeck, owes its existence to the more resistant limestone strata which overlie the shale. Near the modern coast-guard station is a curious square 'chapel', probably of twelfth-century date to judge from the Norman doorway on its north-west side. Some doubt has been expressed as to the exact purpose of the building for the square shape might make worship difficult; it has however a fine vaulted ceiling and arcades. One suggestion is that it served as a beacon or even a look-out post, for its pyramidal-shaped roof is crowned with a cylindrical structure. Whatever its former usage it is worthwhile visiting for from its headland site there are fine coastal views and pleasant cliff-top walks in both directions.

Durlston Head was designated a Country Park in 1973 by Dorset County Council and covers 106ha (261 acres) of relatively wild and unspoiled coastland. The approach can be made by car from Swanage to the Information Centre, or via the Dorset Coast Path from the west. The latter approach is preferable and shows how even this tucked-away corner has been used by man over the centuries. The sides of valleys cut into the limestone plateau have been terraced for agriculture since prehistoric times, especially south of Worth Matravers. But the greatest impact has been stoneworking, with quarries dating back to the seventeenth century, for the easily shaped, cream-coloured freestone of the Portland Beds proved ideal building material. Overland transport from this rather remote area might have been a handicap, but was solved by lowering the hewn stone over

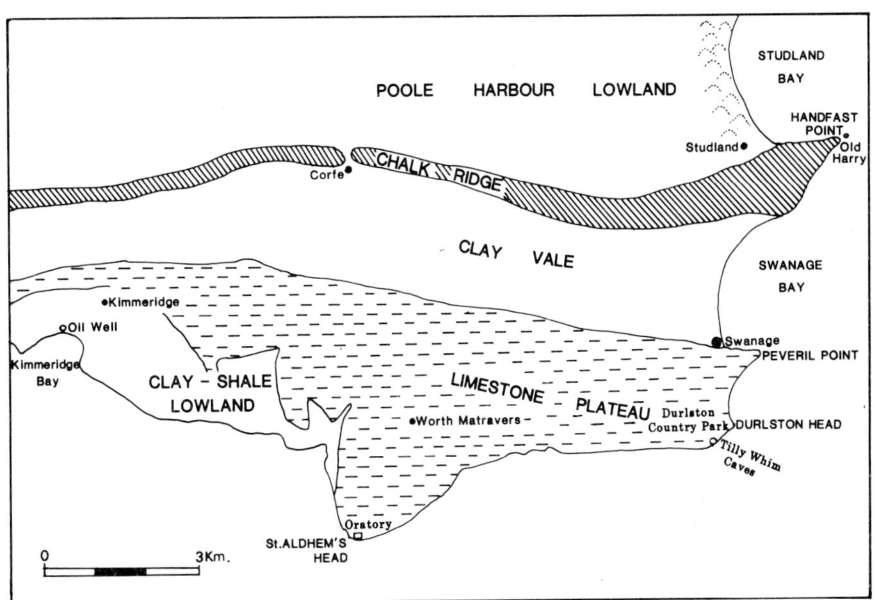

The geology of the 'Isle' of Purbeck

the cliff edge by means of wooden cranes or whims into waiting barges which carried the stone far afield. Particular beds were followed underground so that man-made caves, with pillars left to support the roof, became commonplace along this coastline, the most famous being the Tilly Whim caves close to the lighthouse at Anvil Point. They were once open to the public and became something of a tourist attraction but, after a number of roof collapses, the caves were closed. Even so they make a fine sight from the coastal path just below the lighthouse. They can also be approached from the car park by the Information Centre at Durlston Country Park, within which is Durlston Castle, a late Victorian mansion now used as a restaurant, and a great 40 tonne (40 ton) stone globe built out of segments of Portland stone. At the cliff base at Durlston Head, the sea has exploited many natural joint systems to form small caves.

Swanage nestles in a hollow in the lee of Peveril Point, another limestone promontory. Its sheltered position and fine sandy strand running northward to the chalk cliffs of Handfast Point made it a natural site for both a port and a resort. The port flourished through the export of stone, with the Burt and Mowlem families prominent contractors, and it was from their wealth that some of the unusual features of the present-day town arose. The Town Hall has a façade designed by Wren which came to its present situation through purchase from the old Mercer's Hall in London in 1883. Opposite in the High Street is the Convent of Mercy, built by George Burt in 1875 as Purbeck House, in the grounds of which are several architectural oddities Burt acquired from his uncle's demolition firm, Mowlem & Company who operated in London. These include the archway from Hyde Park Corner, some seventeenth-century statues from the Royal Exchange, and columns from the former Billingsgate Market. But Burt achieved more for Swanage than acquiring curiosities, for it was largely under his guidance that the resort town of boarding houses was built up in the 1880s after the arrival of the railway. This was timely, for by then the stone trade was in serious decline.

Handfast Point is the seaward end of a ridge of chalk which has resisted erosion more successfully than the softer clays and

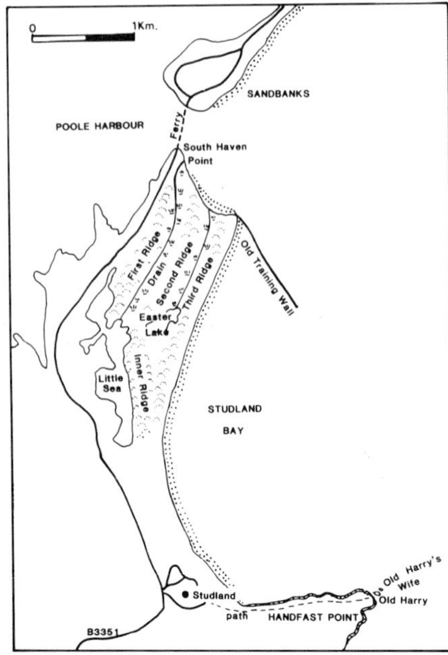

The South Haven Peninsula

sandstones on either side. Where faulting or joints are present the sea exploits the weakness and creates cave systems. These develop into natural arches and when the roof collapses an isolated stack is left, only to be attacked by waves and reduced to a mere stump. All these stages of evolution in the chalk cliff-line can be seen at Handfast Point. Until 1921 the stack known as No Man's Land was joined to the mainland. On its seaward side is the more slender stack of Old Harry's Daughter. Erosion has long since taken toll of Old Harry and his Wife – now mere stumps.

Studland Bay Once over the chalk ridge, the land falls rapidly to the flatness of Poole Harbour and its heathland surround. In the lee of the chalk promontory is the unspoiled village of Studland with its almost complete Norman church built on Saxon foundations. Around are nineteenth-century marine villas like Manor House, now a hotel, and Hill Close, built when this quiet corner of Dorset was beginning to be favoured. Now in the summer months Studland is anything but isolated and quiet for its sandy foreshore, backed by red and yellow cliffs of the Bagshot Beds, is popular for family holidays. Solitude however can still be found in the great spread of sand-dune country forming the South Haven Peninsula which extends northwards to the entrance to Poole Harbour. The peninsula is really built up of three ridges of sandhills with watery hollows in between; one of the hollows contains the Little Sea which, in the late eighteenth century, was in contact with the waters of Poole Bay. Since then two ridges have been built up on its seaward side with sand brought in from the adjacent sea bed. The sand is highly acidic which is remarkable given the nearness of the chalk beds of Handfast Point, and because of this the dune belts are colonised by marram grass, not in itself unusual but, as they become more stabilised, heather and gorse take over. Because of its unusual vegetation the area is managed by the Nature Conservancy but there is access at specific places and a Sand Dunes Nature Trail has been devised. At the extreme tip there is a car ferry across Poole Harbour entrance to the Sandbanks Peninsula on the other side.

Bournemouth was once looked upon as a nineteenth-century upstart which inserted itself on the coast between its much older neighbours, Poole and Christchurch, but now it has eclipsed both and linked with them to form one vast urban spread. Yet the town began only hesitantly when, in 1811, Lewis Tregonwell built a seaside residence close to the mouth of the Bourne brook in an area which at that time was one vast untenanted heath of gorse and bramble. The Tregonwell villa has survived as part of the Royal Exeter Hotel in Exeter Road. Others found the area less attractive for settlement, partly because the deep valleys (chines) cut into the low coastal plateau gave an impression of hilliness. Ultimately the dry soils and high sunshine figures did prove popular, especially for those seeking health cures and convalescence, and it was in this direction that the first real development took place. A local architect Benjamin Ferrey was commissioned to create the Westover Estate, including the original St Peter's church which he began in 1841. Later the more nationally known

Decimus Burton (of Fleetwood, Hove and St Leonard's fame) was brought in, and from 1845 to 1859 pushed ahead with further development. A distinctive feature was the planting of thousands of firs which flourished on the sandy soils and gave the villa residences especially an air of seclusion. All this took place without the help of the railway system which was instrumental elsewhere in creating seaside resorts, but in 1870 the town of 6,000 was finally joined with Ringwood by a branch line and two years later a link was forged with Poole. The present direct route with Southampton and London had to wait until 1888. After that there was no holding back; there was a burst of uncontrolled expansion in late Victorian times and its extension to join Poole in the west and Christchurch in the east took place in the first decades of the present century. With land of little agricultural value there was also considerable growth well inland from the coast. This was to engulf Talbot Village, a model settlement of farms, cottages, almshouses, church and school, all founded by a wealthy Surrey spinster in 1833 in her endeavour to improve the 'condition of the poor'.

Haphazard growth has left its mark on the present Bournemouth which lacks a real centre though the original nucleus around the mouth of the Bourne Valley now functions as such. In recent years many of the Victorian villas have been pulled down and blocks of flats built on their spacious grounds. There has also been considerable office development so that the town no longer relies solely on its visitors. For them the miles of sandy beach have always proved attractive, though erosion has necessitated a recent and successful scheme of beach nourishment with sand pumped ashore from the bed of Bournemouth Bay. Groynes and a promenade help to keep the sand in place and prevent wave action on the base of the cliffs. Erosion has also been a problem at **Southbourne** where the soft sandstone cliffs offer little natural resistance to the waves. Houses have disappeared over the cliff edge, but with the beach-restoration plan now complete it is hoped that further trouble has been averted.

Hengistbury Head stands out as a bastion because layers of ironstone doggers give the cliff-face the necessary 'teeth' to resist erosion. In the past the ironstone has been quarried, but this has long ceased in the interests of coast protection. The furzy-topped headland is a favourite walk for both local residents and visitors, with the approach either from the signposted road near Tuckton Bridge to the car park, or by the foot-ferry across the harbour entrance at Mudeford. Because of its isolated situation Hengistbury was favoured as an early settlement site. There are a number of Bronze Age barrows, perhaps dating from about 1500 BC, and a late Iron Age promontory fort protected on its most vulnerable side by a double bank and ditch.

Christchurch lies on a low site between the rivers Stour and Avon which unite as they enter the wide sheet of shallow water forming the harbour. Once a centre of commerce and fishing, the harbour now is crowded with yachts and other small craft. The original name of the settlement was Twynham, a name which reflects its site on a tongue of land between two rivers; the modern name dates from the founding of the minster church, mentioned in Domesday Book, which became an Augustinian Priory in 1150. Close by are the remains of the twelfth-century Norman castle. Around both castle and priory church a nexus of small streets and passages form the most pleasing quarter of the present-day town, but elsewhere modern estates, built to feed new factories or cater for the retired, cover large areas as in so many south-coast towns. It is the harbour, and particularly Mudeford Quay, that attracts so many summer visitors. At Mudeford the tarred inn and cottages at the harbour entrance form a link with the past and there is still salmon fishing by seine netting in the early months of the year. Formerly a long sandbank from the southern shore forced the entrance channel, known as The Run, to hug the coast as far east as Highcliffe Castle; but since the building of the new promenade and coast-protection works, there is little likelihood of a return to this natural condition.

Christchurch Bay is a small-scale replica of Bournemouth Bay, with its gentle curve, extending from Hengistbury Head round to the shingle Hurst Castle Spit, fashioned out of soft rocks of clay, sand and a gravel capping. Erosion has long been a problem. Water percolating through the upper gravel and sand beds ultimately meets the impervious clay to emerge as springs which act as a lubricant and bring about mudflows, slumps and slides. The result is a jumble of confused strata which gradually moves towards the sea only to be washed away, thus allowing the process to continue from above. Many attempts have been made in recent years to counter the erosion but the cost of protection is enormous if it is to be successful. A series of gravel tracks, like terraces, on the undercliff have helped stabilisation. In the past Hordwell Church and village, lying to the west of Milford-on-Sea, have been lost to the sea. The continuous mass movement of the cliff-face does however open up new exposures, and the cliffs are famous for what the Victorians called the 'Hordwell fossils', of both brackish water and marine origin and including alligator, lizard and other reptilean skeletons.

Hampshire

Milford-on-Sea The idea of creating a resort here goes back to late Victorian times when, in 1887, Colonel Cornwallis West put forward a development plan. It was to differ from the already established south-coast resorts like Brighton in that villas with gardens were to take the place of elegant terraces and spacious squares. The development was not a great success, partly because of the lack of a railway close by, but also because the constant threat of erosion meant that the houses had to be built well back from the sea. After a century of further erosion, the resort still has its ever-narrowing greensward along the cliff top. The original centre of the village lies inland around its Norman church.

Hurst Castle Spit runs out from the mainland into the Solent for about 2km (1½ miles). It is formed entirely of shingle, brought both from offshore and from the retreating cliffs of Christchurch Bay. At its further end the shingle ridge forms a number of sharp recurves, perhaps indicating stages in its growth over hundreds of years. The castle near the outermost point dates from 1541 when Henry VIII was building a system of defence along the south coast in face of possible invasion from the continent. Its position indicates that little lengthening of the spit has occurred over the past 400 years. The main danger now lies in the possible breaching of the narrow neck of the spit which has to withstand the full impact of south-westerly gales, and great rock piles have been dumped near the point where the spit joins the 'mainland' coast close to Milford-on-Sea. The approach to the castle can be made by boat from Keyhaven.

Lymington is to many simply a ferry port to Yarmouth in the Isle of Wight with a short crossing taking 30 minutes. Now it is so crowded with leisure craft that the ferry boat has to pick its way carefully through the anchorages as it makes its way down the narrow Lymington river and out into the Solent. Activity is very much centred around the waterfront and it was here that the original borough of the de Redvers family was created in the mid-twelfth century. The initial site, centred on Quay Street and the cobbled Quay Hill, soon proved inadequate, and in the following century New Lymington began to take shape on the hill-slopes above. The axial street, the present High Street, once contained the Market Hall and at its furthermost end was the town church of St Thomas, originally a mere chapelry of Boldre, in whose parish the new town was placed. The main prosperity of the settlement lay by the quayside where the granaries and saltworks were sited. Around 1800 there were still forty salterns on the mud-flats, the brine being collected in shallow pools and ultimately salt obtained by boiling off the water. Huge piles of ashes once lined the shore but all have now disappeared along with the Lymington salterns. Towards Keyhaven, however, there are still traces of salterns on the marshland fringe.

Buckler's Hard has a fame out of all proportion to its present size. It is an oddity, the creation of the 2nd Duke of Montagu who had plans for developing a major port here on the Beaulieu river to receive imports from his estates on the island of St Lucia in the West Indies. But the plan failed and neither the town nor the proposed docks dug out of the mud banks of the Beaulieu river ever materialised. Only two terraces of red-brick cottages, set on either side of a wide grass verge, were built. At the end of the north row is the master builder's house, and dates from the eighteenth century when pedimented doorways were fashionable. For, although the port failed, Buckler's Hard – hard refers to a layer of gravel and stone to provide a firm foundation on the mud-flats – did become a notable centre for shipbuilding in the eighteenth century, and the small basins which were dug out of the river bank still remain. Its most famous launching was the *Agamemnon* in 1781, a ship that Nelson commanded for several years and that saw service at Trafalgar. It is difficult to imagine that this tiny place could launch a ship of almost 2,000 tons, *HMS Spencer*, in 1800. In the days of wooden warships Buckler's Hard had the advantage of nearby supplies of fine oak timber from the New Forest. Even during World War II it was making wooden vessels which would be immune from sinking by magnetic mines. Now a little upstream there are flourishing shipbuilding yards specialising in leisure craft, a far cry from the original plans for the place. Recently a purpose built museum has become an added attraction.

Calshot Spit marks the final turn of the coastline into Southampton Water. Like Hurst Castle Spit it is a single ridge of shingle broadened at its farthest end, with a castle built by Henry VIII as part of his overall defence scheme. In contrast to the feeling of isolation at Hurst Castle, Calshot is very much overshadowed by the great complex of the nearby Fawley oil refinery. Begun in 1920 and very much expanded since then, the refinery has completely transformed what was once a quiet corner of the New Forest.

Lee-on-Solent, on the opposite shore, and in the approach to Southampton Water, started as yet another late nineteenth-century resort. It even achieved a pier, built in 1885, but this has now disappeared along with its former branch railway link with Southampton. Lee Tower now occupies the site of the former railway terminus which itself was close to the pier entrance. Today the gabled Edwardian villas are swamped by later indifferent housing as Lee concentrated on becoming a residential resort, serving both the retired and the commuters.

Gosport or God's Port, so named by Bishop Henry de Blois in 1158 when he put in here to shelter from a storm, marks the first of a group of 'insular' settlements which line the shore of the eastern Solent. With the older villages which it has engulfed, Gosport has spread over a vast area of the peninsula bordering the western side of Portsmouth Harbour and naturally shares some of the naval history of its near neighbour across the water. The original settlement was at the head of Haslar Creek, around the thirteenth-century church of St Mary, and even today there is still a village atmosphere preserved in the narrow streets to the west of the church. Close by in 1826 the Marquis of Anglesey attempted to create a new marine town, named Angleseaville, by building a crescent of nineteen bays which was intended as the centre piece of the new development. Nearby Anglesea House (now the National Children's Home) was completed in 1830. These apart, Angleseaville never really got off the ground, though the fine crescent, with a central portico and long colonnades of fluted Doric columns, iron balconies extending to end pavilions, still survives, to add a touch of grandeur compared with the later drab urban developments. The only other notable building is Bay House, built to the designs of the eminent architect Decimus Burton and now part of a school. Gosport proper grew out of Alverstoke parish and its church of Holy Trinity started as a chapel-of-ease in 1696, though earlier there had been a fishing settlement here on the low peninsula between Haslar Creek and Forton Creek.

Because of its strategic position in relation

to the naval base of Portsmouth, Gosport has had its share of defensive works. The most notable is a string of forts which run through the area from Elsdon, on the shores of Portsmouth Harbour across to Fort Gomer (now demolished) on the coast. Of those which have survived, some like Fort Rowner and Fort Grange are still in naval hands. All the forts date from the period 1850 to 1860 and were built on the orders of Lord Palmerston who feared a possible French invasion and neutralisation of the naval base of Portsmouth through a back-door entry. Fort Brockhurst is now under the control of the Department of the Environment and as an Ancient Monument has been restored to its original condition. The old town of Gosport had its own earlier defensive system consisting of an elaborate set of ramparts guarding the western approaches to the peninsula, but few traces now remain. Bombing during World War II took its toll of the old town, so that there are tall tower blocks close to the waterside completely dwarfing the parish church with its Victorian campanile.

Porchester occupies the blunt peninsula which projects into the head of Portsmouth Harbour. It is approached from the main A27 road by a twisting street, first through typical twentieth-century suburban housing and then on to the much older village core. A tiny triangular green and grouping of houses, mainly eighteenth century in date, form a real oasis of tranquillity in a coastland which has been swamped with estates and factories. Beyond lies Porchester Castle with its walled enclosure of 4ha (9 acres) next to the waterfront. The fort dates from the third century when the Romans were anxious about possible invasion, and was one of a series built at this time on the coast from Norfolk round to Hampshire. The walls, 3m (10ft) thick and about 6m (20ft) high, are built in typical Roman style of flint work with bonding courses of red tile. After the Romans left it seems to have been occupied periodically during Saxon times, for excavations within the walls have shown up the post-holes of a great timber hall, possibly of early sixth-century date. The greatest change came in the twelfth century when a medieval castle with keep and moat was erected in the north-west corner of the Roman fort. In the opposite corner an Augustinian Priory was founded a few years later in 1133. Both survive to give additional interest to what is one of the finest Roman remains in southern Britain.

Porchester Roman fort and Norman castle

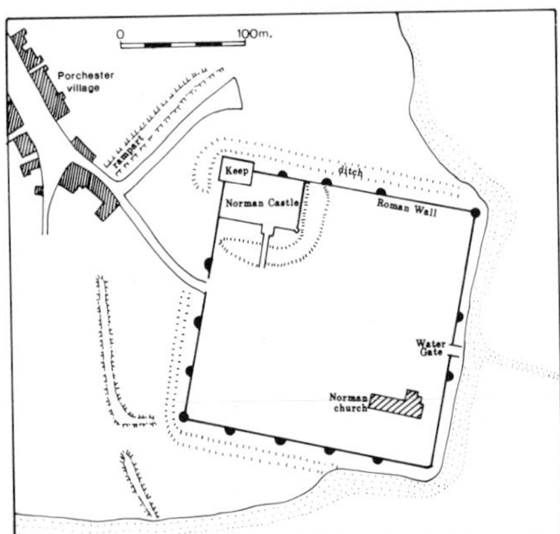

Portsmouth Here the former unbroken coastal plain, as in Sussex, was partly drowned during the rise of sea level which followed the Ice Age, giving rise to the spacious inlets of Portsmouth, Langstone and Chichester harbours. Of the three, Portsmouth has fared best in terms of development. Little by way of settlement existed on Portsea Island until towards the end of the twelfth century when a small port was created by Richard the Lion Heart close to the narrow entrance channel, with a creek in the lee (the Camber) to act as a sheltered anchorage. This newly established town formed the basis of what is today called Old Portsmouth. Streets were laid out in regular fashion, burgage plots demarcated and, in 1194, the town charter gave market and fair rights. At the same time a dock was dug out of the tidal mud to the north of the town. There was already a recently built chapel in existence for John de Gisons, a wealthy merchant, had granted the monks of Southwick Priory 0.5ha (1 acre) of land on which to build in memory of Thomas à Becket. This priory chapel later became

Hayling never really succeeded as a resort, despite the hopes raised by this early-nineteenth-century cresent

incorporated in the parish church, which in turn became the cathedral of St Thomas in 1927.

The new town of the twelfth century was no different from scores of other medieval foundations all over the country, and could easily have languished in succeeding centuries if it had not become an important naval base. This development took place in the fifteenth century with the building of stone defences, ramparts and a dry dock. Growth soon outstripped the land available within the old walled town and a new extension, Portsea, was built and equipped with its own defences in 1780. Later growth, much of it of indifferent character, was to cover virtually the whole of Portsea Island in the twentieth century. The town suffered badly as a result of bombing in World War II and large areas were laid flat. The greatest loss was in the old town where the streets and buildings still retained their old-world character. Rebuilding, including the provision of a new shopping centre, has been uninspiring, so that Portsmouth today is no different from many other English towns. Southsea, its resort suburb, which began to develop between 1810 and 1820, has fortunately more to show for its early period of growth, in particular a number of fine terraces overlooking the open expanse of the common. Here the Clarence Promenade was laid out in 1847, and looks over a shingle beach from which noisy hovercraft make the rapid trip across to the Isle of Wight. Nearby is Clarence Pier, which has been rebuilt in the post-war period to provide the amusements and novelties which seem to draw the day tripper.

Hayling Island still gives a hint of what this coast must have been like before large-scale development took place. The natural setting was a low flat land made fertile by great spreads of wind-blown brickearth, though with patches of infertile gravels in places. This open landscape, now largely hedgeless, is still apparent in the northern part of the island. In contrast, the southern coastal fringe has turned its back on all this and is now a spread of residential housing and seaside villas. Development began in earnest following the bridge link with the mainland in 1824, and a hotel (the present-day Royal) and part of a crescent were built on the seafront overlooking a wide expanse of shingle and tiny sand dunes. It was never followed up and the crescent still forms the only group of buildings of any real character. A few Edwardian villas added little and it was left to the speculative building of the 1930s to impose itself on the island. A railway link had been established with the mainland in 1899, ostensibly to provide a steamer service with the Isle of Wight, and this allowed people to work away from the island. The railway has now closed, although the broken causeway across the strait and the terminal sheds near the former station remain, and the car now takes the commuters to work in the mainland factories and offices. The car also brings in the summer visitors in their thousands. But although amusements and arcades are to be found on a small scale, they do not dominate as in many south-coast resorts. Hayling caters largely for those in search of carefree holidays where full use can be made of the wide shingle expanses of the central Beachland section and the light-coloured sandy strands which appear as the tide falls.

The best section of the coast is in the west at Sinah Common. Here, close to the entrance to Langstone Harbour, there is a succession of curving beach ridges of shingle and curious banks of unbroken shells. Inland the shingle gives way to low dunes capped with tamarisk, gorse and sea lupin which make a colourful show in the summer. In this section the land appears to be extending at the expense of the sea, but elsewhere on the island it is a different story. Prior to the building of the concrete promenade and groynes in 1947 there had always been considerable erosion towards Eaststoke Point. Even with this protection the beach remains low and the newly built expensive villas (a replacement of meaner 1930s chalets) seem very vulnerable to winter storms. In the central section between Beachland and the golf course, the shingle foreland has been pared back as much as 61m (200ft) since 1940. Fortunately it is wide at this point, but it gives an indication of the serious threat of erosion to the southern shore of Hayling Island. The dangers of erosion and flooding have been ever present for a record of 1324 speaks of the flooding and destruction of the priory on the island. Today the whole area still lives with this threat, but nevertheless thrives on its holiday-camp trade which has benefited in recent years from the increasing tendency for families to favour self-catering holidays, either in chalets or caravans.

Isle of Wight

Compared with the nearby Hampshire mainland, the coastline of the Isle of Wight is one of rich variation born out of a succession of different geological strata which run as a series of bands across the island from east to west. The northern part consists of soft Tertiary beds though occasional layers of limestone give more positive features especially around Bembridge. It is the chalk, however, which occurs more than any other single rock type. Inland it gives rise to a narrow ridge of downland running right across the centre of the island; on reaching the coast it projects as the partly dismembered stacks of the Needles in the west, while in the east it forms the prominent Culver Cliff. The rolling over of the beds to form a huge upfold has affected the country to the south and led to the creation of the bays of Shanklin and Brighstone where the sea has worn back underlying softer beds of clay and ferruginous sands. Further south the return of the chalk, this time as a flat slab of downland between Shanklin and Ventnor rising to over 213m (700ft), heralds a new type of coastline, that of the Undercliff with its succession of landslip features. Once this is left behind at St Catherine's Point, the coastline becomes less impressive as waves steadily roll back the clay cliffs. But with the return of the chalk at Freshwater Bay the natural grandeur of the island's coastline is restored.

Cowes is often the starting point for visitors arriving from Southampton, either by boat or hydrofoil. The relatively wide mouth of the river Medina has long associations with yachting and its banks are lined with boatyards, boat-building concerns,

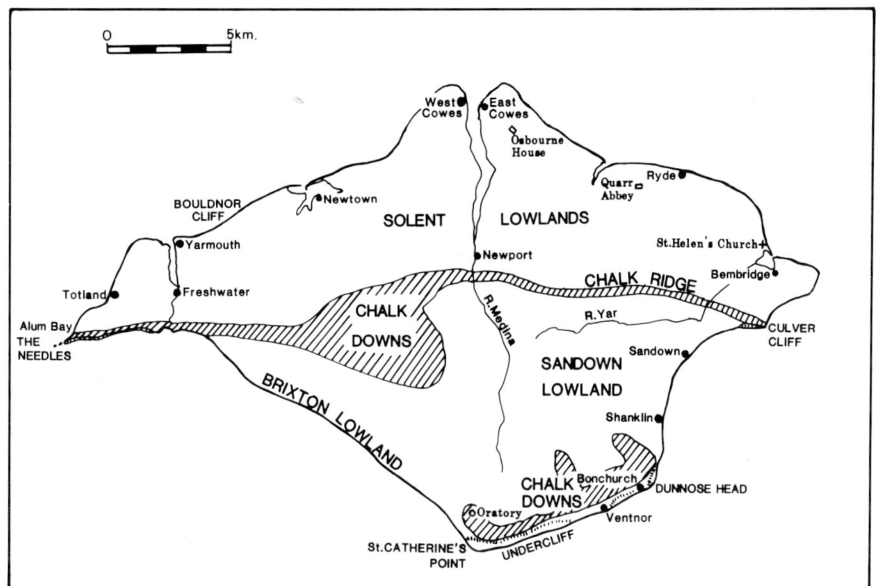

The main elements in the geography of the Isle of Wight

ships chandlers and slipways, some dating back to the eighteenth century when yacht racing first started here. The Yacht Club was founded in 1815 after a successful regatta had been promoted the previous year. Of the two settlements of West and East Cowes separated by the Medina, only the former has the appearance of a town. Apart from sailing activities off the water-front, the town is not without interest. The main High Street is set a little back and in its twists and rises follows the contours of the coastal strip. It ends near the Royal Yacht Squadron's club house which incorporates Henry VIII's coastal fort. Behind there are steep streets like Sun Hill and Market Hill with houses which have remained untainted by modern shop-front development such as has occurred in the High Street. Close by is Northwood House, now the urban authority offices but once a mansion in simple classical style dating from the early nineteenth century.

Across the river and reached by ferry is East Cowes, now largely a residential area, though its waterfront has its boatyards and the like. Beyond lie leafy roads and the two estates of Norris Castle and Osborne House. Formerly there were three major houses here but East Cowes Castle, built by John Nash for his own use, has been savagely demolished. Of the three, Norris Castle was always the largest and most imposing. It was built in a mock-Norman style in 1799 and made to look deceptively grand, especially when seen from the Solent. The surrounding grounds have a parkland setting with lawns running down to the water's edge. Nearby Osborne House, the retreat of Queen Victoria after the death of her husband in 1861, is less imposing and an architectural jumble. The queen bought the original eighteenth-century house in 1845 along with 405ha (1,000 acres) and here the prince consort, with help from the builder Thomas Cubitt, gave full play to his architectural ideas and in the end completely transformed the original structure. Terraces front the house on its seaward side and there is a short esplanade where the queen and her husband could stroll and admire the seascapes of the Solent. Much of the low coastland formed of red and green clays is scenically unexciting, and now largely wooded around the shoreline. Between here and Fishbourne, another ferry terminal, access is limited save where holiday camps have intruded.

Quarr Abbey There are really two buildings, the fragmentary remains of a former twelfth-century Cistercian monastery and its twentieth-century counterpart dating from 1908 when French Benedictine monks bought a Victorian house nearby and then added to it to serve their needs. Unlike the original abbey built of local limestone, they used multi-coloured Flemish bricks to achieve a surprising effect. The name 'Quarr' is said to relate to the nearby limestone quarries (*quararia*) at Binstead, which in medieval times were an important source of building stone. Apart from its use in the early monastery, the stone was shipped to the mainland for cathedrals like Chichester and Winchester. With its broken shell fragments set in a tenacious cement matrix, it was said to resemble the famous Caen stone of Normandy with which it is often confused. The workable stone was of limited extent and the quarries were abandoned over a century ago.

Ryde developed early enough in the nineteenth century to avoid all the excesses of Victorian times and it is this which distinguishes the town from its east-coast neighbours, Sandown and Shanklin. It has always been a point of entry to the island, especially since the building of its first pier in 1813. Much modified, the latter is still used for landing and now the visitor is hustled into waiting old London Underground trains for transport along the long pier to the town of Ryde itself and on to Shanklin – the only remnant of the once extensive rail network of the island. Early Ryde consists of a grouping of streets around the pier which rise steeply up the slope to what later became the Upper Town. Most of the buildings remaining from this early period have a Regency air, even though some are slightly later in date. In the upper town the dominant building is All Saints Church, built in 1867 by Sir Gilbert Scott with a 55m (180ft) high spire. Around are the meaner buildings of the later phase of development. But it is on the Esplanade that the true character of Ryde is apparent, in the seaside villas and fine views across the Solent. There is also a coastal walk round to Seaview with its fine beach and small yacht club.

St Helens, set on the inner edge of Brading (Bembridge) harbour and protected by the broad sandy grassland spit of *The Duver*, was once famed for the great variety of over 250 species of plants. The original church on the coast has been extensively damaged by sea erosion and only the landward side of the tower remains. It would probably have disappeared altogether but for Trinity House who preserved it as a sea-mark. A new church was built inland in 1719 and subsequently enlarged as the former fishing village grew from a population of only 200 to over 2,000 by the mid-nineteenth century, largely through St Helens Roads becoming a favourite anchorage for shipping. At one time the inlet around which the village lies ran inland as far as Brading and there were many attempts at reclamation of the 'muddy swamp', as it was described as late as the 1850s. One early scheme was initiated early in the seventeenth century by Sir Hugh Middleton who, with Dutch labour, threw an embankment across the entrance. As part of the scheme a tide mill, barn and houses were built and crops of rape grown on the reclaimed land, but ultimately the sea breached the man-made wall and so the lands returned to their marshy and brackish state. It was not until 1876 that the present embankment carrying the road, followed a few years later by another causeway for the branch railway to Bembridge, finally sealed off the inlet. Today St Helens still has some character especially around the village green where there are several old houses. Offshore stands St Helen's Fort, one of Lord Palmerston's follies, built about 1860 to protect the eastern Solent from possible invasion by Napoleon III.

Bembridge, a straggling residential area, is sited on a peninsula formed of flint gravel on top of marls. Below lies the famous Bembridge limestone which runs out onto the foreshore as prominent reefs. The impetus to growth came in 1882 when the sailing club was formed so that, with the Royal Spithead Hotel built at the same time, Bembridge quickly attracted yachtsmen who preferred to sail smaller craft. Villas soon followed, and more recently bungalows have spread like a rash across parts of the peninsula. Nearby in Whitecliff Bay there are the same beds of coloured sands which

The church tower at St Helen's. Trinity House requested that it be preserved because of its usefulness as a seamark

have become such a tourist attraction on the other side of the island at Alum Bay (see page 296). Here they are less impressive through being partly covered by vegetation but, where visible, are seen to be upturned in an almost vertical position. To the south they give way to the chalk strata of Culver Cliff, best seen from seaward, where layers of flints clearly indicate the sharp dip of the beds. The obelisk on the downland ridge above was erected in memory of the commodore of the Royal Yacht Squadron, the Earl of Yarborough.

Sandown was described in a guide book of 1865 as 'once a small cluster of fishermen's huts but now rapidly assuming the character of a town and bidding fair to become one of the places of largest resort in the island'. The last hundred years has seen all this come about, not always in the best taste but always able to rely on the natural strand of fine sands to attract visitors. Some of the older buildings of the town which showed such rapid growth at the turn of the century now have a careworn look, especially in the winter months when the masking effect of the droves of summer visitors has been stripped away. There is still the pier and its pavilion with summer shows, concert parties and dancing to attract, while along the Esplanade there are bars, cafés, bingo halls, fun fairs intermixed with guest houses and hotels, together with the odd remaining nineteenth-century seaside villa. In many ways this sums up the present role of Sandown. Fortunately the more natural beauty of the island is never far away for those wishing to seek it out.

Shanklin is now in urban continuity with Sandown, though originally it grew up quite separately and at a much earlier date. This is its saving grace for, although it has its modern 'attractions', there are still corners where the old shows through. Shanklin could well have become a 'spaw' in the Scarborough tradition for at the end of the Esplanade there is a chalybeate spring coming out of the cliff. There is a further spring inland towards the upper entrance of the chine, a deeply cut valley where a small stream drops over 91m (300ft) in a series of cascades to the shore. What was once a winding glen of luxuriant vegetation has now been commercialised though its original character is still discernible. Close by is the old village of Shanklin with its thatched cottages turned into restaurants, cafés and gift shops so that it wears an artificial air when it could so easily have lent character to the resort.

Bonchurch South of Shanklin the coastline of sandstone cliffs gives way to the more tumbled landslip scenery formed as the pervious chalk capping of Shanklin Downs admits water which is then retained by the underlying clay strata. A past slip, comparable in extent with those of the east Devon and west Dorset coasts, has let down strata on the seaward side of Nansen Hill. There are two major areas of slip, upper and lower, and it is possible to walk through the whole tormented area amidst tangled oaks and hazel thickets. Continuing round Dunnose Head, the village of Bonchurch is reached, with its early Norman church something of a surprise since there was little settlement until the nineteenth century. A church had been established on this site probably as early as AD 755 after monks had landed on the shore below (still called Monk's Bay) from the abbey of Lyre in Normandy. The dedication to St Boniface later became incorporated in the names of the settlement and the wide expanse of chalk plateau above. The rudiments of the present building were supposedly the work of Benedictine monks who settled here in 1070 and led to its entry in Domesday Book as *Boncirce.* This is the only glimpse of the past, for present-day Bonchurch dates only from the past hundred years. Amidst the tumbled greenery of the landslip topography Victorian villas and later residential building have now made a considerable impact on the steep slopes with its palms, fuschias and myrtle bushes.

Ventnor If the growth of nearby Bonchurch is unexpected, the development of Ventnor in what must be looked on as a very unfavourable situation is even more dramatic. One man, Sir James Clarke, played a major role through the publication in 1829 of his medical treatise on 'The influence of climate in the prevention and cure of organic diseases'. In this he cited the Undercliff area as having one of the best climates in Britain. Within fifteen years town commissioners had been appointed with the task of creating a town as Clarke had suggested. Today Ventnor is set on a rising staircase of terraces which lead from the shoreline to the cliff overhang of the chalk downs above. Streets progress up the slope in a series of zigzags but even so the gradients are hardly for the retired. This however did not appear to worry the early residents who came here in search of a health resort. Armed with the medical advice of Sir James Clarke and the

Ventnor, south-facing and sheltered by the high downs to the north, has an ideal situation for early holidays by the sea

statistics of the registrar general who declared Ventnor to be the healthiest spot in England (with a death rate of 15.4 per 1,000 compared with 17.1 for Torquay) villas began to appear on the slopes. Fresh impetus came with the opening of the railway link with Shanklin and Ryde, only made possible by a 1.6km (1 mile) long tunnel under the chalk downs. Trees and shrubs were introduced from warmer climes and today the 'riviera' touch is still apparent. A short esplanade was laid out in 1848, later followed by a pier (rebuilt in 1955), so that it was possible to come to Ventnor by steamer from Littlehampton, itself served by the London train.

St Catherine's Point has the most spectacular landslip scenery of the whole island. The well travelled Mrs Radcliffe at the end of the eighteenth century described it in her usual exaggerated terms as having 'a sense of wildness and ruin as we never saw before. The road is close to a wall of rock, frequently beneath enormous masses that lean forward'. It was as well that Mrs Radcliffe made the journey when she did, for the road subsequently disappeared in a great landslip in 1799 when nearly 40ha (100 acres) slipped downwards to the shore. Another more recent slip in 1928 carried away a replacement road and this time it was decided to re-route it inland through Niton village. On top of St Catherine's Down – reached by a field path from the main road – is the octagonal building of an old lighthouse dating back to the fourteenth century and still in a fine state of preservation (National Trust). An adjacent oratory is known only from excavations. Trinity House started a replacement light nearby in 1786 but the scheme was abandoned, after the base had been built, in favour of the present site much closer to the shore.

Blackgang Chine is the first of many such chasms which break up the continuity of this south-western coast, but it is distinguished from the others by its over-commercialisation which seems always to have been its fate. The Victorian predecessor of the present-day visitor, for example, was politely told that 'if he left the chine unvisited he may be consoled with the assurance that he had lost but little', sentiments that some might echo today though the gardens, gnomes, model village and the like have their devotees. The name Blackgang is derived from 'black way', the route up the chine from the shore between walls of black shale. These are overlain by harder sandstone beds which form an upper cliff over which mud glaciers spew onto the tumbled lower slope towards the sea.

The succession of Wealden Beds which make up the cliff coastline as far as Compton Bay near Freshwater are soft and easily eroded, though they prevent access to the beach save at a few points. At both Atherfield Point and Hanover Point harder beds form minor headlands with rocky reefs projecting seawards. In Compton Bay the succession of Lower Greensand, Gault Clay and Upper Greensand finally give way to the chalk which now forms the cliff-line as far as the Needles.

Freshwater Bay A rise in sea level of a few feet would cause the present valley running inland to become a strait. On John Speed's map of 1610 it is shown as such and named the Isle of Freshwater, though it is doubtful whether it was a true island as late as this. The breaching of the chalk wall lies well back in geological time, the result of river action etching out a through valley. The sea then entered the gap to form the present bay with its residual chalk stacks like Arched Rock and the pyramidal Stag Rock. Beyond lies the rounded shoulder of Tennyson Down with its monument on top and the poet's home (now a hotel) at Farringford on its northern slopes. There he tried to lead a normal family life shunning the visitors who came to gaze at the house in which he lived continuously from 1853 to 1867 and thereafter at intervals until his death in 1892. It was as an old man of eighty-one that, on making the ferry-crossing from Lymington to Yarmouth, he jotted down the lines of his poem 'Crossing the Bar' on the inside of an envelope.

The Needles and Alum Bay are two of the great curiosities of the English coastline and on the visiting list of anyone coming to the Isle of Wight. The Needles, a succession of stacks formed of toughened up-turned chalk thrusting out defiantly into the English Channel, are best seen from seaward though good views are obtained in morning light from the look-out station on the end of the sharp promontory. There are three main chalk stacks, though the base of two others is discernible. Formerly there was a prominent cylindrical chimney-stack known as Lot's Wife, the only true 'needle', but this collapsed in 1764. The innermost stack was formerly connected with the mainland by an arch, but this too gave way about 1815. From the Needles it is but a short walk to the contrasting cliffs of Alum Bay. Here, the same earth movements which affected the chalk have turned a succession of younger clays, sandstones and shales almost on end. Though commercialised to the extent of having a chair-lift to carry the thousands down to the shore to view the variegated cliffs, the spot still retains a fascination, especially after rain and in evening sunlight when the range of colours of the closely packed strata are brought out to the full. The shales were quarried for alum in the sixteenth century, hence the name of the bay.

Totland can be looked upon as the seaside extension of inland Freshwater, itself made up of a number of 'green' hamlets which increasing building this century has now linked together. Though a resort, it is much less crowded in the summer months than its east-coast counterparts and consequently more attractive for the permanent residents. The church of 1875 was built at a time when Totland was just beginning to expand, but developing late as it did it still managed a tiny pier. The adjacent Colwell Bay has its holiday camp, with chalets overlooking a fine curving beach.

Yarmouth is of much greater historical interest than the Victorian resorts of the island. As one of the island's three purposely planned towns, it can trace its beginning to about 1170 when it was chartered by the 3rd Earl of Devon. Even though 800 years have passed since its foundation it is still possible to see its grid-plan of streets. The earliest church lay to the the east, but after a French

The hardened chalk at the western end of the Isle of Wight has created a festoon of stacks known as the Needles

raid in 1378 was rebuilt on its present site. The castle came much later as one of the coastal chain built by Henry VIII in 1547, but by then the town was largely in decay with only twelve burgesses remaining. Competition from Southampton, which took away its maritime trade, was the main reason. Even in 1800 there were less than a hundred inhabitants, in view of which it is surprising that the town has survived even in its shrunken state. The once flourishing market square has its tiny Town Hall, built in 1763 by the governor of the island, and the adjacent High Street has its rows of cottages. The causeway across the Yar was only built in 1863. Many visitors only know the town casually as it is the ferry terminal from Lymington.

The north-western coast of the island has little scenic interest with the soft Tertiary beds subject to erosion and landslips. A great mudflow is to be seen at Bouldnor Cliff which, after wet weather, can be very sticky and treacherous. Such falls occur where the flow tumbles over the harder beds in the succession, and there is movement after heavy rainfall rather like that of a glacier. Further east beyond Hamstead the land loses height and the partly drowned marshland and estuary of Newtown river dominate the scene.

Newtown It was in this lowland setting that another artificially created town arose in the parish of Calbourne, the estate of which had belonged to the Bishops of Winchester since AD 826. Anxious to improve the income of what was a purely rural manor, the bishop decided to create a town and thus derive benefit from market and port dues. Called Francheville at the time of its foundation in 1255, it had an inauspicious start for it was destroyed by the French in 1377 and always suffered from competition from nearby Yarmouth. Nevertheless the seventy-three plots in the original borough were largely occupied throughout the medieval period and it managed to hang on until disenfranchised in 1832. A plan of 1768 shows the layout of the plots on either side of High Street and on the north side of Gold Street. In the other street, Broad Street, the Town Hall is one of the few survivals which give a clue to former urban status. For the rest there are only grassy streets and back lanes to hint at the former layout, and even the Town Hall was derelict until rescued in the 1930s and handed over to the National Trust for safe keeping. The present building dates from 1699 and has dramatic simplicity expressed in stone and brick. Of the former harbour nothing remains save a derelict quay looking out across saltings, reeds and bare mud-spreads, with part of the area forming a Nature Reserve with a trail laid out by an enlightened county council who have also prepared an explanatory leaflet. This is a seascape of oystercatchers, curlews and terns winging over the large expanses of sea lavender and thrift, in delicate shades of mauve in early summer. Eastwards from Newtown harbour the coastline is low and largely inaccessible except on foot. It is not long before Gurnard Bay is reached and with it the huts, bungalows, hotels and holiday camp which form the approach to West Cowes.

13 South-east England

Sussex

Bosham combines all that is best in a waterside settlement. Lying at the head of a side creek of Chichester Harbour it has a history going back to Roman times, as red tiles in the church tower proclaim. The church has many surviving Saxon remnants, particularly the 17m (55ft) high tower, and was even stylised in the Bayeux tapestry – Harold sailed from Bosham on his ill-fated encounter with Duke William of Normandy. One of the chief glories of the church is its setting on slightly raised ground overlooking the harbour with its mud-flats covered with green algae and rice grass, rich feeding grounds for swans and eider ducks. It is partly encircled by a moat which once provided water for a mill on its south side. The cottages of the narrow High Street, and those along the waterside, give Bosham a charm which singles it out as perhaps the most exciting and picturesque place on the south coast. Even modern intrusions like the tiny precinct of thirteen shops housed in a converted barn – reminiscent on a tiny scale of the Fishermen's Wharf on San Francisco's waterfront – do not detract from its old-world atmosphere.

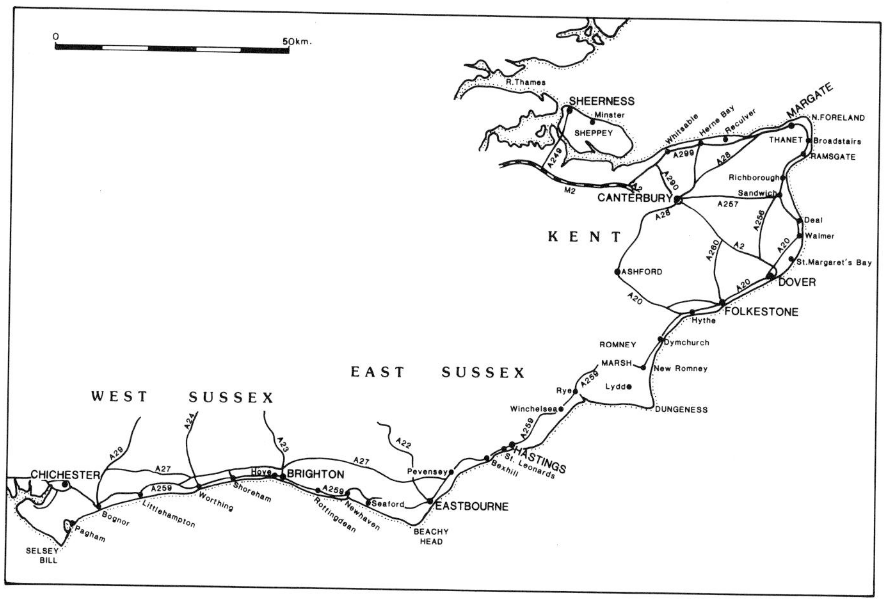

The coast of south-east England

Bosham, with its Saxon church and surrounding cottages lapped by the advancing tides across the saltings of Chichester Harbour

Selsey Peninsula is a flat land of fertile brickearth soils bounded by the sea and the penetrating inlets of Chichester Channel and Pagham Harbour. Before the Romans arrived, Selsey was an Iron Age centre of some wealth for the low cliff of Cakeham, now under constant threat from the sea, yielded a hoard of 200 gold coins, probably needed for trade with Gaul. On the eastern shore there is an Iron Age earthwork at Church Norton. Roman buildings were later erected on the mound and there are many other places where Roman remains and villas have been found eg Sidlesham. A Roman road ran down the backbone of the peninsula from Chichester to Selsey and there was another to the port of Birdham with an offshoot to Bracklesham. After the Romans left the Saxons moved in to form their own kingdom, and one of their landing places was *cymenes ora*, a name which survives as The Owers. This is now a submerged bank lying offshore from Selsey Bill, but tradition asserts that it was once the site of a monastery founded by Saint Wilfred in the seventh century and a later cathedral before erosion took its toll and forced a removal to Chichester. Saxon settlement is also apparent at West Wittering, even though its appearance today hardly suggests that it began with the founding of its church in the eighth century. One rock offshore is called Mixon; this has yielded a shelly limestone which was once extensively used as a building material and can be seen in the old thatched cottages of Selsey.

Selsey Bill Low gravel-topped cliffs have long suffered erosion which led to the building of the present concrete sea wall and groynes in the 1960s to protect the tremendous spread of twentieth-century housing which has all but obliterated the original Selsey village. It began on a large scale after 1907 when the syndicate of Selsey-on-Sea Limited was formed to develop the strip of coastline near the lifeboat station as a resort. Up to that time this had been occupied by a loosely knit community of fishermen with their fish-shops – tarred huts for storing fishing gear – scattered over the backshore. This early development was on a part of the coast which was gaining at the expense of the sea so there was no fear of any buildings being swept away. But this had not always been the case for offshore lies the shallow sea bed known as The Park, associated in legend with the former hunting lands of the bishops of Chichester, supposedly inundated during the stormy fourteenth century.

Pagham Harbour is still a wetland wilderness enclosed by two shingle spits which approach each other from different directions and leave only a narrow gap through which the tide floods and ebbs. The present harbour of mud-flats and saltings stands as a monumental failure by man to control natural forces. In 1876 the narrow entrance was artificially sealed with the intention of reclaiming a vast acreage of good agricultural land, but in the event only marginal inning took place before a storm in December 1910 once more created a gap in the shingle. Pagham Lake, with its holiday chalets, is the remnant of the old harbour exit-channel. Church Norton, on its southern fringe, is the mother church of Selsey and is of interest because of its isolated position. It has been compared with the Welsh *llan* type of foundation, so favoured by Celtic saints in isolated countryside.

Bognor Regis was described as dull or uninteresting or dismissed as a minor watering place in many Victorian guide books. One of these, *Murray's Guide* of 1868, however, was more favourable and adopted a more hopeful note for the future now that an esplanade and pier had just been completed. For all its shortcomings, Bognor can claim one first, namely that it was the earliest resort to owe its origin to one man, in this case Sir Richard Hotham, a London hatter, who invested his considerable fortune in promoting a seaside settlement, which he hoped might be called Hothampton. It all began about 1784 with the building of Hotham House set in a park to the east of the present Bognor. There was also The Dome, the centre piece of Hothampton Crescent, by which it was hoped to wean George III away from Weymouth. Built of local Bognor stone and brickwork, it is perhaps the finest building to survive from the early attempts to found the resort. Sir Richard died in 1799, having lost his entire fortune in the venture. In the early decades of the next century further development took place, including

Erosion rates for the southern coast of the Selsey Peninsula

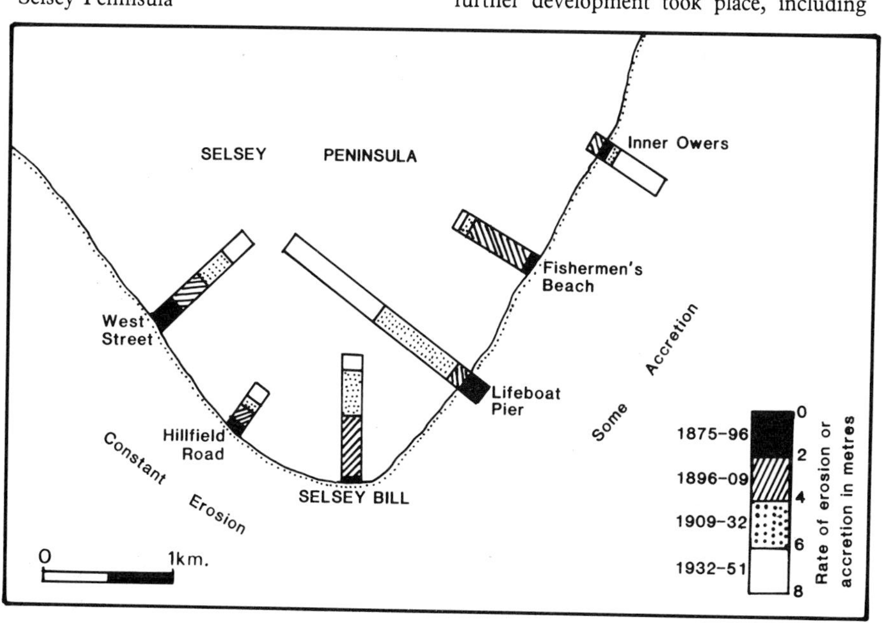

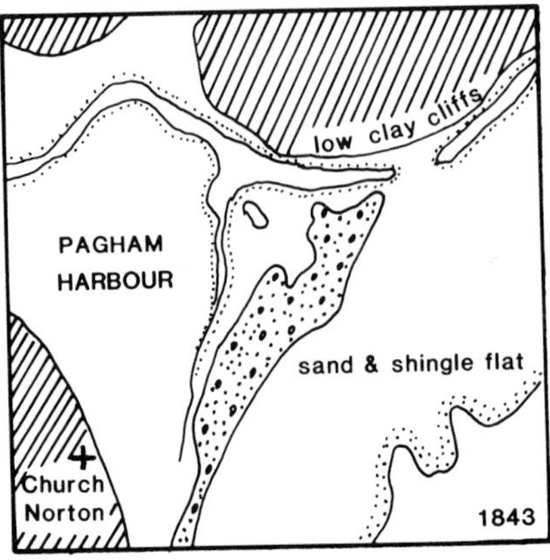

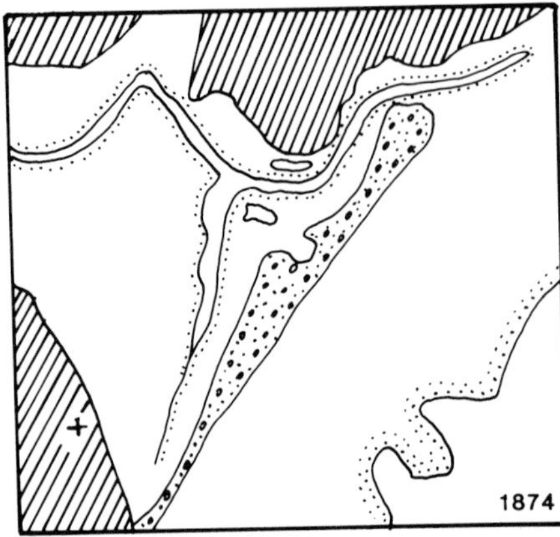

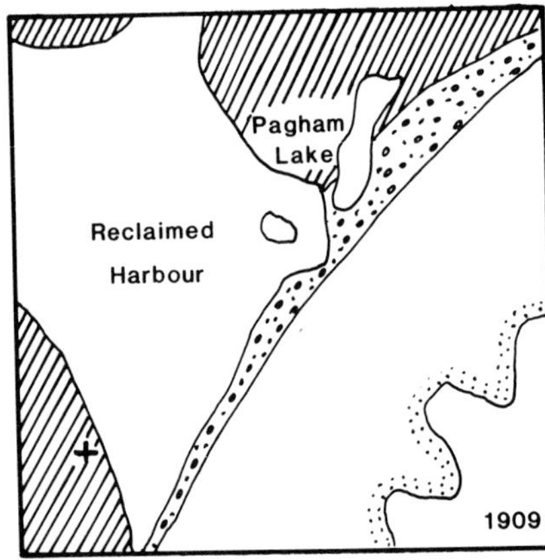

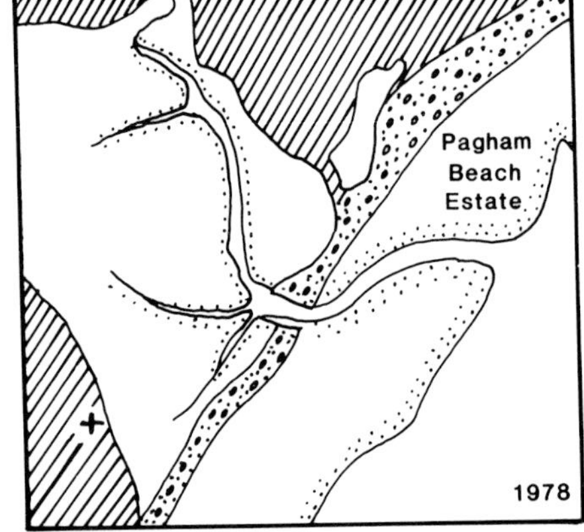

The changing coastline at the entrance to Pagham Harbour

Rock Garden Crescent (1804), Waterloo Square (1811), West Side (1820) and, best of all, The Steyne – a direct import from Brighton. Growth was slow throughout much of the nineteenth century and it was not until after George V stayed at the Norfolk Hotel during his convalescence in 1927 that the title 'Regis' was affixed. Now the town has the usual selection of seaside amenities, including a large holiday camp to the east, although its pier has a severed end and seems unlikely to be rebuilt. Further along the coast there is the exclusive suburb of Middleton-on-Sea, which developed out of a private estate and still has its 'Keep Out' notices. A chapel of 1859 replaced the original parish church of the old village which was lost through erosion. The sea-front houses and bungalows are still waging a ceaseless battle with the sea and novel methods have been employed to prevent further coastal recession (see J. Cartland, *Bygone Bognor*, 1979).

Littlehampton represents the smallest of the group of Sussex ports which has seen an increase in trade and leisure activities in recent years. The harbour is artificial in that the Arun mouth has been controlled ever since a cut was made direct to the sea in 1732 and wooden piers built. The old town is tucked away a little up-river with flint-dressed cottages grouped around the church. The resort lies to the east of the harbour, its centrepiece being the green with a long range of early nineteenth-century terraces as a backcloth. These include Norfolk Place which was intended to become part of a square, and South Terrace, where the differing styles of the houses reflect the long period it took to build. A modern block of flats at the eastern end now completes the picture. **Rustington** and **Angmering-on-Sea** are bungalow resorts of the type so favoured by the retired who want a place by the sea. Angmering has its old village core inland set on two small hills with a green in between. Although building is going on all around there is still an open belt between the village and the modern resort, largely devoted to glasshouses.

Worthing, the next of a whole string of resorts which now completely dominate the coastline of West Sussex, appears at first sight to lack a sense of unity, as if it suffers from the absence of an overall initial plan. It began in 1759 as a seaside fishing hamlet known as Broadwater, and for the next thirty years little happened until the speculator John Luther saw its possibilities as the choice of 'those who prefer retirement and quiet to the hustle and dissipation of Brighton'. He began by building a large house capable of providing lodgings for visiting gentry, which was later purchased by the Earl of Warwick in 1789 – an event which marks the beginning of the resort town. The visit of George III's daughter in 1798 provided a stimulus to development and in the early years of the nineteenth century simple terraces like Bedford Row and Montague Place were built. The latter still retains some old houses with high shallow bow-fronted windows. Another development of this period, the theatre, still survives (though now a warehouse) close to the modern shopping precinct of Warwick Road. With the laying out of the open space of the Steyne in 1807 – the import from Brighton also copied in Bognor – Worthing was deemed to have arrived and in 1812 was granted a chapel-of-ease. Subsequent expansion has filled up the coastal strip both to east and west so that the sea front now looks very much like many other English resorts. The new swimming pool of 1968, with its attendant children's pleasure ground, lies somewhat incongruously next to the pleasant Beach House of 1820, a stuccoed bow-fronted villa that still attempts to maintain its dignity in spite of all that is going on around. (See D. R. Elleray, *Worthing – a pictorial history*, 1977.)

Like so many of the Sussex resorts, Worthing has sand only at low water, so that for most of the time its visitors have to be content with sunning themselves on the shingle backshore. If only some of the fine sandy spreads of lesser-known parts of these islands could be imported to the south-coast resorts, the transformation could be quite dramatic. This may seem a wild dream but it could be done, as witness the beaches threatened with erosion which have been artificially replaced by thousands of tons of sand pumped from the adjacent sea bed.

Shoreham is something of a surprise in that amidst the rash of twentieth-century housing there are features which lend character and distinction to the town. There are really two Shorehams, Old and New. The core of Old Shoreham lies by the banks of the Adur about 1.6km (1 mile) inland with old cottages grouped around the Norman church of St Nicholas. There may well have been a Saxon village here for part of the north wall of the nave of the church may date from as early as AD 900. With the replacement of the nearby timber bridge of 1781 by a new structure as part of the orbital road, Old Shoreham has once again become a pleasant backwater.

This is not so with New Shoreham, nearer the coast and harbour. In spite of past difficulties and destruction, it has survived to become one of the most important of the Channel ports with considerable traffic in coal for the power station, oil, timber and, more recently, diverse cargoes in container ships. It can trace its beginning to the time of William de Braose, the Norman lord who, shortly after the Norman Conquest, created a town of ordered rectilinear streets. As part of the planned layout, the substantial church of St Mary de Haura (of the port) was built out of an original pre-Conquest village church. Set well back from the main street and with a large churchyard around, its sheer bulk is an indication of the importance of the settlement prior to the disasters which beset it in later medieval times. One of these was the complete loss of the southern half of the town through sea erosion sometime before 1401, while another was the deflection of the

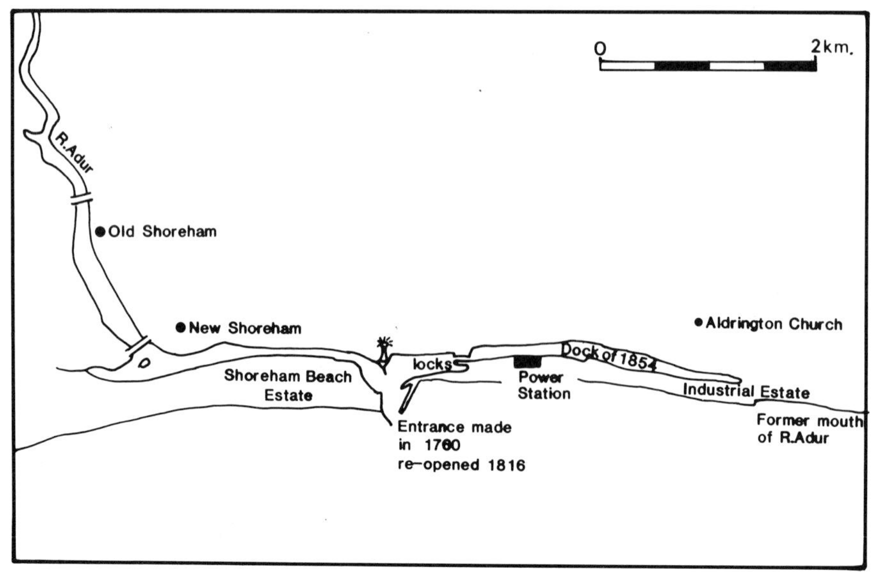

Shoreham harbour

Adur almost 6km (4 miles) to the east by the growth of a long shingle spit which made access to the port difficult. It was in fact several centuries before a solution was found by making a new cut through the shingle bank and, after an unsuccessful attempt in 1762, the present mouth was fixed in 1818. The dismembered section then became a naturally protected canal basin once it had been fitted with entrance locks, and it is in this eastern harbour section that the prosperity of the present port is based. In contrast the river section is largely given over to yachts and other small craft, overlooked by the High Street of the town with its modern shop fronts. Surprisingly some older buildings have survived including the nineteenth-century Town Hall and, more amazingly, the Marlipins, with its chequerboard front of flint and Caen stone, which could well date back to the twelfth century and may have functioned as the Customs House of William de Braose. At a later date it was probably used as a warehouse, but today it provides an ideal setting for a museum and houses an interesting collection of maps which trace the changes in the town's fortunes brought about by the wayward lower Adur.

Hove has for so long been looked on as the poor relation of Brighton and largely developed when the full flowering of architecture had passed, that it comes as a surprise to learn that it once had considerable promise as a coastal spa town, perhaps another Scarborough. The same Dr Russell who put Brighton on the map by advocating the merits of sea-water bathing sent some of his patients to drink the waters of a chalybeate spring located not far away at Hove. As he put it 'bodies labouring under the consequences of irregular living and illicit pleasures were by the water greatly relieved'. The spring, known as St Ann's well, was on the Wick Estate which is now a public park. At the height of its fame a furnished pump room was built around the spring, with a colonnade supported on Ionic columns; but in the 1930s it became a ruin and was pulled down while the well was covered over. Long before this time, however, the impact of the spring on the fortunes of Hove had been minimal.

In the 1820s the first real housing development was begun in the Brunswick area as a western equivalent of Kemp Town which was being laid out at the same time to the east of the old core of Brighton. Both Brunswick Square and Brunswick Terrace were the work of the architects Amon Wilds

Brighton can lay claim to be the premier resort of Britain

and John Busby, and followed the Regency style. Brunswick Terrace, with its horizontal rows of windows separated by Corinthian columns, is still the most impressive feature of Hove and compares well with anything Brighton has to offer. Brunswick Square is equally fine with its bow-fronted houses, though perhaps more subdued. Apart from later work by the architect Decimus Burton, who began building Adelaide Crescent in 1830 although it was not completed until 1850, little of later decades attracts attention today. Much of Hove away from the sea front represents Victorian expansion with a regular pattern of streets running at right angles to the shore. Some indifferent blocks of flats from the 1930s, and the inevitable tower blocks of the post-war period, have done little to improve the architectural image of Hove in the present century (see Judy Middleton, *A history of Hove*, 1979).

Brighton, like so many present-day coastal resorts, began life as a small fishing community, with the name Brighthelmstone. In spite of problems arising from repeated French raids, the original settlement became consolidated as the Old Town, bounded by the sea and East, North and West Streets. Within this small rectangle a compact development of houses, shops and business premises arose amidst a tangle of narrow alleys, the famous Lanes which attract so many of today's visitors in search of antiques, knick-knacks or souvenirs. Although the layout is probably medieval in origin, none of the present buildings of the Old Town is earlier than the seventeenth century, though this does not detract from the fascination of the place, especially the flint-faced cottages which survive as a link with the early fishing community. It was to this small coastal town that Dr Richard Russell came from Lewes in 1753 and decided to settle on its eastern fringe in the area known as the Old Steine (see page 97). Visitors came in ever increasing numbers and this led to the provision of extra accommodation as well as the building of a ballroom addition to the Castle Inn in 1766 and an Assembly Room attached to the Ship Inn in 1767. A great boost to expansion, largely under royal patronage followed the visit of the Prince of Wales (later George IV) in 1783. By 1820 the population had reached 14,000 and a decade later it exceeded 40,000. It is perhaps natural that Thackeray should comment that countless Londoners had George IV to thank for inventing 'the kind, merry and cheerful Dr Brighton'.

The main phase of development came after 1820 when two young architects, Busby and Wilds, designed Kemp Town. They were fortunate in having that foremost builder, Thomas Cubitt, at their disposal, and between 1822 and 1828 no fewer than one hundred fine houses were erected. Time has done little to alter Kemp Town, and its appearance today is enhanced through comparison with later inferior buildings.

Brighton spread quickly in the first half of the nineteenth century, both along the coast and inland towards the Downs, but the later buildings lacked the verve and inspiration of the Regency period so that so much of Victorian Brighton falls far short of the earlier high standard. Because of its size the town was the first along the Channel coast to be reached by the railway, and some measure of the pre-railway growth of Brighton can be gathered from the siting of the station almost 1.6km (1 mile) inland from the coast. With so much to gain it is not surprising that many railway promoters put forward schemes to link the town with the capital. The route finally chosen ran almost due north – south through Croydon, Redhill, Haywards Heath and under the South Downs by means of the Clayton Tunnel to end in what *Meason's Guide* of 1840 referred to as 'a station quite in the northern suburbs'. With the continued growth over the past 140 years the station now enjoys a relatively central position. The coming of the railway soon extinguished the lingering role which Brighton enjoyed as a port and even the packet boat service to Dieppe was abandoned.

On the eastern outskirts of Brighton the South Downs reach the sea and immediately the coastal setting becomes more interesting with vertical cliffs and a rocky platform on the foreshore. Access is difficult except where dry valleys reach the coast, as at Rottingdean, and the visitor has to be content with a cliff-top walk along a greensward. There is also a temporary break in the almost continuous built-up area of the coastal fringe where the prominent Roedean School looks curiously isolated on the lower downland slopes.

Rottingdean, nestling in one of the few dry valleys which break up this section of the coastland, has a Norman church built of flint with an impressive central tower. With its fronting green and pond, the core of the former village has survived as an oasis amidst a desert of more recent housing. **Saltdean** is similar though its modernity lacks the compensation of an old village centre. The worst excesses of twentieth-century housing, however, occur at **Peacehaven**. Here an all-time low is reached in seaside estate development and it is often quoted as the prime example of pre-war ruination of the coastline. Originally named Anzac-on-Sea, the flat downland top was laid out in regular rectangular strips on either side of the main coastal road, where only small parades of shops, strung out at intervals, provide focal points. The original wooden chalets could be bought for as little as £120 plus an excessively high ground rent; many of these poor-standard speculative buildings have now been replaced by modern bungalows, though little can be done to improve the dreary layout.

Newhaven, for all its disorder and air of untidiness which seems to be associated with ferry ports, is not unattractive. In medieval times it was a valley-side settlement called Meeching, consisting of cottages and a Norman church. Below, the river Ouse made its way out to sea well to the east near Seaford, but the deflecting barrier of shingle was prone to breaching in storms and there were a number of different outlets throughout the Middle Ages. In an attempt to drain the Ouse Valley marshes, local landowners in about 1539 decided to canalise the lower section of the river and at the same time improve navigation. Thus the straight lower section which today forms the harbour came into being and with it the name Newhaven. Drifting shingle from the west posed a problem as it blocked the harbour entrance and this was not finally solved until the great west-pier arm was built in the mid-nineteenth century. The foundations of tide mills, built in 1761, remain on one of the

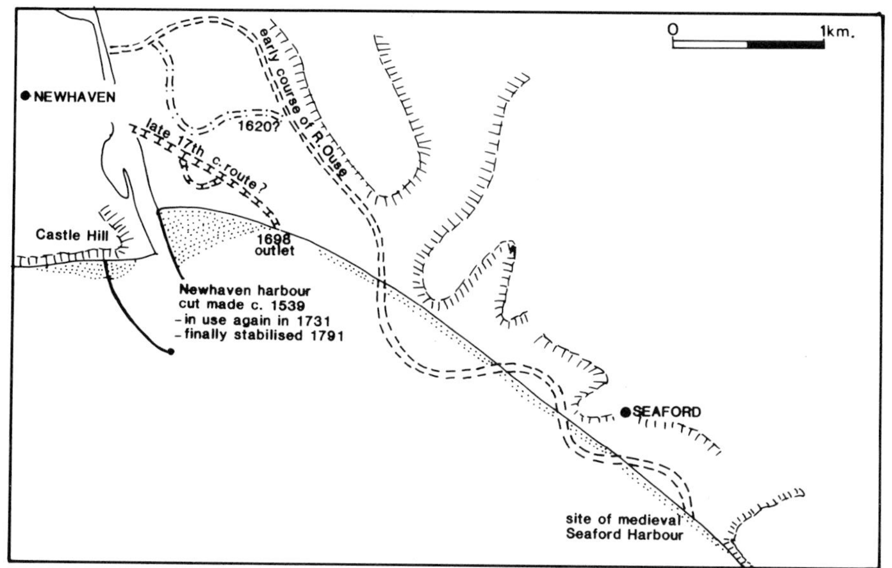

Changes in the lower course of the river Ouse

former distributaries of the lower Ouse. This is a wild area of shingle-loving plants, rather spoilt by concrete remains and old railway sidings. It is land which will be needed for any future expansion of the port, not only as a passenger-ferry terminal but also for freight traffic.

Seaford The changes which took place in the course of the lower Ouse (see Newhaven above), had a profound effect on the fortunes as well as the townscape of Seaford. The town is clustered around the Norman church, but between it and the coast there is a distinct hollow with little or no building and this is usually taken to be a remnant of the former bed of the Ouse when it ran out to sea close to Seaford Head. That Seaford once possessed a harbour is shown from the fact that it was a 'limb' of Hastings, chief of the Cinque Ports, but all this came to an end in the early sixteenth century with the rise of Newhaven. An attempt to become a resort town about 1875 with the building of the Esplanade – a short terrace of substantial houses now badly in need of repair – really never got off the ground. Perhaps this was fortuitous, for every winter Seaford suffers badly from stormy seas which carry thousands of tons of pebbles onto the promenade and coastal road which is often closed. At the end of the Esplanade is a former Martello Tower, the most westerly of a system of defences built early in the nineteenth century when the channel coastlands were threatened with a Napoleonic invasion (see page 145). A much older defensive structure, the ramparted Iron Age promontory fort on top of Seaford Head, looks down on the town and forms an excellent viewpoint, especially to the west. Since it was built, about 100 BC, erosion has laid claim to a considerable slice on the seaward side. Chalk cliffs recede quite quickly, especially where the rock has been shattered by faulting, for the sea can soon exploit the weakened beds to form caves, as at Seaford Head.

From the end of the promenade there is a fine walk along the cliff top to Cuckmere Haven. The route goes through the ramparts of the Seaford Head promontory fort and then keeps close to the cliff edge until it drops into a dry valley running almost parallel to the coast. Beyond the shingle ridge which lies athwart the mouth of the Cuckmere, the distinctive up and down profile of the well known Seven Sisters chalk cliffs appears to perfection. This distinctive

Along with the White Cliffs of Dover, the Seven Sisters, a series of severed dry valleys in the chalk downs, form one of the best-known coastal panoramas of the country

outline came into being over a considerable period of time as the cliff-face has retreated steadily, truncating both the dry valleys and the intervening ridges of the edge of the chalk downland.

Birling Gap is one of the few points where the minor road approaches the cliff edge and where it is possible to get down onto the beach by means of rickety steps. The line of coastguard cottages overlooks a car park and café and presents a dismal scene in contrast to the natural beauty of the chalk cliff-line. There is some sand at the base of the cliffs, though with chalk lumps liable to fall from the face above, sunbathing can be a dangerous pastime. Measurements have been made of the rate of cliff recession here; between 1951 and 1962 it was about 1m (3ft) per annum, most of the losses occurring during the winter months when sub-aerial weathering, including frost shattering, was at its maximum.

Beachy Head, where the chalk cliffs attain their greatest height of over 152m (500ft), has sadly become associated with many suicides. The old lighthouse of Belle Tout lies somewhat west of the headland. It was built in 1830 by Stevenson, the Scottish expert, who brought down Aberdeen granite for its construction. Its original lantern piece has now gone following the building of the new lighthouse in 1902 at the foot of the Beachy Head cliffs; this time Cornish granite was used and the foundation sunk 5m (18ft) into the chalk. As at Birling, the chalk cliffs are retreating steadily, especially during severe winters like those of 1962 and 1979. In spite of the rapid erosion, ephemeral features like isolated stacks occur from time to time. There were formerly seven – the Seven Charles – at the foot of Beachy Head but the last one, after persisting for over a century, finally collapsed in 1853.

Eastbourne With a fishing village and bathing resort called Seahouses located on the shore just to the east of the present pier as early as the eighteenth century, there seems no reason why the town should have waited until the second half of the nineteenth century to develop. But it did, and therefore missed both the Regency style development of Brighton and its modified successor under Decimus Burton typified by early building at Hove and St Leonard's in the 1830s. The probable explanation lies in the unwillingness of the major landowner, the 1st Earl of Burlington, to have his family seat of Compton Place lose its seclusion – a plan was under consideration in 1833 involving Decimus Burton but it came to nothing. It was left to the 2nd Earl, who became the 7th Duke of Devonshire, to bring present-day Eastbourne into being. Along with another landowning family named Gilbert, a programme of major building works was begun in 1851 involving the laying out of the Grand Parade on the sea front, the terrace of bow-fronted houses in Cavendish Place and the later Devonshire Place, with its statue of the town's founder, the seventh duke. There was a further burst of building activity in the 1870s when a great estate of over 1,500 houses was built within a few years. Though the Victorian architecture is not of the highest quality the layout is distinctive and, with an emphasis on open spaces and gardens, still forms an attractive element in Eastbourne's townscape. Titles such as 'Queen of Watering Places' or 'the Gentlemen's resort built by Gentlemen' were now showered on the town and, although it has not quite lived up to this reputation in recent years, it still proves attractive for those seeking off-season holidays. Its high sunshine record, perhaps only exceeded by some of the Isle of Wight resorts, also helps to give it a much longer season than most of the English resorts (see page 117).

Since the war, Eastbourne has seen tower blocks rise, many of them out of harmony with the natural coastal setting. There has also been large-scale estate development inland so that the original village of Old Eastbourne, with its twelfth-century church of St Mary and other old medieval buildings, is now in urban continuity. Further estate building has also taken place at Langney where new housing has now encroached on one of the few remaining natural features of the area, the great shingle foreland of the Crumbles. In its original form the latter

Eastbourne front, dominated by the Burlington Hotel

consisted of a succession of shingle ridges, but many have now disappeared as a result of gravel working. Erosion of the seaward face of the Crumbles has caused a number of the Napoleonic martello towers to disappear (see page 145). Only around Langney Point, with its surviving tower, is there a glimpse of what the shingle foreland must have been like in its natural state when long lines of shingle fulls existed with a scattered covering of plants like viper's bugloss, sea poppy, sea sorrel and other vegetation which miraculously seems to extract some sustenance out of the sterile environment.

Pevensey Bay is reputedly where William I landed prior to the battle which won him the English crown, though he would hardly recognise the present setting of yet another bungalow and chalet resort. There is compensation inland at Pevensey village, dominated by the great walls and bastions of the Saxon Shore fort dating back to the end of the third century AD. The walls, three-quarters complete and of considerable height, were built of greensand with the occasional bond-course of red tiles, all set in a tough pink mortar which has withstood centuries of weathering. The stonework of the castle was sold in 1650 to a Mr John Warr for £40, but its removal proved so difficult that fortunately little was actually taken away. It is only on the southern side that the wall is incomplete and this is due to landslipping. Within the Roman fort the Normans built their own defensive works in the south-east corner and Robert, half-brother of William the Conquerer, was responsible for the keep and inner bailey surrounded by a moat. Now under the care of the Department of the Environment, Pevensey Castle with its two-stage history as a fortification (like Porchester, page 288) has an assured future.

The castle lies on a slightly raised site overlooking the marshland landscape of the Hooe Level to the east. In the Roman period the area was probably covered at high tide, with only a few clay islands (eyes) unsubmerged. In medieval times large tracts of land were reclaimed by local landowners and Battle Abbey, but settlers within the marsh still sought out the drier sites provided by the 'eyes'. This proved fortunate for, when the marshland was periodically drowned during the storms of the thirteenth and fourteenth centuries, they were able to survive, at least for a time. Northeye, the largest, was a limb of the Cinque Port of Hastings and before it was finally abandoned had a chapel, inn and harbour wall. The isolation and sense of tranquillity of the site stand in great contrast to the development which has taken place along the great shingle ridge at Norman's Bay, where easy parking on the upper beach proves attractive.

Bexhill as a resort dates from only a century ago when the De la Warr family began to develop a largely empty coastal strip. As an example of a Victorian town it is pleasant enough without being exciting, and is now largely residential, escaping the great summer invasions of the other Sussex resorts. Much more interesting is the original village located 1.6km (1 mile) inland, where the twelfth-century Norman church of St Peter contains an interesting Saxon coffin-lid, possibly dating back to the eighth century. Around the church and just away from the main coastal road is the manor house and a group of typical Sussex weather-boarded cottages, some with overhangs recalling the domestic architecture of the nearby Weald. At the western end of the resort is the rather exclusive Cooden Beach with a golf course, its *raison d'être*, alongside. The low cliffs of shale here need protection from sea erosion, but at Bexhill itself the Ashdown Sandstone forms low cliffs up to 18m (60ft) high, which are more stable. At Galley Hill there has been considerable landslipping while further on, at Glyne Gap, a sandstone stack is being reduced in size by the sea's action.

St Leonard's, or New Hastings as it was originally called, was started when the London builder, Joseph Burton, purchased an estate a little to the west of Priory Valley. With a sea front almost a kilometre (½ mile) in length there was scope for ambitious planning. With his son Decimus as principal architect, the palatial, stuccoed brick terrace of the Marina, with the Victoria Hotel as the focal point, was built in a space of a few

The three-storey sheds – known as 'deezes' – of Hastings were used for drying nets and storing fishing tackle

years. An Assembly Room, chapel, hotels and shops quickly followed, and although so close to Hastings the new resort remained an independent authority until 1875. With St Leonard's Gardens, built on the site of a quarry which lent itself to landscaping, and Warrior Square dating from 1853 to 1864, yet another resort was born.

Hastings has perhaps the most exciting topography of all the Sussex coastal towns for the sandstone ridges of the Inner Weald reach the sea at this point and form high cliffs broken by deeply cut valleys. It was in one of these valleys, the Bourne, that what is now known as the Old Town was laid out to a definite plan in the twelfth century. Within the narrow confines of the valley there was only room for two axial streets, Market Street (now High Street) on the western side and Fisher Street (now All Saint's Street) to the east. Burgage plots with a narrow frontage were offered for sale and can still be seen in the present-day plan. The original medieval town suffered severely from attacks by the French so that the earliest buildings to have survived are a number of timber-framed cottages dating from the mid-fifteenth century. The area at the mouth of the Bourne Valley, known as the Stade, functioned as the harbour quarter and today still has its fishing luggers drawn up on the beach. Many attempts have been made to build a breakwater but all have failed; the present broken pier dates from 1890 but even this only lasted twenty years before being shattered by the sea. It is in this same quarter that the unique tall three-storey weatherboard sheds are found; known as 'deezes' they were used for drying nets and storing fishing tackles. Some of the black tarred sheds date back to the seventeenth century though their design could even be Norse in origin. Although still there, the fishing industry is no longer the mainstay of the town. Whereas at one time more than a hundred boats were based on Hastings the number has now dropped to less than a score. Once the leading member of the Cinque Ports confederacy, the town now suffers the indignity of having its boats registered at Rye.

In spite of its name, the Old Town,

nestling in the narrow confines of the Bourne Valley, was not the earliest settlement in this area. That distinction goes to the Priory Valley, a little distance to the west. Here a Saxon settlement was founded and, by AD 928, it was sufficiently important to have its own mint. Still later in the tenth century the town became closely linked with the Abbey of Fécamp in Normandy, which may have been the reason why William the Conqueror chose this spot on the south coast as a base for his invasion. Although he landed on the shores of Pevensey Bay William quickly advanced further to overcome the Saxon town of Hastings and built a temporary wooden fort on the hill top above. At a later date this same commanding site on East Hill was used for building the present stone castle. After the Conquest the main settlement moved from the Priory to the Bourne Valley where the newly planted town (as outlined above) arose.

One reason for the change of site might have been the greater liability to flooding of the low-lying Priory Valley. When this problem was solved in the eighteenth century the town gradually re-established itself on its earlier site in the Priory Valley, where it grew into the modern town. One man, John Collier, was closely associated with this final phase of development. From 1707 until his death in 1760, Collier held various offices – town clerk for thirty-nine years and mayor on five occasions – and built himself a mansion at the top of the High Street of the Old Town and which survives as Old Hastings House. It was here that he entertained his wealthy London friends and ultimately persuaded them to assist in developing Hastings as a health resort. Collier was to die before his scheme was fully implemented, but in 1771 Thomas Howard took over the Swan Inn and built an adjoining Assembly Rooms to attract visitors. Bathing machines appeared on the beach and, with a marked shortening of the journey time from London, visitors now came to the resort in increasing numbers. This prompted further expansion in the early nineteenth century, so that lodging houses were built in The Croft in 1805 and Wellington Square was laid out about 1815 around a sloping green at the foot of Castle Hill. The finest development came after 1825 when Joseph Kaye designed and built the curving Pelham Crescent at the foot of the castle cliff. With its flanking terraces of Breeds Place and Pelham Place and the central church of St Mary, set back into the sandstone cliffs, the whole grouping is a fine example of Regency architecture.

The arrival of the railway in 1851 led to further growth. At the mouth of the valley lay a wide shingle spit, known as America Ground – a desolate area occupied by squatters and occasionally swept over by the sea. Earth and stone removed from the many tunnels north of the town were dumped to make the land free from flooding, and on the reclaimed land Carlisle Parade and Robertson Terrace were built between 1850 and 1860 with the Queen's Hotel at the eastern end. With this growth in the Priory Valley, businesses were now moving out of the Old Town and occupying premises in, for example, Wellington Square. A new parish church of Holy Trinity was built in 1858, curiously close to the site of the original Saxon priory. Farther up the valley old brickfields were cleared away and laid out as Alexandra Park. With the opening of the unmistakably Victorian Town Hall in 1881, the transfer from the old town to the new was virtually complete.

The cliffs of pale-yellow Ashdown Sand which make such an impressive feature at Hastings, continue further east towards Fairlight though increasingly there are clay beds within the formation. Where joints are present they have often been eroded by the sea to form caves, but some of the sandstone beds are tough and small valleys like those of Ecclesbourne and Fairlight 'hang' as they reach the sea. There have also been many slips where clay beds hold up water which has percolated through the overlying sandstone. Much of this stretch of coastline is inaccessible except on foot and in contrast to all that has gone before, forms a quiet, unspoiled and undeveloped section. At Cliff End there is an abrupt change to marshland, and with it the inevitable caravan sites and less attractive bungalow estate development. Near the low-water line, stools of trees set in clay form a well known submerged forest. From Cliff End round to Hythe the original cliff-line runs inland in a gentle curve

Camber Castle was built by Henry VIII in 1538 to protect this low-lying coastline from invasion by the French: it was then much nearer the sea than at present

although at one time it was lapped by the waters of the English Channel. Over the past two thousand years, there has been a gradual accumulation of sediment in this shallow bay and, aided by man, considerable areas have been reclaimed from the sea to form Romney Marsh and the pointed shingle foreland of Dungeness (see page 65).

Winchelsea, set on a flat-topped hill above the Brede, is a remarkable example of fossilised urban development. It all began in the late thirteenth century when storms destroyed the original Winchelsea which lay somewhere offshore in what is now Rye Bay. That great founder of new towns, Edward I, then decided to create another in this corner of south-east England; land was purchased at Iham in 1280 and plots set out in a regular street system. There were thirty-nine plots in all, each with a frontage of 15m (50ft), and burgesses were then brought from Old Winchelsea which by then was rapidly falling victim of the sea. Building went on rapidly at the turn of that century and a new church of St Thomas was begun soon after. But then something went wrong; not all the available plots were taken up by the burgesses and only the chancel and side chapels of the church were completed and this is its state today. Sheep graze on plots that were left unoccupied and the whole town might have disappeared but for considerable rebuilding which took place in the nineteenth century and gave it a Georgian appearance. It is a fascinating place to visit with its great central churchyard, wide grass-verged streets with weatherboard houses, ancient wine cellars of the former medieval houses and three surviving gates of the walled town.

Present-day Winchelsea lies so far from the sea that it is difficult to believe that it was once one of the Cinque Ports. Since medieval times a great area to the west of the river Rother has been added to the coastline. At the close of the thirteenth century a large bay existed here perhaps along the line of the Daneswall near Castle Farm, but when Henry VIII came to build Camber Castle in 1538 the coastline had already built out. This process continued at an ever increasing rate, helped by the growth of great shingle ridges like the Nook. In all between 1.6 to 2.4km (1–1½ miles) of land have been added to the coastline since medieval times, though the pace has slackened considerably over the past century and some erosion has even occurred at Winchelsea Beach.

Rye is often linked with Winchelsea because of its similar history as a rising Cinque Port and its subsequent decline. It was probably

The shingle spreads of Dungeness Foreland, with a scattered cover of vegetation. The new lighthouse rises like a slender rocket out of this wasteland

founded during the mid-eleventh century, for Domesday Book records it as 'a new borough, and there are 64 burgesses returning 9 pounds and 2 sh'. That it flourished in the century following its foundation is shown by the fact that it had a mint in 1142 and became a member of the Cinque Port confederation in 1156. Standing on a sandstone hill a rough rectangular plan of streets was laid out and the whole was later surrounded by a wall. The centuries since have brought changes, principally the disappearance of a former large market place so that the town church of St Mary is hemmed in by later buildings. Many old buildings survive, particularly in Mermaid Street and Church Square. As at Winchelsea there has been some attractive Georgian rebuilding, for instance in West Street where Henry James lived for many years. With its varied range of building materials and different architectural styles combining harmoniously, Rye is a pleasant place in which to live. Its port activities are now largely a thing of the past, but the great warehouses down by the quayside tell of its more prosperous days. Port activity, mainly fishing, has now moved down the Rother to nearer the sea.

Kent

Romney Marsh is one of the great reclaimed lands of coastal Britain (see page 65). When the Romans landed in Kent the area of the present marsh was covered by a shallow sea. A drop of sea level in post-Roman times meant that the area became less subject to inundation by the sea, and over the centuries continued siltation behind a barrier of coastal sandbanks near to present-day Lydd and New Romney converted the area into a brackish water salting. From the ninth century onwards reclamation was put in hand, largely by monks of abbeys who had been given grants of land here. With a falling water table, former saltings became rich pastureland and the home of the famous Romney breed of sheep. In recent years, as drainage has improved, former pasture lands have now been ploughed and carry 'crops' like strawberries and daffodils.

Lydd grew on an 'island' whose slightly raised site kept it free from flooding even when Romney Marsh was still covered by the occasional high tide. Although it is first mentioned in a charter of AD 740 it is probable that the original settlement is even older. The fine church certainly has some early Saxon, some say late-Roman, building incorporated in the present fabric which is largely fifteenth-century in date. The elongated plan of the town with axial streets like High Street, New Street and Queen's Road, perhaps reflects the outline of the raised sandbank on which the town first developed. At the outset, and well into the Middle Ages, Lydd was a port with open water to the north east but subsequent silting brought about its decline and the town only survived because of its wool market. The fine church, largely rebuilt in the fifteenth century, was possible because of the fortunes made out of wool from the Romney sheep.

Dungeness The great expanse of wilderness running south-east from Lydd to the ness has been moulded out of a succession of shingle ridges piled up by the sea during the past thousand years or more. Certain plants are able to survive in the loose shingle by building up a limited humus content around them (see page 21), so that patches of green lighten the scene of barren desolation. Man himself has not improved on the natural landscape. Old fishermen's cottages and shacks now put to a multitude of uses, the huge atomic power stations destined to become useless concrete monuments of the twentieth century and the lines of pylons which march across this flat landscape, all tend to detract. It is only by joining the score of fishermen who cast their lines into the English Channel, summer and winter, and turning one's back on the succession of eyesores, that Dungeness can be tolerated. The constant stream of shipping sailing close to the point, for there is deep water within 90m (100yd) of the beach, is a reminder that before Trinity House erected the first lighthouse in 1792 many were shipwrecked on this lonely shore. A replacement lighthouse of 1904, built of brick but painted black, is open to the public and gives good views over the whole of the shingle foreland. The most recent lighthouse, dating from 1960, is closer to the point and has a most pleasing design with its slender column and spreading top. The changing position of the various lighthouses has been in response to the shoreline alterations over the years. The coast to the west of the point, where the power stations lie, has been liable to erosion; in contrast the east coast has been steadily building out as new shingle ridges have been added. Together these changes have altered the exact position of the point which has migrated slowly to the east, hence the step-by-step movement of each succeeding lighthouse.

New Romney, on a raised site on a former sandbank similar to Lydd, has had a closely comparable history. Until the late nineteenth century there was a great bay to the east of the town known as Romney Hoy so that in medieval times vessels were able to sail into the bay and anchor alongside St Nicholas's church. But even then the town, another Cinque Port, was experiencing difficulties with the silting up of the harbour and the situation became acute after 1287 when a storm forced the river Rother to change its mouth from near New Romney to its present position. The Rhee Wall, really an artificial channel running across the whole width of Romney Marsh, was built some time prior to 1257 to carry water to flush out the accumulating silts and sand in New Romney harbour. Like so many similar schemes it failed and so New Romney joined other Cinque ports in losing its sea trade. The town, however, survived because of the farming of the rich lands of Romney Marsh and became a great sheep market with thousands of sheep being sold at fairs held in the broad High Street. The threat of flooding was always present and so development was kept to the elliptical shape of the higher ground of the original island sandbank. Even today this is still apparent in the layout of the town. Four parallel streets, Church Road, High Street, St John's Road and Sussex Road, run down the long axis of the sandbank and still form the nucleus of urban development.

With the infilling of Romney Hoy early in the nineteenth century the sea now lies over 2km (1½ miles) to the east. On the coast **Littlestone-on-Sea** was laid out in 1886 as a specific Victorian 'marine town' with a row of hotels and boarding houses looking out over the waters of the English Channel. The whole idea never came to more than this and it is only in the last twenty years that empty plots have been taken up. This same period has seen an expansion of villa-dom to the south to form the uninspired (both in name and appearance) **Greatstone-on-Sea**. With a shingle base for the front garden, it can only be the view of the sea that attracts and persuades people to invest in very elaborate and out-of-place holiday homes. These are now rapidly replacing the more modest chalets and beach bungalows that characterised development at Greatstone in the inter-war years.

Dymchurch was always vulnerable to flooding whenever the sea poured over into the Romney Marsh, particularly during the stormy thirteenth century, and this led to the building of the medieval Dymchurch Wall. This has been replaced on several occasions, the last after the storm-surge of 1953. During rebuilding in 1847 the engineer-in-charge, J. Elliot, found an extensive layer of fragmentary pottery mixed with broken tiles, scoriae, whetstones and a few coins. The remains are taken to indicate that there was an important Roman pottery site here and implies that in the second century the site was free from flooding. Apart from the Norman church and the nearby New Hall, where the Lords of the Level used to adminster the affairs of Romney Marsh, the old Dymchurch is gradually being overpowered by new houses and swamped with holiday camps. Inland runs the Romney & Dymchurch narrow-gauge railway – a slight misnomer for it runs from Hythe in the north almost to Dungeness in the south. A tourist attraction, it also provides a service for the local communities, though its future is now very much in the balance, certainly as a privately run venture.

Stutfall Castle Some idea of the extent of coastal change can be gathered from the fact that this Roman coastal fortress, dating from the late third century when it was called *Portus Lemanis*, was once on an arm of the sea. It was another of the system of castles (including Porchester and Pevensey) built as naval garrisons where ships could anchor and then sail out to repel any threatening invasion of the south-east coast. Stutfall has less to offer than the other fortresses of the defensive chain for it was built on the side of

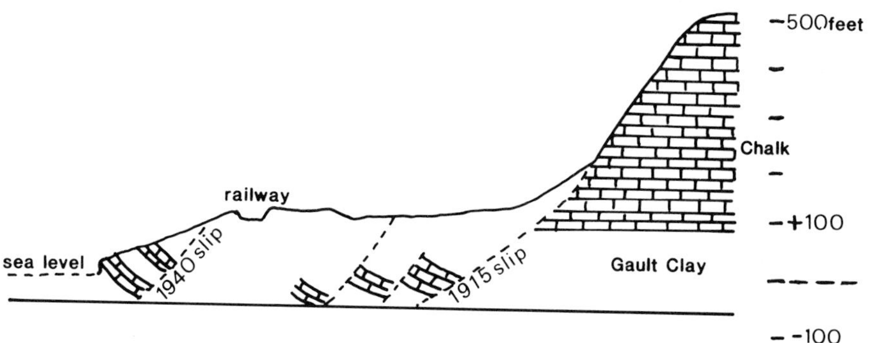

Cliff section of Folkestone Warren (*after Muir Wood*)

a hill overlooking Romney Marsh and has been partially destroyed by subsequent landslipping with the result that the ruins are disjointed and scattered. The approach is best made along the banks of the Royal Military Canal, then across a small stream and up the slope which represents the ancient cliff line on the inner edge of Romney Marsh. The great lumps of flint masonry of the castle lie at odd angles as a result of slipping, but a broadly rectangular plan for the former fort walls is discernible. At the foot a re-entrant in the slope may represent an artificially excavated dock basin, but to make anything of the present site requires some imagination.

Hythe is a coastal town of two parts – a centre around the banks of the Royal Military Canal, and the resort nearer the coast. The huge spread of shingle to the south west of the town is a military firing range, which has abruptly limited growth in this direction. A few fishing boats and tarred huts sit on the shingle beach at the end of the promenade close to the martello towers, one of which has been adapted as a house. At the other end of the town there are huge hotels, which cater for the golfing fraternity, dominating the shore-line. Along this stretch of coastline there is a need for artificial protection for there is now little by way of natural shingle ridges. Coastal changes over the centuries have been so immense that it is difficult now to realise that Hythe was once a major Cinque Port, reaching the height of its prosperity in the twelfth to thirteenth centuries. By the time the Kentish topographer William Lambarde wrote about the town in 1570 the sea had destroyed the harbour and considerably diminished the importance of the town which once had four parish churches.

Sandgate, almost continuous with Hythe, continues the theme of coastal defence and military establishments. On the concrete-protected front lie the remains of yet another of Henry VIII's coastal castles, the front and outer section having been claimed by the sea. Built originally in 1539 of greensand blocks at a cost of £5,543, it was adapted in 1806 to meet a new threat from across the Channel, the centre core becoming, to all intents, a martello tower.

Folkestone is something of a delight for it could so easily have been yet another Kentish resort and Channel ferry town. It is both, but its history makes it distinctive, particularly regarding the laid-out West Cliff. This area of flat land above the terraced slopes of the cliff-face, the Leas was developed following a plan prepared by Decimus Burton in 1843. The earliest building was in the east with four-storey terraces like Longford Terrace, Cheriton Place and Shakespeare Terrace all running at right angles to the cliff top and dating from about 1855–60. Further west Clifton Terrace, with its gentle curve and first-floor iron balconies is later, and there has been some rebuilding with modern flats, fortunately in a tasteful style. Dominating this part of the town is the huge, red-brick Grand Hotel dating from 1899 and the New Metropole of the same period. The original town nestles in the valley near the harbour though little now remains save the twelfth-century parish church of St Mary and St Eanswythe, and a network of narrow streets. Now modern shopping precincts take up much of the area. The transformation from a fishing town to a modern port dates from 1842 when the old harbour was purchased by the South Eastern Railway Company which had just reached the town. Immediately plans were put in hand for a link with France, the first passenger steamer making the crossing to Boulogne in June 1843 in four hours and so inaugurating a service which has expanded considerably, especially as a car ferry, in post-war years.

The East Cliff stands out in complete contrast to the Victorian development of the Leas to the west. Small houses dominate, but all are set well back from the cliff edge where there is a spacious greensward. Erosion has always been a problem especially in the area of Folkestone Warren, the difficulty here, as in Dorset and east Devon, arising through the chalk overlying a bed of impervious Gault Clay. Great slips have occurred at intervals in the past and, with the main railway line to Dover running along the foot, maintenance has been difficult. While chalk cliffs tower above, below is a jumble of dislodged strata, partly vegetated but always liable to further movement. One of the largest slips occurred during December 1915 when a whole section of the railway line was carried away and a great toe of clay rose from the sea bed. The slips are rotational and seem to occur at intervals of about twenty years, though some dispute that there is any regularity in the sequence. At one time it was thought that the slips were due to water seepage at the chalk-clay junction, but it is now believed that super-saturation of the beds after periods of heavy rain can reduce the natural effective shearing resistance of the strata. It has also been suggested that the slips at the Warren have increased considerably since the building of the harbour breakwater in 1875, which effectively cut off the supply of shingle from the south and thus lowered the beach. Whatever the cause, and there are probably many related factors involved, it has had the effect of creating a natural wilderness along a stretch of coastline that would otherwise have shared in the development which has gone on all around.

Dover Packet ports like Dover are often overlooked simply because visitors are hurrying through to more distant destinations. Yet Dover as a town is of great historical interest with some of the finest monuments to the past to be found anywhere in Britain. Its site in the floor of the narrow valley of the Dour stream, hemmed in by imposing chalk cliffs on either side, was sufficient in itself to claim attention from earliest times, especially because of its closeness to the continent. Considerable quantities of finely worked flint implements and flakes of the late Neolithic period have been found and point to an extensive settlement on the lower slopes of the western heights above the Dour valley about 2000 BC. But it is to the Roman period that Dover owes its pre-eminence, and it has been claimed that under the present town there are remains which parallel those of Pompeii. Even if this is an exaggeration, the Roman remains which have come to light in the last ten years as a result of redevelopment of the town centre, are outstanding for this country. The Roman pharos set on Castle Hill and dating from the first century AD has long been known and to some represents the most remarkable surviving Roman building in Britain. The lower 12m (40ft) of this octagonal structure, built of greensand and tufa and typical courses of red tiles, is in a remarkable state of preservation. It stands within the castle compound next to the Saxon church of St Mary and could have functioned as a bell-tower at one time (see page 136). A second pharos, to guide shipping in the Channel, existed on the western hill until the seventeenth century, but is now only a heap of rubble. Down in the Dour Valley the Roman remains are no less remarkable, though largely buried under the later buildings of the town. A great second-century naval port had long been suspected from the many tiles marked CL. BR. (*Classis Britannica*) and was clearly the headquarters of the Roman Fleet in British waters. It has recently been excavated though unfortunately no longer visible as it mainly underlies the new dual carriageway on the western side of the valley. At the end of the third century another naval fort was built as part of the 'Saxon shore' defensive system. Close by lay a civilian area of which a remarkable town house of about AD 200, with painted plaster walls, was discovered by chance in 1970; a rescue dig showed the importance of the find and the whole has now become the core of a fine museum. The painted walls of the house survived largely because in building the wall of the third-century fort an earthen rampart was banked against it. Altogether about 37m^2 (400sq ft) of painted plaster remains *in situ.*

Later centuries have not produced such a wealth of finds though Dover remained an important place in Saxon times as witness the church of Mary de Castro dating from about 1000 and the Saxon hut found over the site of the 'Painted House'. Although a timber castle existed on the eastern heights at the time of the Norman Conquest, the huge works we see today date from the reign of Henry II who began the present building in 1168. By twelfth-century standards the keep is massive and dominating, and succeeding centuries have added to the works so that today's visitor approaches through a vast complex of defences and other buildings. The view over the harbour and town can be breathtaking on a clear day.

Dover still retains her pre-eminent position as a cross Channel port. The problem in medieval times was always to prevent blocking of the valley mouth by shingle and this led in 1595 to the building of a large enclosed basin, the Great Paradise which, when the present enlarged harbour was built in the 1860s, became the inner harbour. Today the great outer harbour is shared by train-ferry, car-ferry and hovercraft services to the continent.

St Margaret's Bay was described in the 1960s (*Kent: A Shell Guide*) as 'undesecrated because the approach is so steep for motor cars'. This no longer applies, for the modern petrol engine can easily take the steep incline in its stride. The bay is formed because here the chalk cliffs recede a little inland, and at their foot is a huge car park and an inn. Their attraction is obvious, for most people are content to simply sit in their cars and watch the constant to and fro of the cross Channel ferries and hovercraft. For the more adventurous there is a walk along the foreshore around the chalk headlands, on a smoothed-off platform cut by the sea. Much of the development on the cliff top above dates from the inter-war years when St Margaret's was looked upon as an exclusive resort for the rich and influential who owned substantial seaside villas as weekend retreats. Now they go abroad where a sun tan is more assured.

Walmer Beyond Kingsdown, formerly a small fishing hamlet but rather swamped by inter-war villa development behind the wide shingle strand, the chalk cliffs lose height so that at Walmer they are no longer a coastal feature. Dominating the shore, though now lying some distance inland from it, is yet another castle in the chain built by Henry VIII in the 1530s. With its surrounding spaciousness it is perhaps the most impressive of the group and is still the official residence of the Lord Warden of the Cinque Ports. The fort was the southernmost of three set just over 2km (1 mile) apart along this stretch of the coast, the reason for the closeness being the important anchorage of the Downs which lies just offshore within the protective arm of the Goodwin Sands. Walmer still has a nineteenth-century charm about it and, with a wide green strip lying between the coastal road and the shingle beach, has an open appearance. There is still some fishing from the beach and the shingle backshore has the inevitable paraphernalia of winches, duck-boards and tarred sheds.

Deal is in urban continuity with Walmer and is similar, though larger. Its Tudor castle lies much closer to the shore, for the shingle beach is narrowing towards the north. The town consists of the three long streets running parallel to the shore with linking narrow alleys – the sort of compactness typical of many exposed coastal settlements and which finds its fullest expression in the 'rows' of Yarmouth. Houses facing the sea are basically late-eighteenth century in date while the main shopping centre of the town, with Town Hall and parish church of 1706, occupies the inner of the three axial

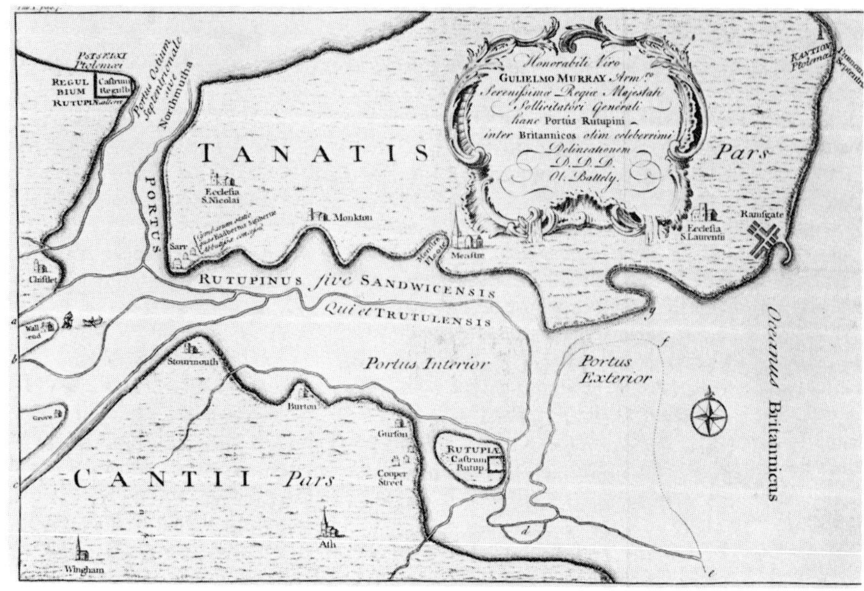

The Wantsum Channel on an early map (illustrating a much earlier period)

streets. At the northern end is Sandown Castle of 1539, the least complete of the three fortresses, for sea erosion has taken its toll and the site is now a rock garden. Inland is Upper Deal, the original settlement from which the seaside resort developed at the beginning of the eighteenth century. Although the brick church of St Leonard looks unimposing, it does have a Norman arcade which establishes the antiquity of the settlement. Apart from this, Upper Deal has a few eighteenth-century houses.

Wantsum Channel is the old name given to the former sea strait which once separated Thanet from the mainland and made it an island in reality and not solely in name as at present. In Roman times, and for some centuries afterwards, the strait offered a safe passage for ships bound for London, but subsequently the Wantsum silted up and, by the tenth century, could only be used at high water. By then large areas were natural salting and the southern part was reclaimed by the monks of St Augustine's Abbey at Canterbury from the twelfth century onwards. A sea wall of sand and stones, believed to have been built in 1280, still exists around Minster and is still known as the Abbot's Wall, while further south near the present industrial estate of Stonar there is also the Monk's Wall. Reclamation at the northern end of the Wantsum came later. There has always been a crossing, either by ferry or shallow ford, between Sarre and Upstreet and this later became the Sarre Wall, with considerable reclamation put in hand at the end of the fifteenth century, again largely under the influence of the Church. One wall named after Cardinal Morton was built in 1486 to reclaim a large area east of St Nicholas while, further north, Chamber's Wall (still in existence as a farm name) took in another huge slice of former marshland. The whole was completed with the building of the predecessor to the present sea wall between Reculver and Minnis Bay in the late eighteenth century. With this straightened north coast the sealing of the old sea strait was now complete, but nature can still have her say and during the great

A journey along the railway between Ulverston and Arnside provides fine views of Morecambe Bay and the Kent and Leven estuaries: Grange-over-Sands looking east (*G. R. C. Lomax*)

TRAVELLERS' REST

storm of January 1953 a large section of the sea wall was breached and for a time the sea again covered a huge area of the old Wantsum Channel.

At the eastern end of the former channel the growth of two spits – an inner one at Stonar consisting of shingle, and an outer one of sand running northwards into Pegwell Bay – have tended to seal up the entrance to the Wantsum from an early date. The Stonar spit, along the line of the main road between Sandwich and Ramsgate (A256), was certainly in existence in Roman times for coins and pottery have been found. The outer spit developed later, lengthening and broadening from the ninth century onwards; much of it is now taken up with the Royal St George and Prince's golf courses.

Sandwich remains one of the more fascinating towns of the south-east coast and is even more attractive now that the western bypass has taken away the traffic which once cluttered its narrow streets. It grew up as a dry-point site, formed of a low bench of sandstone overlooking the Wantsum Marshes, possibly as early as the seventh century. In the tenth century both the port and town were given by the king to the monks of Christ Church, Canterbury, an association which had a lasting effect on the town. At that time it was growing so rapidly that when the Domesday Survey was compiled there were 383 houses, its prosperity depending partly on the rich sandy loams of the countryside around – which are still intensely cultivated for market gardening produce – and, more especially, on its role as a port. The haven was close to the present quay but much larger in size; the Saxon town lay nearby and is represented by the maze of unplanned, narrow streets around St Peter's church. The later Norman quarter of the town with its more regular street plan lies east of the Saxon core near the church of St Clements, the square tower of which is built of Caen stone imported from Normandy, always a sign of a prosperous town. A very pleasing feature of Sandwich is the surviving medieval houses with their timber framework and plaster infilling, particularly in Strand Street, while another survival from the past is the town's enclosing wall, variously known today as the Rope Walk and The Butts. Originally there were five gates to the town but only two now survive – the Barbican next to the river crossing, and Fisher Gate which opens out onto the quay.

As a Cinque Port, Sandwich had a fleet of ships variously engaged in the herring fishery, and in carrying wool to Flanders and Mediterranean countries to return with cargoes of wine. The prosperity was not to last indefinitely, for the silting up of the river Stour and the continued growth northwards of the already mentioned sand spit into Pegwell Bay dealt a death blow. One proposal was to make a direct cut to the sea south-east of the town, but although work was begun in 1548 it was never completed. Another attempt was made in 1727 but again came to nothing and, with the building of Ramsgate Harbour in 1755, all hope for a return to past glory faded. Now it is mainly leisure craft which tie up at the river quay near the Barbican. Trade on the nearby industrial estate north of the town is now conducted almost entirely by road, while the great Richborough Power Station beyond relies on a rail link to bring in coal from the nearby collieries of the Kent coalfield.

Richborough, though close to Sandwich, is still a lonely place with only massive flint walls to remind one of the time when this great Roman fortress of *Rutupiae* commanded the approach to the Wantsum Channel and functioned as a naval base in the chain of Saxon Shore forts. It was at Richborough on an isolated hillock of sandstone that the Roman legions under Aulus Plautius assembled in AD 43 as part of the Claudian invasion that was to ultimately conquer Britain. This took about forty years and, when complete, it was decided to build a prominent monument to commemorate the feat of arms in the form of a massive stone column, perhaps 24m (80ft) high, carrying bronze statues of the emperor and his generals. This has long gone, but its massive concrete base, sunk for 10m (35ft), still

Chesil Beach from its southern end at Portland; it extends 12 miles before reaching the mainland at Abbotsbury

Sandwich Haven was once one of the Cinque Ports, but is now reduced to a wharf alongside the banks of the river Stour

survives within the fort perimeter. The present remains are largely of the later third-century fort with massive walls of squared stones and layers of red bonding-tiles with rubble infill; only on the eastern side, where the river has undercut the cliff, has the wall fallen away. Richborough remained important until the last Romans sailed away in AD 410, and even then the site was occupied for a time, for a small Saxon Chapel has been found within the fort. Today all is quiet save for the custodian and museum keeper, and those Department of Environment staff who carefully tend the lawns and keep the walls under constant repair. From the fort there is a view across the quiet landscape of the Wantsum Marshes to the north west, or to the busy factories of the industrial estate, the massive cooling towers of the power station and the great flats of Pegwell Bay to the east.

Ebbsfleet, on the northern fringe of the former Wantsum Channel, is the traditional site of the Saxon landing in this country in AD 449, followed by St Augustine in 597. Both are commemorated in different ways – the Saxon landing by a replica of a ship sailed across from Denmark in 1949, and the later Christian mission by a simple cross near the entrance to the golf club. The whole setting has been rudely disturbed by the development of the hoverport on the nearby Pegwell Bay shore. At Ebbsfleet cliffs reappear, formed of the Thanet Sand beds which gradually give way to the underlying chalk strata as they edge their way round the southern fringe of the Isle of Thanet.

Ramsgate, the first of a clutch of resorts which now occupy nearly the whole of the Thanet coastline, is by far the most interesting and engaging for it has the advantage over its rivals in having a busy port and flourishing marina. Like so many similar resorts the original settlement was inland, in this case around the parish church of St Lawrence. With the increasing popularity of sea bathing in the closing years of the eighteenth century, a chapel-of-ease was built in 1791 to serve the ever-expanding coastal community which had grown up round the harbour. On this dangerous coast, with shoals like The Brake and Goodwin Sands posing a constant threat to coastwise shipping, it was decided in 1749 to make a new 'harbour of refuge', and in the following year John Smeaton, of Eddystone lighthouse fame, designed a new pier. Progress of the port always remained painfully slow with only the fishing industry taking root; but this changed dramatically in the post-war years when small ports like Ramsgate, without labour problems, were favoured by importers from the continent, especially for specialist products like cars. New space is continually being sought for expansion, and Ramsgate is fortunate in having room for further development below the West Cliff. Added to commerce is the attraction of the marina in the inner harbour, now crowded with leisure craft of all shapes and sizes. From the West Cliff the view of the moored boats against the backcloth of Marine Parade has a distinctly continental flavour on a sunny day.

As a resort Ramsgate can trace its beginning to the first years of the nineteenth century when the gently curving Nelson Crescent of 1798–1801 was completed. The yellow brick terrace of The Paragon followed in 1816, but afterwards the early impetus was lost and only humbler buildings were erected. A similar pattern of development occurred on the other side of the harbour on the East Cliff, the earliest terraces like Albion Place with its iron balconies being far superior to those which followed later. The arrival of the railway in 1846 led to further expansion but this too lacked the distinctiveness and style of the first Regency terraces. There was much infilling between the early village centre of St Lawrence and the resort town, largely because the railway took a course well inland and the station was over 1.6km (1 mile) from the harbour.

Broadstairs has tried hard to remain rather more select than its neighbours, catering more for middle-class visitors and permanent residents. A fishing village grew up in the eighteenth century around a pier at the northern end of Viking Bay, one of the few places where the chalk cliffs recede. Although the early pier was destroyed in 1792 and there is a present-day stump as its successor, it tends to shelter only a few pleasure craft; but Viking Bay has a fine sandy beach and, with cliff walks and gardens, still proves attractive. Broadstairs has also a strong Dickensian association in that Bleak House, though not the setting for his novel, was, as Fort House, where the author lived in 1850. He did write *David Copperfield* while in residence and some of his other novels were conceived on his regular annual visits to Broadstairs from 1837 to 1851.

Today the town makes much of the association and an annual festival is held every October. Broadstairs has now turned its back completely on its original core village of St Peters over 1.6km (1 mile) inland where the mother church, parts of which date back to 1070, is situated. Northwards, just as the urban villas begin to peter out is the North Foreland lighthouse on the inner side of the coastal road. Although an early lighthouse probably occupied the site – the earliest recorded date is 1505 – the present building dates from the late-seventeenth century though it was heightened in 1793 when its flint and brick facing was covered. It was subsequently lowered once again last century, but its light can beam out across the busy shipping lanes for over 32km (20 miles).

Margate is now the largest and loudest of the Thanet resorts with emphasis on providing a wide range of entertainment, much of it now under cover in Dreamland and a whole succession of amusement arcades and bingo centres. All this is centred along the seafront west of the harbour on the fringe of a shallow bay with a fine sandy beach. Two events combined to give Margate an early start as a Kentish resort. One dates from about 1753 when Benjamin Beale, a Margate Quaker and glover, invented the covered bathing machine which could be pushed into the sea to allow the bather a privacy 'consistent with the strictest delicacy'. By 1775 Margate could boast thirty of these machines in use during the summer months. The other influence was the regular passenger service from London provided during the summer months by the Margate hoys. Before roads were improved and the railway arrived in the 1840s, it was the only sensible way to reach the town, though many of the holidaymakers must have had an uncomfortable trip when a northerly onshore gale was churning up the shallow waters over the Kentish Flats. They landed in their thousands at the end of the stone jetty which encloses the harbour, built by the engineer John Rennie between 1810 and 1815. By this time the town had begun to take shape starting with Cecil Square, dating from 1769 but now with much modern infilling; Hawley Square, close by, dates from the 1790s and has a predominance of yellow brick. The parish church of St John the Baptist, largely rebuilt in 1875, has parts dating back to the fourteenth century. This is not the oldest building in the present town for in Nash Road is Salmestone Grange, restored but dating back to the thirteenth century. Cliftonville, the suburb to the west of Margate, has always been looked upon as being more select. A truer assessment would label it less brash, for its boarding houses and hotels do not create the same impression as those of more genteel resorts like Eastbourne or Bournemouth. To the east the urban development continues to Westgate-on-Sea and Birchington, both great spreads of inter-war and post-war estate housing with a rash of bungalows to cater for the retired, and 'semis' for the London commuter. The coastline is formed of low chalk cliffs throughout, with fine sandy bays where the sea has attacked weaker beds. Erosion is a problem and the more vulnerable gaps have been plugged with great concrete bastions. Even these are not immune from attack and at the western bay of Westgate there has been a considerable concrete-cliff fall.

Reculver After the succession of resorts and residential development along the north coast of Thanet, the break provided by the low marshland pasture of the former Wantsum sea-strait comes as something of a relief. The storm surge of 1953 almost completely wrecked the sea defences so that a new sea wall had to be built, and although this has so far prevented a repetition of the flood disaster, the wall has to be kept under constant repair. The same applies to the great apron of concrete which protects the seaward side of the abbey church of St Mary set within the flint walls of the third-century Roman fort of *Regulbium*. The fort has suffered considerable reduction in size due to erosion so that only about half the original area within the walls now remains. The church has suffered similarly so that only the western twin towers are reasonably complete, this limited preservation being due to the efforts of Trinity House who in 1810 rescued them as a sea-mark to safeguard navigation along the north Kent coast. The towers had been part of the thirteenth-century St Mary's which had been built over the site of an earlier Saxon church dating back to 669 when King Egbert gave land here for the site of a monastery, the Roman fort providing much of the building material, especially the bonding course of red tiles. The plan of this seventh-century church shows it to be quite small and of similar design to those of Rochester and Lyminge. The whole site is now cared for by the Department of the Environment, but the tragedy of Reculver lies in the immense caravan site which surrounds this Roman fort and Saxon church. Caravans on a low coast can be unsightly, but this particular site is made worse by the amusement and bingo sheds which line the approach road. Thirty years ago Reculver was peaceful with only an inn and the odd cottage; the transformation to today's scene is a grave indictment of recent planning policy for here was one of the few accessible stretches of this coastline which had not been developed in the inter-war years.

The gap of the northern entrance to the Wantsum Channel also marks a major break in the rock types forming the coastline. The chalk of Thanet gives way at Reculver to low sandstone cliffs. Further east, on the outskirts of Herne Bay, these in turn are replaced by the London Clay and immediately the coastal setting changes for, apart from the greater height of the cliffs, there is a more jumbled pattern to the sloping face. The sticky clay is subject not only to attack by the sea but also to sub-aerial weathering by land drainage. Slumps, often rotational in character, and major slips and slides are liable to occur, especially at **Beltinge**. It was here in 1953 that a major slip occurred following the January storm-surge when a great slice of the upper cliff-face 200m (660ft) in length and 50m (160ft) wide was let down 10m (33ft) and rotated so that its outer upturned edge trapped a temporary lagoon between it and the new cliff top. Gradually weathering reduced the slip to a vast area of disturbed ground: little can be seen today for the dramatic events of that January night caused the coastal authorities to restore the cliff-face to prevent similar occurrences in future, especially as property was now threatened. The entire face has been graded to a more gentle slope of about 30 degrees which is the natural angle of rest for the clay; a herring-bone pattern of landwater drains inserted on the slope carries away surplus water and the whole is now stabilised by vegetation while, at the foot of the cliff, a concrete promenade and groynes prevent the sea from attacking this vulnerable section. Now, thirty years since the event, there is apparent stability making it difficult to imagine the magnitude of the cliff disturbance. Questions as to the cause of the great slump and its relationship to the exceptional tides of that January night have even now not been fully answered. One view is that it was due to the exceptionally low tide which followed the storm surge – without a great weight of water on the beach there was nothing to hold up the clay cliff above.

Herne Bay A combination of developer and railway accounts for the growth of this new seaside resort of the 1830s. The original village of Herne lies 3km (2 miles) inland to the south and even now is not entirely joined to its offspring. In 1830 Samuel Hacker of Canterbury began to lay out his new resort along the coast with a parade and a wooden pier. Parallel streets behind and a number of squares were all part of the plan but the whole development ran out of steam and the present layout only shows glimpses of what might have been. The collapse of the grandiose idea is all the more difficult to explain in view of the arrival of the railway in 1833 so that Herne Bay must be one of the earliest resorts to have benefited in this way, although perhaps the extension of the railway into Thanet, with an altogether more attractive coastline, proved Herne Bay's undoing. However, in its brief period of glory there were notable terraces built; the Central Parade dates from 1831, the parish church in Hanover Square from 1834 and the Clock Tower of Portland stone, the centrepiece of the scheme, from 1837. The Pier Company also set about their work with vigour and soon the Margate steamers were calling. The pier itself had been designed and erected to Thomas Telford's design in 1832, and ran out for 1,066m (3,500ft); it was subsequently replaced in 1873 by a shorter structure, which in turn was lengthened in 1899 to over 1,219m (4,000ft). During the war it was severed in two places and the final blow came in 1969 when its Pavilion was burned down. Urban growth in the twentieth century has been undistinguished and has taken place both along the coast and inland. Studhill estate was put up in the inter-war years to provide cheap retirement homes, but alas many purchasers saw them destroyed by the coast erosion which was particularly severe along this section of the clay cliff before the present defences were built after the 1953 floods.

Whitstable After the glut of resorts of Thanet and the adjacent north Kent coast it is pleasant to arrive at an older and less formal town. Whitstable has its active working harbour, its varied industries based on the sea and streets which still have character, with weatherboarding very much in evidence on a number of houses and cottages. By the beach, Island Wall and Middle Wall have several late eighteenth- and early nineteenth-century cottages, originally occupied by fishermen who worked the profitable oyster industry. This is now no more than a name, and oysters have to be imported from elsewhere. Whitstable was once the port for Canterbury and one of the first railways in the country, opened in 1830, linked the two. Now it is the commuter service to London which is the essential link. One other notable feature, entirely natural, has helped to put Whitstable on the map. Running out from the 15m (50ft) high cliffs of London Clay at right angles to the coastline is the narrow pebble ridge of **The Street**. It looks almost artificial, as if it were a specially built 'hard' running out into deeper water to serve bigger-draught vessels; this is unlikely although it is difficult to find a satisfactory explanation to account for a natural origin. Similar, though much larger pebble ridges in Cardigan Bay, known as sarns, arose as a result of glacial deposition, but this explanation is inapplicable here because this part of the coast has no record of former ice invasion. It could however have been a feature within the London Clay deposits which has remained while the clay cliffs have been steadily worn back over the centuries. That coastal retreat was on a large scale before the present defensive measures were put in hand is undoubted, for the result is a wide shallow area offshore known as the Kentish Flats, formed entirely of a clay bed, where the depth of water is everywhere less than 3 fathoms. There are occasional banks like Pudding Pan, Studhill and Clite Hole formed of cement boulders which occur as concretions within the London Clay (see page 59).

East of Whitstable the clay cliffs turn inland and the coastline has a backing of marshland. There are broad flats offshore while the beach is formed of shingle and shell fragments which increase towards Seasalter where there are fulls formed entirely of shell. Apart from the 1953 storm, earlier similar events have flooded the marsh landscape on several occasions, and the Old Sportsman Inn has marks cut into its brickwork showing past flood levels. There are a number of clay islands within the marsh which function as cattle refuges during floods and some may have been specially built, rather like the *terpen* of the Low Countries.

The Isle of Sheppey

The Isle of Sheppey stands as a detached block of London Clay which, because of its height – not less than 73m (241ft) near the north coast – has resisted complete wearing down by the sea. The island consists of two contrasting halves, the northern clay ridge which has been trimmed back to form high cliffs especially near Warden Point, and the southern marshland fringe running alongside the Swale Channel. In the extreme south-east there is another detached block of London Clay forming the core of the 'Isle' of Harty which is now completely joined to the main island. The approach to Sheppey (sheep's island) is across the concrete Kingsferry Bridge built in 1960 which can be lifted to allow shipping through the Swale. The bridge effectively ended the last remnants of isolation and allowed industrialists to move in and save the island from becoming a depressed backwater, especially after the closing of the dockyard at Sheerness.

Queenborough is a planned town dating from 1366 when Edward III decided to build a castle to defend both the Medway entrance and the Swale 'backdoor' into the Thames, and is named after his queen, Philippa. The castle was built .5km (1/3 mile) inland but virtually nothing remains save a few grassy mounds; the town church, originally a chapel-of-ease to Minster, was built nearer the coast. Only one main street, the broad High Street, formed the original town with its burgage plots - 50m (160ft) long and the width of a house - on either side. In order to attract population to his town, Edward granted borough status, two markets a week, two annual fairs and independence from the jurisdiction of the Cinque Ports; all of which is very reminiscent of the help given by Edward I when he set about his town plantations in north Wales from 1280 onwards. The town also became a wool-staple port and retained its two MPs until 1832. Now it is in need of a face-lift and hope must lie on the new industries and laboratories which have been set up nearby.

Sheerness, after becoming a dockyard town in 1665, took over from Queenborough as the urban capital of Sheppey. The docks were rebuilt in 1813 and later extended and modified, but in 1960 the Admiralty closed them in spite of fears that great hardship would be caused to the town. Fortunately commercial interests took over and with a car-ferry terminal and new industries, the worst fears have been unfounded. The old naval quarter, named Blue Town after the extensive use of naval-dockyard paint on most buildings, has been largely demolished. Marine Town, where resort development took place, has remnants of a late Georgian hotel and some ordinary boarding houses. The esplanade was severely damaged during the storms of January 1978.

Minster The name suggests a religious foundation and, although the present appearance of the place is disappointing, it has an interesting history largely centred on its church. A nunnery was established here as early as AD 670 and, though later destroyed by the Danes, formed the basis of the abbey church built in 1130 when parts of the Saxon building, with its courses of Roman tiles, were incorporated and are still prominent. There are really two churches existing cheek by jowl for, in addition to the abbey church, a parish church was erected alongside in the thirteenth century.

There has been considerable building nearer the coast in the present century but there is no coastal road running along the cliff edge due to considerable erosion of the clay cliffs. Warden Point with its clay cliffs over 50m (160ft) high shows the effects of erosion to the full, with great slides and slumps visible on the unstable cliff face. Although the erosion is largely natural and due to both weathering and sea attack, man has in the past accelerated the process by removing septaria and pyrites from the foreshore; the practice was ended in 1914 after about 3,500 tons had been taken away annually. The storm surges of 1897 and 1953 accelerated erosion by weakening the cliff base and allowing the upper part to slip seaward, but protection of such high cliffs would involve considerable expense and much of the land towards Leysdown-on-Sea has been left to holiday camps, caravans and other temporary occupants. Beyond Leysdown there is a return to a marshland landscape with a protective sea wall preventing flooding of land which is becoming increasingly valuable because of improved drainage and deep ploughing. Outside the wall lie natural saltings where the steady accretion of silt goes on, aided by salt-loving vegetation, until such time as the land is ripe for reclamation.

14 England: The East Coast

Essex

Beginning in the south at the entrance to the Thames at Southend, the Essex shoreline, though not of the highest scenic quality, is unique. This is a watery landscape of channels, creeks and saltings. Arms of the sea, often drying out completely at low water, penetrate deeply and have been navigated by flat-bottomed boats from the earliest times. Small ports, often with shipyards, grew up at the heads of the creeks at the limit of navigation which often coincided with the lowest bridging point. Trade in grain, especially from the Essex claylands of the interior, has always been a feature, and in the nineteenth century many broad-beamed spritsail barges used the Essex rivers and creeks on their way to the London market. A few of these impressive craft with their large red sails still remain, though now they are regarded as museum pieces.

River estuaries like the Blackwater, Colne and Orwell have always proved a barrier to land communication thus re-inforcing the importance of sea routes. They have also isolated communities in the long peninsulas so that an independence of spirit and outlook has arisen; the people of marshlands, in particular, were for long looked upon as a race apart, with a distinctive way of life and a suspicion of the outside world. The railway age made little impact on these peninsular communities and it is only in the past half century that their isolation has been broken by the motor car. Roads have been steadily improved though the journey time can be long because of the succession of bends, especially in the marshland areas where major drainage lines often dictate the exact route to be followed. Each of the peninsulas has the same structure of a core consisting of a low clay plateau, perhaps rising to over 30m (100ft), which at one time was much more extensive but was denuded and broken up as the river valleys developed. During the rise of sea level which followed the end of the Ice Age, these low-lying river valleys were flooded to become the present estuaries and creeks, with an intermixing of land and water typified by Hamford Water, south of Harwich. Now another change is taking place for the creeks are gradually silting up, saltings are extending beyond the present sea walls, and in time more land will become available for reclamation.

Southend-on-Sea The full name denotes the founding of the resort at the south end of Prittlewell parish; the name 'Sowthende' had originally appeared in a will of 1481. It developed more than half a century earlier than the other Essex resorts and dates from the visit of Princess Charlotte of Wales in 1801, an event which gave the previously struggling collection of boarding houses set up alongside the oyster-fishermen's huts a standing in society which it had previously lacked. In less than a generation Southend was to grow up as a watering place of the wealthy. Its advantages over many of its rivals soon became clear. Not only was it close to London but it also had good links by sea and, once the problem of landing had been solved by building a long pier across the wide mud-flats of the Thames shore in 1838, a whole fleet of steamers sailed to and from the capital. This early wooden pier, built at the enormous cost of £42,000, soon gave problems over maintenance, and had

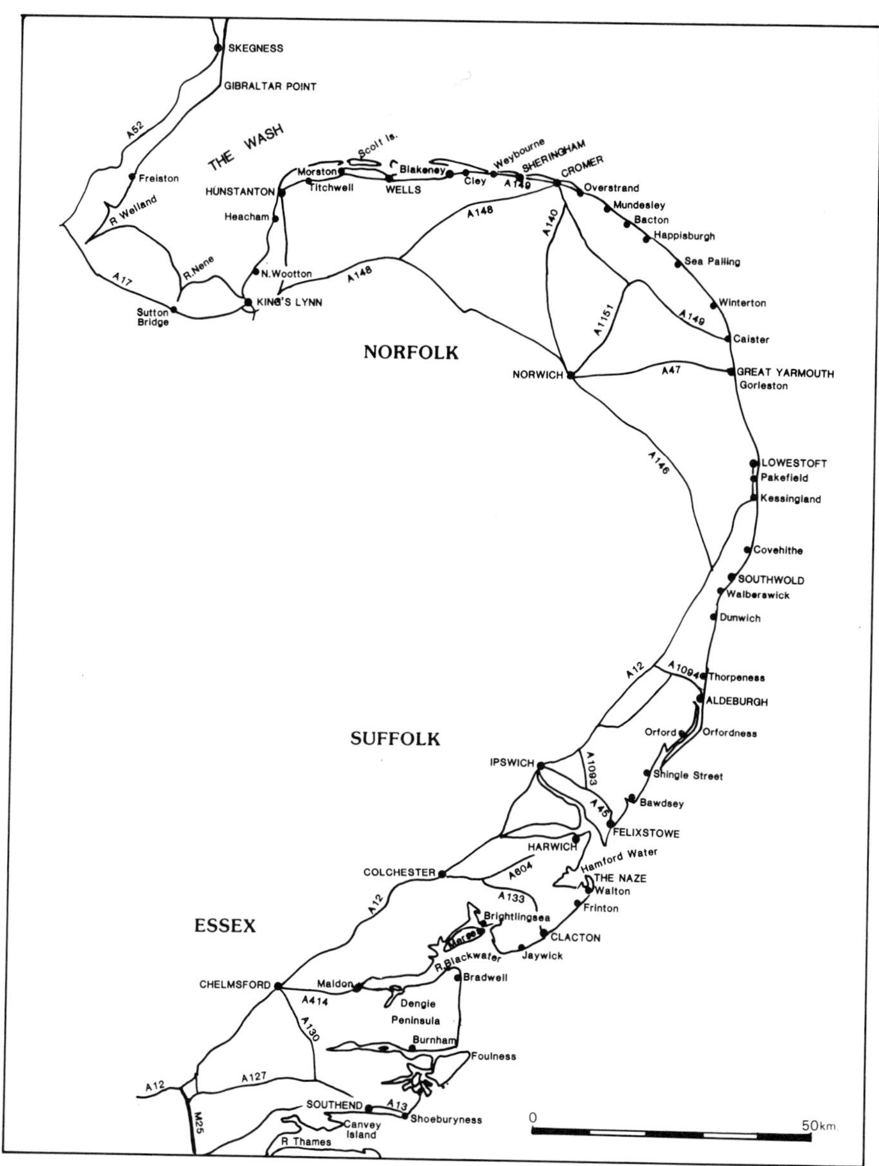

The coast of East Anglia

later to be replaced by an iron structure, the predecessor of the present 2km (1¼ mile) water-lapped promenade with its former railway and plethora of amusement centres. The other advantage claimed by Southend was that its bracing sea air, common enough to many resorts, was accompanied by the lowest annual rainfall in the kingdom.

Since the first hotels and boarding houses sprang up in the early nineteenth century, Southend has engulfed many of its former village neighbours. The built-up area now extends for 11km (7 miles) from the finely sited Hadleigh Castle in the west to the artillery ranges of Shoeburyness in the east. Leigh-on-Sea, Chalkwell, Westcliff,

Southend, for all its attempts to attract the day tripper, still has some fine terraces

Prittlewell, Southchurch and Thorpe Bay have all been swallowed up as Southend has grown into the biggest town in Essex outside the London fringe zone. The raised site, where the clay plateau reaches the Thames to end in cliffs with fine views across the Thames Estuary, is a good one. The basis of the town was already well established by 1856 when the first railway, the London, Tilbury & Southend, arrived. A second rail link via Shenfield in 1889 offered a much shorter journey to the capital and led to further urbanisation while, in the 1930s, the availability of cheap land and the possibility, readily seized upon, of working in London but living by the sea, brought about a housing explosion which is still going on. The railway also brought in the excursionists in thousands during the inter-war years and Southend was able to outdo even Brighton as a resort for the day visitor. And with this fame and a certain notoriety as a popular resort, the whole town became geared to the needs of its fleeting visitors.

Swamped though it is by twentieth-century development, one can still seek out evidence of the early history of the town. The original fishing hamlet of oystermen's huts with the associated two-storied terrace, named Pleasant Row, has gone. The oldest surviving feature is the Royal Terrace, so re-named in 1804 in honour of the Princess of Wales. Although forming a whole, the individual houses vary in detail but have the first-floor iron balconies typical of the period. At the eastern end is the Royal Hotel, dating from the same time as the terrace but considerably extended in later years. A few houses in Marine Parade also belong to the early nineteenth century but, as in many other resorts, considerable later infilling has given a hotch-potch assemblage of architectural styles. The most recent development has been the growth of multi-storied office blocks, for Southend has set out to attract firms who can recruit staff wishing to live and work by the sea, instead of facing the irksome commuting to the London office. A new sense of entity followed the building of the Civic Centre in the 1960s so that the town is now gradually throwing off its image as simply a resort and dormitory for London. The one real surprise is the surviving former manor house, known as Porters, in Southchurch Road. Dating from the seventeenth century and built of brick it is now used as the mayor's parlour. Some of the former village centres also provide glimpses of the past. The High Street of Leigh, for example, dates from the time when it was a simple fishing village. Prittlewell Priory, founded shortly after 1100, has remains dating from the fifteenth century. More important, it still retains an air of tranquillity which is so lacking in the brick and concrete jungle around.

Dengie is a long low peninsula of London Clay that has been enlarged by coastal reclamation on its seaward and river margins. Although it once had a railway link from Southminster via Burnham-on-Crouch to the main Southend–London line at Wickford, this never really helped it to develop. The Dengie marshes, with a network of twisting natural drainage channels and the more recent man-made straight watercourses, has a scattering of isolated farms, many lying on a low ridge of gravel and shell fragments which runs from north to south across the area. These shell banks also occur outside the present sea walls where they are developing within the saltings. One prominent ridge, known as Cockle Spit, lies off Sales Point, the northern extremity overlooking the Blackwater entrance (see page 86).

Bradwell-on-Sea, so named to distinguish it from a similar settlement near Coggleshall, is no longer near the sea but 3km (2 miles) inland. The original site – that of a Roman Fort, *Othona* – lay near the mouth of the Blackwater at Sales Point. The fort dates from the end of the third century AD and was one of a series built when the usurper and self-styled 'Emperor' Carausius temporarily seized power and established naval bases in preparation for the inevitable counter-attack from Rome. History shows that it was not needed at this time but proved useful at a later date when Saxon raiders were attacking the coast and it became one of the Saxon Shore forts. Very little remains save a fragment of the south wall. The eastern face perished as the result of wave erosion, but greater destruction was done by man over the centuries when the much valued stone was robbed for later buildings. One to benefit in this way was the church of St Peter's-at-the-Wall built across the west wall of the fort (see page 89). This fine high building dates from the beginning, in AD 654, of Bishop Cedd's mission of converting the people of East Anglia. That the mission was successful and that the settlement flourished is shown by Bede's reference to the 'city' of *Ythancestr*, the Anglo-Saxon name for *Othona*. It was later mentioned in the Domesday Book and by 1212 became known simply as *Walle*, perhaps an indication that the settlement had now been abandoned in favour of the less exposed site of the present village, 3km (2 miles) away along the straight Roman road. North of the village, on the low shores of the Blackwater stands the huge concrete pile of the Bradwell-on-Sea Nuclear Power Station, begun in 1957 when isolation was of paramount importance for siting such structures.

Mersea Island is something of a topographic oddity in that while other Essex islands like Foulness (a prohibited army area) are flat, Mersea has a backbone of clay rising to 21m (70ft) in the centre. Only the inner fringes need embanking to keep out the tide from the reclaimed marshland; the seaward face consists of a long low line of clay cliffs. West Mersea is the principal settlement, and has more history than its modern appearance might indicate. The focal point is the church which stands in a circular churchyard within sight of the sea; its foundation could be as early as the seventh century and it stands on the site of an earlier Roman villa. Grave diggings at the eastern end of the churchyard have uncovered a tessellated pavement at a depth of about 1m (4ft) and Roman tiles are extensively used as quoins in the church tower. From the churchyard it is but a short distance to the saltings fringing the Blackwater. Boat homes, each with its own electricity supply, lie in Dickensian fashion in separate compartments dug out of the mud of the river bank. Mersea has one other feature of interest to the historian – the impressive tumulus of Mersea Mount at Barrow Hill Farm. Looking very much like a

Bronze Age feature, excavations have confirmed a surprisingly late Romano-British date of the first century AD. Inside the mound there is a small chamber built of Roman tiles which once held a lead casket containing the cremated remains of an adult. The passage from Mersea Island to the mainland is made across an ancient causeway known as the Strood where the salt-loving vegetation, particularly red-tinged marsh samphire, covers the flats.

Brightlingsea was formerly a Cinque Port attached to Sandwich, but betrays little of this in its present townscape. Even the waterfront, with its wooden jetty and gravel hard, lacks the expected picturesqueness of an ancient port. The out-of-place Anchor Hotel and shipyards with rusting corrugated-iron sheeting do not harmonise with the natural beauty of the creek and saltings and the town, in general, lacks character, perhaps because the parish church lies 2km (1½ miles) away on the approach road. Its eleventh-century tower of flint and flushwork owes much to the local Dorrien-Magen family. Brightlingsea's fame once rested on its oyster fishery for the sheltered St Osyth Creek provided ideal nursery grounds for the famous 'Colchester natives'. There is still fishing here though increasingly leisure craft are taking over the moorings.

Clacton-on-Sea No development took place until 1871 when a sale plan showed a proposed layout for a resort. The main feature was to be a convergence of roads on the pier-head, with substantial villas extending along the marine parade eastwards from the already existing martello tower, the whole operation in the hands of the Clacton-on-Sea General Land Building & Investment Company. While the resort did not develop quite according to the plan, some of its basic provisions can still be seen. The Royal Hotel, still the best building in the town, came in 1871 with the pier quickly following and this allowed passengers to land from the Woolwich steamboats. The Great Eastern Railway did not arrive for a further decade, but after a station was built on the edge of the town it brought about a population explosion so that between 1881 and 1901 the population increased four-fold. Gradually the expanding resort took in the village of Great Clacton, 1.6km (1 mile) inland. With such rapid growth there was little time for architectural niceties, so that even the town

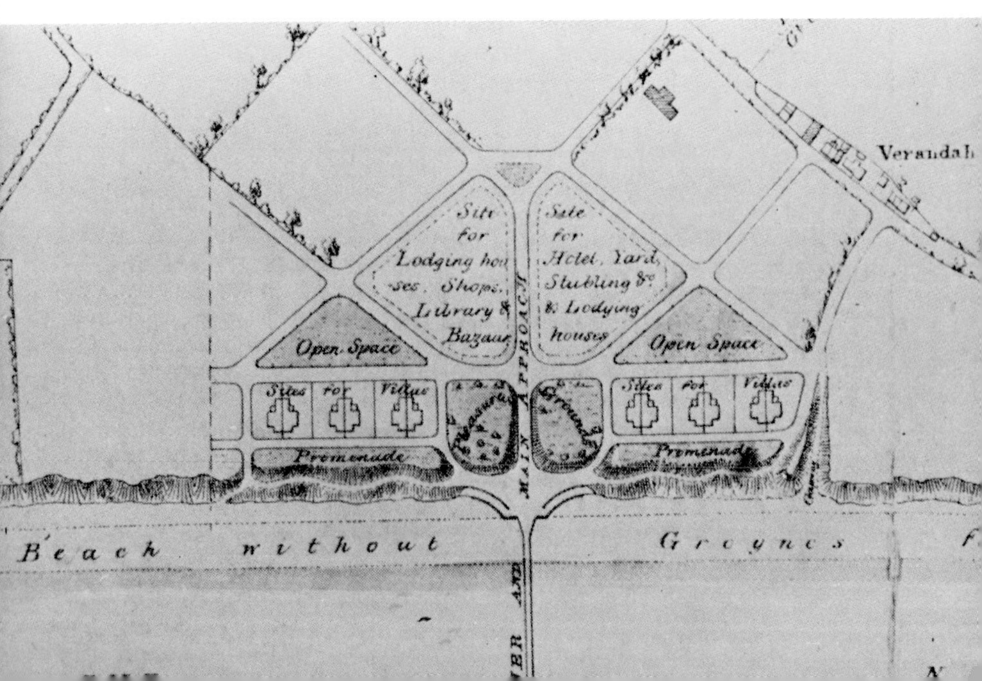

The proposed layout of Clacton (1871). Only part of the development was adopted

centre lacks buildings of note and today is swamped with the inevitable supermarkets, cafés, gift shops and amusement arcades. The best part of Clacton is the sea front with its laid-out gardens on the low cliff overlooking the sea. Away on the low ground to the west is Butlin's holiday camp while further along the coast lies Jaywick, a 1930s' shanty town of wooden bungalows where for £100 it was possible to buy a dwelling by the sea. Many of the original bungalows have gone and have been replaced by more substantial structures but the place still has a careworn appearance stemming from lack of initial capital investment on the layout and services. Fortunately and in complete contrast 3km (2 miles) inland to the north is St Osyth with its fine flintwork gatehouse of the priory and other buildings of note. Across the road lies the parish church and narrow streets with weatherboarded cottages which miraculously have survived the pressures of the twentieth century.

Frinton-on-Sea In 1885 Sir James Harman, one of the promoters of Clacton a decade earlier, turned his attention to another stretch of the Essex coast where the clay plateau reached the sea. A plan issued by the Marine & General Land Company described the place as Frinton Haven, but this was quickly changed to the more appealing Frinton-on-Sea. Within a few years streets were laid out, a first-rate hotel built and a rail connection established. The glory of Frinton, and which was to set it apart from other Essex resorts, was the open grassland of the cliff top known as the Greensward. The whole layout was more spacious with wide roads and grass verges, substantial detached villas and a policy of planting trees and shrubs which quickly masked the newness of the resort. This has survived right through to the present day so that Frinton, with its many-starred hotels, still retains an air of exclusiveness, preferring to cater for the discerning few rather than the masses. But even Frinton has not escaped the tower blocks on the cliff top any more than Eastbourne or the other south-coast resorts.

Walton-on-the-Naze, although now in urban continuity with Frinton, is of an earlier age. Development began with Barker's Marine Hotel in 1829 (still standing) and the building of the Crescent (now Marine Parade) a few years later. The pier is of the same date for it was essential to have steamer connections to attract the visitor. The erosion of the clay cliffs has always proved troublesome and in 1796 led to the loss of the parish church. Now coastal defence works have lessened the danger and gradually these are being extended to protect property on the Naze headland to the north. Land drainage is essential, and to this end a pattern of gravel-filled trenches now covers the jumbled cliff face. Dominating the Naze is the red-brick tower built by Trinity House in 1720 as a sea-mark.

Hamford Water comprises a wetland archipelago lying within the protective arm of the Naze. Numerous islands, some farmed like Horsey but others given over to natural saltings, project only a few feet above the high-water level. The sheltered waters provide ideal nursery channels for the would-be yachtsman, with Walton Channel most used as it leads seawards from the main moorings at Walton. A slight change in the relative levels of land and sea could completely alter the character of Hamford Water. For the moment it is a partly drowned, lonely landscape with an explosives factory making full use of the isolated site. The gentle slopes around are being increasingly used for fruit growing.

Harwich, set at the flat tip of a peninsula which projects out into the Orwell Estuary, though an obvious site for a port, did not develop until about 1210 when a planned town was laid out here within the old parish of Dovercourt. The town consisted of four parallel streets – still apparent in the present plan – and later the whole was enclosed with a wall and ditch. The wall has now gone though it is not difficult to trace its former position. A water-gate lay at the northern end overlooking the sea front, while another approach gate lay where the tall lighthouse now stands. Throughout late medieval times and succeeding centuries Harwich depended on its waterside position for prosperity, with the choice of the site for a naval dockyard in

1666 helping considerably. The old wheel-crane of the dockyard has survived and now stands, rather self-consciously, on the green bordering the eastern sea front. With the arrival of the Great Eastern Railway in the 1860s the packet-boat service with Holland, which had run since the beginning of the eighteenth century, was consolidated. The massive yellow brick building on the sea front was once the Great Eastern Railway Hotel but proved to be a white elephant and later became the Town Hall. Harwich lost its borough status in the local government re-organisation of the 1970s so the building now serves the Tendring District Council.

Although valiant efforts have been made by the local Harwich Society, the town has a careworn look with many buildings still needing renovation. Weather-boarded cottages and old inns are still to be found in odd corners but the town lacks the bustle of former ages as shopping is now concentrated in Dovercourt. Only on the waterfront, where Trinity House have a depot and yard stocked high with replacement buoys and beacons to cover the seaways of the Thames Estuary and Strait of Dover, is there any great activity. Pilot boats are continually coming and going to serve the ferry ships as well as the increasing amount of container traffic now using the port; the passenger terminal for the continental ports now occupies the old naval yard. Some of the passenger traffic uses Parkeston Quay, 1.6km (1 mile) upstream on the bank of the river Stour. This was a development of the Great Eastern Railway Company shortly after 1883 to allow passengers easier transfer from train to ship, the name being taken from the then chairman of the railway company. Resort activities are concentrated at Dovercourt where the local MP, John Bagshow, encouraged development from about 1845 onwards when he built Cliff House as his own residence. Two former iron light-houses stand on the foreshore to the south, but it is doubtful for how long as their rusting frameworks no longer support light towers. When first built in the last century they were movable to allow for changes in the leading-line approach to Harwich Harbour (see L. T. Weaver, *The Harwich Story*, 1975).

Suffolk

Felixstowe is an upstart compared with Harwich lying facing it across the Orwell Estuary where the shingle and sands of the Suffolk coastlands replace the Essex clays. This is yet another resort which owes its origin to the ideas and energy of one man, Colonel George Tomline, who was Lord of the Manor. In 1877 he brought the railway from Ipswich to the Beach Station, but it was another twenty years before the resort really developed, when the two foremost hotels, the Cliff (now Fisons) and the Felix, were built in 1903. The pier (now only a short stump) appeared a year later. The site of the town is excellent – it lies on a low cliff of Red Crag with a flat expanse on top for laying out the streets and a broad strand below for developing the resort. The two parts of the town have tended to remain separated by this physical divide right up to the present day. The original settlement which gave the resort its name lies inland and is centred on the fourteenth-century church with its fine tower built of local septaria. South of the town the shingle beach broadens towards Landguard Common which, commanding the entrance to the Orwell, was a natural site for a fort. The original defensive structure dates from the time of Henry VIII, but it has been modified and rebuilt many times. Now it lies almost submerged by a gravel-working plant and the compounds of the container port. A private road leads down to the common, now a nature reserve with sea poppy, sea cabbage and tamarisk growing on the shingle spreads. Nearby is a viewing bay for the harbour with its sea ferries and container ships plying to and fro. The port was another of the creations of Colonel Tomline, who built the first dock in 1885, but it is only in the past fifteen years that it has grown at a tremendous pace, partly because it did not suffer from the labour problems of the larger ports. Many firms now use Felixstowe for their route to the continent and sea ferries to Zeebrugge and Rotterdam are increasingly popular.

The Red Crag cliffs between the Orwell and Deben have been subject to erosion in the past and Walton Castle, one of the Roman coastal forts like *Othona* at Bradwell,

Felixstowe has become one of the most active and successful of the east-coast ports

had a site which now lies over 182m (600ft) offshore not far from the Deben mouth. Part of the cliff erosion was due to the extraction of coprolites from the crag formation. The coprolites contain 56 per cent phosphate and were eagerly sought as a fertiliser in the nineteenth century; many thousands of tons were extracted before the consequential damage put a stop to the industry.

Bawdsey (Woodbridge Haven) lies near the mouth of the Deben where huge banks of shingle and sandbanks restrict the entrance. On the Felixstowe side there is a motley collection of fishermen's huts where fresh fish can be bought and from here there is a foot ferry across the river. The sea banks are high for this area suffered considerably during the 1953 floods, but the sea wall built subsequently has now been encircled by a huge accumulating bank of shingle. On the north side of the river Deben lies the RAF station (where radar was first developed) which effectively shuts off a section of the coast. Access is possible down East Lane from Bawdsey church between hedgerows filled in spring with wild celery. The coast itself is uninviting except on a fine day. The surviving martello tower to the south of the lane end shows that there has been little coastal erosion here since the beginning of the nineteenth century.

Shingle Street, once a collection of fishermen's cottages but now smartened up for summer visitors and weekenders, lies close to the mouth of the Alde where the river finally breaks out to the sea. Shingle is piled high but there are deep lagoons, some marking former river courses, on the landward side. On the shingle ridges the sea pea flourishes more than on any other part of the Suffolk coast.

Orford, not really on the coast but a former river port 8km (5 miles) from the mouth of the Alde or Ore. Now sleepy and rather cut off, Orford began life as a planned town of the twelfth century within the parish of Sudbourne. The dominant feature is the castle keep built at the time of Henry II in 1165. It was to a new design with three

Orford, a medieval coastal town, is now many miles from the sea

projecting square turrets built onto an internal circular core to enable it to be much more effectively defended. Its height, for it was built on a raised mound, made it a prominent landmark and sea-mark, so that a proposal by the owner, the Marquess of Hertford, to pull it down in 1805, was resisted by the government on the grounds that it was too useful as a shipping mark. Today it is under the care of the Department of the Environment and, though a ruin, has sufficient remains to make a visit worthwhile.

Close to the castle, across the wide market place, lies the church dating from about the same time, and originally a daughter chapel to the mother church at Sudbourne – a not unusual occurrence in a planned town. From the church a long raised causeway leads down to the water front, by the side of which is a sunken area which may have been the site of the harbour of the town prior to silting up, one of the main reasons for its later decline. Another factor was the lengthening of the huge shingle spit of Orfordness which meant that the port lay at an ever-increasing distance from the open sea. Orfordness is now largely under the control of the War Department and so subject to restriction. The spit, which deflects the river Alde for a considerable distance southwards, is a remarkable and in many ways a unique shingle structure. Built up from a succession of pebbly ridges which give it a desolate character, at times in the past it has been even longer than at present. This was the case in 1897, for example, before a storm cut off a long length at North Weir Point and piled up the shingle onto the landward side of the river mouth. It must be a feature of considerable antiquity, perhaps dating from the time when the rising sea level of the post-Ice Age period brought considerable quantities of shingle ashore along this stretch of the coast, and then waves completed the work of fashioning it into huge ridges. The best way to see the spit is not from Orfordness but by walking southwards from Aldeburgh to Slaughden Quay and beyond.

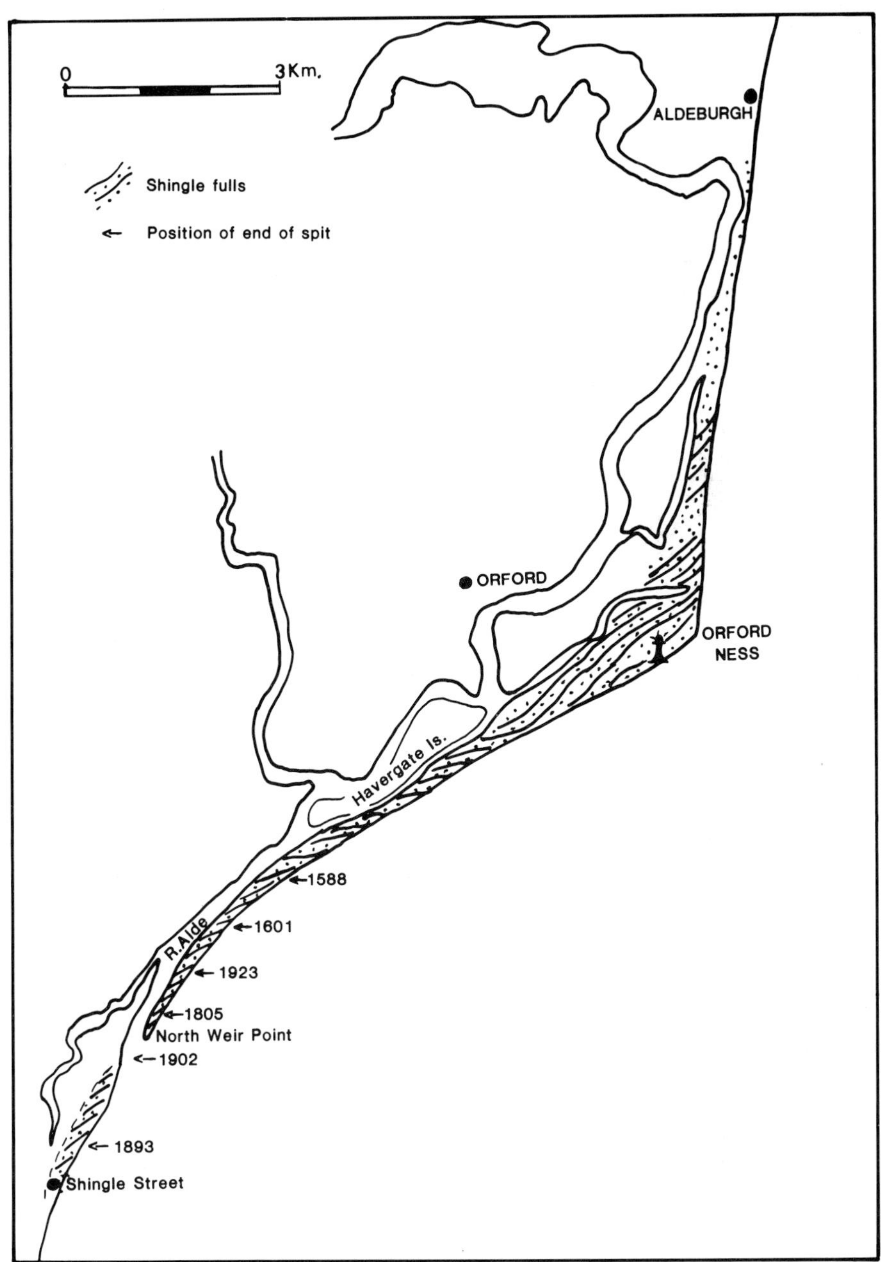

The great shingle spit of Orfordness, with the movement of its southernmost point

Aldeburgh is another disenfranchised borough like Orford, though not decayed to the same extent. Lying as it does on the open coast, it still retains an active fishing interest and has a quiet charm as a small resort. Its association with the poet George Crabbe and more recently the composer Benjamin

Snape Maltings, with its newly built concert hall which has close associations with Benjamin Britten and the Aldeburgh Festival

Britten, have helped to fashion a new image. The Aldeburgh Festival of Music and the Arts, founded by Britten in 1948, has become an annual event in the music lover's diary, and for a week in June thousands flock into this small coastal town to participate in the activities, though the main events now take place at the recently rebuilt former maltings at Snape, a few miles inland to the south east. Britten, a Lowestoft man, was able to make considerable use of local colour especially in his first opera *Peter Grimes* which was derived from one of the verse stories 'The Borough' written by Crabbe. Of its early history present-day Aldeburgh can tell us little, for coast erosion has wiped the slate clean. An Elizabethan map in the Moot Hall, the finest surviving medieval building, shows that since 1594 the sea has claimed further parts of the town, especially in the north. The church has escaped for it lies on a raised site a little inland. Although not as impressive as other coastal churches in Suffolk, the fourteenth-century tower has always provided a prominent navigation mark. The present town lies mainly to the south, strung out along the length of the coastline as it runs towards Orfordness spit. High Street, wide and much rebuilt in Victorian times, forms the principal axis though other streets on either side give width. As the river Alde is approached, the character of the town changes, particularly at Slaughden Quay where there was considerable shipbuilding activity in the sixteenth and seventeenth centuries. Now the sheltered river waters provide a haven for leisure craft of all shapes and sizes. Across the river lies the marshes, a scene which Crabbe described so vividly in 'The Borough':

Here samphire banks and saltwort bound the flood,
There stakes and sea weed withering in the mud:
And higher up a ridge of all things base
Which some strong tide has rolled upon the place.

The narrow neck of shingle at Slaughden seems to invite breaching and there was great concern felt during the 1953 floods that the river might find a permanent outlet to the sea at this point. Now bulldozers can roll back the shingle which the waves distribute so that the threat is less today than in earlier centuries (see H. P. Clodd, *Aldeburgh* 1959).

Thorpeness The emptiness and unspoiled character of much of the Suffolk coast at the turn of the century encouraged Stuart Ogilvy to design and promote a new concept of coastal resort here at Thorpeness (see page 93). Work began in 1910 with the making of an artificial lake called The Meare and then adding a country club, followed quickly by a collection of weatherboard seaside villas on the sand dunes. Follies abound in the area like the House in the Clouds, in reality a water tower, and the re-erected windmill nearby. Some would add the huge concrete lump of the Sizewell Nuclear Power station, 1.6km (1 mile) to the north, utterly dwarfing the huts of the fishermen on the sandy beach. The warm water of the station outfall proves attractive to fish and local fishermen often go no further than this.

Minsmere The present straight coastline is deceptive for at one time there was a large bay here which has been replaced by a reed-choked wetland with some open water. This is now a reserve run by the Royal Society for the Protection of Birds. One approach is from the north across the National Trust lands of Dunwich Heath, and this leads to two public hides on the sea wall. This is the most important bird reserve in Britain with over a hundred species using the lagoons, islets and surrounding woodland for breeding or as migrants.

Dunwich is perhaps the most famous historical example we have in Britain of the disastrous effects of sea erosion (see page 57). The original settlement, dating from the creation of the East Anglian see here by St Felix in AD 632, grew into a sizeable town by the twelfth century. But already documents were telling of land lost to the sea and the need for coastal defences to prevent further inroads. All proved useless and by 1753 two-thirds of the town, including six churches and three chapels, had disappeared without trace. Further cliff retreat was to occur over the next two centuries so that today only a tiny, somewhat melancholy settlement remains, hardly enough to convince the sceptic of its past glory. The ruined Franciscan friary with its fine gatehouse remains, but there is little else of note in the town. Because of the nature of the erosion there is no chance of the lost town lying under the waves for the marine archaeologist to explore. A few fishermen still put out from the open beach at the northern end of the cliffs and at times the visitor can take advantage of their catch. The only church remaining is that of St James, built in the nineteenth century, but alongside is the ruin of a much earlier Norman church, with a massive tomb set inside its crumbling walls.

Southwold could lay claim to be the pleasantest of the Suffolk resorts and perhaps even of East Anglia. The attraction is not the beach, which is predominantly shingle and rather exposed to the biting chill of the easterly winds even in summer, but the town itself. After much of the town had been destroyed by fire in 1659 it was decided to rebuild the houses with a much more open plan centred on a large green close to the Market Place, though some accounts state that the green was in existence earlier. Many of the buildings, including those on the sea front, date from the first half of the nineteenth century; the boarding houses of the Centre Cliff for instance date from between 1820 and 1830 when the first stirrings of resort development took place, long before any railway arrived. The railway, when it did come, had little effect for Southwold never went out of its way to attract the masses. Today, in spite of the motor car, it has retained an exclusive air although recent developments at the northern end might be a prelude to a change of emphasis. The approach to Southwold is from Blythburgh, when the town is seen to be set high on a hill. The townscape is dominated by the fourteenth-century church tower and the lighthouse, built in 1892 and set within the streets of the town. Down by the harbour, which it shares with Walberswick on the south side of the Blythe Estuary, there are tarred fishermen's huts

The 'denes' of Lowestoft, with the wooden posts used for drying nets

and tiny boats in which they bring in their catches of plaice, flounder and whiting.

Covehithe A narrow lane leads down to the crumbling sandy cliffs from the church which, before being largely destroyed during the Civil War, must have been of magnificent proportions. The ruins were the subject of a watercolour by the Norfolk artist, J. S. Cotman. The walls now completely dwarf the Charles II thatched chapel at its side. The massive tower of flint has been preserved as a sea-mark but the question remains as to why such a huge church was built in the first place as there is virtually no village.

Kessingland Beach is a prime example of a twentieth-century invention – making full use of a beach by building holiday huts and laying out a caravan site although the effect is disastrous to the natural setting. The sea once threatened destruction here and a sea wall was built to protect the low-lying ground. In the event it proved unnecessary as the shingle and sand returned to form a wide natural beach protection, the surest defence against erosion. The cliffs to the north were equally vulnerable and substantial sea-defence works have been erected.

Pakefield has two former churches – St Margaret and All Saints – both in one. Until the mid-eighteenth century there were two parishes and two churches adjoining here. The solid dividing wall was then broken down to form a single unit. Its more recent history has centred on its partial destruction by bombing in World War II and the threat of sea erosion. The erection of beach defences and the provision of a greensward has thwarted further depredation so that the area around the church is a haven of peace on an increasingly noisy coast. The story of Pakefield is well told in the delightful book *Flinten History* written by the rector, B. P. W. Stather Hunt.

Lowestoft is a town of contrasts which reflect different stages in its growth. It had an early history based on herring fisheries, and the medieval church of St Margaret, dating from about 1480, indicates considerable prosperity. But one wonders why the church is so far from the present town centre for there is no indication of a medieval settlement around its inland site. The present town centre is formed by the axial High Street which climbs steadily north of the harbour. Narrow passages or 'scores' (Anglo-Saxon *scoren*, to cleave) are a feature, though many have disappeared through rebuilding of the frontages. On the seaward side the scores descend steeply down what was once an old sea cliff to the grassed-over sand-flats known as 'denes', now occupied in part by a huge and unsightly frozen food factory and storage depot. Formerly the denes were the preserve of fishermen, and the posts on which they strung their nets to dry survive as well as some of the old herring-curing houses tucked under the cliff edge. At one time the denes were steadily accumulating and pushing Lowestoft Ness, the most easterly point of Britain, further seaward. This has changed in the present century and now the point has to be protected.

The fortunes of the medieval port declined considerably as the harbour entrance silted up. In 1844 the local Lord of the Manor, Sir Samuel Peto, purchased the harbour and straight away undertook improvements including the construction of the two entrance piers. He also brought the railway into the town as early as 1847, and this had the immediate effect of increasing trade because it ensured quick transit of fish to the London market. Peto was also responsible for laying out the resort quarter of the town on the low cliffs south of the harbour. Marine terraces of boarding houses, hotels and more humble dwellings grew up in this suburb which is still the resort quarter today. The traditional type of holiday is rapidly changing so that camps and caravan parks, like those of Corton and Hopton, have sprung up north of the town and prove more attractive than the old seaside lodging house. Lowestoft's answer is to turn more and more to industry, including a very flourishing shipbuilding enterprise on Lake Lothing.

Norfolk

Great Yarmouth is in many ways a more interesting town than Lowestoft, its near neighbour in Suffolk with which it is often linked. It grew on a broad spit of sand and shingle which deflects the lower course of the river Yare to the south for 6km (4 miles). Some argue that the spit was once a bare sandbank lying athwart the entrance to a wide bay, now Breydon Water with Roman stations at Burgh and Caister located on either side. If this is so, the emergence of Yarmouth as a town probably came as sea level fell in the post-Roman centuries and made the original sandbank habitable, the

Medieval Great Yarmouth and the former mouths of the river Yare

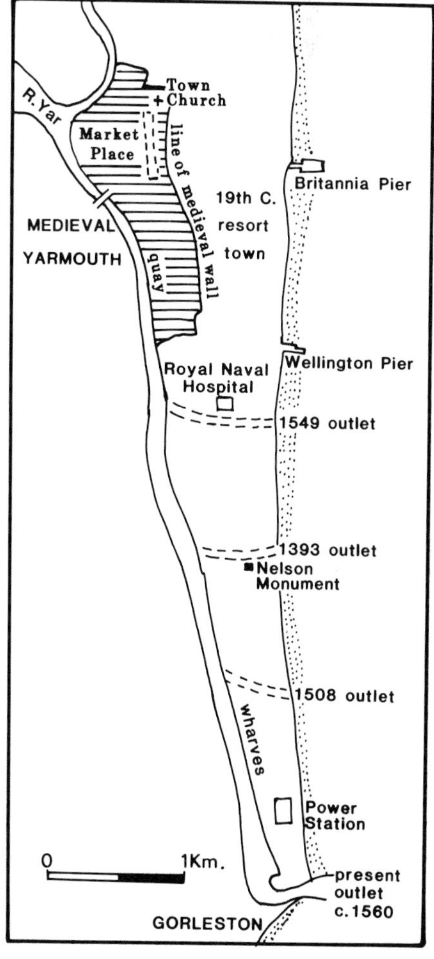

town plan of the present day reflecting the elongated site. It is shown thus on the Hutch map of the sixteenth century, said to depict conditions as they were in the tenth. Whatever the authenticity of the map it is clear that the setting has changed considerably in historic time. By medieval times the harbour entrance had shifted from a northerly outlet (Grubb's Haven) to a southerly position near Corton. This southerly entrance, however, became blocked in 1337 and the burgesses sought help in making a new entrance nearer the town. The present harbour mouth dates from 1559 to 1567 when pier arms were built to prevent the sand-drift choking the entrance.

The medieval town covered a relatively small area to the south of the fine parish church of St Nicholas, of early twelfth-century date. It lay on the river side of the spit so that when the town walls were built, shortly after 1260, they were absent along this waterfront. The rest of the walls survive to a remarkable degree and can be followed as they run north to south a little seaward of the market place and King Street, where they have been specially preserved close to the rear entrance of the new shopping precinct. Within the walls there were three axial streets with a broad waterfront widening into The Quay close to the present Town Hall. A feature of the walled town were the narrow passages or 'rows' (cf the 'scores' of Lowestoft), probably dating from the late sixteenth century. Their origin and purpose has given rise to much speculation but similar features occur in other coastal towns. Possibly they were built as an aid to defence or simply as gaps narrow enough to keep out the biting easterly winds. There were originally over 140, but rebuilding in the town centre after bomb damage during World War II, has eliminated most of them. Many of the ancient buildings also perished at that time, but fortunately some notable ones survive. At the Priory School in Priory Road at the end of the market place is a surviving portion of the Benedictine priory founded in 1101. Another monastic site, the Greyfriars on the South Quay, has fared less well though its scanty ruins have been opened to view. In this quarter is the Old Merchant's House, seventeenth-century in date and now used as a museum. This area of the South Quay is the most interesting part of the town and though considerably redeveloped it includes many fine houses. One built in 1720 by John Andrews, the greatest herring merchant in Europe, is now used as the Customs House. Herring is the clue to the great prosperity of the town over many centuries until the great shoals were no more, partly through over-fishing. Fortunately the new products of the North Sea – oil and gas – came just in time, so that the waterfront hums with activity connected with servicing the offshore installations.

The resort quarter lies on the seaward side of the medieval town and outside its walls. Largely a nineteenth-century creation, it grew as Londoners flocked here to take advantage of the long stretch of clean sands. There is just a hint of Regency development in the odd surviving villa, but most are of later date. The Wellington Pier in the south dates from 1853, the Britannia Pier followed five years later but its new Pavilion dates only from 1958. Recently further additions have been made to attract the visitor, including bowling greens, swimming pools, fairgrounds and a new indoor entertainment centre. Although the day of the rail excursionist has long since passed, seaside Yarmouth has managed to retain its popularity. It is very much a centre for the thousands who come to the camps and caravan sites which have grown up in the 16km (10 mile) stretch of coast towards Winterton, engulfing the former Roman town of Caister. Fortunately the other Roman site of Burgh lies very much in a backwater; as *Gariannonvm* it was one of the chain of Saxon Shore forts dating from the end of the third century. There is much by way of tangible remains, including a substantial length of wall built of flint with layers of red tiles, up to 3m (10ft) thick and 4m (14ft) high. Its position as a coastal fortress, built on a low plateau of silty soil overlooking the marshes bordering Breydon Water, is curious until it is remembered that the natural setting of the coastline has changed considerably during the past two thousand years. The same is true at Caister, north of Yarmouth where, during the post-war years, excavations have partially uncovered a considerable Roman town and trading port with foundations of buildings built of flint, tiled floors and a wide pebbled road. The site has been laid out by the Department of the Environment and is open for viewing.

Winterton It is only when this relatively unspoiled village is reached that the Norfolk coastline becomes free from the succession of camps, caravan sites, wooden bungalow settlements – all there to take advantage of the fine sands. Winterton is different; its recent development has been more tasteful and overlooking a wide dune belt which forms part of the ness feature, there is a succession of white-washed 'kraals', providing individual family accommodation for the nearby Hermanus Hotel. The village itself has character and is very much dominated by the tall church tower which acts as a prominent sea-mark. The ness point has been steadily moving down-coast in the past, so that it now lies opposite the village. In the mid-nineteenth century it lay almost 2km (1 mile) to the north west and is so marked by name on the latest editions of Ordnance Survey maps. The belt of sand dunes, wide in front of the village, narrows considerably further along the coast and has in the past been very vulnerable to breaching. A storm in February 1938 tore a huge gap in the dune wall and flooded extensive areas of low-lying farmland, as it did again in 1953. At Horsey Mere, the Broads come closest to the coast and these artificial peat diggings have been the subject of many drainage schemes.

Waxham with its partly ruined church and hall with fine fifteenth-century gatehouse, and Sea Palling with its caravan site, are equally vulnerable should the sea defences fronting the dunes give way in a severe storm of the magnitude of February 1953. At Eccles the former village and church of St Mary succumbed in the nineteenth century. In 1858 the church tower was close to the high-water mark having already been partially buried by the advancing sand dunes, although it was another thirty years before the church was finally wrecked in the storm of January 1895. Now only jumbled masses of flint masonry lie littered halfway down the beach. Earlier the gales removed sand and exposed the footings of cottages of the former village inland.

Happisburgh has clay cliffs up to 15m (50ft) high which bring a change in character of the coastal scene; but erosion continues, as sub-aerial weathering combines with wave attack to bring about a steady retreat. Both the tall church tower 33m (110ft) high, and the lighthouse built in 1791, form prominent features and invaluable navigational aids to shipping as it makes its way through the succession of sands known collectively as the Norfolk Banks.

Bacton has achieved some publicity as one of the North Sea gas terminals, but the site has been landscaped to minimise the impact on this flat coastland. Bacton's early history centred on Broomholm Priory, standing aloof amongst farm buildings on the inner side of the village. All the remains, including the gatehouse, chapter house, dormitory and refectory, are on private land.

Mundesley cliffs are even higher than those to the east and seem more vulnerable to attack. Great slips have occurred and led to huge circular bites being taken out of the cliff-face, and efforts to arrest this seem puny and ineffective. For a brief period at the turn of the century Mundesley had hopes of becoming a resort to rival Cromer. The late-Victorian Hotel Continental was built in 1892 and the Manor Hotel followed in 1900, but then development came to an abrupt halt.

Overstrand repeats the story of retreating clay cliffs which have swallowed up bungalows erected by speculative builders in the inter-war years. The continuous threat seems to cast a shadow over the place, with roads ending nowhere amidst a tangle of bramble and thicket. Yet, at the beginning of the century hopes were high and the most famous of architects, Sir Edwin Lutyens, was persuaded to design both Overstrand Hall and The Pleasaunce, both exemplifying his own distinctive inventiveness. He was also responsible for the simple Methodist church at the eastern end of the village – perhaps the only nonconformist chapel Lutyens designed.

Cromer is mentioned in Domesday Book as being in the parish of Shipden where there were two churches – Shipden-juxta-mare and Shipden-juxta-Felbrigge. The former was lost through sea erosion some time in the fourteenth century, its supposed site being 365m (400yd) offshore in the vicinity of Church Rocks. The present town church of St Peter and St Paul dates from the reign of Edward III when the king gave 5ha (1 acre) of land for the purpose of replacing the old church of Shipden-juxta-Felbrigge, which in late medieval times was a place of importance, having been granted a fair and weekly market in a charter of 1285. The name Shipden gradually fell out of use and Cromer succeeded it. The old town clustered around the church still retains some character with little shops serving dressed crab, a Cromer speciality. For the rest Cromer has a shabby appearance and is badly in need of renovation. Early nineteenth-century resort development still shows in Brunswick Terrace on the East Cliff but the waterfront is now dominated by later, less successful additions, including the massive Hotel de Paris dating from 1895. To the east, and giving a good view of town and pier, lies the lighthouse dating from 1832 after a large coastal fall carried away the original structure. By siting the new light well inland, Trinity House were taking no chances with future erosion.

West Runton Gap is one of the few breaks in the continuous wall of glacial sands, clays and huge lumps of transported chalk which make up the high cliffs between Cromer and Sheringham. Though very much dominated by camp sites, this section of the coast is of great interest because at certain times the black peat of the Cromer Forest Bed is exposed at the foot of the cliffs, taking us back in time to a warm interglacial period before the onset of arctic conditions which led to the dumping of the great mass of boulder clay forming the cliff-face.

Sheringham A drop in the high cliffs allowed a fishing hamlet to develop with easy access to the beach – the best that could be hoped for on this harbourless coast. Some of the fishermen's cottages with flint and pantiles still survive. It tried, perhaps half-heartedly, to become a resort in the 1890s after the arrival of the railway; and two of its major buildings – the Grand Hotel and Sheringham Court (formerly Hotel) – date from this time. The town still retains the air of a self-contained community with its own theatre, and does not completely die when the last of the summer visitors has departed. There are pleasant cliff-top walks and others inland to Upper Sheringham, the original settlement which lies huddled under the northern wall of the great Norfolk end-moraine which dominates the landscape hereabouts.

Weybourne marks the end of the cliffs and the beginning of the shingle bank of Blakeney spit. Behind the shingle lies a belt of saltings which in turn gives way to flat marshland pastures with their network of straight drainage ditches. Access is possible down a lane from the village with its fine thirteenth-century priory and church.

Salthouse is set on a low platform fronted by saltings and pastures running out to the great shingle bank on the coast. This is a great bird-watching area for the retired who use the laybys of the coastal road and fix their binoculars on the marshes. The coastal shingle bank is very vulnerable to breaching and the events of 1953 were simply a repetition of similar inundations at regular intervals in the past. There was once a small port here with a channel running eastwards into the Glaven at Cley and thence out to sea, but seventeenth-century reclamation works abruptly brought its life to an end, though natural silting may also have been a contributory factor. According to W. G. Hoskins, the name accurately records one of the early industries of this coast, namely the collecting and distribution of the valuable commodity, salt, which dates from the eleventh century when the first warehouse was built.

Cley-by-the-Sea lies 3km (2 miles) further along the coast and has a good site for a port as it lies on the banks of the river Glaven. The original village and port lay well upstream around the church at Newgate Green and is shown as such on a map of 1586. Marsh reclamation which restricted the capacity of the channels and increased silting, combined with the ever-increasing size of ships, meant that the Glaven was no longer navigable as far as the church – a new quay had to be built downstream, near the present mill, and this became the new port. In 1570 Cley had thirteen ships and sixty-five mariners making it second only to Lynn in importance amongst the ports of this coastline. After the export of cloth had taken the place of the wool export of earlier times, prosperity was assured and is best seen in the size and grandeur of the church. As the centuries passed so the character of the trade changed, with coastal shipments rather than continental traffic now to the fore. The building of the coastal road in 1823 led to the present Cley becoming centred near the bridge and mill with warehouses of flint and pantile, rather than round the church at Newgate Green. The old centre gradually acquired the charm and isolation of a backwater, which it preserves today.

Blakeney is very much sheltered by the great shingle spit to the north with an approach from the sea along a tortuous channel of several miles. The shingle spit is narrow at its inner end where it takes off from the coast at Cley Eye – a raised clay bank common on these marshes. At its western end the spit broadens considerably and a succession of recurves of sand and shingle splay out into the harbour entrance. Over the past thousand years the spit has been growing westwards, though at a decreasing rate, as a result of wave-drifting of the shingle but where the material came from originally is uncertain; one possibility is that it is glacial debris left offshore at the end of the Ice Age and then carried to its present position on the coast as sea level rose. On the inner side of the spit the flats have been colonised by salt-tolerant vegetation. Succulent annuals like glasswort (*Salicornia*) and seablite (*Suaeda*) are amongst the earliest colonisers of the bare sand and mud, but as the level rises so other plants like the sea aster, sea plantain and sea manna grass make an appearance. At an even higher level and therefore not submerged at every tide, sea lavender colonises and in areas like Stiffkey Marsh can make a glorious show of colour in late June and July. The best way to visit Blakeney spit and its marshland fringe is to take a boat from either Blakeney or Morston Quay when the tide is suitable. Alternatively there is a long walk along the foreshore from Cley Eye. Blakeney village, formerly called Snitterly, is typical of many of the smaller centres on this coast. Like Cley it once had a considerable coastal trade though today the quay is jammed with pleasure craft. Although the place is thronged with visitors in the summer and the narrow streets choked with cars, its flint-faced cottages give it an old-world charm and are much sought after for retirement.

Wells-next-the-Sea is the largest of the clutch of ports on this sand-choked north-Norfolk coastline. Its long waterfront, dominated by a big granary, is the centre of activity in the summer months, and from it a long straight channel leads to the sea. On one side there is reclaimed land with a big caravan site near the dune belt, but on the east natural salting remains. The port of Wells was looked upon as sufficiently important for it to be linked by rail with Dereham in 1857, and by 1866 the line had been extended to Heacham where it joined with the King's Lynn to Hunstanton branch. Both railway links are no more, but this does not seem to have affected the popularity of Wells. The town has simple, almost grid, layout on the north side of the main coastal road with the pleasantest area around the church, rebuilt in 1875 after a fire. Close by there is an open green, the Buttlands, and a group of Georgian houses.

Holkham The approach to the shoreline is by a private road which leads to Holkham Gap, where duck-boards have been laid to prevent the erosion of the dunes. The wide sandy beach follows a gentle curve and is protected save when the wind is in the north, and behind it a belt of planted pines forms a backcloth. On the beach itself there are dune ridges colonised by bushes of perennial seablite. Something of a surprise are the extensive ramparts of an Iron Age fort near Burrow Gap on a slightly raised site in the nearby marshes. Back on the coastal road there is the estate village and hotel at the entrance to the Holkham estate. Developed in the early eighteenth century by Thomas Coke, the centrepiece is the Palladian style mansion built of a yellow-grey brick and stuccoed. His great nephew, created Earl of Leicester in 1837, achieved fame as an agricultural pioneer responsible for transforming what had always been considered wasteland by a system of crop rotation and animal manuring. The family still own the estate and the house is open to visitors on certain days in the summer.

Overy Staithe, the port for the Burnham group of villages, attracts because it is unspoiled, with an old warehouse used as a shop. It must have been familiar to Nelson who was born in the nearby Burnham Thorpe. The channel from the quay to the open sea is tortuous and liable to shift. West of the entrance lies Scolt Head Island, a nature reserve of dune and marsh, not unlike parts of Blakeney spit but much less visited, though there are sailings to it from Brancaster Staithe. From Overy there is a pleasant walk along the top of the sea bank to the Holkham Nature Reserve and the dunes which form the eastern side of the entrance to Burnham harbour. The sand and shingle beach has a wealth of shells including scallop, oyster and cockle.

Brancaster is yet another village lying on the coastal road which clings to the higher ground around the marshland fringe. Interest here is centred on the Roman fort of *Branodunum* 1km (½ mile) to the west which had walls 3m (10ft) thick and dates from the second century AD. Although it later became incorporated in the system of defence known as Forts of the Saxon Shore, this was not its initial function. Possibly it was the terminus of a route running across Norfolk – the prehistoric Peddars Way is close by – with a ferry connection across the Wash into Lincolnshire. There is little to see of the fort today. Brancaster Staithe has its mussel gathering in the many creeks and is a port for Scolt Head. A recent addition nearby is the Royal Society for the Protection of Birds reserve of Titchwell.

Hunstanton is a town with two faces. Along the cliff top to the north there is a substantial town of well-built houses, mainly of dark-brown carstone brought from a nearby quarry at Snettisham. The town centre occupies sloping ground around a green and it was here that the first hotels and boarding houses were built following the arrival of the Great Eastern Railway to the area in 1862. The idea of the resort town came from the local Lestrange family who for generations had lived in nearby Hunstanton Hall. The railway encouraged such development and, in a matter of a few years, the railway-owned Sandringham Arms (now council offices), the church of St Edmunds, the pier and streets of four- and five-storey houses appeared. For a time the new resort was called St Edmunds to avoid confusion with the original village of Hunstanton (now Old Hunstanton) lying further north along the coast, but this was later changed. A unique feature of the resort is the striped cliffs of dark-brown carstone at the base followed in turn by red and white chalk. The other part of the town has a different setting for it is low lying and was therefore less attractive to the early builders. The railway station lay here and was quickly surrounded by amusement arcades and other entertainment facilities likely to attract large numbers of people from the industrial towns. The distinctiveness of this quarter persists at the present day, and the clearing away of the old railway station and sidings has released more ground for similar development. The two contrasting sides to Hunstanton obviously worried the writer of *Murray's Guide* in 1892 who wondered whether he could recommend the resort to the genteel visitor because 'It must be remembered that Hunstanton during the summer is exposed to constant forays of excursionists, who are brought here hundreds at a time from Cambridgeshire, Lincolnshire and elsewhere. Their visits do not lead to an increase in the comfort of the inns or of the beach.'

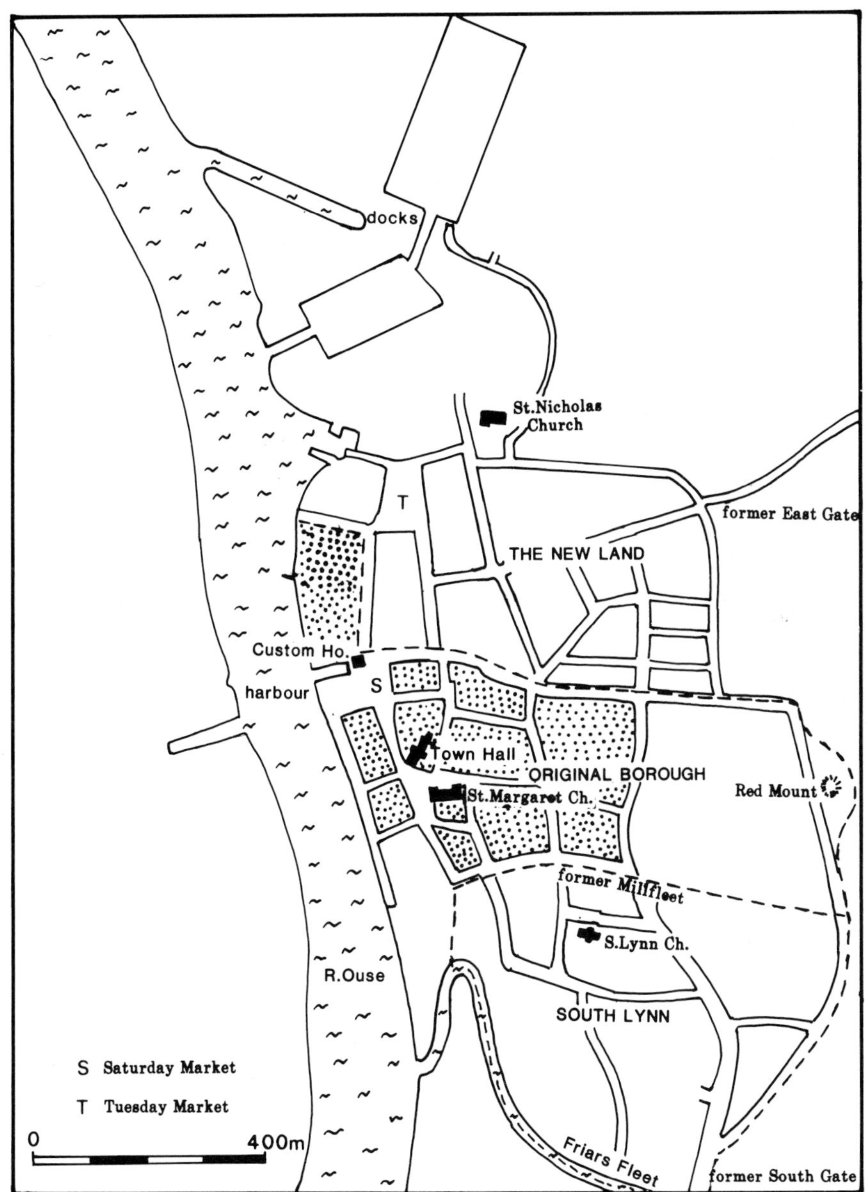

Plan of King's Lynn showing the expansion from the original core (*after Hoskins*)

North Wootton The edge of the Wash is too flat to provide much by way of scenic attraction and has been made worse by the development of huge caravan camps at places like Heacham. As King's Lynn is approached the situation changes and we enter a landscape of reclamation, best seen by taking the lane beyond the village of North Wootton where over the past centuries vast tracts of former sand-flats and salting have been reclaimed in huge embanked enclosures. The sandbank of Vinegar Middle, once beneath the waters of the Wash, now forms part of a rich agricultural expanse, exemplifying the piecemeal reclamation which is the only possible method for this area. Schemes like that undertaken in the Zuider Zee in Holland cannot be entertained because of the very different physical conditions (see page 61).

King's Lynn It is not known when the first settlement of fishermen and traders established themselves on this relatively dry site on the eastern bank of the river Ouse. But by the end of the eleventh century the church of St Margaret and the Priory had been founded by the Bishop of Norwich, together with a Saturday market 'at the request of the men of the town of Lynn'. A century later in 1204 we learn that another Bishop of Norwich had granted a charter to the town, for in the intervening period Lynn had grown considerably and had acquired another suburb, centred on the chapel of St Nicholas, to the north. A second market place was laid out and market rights given for Tuesdays. Even 800 years later these medieval concessions influence the layout and activities of the present town. As a trading centre for much of the Fenland and north Norfolk, Lynn is a bustling place at all times of the year; it is also a considerable port with continental and coastal traffic. The straightening of the lower course of the Ouse in 1850 and the building of the dock in 1869 were acts of faith at the time, but have been fully justified in recent years. Previously shipping had tied up at the open wharves along the river bank, and it is here that one of the town's noblest buildings, the Customs House, originally a Merchants' Exchange, was built in 1683 with stone brought down the river Nene from the Midlands. Former merchant houses are found in odd corners of the town; the best is probably Clifton House in Queen Street. Opposite St Margaret's church is the Steelyard or Hanseatic warehouse, while to the north is the open space used by the Saturday market. This is overlooked by Lynn's most famous building – The Guildhall built for the Guild of Holy Trinity in 1421. It stands out not only because of its antiquity but also for its fine chequerboard facing of flint and freestone. But perhaps the most remarkable building in this town of many prized assets is the twelfth-century Norman house at present being restored by the King's Lynn Preservation Trust. Here is tangible proof of the continuous prosperity enjoyed by the town and port throughout its long history.

Lincolnshire

Sutton Bridge, on the main and busy trunk road linking King's Lynn with Boston, makes an ideal starting point from which to explore the fenland country along the southern margin of the Wash. The winning of new lands by reclamation has gone on over the past century and a half at the mouth of the Nene (see page 000), beginning with the cutting and embanking of a straight outfall between 1826 and 1830. A new bridge was designed and built by Rennie and Telford at the lowest crossing of the new cut and this forms the present Sutton Bridge. A pair of lighthouses was built as beacons at the seaward end (Guy's Head), on land owned by Guy's Hospital. Sea banks, now followed by the twisting marshland road around the coast, began to appear from 1824 onwards, but more recent innings have extended the land frontier and created first-class arable fields. Outside the sea banks scurvy grass, sea lavender and sea aster are gradually building up the natural saltings which in time will allow further reclamation. Offshore, on Breast Sand, lies an artificial island made as part of the Hydraulic Research Station's feasibility study relating to water storage and reclamation works in the Wash. Part of the area is a bombing range, so that even in the loneliness of the saltings it is impossible to escape from the realities of the late twentieth century. Sutton Bridge is very much a roadside settlement but at one time it seemed destined to become a river port to replace Wisbech. A dock with lock gates was dug out on the present site of the golf course, but it was never flooded and the whole project was abandoned.

Boston was once the premier medieval wool port of the country and later had Hanseatic

---

The coast of Lincolnshire and the East Riding of Yorkshire

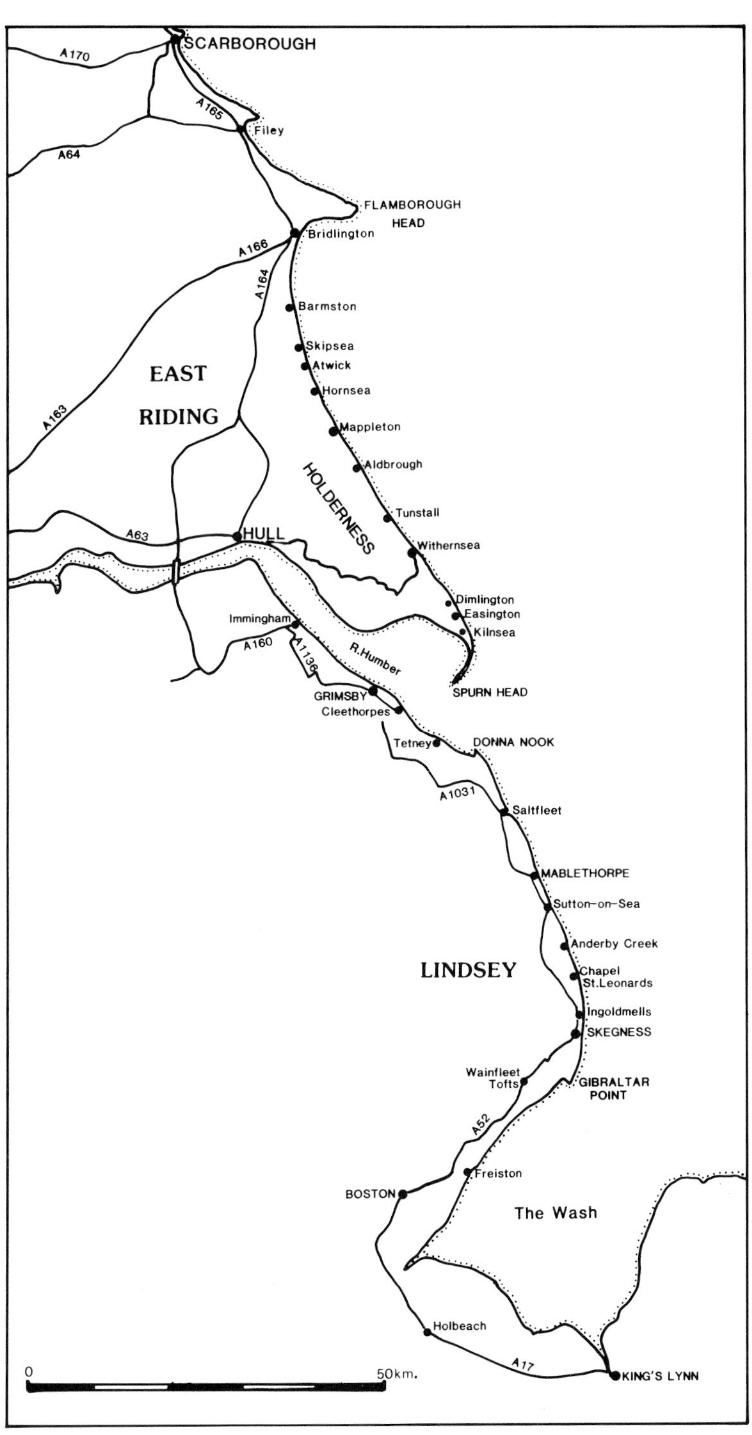

SCARBOROUGH
A170
A165
Filey
A64
FLAMBOROUGH
HEAD
Bridlington
A166
A164
Barmston
Skipsea
Atwick
Hornsea
EAST
RIDING
A163
Mappleton
Aldbrough
HOLDERNESS
Tunstall
HULL
A63
Withernsea
Dimlington
Easington
Kilnsea
Immingham
A160
A1136
R.Humber
SPURN HEAD
GRIMSBY
Cleethorpes
Tetney
DONNA NOOK
A1031
Saltfleet
MABLETHORPE
Sutton-on-Sea
Anderby Creek
LINDSEY
Chapel
St.Leonards
Ingoldmells
SKEGNESS
Wainfleet
Tofts
GIBRALTAR
POINT
A52
Freiston
BOSTON
The Wash
Holbeach
A17
KING'S LYNN
0
50km.

Boston, on the river Witham. Its famous 'Stump' dominates the town and surrounding countryside

League associations before lapsing into obscurity through the inability of ships to navigate the rapidly silting lower part of the river Witham. The building of the docks in a bend in the river in 1882 and the cutting of a new channel to the sea renewed Boston as a port, and since the recent link-up with Europe it has grown in stature so that today ships jostle for wharf space in the dock. Goods mainly arrive by lorry and this can cause congestion in the town; fortunately the old town lies upstream from the docks and bridge so that it enjoys a partial immunity. Its dominant feature is the fifteenth-century church of St Botolph and the huge triangular market place alongside. The best view of the church with its tall tower crowned by an octagonal lantern – the famous Boston Stump – is from the upper-bridge parapet where it is seen standing proudly above the muddy margins of the Witham. Almost contemporary with the church is Boston's other remaining medieval building – the Guildhall dating from 1450. Now a museum extending back along the length of a former burgage plot, the building was once the home of the trading guild of St Mary. Next door is a fine eighteenth-century residence, Fydell House, dating from 1726 and almost opposite a huge brick warehouse, a reminder of the town's trading past.

Freiston Shore, one of the more accessible spots along the Wash margin, and 6km (4 miles) south east of Boston, is approached through a maze of twisting lanes. The settlement, consisting of an inn and roadside cottages, crouches behind the huge sea bank, beyond which lie newly reclaimed pastures and others in process of being snatched from the sea (see page 64). This Wash margin of protective sea banks fringed by natural salting and sand and mud flats, runs north east as far as Gibraltar Point. Throughout it offers considerable potential for future land reclamation by piecemeal inning; nature cannot be hurried however.

Wainfleet Tofts, now 2km (1½ miles) from the coast, was once very much in contact with the open sea. In a pasture by the main road is the unmistakable hummocky ground of mounds and ridges of former salt-workings; their age is not known but is likely to be medieval rather than Roman. The

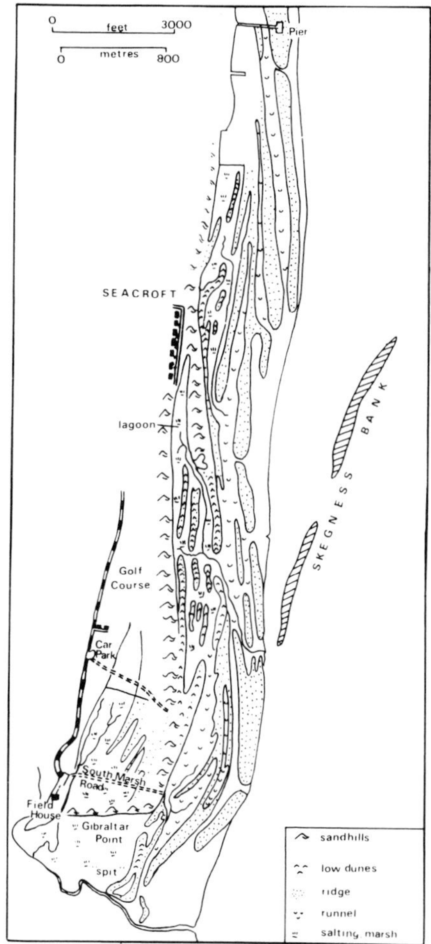

Between Skegness and Gibraltar Point: sand ridges and salt marsh

method of extraction was crude but effective. After high spring tides a thin veneer of silt was left behind near the high-water line and this was scraped up and placed in a trench. Water was added to carry off the salt, and the brine was then heated over peat fires to extract the valued commodity. The original silt, 'muldefang', was thrown into waste heaps, hence the hummocky nature of the former salt-extraction sites today (*Lincolnshire Architectural and Archaeological Society Report* No 8, 26-112).

Gibraltar Point Nearness to Skegness once posed a threat to this natural area of salting and dune landscape, but the area was saved by establishing a conservation reserve run by the Lincolnshire Naturalists' Trust. There is field-study accommodation for students and, for the ordinary day visitor, a newly built centre with displays showing the evolution of the coastline, marsh and dune vegetation, bird life etc. The path across the marsh to the beach gives a good insight into the character of the salt-marsh vegetation as the main plant associations are labelled. Sea couch grass and sea arrow grass grow in patches along with the sea lavender, while bordering the creek margins there is the sea purslane and sea aster. The coastal dune belt is dominated by the spiky, orange-berried sea buckthorn and the ubiquitous marram grass. On the beach new sand ridges are continually forming with salt-marsh patches in the muddy enclaves. Here the salt-tolerant rice grass (Spartina) and samphire, a vivid red in autumn, quickly take hold. An excellent *Walkabout Guide* is available at the Visitor Centre.

Skegness, a name meaning Skaeggi's nose or promontory, tells us that the first settlement here in the ninth century was on a coastline different in shape from that of today. The headland which protected a harbour to the south was subsequently destroyed by erosion and Leland, the antiquary who wrote in the early sixteenth century, described the place as 'sumtyme a greate haven towne'. The town we see today is very much a Victorian creation and dates from the Earl of Scarborough's decision in 1870 to create a new resort in anticipation of the railway reaching the coast within a few years (see page 104).

Ingoldmells, north of Skegness, seems to have every available field near the coast occupied by caravans or holiday chalets, possibly more to the acre than the sheep they displaced on the marshland pastures. The holiday industry started in the 1930s with Butlin's camp, quickly followed by miners' holiday homes and some retirement bungalows. The name is Norse and incorporates the element *melr*, referring to the marram grass which covers the dunes. The latter suffered badly during the 1953 storms and concrete facing, together with groynes, was found necessary to trap the beach sand.

The submerged forest at Sutton-on-Sea, only seen at very low tide

Chapel St Leonards, originally Mumby Chapel, indicates by its name that here was a daughter settlement of an inland mother church. It has suffered from past erosion like so much of this Lindsey coast, with the high sand dunes proving vulnerable in 1953. During a 'tempest of wind and rain' in 1571 'the whole towne was lost except three cottages . . . the church was wholly overthrown, except the steeple'. Now the concrete promenade and groynes give a sense of security to the retirement bungalows and holiday chalets.

Anderby Creek represents a pre-war attempt to create a more substantial settlement with a group of villas perched precariously on the dune top. It was unsuccessful, so this small area, close to one of the major drainage outfalls, is like much of this coast, swamped with caravans.

Sutton-on-Sea has tried, with some success, to remain small and exclusive in contrast to neighbouring Mablethorpe; and two hotels cater for those content with the fine sands and bracing air. It could have been so different if an ambitious scheme of the Lancashire, Derbyshire & East Coast Railway Company to build a huge artificial harbour jutting out into the open waters of the North Sea had succeeded. Fed by rail traffic from both Lancashire and the Midlands, the new port was to become the Liverpool of the East Coast, but nothing came of the project and it was abandoned in favour of Immingham on the Humber, developed by the Great Central Railway in 1907. Sutton had to be content with a branch loop but even this closed in the 1960s. The beach here can claim distinction in that it is one of the few places on the Lincolnshire coast where it is possible to see the remains of stumps of trees of a submerged forest near the low-water line of spring tides, after longshore currents have swept away a superficial covering of sand. The stumps – lime, hazel and alder – project through a layer of peat and are set firmly in clay. The forest dates from about 2500 BC when sea level was much lower, and was the subject of a paper to the Royal Society by Correa de Serra in 1796, who also spoke of a belief among old inhabitants that their parish church once stood on one of the clay islets offshore. Certainly the original parish church had perished through sea erosion by the mid-sixteenth century. Its present humble successor, near the main coastal road and well inland, dates from 1818, but

Seaford Head, looking west

judging by its leaning tower seems destined to fall into the marsh at some future date.

Mablethorpe like Skegness was largely the creation of the railway, but failed to take advantage to the same extent. A late Victorian guide book spoke of it 'as a much frequented watering place with fine sands, it is nevertheless wanting in energy for creating popular attractions which have been conspicuous at Skegness'. Throughout this century it has never been able to make up its mind whether to become loud and gaudy to attract the masses or to simply remain quiet and impassive so as to appeal to those seeking retirement by the sea. The building of a self-catering chalet complex to the north of the town suggests compromise between two opposing factions. Certainly the fine sandy beaches and fringing dune belt represent natural assets which many greater resorts would look on with envy. Mablethorpe's chalet park marks the last outpost of major holiday development on the Lindsey coast, for beyond lies the Theddlethorpe Gas Terminal, a development which alarmed conservationists but which makes surprisingly little impact on a coastline which had already suffered from the excesses of caravan growth.

Saltfleet Between Mablethorpe and Saltfleet the main coastal road (A1031) pursues a tortuous course some distance inland through Theddlethorpe with its RAF bombing-range base. For the last 1.6km (1 mile) it runs alongside the straight course of the Withern Eau – a small waterway which formerly ran directly out to sea beyond Cloves Bridge along a course still marked by the parish boundary. Towards the end of the thirteenth century the silting up of the muddy creek forming Saltfleet Haven threatened the usefulness of the harbour, and the solution lay in diverting the Withern Eau into the head of the creek and using its waters to scour out the mud. The whole undertaking, a considerable engineering feat, probably took place sometime before 1330, and is similar to a scheme for flushing out the silt of New Romney harbour in Kent about the same time. Once the harbour had been secured, Saltfleet enjoyed a considerable increase in trade, principally the export of wool, from Louth Park Abbey, and corn. Fish and wine were the main imports in these late medieval times, when a local landowner, John Willoughby, carried out improvements to the harbour by levying quayage dues. The threat of silting always remained, and in the nineteenth century, when Saltfleet was a useful coal-importing port, the approach was straightened. Trade declined following the opening of the Louth Canal and the coming of the railway. Only in the last twenty years has there been an upturn in the fortunes of the port as boating and sailing have increased in popularity, but the muddy creek still poses problems both for navigation and mooring.

Famous beauty spot Robin Hood's Bay, near Whitby, is noted for its fossils (*R. L. White*)

Donna Nook, where the coast turns into the Humber, forms an extensive sand-flat up to 2km (1½ miles) wide. The inner part is colonised by sea grass and marsh samphire which has succulent leaves excellent for pickling. Access to the flats is restricted as part of the area is a bombing range. Even though the wide foreshore helps to break the power of the waves, there is erosion of the outer face of the low dune belt and brushwood bundles have been laid to arrest this, as in Holland. The approach to Donna Nook is down a long straight road from North Somercotes through rich farmland. Reclamation here dates from 1632 when Endymion Porter, of London court circles, became an 'adventurer' willing to risk capital on drainage and embanking works. Some 200ha (500 acres) were reclaimed in this way and the area is still known as Porter's Marsh. Another significant place name is 'fitties', the local name for salt marsh – lands where salt extraction was once practised. Seaward of the coast road running through Grainthorpe and Marsh Chapel is an area of hummocky ground, the result of salt extraction.

Tetney Haven The building of the Louth Navigation between 1765 and 1770 led to extensive areas being reclaimed around the canal outfall into the Humber at Tetney

Haven. The canal was a great success commercially for it enabled Louth, some miles inland, to export corn and import coal and fertilisers. From Tetney, there was even a passenger steamer twice a week to Hull, and remarkably this continued into the present century. The curious Tetney blow-wells are described on page 85.

Cleethorpes is a resort dating from the 1860s when the Great Northern Railway established a connection with the coal and steel-making areas of south Yorkshire. The railway company not only brought in the excursionists but also catered for their needs. They built the sea wall and promenade and the 366m (1,200ft) long pier. The site chosen was on a low clay cliff (hence the original name of the settlement, 'Clee'). Whereas Skegness catered for Leicester and Nottingham, Cleethorpes' visitors have tended to come from Sheffield and the Don Valley towns because of the direct rail link. The past decade has seen a complete change of emphasis with the resort function of the town now fading and giving way to a role as a residential suburb for nearby Grimsby. The pier, save for a tiny stump, has gone and the nearby station no longer has to deal with the teeming masses pouring off the excursion trains.

Yorkshire

Sunk Island was once a true island, but since the early nineteenth century it has been joined to the mainland. It started life as a partly submerged sandbank close to the north shore of the Humber, but the gradual accumulation of warp (layers of mud brought in by the tides) created the basis of the present rich agricultural land. The island was originally Crown land but was later given to Colonel Gilby, Governor of Hull, by Charles II. Its growth, as a result of warp accumulation and aided by artificial reclamation, can be seen from the accompanying map. A chapel, built in 1802 to serve the few families living on the island, later became the parish church when Sunk achieved parish status in 1831. Although no longer a backwater, it is still a place of open skies and wide horizons where solitude is easy to find.

Spurn Spit consists of a long narrow ridge of sand running for 4.5km (3 miles) in a curve from the 'mainland' of Holderness at Kilnsea. Controversy rages as to whether the

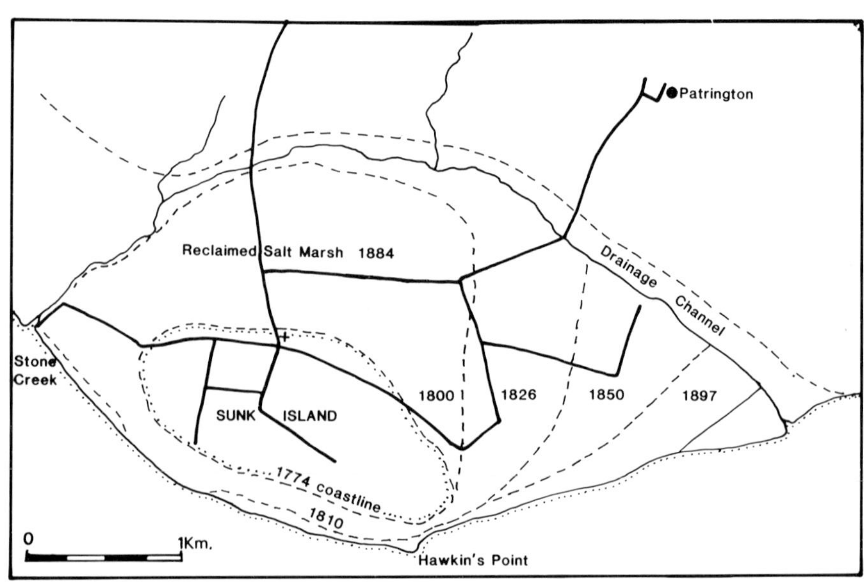

Sunk Island with the successive stages of its reclamation

The present lighthouse at Spurn Head. Constant vigilance is needed because of the danger of erosion on its seaward side

spit has grown in length from Kilnsea during the past 400 years, a repetition of earlier similar growth cycles. Evidence quoted in support, and especially the use of old (and inaccurate) maps, is not wholly convincing. What is clear is that throughout its history Spurn has been characterised by a broad spatula-shaped southern end, Spurn Point. Until the long narrow tail connecting the ridge with the mainland was stabilised in the middle of the last century by coastal protective works, Spurn Point was often an island. It was shown in this form on the first large scale Ordnance Survey map of 1852, and would undoubtedly have reverted to an island but for man's involvement in providing defence works. The narrow tail is still breached on occasions, the last being in January 1978 when part of the spit road was broken up. At its narrowest point it is only about 50m (165ft) wide, and great concrete walls are necessary to withstand wave attack. Erosion is likely to occur throughout its length and a great concrete bastion has been built in front of the lighthouse, for without it the dune fringe readily succumbs to storm wave attacks.

The most stable part of the spit is the broad southern end. Colonised by marram grass and sea buckthorn (orange berries) it has retained its present form, though not its exact position, over the centuries. Erosion on the outer and vulnerable face is balanced by accretion on the inner and more protected side. As a result the broad width remains, but at the same time the whole feature is gradually moving bodily to the west. It is maintained by a complex current system operative at the mouth of the Humber. The Admiralty chart is a better guide here than the Ordnance Survey map, for it tells us about the underwater features as well as the form of the spit above sea level. The Spurn spit we see today is really only the raised part of a great parabola of sand and shingle in the north-east approach to the Humber. The mainly submerged portion lies offshore, where it forms the bank known as The Binks. At low water spring tides it is possible to walk onto the narrow neck of The Binks, though care must be exercised to avoid being cut off by the rising tide. Swift currents have

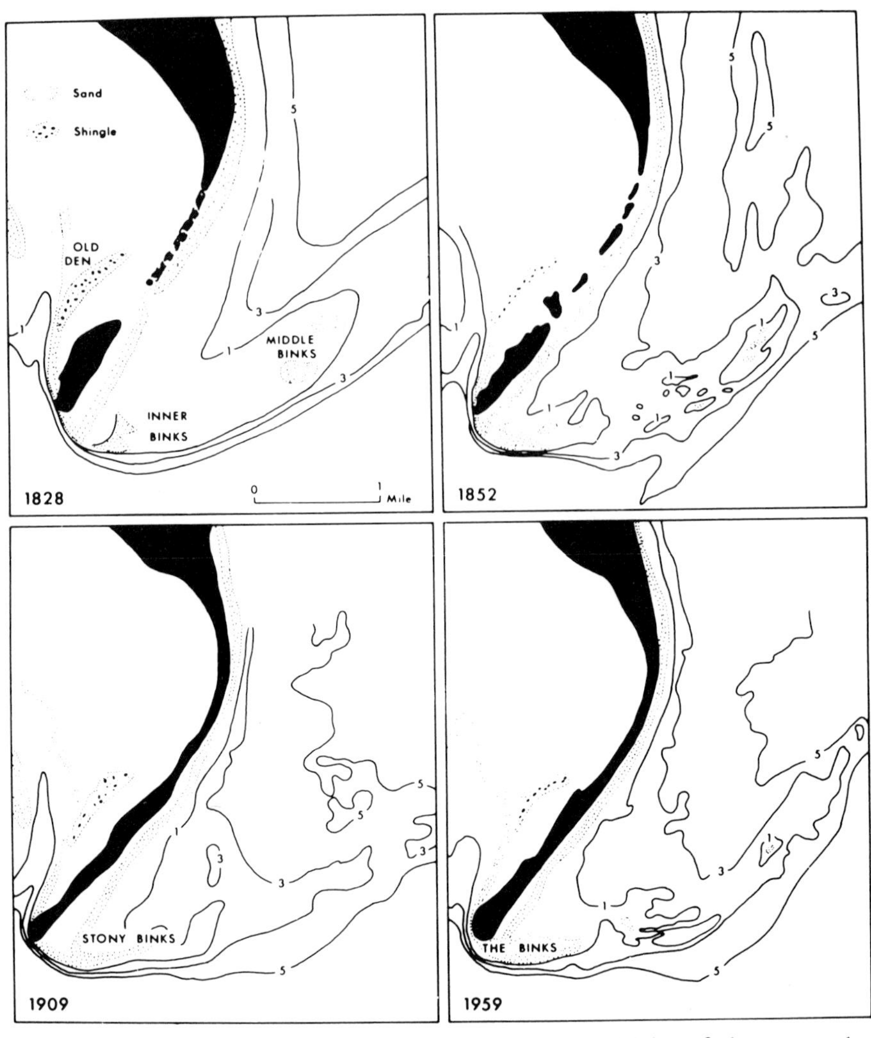

Changes in the form of Spurn Spit since the early nineteenth century

created a sand and shingle surface deeply scoured with hollows which indicate highly turbulent conditions.

Spurn spit of past centuries is equally fascinating, and again there is a certain amount of controversy as to the exact interpretation of the evidence available. The main source of information is the documents of Meaux Abbey, and it is almost a century since J. R. Boyle in his *Lost Towns of the Humber* drew attention to the story these papers told. There were two earlier settlements in the vicinity of the present-day Spurn Point. The earliest was Old Ravenser, mentioned at least three times in old Icelandic sagas. This place name is Norse in origin: the first element comes from the Danish standard, the raven, while the latter portion of the word, *eyr* or *ore*, tells of a narrow strip of land between two waters, undoubtedly a reference to Spurn spit. We thus have evidence of a settlement here, possibly on an island-sandbank site, at least as early as the eleventh century. Another town, which appears in the Abbey records of the thirteenth century, is Ravenser Odd or alternatively Ravenserodd. Its origin is described in the Hundred Rolls of Edward I, which tell of the events of around 1235, when 'by the casting up of the sea, sand and stones accumulated, on which accumulation William de Portibus began to build a certain town which is called Ravenserodd: and it is an island: the sea surrounds it.' From this and other similar references it looks as though Ravenserodd must have been situated in the Humber entrance, in a similar spot to the present-day broad end of Spurn, though not in the same geographic position, due to the westerly migration of the spit. It became a place of considerable importance, both as a port and market town, as is clear from the charter which it received from Henry III in 1251, and the rights of a free borough in 1299. But although the thirteenth century had been a time of advancement for Ravenserodd, the following 100 years saw its complete eclipse; the Meaux Abbey Cartulary, written between 1394 and 1400 tells us that by then there was scarcely anything left of the former town. To stand near the lighthouse at Spurn Point today during a winter storm, such as occurred in 1978, leaves no doubt as to the vulnerability of the fragile sand spit. The same must have been so in the late fourteenth century, a period of tremendous coastal storms, and both Ravenserodd and its near neighbour, Old Ravenser, would have perished with little trace.

The later history of the spit is very much tied up with the building and maintaining of lighthouses. In 1676 a patent was granted by Charles II to a Mr Angell for the erection of lights at Spurn Point. A lengthening of the spit over the next 100 years made Angell's lights useless, and they were ultimately replaced by a pair recommended by Smeaton. The outer light proved vulnerable as the high-water line moved steadily westwards at the rate of 3m (10ft) a year and so the present lighthouse was built in 1895. The old light, on the inner side of the spit close to the row of coastguard cottages, still stands with its feet in water and is used as a magazine store. The whole area now has an untidy appearance for the army gun emplacements dating from both wars have never been cleared away. Those on the seaward side are occasionally prised out of the dunes by the erosive action of the sea. Today the spit, including the road running down to the lighthouse and coastguard cottages, is managed by the Yorkshire Naturalists' Trust, who maintain a small centre near the entrance. It is a wild and windswept place during the winter, but is never without the odd beach angler or bird watcher. Brent geese frequent the mud-flats on the inner side in late November, and other seabirds nest in the dunes.

Kilnsea, the last place on the 'mainland' at the base of the spit, has a history which typifies most of the Holderness settlements. For the past 700 years at least, it has been virtually powerless to prevent the relentless encroachment of the sea, and huge areas of the parish have been swallowed up. At Kilnsea the clay cliffs are low but very vulnerable to erosion (see page 51). In 1822 the village consisted of the church and about thirty cottages arranged around a wide village street which also contained the 'towne' well. But in a matter of a few years the church had been swept away and the cottages were engulfed one by one by the advancing cliff line. Today, in spite of concrete defence works, the erosion goes on. A plaque set into the wall of the former Bluebell Inn (now a shop) records that in 1847 the sea was 488m (534yd) away, but it is now only approximately half that distance.

Easington is situated far enough inland to ignore any future threat of destruction, for at least the next 100 years. The village is centred on the church, and there are groups of cottages built of rounded cobbles. It has changed little in recent years, even though there is now a gas terminal situated nearby. Easington Beach, with its inevitable caravan park, lies 1.7km (1¼ miles) away at the end of Sea Lane. The cliffs are low and a sloping ramp cut into the clay gives access to the sandy beach, still with its concrete defence works built during the last war. A pill box, formerly sited on the cliff top, now sits precariously two-thirds of the way down the beach, showing the rate of cliff retreat over the past 40 years.

Dimlington, the only traces of which are the outbuildings of an abandoned farm, has the highest cliffs of the Holderness coast, over 30m (100ft) high, but formerly even higher. Erosion rates over the past 100 years have tended to be greater here than elsewhere, for, because of the height of the cliff, when a great slide takes place thousands of tons of clay are removed from the cliff top. At nearby Holmpton great circular bights into the cliff face in recent years are now threatening yet another of the coastal farms, which each year sees more fields disappearing into the sea.

Withernsea had ambitions of becoming a resort after a Hull businessman, Anthony Bennett, took the railway there in 1854 and built the imposing and restrained Queens Hotel. Development was slow and, although a pier was built, a guide book of the 1890s dismissed the resort as 'a dreary watering place'. The pier has now gone, and only the castellated gateway remains on the promenade. New housing estates have encouraged both commuters and retired people to move to Withernsea in recent years. Extensions to the sea defences in the south have arrested erosion for the time being, but the town has obviously suffered in the past, and the present lighthouse was erected well back from the coast amongst the houses in 1894 (cf Southwold).

Tunstall lies off the main coast road but is situated on the original route which has been broken up by the retreating cliff-line. Its church dates from the thirteenth century and is built mostly of cobbles, and, like many old buildings, forms a useful marker to measure erosion. Between 1786 and 1895 the distance to the cliff edge decreased from 845 to 632m (924 to 681yd), but has now dropped to only 512m (560yd).

Aldbrough is one of the largest of the Holderness coastal villages. Its cottages are arranged neatly around a rectangle of streets close to the church, which has a circular churchyard. Although now about 2.5km (1½ miles) away from the coast, the church and village must be of late medieval date, replacing a Saxon settlement which now lies beneath the waves. We know this from a Saxon inscription inserted above a massive round pier in the south aisle of the church which records that 'Ulf ordered this church to be built for the souls of Hanum and Gunthard'. Ulf is recorded in the Domesday record as lord of Aldbrough in the days of Edward the Confessor. As we know that the present church of St Bartholomew was built between 1353 and 1377, the original Saxon church must have perished some time during the twelfth and thirteenth centuries, a period of very bad coastal weather. Erosion continues to the present day, and in the last few years substantial houses have gone over the edge.

Mappleton, a compact roadside settlement, is unlikely to develop as land between the churchyard and the cliff top is fast disappearing. Nearby Great Cowden (or Colden) has already suffered severely and its church has been destroyed, while its twin, Little Cowden, lost its chapel about 1690.

Hornsea has a very similar history to Withernsea, in that it grew as a resort following the arrival of the railway from Hull in 1864, largely under the influence of Joseph Wade, a Hull timber merchant. Some lodging houses and a hotel had been built already, to take advantage of the attractive inland mere nearby; and there was a chance that it might become a spa, following the discovery of a chalybeate spring. The closing of the railway in the 1960s (the red brick terminus still survives) did not affect the fortunes of Hornsea to any great extent, for it had already become a town of commuters and the retired. For many years erosion has posed problems, and great sea defences have had to be built to protect the low-lying land. This part of the town has remained largely undeveloped, and has been given over to amusement arcades, bingo halls and seasonal shops. Fortunately the main part of the town, with its curving main street following the eastern shore of the Hornsea mere, still gives Hornsea the character and function of a small country town and make it less dependent on the summer day-trippers.

The mere, with its boating and fishing, is another tourist attraction. It is the largest area of natural water in Yorkshire and dates from the time of the Ice Age when a depression formed in the thick deposit of boulder clay found throughout Holderness. Now it is silting up quite rapidly, and could eventually disappear, as has happened at Owthorne, near Withernsea. In medieval times Hornsea mere was of great economic value because of its fish, and there was a prolonged argument about its ownership between the Abbey of Meaux and St Mary's Abbey in York, the latter eventually winning the day. Hornsea was very much influenced by the Abbots of York for they obtained a market charter for the town in 1257.

Today Hornsea is perhaps best known for its distinctive brown-glazed pottery. The enterprise of two brothers who in 1949 established a small kiln off the main road on the south side of the town, has led to the development of a considerable industry and given the holidaymaker another place to visit on a wet day. An extensive car park, garden shop and children's amusement centre lie alongside the original pottery.

Atwick, 3.2km (2 miles) north of Hornsea, has a road down to the coast but access to the beach is made difficult by the continuous erosion of the clay cliffs. An infilled mere has produced remains of the Irish elk and a fine elephant's tusk, a reminder of the great changes in climate and landscape which have taken place in the past.

Skipsea Although it has rather unattractive modern caravan sites, Skipsea is a place of history. In a field to the west of the church is the huge mound (motte) of a Norman castle, once known as Albermarle Hill. The castle dates from the eleventh century and was built by Dru de la Beuvrière, who came to this country with William the Conqueror. The mound is 12m (40ft) high, and must have looked very impressive as it rose above the waters of a typical Holderness mere, now drained. It has been suggested that the mound is largely composed of gravel, and could therefore be a depositional feature of the Ice Age. Even though de la Beuvrière was given the title of Lord of Holderness, it is not easy to understand why he should have sited his castle here; it might be an example of continued use of an existing site, as there are indications that the church (with its eleventh-century nave, and chancel with herringbone-patterned walls) may be built on the site of an earlier structure. Its circular churchyard recalls the Celtic *llan*, with its rounded enclosure of ditch and rampart. Whatever its pre-Norman history, its subsequent owner obviously hoped that the castle–church relationship would lead to the development of a market town. The fact that this did not happen is probably due to the proximity of Hornsea, which acquired market rights in the thirteenth century.

Barmston can claim distinction as one of the few places on the Holderness coast where sand rather than clay appears in the cliff-face. Erosion is no less intense, and during the 1970s a row of detached bungalows was picked off by the sea, one by one, until only one now remains in 1982. Previously pathetic attempts had been made to keep the sea at bay but to no avail. The tragedy lies in the fact that the buildings were erected in the first place and willing buyers found, doubtless attracted to the site on a fine, calm summer's day. Barmston has more to it than the motley collection of wooden shacks and caravans by the sea, for the true heart of the village lies safe inland. After the eclipse of Dru de la Beuvrière at Skipsea, Barmston took over as the seat of the Lord of Holderness. A moated enclosure and the remains of one wing of the old hall, south of the church, tell of the influence of the Boynton family, prior to moving to their fine house at Burton Constable. In the adjacent village of Ulrome a former dried-out mere yielded remains of prehistoric lake dwellings consisting of a huge platform resting on oak piles.

Bridlington has often been dismissed simply as a nineteenth-century seaside resort, and its many summer visitors may only see this side of it. But the original village grew up inland around the Augustinian Priory founded between AD 1115 and 1120. This formed the core of the settlement, with its cluster of narrow streets, and it still survives in part today to form what is known as the 'Old Town'. Following the dissolution of the monasteries by Henry VIII in 1537, the eastern half of the chancel of the priory church was pulled down, but the rest survived to become the parish church. The only other medieval building to have remained is the Bayles Gate, dating from 1388 when permission was given to fortify the priory site. The rest of the old town consists of the narrow curving High Street, with its seventeenth-nineteenth century bow-fronted buildings, and the more spacious Market Street, possibly laid out in the early thirteenth century when the priory was granted the right to hold a weekly market and occasional fairs.

The Quay, the area around the harbour, was originally quite separate from the rest of Bridlington. Situated at a break in the almost continuous line of cliffs where the Gypsy Race from the Wolds enters the sea, it was natural for some sort of haven to grow up on this harbourless coast. The present harbour walls, dating from the mid-nineteenth century, are the successors to much earlier medieval piers. They give shelter to a fishing fleet of keel boats as well as a varied collection of leisure craft. As in so many harbour-resorts this corner of the town is a mecca for summer visitors who are content to watch impassively the continuous activity of the boats.

The last part of the town to be built up followed the arrival of the railway from Hull in 1846. Although Bridlington was regarded as a watering place as early as 1770, with lodging houses around the harbour, the main phase of resort building took place between 1850 and 1880. Street after street of substantial terrace houses were built on the flat land alongside the north cliff, in an attempt to copy similar development at Brighton. Dominating all was the ornate Alexandra Hotel dating from 1866; churches and other public buildings followed, as well as a range of activities to attract the summer visitor. By the turn of the century Bridlington's three parts had largely coalesced to form the present town, and, with a population of almost 30,000, it is by far the largest of the resorts of the East Riding.

Flamborough consists of a great promontory of chalk which projects eastwards from Bridlington and gives protection to shipping in the bay. To anyone used to the crumbling, soft chalk cliffs of Sussex, the more resistant rock of Flamborough is something of a surprise. The pore spaces of the original chalk have been infilled by secondary deposition of calcium carbonate so that the resulting rock has a toughness and resistance to erosion comparable to limestone. The sea does attack along weakened joint zones, and the cliff-line all around the headland is very indented. At the headland itself the isolated Green Stacks stand defiantly against the full onslaught of the waves while at the nearby Pigeon Hole a collapse of the surface strata has created an impressive blow-hole feature. Close by, as though guarding the flanks of Selwick Bay (just below the lighthouse) were the twin stacks known as Adam and Eve. Eve, alas, has now collapsed, a common fate for these vulnerable isolated rock pillars. The same thing has happened to the stack known as The King, 1.5km (1 mile) further west along the coast towards Flamborough North Sea Landing. This section of the coastline is fascinating for, apart from the stacks, there are geos (long narrow fissures in the cliff face), natural arches and a multitude of caves, many of which can only be explored by boat. It was this fretted cliff-line that R. D. Blackmore used for the setting in his novel *Mary Aneley* where the principal character, Robin Lyth, was brought up and ultimately became a smuggler. During one of his exploits, he took refuge in one of the caves just east of the North Landing, now known as the Robin Lyth Cave.

Flamborough Head itself, like so many of the 'end' points of the British coastline, has become rather trippery with gift shops and cafés. The great New Lighthouse (built in 1806) towers above all. The old lighthouse, an octagonal stone tower built of chalk and dating from about 1674, lies alongside the road on the approach to the headland. At one time it was suggested that the name Flamborough was derived from the flame of the open coal brazier of the old lighthouse but this is wishful thinking. It is more likely to derive from the Saxon *flaen* meaning arrow head, and related to the shape of the whole promontory. The only way to appreciate the intricacy of this unique chalk coastline is to walk the cliff top from North

The collapsed cave feature, known as the Pigeon Hole, near Flamborough Head

Sea Landing at least as far as the Green Stacks. A multiplicity of features abounds, for both the chalk and the boulder clay have been sculptured by the force of the sea.

Any approach to Flamborough village, 3km (2 miles) inland from the headland, has to cross Danes' Dyke, a great ditch crossing the whole width of the promontory. The northern half is completely man-made, but the southern section makes use of a natural valley cut in the chalk. The date of the man-made feature is uncertain; some believe that it belongs to the early Bronze Age, while others think it is an Iron Age creation. It is definitely of prehistoric date, and nothing to do with the defensive perimeter of a later Danish settlement which is supposed to have occupied the 13km^2 (5 square miles) of the headland. Bempton Cliff, a bird sanctuary with the only mainland gannetry in Britain, is further to the west and is worth a visit as the RSPB has provided viewing platforms to study the nesting seabirds (see page 34).

Filey Beyond Bempton the chalk cliffs give way to clay, and the appearance of the coastline immediately changes. Weathering and marine erosion have combined to create a complex coastline, and have led to the development of Filey Bay. It was at the northern end of this bay, under the shelter of a long Calcareous Grit promontory, that the resort of Filey grew up in the nineteenth century on the site of a small fishing village. The original village consisted of two streets, Church Street and Queen Street, on the south side of a deep ravine cut into the boulder clay infill of the bay. Curiously the twelfth century Norman church of St Oswald (Pevsner rates it the finest church in the north-east corner of the East Riding) lies quite separate on the other side of the ravine. Although many of the original cottages have been replaced by modern housing, there are survivors in the cobbled Church Street. The nineteenth-century resort town lies immediately to the south, and development began shortly after 1830, when the first villas were built. The greatest period of development coincided with the rail link-up with both York and Hull in 1846–7. Six classical-style stuccoed blocks of buildings were erected in The Crescent between 1844 and 1860 and now give Filey a slightly superior air over other northern resorts. Further expansion to the south was prevented by

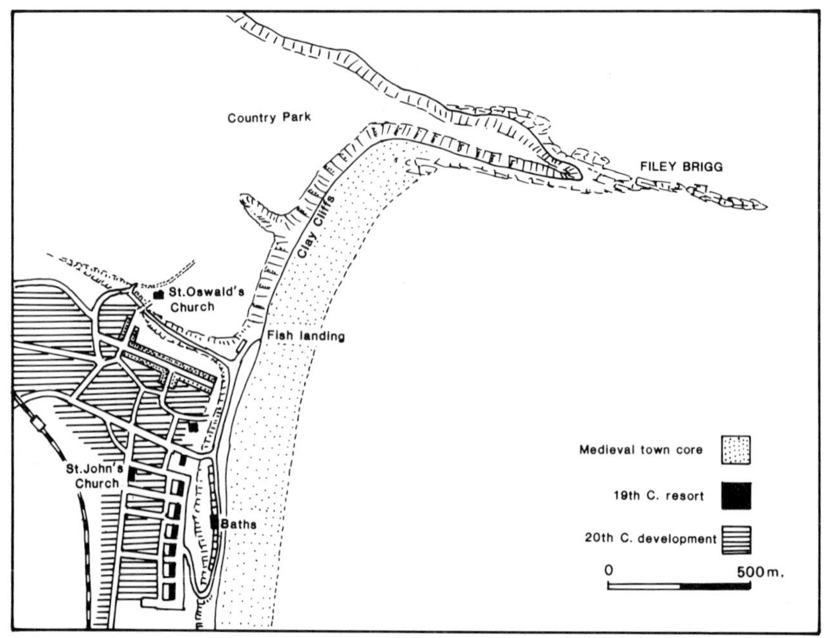

Filey: the nineteenth-century resort town was sited away from the medieval settlement

another deep ravine, which has luckily kept Filey small and compact. Some urban expansion has taken place with the development of bungalow estates. Butlins holiday camp along the coast to the south towards Reighton absorbs hoardes of holidaymakers and has helped to preserve the Victorian flavour of Filey.

Filey Brigg, a natural breakwater of hard grit, can be approached by a cliff walk through the Country Park near the parish church. It is only at the seaward end that the hard rock emerges from beneath its cover of boulder clay which makes up more than half the promontory. The clay overlay has been deeply runnelled by rainwater so that it resembles the 'badland' topography of parts of the United States or Central Italy. The Brigg proper of Calcareous Grit is a jumble of rocks, hollows and ledges which the sea has selectively eroded.

The coastline between Filey Brigg and Scarborough is accessible only on foot for the coast road, except at Cayton Bay, runs some distance inland. The cliff-top walk of about 8km (5 miles) from Filey to Cayton is full of interest and a geologist's paradise because of the varied succession of different rock types which make up the Jurassic formation. Harder beds like grits stand out as promontories or nabs, while the softer formations have been eroded to form bays like The Wyke. Details of cliff form also reflect the rock type, and the grits give rise to vertical or even overhanging faces, often with supporting buttresses. At Cayton Bay a cluster of shacks and huts obscures the natural coastline. The bay has been formed by structural faults which have caused the hard and resistant Millepore Bed to drop to sea level, resulting in a wide, low-lying sandy beach.

Scarborough has a history extending back over a thousand years. What is even more remarkable is that in spite of recent development it is still possible to discover the main stages of that history in the buildings, layout and appearance of the present town. Although a Roman signal station was sited on the rocky promontory which dominates the town to the north, there is no evidence of a true settlement here at this time, nor even later in the Saxon period. The usually accepted date for the town's foundation is AD 966, and the name *Skardi's burgh* suggests a

Filey Brigg is a long finger of boulder clay intensely runnelled by rainwash

Danish stronghold. This did not survive Harald Hardrada's attack of 1066, so the present town really dates from the time of the building of the castle by William de Gros in 1136. Twenty years later the urban growth had been so swift that the town was granted a borough charter. This early development took place in the area immediately around the foot of the castle in what became known as the Old Borough, with streets forming a grid pattern. Town walls once surrounded this quarter of the town, but they were taken down in 1817. Part of this earliest settlement can be identified by the twelfth-century church of St. Mary, and by the succession of narrow streets and twisting alleys, some of which run up from the quay and are known as The Bolts (cf The Rows of Yarmouth). Later development, in what became known as the New Borough, occurred in the thirteenth century; a new charter of 1256 makes a distinction between the two areas, and, even today the original division is recalled by the name Newborough Street. Few medieval buildings have survived, but King Richard III's House was built on Sandside about 1350, and the nearby Newcastle Packet Inn is said to date from the middle of the thirteenth century. Coastal trade was the lifeblood of the town at this time, and the charter of 1256 granted permission for the burgesses to 'make a certain new port with timber and stone towards the sea', the first reference to the building of the old harbour.

Scarborough might simply have remained another east coast port, but for the chance discovery of a medicinal spring coming out of the South Cliff by a Mrs Farrow in 1626 (see page 95). The transformation from spa town to bathing resort took place in a relatively short time in the early eighteenth century but the greatest phase of growth occurred a century later. As so often happened, the opening of the York to Scarborough Railway in 1845 acted as a catalyst, and in the next twenty years there was a remarkable expansion of the town as a health and holiday resort. Harbour works, including the construction of a more commodious outer harbour, also added to the prosperity of the town. Today Scarborough claims to be able to meet all the requirements of the visitor, whatever his taste or fancy.

Between Scarborough and Whitby the

scenic quality of coastline improves, partly because of a rich variation of rock type within the Jurassic sequence, but also due to having escaped the development of extensive camping and caravan sites. Access is by foot along the Cleveland Way which runs close to the cliff edge. From Scalby to Cloughton Wyke a huge boulder clay infill replaces the normal solid rock sequence, but north of the wyke (Norse for creek or bay) the sandstone, grits, oolites, shales and clays of the Jurassic succession take over. Softer strata are quickly eroded to form the wykes while the harder beds stand out as promontories or nabs. Some beds were of great economic value in the past, and between Cloughton and Hayburn Wykes a thin bed of coal was worked in the cliff-face during the nineteenth century. Farther north, close to Petard Point near Staintondale, beds of soft jet (inferior to the Whitby product) were sufficiently valuable to be worked in the nineteenth century. Alum was also extracted from the shales of the cliff-face at Old Peak, the southern bastion of Robin Hood's Bay. The biggest alum quarries lay beyond Whitby at places like Kettleness and Boulby, but all have long since closed down.

Ravenscar was the proposed site of a superior planned seaside resort in the early part of the present century (perhaps similar to Thorpeness in Suffolk), but it all came to grief after the roads had been carefully laid out, and only the hotel and golf course were completed. During the building of the Raven Hall House in 1774 the foundations of a Roman signal station were uncovered along with an inscribed stone. Ravenscar is perhaps best known today as one end of the famous Lyke Wake Walk, which crosses the North Yorkshire Moors.

Robin Hood's Bay has become the haunt of the retired and week-enders with their much sought-after pantiled cottages. Today an artist's paradise, it was once a flourishing fishing community. The existence of the bay is due to an upfold in the Jurassic strata which brings softer and easily erodable clays to the surface. Steep slopes running down to the sea are unstable and the houses of the lower town (Bay Town) cling precariously to the edge like the nests of the sand martin, each buttressing the one above. The 1 in 3 hill down to Bay Town discourages most motorists, but it is worthwhile making the journey down to the shore on foot. Apart from the main street of shops, there are terraces set high above the deeply cut valley. Many of the cottages date from between 1650 and 1750 when there would have been up to twenty fishing boats reaping the harvest of the North Sea. Later, retired sea captains, who had been successful in the whale fishery, built modest villas in the upper town (cf New Quay in Cardiganshire). There are still fishermen on the beach with tractors to haul in the boats, for there is virtually no natural harbour.

The coast between here and Whitby is scenically exciting with Saltwick Nab, the site of former alum quarries which were closed down in 1821, being the dominant feature. This stretch is under the ever-increasing threat of being swamped by caravan and camping sites.

Whitby Two things should immediately strike the visitor to this fishing town: the deep gorge-like character of the Esk Valley as it reaches the sea – it forsook its original course in glacial times for the present one – and the gaunt remains of the Abbey standing on the eastern cliff top. This was founded by St Hilda in AD 657, but there are no visible remains of that Celtic monastery today, and the present picturesque ruins date from the thirteenth century when the monastery had been re-established after years of neglect. Close by is the parish church of St Mary, with its squat Norman tower. The approach from the town is up a steep flight of steps from the south quayside. The old town of pantiled houses lies nestling beneath the steep river cliffs, principally on the west bank. Narrow curving streets like Flowergate and Baxtergate have been in existence since before Domesday, and their names indicate a Danish foundation for the town, as at Scarborough (*gat* = street).

The seaside town stands aloof from the bustle of the fishing port, and was laid out in the mid-nineteenth century largely under the influence of the railway king George Hudson, who bought the West Fields in

The imposing Grand Hotel, built of brick, helped to make Scarborough the premier resort of the north-east coast. One of two cliff railways run alongside

1848. A formal network of streets, including the East Terrace designed by John Dobson of Newcastle fame, followed in the next twenty years. At the end of East Terrace is the memorial to Whitby's greatest son, James Cook who, although he was not born in the town, learned his seamanship here and lived in a house in Grape Lane, on the south side of the river.

Runswick Bay Faulting and the presence of boulder clay are responsible for this major break in the coastline. Both have caused problems for the settlement at the western end of the bay which clings precariously to an unstable cliff. The village was supposedly swept into the sea, save for one cottage, by a major slide in 1682. Like Robin Hood's Bay this is a place to be explored on foot, and the most striking view of the settlement is from Kettleness at the eastern end of the bay, where it is possible to park the car near the farm on the cliff top. At the headland itself there are traces of alum quarries whose activities were brought to an abrupt halt in 1829 by a great cliff slide which carried away the workers' houses. Now only a scene of grey desolation exists.

Port Mulgrave The former harbour works here now lie in ruins, though the great sandstone blocks used in their construction remain as a fitting monument to a great enterprise. The prize was iron ore, yet another of the economic products of this coastline. The iron mine tunnelled into the cliff above the harbour and in the mid-nineteenth century vessels were loading the ore for transport to Jarrow and the works of the Palmer Iron Company. In 1854 the Company built a row of substantial houses on the cliff top, including an imposing manager's house, and these have survived. A mile away along the coast towards Runswick Bay the Company also built an ironworks in 1856 known as Wreckhills (from wrack or seaweed formerly dried here and used as a fuel in the alum industry at Kettleness). It was a short-lived enterprise, for in March 1858 a great landslip wrecked the blast furnaces and reduced the site to rubble. It never recovered and so Port Mulgrave continued to export all the locally-produced ore.

Staithes is a place which the guide books insist should not be missed, but the best time to visit is out of season when the narrow streets around the harbour are less choked with cars and people. Set at the entrance to a narrow valley in the lee of Cowbar Nab, Staithes resembles Cornish fishing villages like Polperro, but here the buildings are of sandstone and roofed with pantiles. A twisting, cobbled High Street wends its way steadily to the sea front and harbour. The latter is small, making it difficult to imagine the time in the last century when it sheltered a large fishing fleet. Though reduced in size fishing still goes on, for the reef-strewn offshore waters prove ideal habitats for crabs, lobsters and cod; but many of the inhabitants have turned their backs on the sea and now look to the iron and potash industries for a living. Two miles away at Boulby a great new potash mine was opened in 1972 to tap the rich deposits at depth, but problems of water seepage have bedevilled the operation and a pumping station sits conspicuously on the cliff top.

15 North-east England

Cleveland

Skinningrove, although decayed, with its mines and blast furnaces no longer operating, still retains a certain fascination. The small fishing community was swamped by the ironworks in 1864, but many people are now returning to fishing, and their boats can be seen drawn up on the stony beach. The village consists of two streets of terraced houses, a shop, club and Wesleyan chapel.

Saltburn was another creation of the iron industry, but here the emphasis was on leisure and recuperation. A Quaker iron-master, Henry Pease, provided the impetus for the town's development following the arrival of the railway in 1861, and he built the imposing Zetland Hotel overlooking the deep gorge. The Victorian town developed on flat land to the west, with its parallel terraced rows running down to the sea. The original fishing hamlet survives by the inn at the mouth of the beck.

Redcar has industrial Teesside on its doorstep, but still continues to attract visitors with its fine stretch of golden sand and leisure park. Ore is brought in to the long jetty to supply the great steelwork complex at Tod Point now that the local Cleveland ores are no longer worked. Redcar is set apart from its neighbour, Marske-by-the-Sea, by a stretch of shore backed by sand dunes which has so far escaped development.

From the Tees to the Tyne we have one of the most industrialised coastlines in the country; a succession of harbour towns and urban sprawl, with the intervening stretches riddled with coal mines or other industrial works. The offshore area is widely used as a convenient dumping ground for coal waste and the beaches inevitably suffer. Teesside sets the scene; new steelworks, oil terminals and refineries, chemical works (on reclaimed land of the former Seal Sands) and power stations developed during its rapid industrial advance in the 1970s.

Hartlepool consists of the old town set on a low, rocky peninsula with a sheltered harbour in its lee, and its later upstart, usually referred to as West Hartlepool. Since 1966 the two have been joined into one administrative unit following a century of 'feuding'.

The old and original Hartlepool's history extends back over at least 1300 years and its age is beginning to show, making it a prime target for twentieth-century redevelopment. As early as AD 640 a monastery, Hereteu, was established here by St Bega (of St Bees in Cumbria), though the first actual settlement is associated with St Hilda, prior to her removal to Whitby in AD 657. The monastery lasted until AD 865 when it was destroyed by the Danes. Nothing is heard of Hartlepool again until a reference in a charter of 1162; at that time the manor was held by Robert de Brus, whose father had fought with William the Conqueror and had been suitably rewarded with lands, including the manor of Hart. The present village of Hart, with its ancient church, lies 4.5km (3 miles) away to the north-west, but it was in this parish that a new planted town of Hartlepool was created by the de Brus family, together with the chapel of St Hilda. The present church is the only real tangible link with the medieval past and is reckoned

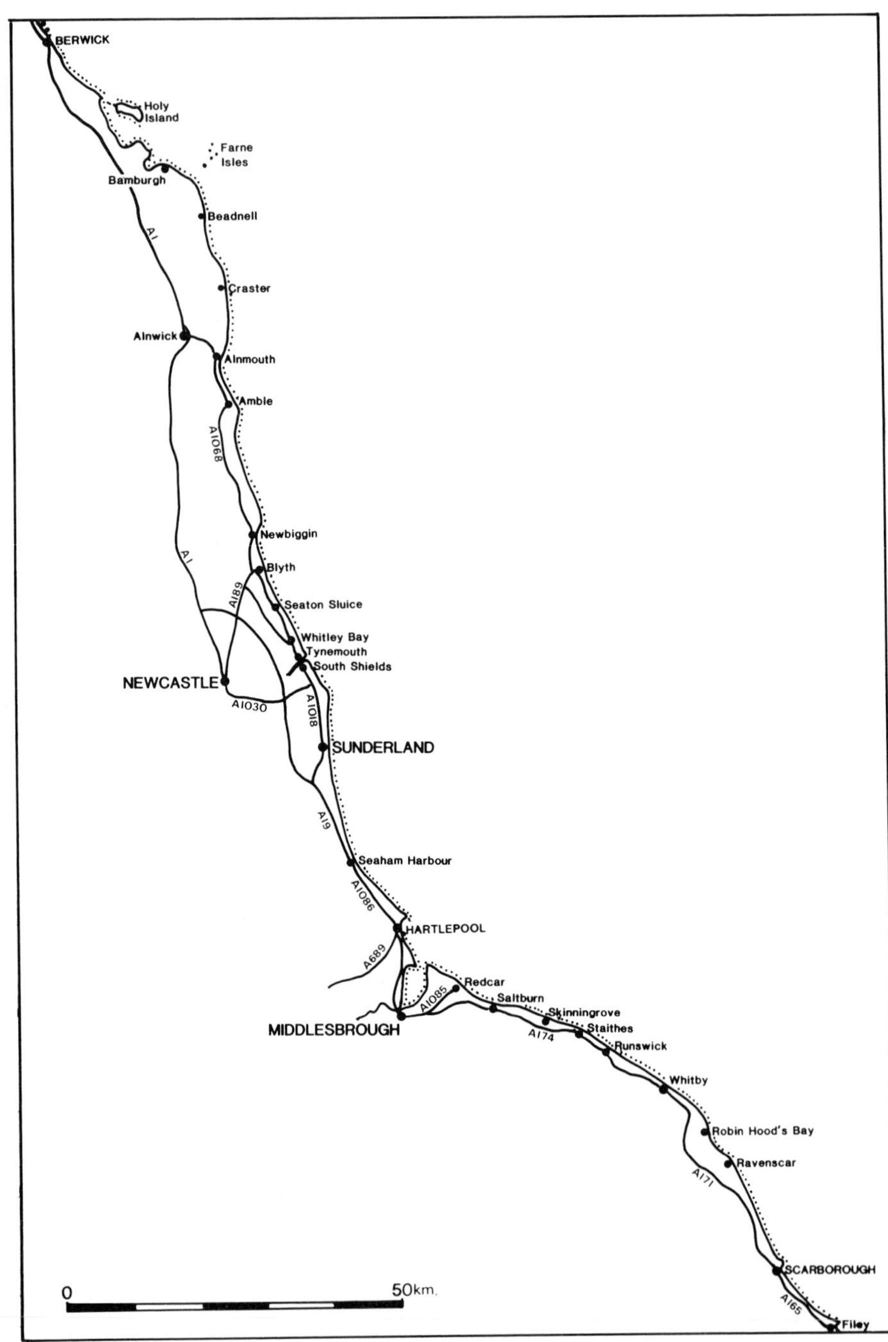

The coast of north-east England

to be one of the finest in the county. A fragment of the medieval wall that once surrounded the town, including the Sandwell Gate, remains to the south-west of the church. Only burgesses were allowed to live inside the walls; fishermen were excluded and they settled on the town moor which became known as the Far Field. Until the early part of this century they remained independent and maintained their old customs and habits through intermarriage.

West Hartlepool owes its birth to a quarrel and the subsequent energy of a Stockton solicitor, Ralph Ward Jackson. Considering the Hartlepool harbour charges too high, he decided to promote a rival port in 1847, served by the Stockton to Hartlepool Railway. Within twenty years a new harbour complex and rigidly laid-out town had grown up. The port took the coal from the South Durham field in such quantities that it became the fourth largest port of the country in the latter half of the nineteenth century. Although the coal trade has now collapsed, the West Hartlepool docks still handle considerable quantities of timber, iron ore and oil. Jackson created a Town Improvement Company to ensure that good standard housing was built, but the growth in the 1850s and 1860s was so rapid that few notable buildings emerged. The centrepiece was Christ Church, built in 1854 on an 'island' site in Church Square. Nearby stands the statue of Ralph Ward Jackson looking down on the scene for which he was almost entirely responsible.

The resort for the Hartlepools (and for Stockton) lies a short distance along the coast at Seaton Carew. With its fine level stretch of clean sand - no coal waste here - a resort began to develop in the late eighteenth century, when the wealthy Quakers of Darlington organised a twice-weekly coach service to the coast in 1783. Ten years later the first hotel appeared, the New Inn, and this acted as a catalyst for further growth, though rival towns like Redcar and Saltburn soon developed on the other side of the Tees (see *West Hartlepool - the rise and development of a Victorian New Town*, R. Wood, 1967).

The coastline between Hartlepool and Seaham Harbour (Durham) combines the disastrous effects of industrialisation with a natural charm that has miraculously survived in limited areas. Close to Hartlepool are the factory buildings and storage tanks of the Steetley Magnesite Company. Its coastal situation is essential, for it extracts magnesium directly from sea water. Then at Crimdon Dene we come to a number of deeply cut rejuvenated valleys that give variety to the Durham coast. The natural setting here has been marred by a massive caravan park and its related development. Further along the coast, at Blackhall Rocks, the limestone headland has been honeycombed by caves as the sea has attacked weaker strata. Unfortunately the beach has been ruined by the coal waste dumped from the nearby colliery. The same is true at Easington and Horden where beachcombing for coal is a popular pastime, and even a lucrative business for some.

Durham

Seaham Harbour, founded by the Marquess of Londonderry in 1828 and designed by John Dobson of Newcastle fame, developed with great speed. Within a generation warehouses, brass foundries, bottleworks, gasworks and other industrial enterprises had sprung up. The main function of the port was the export of coal, and the dock was fitted with coal drops to allow direct loading into the ship's holds. Until recently one still existed at Seaham but it has now been dismantled for re-assembly at the Beamish Outdoor Museum.

Tyne & Wear

Sunderland is one of the largest of the north-east coastal towns, with a population approaching 200,000, and so has greater municipal status and functions. A sense of civic pride has returned to the town after the grim years of the 1930s, and although now part of the bigger authority of Tyne & Wear, the people are completely different in speech and attitudes from their Tyne neighbours. After a spate of new building the town's appearance has completely altered in the post-war years. The nineteenth-century guide-book description can no longer find general application though, as with other industrial towns, there are depressed quarters. In the 1890s the town was painted as being 'black and gloomy in the extreme with the atmosphere so filled with smoke that the blue sky is seldom seen. Dirt is the distinctive feature: earth, air, and water are alike black and filthy.' This was hardly the sort of description that would bring visitors flocking to the town.

The present town is really an amalgamation of three originally distinct settlements: Monkwearmouth, north of the river, Sunderland (the south land) and Bishopwearmouth on the south bank. All lie close to the mouth of the river Wear, here deeply incised and not unlike the Tyne at Newcastle. Coal staithes fed by waggonways once tapped the Durham coalfield. It was shipbuilding, however, that made the town famous and provided the greatest single source of employment. Even today, when the industry is suffering a world-wide decline, Sunderland Shipbuilders can hold their own, having already undergone the torments of rationalisation. Glass has long been produced in the town and the Hartley works were the first to produce rolled plate glass, and the glassmaking tradition continues today with the manufacture of Pyrex. In order that industrial development could flourish, the port authorities had to build artificial docks at the river mouth. Fortunately the Midland Railway king, George Hudson, became MP for the town in 1845, and used his financial wizardry to have the South (Hudson) Dock excavated out of solid limestone between 1846 and 1850; this, with the addition of later docks, gave the town considerable advantages over its rivals throughout the remainder of the century.

Of the three historical divisions of the town, it is Monkwearmouth that claims most attention through its association with the Venerable Bede. A monastery was established here in AD 674 by Bishop Biscop under whose tutelage the young Bede grew up. Nothing has survived of the initial foundations but a ninth- or tenth-century tower above the porch has been described by Nikolaus Pevsner as 'a precious relic . . . in a sordid setting'. Monkwearmouth has another outstanding architectural feature, of a completely different age, for close to the church was the former railway terminus of the line from Newcastle; the station (usually attributed to Dobson) is in neo-Greek style with Doric columns, quite one of the best offerings of the early Railway Age.

Seaside Sunderland lies north of the river and is now concentrated on Seaburn, though formerly Roker, with its Holey Rock, was the main beach used by the townspeople. Beyond lies Whitburn, still an interesting village, and then Marsden. Here the limestone rocks have been under constant attack by the sea which has cut deep caverns into the cliff-face; one, the Grotto, has been an inn since the last century. Parts of the former cliff now lie isolated as stacks, including the massive bulk of Marsden Rock with its pierced arch at the base.

South Shields holds a surprise for those who regard this coastline as dominated by the coalfield and industry. A Roman fort in Baring Street has been excavated since the war and is now laid out for all to view. The fort is unusual because of the presence of nine granaries, and it has been suggested that grain was stored here as a supply base for the armies guarding the Roman wall north of the Tyne. After the withdrawal of Rome early in the fifth century, there is no record of any settlement on the south bank of the Tyne entrance until St Hilda established a chapel in the seventh century. The Bishop of Durham eventually built a manor here (cf Bishopwearmouth in Sunderland) and, in keeping with the spirit of the age, he decided to plant a town here in 1235. The chapel of St Hilda remained attached to its mother church, the monastic church at Jarrow dating from AD 684, until 1854. Bede lived at Jarrow for most of his life, and parts of the chancel and tower of the present church date from the original building, a miraculous survival considering its proximity to the coast and the ever present threat of destruction by sea-borne raiders in the Dark Ages.

Throughout medieval times the south bank of the Tyne was a great producer of salt, and duty payments alone exceeded £80,000 in some years. Later, alkali manufacture took over and led to the

The artificial cut made at Seaton Sluice in the 1760s in an attempt to improve the harbour

building of the first glassworks here in 1619. Today, South Shields is a multi-industry town and no longer so isolated since the building of the Tyne Tunnel in the 1960s.

Tynemouth dates from the seventh century when a small monastery was built on a limestone peninsula overlooking the river mouth. Though nothing now remains, there are ruins of a later Benedictine Priory founded in 1090 covering the site. The so-called castle, with a substantial gatehouse and walls, dates from about the early fourteenth century, and within the walls are the fragmentary remains of a Norman church. A market place arose at the castle gates.

Tynemouth as we see it today dates from a much later period, for it was only after 1800 that it became fashionable for the Newcastle traders and shopkeepers to own a villa by the sea. A succession of terraces like Huntingdon Place and Dawson Square were built, many of the houses with iron balconies. Once Tynemouth was linked by rail with Newcastle (especially after it was electrified) the ordinary citizens of Newcastle moved to the seaside, not only to Tynemouth, but also to its urban neighbours like Cullercoats and **Whitley Bay**. In the present century Whitley Bay has become the main resort for it has a fine stretch of sand, and even in pre-war days considerable efforts were made, through the erection of boarding houses, hotels and the gigantic funfair, to attract both the short-stay and long-stay visitor. Today Whitley Bay still remains a favourite destination for the Scottish holidaymaker, who returns year after year. **North Shields**, slightly up river from Tynemouth, still retains some buildings which indicate its growth during the Regency period, although it is best known for its fishing interests. Fishing has been important here for centuries, for the very name comes from *shiel* meaning fisherman's abode (cf shieling = summer dwelling).

Northumberland

Seaton Sluice is so named because of the sluice erected across the mouth of the Seaton Burn by the Delaval family, great landowners who lived nearby in the eighteenth century. The object was to pent up the waters of the river before releasing them to flush out the silt and sand of the harbour. Although the idea was sound, it did not actually work, and instead a great cut was made through solid rock in the 1760s to reach the sea, a sort of miniature Corinth Canal. This became the harbour, often with as many as a dozen small colliers waiting to sail. Now it lies abandoned with great sandstone boulders blocking the entrance. The Delaval family employed Vanbrugh as architect and built their fine Palladian style house nearby in 1729. When the family was at the height of its power it was the scene of extravagant revelry and guests were often subjected to practical jokes by Sir Francis Delaval. Although Seaton Sluice is now well within the orbit of the Newcastle commuter, the Delaval influence still survives in the landscape.

Blyth was once one of the greatest east coast coal-exporting towns and was built for that purpose, though now the trade has collapsed and the abandoned staithes line the harbour. Development began in the early eighteenth century following the opening up of this northern part of the coalfield. The pits were connected by wooden waggonways to staithes on the River Blyth, one of the earliest examples of goods travelling by rail. The harbour was built after 1850 and the great long piers were not completed until after 1880, by which time more than 4 million tons of coal were being shipped each year. Now the red brick town is suffering depression, and the coal goes to the power station which dominates the north bank. Instead seaborne trade revolves around importing bauxite, stored in three large conical containers, destined for the nearby Alcan aluminium smelter at Lynemouth. Timber, in the form of pit-props, is another item of trade.

Newbiggin, literally the 'new building', can trace its origin to the twelfth century when development began at the southern end of the parish of Woodhorn. A fair and market were granted in a charter of 1203 and the church of St Bartholomew was built as a chapel to the mother church of Woodhorn. Hopes that the planted town on the coast might flourish came to nothing, and it became a colliery village and a small seaside resort during the nineteenth century. The church stands aloof from the town and sits on a sandstone promontory, and its coastal site and isolation make it an obvious seamark for those sailing these dangerous waters. To the north lies the massive aluminium works but these mark the end of the industrialised coast, and henceforth we can enjoy unspoiled sandy beaches backed by dunes, rocky headlands fronted by great platforms or carrs and smaller settlements.

Amble, like Blyth, was once a small coal port which developed in the nineteenth century when a rail link was forged with the Broomhill Colliery, inland to the south. Now fishermen cast their lines from the former wooden coal staithes and yachts sail the open waters of the harbour. Two miles up the Coquet lies **Warkworth**; a great meander loop in the river gives a natural defensive site and it was here that the Saxons established a stockade, *Wercewode*, in AD 737. The present town represents a twelfth-century plantation in the reign of Henry II, when 77 burgage plots were set out on either side of an axial street running the length of the meander loop. The castle at the southern end was built from 1139 onwards, while the church of St Laurence, close to the river, is of about the same date. Warkworth's attraction today lies in the fact that although rebuilding has taken place in later centuries, it still has character and style with the elements of the initial, simple town plan showing through.

Alnmouth was a favourite quiet resort for Newcastle people in the 1930s when a 30-mile journey by rail was looked on as something of an adventure. The town is yet another example of a planted medieval settlement, created out of the parish of Lesbury in AD 1147. Sixty years later the new borough was given permission to hold a market and establish a port. The church of St Waleric, which predated the town, lay at the extreme southern end, but in 1806 the river Aln changed its mouth and left the church stranded amongst the sandhills of the southern shore. Only the foundations of this Saxon church now remain. As with so many planted towns little subsequent growth has taken place so that even today it consists of little more than a single main street. Its harbour was too shallow to develop more than as a small outport for Alnwick and an attempt by the Duke of Northumberland to establish an oyster bed here came to nought. Today its summer visitors bask amongst the sandhills or sail their boats in the river mouth.

Craster There is a complete change of coastal scene just south of Craster, where the dark rock of the Whin Sill replaces the sandstones and red grits which occur around Boulmer Haven. The result is that the coastline northwards to Bamburgh is one of the finest in the country. Though not high, it has spectacular columnar cliffs, beaches of huge, dark, rounded cobbles and narrow gashes marking faults where the sea has been able to scoop out the crushed rock. Craster is a small fishing village set around a small harbour which was made safer when a pier was built in 1906. Previously the local fishermen had the tricky problem of bringing their boats in between two limestone islets, Little Carr and Muckle Carr. The place is famous for its kippers - a curing shed stands nearby - and dressed crab and lobster are sold from huts in front of the cottages. Its picturesque setting has long been a favourite subject for artists, but the small village is liable to become swamped by cars in the tourist season.

The walk northwards for 3km (2 miles) to Dunstanburgh Castle along the grassy path bordering the shoreline is full of interest, for there is evidence of the longstanding conflict between the sea and the tenacious dolerites of the Whin Sill formation. Dunstanburgh Castle, like its near neighbour Bamburgh to the north, was sited to take every advantage of the natural defences afforded by the Whin Sill. The castle, now a ruin under the care of the Department of the Environment, dates from 1314 when, at a time of border raids, the Earl of Lancaster was given a licence to turn his manor house into a castle. A great gatehouse was built immediately and the walls quickly followed, with the Lilburn Tower (almost like a Norman keep in its size and proportions), outstanding.

Beadnell is a pleasant village, though in danger of being overrun by caravans and camps. Half a mile down the coast the rebuilt harbour has more character. A glimpse of the past, when this whole coastline depended on sea traffic for the necessities of life and trade, is provided by the huge eighteenth-century lime kilns, built of great sandstone blocks, and now under the care of the National Trust.

Seahouses is now the biggest harbour on this northern section of the Northumberland coast, with many registered fishing boats and a flourishing tourist industry when thousands of summer visitors are carried to the neighbouring Farne Islands. Formerly called North Sunderland, a name now restricted to the more inland settlement, Seahouses has become somewhat commercialised in recent years and saturated with cafés, gift shops and bingo halls. Interest still focusses on the activity around the harbour, which was originally built at the end of the eighteenth century, but considerably enlarged in 1889 by the Crewe Trustees. The coastal road towards Bamburgh runs close to the shore, here dominated by sandhills covered with marram grass. Halfway along is Monks House, a group of buildings whose origin goes back to 1257 when Henry II granted the monks of Farne Island a small plot so that they could store provisions awaiting shipment. In the nineteenth century one of the buildings became St Cuthbert's Inn.

Bamburgh is still a village of engaging simplicity with a widening green running between the church and the great wall of the Whin Sill, crowned by Bamburgh Castle. Although the Bamburgh we see today was largely created by the Crewe Estate from about 1800 onwards, there are many visible features of the past. A triangular green was the site of the medieval market. The history of Bamburgh goes much further back to the time when it became the capital of the kingdom of Northumbria in AD 547. This original Anglian settlement was most likely restricted to the top of the elongated Whin

Beadnell lime kilns, set alongside the small harbour where small coasters once put in with their agricultural cargoes

Sill outcrop; but even this fine natural defensive site did not give complete immunity during the Danish raids of the tenth century. After the Norman conquest the castle became less important with the development of castles at Alnwick and Warkworth. Bamburgh remained small because of its restricted site and, even when the settlement moved to the lower ground at the foot of the dolerite cliff, there was no urban explosion. The church of St Aidan dates mainly from the thirteenth century, though is probably on the site of an older building. The medieval history of the town, which returned two members of Parliament in the reign of Edward I, is one of a continuous fight for survival. By 1704 the castle was in ruins when Lord Crewe, then Bishop of Durham, took over. After his death the Crewe Trustees made the keep sound and used it to provide accommodation for a school, hospital and a rest home for ship-wrecked sailors. More drastic restoration followed at the end of the nineteenth century when the castle came under the ownership of Lord Armstrong. It is his building, rather than that of preceding centuries, that we see at Bamburgh today. Whatever views one might have about the Victorian restoration there is no doubt that it still possesses a certain magic stemming from its elevated position on a bare rock crag, with dunes whipped up against its seaward face and the bare clean sands of the bay below.

Farne Islands Although a visit to the islands is usually made from Seahouses, the group lies closer to Bamburgh, and the largest, Inner Farne, lies nearest the coast, about 3km (2 miles) due east of Bamburgh. It is also the most interesting historically, for St Aidan used it as a retreat about the year AD 651, and St Cuthbert had a monastic cell and ultimately died here in AD 687. Nothing remains of this, although St Cuthbert's Chapel (built about 1370) at the north end is probably on the same site. A short way off to the west is the tower built by Prior Castell about 1500. The only other building is the High Lighthouse (there was formerly a low light as well). Of the other islands perhaps the best known is Longstone because of its association with the heroism of

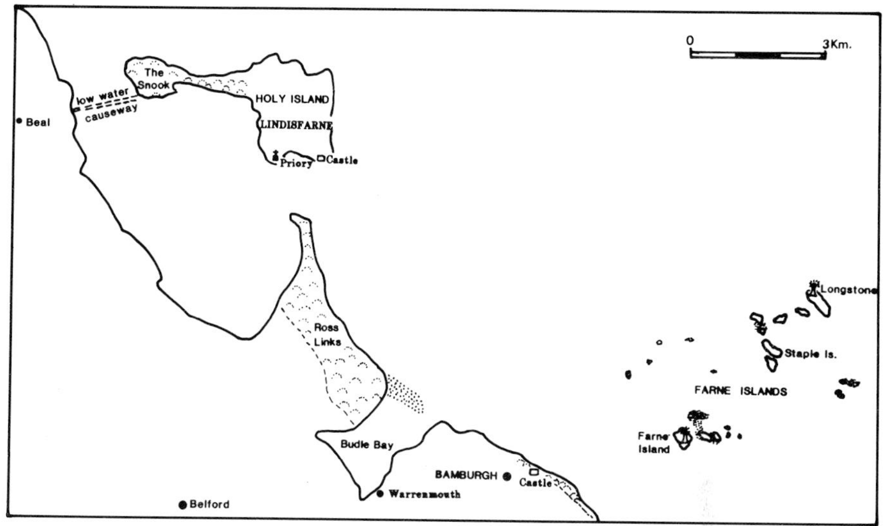

Lindisfarne, the Farne Islands and Bamburgh

Grace Darling in September 1838 when, with her father, she rescued some of the crew of the *Forfarshire* and overnight became a national heroine. The remaining islands are all uninhabited and today the whole group is famous as a bird sanctuary, particularly for the eider duck, cormorant, shag, various gulls and terns and the ubiquitous puffin, known locally as 'Tommy Noddies' from their head movements when walking. The Farne Islands are the only place on the east coast where the grey or Atlantic seal breeds but they have increased so alarmingly in recent years that periodic culls are necessary in the interests of the livelihood of local fishermen (see *Birds of the Farnes*, R. Embleton and P. Hawkey, 1973).

Holy Island is mainly formed of the slightly raised sand flats and dunes which characterise this coast, but at its south-eastern end there is an outcrop of dolerite (Whin Sill) every bit as striking as at Bamburgh. It was here that Edward Hudson, owner of *Country Life* bought the ruin of a sixteenth-century fort and engaged Sir Edwin Lutyens to create a twentieth-century castle residence. The much earlier priory church and other monastic remains belong mainly to the thirteenth century, and lie at the southern end of Lindisfarne village. The approach to the island can only be made for a few hours on either side of low water when the causeway is not covered. Formerly the crossing was made along a track, marked by poles, but now there is a metalled road which leads to the Snook, the long western peninsula formed of sand dunes up to 12m (40ft) high, resting on a base of boulder clay. Apart from the historical interest of the monastic remains the island is famous as the home of the Lindisfarne Gospels, now preserved in the British Museum.

Due south the tip of the Ross Links on the mainland approaches to within 1.5km (1 mile) of Lindisfarne village. They form a fine stretch of unspoiled sand-dune coastline, fortunately spared the caravans and camping sites which have crept into some areas. The links were obviously a favoured site for early settlement, and examples of Bronze Age pottery have been found under 2.4m (8ft) of sand. Further south lies the sand-choked inlet of Budle Bay which, although quiet and largely unvisited by the thousands who invade nearby Bamburgh, has a long-forgotten history. In 1247 Henry III founded a new borough which he called Warenmouth, and granted it the same rights as Newcastle. It was built by the water's edge so that it could function as the port for Bamburgh. Although nothing now remains, for the new plantation was unsuccessful, the most likely site is the cove at Heather Cottages. The name was later changed from

Lindisfarne is yet another of the Northumberland coastal fortresses set on an outcrop of the dolerite of the Whin Sill. The castle is now owned by the National Trust

Warenmouth to Newtown for it is referred to in this way as a desolate town in 1621.

Berwick-on-Tweed The approach to this border town is more exciting by rail than by road, for the railway hugs the coast for several miles before giving a fine view across the mouth of the River Tweed. The Lower Carboniferous rocks give rise to cliffs with a rock platform below, and are mainly sandstones and shales, though they include the Scremerston coal seams which were once worked in the vicinity. Further south at Cheswick Rocks there is red sandstone which was used in the building of Lindisfarne Priory and carried by cart across the long spit of sand and thence across the flats at low water.

Due to its position on the border between England and Scotland (there has always been doubt as to which country Berwick is in), defence was a prime consideration and there is evidence of this in the town today. The town walls, dating mainly from the reign of Elizabeth I, are as well preserved as any in England. Prior to the Tudor defences, Edward I had provided the town with a wall at the end of the thirteenth century; he also built a castle of which little remains, as most of it was swept away to make room for the railway station. It is the Elizabethan walls that claim attention (actually begun under Mary Tudor in 1555) for the inclusion of angled bastions indicated the adoption of a completely new style of fortification in this country. Only one of the gates survives and even this was enlarged in the nineteenth century. It is still possible to walk around the town wall, a rewarding exercise for it gives good views of the town and its setting at the mouth of the river. Three bridges now span the Tweed, an old early seventeenth-century bridge with its 1925 replacement alongside, and Stephenson's railway bridge of 1850 further upstream. Although there are no buildings of exceptional merit within the town, it is the harmony and composition of the whole which makes Berwick so attractive. It seems strange that at the turn of the century the author of *Murray's Guide* felt unable to recommend it to visitors because it was mean and dirty, with unswept streets and a general air of decay. Although the harbour is commodious it is not particularly deep and therefore can only be used by small fishing boats. For many years the salmon fishing at the river mouth has proved remunerative, and even today it employs over fifty men. At one time the salmon were kept on ice and many ice-houses were built in the town, but they disappeared once the railway provided quick transport to both Newcastle and London markets.

16 South-east Scotland

Between the Border and the Firth of Forth

The frontier between Scotland and England became established along the line of the river Tweed in 1157. Northwards from the border to the Firth of Forth – the Scottish Sea, as this wide estuary was once called – the coastline exhibits many varied topographical features, colours and moods. St Abb's Head projects into the North Sea from one of the finest cliff-lines in the whole of Britain. This is a wild grey scene of gullies, coves, hidden waterfalls, reefs and skerries that are constantly awash, and cliffs that hang sheer above the sea from 152m (500ft). Westward, the igneous rocks of St Abb's Head – a mass of felsite – give way to a lower line of cliffs about Cockburnspath that expose the warmer colours of Old Red Sandstone. Towards Dunbar, the coast is carved out of limestones of Carboniferous age. The Barns Ness lighthouse marks the site of a wide limestone reef; inland, close beside the A1 trunk road, tall smoking chimney stacks and the deep quarries of a cement factory signal the intrusion of heavy industry upon the coastline.

From the border to St Abb's Head and beyond as far as Cockburnspath stretches one of the finest pieces of Britain's eastern coastline. It begins in a simple mood with sheer cliffs carved out of the horizontal strata of the Lamberton Limestone, a rock of Carboniferous age. As far as the deep gash

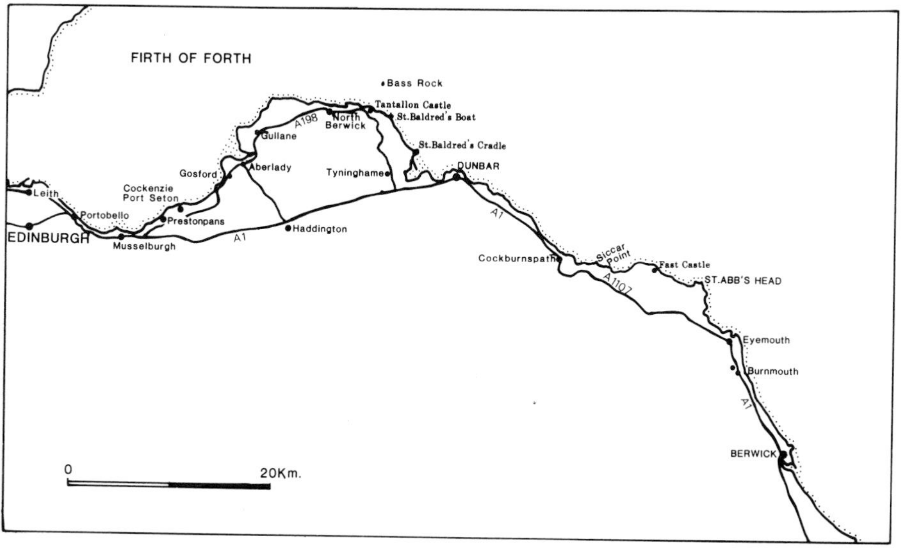

The coastline, with features of special interest, between the Tweed and the Forth

Felsite cliffs and colonies of nesting seabirds at St Abb's Head

where Burnmouth Harbour nestles, the main line of the Eastern Region runs close to the cliff-edge and provides the railway traveller with a fine brief prospect of this section of the North Sea coast. Westward of the little holiday resort of **St Abb's** with its good sandy beach the coastline presents a huge wall of jagged rock to the North Sea.

Eyemouth, a cluster of grey warehouses and narrow streets where the wooded gorge of the Eye Water opens to the sea, is the most important place on this piece of coastline. The harbour stands severely exposed, wide open to the worst gales and tempestuous seas from the north-east. And the North Sea has exacted its own tribute from Eyemouth for, in a sudden storm on 14 October 1881, 24 boats were sunk and 129 fishermen drowned. Eyemouth achieved the status of a free port and consequently the reputation as a base for smuggling in the eighteenth and nineteenth centuries. Fishermen still go out from Eyemouth and it is also a popular holiday resort.

The high cliffed coast between St Abb's Head and Fast Castle Head presents spectacular scenery. The surroundings of Coldingham Loch were the site of a prehistoric village some 2,000 years ago. Fast Castle, a battered wreck of stone, is perched 21m (70ft) above the sea. The approach to this fourteenth-century stronghold of the Homes is made by a track that winds down the bare windswept slopes above the cliffs. Scott was attracted by the romantic wildness of Fast Castle – it is Wolf's Crag, the tower of Edgar of Ravenswood, in *The Bride of Lammermuir*.

To the west of Cove the warm-coloured Old Red Sandstone gives way to low blunt promontories of grey limestone such as Barns Ness and Torness Point. Volcanic rocks intruded into the sandstones, and limestones begin to play an important part in the shaping of the landscape.

Dunbar Its name, Gaelic by origin, means 'the fort on the point'. Warfare occupies a place in Dunbar's history until 1945 when it ceased to be a garrison town. Of the medieval castle, on a rocky peninsula to the west of Victoria Harbour, little survives apart from a shaggy obelisk of red sandstone masonry.

Much of the townscape of Dunbar today dates from the two centuries of prosperity gained from its fisheries and North Sea trade. The High Street was laid out in the seventeenth century on higher level ground above the Old Harbour. There is a fine spaciousness about the High Street and its three- and four-storeyed Georgian tenements, a fact noted by Cobbett in 1832 when he described it as 'so wide as to be worthy of being called an oblong square instead of a street'. Down by the Old Harbour at the foot of Victoria Street a vanished epoch in Dunbar's history is recalled by the deep-red sandstone walls of warehouses that stored the grain and potatoes of the export trade.

Dunbar developed as a holiday resort at the end of the nineteenth century. The railway brought the town within easy reach of Edinburgh and its reputation was enhanced by the fact that this is one of the driest and sunniest places in Scotland. Westward of the High Street towards Belhaven are villas built in stone and that austere classical style that contributes so much character to Scottish towns of the nineteenth century. In the redevelopment of a congested slum in the oldest part of the town close to the old harbour are some attractive colour-washed houses designed by Sir Basil Spence.

East of Dunbar, at Oxwell Mains, the quarries that were opened to provide limestone as flux for the ironworks of Lanarkshire now provide the raw material for a huge cement-works. At Torness Point, an even vaster industrial project is under way with the building of an atomic power station.

Tyninghame The unique landscape of Tyninghame owes not a little to the creativity and care of its landlords, the Earls Haddington. In the early years of the eighteenth century the 6th Earl of Haddington introduced the ideas and new farming methods of England's agrarian innovators to his estate. Part of these revolutionary changes involved the planting of woodland. In 1761, the village, close to the now ruined parish church of St Baldred, was cleared to make way for the park where, in 1829, a romantic turreted Scots baronial

Mature woodland reaches down to the seashore in the John Muir Country Park at Tyninghame

Tantallon Castle, looking down the precipitous face of volcanic cliffs

mansion was built. Tyninghame village was refounded towards the end of the eighteenth century, 'the very model of an estate village', at the western entrance to the park. Diamond-shaped windows, a rosy pink building stone, cottage gardens and a richness of trees all make a scene that is notably out of tune with the austerity and harshness that seems to belong to Scotland's landscapes.

There is no free access for the tourist to Tyninghame House and its park, but as an attractive compensation the John Muir Country Park has opened acres of pine woodland and a stretch of this beautiful coast to the public. There are nature trails, picnic areas and opportunities for horse-riding and sea-fishing. Cars cannot enter the park beyond the main parking places at Linkfield, West Barns and Tyninghame Links, but the woodland walk from there to the sea-shore and on to the low jutting headland of St Baldred's Cradle is among the great attractions of south-east Scotland's coastline.

Tantallon Castle Here a huge wall of red sandstone and dark green basalt some 15m (50ft) in height stretches across the neck of a blunt, cliff-bound headland. Visually, Tantallon ranks among the most exciting of Britain's castles. It was built probably about 1370, but its much older Celtic name hints at the presence of a fort or enclosure at this place centuries earlier. In 1529 Tantallon surrendered to James V and another phase of building followed with the repair of the central tower. Tantallon Castle was removed from the stage of national history in 1651 when General Monk and 3,000 of Cromwell's troops laid siege for twelve days. Ruined and abandoned, Tantallon was used as a quarry throughout the eighteenth century. At the close of the nineteenth century the restoration of Tantallon began under its owner Sir Walter Hamilton Dalrymple. In 1924 the Office of Works took over the site and further deterioration of the ruin has been prevented.

North Berwick This little resort with a population of over 4,000 is overshadowed from the south by the 187m (613ft) volcanic bastion of North Berwick Law, which ranks

(*above*) The curtain wall of Tantallon Castle, raised across the narrow neck of a headland; (*below*) The Law, a volcanic plug, rears above the resort of North Berwick

The Bass Rock is a volcanic plug in the Firth of Forth. Its cliffs splashed with guano indicate the island's role as a bird sanctuary

as one of the most dramatic sites for an Iron Age fort anywhere in Britain. Apart from the fragmentary wall that encloses the summit there are terraces and enclosures on the southern flank; the lowest area contains the foundations of a settlement. The remains of the Auld Kirk, the first parish church dating from the twelfth century, occupies a tiny island that is linked to the town by a causeway. The roofless shell of the second parish church, built during the seventeenth century, stands in Law Road. In the Middle Ages North Berwick was an important ferry terminal for pilgrims crossing the Forth to St Andrews. During the eighteenth century it rivalled Dunbar as a fishing harbour and exporter of grain from the rich farmlands of Lothian. North Berwick had become a fashionable seaside resort as well as a residential suburb for Edinburgh by the end of the nineteenth century. Golf was a dominant element in the life of the town. Apart from the West Links, the Town Council bought land to the east of the burgh to lay out the East Links course. North Berwick is no longer a port. Its eighteenth-century warehouses have been converted into flats or taken over by the East Lothian Yacht Club. The main traffic from its harbour is of summer pleasure cruises.

Out to sea a chain of reefs and islands of volcanic rock culminate in the 128m (420ft) precipices of the Bass Rock whose guano-white cliffs lead upwards to a grassy sheep pasture. In medieval times St Baldred's Chapel served as a parish church. There was a castle of the Lauder family at the southern tip of the island. In the seventeenth century the rock was used as a state prison. Now, uninhabited apart from the little colony at the lighthouse, the Bass Rock is a wildlife reserve.

Dirleton, reckoned among Scotland's most attractive villages, has a wide tree-lined green dominated by a twelfth-century castle. The Archerfield Estate extends from Dirleton village to the sea coast. Archerfield House, built early in the seventeenth century and extensively redesigned by Robert Adam in the 1790s, is now derelict and the estate, too, has suffered change. At Yellow Craig, where the estate comes down to the coast, there are parking facilities, a picnic site and a nature trail, as well as a beautifully landscaped caravan park. Yellow Craig also has a claim to fame in the literary history of Scotland as the inspiration of Spyglass Hill in Stevenson's *Treasure Island.*

Gullane The gentle arc of Gullane Bay is overlooked by a complex rim of tumbled dunes. Serious erosion and wind drifting of sand has here presented some difficult problems. Blown sand invaded the churchyard and in 1612 the Scottish Parliament allowed the removal of the parish church from Gullane to Dirleton, from 'a decaying place' to 'a flourishing town'. But if sand has menaced Gullane, it has also been an advantage. Since the formation of the Gullane Golf Club in 1882 it has become one of the most famous of Scotland's golf resorts, with three first-class courses. It is the most expensive of Edinburgh's dormitory suburbs, and the half-timbered fronts of its mock-Tudor villas run counter to all the architectural traditions of Scotland.

Aberlady This former burgh is sandwiched between the estates of Luffness and Gosford. Luffness House, a sixteenth-century tower-house, was extended in a full-blooded Scottish baronial style in the 1840s. Gosford, the work of Robert Adam and one of the great houses of south-east Scotland, was completed in 1800 for the Earl of Wemyss. Its great glory is the Marble Hall, a room of polished Caen stone and pink and white Derbyshire alabaster, all under a great central dome. Until the coming of the railway Aberlady was a port of some consequence. The port settlement stretched along the shore towards Kildpindie Point, where now a private road leads to the golf course.

From Cockenzie westward to the green acres of Dalmeny House, beyond Edinburgh, man and his works have created a complex townscape out of the coastline of the Forth. Beneath the miles of streets, coal bings, power stations and harbour works we find the '25-foot raised beach' shaped during a period of higher sea-level between 9,000 and 8,000 years ago.

Port Seton The huts and caravans of a large holiday camp mark the eastern approach to Port Seton. An open-air bathing pool, fairground, children's paddling-pool, and putting and bowling greens, largely the work of the 1930s, signalled its transformation into a conventional holiday resort. The outstanding feature of the coastal scene is the power station built in the early 1960s. Its soaring twin chimneys and the vast steel and glass generating hall are a landmark and a guide to shipping in the Forth. The construction of Cockenzie power station achieved a considerable tidying up of the landscape hereabouts because it conceals the old spoil heaps and dumps of the Prestonlinks colliery.

Prestonpans is composed of a former fishing settlement on the raised beach and a cliff-top burgh where the seventeenth-century mercat cross – perhaps the finest in Scotland – marks the place where markets and fairs were held 200 years ago. Coal-mining and the extraction of salt from sea water by evaporation have been the occupations of Prestonpans for many centuries. The monks of Newbattle Abbey were engaged in both industries as early as the twelfth century. The salt pans at the priests' town (Preston) were active until the first quarter of the nineteenth century when the industry was destroyed by the repeal of the salt duties. Mining reached its peak in the later years of the last century with collieries at Prestongrange and Prestonlinks. The workings at the latter crept out for 3km (2 miles) under the Firth of Forth. Near the coast road at Prestongrange colliery, now closed, one can still see the stone engine house with the protruding beam of a Cornish-type engine that was installed in 1874 and worked until after World War II.

Musselburgh At the mouth of the Esk, history begins here with the Romans. At Fisherrow, where the Esk empties into the sea, there was a Roman port. The site of a Roman fort on the west side of Inveresk church was found in 1946, since when evidence has accumulated of a town with stone buildings laid out along streets to the south and east of the fort, and aerial photography has revealed a hidden pattern of fields, tracks and enclosures beyond. Little remains of Roman Inveresk above ground, only a fragment of a building of the civil settlement in the garden of Inveresk House.

Musselburgh can also offer a sixteenth-century tolbooth, one of the earliest surviving in Scotland of this peculiarly Scottish kind of municipal building. The constant traffic of the A1 is carried across the Esk by John Rennie's bridge of 1806, widened in 1924. Upstream stands the old crossing of the river, a bridge that was there three centuries before Rennie set about his design, while downstream towards the sea are two bridges of the 1960s. The pride of Musselburgh and one of its oldest buildings is Pinkie House – a sixteenth-century tower-house of the abbots of Dunfermline that was acquired by Alexander Seton, 1st Earl of Dunfermline, in 1597. The house was vastly extended in the early years of the seventeenth century. Pinkie is now one of the boarding houses of Loretto School, whose name derived from a medieval chapel, demolished about 1590.

Musselburgh is equally interesting for the relics of the Industrial Revolution in a cluster of mills contained by a loop of the Esk above the town. Brunton's Wireworks is recalled by the latest notable addition to the townscape of Musselburgh, the Brunton Memorial Hall and Municipal Offices, clad in shining white aggregate slabs, a late twentieth-century foil to the grey stone of Georgian and Victorian Musselburgh.

The 16km (10 mile) coastline between the mouth of the Esk at Musselburgh and Cramond where the Almond empties into the Forth are part of the city of Edinburgh. Few natural features remain; the coast itself is entirely artificial, built out beyond its original limits with breakwaters, piers, dock-basins and promenades. Places that were once distinct settlements – North and South Leith, Portobello and Granton – have been swallowed up by the growing conurbation.

Portobello The grey-green sandstone terraces of this Regency resort recall something of the character of Edinburgh's new town. Perhaps the anonymous observant author of Murray's *Handbook for Scotland* at the end of the nineteenth century was able to measure a century of change at Portobello 'a second-rate watering-place with Promenade Pier and extensive sands crowded in summer with bathing-machines, donkeys and day-trippers. The proximity of a big city and cheap railway travel transformed the resort that began as a "Scottish Brighton".'

Leith Its earliest record appears in a charter dated 1329. Down the centuries Leith has struggled to express its individuality, but lacking the privileges of a medieval burgh it was unable to establish markets or engage in trade free of the tolls imposed by Edinburgh's council. Leith was made a parliamentary burgh in 1833, but since the 1890s the capital city has relentlessly swallowed its close neighbours. The Victorian decades saw the growth of Leith into the second port of Scotland and the most important on the east. Andrew Lamb's House, 13 Waters' Close, is considered to be the finest of the historic houses of Leith. Its tall four storeys of grey harled stone with a projecting turret staircase on the front face reflect Leith's seventeenth-century merchant town. Today, Andrew Lamb's house is a day-centre for old people. St Mary's Church, Kirkgate, a medieval cruciform building as great as St Giles in the capital, was entirely rebuilt in 1848. From the close of the eighteenth century there survives the Exchange Building in Constitution Street, built as a meeting place for merchants. The industrial hinterland that lies behind Leith and Granton is a place of railway sidings, many now closed, of coalyards, scrap-metal dumps and working-class tenements. Large areas have lately suffered redevelopment. The town-planners' wastelands have sprouted tower blocks, while in dockland are the bonded warehouses of the whisky industry: some of them twentieth-century, clad in white-painted steel; others, built by our Victorian forefathers, in austere dark grey stone, their tiny iron-grilled windows reminiscent of some Muslim fortress in southern Spain.

Newhaven, as the name implies, began as a fresh foundation – a rival for Leith – when in 1506 James IV founded a dock and ship-building yard there. Edinburgh, fearing this close competitor for its harbour at Leith, bought Newhaven from the crown five years later, 'with all its privileges'. Newhaven

Cramond, at the mouth of the river Almond, is a favourite Edinburgh resort for tourists

settled in the seventeenth century for the exploitation of the fishing banks in the North Sea. Today, the well-restored fishermen's quarter of Newhaven is one of the more attractive fragments of this industrialised coast.

Granton came into being in 1835 when the Duke of Buccleuch invested in the making of an artificial harbour on a shelterless piece of the coastline. A pier, almost 0.5km (⅓ mile) long, is screened by breakwaters on every side except for a narrow access to the firth. Accessible at any state of the tide, Granton enjoyed half a century of prosperity before the building of the Forth railway bridge. From the railway station on the pier passengers embarked for Burntisland and the Fife shore. Ferries to Fife and fishing no longer exist and the harbour is a marina for Edinburgh's yachtsmen.

West of Granton the coastal scenery changes. The works of man belong largely to the latter half of the twentieth century: first, oil-storage tanks and then the long, low single-storied factories of an industrial estate amid grassy lawns. Further west a new residential district takes over in Pilton with its suburban bungalows, wide boulevards and roundabouts served by the double-decker buses of Edinburgh's city transport. All this development is stopped in its march towards the coastline by golf courses that stretch inland for more than 3.2km (2 miles) from the shore at Muirhouse. The dullness of the motorist's route through the housing estates between Granton and Cramond can be avoided, on foot, by taking the attractive coastal path to the mouth of the Almond with its views across the Forth estuary to Fife, the firth here broken by a girdle of volcanic islands – Cramond Island, a sill of igneous rock, Inchmickery, Cow and Calves, Oxcars and Inchcolm.

Cramond The steeply sloping street of white-washed cottages at the mouth of the Almond's wooded gorge is one of the most frequented tourist spots of suburban Edinburgh. The remains of slit mills and the seventeenth-century bridge, higher up the gorge, belong to Cramond's forgotten industrial past. In Roman times, Cramond, with its fort (on a site near the church), granaries, storehouses and workshops, must have been a vital port in the brief campaign to push northward the imperial frontier.

Beyond Cramond the messy coastal townscape of Edinburgh is largely left behind. Dalmeny Park, the extensive estate of the Earls of Rosebery, occupies the whole coastline between the Almond gorge and Queensferry. Rolling parkland and mature planted woodlands reach down to the shores of the Forth.

Queensferry acquired its name after Queen Margaret, wife of Malcolm Canmore, who crossed the Forth on a journey from Edinburgh to Dunfermline in 1070. By the early fifteenth century it was already on record as 'the town of the ferry'. The building of the Forth Bridge by the North British Railway between 1883 and 1890, achieved a link between the Lothians and Fife that had been in the mind for almost a century. In 1805 the boring of a double tunnel beneath the waters of the Forth had been proposed, but South Queensferry was to find even greater prosperity as a ferry port in the age of the motor car. The continuous traffic from the slipway close beneath the southern approach to the railway bridge came to an end only in 1964 with the opening of the road bridge.

The High Street, gently twisting along the narrow shelf of raised beach between the towering approaches of the two bridges, is a notably satisfying piece of townscape. There are two levels of pavement with a good Georgian terrace, old-fashioned Victorian shop-fronts, crow-stepped gables and a solid bank in the best baronial style. At the west end of Queensferry, St Mary's Episcopal Church survives from the early fifteenth century when it was the chapel of a Carmelite friary; and in the High Street there is a seventeenth-century tolbooth. But the excitement of South Queensferry rests in the overpowering presence of the great bridges.

The bridges isolate the inner part of the Firth of Forth from the North Sea. Even so, a deep navigable channel stretches 19km (12 miles) westward of the road bridge to Grangemouth. This is not tourist country, even though there is much to enjoy between the M9 motorway and the muddy shore of the firth. Outstanding is the succession of great houses that have arisen in this fertile countryside. Their estates, reaching to the waterfront, have done much to preserve several miles of coastline from haphazard urban and industrial development. Hopetoun House, Midhope Castle, The Binns, Carriden House and Kinneil House succeed each other westward. Hopetoun House is one of the finest works of William Adam and his sons John and Robert. Today, one can wander through the deer park of the vast estate and there is a nature trail laid out by the Scottish Wildlife Trust. Kinneil House, now part of a municipal park on the western fringe of Bo'ness, was founded as a palace of the Earls of Arran in 1553. The time-span of Kinneil's historic associations is immense. Apart from the gaunt seventeenth-century centre block of the house, the site of a fort of the Antonine Wall lies close by, and in the grounds are the remains of an out-house where James Watt developed his steam-engine in 1765.

Around the Fife Peninsula

Fife lies between the firths of Forth and Tay. It has been described as 'a beggar's mantle fringed with gold'. A phrase that notices the concentration of population and wealth-producing economic activities close to the coastline. Beside and beneath the Forth in west Fife are Scotland's richest reserves of coal and a string of modern mines that produce almost half the output of the country. The wealth of Fife's coastline belongs not only to the twentieth century. The ports of the East Neuk, the eastern corner of the peninsula, engaged in trade with the Baltic and the busy commercial cities of the Netherlands and Flanders before the Industrial Revolution. Forgotten industries – the building of wooden ships, the fisheries in the firths, the extraction of salt by evaporation from sea water – all added to the wealth of this coast, and no other part of Scotland saw the creation of so many royal burghs in the Middle Ages. Eighteen towns were granted special trading privileges, and of these royal burghs all but

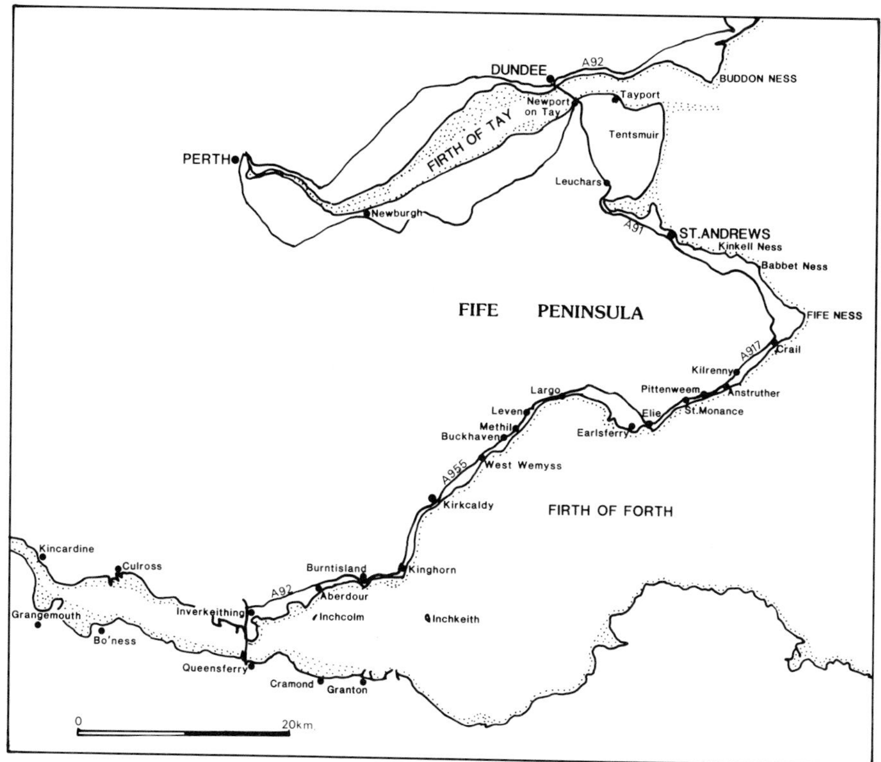

The Fife Peninsula

five are located on the northern shore of the Forth. Another less well-known epithet has described Fife as 'the concentrated essence of Scottish history'. Not only was the peninsula a stronghold of the Picts in late prehistory, but during the Middle Ages Dunfermline and St Andrews were the civil and ecclesiastical capitals of Scotland.

The southern coastline of Fife may be described as a northern riviera. Tiny sheltered bays and sandy beaches look southward across the Firth of Forth into the eye of the sun. Resorts such as Elie and Aberdour can boast above-average sunshine figures for Britain and average annual amounts of rainfall between 560mm (22in) and 760mm (30in) that rank among the lowest for Scotland. From early spring to midsummer, however, raw sea fogs, the 'haar', frequently envelop the shores of the firths. Then temperatures are held at about 10°C (50°F) while the interior of Fife, perhaps as little as 4-5km (2-3 miles) from the sea, basks in warm sunshine. The haar has been described as the blight of Fife, and its cold clinging greyness makes even the most ardent golfers give up as it closes in upon them.

Kincardine provides a notable illustration of the way in which an ancient burgh adjusts to time and its changes. An isolated seafaring community a century ago, it is now a busy centre of road traffic. The opening of the bridge across the Forth in the 1930s put Kincardine in the line of much traffic between the Clyde valley and eastern Scotland. The opening of the Forth Road Bridge in 1964 has done nothing to diminish the volume of traffic at Kincardine now that the western exit of the bridge feeds into the motorway system of central Scotland. Power stations have transformed the landscape of the sea-shore on either flank of the town. Longannet stands out in the firth on reclaimed land, a generating station that itself consumes 6 million tons of coal a year.

The fishing fleet is no more, the steamers that once plied up-river to Stirling and down to Leith have gone.

Culross With a population of little more than 500, Culross is the third smallest burgh in Scotland. Its steep, narrow, cobbled streets, crow-stepped gables, pale-red pantiled roofs and white-washed walls make it the gem of this part of the coast. The attractiveness of Culross owes as much to the restoring care of the National Trust for Scotland and the Ministry of the Environment as to its legacy of seventeenth-century buildings. A charter of 1588 dates Culross as a royal burgh, but its history reaches back centuries beyond the Middle Ages. A Cistercian abbey was founded here in 1215. Part of the monastic buildings now forms the parish church of Culross. Earlier still, in the fifth century, the tradition survives of a monastery at Culross associated with the name of St Mungo. But the visual delight of Culross today lies in its houses and streets dating from the prosperous decades of the seventeenth century. In this little town we can enjoy a brief phase of Scottish domestic architecture in which ideas and motifs borrowed from the trading cities of the Netherlands and Flanders contributed to a distinctive national style of building. Outstanding is the area around the mercat cross. Restored by the National Trust for Scotland is The Study, a tall, L-shaped tower-house with tiny rooms and corkscrew stair-turrets dating from the turn of the seventeenth century. It contains a museum of early life in Culross.

East of the Forth Bridge and the rugged quarried outline of the volcanic Ferry Hills the southern shore of Fife stretches with several bays and indentations towards Kirkcaldy's mines and linoleum mills. Industry may dominate, but there are quiet, beautiful and unspoilt places to be found. Bathing beaches occur cheek by jowl with coal bings.

Inverkeithing, tucked into a sheltered bay behind the Gibraltar-like peninsula of Ferry Hills, held out the possibilities for twentieth-century tourism that have been so successfully exploited at Culross. Its earliest charter as a royal burgh was granted by William the Lion in 1165. A medieval church tower survives at St Peter's and there is a mercat cross, among the finest in Scotland, dating from the end of the fourteenth century. Inverkeithing inevitably suffers by its location on the map of the communications geography of the twentieth century. The main railway line from the Forth Bridge snakes around the Inner Bay and tunnels beneath the town. Close by, the new road bridge debouches its constant stream of traffic northwards to the Perth motorway. Rosyth dockyard, with its call for accommodation for thousands of employees at the height of two world wars, inevitably shaped the growth of Inverkeithing.

Aberdour has successfully resisted the incursion of industry; as a result, its beaches and especially the wooded shore of Silversands Bay have long been the object of day-trippers from nearby industrial towns. Before the bridging of the Forth, this wide arm of the sea was busy with ferries that plied between the shores of Lothian and Fife. Aberdour emerged as a Victorian resort where boats called on the route between Granton and Burntisland. Edinburgh businessmen and their families retreated in summer to villas along the sea-shore, a riviera facing south and screened from the north by gentle wooded hills. There is good sea-bathing here and Aberdour has become a popular sailing centre. The castle has a late-medieval tower and parts of St Fillan's Church, restored from ruin in the 1920s, date to Norman times.

Inchcolm, scarcely 1.6km (1 mile) in length, is one of the scattered tiny islands, untouched by the development of the Fife coastline, that look like stepping-stones across the firth to Edinburgh's shore. It is composed of a gently sloping slab of igneous rock which displays a fine columnar structure close to the island's landing place at Swallow Craig. Inchcolm has been described as 'the Iona of the east', and the name means Columba's isle. On this lonely horseshoe-shaped volcanic rock was a Dark Age hermitage, and later an abbey was founded by the Augustinian order. An echo of this

The church at Burntisland was the first to be built in Scotland after the Reformation

medieval holy island finds its way into Shakespeare's *Macbeth* where Inchcolm is mentioned as 'an island close to heaven'. Inchcolm may be visited during the summer months by boat from Aberdour.

Burntisland, a grey stone-built town, is another of Fife's royal burghs whose long history has been overlaid and obscured by the works of the Industrial Revolution. Above the town, the walled enclosures of a prehistoric fort or settlement on Dunearn Hill hint at man's presence here 2,000 years ago. The medieval church built by David I in about 1120 has vanished and in its place is the first church to be constructed in Scotland after the Reformation. It is a grey shaggy building, modelled after the Old North Church in Amsterdam, square in plan and surmounted by an octagonal tower. Inside the galleries, the Trades' Lofts, installed in the seventeenth century, are elaborately carved and painted. Burntisland suffered severely from the opening of the Forth Bridge in 1890. For less than half a century it had been the chief ferry port for the railway link across Fife to the Tay ferry and thence to Aberdeen. The ferry across the Forth to Granton lingered long after the making of the direct railway link to Edinburgh; it stopped finally in 1939. Burntisland has lost much else. The whaling fleet that once ranged the North Atlantic from Greenland to Spitsbergen has vanished and the limestone quarries on the eastern edge of the burgh are now occupied by a golf course. However, Burntisland's good harbour and presence of coal has attracted new industries. The British Aluminium Company set up a plant at Burntisland to convert bauxite clay, imported from West Africa, into aluminium oxide. Since 1960 shipbuilding has given way to the construction of oil rigs for the North Sea oil- and gas-fields.

Eastward of Burntisland, for more than 19km (12 miles), the coast road of south Fife – first the A92 and later the A955 – follows a traffic-cluttered course through a string of industrial towns. Kirkcaldy, now the busiest town in Fife, lies at the heart of this conurbation with a population of 50,000.

Although the present landscape is dominated by coal mines, docks, linoleum mills and vast stretches of local authority housing, here and there survives evidence of a past before the blight of the Industrial Revolution.

Kinghorn, with its pair of now derelict harbours, straddles a headland of volcanic rocks. The chain of tiny islands lying close to the shore between here and Kirkcaldy – West Vows, East Vows and Long Craig – is composed of volcanic sills, and Black Rocks, in the wide sandy bay to the west of Kinghorn, are made of basalt. Kinghorn was made a royal burgh by David I eight centuries ago. The stream that drains seaward from Kinghorn Loch, 1km (½ mile) inland, provided power for the first flax spinning-mills here in the early nineteenth century. Today, Kinghorn lives mainly as a seaside resort whose amenities include a good sand beach and a golf course.

Kirkcaldy 'The Lang Toun', as it is known, evolved from a 6.4km (4 mile) long street that runs close to the shore along the level surface of a raised beach. Kirkcaldy's most distinctive industry is the manufacture of linoleum. It is almost a speciality of Fifeshire where more than 50 per cent of Britain's linoleum workers are concentrated. Linoleum has stamped Kirkcaldy with the pungent smell of linseed oil. Here is the greatest concentration of industry in Fife – carpets, clothing, flour-milling and electrical engineering. In addition, Kirkcaldy lies astride the rich coal seams of the Fife coalfield where the Carboniferous rocks dip beneath the Forth. The Frances Colliery stands on the shore at Dysart. The Seafield Mine marks the approach to Kirkcaldy from the west. This recent sinking, with an output of more than 1 million tons a year, exploits 20 different coal seams at depths of 610m (2,000ft) far out to sea beneath the Firth of Forth. Tall concrete blocks have replaced pleasant rows of seventeenth- and eighteenth-century houses in Kirkcaldy, but in Sailors' Walk buildings from this period have been restored. The museum and art gallery are situated above the gardens near the railway station. The history of the Firth of Forth is expounded through ship models and there is an industrial museum that illustrates the history of coal-mining and the linoleum industry.

A quiet wooded haven, Ravenscraig Park, suddenly intrudes on this busy built-up coastline between Kirkcaldy and Dysart. Here stand the ruin of a castle raised in 1460 by James II. It is notable as one of the first castles of northern Britain designed for defence by cannon. Ravenscraig contains a nature trail and picnic places.

Dysart is the most rewarding piece of Kirkcaldy's coastline. The harbour, reached by a steep twisting lane from the 'upper town', is quiet and deserted; once it exported up to 100,000 tons of coal a year to the continent. A comprehensive rehabilitation scheme has produced a place of great charm. In the quiet unhurried quarter of the 'seatown', close by the harbour, we find renovated seventeenth-century houses and the gaunt fortified tower of the ruined church of St Serf. The upper town with its Civic Centre and High Street has a sixteenth-century tolbooth and a number of houses with characteristic crow-stepped gables, among which the Towers, dating from 1587 and now restored as an old peoples' club, is the most important. The name 'Dysart' refers to the *desertum*, the lonely isolated place of a Dark Age hermit – possibly St Serf who occupied one of the large caves of the cliffs above the raised beach.

West Wemyss This attractive secluded village, screened by its inland plantations, is a place of red pantiled roofs and favoured for retirement. Three centuries ago West Wemyss boasted a weekly market and six annual fairs, but the peak of its commercial prosperity came towards the end of the nineteenth century when coal, exported from the Victoria Pit to the Netherlands, reached the shore by a mineral railway that tunnelled through the wooded face of the raised beach cliff behind West Wemyss. The place-name Wemyss descends from the Gaelic *uamh*, a cave. It refers to the succession of caves in the raised beach cliff-line. There are ten caves along this section of the coast, some containing primitive rock drawings.

The ruined church of St Serf in Dysart, with its fortified tower

Coaltown of Wemyss with its red roofs, crow-stepped gables and brightly coloured gardens and the brilliant seaside light of early summer, has been described as 'the prettiest mining village in Scotland'. It is as much an estate village as a mining settlement, associated with a family that has exploited the coal seams of its lands in Fife for more than five centuries. Wemyss Castle, a sumptuous Victorian mansion of 1876, was built in the boom years of coal-mining.

Buckhaven underwent an astonishing transformation of its economy and landscape in the latter part of the nineteenth century – a fishing village was transformed into a mining town. In 1878 almost 100 fishing boats used the harbour at Buckhaven; by 1914 only five boats fished the Forth and the North Sea. Soon the harbour itself was to vanish as the entrance became blocked by waste from the Wellesley mine. A storm in 1932 destroyed the east breakwater, and the lighthouse was reduced to a heap of stones. The deposit of mining waste along the shore also ravaged Buckhaven's fine beach of yellow sands. In its active life the vast bing of Wellesley Colliery on the foreshore was a menace to the life of Buckhaven with its 'eruptions and poisonous fumes'. One oddity in the townscape is St Andrews Church, formerly the Episcopal church in St Andrews, ecclesiastical capital of Fife, that was dismantled and transported by sea to be re-erected in the expanding mining settlement of Buckhaven.

Methil In the closing years of the nineteenth century Methil overtook all the other harbours of the Forth in exports of coal. By 1900 its docks were handling 2–3 million tons of coal and by the 1930s coal formed 93 per cent of the value of Methil's exports. Now, coal exports are a negligible part of its activities. It is engaged in oil-platform construction and acts as a servicing base for the rigs of the North Sea oilfields; fertilisers are manufactured and there is a marine-engineering plant.

Leven A notorious bottle-neck in the roads of Fife is the bridge across the river that connects Methil and Leven. As a shopping centre Leven draws its customers from Methil and Buckhaven as well as the string of fishing burghs in the East Neuk. It has an industrial quarter, compact and adjacent to the shopping streets on the banks of the river Leven, with general engineering, timber yards and a paper mill. Leven also has some reputation as a resort with a minimum of amenities for the summer visitor – a promenade, beach pavilion, children's playground and paddling pond. Perhaps Leven's main attraction lies in its location at the eastern limit of several miles of built-up, industrialised and polluted coastline. Beyond lies the wide arc of Largo Bay, its vast sandy beach backed by the shapely outline of Largo Law, a conical hill of volcanic rock congealed in the neck of an ancient volcano.

Leaving Leven by the A915 one of the most attractive sections of Scotland's coastline lies ahead. The attraction lies in the close succession of harbours, most of them medieval burghs, between Earlsferry and Crail. Each presents the same charming picture of harled, white-washed houses, pantiled roofs, narrow steeply twisting wynds that focus on a tiny harbour confined behind the grey curving arm of a breakwater. The disused quays and empty moorings, except for the yachts and small pleasure craft of high summer, speak of the bustling trade with continental ports and the fishing fleets that are now no more. The herring fisheries off the Fife coastline are recorded as long ago as the twelfth century. A century ago fishing was the predominant occupation of the little towns of the East Neuk; it occupied more than 4,000 men. By 1950 less than 500 gained their living from the fisheries. World War II with the commandeering of drifters for mine-sweeping and other purposes by the navy meant that the fleets were not restored when peace returned. In 1947 and 1948 the shoals of herring disappeared completely from the Forth and over a long time there has been a drift of young people from the East Neuk to less hazardous, more secure jobs in the industries of West Fife.

From the wide sweep of Largo Bay to Fife Ness a straight-edged cliff-line runs for miles broken by shallow indentations where the tiny burghs crouch around their man-made havens. Abruptly at heights of little more than 15m (50ft) above the sea the sharp-edged cliff tops of limestone or Calciferous Sandstone give way to the monotonously level surface of the coastal plateau of the East Neuk, its farming on fertile loamy soils among the richest in Scotland. Treeless, windswept fields with crops of oats, potatoes, wheat and barley speak of a way of life completely remote from the sea.

Largo consists of three settlements, loosely grown together as a once important fishing port transformed itself in this century into a holiday resort and a favoured place for retirement. Upper Largo or Kirkton of Largo, lies 1km (½ mile) from the sea-shore where the land begins to rise gently from the level surface of a raised beach towards the steeper slopes of Largo Law. There was a church here in the thirteenth century and a Pictish cross-slab in the churchyard speaks of a settlement almost 1,000 years earlier. Largo's main claim to fame was the birth of Alexander Selkirk in 1676. For several years stranded on a desert island off the coast of Central America he became the prototype of *Robinson Crusoe.* A memorial statue may be found in front of his cottage birthplace in Lower Largo. Largo Bay, a place mentioned in the fishing songs of Fife, no longer puts a fleet to sea. The last fishing boat at Lower Largo was sold in 1948, and the place has seen the demise of the steamer services of the Firth of Forth. Largo now is a sedate seaside resort whose sands, golf course and 'the beauty of Kiel's Den' – a shallow wooded gorge on the burn that empties into Largo Bay – have long been considered to provide sufficient amusement for the visitor. Lundin Links has been favoured by retired professional people from Edinburgh since the latter years of the nineteenth century and Lundin Links golf course is the greatest asset of the parish. Here, just north of the A915, as one enters Lundin Links from the west, are two standing stones. Astroarchaeologists have argued that Lundin Links was the site of a lunar observatory in the Early Bronze Age. Seen from the stones, the moon rising at its most southerly position would be observed to graze the Bass Rock 24km (15 miles) away across the Firth of Forth.

The fourteenth-century parish church in the Fife-coast fishing port of St Monance

Earlsferry The place-name records the dark side of Scotland's medieval history, for it is from here that Macduff, Earl of Fife, in flight from Macbeth was ferried across the 'Scottish Sea' to Dunbar. Earlsferry is a minor paradise on those cloudless, brilliantly clear days that are not so infrequent on the east coast of Scotland. Narrow lanes run down to the sands between glistening white-washed single-storey cottages.

Elie has a long reputation as a resort. The first *Statistical Account*, published in 1798, noticed the three sheltered, south-facing beaches: 'The shore is sandy, and shelving gradually; is remarkably well adapted for sea-bathing, and is, of late, much resorted to for that purpose.' The coming of the railway hastened Elie's transformation into a resort, a place that was valued by Edinburgh's well-to-do for its golf courses and the reputation of its climate.

St Monance has two distinct parts – a cliff-top town of bungalows, municipal housing and caravans, and a sea-town of crowded, colour-washed eighteenth-century houses round a narrow winding quay. The steep cobbled wynds lead down to two harbours nestling in the crook of stout breakwaters. At low tide they are completely drained of water and even the smallest craft is unable to enter for a space of two hours at the turn of the tide. Nevertheless, St Monance looks back to a prosperous history as a fishing port. In 1900 more than 100 brown-sailed boats fished from here and the whole population was occupied by the fisheries. St Monance successfully overcame the technological challenge that came with the steam drifter and, later still, the motor vessel. Now there is only a handful of motor vessels. St Monance's other occupation is shipbuilding in yards that were once famous for luxury yachts, but since World War II have concentrated on small wood-built fishing craft. The fourteenth-century parish church, dramatically sited on a rocky head-land across the shallow gorge of the St Monance burn, is sometimes isolated from its congregation at the time of high spring tides.

Pittenweem About 1.6km (1 mile) along the coast road between the fields of barley and potatoes on the East Neuk bench above

Vernacular building in St Monance

the cliffs lies Pittenweem whose place-name is Pictish by origin. Although Pittenweem displays themes in its history common to the other coastal burghs of the East Neuk – the loss of its North Sea trade, declining fisheries and a picturesque attractiveness of its buildings and harbour – some original elements in its evolution have left their mark on the townscape. The town, granted a burghal charter in 1542, grew up in the shadow of an early twelfth-century priory. The priory ruins still stand close by the parish church, and from the garden of a seventeenth-century house that incorporates some of the priory building, steps lead down to the cave of St Fillan in the cliff-face below. Until its rededication as a shrine in 1935 the cave had been used as a store for fishing gear. The harbour at Pittenweem is lined with some of the handsomest seventeenth- and eighteenth-century houses in Scotland. They were built by merchants who engaged in trade with the Netherlands, exporting salt, malt, white fish and herring.

Anstruther Easter and **Anstruther Wester**, two royal burghs with sixteenth-century charters, face each other across a shallow embayment where the Dreel Burn enters the Firth of Forth. Anstruther Easter, where the most recent harbour improvements were made in the 1930s, ranked among the leading fishing ports of the Fife coast. Even though it accepted the technical revolution of the steam drifter and the introduction of diesel power, fishing has experienced a long decline throughout the twentieth century. From a pre-war fleet of nineteen drifters, only three returned after World War II. On the site of St Ayles Chapel – a fifteenth-century building of which some fragments remain – is the Scottish Fisheries Museum. A display explains the defunct whaling industry; there are ships' logs from the early years of the nineteenth century and exhibits that illustrate the working of radar. Near the museum is a sixteenth-century building that was the residence of the abbots of Balmerino, a monastery beside the Tay on the northern coast of Fife.

The **Isle of May** which lies some 8km (5 miles) distant in the firth is counted as part of the parish of Anstruther Wester. Little more than 1.6km (1 mile) in length, it consists of a gently sloping volcanic sill of dolerite. The west coast of the island, rising to 46m (150ft) above the sea, is marked by steep cliffs in which the dark volcanic rock has solidified in column-shaped forms. The island was an important strategic target in wars between England and Scotland before the union of the parliaments in the eighteenth century. There is the ruin of a twelfth-century Benedictine priory, and the Beacon, a small battlemented building now ruined, was the first lighthouse erected in Scotland, in 1636. The present lighthouse, dating from 1816, was built by Robert Stevenson. The island provides a nesting place for migrant birds and has been designated a National Nature Reserve.

Crail has much in common with the other ports of the Fife coast: the clutter of chimneys and orange pantiles as one looks down on the harbour, the many well-restored seventeenth-century houses, a prosperous port history that petered out in the eighteenth century, and a fishing industry that in decline is now mainly concerned with crab and lobster. Now it is a holiday resort with a ring of caravan sites on the northern fringe of the town. Crail's origin as a royal burgh dates to the twelfth century, but the legacy of that period is perhaps more apparent in the town's layout than elsewhere. The wide streets of the cliff top, Nethergate and Marketgate, are reminiscent of the planned new towns that were established in England during the two centuries after the Norman Conquest. By the end of the twelfth century Crail was a walled town. St Mary's, at the east end of the town, has the oldest church tower in Fife, dating to the time of the burgh's foundation. In the entrance to the church is evidence of a much older culture, a Pictish cross-slab from the eighth century.

Fife Ness marks an important turning point in the coastline of Fife; thence, as far as the sandy promontory of Tentsmuir, the peninsula looks into the empty spaces of the North Sea. There are some remarkable contrasts in the physique of this exposed piece of coastline between Forth and Tay. To the east of St Andrews lies a coastline of reefs and rocky platforms carved out of the Calciferous Sandstone Series. Scenically, it offers nothing spectacular, high cliffs are lacking and there are no deep sandy bays. Extensive raised beach platforms stretch inland from a rocky shore. The interest here lies in the intrusion of volcanic rocks among the sandstones. The eternal gnawing of the sea at these rocks of differing hardness and texture has produced an intricate pattern of coastal forms. For instance, at Kinkell Ness five volcanic vents can be picked out on the foreshore amid a complex of faulted and folded sandstones. They stand out as worn-down stacks on the raised beach platform.

North of St Andrews the character of the coastline changes dramatically. The 25ft (8m) raised beach forms a broad platform. There are several miles of fine sand along the foreshore on either hand of the Eden estuary and the gloomy plantations of Tentsmuir Forest have taken over one of the most extensive tracts of dunes on the east coast of Scotland. This section of low sandy coastline is subject to rapid change. The outfall of the River Eden shifted in the early years of this century and as a result 30ha (75 acres) of dunes vanished from the south end of Tentsmuir.

St Andrews, with a population of just over 13,000, ranks as one of the most attractive towns in Great Britain. Although it has the immense advantage of being passed by in the Victorian years of industrial growth, it is much more than a fossilised North Sea fishing community. This neatly planned, grey stone town, focused on three parallel streets with their visual echoes of Edinburgh's New Town, still displays some of the glories of the medieval centuries when it was the ecclesiastical capital of Scotland. Here, at the beginning of the fifteenth century, Scotland's first university was founded. At the east end, above the disused harbour, are the spectacular ruins of the cathedral and priory, a site close above the sea that was enclosed by a 1.6km (1 mile) long wall with thirteen round towers in the early years of the sixteenth century. Founded in 1161, the cathedral was substantially complete after 70 years, but 300 years of

neglect after the Reformation brought it to ruin. The buildings served as a rich quarry of dressed stone for development in the town until, in 1826, the preservation of what was left of this incomparable building was ordered. Today, the only standing remains are parts of the west and east elevations and the south wall of the nave. Excavation has revealed the foundations of the whole of the buildings. Close by are the remains of the priory, founded in 1144, as well as the twelfth-century church of St Rule, a Romanesque building, the first church of the Augustinians in Scotland. The nave has gone and only the slender, square tower, over 30m (100ft) high, remains. Priory and cathedral, on the low bluff overlooking the harbour, together compose one of the most impressive ruins in the British Isles. The very desolation of these imposing buildings recalls a long-lost medieval Catholic Scotland.

The attraction of St Andrews lies largely in its remoteness from so much that belongs to twentieth-century Scotland. It is far removed from motorways and railways and has had no connection with the development of the North Sea oil industry. Education and golf dominate its life. On the Pilmour Links that stretch northwards along the shore to the mouth of the Eden, golf was played as long ago as the sixteenth century. In 1754 a group of local gentlemen formed a golfing society that became the Royal and Ancient Golf Club – a body that has long acted as the leading authority on the rules and practice of the game. St Andrews Links, the Old Course, is the venue for the Open Championship.

Guardbridge was the medieval port of St Andrews, a safe haven from North Sea storms. After 1873, when a large paper mill was established on the property of the Seggie Distillery and Brewery, the character of Guardbridge was changed profoundly. It became virtually a Victorian company town with a population of 1,000 and 200 company houses. The once famous salmon- and sea-trout fisheries of the estuary were destroyed by pollution from the mill.

The gaunt ruin of the medieval cathedral in St Andrews

Leuchars The chief attraction here is a parish church founded by a Norman baron, Saier de Quincy, whose twelfth-century fortress, Castle Knowe, survives as a few enigmatic bumps in a field close beside the embankment of the closed railway from Leuchars Junction to Tayport. The chancel and the tiny semi-circular apse rank among the finest examples of the Romanesque in northern Britain. In this dark stone interior one may sense the mystery of Scotland's medieval centuries – a world remote from the tall pulpits and polished pine benches of most of the north's Presbyterian sermon houses.

A military aerodrome was established here in 1917 on the level farmlands of the wide raised beach. Now the huge runway of this RAF base stretches to within a few hundred yards of the sea-shore and the air is filled with a deafening roar of jet aircraft.

Tentsmuir Forest Between the mouth of the Eden and the wide estuary of the Tay stretch hundreds of acres of forested sand dunes. Tentsmuir was taken over by the Forestry Commission in 1922 and from its nurseries at Fetterdale the transformation of a whole landscape has been achieved within half a century. The area was once a wilderness of treeless dunes and intervening marshy depressions. The *New Statistical Account* of 1848 tells of a scattered isolated population, 'a race of people who lived a life apart from other parishioners – descendants of shipwrecked Scandinavian sailors engaged in wrecking, smuggling and poaching'. Today, Tentsmuir is a different kind of wilderness, for the oppressive gloom of a man-made forest stretches to within sight of the sea. Tentsmuir Point Nature Reserve is a sanctuary for sea birds and marine life. Eider duck and terns abound; seals bask on the off-shore sandbanks; and the call of the curlew can be heard. At Morton Farm among the sand dunes, an important early archaeological site has come to light. The floors of huts, hearths and a chipping floor with waste flint flakes have survived as the remnants of a Mesolithic hunting settlement. Radio-carbon dating of material suggests that the site was occupied between 5400 and 4400 BC.

(*above*) The parish church in Leuchars is a rare flowering of the Romanesque in Northern Britain; (*below*) The Forestry Commission conifers of Testsmuir Forest have obliterated a wilderness of dunes

The coast of northern Fife looks across the sandbanks of the Tay to Dundee. Visually, this is a landscape of the highest quality. A line of dark shapely volcanic hills rises steeply from the shore, broken here and there by depressions that lead to the interior of the Fife peninsula. Steep hillsides emerge from a coverlet of woodland to summits crowned by Iron Age forts and other evidence of prehistoric settlement.

A cluster of settlements stretches for 10km (6 miles) along the Fife shore, facing Dundee across the Firth of Tay. Their development and life is bound up closely with the city across the water. It has been argued that Dundee's monopoly of the traffic of the Tay Estuary, established by a decree of the Court of Session in 1602, did much to prevent the growth of a major port on the Fife coastline, despite the location of a deep navigation channel close to this shore.

Tayport flourished briefly for half a century after the Edinburgh and Northern Railway, later part of the North British system, acquired control of the ferry across the Tay to Broughty Ferry in 1842. This became a vital link in the railway to Aberdeen. Here passengers trans-shipped, and huge freight ferries carried goods wagons across the Firth. Tayport, its name given by the railway company, achieved burghal status in 1888, but that political promotion was not to save it from decline, for in the same year the second Tay Bridge was opened. The ferry service was closed during World War I.

Newport on Tay, composed of **East Newport, West Newport, Woodhaven** and **Wormit**, is a ribbon of white-washed terraces and spacious stone-built villas on the steep hill-slopes between the two bridges. The new Tay Road Bridge, finished in 1966, points directly across the water to the heart of Dundee. It is visually uninspiring, more like a huge dam raised 30m (100ft) above the firth as the concrete supports of its forty-two spans merge in the distance. The graceful ironwork of the second railway bridge climbs and curves across the sea into Dundee 3.2km (2 miles) west. Forever in the history of Scotland this triumph of the Industrial Revolution will be associated with its predecessor, destroyed on a night of a severe gale, 28 December 1879, when thirteen girders of the high span were swept away and a train carrying ninety passengers went to its destruction. Until the opening of the railway bridge in 1888 changed the life and had been the chief stage-coach terminus and ferry for Dundee; Woodhaven, too, was a coach terminus. The opening of the second railway bridge in 1888 changed the life and function of Newport. A new suburb of Dundee appeared at Wormit and this seaside of Fife, remote from the factories and close-built tenements of the jute city, became a favoured home for commuting businessmen. Solid, square-built, eight- or ten-roomed villas took over sites with fine views across the water.

Balmerino is the site of a Cistercian abbey founded in 1226 which began as a daughter house of Melrose. Today, little remains except the entrance to the Chapter House. What Balmerino lacks in visible remains is made up by the atmosphere of the place on a fine summer's day – the neighbouring woodlands that stretch to the shore and the feeling of a North Sea tamed in this quiet estuary. In the precinct at Balmerino stands a hoary Spanish chestnut, held together by chains. Planted by the Cistercians, it is claimed to be the oldest tree of its kind in Scotland.

Westward of the Tay railway bridge there is no continuous coastal road and for over 19km (12 miles) there is no settlement of any size until Newburgh. The volcanic hills fall steeply to the wide raised beach platforms where, in springtime, clouds of gulls follow in the wake of tractors ploughing some of Scotland's richest soils. This narrow strip of highly fertile land has long been famed for its early potatoes.

Newburgh On the outskirts of the town are the ruins of the twelfth-century Benedictine abbey of Lindores. An arch of its main entrance and part of the west tower are its only important standing features. The rich farmlands of the Tay shore-line may owe not a little to the pioneering achievements of the monasteries before the Reformation. For instance, the cultivation of fruit trees was first introduced by the monks at Lindores

Dundee: the Law and its girdle of tower-blocks show through a gathering *haar*, with Wormit and the Tay Bridge in the foreground

and it is claimed that old fruit trees may still be found in the surrounding countryside. Newburgh's charter was granted by Alexander III in 1266. The town's steeply curving main street and the continuous frontage of built-up burghal plots reveal the layout of a planned town of the Middle Ages. Today, its quiet, almost derelict air, is a reminder that it has seen busier and better times. Until the early years of this century Newburgh was a port with a steam passenger service to Perth and Dundee. The quarries in the volcanic rocks above the town, where the whinstone is now crushed for road metal, supplied the building material for the piers of the Tay Bridge. Salmon fishing was an important and profitable trade in the last century and, briefly, Newburgh was touched by the Industrial Revolution when an outlier of the Kirkcaldy linoleum industry opened a factory here in 1891.

On the hills above, there is situated one of the most impressive prehistoric sites of Fife – a complex hill-fort with features of three stages of construction. The main oval-shaped ramparted enclosure as well as four outer ramparts all date from before the Roman intrusion into Scotland. The latest work dates from the sixth century AD. Pottery, made in western Gaul, has been found there; it shows that the Picts living on the shores of the Tay were engaged in trade, most likely the import of wine, with the continent.

From the Tay to Aberdeen

Above the Tay Bridge the wide sand- and mud-banks with such fascinating names as Eppie's Taes Bank and Sure as Death Bank give way to the low coastline of the Carse of Gowrie. This former marshland, extensively reclaimed over the last 200 years, ranks as the richest, most fertile tract in the whole of Scotland. Over 10,000 years ago, in a much wider embayment of the Tay, thick deposits of marine clay were laid down. Subsequent uplift of Scotland's land-mass, the result of recovery from the weight of the vanished ice sheets that had covered northern Britain in the Ice Age, led to the extensive emergence of these rich clays above present sea-level.

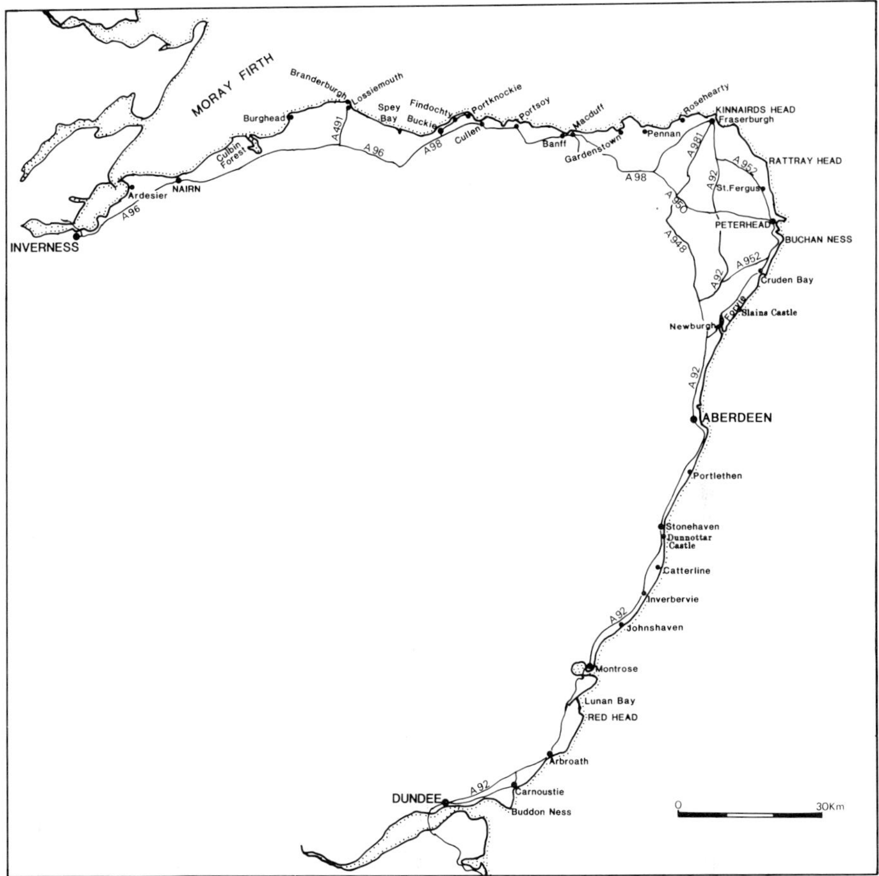

The coastline of the north-east shoulder of Scotland between the Tay and Moray Firths

For instance, the main raised beach stands at 8m (28ft) above mean sea-level at Dundee, and the channels of rivers that cross the flat clay lands of the Carse of Gowrie to empty into the firth are deeply incised. The place-names of this rich coastal lowland of the inner firth reveal something of its wilder landscape that has now disappeared. Carse itself derives from the Scandinavian *kjerr*, 'a marsh'. 'Inch' means an island; it occurs in Inchture, Inchmartin and Inchmichael and recalls the higher, drier patches of ground that nurtured the earliest settlements of this marshland.

Dundee Invergowrie marks the eastern limit of the Carse of Gowrie and signals the approach to Dundee, the fourth city of Scotland with a population approaching 200,000 and a certain Victorian grandeur that has done little to make its name in the tourist guides. Dundee's dramatic site is best appreciated in the wide panorama across the Firth of Tay. The city clusters around Dundee Law, a volcanic plug rising 174m (571ft) within 1.6km (1 mile) of the sea that marks the presence of an Iron Age community on this northern shore of the Tay 2,000 years ago with the remains of a vitrified fort. By the closing years of the twelfth century an urban settlement existed at Dundee. A burgh charter was granted by William the Lion in 1180 and St Mary's Church was founded in 1198. By 1600 Dundee was second in importance only to Edinburgh among Scotland's towns. For over 200 years it was busily engaged in

North Sea trade. Little survives of medieval Dundee. The skeleton of main streets at the heart of the city – Nethergate, Marketgate, Seagate and Cowgate – was determined by the earliest development of the town. The only important visible relic – a striking landmark – of those centuries is the tower of St Mary's, 49m (160ft) high. The latter half of the fifteenth century saw the rebuilding of St Mary's and this was the time when the still standing Gothic tower, the Old Steeple, was raised. The medieval castle that stood close to the centre of the town was destroyed in 1314. The site is now occupied by the Episcopal cathedral, built in the 1850s. Its 60m (200ft) spire looks strangely dwarfed against the tilted urban backcloth of the steep slopes of the Law. The first castle was succeeded by Dudhope Castle, above the medieval streets and harbour where the hill-slopes begin to climb steeply to the summit of the Law. But the most interesting castle within the boundaries of the twentieth-century city may be discovered entangled in a modern housing estate close to the A92 trunk road in West Ferry. Claypotts Castle, a Z-shaped tower-house, was built by John Strachan between 1569 and 1588. Two squat round towers stand at opposite corners of a central keep. The dark eyes of gun ports peer out at ground level in this defended dwelling house and atop the solid stone-built circular towers are perched living quarters, cottages, with tiny windows and crow-stepped gables. The tower fortalice, the term for the defended mansions of rich lairds in late medieval times, is a relic of Scotland's unruly centuries; Claypotts Castle is about the most complete of its kind.

Nothing is left of the fine eighteenth-century merchant houses. Particularly regrettable is the demolition of the Town House, an arcaded classical building designed by William Adam in the 1730s. This was pulled down in 1922 to make way for Caird Hall and city offices. A handful of terraces and three public buildings – St Andrew's, Cowgate with its graceful steeple, the Custom House of 1842 and the classical buildings of the High School – alone contribute a Georgian flavour to the townscape of Dundee.

One industry more than any other was responsible for the growth and transformation of Dundee in the nineteenth century. A sample of jute first reached Dundee in 1822, sent by the East India Company as a raw material in the manufacture of textiles that might rival cotton. Juteopolis, as Dundee became known, flourished on the manufacture of sacking and the base for linoleum. By the latter half of the nineteenth century the city was the world centre of the jute industry. Although the numbers employed in the industry have declined considerably, the acceptance of technological change has left the jute industry as the dominant occupation of Dundee. Bags with plastic linings have become an important commodity and jute backing for carpets is a recent development.

Of outstanding interest are the mills built between 1850 and 1870 – 'the golden age of mill-building'. Lochee, lying to the west of Dundee Law, emerged as an industrial suburb at this time. Today, Camperdown Works, the most notable monument to the era of Juteopolis, is an outstanding object for the industrial archaeologist. Its brick chimney, 86m (282ft) high and in the shape of an Italian campanile, is a remarkable part of the townscape.

The twentieth century has seen the inland growth of Dundee as well as an eastward expansion of the conurbation to swallow up Broughty Ferry and Monifieth. The axis of inland development is marked by the construction of a ring road, Kingsway, to the north of Dundee Law. Here, since 1948, a large industrial estate has been established that has changed the pattern of Dundee's industries. Several new factories are given over to business machines. There is Britain's largest publisher of calendars, picture postcards and greetings cards, and other new industries include watches, refrigerators and cameras. Shipbuilding has long been located in the harbour district of the city. For instance, the ships for Scott's Antarctic exploration, *Discovery* and *Terra Nova*, were built here and of late a valuable development has appeared in servicing the oil- and gasfields of the North Sea. In the medieval town where it reaches the shore the building of the Tay Road Bridge in the 1960s suddenly and drastically realigned the links of Dundee with the world beyond. The new bridge provided a main artery to the south that debouches an immense volume of traffic into the heart of the city. Consequently, a complex figure-of-eight of new roads has been built to ease the flow of vehicles. Adjoining this jungle of traffic lanes is the new shopping centre and pedestrian precinct that occupies the site of Overgate.

The most impressive public open space, Camperdown Park on the western edge of Dundee, was acquired in 1946. Previously the estate of the Earls of Camperdown, this 280ha (700 acre) tract of wooded parkland houses an eighteen-hole golf course, picnic places, facilities for football and tennis, nature trails, a children's zoo and an aviary. Camperdown House contains the Spalding Museum that displays a history of golf. The chief museum and art gallery is the Albert Institute, in the square of the same name. The building houses collections of symbol stones to illustrate the important role of the Tay's coastlands in the Pictish kingdom. In the Barrack Street Museum the visitor can find displays of local history and ecology as well as exhibits and relics of Dundee's sea-faring history. A valuable part of the cultural life of Dundee is expressed by the university that gained its charter as an independent degree-giving institution in 1967.

Buddon Ness is the most striking feature of the dull shore that stretches eastward along the Tay towards Arbroath. This low, triangular-shaped foreland projects seaward, a wilderness remote from the bustle of Monifieth and Carnoustie, overgrown outliers of Dundee that lie to its landward side. Wild geese gather here and at times of North Sea gales sand-storms swirl among the extensive clusters of dunes. Two military camps, Buddon and Barry, and five marked danger areas reveal that much of this wilderness is the property of the Army, used as an artillery range and closed to the public. Hutments, military roads and light railway tracks disfigure much of its landscape. The High Lighthouse and the Low Lighthouse towards the blunt tip of the Ness are historic objects in this desolate landscape. The former, over 30m (100ft) high, was built by Robert Stevenson in 1805–6. The Low Lighthouse was raised in the 1860s. The presence of two lights speaks of the difficulties of navigating the entrance to the Tay with its sandbanks and shifting deep-water channels. In fact, the shifting sandbanks in the mouth of the firth have rendered both lighthouses useless; they have been replaced by the Abertay lightship.

No clear answer has been found to the question why Buddon Ness grew in its present position. J. A. Steers, in his important pioneer survey, *The Coastline of Scotland*, concludes that this is a very stable feature of the coast. The foundation beneath the thin skin of dunes and sparse shingle ridges seems to be a platform composed of the 25ft (8m) raised beach or perhaps a more ancient rocky reef. It is most likely that Buddon Ness was shaped by tide streams and wave action at a time of higher sea-level, in a wider Tay estuary, some 10,000 years ago.

Carnoustie On the north-eastern edge of Buddon Ness is a golf course that has been described as one of the three best in the world. Golf and a fine sand beach have acquired for Carnoustie a reputation as a family holiday resort. But like that other resort, Monifieth, on the western flank of the Ness, Carnoustie has not been able to avoid Dundee and its industries. Both Carnoustie and Monifieth have seen much housing development as commuter settlements for Dundee and with no bypasses the axial roads of these little resorts hum with traffic.

Arbroath, with a population of 20,000, is a pleasant, plain stone-built Scottish town whose attractiveness has been enhanced of late by the making of a long pedestrian precinct in the main shopping quarter – not a 1960s precinct of glass, concrete, and those artificial stones that look like *tutti frutti*, but a place of grey and red sandstone and the solid façades of Victorian banks.

Historically, Arbroath could lay claim to a role as the capital of Scotland for on 6 April 1320, in the abbey that William the Lion had founded towards the end of the twelfth century, a gathering of noblemen, the Scottish Estates, made a declaration of independence which was despatched to the Pope at Avignon. The abbey, apart from its historic associations, is one of the most striking ruins in the British Isles, despite the sale of its stone by the Town Council as building material during the eighteenth century. Traffic still passes under the Abbey Pend, the gateway that controlled the entrance to the monastery. The walls of red sandstone masonry of its huge church form a jagged line against the sky and in the south transept one can trace the outline of a huge circular window – the round O of Arbroath – that was probably used as a light to guide ships. The Abbot's House, a building of the late-fifteenth century, now shelters a museum of works of Scottish medieval art. Arbroath's charter as a royal burgh was not granted until the sixteenth century. The early history of the town is that of an urban settlement, a port established by the monastery, within the large coastal parish of St Vigeans. The parish church at **St Vigeans**, lying only 1.6km (1 mile) inland in the valley of the Brothick Water, is worth a visit. It stands on a huge mound where the dedication to St Fechin, a seventh-century Irish saint, indicates that he was the probable founder of an early Christian community here. The proof of that Dark Age settlement may be found in the little museum in a cottage close by which houses a collection of thirty-two sculptured stones found on the adjacent church site. Among them, a ninth-century cross-slab, the Drosten Stone, depicts a stag hunt, and at the base of one of the narrow sides are the names of three members of the southern Pictish kingdom.

Towards the end of the past century Arbroath was 'bristling with chimneys of large factories'. The relics of this period, three fine spinning mills, are now objects of interest for the industrial archaeologist. Engineering is still an active industrial interest with the manufacture of printing and adding machines, clutches and gears, lawn mowers and road-making equipment.

Fishing began in the 1830s when families from the hamlet of Auchmithie settled in a new fishing village established by the town council of Arbroath on the West Common. 'Smokies', haddock cured with hardwood chips in the backyards of the cottages of the fishermen's quarter, became one of the most famous products of Arbroath. The fishing hamlet with its narrow lanes and long rows of cottages forms a distinctive quarter in the townscape of the burgh and the pioneers from Auchmithie may still be distinguished in the surnames of Arbroath the Cargills, Spinks, Beatties and Swankies.

The scenery along the coast north and east from Arbroath is some of the finest in eastern Britain. Fine cliffs coincide with the more resistant rocks – basaltic lavas and intrusive dykes or the resistant conglomerates and grits of the Old Red Sandstone. Where weaker rocks abut on the coastline – soft sandstones, shales or deposits of the Ice Age – bays have been carved out by the action of the sea. The cliff-line between Arbroath and Ethie Haven is almost continuous and the details of the scene are varied with stacks, fearsomely narrow inlets, caves noisy with the incessant groan of the North Sea and sudden blow-holes amid the pastures of the cliff top. On the eastern outskirts of Arbroath this fine cliff landscape may be explored along a nature trail established by the Scottish Wildlife Trust in 1971. The Needle E'e, a natural arch on the cliff-face, is situated along the trail and further on, the coast path skirts the edge of Dickmont's Den, a deep narrow inlet or *geo* cut along the line of a joint plane with the pinnacle of a stack at its mouth. Later, Deil's Heid is reached, a bulbous-topped pillar of rock that was shaped as a stack at a time of higher sea-level. The Mermaid's Kirk is a blow-hole connected to the sea by a cave passage that runs for some distance parallel to the general line of the cliffs.

Auchmithie is the only settlement on the cliffed coast between Arbroath and Lunan Bay. A fishing village, it is located just below the cliff top, 46m (150ft) above its little used boat-strand. The most striking coastal feature is Gaylet Pot, a blow-hole that opens into a field some 183m (200yd) from the sea, 36m (120ft) in depth, and from its floor a long cavern reaches to the shore. In summer there are boat trips from Auchmithie to the several sea caves along this cliffed coast.

Northwards from Auchmithie the cliffs come to a fine climax in Red Head a 76m (250ft) high cliff carved out of basalt lavas.

The cliffs come to a sudden end in this rough-hewn promontory of volcanic rocks; beyond lies the long gentle arc of Lunan Bay, its fine sand beach a forerunner of so many of the beaches of eastern Scotland. The Lunan Water winds placidly across a richly farmed countryside to reach the sea through a high barrier of dunes at Red Castle. Apart from the belt of sand dunes, the most striking feature at Lunan Bay is the extent of the 8m (25ft) raised beach, a platform carved out of loose glacial material, clays and sands, at a time of higher sea-level.

Beyond Lunan Bay to the estuary of the South Esk at Montrose a coastline of hard volcanic rocks, of andesite and andesite-basalt, is resumed. But here the cliffs are of no great height. The landscape offers no great excitement, except perhaps that of the North Sea in turmoil among jagged black reefs. The only places of access for the motorist to this little-visited piece of coastline are by minor roads to **Boddin Harbour** and **Fishtown of Usan**. The former has the ruins of a limekiln built by the lairds of Rossie three centuries ago and an extensive prospect across Lunan Bay to the long projecting peninsula at Red Head. Fishtown of Usan is a deserted fishing haven, a boat-strand with the remains of a vaulted ice-house among the rocks for the storage of fish. Its only life is around the coastguard station.

Montrose is an attractive, solid, stone-built town which has grown on a wide shingle spit. To the east of the peninsula lie the links of Montrose, a large tract of blown sand, and beyond is a 6.4km (4 mile) long sand beach. Inland, the town looks out across The Basin, a lagoon of 5sq km (2 square miles) through which the river South Esk drains to the North Sea. At high tide The Basin forms a miniature inland sea; at low water it is a maze of drying mud-banks flanked by a rim of salt-marsh, a gathering place for pink-footed geese at the time of their migration.

The High Street, a wide boulevard flanked by warm grey stone buildings, is not only the focus of the medieval royal burgh but also, as part of the A92 trunk road, a main line of communication in eastern Scotland from the south to Aberdeen. Parallel to the High Street lie the Mid-Links – lawns, gardens and recreation areas developed in about 1800. Montrose Academy, built in the classical style, is a notable piece of architecture. From the Mid-Links, the nineteenth-century residential town and resort reaches out towards the sea. Montrose is attractive with many seventeenth- and eighteenth-century houses, good doorways, pleasant courts and hidden gardens. Its character, marred only by the incessant stream of heavy traffic through the High Street, largely derives from its past function as a winter resort for the rural aristocracy of Angus. Here the local lairds had their town houses where they organised a social round to pass away the wild winter months. Today, the Department of Employment occupies the town house of the Earls of Montrose in Castle Place and another aristocratic home is a newspaper office.

Montrose and its population of less than 11,000 find a living in a varied range of industries. In the eighteenth century tobacco, claret and Baltic timber and flax were its main imports. Today, the docks are still active in the timber trade with Scandinavia, seed potatoes form an important export and Montrose has participated in some unusual and temporary items of trade such as the export, in the 1960s, of disused railway track to the iron-works of the Netherlands and Belgium. The newest activity of this little port is the servicing of the North Sea gas- and oilfields. As a resort, there are 2 golf courses, 5 caravan sites, yachting in the basin, a children's adventure playground, 6.4km (4 miles) of clean sand beach and the sunshine and bracing air of the North Sea coast.

Montrose stands between two rivers, the South and North Esk. The estuary of the North Esk with its sand dunes and salt-marsh forms a notable piece of the Scottish coastline, a place where one of nature's recent catastrophic events may be seen written on the present landscape. Until 1879 the river emptied into the sea 3.2km (2 miles) north of its present mouth.

A flood in 1879 broke through the shingle spit that divided the estuary from the open sea at the present mouth of the North Esk. The former lower end of the river towards St

Cyrus is now occupied by a tract of salt-marsh. The settlement that once flourished at the former river's mouth, known as Ecclesgreig, is marked by a ruined church.

Also to be found on this forlorn shore are the white-washed cottages of a salmon-fishing station, with its thin forest of net-posts standing at drunken angles. The whole coast from the North Esk to St Cyrus is now a National Nature Reserve with a variety of environments contained in its restricted space – a sand beach backed by dunes that reach heights of 15m (50ft), salt marsh and pasture inside the dune barrier, and a cliff-face of rocky ledges, stony aprons and sandy slopes.

Rounding Milton Ness one reaches Tangleha', a relic of a former fishing hamlet with a boat-strand, the ruins of a limekiln and four cottages. Seagreens, across the bay to the north, is another remnant of a once active fishing settlement with a limekiln near the quay and an ice-house that was used for the storage of fish. Most intriguing of all is the lost village of Miltonhaven. Until the end of the eighteenth century it lay on the foreshore, astride a shingle bank that was sheltered from full exposure to the North Sea by a reef of limestone. The quarrying of the limestone led to the destruction of the village when, in 1795, the sea broke through in a storm. Earlier still Miltonhaven had been a prosperous place, a burgh of barony where markets were held and fairs gathered twice a year. Now it is known only as a caravan site close to the shore below Milton of Mathers Farm.

Johnshaven, a place that less than a century ago possessed a fleet of sixty fishing boats. Its terraces of harled cottages, separated by narrow lanes and huddled around little squares, stretch out for more than 1.6km (1 mile) beside a rock-ribbed beach. The track of a long-disused railway from Montrose to Inverbervie winds its way through the village, and at the north end is a caravan site.

Gourdon is the harbour and fishing port of the medieval burgh of Inverbervie, 1.6km (1 mile) north. Sheltered by lofty cliffs to the north, this good harbour developed into an important east-coast fishing port by the middle of the nineteenth century when 100 fishing boats would make for the harvest of the North Sea. Gourdon, in its busy prosperous years, also exported much of the grain harvest of the Mearns.

Inverbervie was founded by a royal charter of David II in 1342. The A92 as it climbs steeply away from the crossing of the Bervie Water forms the main axis of the town, King Street. Inverbervie is coloured by the deep reds of its sandstone cottages, the red sandstone tower of its Victorian church and a raised beach on the seaward side of the town covered with post-war bungalows and caravans.

Catterline is a fishing settlement of single-storey terraces on the cliff's edge. Inland, the Den of Catterline, a steep-sided wooded valley, runs parallel to the coast to leave the village facing the North Sea from a windy, exposed spine. From this high, wedge-shaped bluff Catterline looks down to a crescent-shaped bay of boulders and shingle; out to sea an isolated stack, Forley Crag, stands up from a rocky reef. Caterline gained its reputation as a 'delectable fisher town' after an artists' colony, led by John Eardley of the modern Glasgow School, settled here.

The approach to the fortress of Dunnottar must be one of the most impressive in Scotland. A path drops steeply towards the sea from a parking place beside the A92 trunk road. The fifteenth-century castle raised by the Earls Marischal lies spread out across the summit of its huge cliff-bound rock. One descends by a deep ravine to the foreshore before climbing steeply to the interior of Dunnottar through the gate-house, a solid wall of masonry, 11m (35ft) in height, built into the natural wall of Dunnottar's conglomerate cliff. This is much more than an impressive medieval castle. Dunnottar was the site of an Iron Age fort and, later, an early Christian chapel, dedicated to St Ninian, was built here. By the thirteenth century this was the site of the parish church of Dunnottar, a parish that contained within its bounds the oldest part of the burgh of Stonehaven. It was only the fifteenth century that saw the conversion of Dunnottar into the huge defended site that we know today.

Stonehaven has grown up where two rivers, the Carron Water and the Cowie Water, enter a deeply indented bay between two rocky headlands, Downie Point to the south, composed of conglomerates of Old Red Sandstone age, and Garron Point to the north. Stonehaven was the work of two individuals who engaged in urban development at different periods of time. The Old Town, known as Old Steenie, was the creation of George Keith, 5th Earl Marischal, in the early years of the seventeenth century. Here a harbour was developed in the shelter of Downie Point. The new town of Stonehaven was founded by Robert Barclay of Ury in 1795. With its spacious market square and a connecting grid-iron of streets, the formal pattern of New Stonehaven bears all the marks of a planned town.

After the founding of Robert Barclay's new town and the encouragement of settlers by the granting of plots of land in perpetuity, the greatest step forward in the development of Stonehaven came in the nineteenth century when the harbour was improved by Robert Stevenson. He demolished a rock, Craig-na-Caer, that impeded the harbour entrance, constructed a new sea wall and designed a pair of basins that gave shelter from the North Sea's winter gales. By the end of the century 120 fishing boats worked from Stonehaven. Today, the fishing is no more and only in the holiday season are the harbour basins alive with yachts and pleasure craft. For the holiday-maker, there is a 1.6km (1 mile) long sand beach, a caravan park and camping sites, an eighteen-hole golf course beside the sea, a heated open-air pool and a substantial residential quarter in the high part of the eighteenth-century New Stonehaven with hotels and guest-houses.

Across the Highland Line at Garron Point the deep red cliffs and warm-looking sandy beaches that have coloured the coastal scenery for miles give way to the grits, schists and gneisses of the Dalradian Series. From Stonehaven northwards to Aberdeen a bleak, shelterless cliffed coast meets the North Sea. For several miles the A92 trunk road and the main-line railway run close to the cliff tops and in places one is given passing glimpses of a wild and not easily accessible shore below. The chief settlements are a string of former fishing villages, located usually on the cliff's edge with a boat-strand on the rocky foreshore below.

Muchalls already gives warning that the fast-growing city of Aberdeen lies not far away because several of its fishermen's cottages have been taken oven and restored by commuters. Muchalls Castle, lying 1km (½ mile) inland among wind-blown trees, is a perfect example of a Scottish laird's house of the seventeenth century, with its tall harled walls, angle turrets, steep roof and crow-stepped gables. Inside, the plasterwork ceiling of the Great Hall with the coat-of-arms of the Burnett family ranks among the finest of its kind in Scotland.

Newtonhill, Downies, Portlethen and **Findon** are all practically defunct as active fishing villages. Their exposed tiny shingle beaches where boats were raised out of the water on wooden rails did not favour the survival of an occupation that became concentrated on Aberdeen and Peterhead with their large trawler fleets and fish-processing plants. Of late, all have become outliers of Aberdeen.

The linear, cliffed coastline continues towards Aberdeen, but at Greg Ness, on the very threshold of the city, a deep embayment, Nigg Bay, causes a break in the long rock-bound façade of Kincardineshire. The minor road that runs close to the sea from Cove Bay, encircling Nigg Bay and Girdle Ness, makes an attractive approach to Aberdeen. The Bay, with some 20ha (50 acres) of land behind the foreshore owned by the city, is reckoned among the public open spaces of Aberdeen. Its main interest is the ruined medieval church of the seventh-century hermit St Fittick and, just below the unfenced road where it skirts the sea-shore, is the site of St Fittick's Well.

Aberdeen Rounding Girdle Ness, crowned by the 40m (130ft) high stack of Robert Stevenson's lighthouse raised in 1831, Aberdeen comes into full view across its harbour, busy with the constant traffic of supply vessels to the oilfields scattered across the North Sea. Across the three dock basins, a jumble of warehouses, fish-processing and ice plants, rise the pinnacled towers and modern office-blocks of this silver-grey city. Aberdeen displays bright, untarnished harshness on its unsheltered North Sea shore between the mouths of Dee and Don. Only the grey haar that drifts inland from the cold sea on the days of early spring and summer is able to soften the harsh clear lines of this granite city.

This is Scotland's third city, with a population of 185,000. As the main focus for the exploitation of the new-found energy resources under the North Sea, Aberdeen seems set to become the economic capital of northern Britain. The earliest firm evidence of a town at Aberdeen goes back to 1179, the year when a royal charter was granted by William the Lion, although the terms of William's charter show that an urban society was already in existence. The most important links with Aberdeen's past are the cathedral of St Machar and the oldest buildings of the university. All that remains of St Machar's Cathedral, situated in the quiet, cobbled, tree-shaded lanes of the Chanonry, is the nave. The choir was demolished in the Reformation and the central tower, weakened by the destruction of the choir, collapsed and crushed the transepts during a storm at the end of the seventeenth century. Today, St Machar's consists of the nave of the medieval church that itself was the successor to more than one earlier place of worship at this site. The great treasure of St Machar's is the high wooden ceiling decorated with forty-eight heraldic shields. Bishop Elphinstone, the founder of King's College, secured a papal bull for the creation of a university at Aberdeen in 1494, the fourth oldest university in Britain. The chapel from that date survives. Above its fine timbered and vaulted roof rises the Crown Tower, a sculptured stone crown in the shape of that of the Holy Roman Emperor to show that the university belonged to the whole of Christendom.

New Aberdeen, above the harbour, also has its historical roots in the fourteenth century, when it was a fishing hamlet. The critical years in the shaping of Aberdeen were at the beginning of the nineteenth century. In 1800 an Act of Parliament authorised the making of Union Street, so named to commemorate the Union of Great Britain and Ireland. To make this mile-long street – the shopping centre and axis of modern Aberdeen – a densely built quarter of the old town was cleared and a hill was also removed. Even so the topographical problems involved in the making of the new street were immense. It is built on a succession of bridges, the finest of which, designed by Telford, carries the road across the ravine of the Denburn. The ambitious development of Union Street bankrupted the city to the extent of £¼ million. Marischal College, the other part of Aberdeen University, was founded in 1593 by George Keith, 5th Earl Marischal, as a Protestant counterpart to the Catholic King's College. In 1860 the two colleges were united to form the University of Aberdeen. The building of Marischal College was started in 1844 by the famous local architect Archibald Simpson who had a vision of 'a planned silver city by the sea'. It was completed only in 1905 with Marshall Mackenzie's 'thrusting spires and buttresses'. Opinion about the aesthetic qualities of Marischal College have varied widely. It has been described as 'a wedding cake in indigestible grey icing'; to others, this grey mountain of sculptured granite at the heart of the city justifies itself as 'the second largest granite building in Europe after the Escorial'.

Aberdeen, small as it is, stands richly endowed with churches. St Nicholas, the mother church of New Aberdeen, has a huge graveyard that runs down to Union Street from which it is screened by an Ionic colonnade, a replica of that at Hyde Park Corner in London. At the Reformation, St Nicholas Church was divided into two – the East Church in the former medieval choir and the West Church in the nave. Today, St Nicholas represents a compact example of different periods and styles of ecclesiastical architecture. The crypt is the only surviving part of the medieval church. The West Church, known as the Auld Kirk, was rebuilt in 1751 by the Aberdeen architect James Gibbs. With its dark oak box pews and galleries, it is the place where civic dignitaries gather to worship on public occasions. The East Church was demolished and rebuilt in Gothic granite by Archibald Simpson in 1834. Aberdeen has two other cathedrals – the Episcopal Cathedral in King Street, built in 1817, and the Roman Catholic Cathedral of St Mary of the Assumption.

The harbour, the economic focus of Aberdeen, grew at the outfall of the Denburn into the sandy estuary of the Dee. The shape of the coastline hereabouts has been changed radically down the centuries by the forces of nature and at the hand of man. In about 1800 work began on the improvement of the harbour whose chief defect, apart from the need for proper wharfage, lay in the sandbanks that choked the Dee Estuary. Three dock basins now reach from the lower river towards the heart of the city. One of the main objects in their design was to isolate shipping from the turbulent floods of the Dee. The Albert Basin is the headquarters of Aberdeen's fleet of long-range trawlers. Here are the fish-meal processing plants, fertiliser works, kippering sheds, fish-box factories, boat-, net- and rope-yards and ice plants that serve the industry of the North Atlantic. The Victoria Dock is the terminus for ferry services to Shetland.

The long sandy beach that stretches between Dee and Don fulfils an equally important function in the life of Aberdeen, and also of Scotland as a whole. With its beach amusements park, ballroom, playgrounds and links, as well as all the nearby amenities of the city, here can be said to be one of the leading holiday resorts in the northern part of Britain.

It is worthwhile to visit the western suburbs of the city to see the Rubislaw quarries that were opened up during the eighteenth century and which closed in 1970. The building of Aberdeen and the export of granite for the street paving of many other towns has left a hole 137m (450ft) deep in the ground.

17 North-east Scotland

A straight low shore-line of wide sandy beaches and a continuous belt of dunes stretches northwards for 19km (12 miles) from the Dee estuary. This is one of the longest unbroken line of dunes in Highland Scotland; in places the wind-sculptured sand-hills of the succession of links – Balgownie Links, Blackdog Links, Eigie Links, Foveran Links and the Sands of Forvie – reach to over 21m (70ft) in height. North of the Ythan Estuary, in the Sands of Forvie, the summit of the highest dune touches 57m (187ft) above sea-level. Behind and among the dunes are found marshy hollows, richly coloured with wild flowers in summer and often flooded in winter. Although this fine stretch of sea-shore lies so close to a large and busy city it has seen very little development, apart from a golf course at Balgownie, a caravan park at Balmedie and a rifle range on the Blackdog Links. The only important break in the wall of dunes occurs where the river Ythan empties into the North Sea. Its eastern shore is flanked by the wasteland of the Sands of Forvie, 'a miniature Sahara', as it has been described. To the west, fields and woods reach down to the quiet estuary that is one of the chief resting grounds for migrant greylag geese. It is a prosperous, well-formed landscape, the outcome of the Improving Movement – the revolution in agriculture that deeply affected the life and economy of eastern Scotland from the early years of the eighteenth century until the 1880s. The new farms that arose during this period may be recognised by the place-name 'mains'.

Newburgh, as the name implies, is a newly founded settlement within the older established parish of Foveran. However, this pleasant little place, on an inlet of the Ythan's estuary made by the Foveran Burn, was already in existence at the end of the eighteenth century when *The Old Statistical Account* of 1793 described it as 'a dirty place in pleasant and commodious situation, with six or seven alehouses'. Lying scarcely 1.6km (1 mile) from the open sea, Newburgh came into existence as the port of Ellon – the little inland burgh of the Ythan valley that lays claim to an historic role as the capital of Buchan. Today, an old vaulted ice-house remains from former days of the salmon fisheries and down on the point of Inches that reaches out among the mud-banks of the Ythan estuary are the only remains of a pre-Reformation chapel in the burial vault of the Udny family. At the northern end of this straggly village is a field centre belonging to Aberdeen University for research in zoology and ornithology.

The massive dune hills of the Sands of Forvie reach northwards to the outskirts of Collieston. The oldest, longest and most northerly dunes have been fixed by vegetation and seem to be no longer on the move. Periods of great gales bring about a considerable amount of movement and sand-drifting among the younger dunes at the south end of the peninsula. Sand has gathered over the peninsula for at least 4,000 years. In recent times the shifting sands have uncovered evidence of prehistoric man. Over 6,000 years ago a community of hunters lived here and there is evidence of Bronze Age and Iron Age settlers. The remains of a medieval chapel, dedicated to St Fidamnan, who died in AD 704, have also been uncovered. By the end of the sixteenth

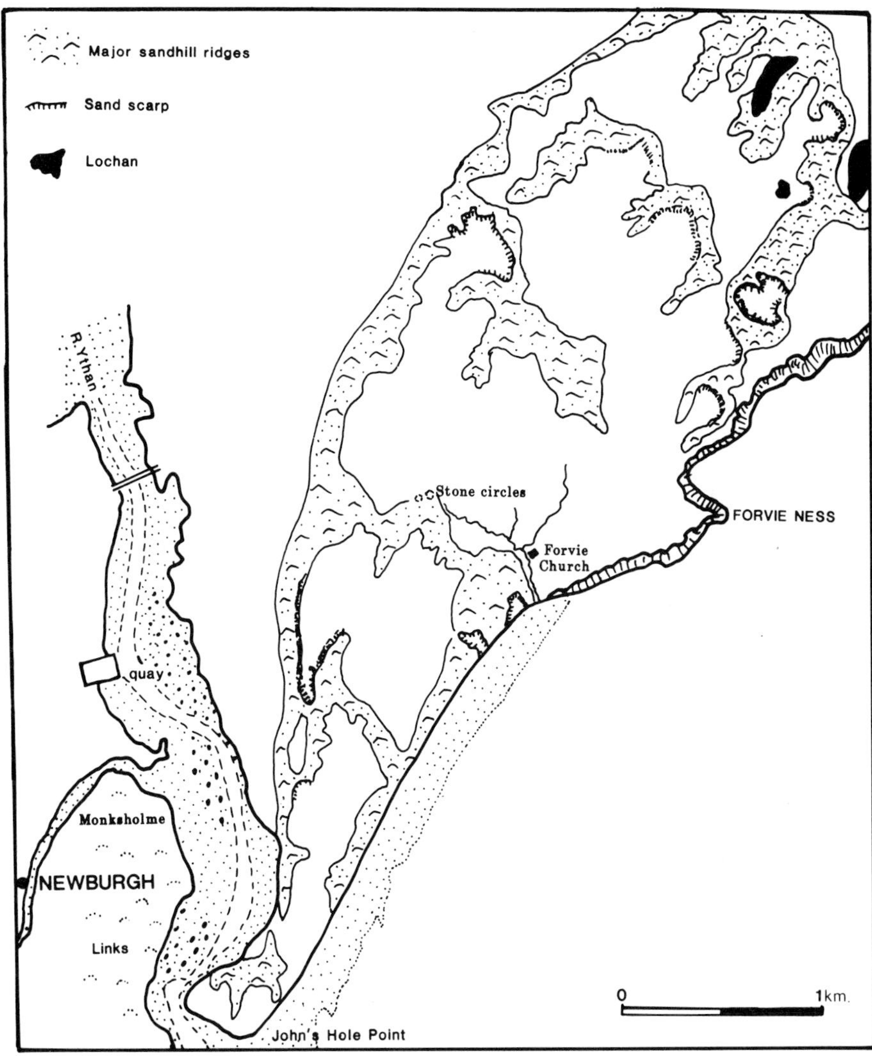

The Sands of Forvie (*in part after Landsberg*)

century Forvie's chapel was united with the neighbouring parish of Slains and a century later it was lost without trace beneath the sands. Today, Forvie is a National Nature Reserve managed by the Nature Conservancy Council. It boasts the largest concentration of eider duck in Britain and there are colonies of terns, kittiwakes, fulmars, shelduck and oystercatchers. To reach the Sands of Forvie take the track that winds through the dunes from the A975, starting close to the bridge across the Ythan. There is no access to the south end of the peninsula during the breeding season from April to July.

At Collieston the seemingly unending sand beaches and links of Aberdeen Bay give way to a harsh cliff-bound coast of ancient schists and granite. Between Collieston and Cruden Bay Dalradian schists form a coastal plateau at a height of about 61m (200ft) above present sea-level. Where the Buchan plateau meets the coast, Buchan's dullness gives way to an exciting landscape of cliff-bound coves, stacks, rocky cauldrons and caves. At Skares

Reef, at the southern flank of the Bay of Cruden, Dalradian schists are replaced by the pink granites that reach northwards to Peterhead. The granite coast is if anything wilder and more spectacular than the schist cliff-line to the south. The joint planes in the pink rock provide zones of weakness for the erosive action of the sea. Intruded dykes of igneous rock - dolerite - form another weakness in the granite armour that has been exploited by wave action. One of the most striking sections of this coastline, and easily accessible, is the huge cauldron 46km (150ft) in depth, known as the Bullers of Buchan, that reaches out to the open sea through a fearsome arch in the granite cliffs. The main A975 road from Aberdeen to Peterhead runs close to the cliff top at this point and from a car-parking place a path leads to the cliff's edge. On stormy days with the wind set from the north-east the sea spouts in this huge granite cauldron, hence the name - 'the boilers' of Buchan.The place has achieved fame by its entry into literature. Boswell and Johnson came as tourists when they stayed at New Slains Castle. It is said they followed the vertiginous footpath around the lip of the cauldron and also entered the Buller by boat. Johnson, with a characteristic phrase, described the place as 'a rock perpendicularly tubulated'. Scott, too, who wove so much of Scotland into his romances, put this fragment of the coast into *The Antiquary.*

Collieston has changed over the years from a fishing harbour to a quiet seaside resort. The harbour is safe for bathing and many of the cottages are now holiday homes.

Cruden Bay The earliest settlement here, known as the Ward of Cruden, was located on the north side of the low headland that shelters the present harbour of Port Erroll. Here a tortuously narrow inlet is situated beneath the ruin of New Slains Castle. Through this winding narrow inlet in the granite cliffs the Water of Cruden emptied into the North Sea. Access to the harbour and to the fishing hamlet was perilous in all but the calmest seas. It was the 19th Earl of Erroll who decided, in 1875, to develop a safer harbour, named Port Erroll, within the northern arm of Cruden Bay. In 1899 The Great North of Scotland Railway opened a luxurious hotel, built of Peterhead granite, at Cruden Bay. For forty years Cruden Bay maintained a fashionable reputation for golf and sea-bathing. The hotel was taken over by the Army in 1939 and was demolished in 1947. Port Erroll is now a picturesque deserted harbour and Cruden Bay is a place of holiday chalets and caravans. This sandy, dune-fringed bay has found a new role, for the pipeline from the Forties oilfield has been brought ashore here owing largely to the ease of driving an underground pipeline through the loose sands.

Peterhead With a population of 13,500, Peterhead is the largest town of eastern Scotland between Aberdeen and Inverness. Peterhead came into existence as a burgh of barony, founded by George, 5th Earl Marischal, in 1593. The burgh with its tall castle was confined to the off shore granite island of Keith Inch. Nothing now remains of the original Peterhead. The castle has vanished; it has become a place of warehouses and all the clutter that belongs to a busy harbour. In its latest transformation Keith Inch has become the base for the numerous service facilities of the oil and gas industries.

During the eighteenth century Peterhead expanded across its narrow harbour channel to the mainland when the severely regular grid-iron plan of the streets in this red granite burgh was laid down. The Town House at the top of Broad Street, designed by John Baxter, symbolises the period of expansion. At the foot of Broad Street stands the handsome Georgian Arbuthnot House, now, with its ship models and harpoons, a museum of the extinct whaling industry.

The seventeenth-century town of Peterhead contented itself with the natural shelter given by the North and South Harbours between Keith Inch and the mainland. Improvements were made during the eighteenth and nineteenth centuries, but the construction of a harbour of refuge at the end of the nineteenth century made Peterhead the most important port in Buchan. A prison was built at Salthouse Head on the southern shore of the bay in 1886 and convicts were set to work on the

914m (3,000 ft) long granite barrier of the South Breakwater. In 1956 the waters of Peterhead Bay became even safer with the completion of the North Breakwater that reaches out from Keith Inch.

From 1793 to 1893 Peterhead was more important as a whaling port than Aberdeen. Failure to adopt the steam-driven whaler, new harpoons and to embark on long voyages to the Antarctic led to the extinction of the industry. Since the 1820s the prosperity of Peterhead has rested mainly on herring fishing, although by 1955 the output of the North Sea herring fisheries had fallen into a steep decline. However, since 1972 the town has become a focus for the exploitation of the oil and gas fields of the North Sea, with pipe laying industries supplying materials and servicing derricks and production platforms far out to sea.

Between Peterhead and Fraserburgh the coastline is again of long sand beaches backed by miles of mountainous dunes. Kirkton Head, Scotstown Head, Rattray Head and Inzie Head project forward from the long curving arcs of tide-washed sands. Between 1871 and 1873 the long ridge of low-lying rocks at Rattray Head, scarely awash at any state of tide, claimed twenty-four wrecks. In 1895 this danger point of Buchan's coast was marked by the building of a lighthouse on the Ron Rock. For miles between Peterhead and St Combs this is an utterly deserted shore with no easy direct access from the A952 trunk road.

At **St Fergus** bare, treeless fields lead down to a barrier of sand-hills and a 10km (6 mile) long beach. On the edge of the sandy links stands the ruin of a medieval chapel, dedicated to St Fergus. The twentieth century has made its mark on this lonely coast for a terminal for the Frigg and Brent gasfields has been built here. One piece of this coast not to be missed can be reached by the lane that leads towards Rattray Head from the A952 1.6 km (1 mile) south of Crimond. The road skirts the marshy shore of the Loch of Strathbeg at Old Rattray; a rough track then leads through a mountainous range of dunes to reach the foreshore close to Rattray Head. This part of the Scottish coastline has profoundly changed its shape and its value for mankind over the past few thousand years. In Late Glacial times a wide bay occupied the present site of the Loch of Strathbeg, stretching inland as far as the line of today's trunk road between Peterhead and Fraserburgh. A shingle spit gradually built up across the mouth of the bay from its northern flank at Inzie Head. Professor J. A. Steers observes that this dune-covered shingle bar stands well above present sea-level, an indication that its formation began several thousand years ago at a time when the sea stood 6m (20ft) and more above its present level. The final closing of the lagoon behind the shingle bar and its conversion into the freshwater Loch of Strathbeg took place in the eighteenth century. Until then passage to the sea led through a tortuous sand-choked channel around the southern end of the spit, close to the present site of Old Rattray. Tradition remembers a great easterly storm in 1720 that finally closed the entrance to the lagoon; and it is said that a ship, loaded with a cargo of slates, was trapped in the harbour of Old Rattray.

Within 10km (6 miles) of Fraserburgh are five fishing settlements whose fisheries have died with the concentration of the industry in the burgh. **St Combs**, **Inverallochy** and **Cairnbulg** occupy the blunt headland eastward of the curving arc of sands in Fraserburgh Bay. None of them possesses a man-made harbour; boats were drawn on to the foreshore under the gable-ends of the single-storey cottages. St Combs still has a fragment of a ruined medieval church, abandoned in 1607, dedicated to St Columba. The fishing village itself, a score of cottages along the shore, was founded in 1771 by the Laird of Cairness. Today, these are commuter settlements for fishermen employed in Fraserburgh and Aberdeen.

Fraserburgh belongs to those numerous sea-shore burghs that came into being on the initiative of a landowner. Sir Alexander Fraser, 7th Laird of Phillorth, obtained a charter in 1546 'to build a harbour in which ships overtaken by storms may find refuge' and to 'erect the town of Faithlie into a free burgh of barony'. A quarter of a century later Alexander Fraser's grandson was engaged in laying out the town and in building a castle.

The Castle of Dundarg, 'the red fort', perched on a promontory of Old Red Sandstone

Kinnairds Head Castle still stands at the head of a street of grey warehouses and terraced houses. Its keep has survived because in 1787 the Commissioners of Northern Lights used the derelict building as the base for the lantern chamber of one of the earliest lighthouses in Britain. Fraserburgh has not achieved all that its guiding lairds of the sixteenth century intended. In 1592 a charter to establish a university was granted by King James VI. Failure followed within a decade and the place where a university might have been is known today only in a street name, College Bounds. In the eighteenth century the Frasers rose to the title of Lord Saltoun. In the heart of this grey, windy, Georgian town, remain the mercat cross in Saltoun Square, a statue of a Lord Saltoun in a high domed tower over the Victorian Town House, and on the south side of the parish church the Fraser mausoleum, a stepped pyramid of stone.

Fraserburgh has escaped the direct impact of the modern energy industries. Its chief occupation is still with fishing. In 1900 it had a fleet of 800 sail-boats, but it moved with the technical and economic changes and in the 1930s her fishermen took up the seine net and entered the white-fish trade. Her complex group of harbours – Faithlie, Outer, Inner and Balaclava – with their fish-processing and cold-storage plants attracted fishermen and their boats from the dying villages along the adjacent coastline. Fraserburgh can boast one link with the history of communications for it was here that Marconi set up an experimental station that made contact with a transmitter at Poldhu in Cornwall, and on the municipal housing estate we find Marconi Road and Marconi Terrace.

The Moray Firth

Along the southern shore of the Moray Firth between Fraserburgh and Inverness are 91m (300ft) cliffs where secret coves shelter fishing villages that have been compared with those of Cornwall. To explore some of the features of this coastline, the 'Banffshire Riviera', take the B9031 out of Fraserburgh

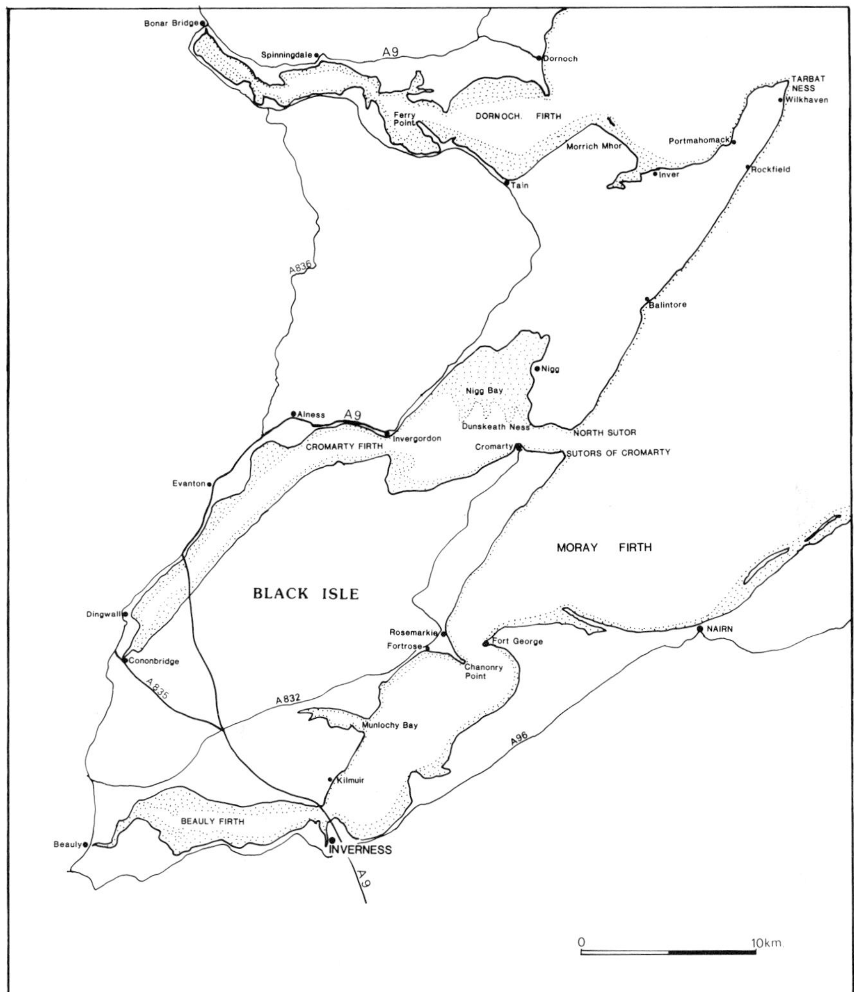

The 'firths' coastline and the Black Isle

for Macduff and Banff. 'Riviera' seems hardly the right word to describe a shore that looks directly into the eye of northerly gales and which turns its back on the sun. 'Rivieras' bask in the sunshine beneath their sheltering cliffs; here one feels that a fresh meaning has been added to the term, one that is in keeping with the harsh puritanism of the fishing communities that found little shelter beneath these cliffs. Riviera or not, it is certainly true that this is 'one of the least known and most underrated of Scottish coasts' (J. B. Whittow).

Rosehearty is typical of the seventy and more fishing villages that are strung out along the 241km (150 miles) of Scotland's east coast. Fishing as a local industry is now almost extinct for Fraserburgh has eclipsed its neighbours since the beginning of this century. Before the onset of its decline, almost a century ago, 130 boats worked out of Rosehearty. And that decline seems to be written on the landscape as one looks across the empty harbour to the breakwater where a huge gash made by some winter storm remains unrepaired. The Castle of Dundarg, perched on a sea-bound promontory of Old Red Sandstone, is well named for *dun dearg* means the red fort. It was a stronghold in

Iron Age times, one of the sea defences of the kingdom of the northern Picts. Later, a Dark Age community of monks took over the Pictish fort. The thirteenth century saw the building of a strong castle within the earthworks of the Dark Age fort by the Comyn Earls of Buchan. Today, as we follow the narrow footpath down to Dundarg with a wide sea horizon before us, we can see few remains of this long history. There are the grass-grown foundations of the medieval castle, blurred imprints of lost centuries, the ditch of a Pictish fort that was widened into a moat by the castle-builders of the thirteenth century.

The villages of Pennan, Crovie and Gardenstown raise images of Cornwall, but analogies are superficial, perhaps odious. Most of Cornwall's fishing villages secrete themselves in long quiet estuaries; here a rim of stone cottages, gable end to the sea, may cling to the edge of a narrow raised-beach platform full in the face of the battering North Sea. Latitude and climate also play their part in shaping the personality of this coast. This is northern Britain, where winter reigns for almost three-quarters of the year and the aurora borealis can be expected to light up a polar sky undimmed by the glare of cities. Fishing communities everywhere in Britain may have been closed, specialised, inward turning groups, at least before modern technology concentrated our fisheries in a few large centres, but in north-east Scotland religion has added a special flavour to the social geography. Where else may one find a harbour entrance with the inscription 'God is Love' in bold white letters?

Pennan The little used harbour of this picturesque fishing village cowers beneath the vertical red sandstone cliff of Pennan Head. Once it employed forty boats and her fishermen reached out to the Hebrides and the fishing grounds off western Norway. Today, several of the brightly painted cottages, built of huge roughly shaped blocks of red sandstone with pale-pink pantiled roofs, serve as holiday homes. By the beginning of October, the staple occupation of fishing long since vanished, the place dies. At the Lion's Head, 1km (½ mile) along the coast from Pennan, a deep cave reaches

Hell's Lum, a spectacular blow-hole near Pennan

Forty fishing boats once crammed the now largely deserted harbour of Pennan

under the promontory to end in a blow-hole known as Hell's Lum. At times of strong on-shore winds columns of spray are blown upwards through this vertical chasm, looking like smoke from some subterranean fire.

Two fishing villages, separated by a crumbling footpath of only a few hundred yards, crouch at the edge of Gamrie Bay, a precipitous ring of red rock.

Gardenstown is a laird's creation, founded by Garden of Troup in 1720. A lane from the main coast road, the B9032, falls through a series of hairpin bends where the terraced cottages and warehouses cling to the cliff-face.

Crovie, of a much simpler plan, consists of a line of forty cottages that cling to the shore-line without space for a street. The oil lamps in the little windows of gable-ends facing the sea have no need to burn now on dark winter nights because the fishermen have largely migrated to Fraserburgh and Macduff. Crovie now is given over to holiday cottages, some occupied throughout the year. On the very brink of Gamrie Bay Gardenstown and Crovie are not immune to the ravages of the North Sea. The storm surge that swept the coast of eastern Britain at a time of high spring tide in late January 1953 destroyed two cottages in Gardenstown, battered the sea-wall and demolished part of the cliff-foot path that leads to Crovie.

Macduff Until 1783 this former fishing and farming township was known as Doune; then the 2nd Earl of Fife, developer and owner of the harbour, attached his family name to the growing port. Macduff possesses the largest harbour between Fraserburgh and Buckie. Unlike its neighbouring fishing villages, Macduff succeeded in keeping abreast of the changes that faced the industry at the turn of this century. It is claimed that Macduff is now the safest haven for fishing boats among all the ports of the Moray coast and that her fishermen lose only one month of the year through bad weather.

Macduff has a modest claim as a holiday resort. There is a sand beach at the mouth of the Devoran in Banff Bay, an eighteen-hole golf course, the Royal Tarlair, from

The cottages of Crovie, built along the inner edge of a raised beach protected by a sea wall

which fine views open up along the high cliffed coastline towards Troup Head. Tarlair, a rocky bay 1km (½ mile) to the east, had some reputation as a spa in the last century. Now it is the site of an open-air swimming pool in the natural frame of the rocky bay.

Banff Visually, Banff is an almost perfect realisation of Georgian eighteenth-century Scotland. Its two main streets, at the top and the foot of a steep slope parallel to the shore, are composed of ranges of stone-built houses from the seventeenth and eighteenth centuries. A plain classical style pervades the town's buildings. St Mary's parish church at the east end of High Street was built in 1790 and based on the design of St Andrew's, Dundee. The former Free Church in Castle Street displays a cupola and pillared portico characteristic of the classical revival of the early years of the nineteenth century. The Town House dates from the same years at the close of the eighteenth century when Banff was a prosperous country town, a place where the lairds of country estates came to build their town houses and gathered for the social life of the winter months. Classicism of the early nineteenth century is the theme that runs through the buildings of Banff. The richest architectural treasure is Duff House whose estate occupies the left bank of the Devoran above Smeaton's seven-arched bridge. This is one of the great houses of Scotland, built between 1725 and 1740 from the designs of William Adam for William Duff, later 1st Earl of Fife and Viscount Macduff.

The first charter, as a royal burgh, was given to Banff by Malcom IV, in 1163. As a medieval port it was a member of the Hanseatic League. Of the medieval burgh little is left. Castle Street recalls the site of the medieval castle, and all that remains of the first parish church, near the harbour, is the sixteenth-century burial aisle of the Ogilvies of Dunlugas.

With a population of less than 4,000, Banff acts as a shopping centre for a wide countryside. It has much to offer as a select holiday resort – the Royal Duff House Golf Club, fishing for salmon and sea trout in the

Devoran, water-skiing, good sands, and a town built in perhaps the greatest period of architecture in Scotland.

Portsoy was created a burgh of barony in 1550 and the first harbour was built by Sir Patrick Ogilvie of Boyne before the end of the sixteenth century. In 1825 the Earl of Seafield constructed the new harbour alongside the old one; it was destroyed by a storm in 1839 and was only rebuilt in 1884 at the time of the North Sea's herring-fishing boom. Portsoy has lost its fishing fleet to Buckie and Macduff; now the harbours are filled with yachts and a few lobster boats. The old harbour with its cluster of warehouses and eighteenth-century buildings has recently been much restored, and its harled and white-washed houses have won a Saltire Society Award for the careful renewal of a fragment of Scotland's past.

Cullen with its 3.2km (2 miles) of white sand beach is a most attractive place. It has three distinct parts: Seatown, where the cottages stand gable-end to the street; New Town, a planned settlement of the 1820s; and Old Cullen, close to the old parish church and Cullen House, the site of the medieval royal burgh that was destroyed at the making of the New Town. In 1817 the Earl of Seafield built the harbour that became the base for a large herring fleet by the latter half of the century. By 1822 he decided that the town that had been granted a charter from William the Lion before the end of the twelfth century should be removed from the precinct of Cullen House. The plan for the new town with its wide streets and central square was designed by George MacWilliam. A seventeenth-century market cross that had stood on Castle Hill within the bounds of the Seafield estate was moved to the square in New Town in 1871. A new church was built in the main street in 1839.

St Mary's Church, the only visible relic of the medieval burgh, stands close to Cullen House. The majority of pre-Reformation church sites stand roofless in their graveyards in windy places – witnesses not only to changing patterns of settlement but to a form of Christianity that no longer expressed itself in chancel and nave but through the tall pulpit squarely set among its congregation. Inside, St Mary's shows itself not only as a parish church, but also as the memorial chapel of an aristocratic family who were the makers of national as well as local history.

Today, Cullen lives mainly as a holiday resort. To the west, a long sandy beach is flanked by a fine eighteen-hole golf course. There are two caravan parks – the burgh park on the cliff top to the east and another occupying a wooded ravine on the Seafield estate.

Portknockie The first settlement was made here in 1677 by fishermen who had migrated from Old Cullen. In the hey-day of the herring fisheries Portknockie owned 140 boats and in 1888 the Earl of Seafield built a harbour to replace the natural shelter that had been used among the rocky clefts. The owners of Portknockie's fishing boats all work their craft out of Buckie and the abandoned harbour has use only as a paddling pool.

Findochty was founded in 1716 as a haven for fishermen from Fraserburgh. In 1833 improvements were made to Findochty's harbour and a new estate town was laid out to the design of George MacWilliam, who, as we have seen, was also employed by the Earl of Seafield in the planning of New Cullen. By the 1880s over 100 fishing boats were based here; now the harbour is used only by lobster boats and pleasure craft. The harbour quarters belong to the picturesque, but their late development over a restricted span of time in the years about 1800 means that they lack the variety of townscape of the ports of the Fife coastline. Here the neat rows of cottages, painted in glistening greys and black with the courses of mortar outlined in white, blues and greens, provide some diversity in a string of monotonous villages planted beside a grey sea.

Buckie At the approach to Buckie the long section of coast shaped out of the Dalradian rocks gives way to a line of cliffs carved out of horizontal beds of the Old Red Sandstone at a time of higher sea-level. A rim of raised beach lies at the foot of the cliffs where the long harbour settlement of Buckie and its adjacent hamlets has grown up. Buckie achieved burghal status only in 1888. A string of coastal fishing hamlets already in existence in the eighteenth century – Buckpool, Seatown at the mouth of the Buckie Burn, Gordonsburgh, Ianstown and Portessie – were gathered together in the late Victorian burgh. Portessie was established in 1727 by the laird of Rannas, and the 4th Duke of Gordon founded the harbour of Portgordon in 1797.

Buckie owes its success and survival as a fishing port to the initiative of Gordon of Cluny who created a harbour of refuge here in 1872. Cluny Harbour with its four basins and outer haven finds accommodation for some 400 vessels, and associated with the harbour are ice-works, curing establishments, ship-chandlers, boatyards and fish-market sheds. Buckie has survived all the technological changes of the fishing industry, drawing to itself fishermen from declining harbours along the Moray coast. Buckie is divided in two by the line of the fossil cliff carved at a time of higher sea-level. The main A990 road threads its way along the raised beach at the cliff's foot through the former fishing hamlets and the industrial clutter of the modern port. On the cliff top above the harbour stands an orderly plan of a Victorian town. Here is the main shopping street, West and East Church Street linked by Cluny Square. The only landmarks in Buckie are two churches – the North Church, built in 1835 and rebuilt in 1880, and the impressive twin-spired Catholic church at the west end of the town. There is a small maritime museum with an exposition of a history of the fishing industry, as well as a collection of the paintings of Peter Anson who took his themes from the fishing ports of the north-east.

At Portgordon the cliffed coastline that has been the dominant scenic element for many miles comes to an abrupt end. Westward the shore of the Moray Firth is mainly composed of wide sandy bays where thousands of acres of planted woodland come close to the sea in Lossie Forest, Roseisle Forest and the Culbin Sands. From Portgordon to Lossiemouth the ruler-straight shore of Spey Bay is marked by parallel ridges of shingle, ridges constructed by wave action over the past few thousand years. Two considerable rivers, the Spey and Lossie, enter the sea here, and the changes in their courses during recent times through the coastal wilderness of shingle and sand-dune suggests the complexity of the processes at work in the making of this part of the Scottish coastline. Steers, in his comments on the mouth of the Spey, has written of 'a short stretch of coast that changes as much as, even if not more than, any other section of the coast of these islands'. Floods, sometimes of great violence, cause the river to reshape its channel, especially in the final mile where the Spey breaks through a succession of shingle ridges towards the sea. As recently as 1960 a severe flood washed away two houses in Kingston and in 1962 this uncertain river broke through the spit, at its mouth, to find a yet different exit into the North Sea.

Garmouth, a pleasant place of narrow winding lanes and white harled cottages, was a small medieval port raised to the status of a burgh of barony by the Laird of Innes in 1587. The fickleness of the Spey has helped to determine the decline of Garmouth as a port, where a nine-hole golf course now occupies the site of the medieval harbour. But Garmouth's decline is also connected with the rise of **Kingston**, founded in 1784 by migrant shipwrights from Kingston-on-Hull who settled here to make use of the abundant supplies of timber that were rafted down the Spey from the Highland forests of Abernethy and Rothiemurchus. An 1862 directory shows that Garmouth and Kingston had 25 shipowners, shipbuilders and ship masters, and that 57 carpenters and joiners lived and worked here. Kingston as an industrial centre died with the passing of wooden ships, but at its height there were 7 shipyards and in all more than 300 ships, clippers and Cape-Horners were built here. Today, Kingston is a desolate place – a shingle-shore with parallel lanes of single-storeyed cottages, corrugated-iron roofs, an untidy tangle of wires. There is no trace of the shipyards of a century ago – storms and shifting shingle have erased all traces from the open foreshore where the industry was located.

Lossiemouth The expansion of the fishing industry in the nineteenth century is written on the landscape with the building of a whole new town on the fringe of an older settlement. The oldest part of Lossiemouth, Seatown, dates to 1698 when the Town Council of Elgin acquired 32ha (80 acres) of land at the mouth of the Lossie for the development of a port. Today, this fishermen's settlement is an isolated huddle of whitewashed cottages on a sandy neck of land at the mouth of the Lossie. The name Lossiemouth was not attached to the new port until 1764, when the streets of a new quarter – a grid-iron plan of four main streets, crossing lanes and a market place – were laid down on the rising ground to the west. In 1834 a new harbour was carved out of the rocky headland to the west of the sandbank-choked mouth of the Lossie. At the same time a new settlement, **Branderburgh,** was founded by the owner of lands adjacent to the new harbour, Colonel Brander of Kinnedar. Branderburgh's spacious streets and solid stone villas rise from the shore to a central St James Square.

The period of fastest urban growth coincides with the peak decades of the herring fisheries between 1840 and 1890, and the summit of Lossiemouth's prosperity belongs to the years before World War I with the rich harvests brought by the steam drifters. Since the 1930s Lossiemouth's fleet of some fifty seine-net boats has been concerned solely with white fishing in grounds as far away as the Hebrides and the coasts of Northern Ireland, as well as the North Sea. After Buckie, it is the busiest harbour of this coastline. The present population of the burgh – a status which was acquired in 1890 with the amalgamation of Lossiemouth, Branderburgh and Stotfield – approaches 6,000.

Apart from fishing, its service industries and marketing, Lossiemouth has a reputation as a holiday resort. It is not the only place to claim the lowest rainfall in Scotland, but apart from its exhilarating climate Lossiemouth offers fine sand beaches and sea-bathing, two caravan and camping sites and the championship course of the Moray Golf Club.

The two headlands at Branderburgh and Burghead are separated by some 10km (6 miles) of low sandstone cliffs. When sea-levels stood higher, caves were eroded along the line of cliffs. The Sculptured Cave, a couple of kilometres (one mile) west of Covesea, is known for a dozen incised symbols in its soft sandstone walls that date from the centuries of the Dark Age Pictish kingdom.

Hopeman stretches from the Lossiemouth–Burghead road (B9040) towards a tiny exposed harbour – a dull, grid-iron pattern of terraced cottages. The fishing settlement was established in about 1800 when peasant communities were cleared from the good lands of the interior to make way for the efficient, isolated farms of improving landlords. Hopeman still possesses a handful of fishing boats that take their catch to the Lossiemouth market, but now its harbour largely serves summer holiday craft. The most notable landmark is the tall clock-tower of the church by the main road at the top of the village, a gift in 1923 from an Elgin distiller who worshipped here.

Burghead The approach to Burghead is marked by the 152m (500ft) masts of a BBC transmitter. The long streets of grey cottages that reach down the peninsula indicate a planned nineteenth-century settlement. In 1807 a group of local landowners formed a company to build a harbour and lay out afresh the village known as Burgsea until that time. Building stone was at hand, quarried and ready shaped, in one of Scotland's most important prehistoric sites – a triple-ramparted earthwork at the tip of the peninsula that has strong claims to be the capital of the Picts in the sixth century AD. Today, it is hard for the traveller to make sense of the jumbled ground at the tip of the peninsula. The most exciting feature is a well, discovered in 1809, at a depth of 6m (20ft) below the general level of the ground, in a chamber – 'an artificial cavern' as it has been described – carved out of the living rock. The pool is reached by a flight of stone steps. Recent speculation about Burghead's past places the well in the Pictish centuries when it is believed to have been a Christian baptistry. It is on record that Columba

The warehouses of Burghead, for which the stone was quarried in the ramparts of Scotland's finest Pictish fort

visited the ruler of the Picts, King Bridei, in the sixth century. This holy well may survive as a memorial of his mission. Fortunately, the former splendour of the earthworks at Burghead may be gauged from the plan drawn by General Roy a half century before their destruction. It shows the rocky end of the peninsula straddled by three ramparts each of 240m (800ft) in length. The quarrying of stone from the ramparts to provide building material for the warehouses beside the new harbour in 1807 has all but obliterated this ancient earthwork. Burghead was a capital of the Northern Picts. Pity it is that a Mr James Young, engaged in the building of nineteenth-century Burghead, received a contract in 1808 'for the removal of 20,000 cubic yards of rampart'!

Burghead Harbour is a quiet place with a handful of fishing boats and an Outward Bound boat centre that has been established under the aegis of Gordonstoun School. At the south end of the town, the chief landmark is the maltings of Scottish Distillers where barley is imported and stored for several of the inland distilleries.

From Burghead westwards, seemingly endless sand beaches rise imperceptibly to a wilderness of dunes, salt-marsh and shingle ridges. Natural and man-made changes have been a feature of the history of this coast. Across a narrow, salt-marsh-filled channel from the Culbin Forest a long narrow island of shingle and sand dune, The Bar, is migrating westward at the rate of a mile a century. Man, too, has drastically changed this coastal landscape during the past half century. Before the planting of the Culbin dunes by the Forestry Commission in the 1920s, this was the finest and most extensive tract of sand dunes in the British Isles; at their highest the shifting sand-hills reached to 30m (100ft) above sea-level. Today the Culbin Sands are a vast coniferous forest that covers 2,000ha (5,000 acres) and stretches for almost 11km (7 miles) along the coast.

The afforestation of the Culbin Sands is only the most recent stage in the evolution of this attractive piece of the Scottish coast. Seven thousand and more years ago, in the period of post-glacial higher sea levels, a wide, shallow bay stretched inland for

3–4km (2–3 miles) beyond the present shore. Seawards from this prehistoric shore wide sand flats existed at low tide. They provided the foundation for the building of a complex series of shingle ridges. In turn the accumulations of shingle, raised by storm waves above the level of all but the highest and most destructive tides, became the platform for the accumulation of dune sand. The evolution of the projecting Culbin foreland was favoured by the falling sea-levels of later prehistoric times, a process that exposed greater areas of sand to nourish the growing dunes.

Until the seventeenth century the sands of Culbin were confined to a comparatively limited belt close to the sea. Archaeological finds show that the region was inhabited in the Bronze Age. During the seventeenth century the Culbin estate was gradually overwhelmed by sand. At times of gales from the west and north-west sandstorms raged, leaving a deposit thinly spread over the fields of Culbin. Farming ceased as the blown sand buried formerly fertile soils. Eventually, with the abandonment of the estate, Culbin House and its adjacent cottages were lost beneath the mountainous dunes. Much argument has been spent over the reasons why the sand of Culbin spread inland in the seventeenth and eighteenth centuries. Increased storminess in the climate of northern Britain may have triggered off this landscape change, but there seems little doubt that man also played a vital part. The culling of marram grass, a notable stabiliser of dunes, for thatching purposes may well have intensified the movement of sand. It may be regretted that the unique sand desert of Culbin that had been in existence for scarcely 200 years should be transformed within a generation into another state forest, but even so the miles of silent woodland tracks that lead to an undeveloped shore of sand and salt-marsh rich with wild birds and flowers is one of Scotland's most prized environmental assets.

Findhorn has suffered much change at the dictates of nature and the hand of man. Until the beginning of the eighteenth century the Findhorn river emptied into the Moray Firth 5km (3 miles) to the west of its present mouth. Guided by a long shingle bar it followed a course in the Culbin Foreland now marked by the marshy depression of the Buckie Loch. On 11 October 1702, storm waves breached the shingle barrier at the site of the present mouth of the Findhorn. The new direct channel to the sea was the motive for the abandonment of the old town of Findhorn that stood about 4km (2 miles) to the west of the present port. Findhorn's quays, warehouses and former custom house are the evidence of a once flourishing port. Trade with continental ports has ceased long ago and the shipbuilding industry is dead. Findhorn is now a summer holiday resort, its sheltered bay favoured by yachtsmen and water-skiers. Of late, the name of Findhorn has become known as the centre of a religious 'new age' community in one of its caravan parks where the sterile sandy soils have been made to yield rich harvests of vegetables and fruit.

Westward from the mouth of the Nairn river the coastlines of the Moray Firth close rapidly towards each other, until between Fort George and Chanonry Point they are separated by a deep, tide-swept channel less than a mile in width. Beyond, sheltered waters lead to Inverness and the innermost recess of Beauly Firth. This coastline is shaped out of weak, loosely consolidated glacial deposits. Most of the coastal features are of recent origin, shaped over the past 15,000 years in a period of falling sea-levels, as the land-mass of Scotland recovered from the weight of the vanished ice-sheets. Raised beaches reach inland for up to 5km (3 miles). The latest advance of the ice into the coast-lands came only some 13,000 years ago when a moraine was deposited at the sites of Fort George and Fortrose. The glacial deposits of this moraine provide the foundations for the foreland at Ardersier, a foreland that has been shaped down to the present time under the force of waves and tidal currents on the flood and ebb circulating through the narrow strait off the Ardersier Foreland and Chanonry Point. Ardersier Foreland is composed of a succession of four main raised beaches at 100ft, 50ft, 25ft and 15ft (30m, 15m, 8m, 5m) above present sea-level.

At Ardersier man, of late, has proved to be an even more potent factor than nature in

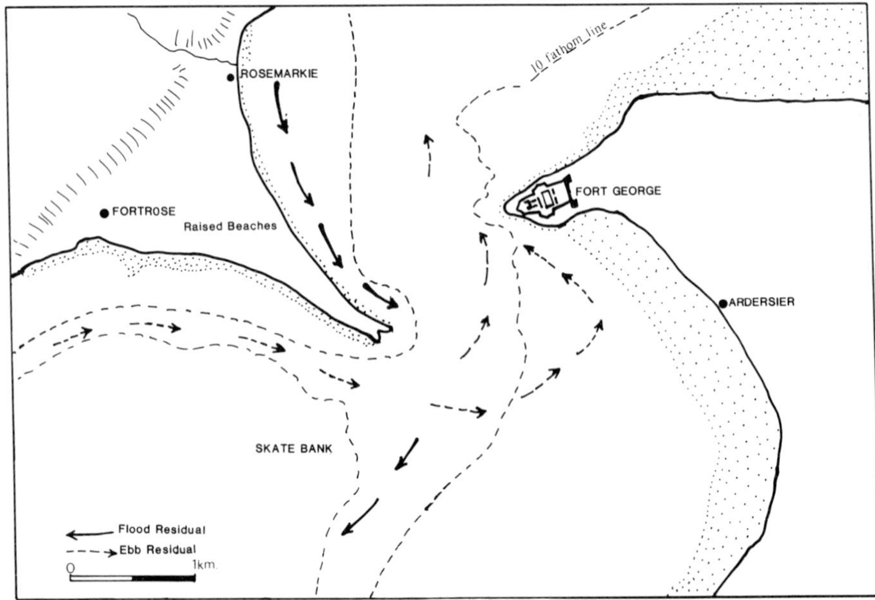

Illustration of the paired spits across the Moray Firth (*after Ogilvie*)

environmental change. Whiteness Head was chosen by an American company in the early 1970s as a site for the construction of oil-rig platforms. It provided favourable conditions in the flat land of an extensive raised beach with deep water close inshore, necessary when the time came to float such huge structures out to oil-fields beyond Shetland. Ardersier, the place-name, means the 'headland of the carpenter'; today the carpenter works in steel and on a gigantic scale.

Nairn, with a population of about 5,000, is the leading holiday resort of the north-east. There are several good hotels and guest-houses in a pleasant residential quarter to the west of the town – a suburb of quiet roads of late-Victorian villas hidden behind stone walls and spacious shrubby gardens. Towards the shore a fine prospect of the Black Isle opens up across the Moray Firth and further still on clear winter days the bulk of Ben Wyvis rears up behind the nearer peninsula. Nairn owes some of its success as a resort to a Dr Grigor who practised there during the 1850s. He recommended the cool, dry summer climate of Nairn to his patients. By 1888 Nairn held a place in a book called *The Baths and Wells of Europe* where it was described as a 'flourishing watering place with first-rate arrangements'. Nairn has two golf courses – to the west the championship course of the Nairn Golf Club and beyond the harbour to the east the eighteen-hole Dunbar Golf Course. There is also a large municipal caravan and camping site by the east beach. In August the Open Golf Tournament takes place, as well as the Highland Games which attract some 20,000 spectators.

There are no visible remains of the medieval burgh, that received a charter in the twelfth century, apart from the line of the High Street that must have formed the focus of the early settlement. At the end of the High Street, overlooking the river, stood the castle – a twelfth-century motte with a strong stone keep such as the Normans brought to Britain. Now there is not a trace of what was one of the great medieval castles of northern Scotland where the Thanes of Cawdor held the post of governor. High Street was entirely rebuilt during the late-Victorian decades. At the western end of the town are a cluster of spired churches and the Academy. By the harbour is the former fisher town, a place of narrow streets, back lanes and attractive white harled cottages.

Nairn now is caught up with the oil-platform yard 5km (3 miles) along the coast at Ardersier.

Fort George was built between 1747 and 1767. It was intended to replace the castle that General Wade had built at Inverness earlier in the century. With six great bastions facing the sea and a huge ditch to the landward side, Fort George has remained the chief centre of military activity in northern Scotland. This military stronghold, almost the last product of centuries of castle building, long ago lost the original purposes of its design 'to overawe the Highland population and to repel any invasion from the sea'.

Inverness With a population of 36,000, Inverness straddles the fast-flowing river Ness where it empties across a delta at the Kessock Narrows. Around the site of this capital of the northern Highlands the evidence of man reaches back to prehistoric times. Neolithic burial places, unique of their kind to this part of north-east Scotland and known as the Clava Cairns, have been shown by radio-carbon dating to have been built 5,000 years ago. Equally striking visual evidence of the long history of settlement is found on the summit of Craig Phadrig, a wooded hill 152m (500ft) high, on the western outskirts of Inverness, crowned by a stone-walled Iron Age fort. Craig Phadrig was the prehistoric forerunner of Inverness. The latest excavation at the site, in 1971 and 1972, produced a date, by radio-carbon analysis, for the building of the fort in the fourth century BC. But Craig Phadrig was occupied during the centuries when the Picts held sway over northern Britain. Pottery from between the fifth and eighth centuries AD has been found there – drinking vessels, bowls and pitchers, manufactured in western France, and probably having reached the north as part of the Dark Age trade in wine. Even more striking, though hard to establish, is a reference in a *Life of St Columba*, written by Adomnan, ninth Abbot of Iona, towards the end of the seventh century. Adomnan describes how Columba in his mission to the Picts visited King Brudei about the year 565 at his 'fortress' near 'the Ness'. When the saint comes to leave the province of the Picts he 'is borne along the long lake of the River Ness'. Craig Phadrig from the bare references of Adomnan's *Life* seems the most likely site for the capital of the Northern Picts. But one must remember that the great promontory fort at Burghead puts forward an equally strong claim as the capital of Pictland in Brudei's time.

Although a town has stood here for almost 1,000 years there is scarcely any visible evidence of its medieval past. There are two castle sites. One, a huge castellated theatrical building of brilliant red sandstone looks down a grassy river cliff to the Ness. Raised on the ruin of General Wade's fortress, built there in 1726 and destroyed by the Jacobite army at the time of Culloden, 1745, the present buildings were designed by William Burn in 1835. Today, they house the Sheriff Court and the headquarters of the County Police. The other castle site lies to the east of the river in the pleasant residential district known as The Crown. Here an eleventh-century fortress is remembered only by the name of Auldcastle Road. The only relic of medieval Inverness is a single pillar of the Blackfriar's that stands in a small graveyard off Friars Street.

In Church Street, at the busy junction with Bridge Street, the 40m (130ft) tower and spire of the Town Steeple, built in 1791, stands on the site of an earlier tolbooth. Further along stands High Church, site of the original parish church of Inverness on a mound between the street and the river. Today, the building, save the older parts of its tower, dates from the end of the eighteenth century. Nearby stand the tall-steepled St Columba High Church and the Free Greyfriars, where for over three centuries worship was in Gaelic. When seen across the river Ness from the west bank the clustered steeples of Church Street present perhaps the most memorable impression of the town – a visual image of the stillness of the Scottish sabbath when seen under the clear light of a North Sea sky. The white-washed harled walls, crow-stepped gables and circular stair tower of Abertarff House are characteristic of the town houses built by wealthy merchants and country lairds at the time of the Reformation and after. Today,

Classical Inverness

Abertarff House is an Information Centre, a craft shop and the home of the Highland Association, An Commun Gaidhealach.

The Episcopal Cathedral of St Andrews raises its twin red sandstone towers on the west bank of the Ness. It was the first Anglican cathedral to be built in Britain after the Reformation; Gothic and solidly Victorian it is now more than a century old. The heart of the town – the shopping and business quarter of Union Street, Queensgate, Station Square and part of Academy Street – is a sombre, dignified piece of Victorian town planning, by a local architect, William Ross. Part of the scheme involved the conversion of an open market-place into covered arcades – an amenity of no mean value in the severely stormy winters of the north-east coast. Its little shops – permanent stalls – have preserved the original character of a market.

Towards the mouth of the river Ness, Shore Street leads abruptly from the town centre into a squalid harbour district and the Longman Industrial Estate. Longman refers to a long-since vanished Viking burial cairn that once stood hereabouts on the shore of the Inverness firth. Among the oil-storage tanks there still stands a clock-tower that belonged to a fort, the Sconce, built by Cromwell's troops, near the river mouth in 1648. On the west bank, beyond St Andrew's Cathedral, lies the Northern Meeting Park – a place of great open-air gatherings, Highland games and military tattoos. Further still, stands the Eden Court Theatre – a finely equipped and designed modern theatre that fulfils a long-felt need in the north for the proper presentation of opera, ballet, local productions and a summer holiday show. On the southern edge of the town are two parks. Bught Park, beside the A82, has a sports ground and a large municipal caravan site. The Ness Islands Park ranks among the most attractive parts of Inverness. It consists of a stretch of riverside on both banks of the Ness as well as a number of wooded mid-stream islands linked to each other by bridges. In summer there are illuminations and open-air concerts on one of the islets.

Finally, leaving Inverness for the north by the A9, one crosses the Caledonian Canal.

Built by Telford between 1803 and 1822, it provides a shipping route between the Atlantic and the North Sea. It is one of the great monuments of the Industrial Revolution – an imaginative development of landscape in the connecting of the lochs of the Great Glen, but one that lacked a proper economic motive. Fishing fleets, moving from east-coast ports to western waters, have made use of the Caledonian Canal, but now it is mainly summer pleasure craft that pass through the locks. Scenically, this must be one of the finest canal cruises in the world.

From Inverness to the Pentland Firth

Westward of the new Kessock road bridge and the now deserted staithes of the disused vehicle ferry between South and North Kessock stretches the innermost reach of the North Sea in Beauly Firth. Towards the head of Beauly Firth the wide expanse of mud-flats provide a rich winter feeding-ground for wild birds. Mallard, teal, wigeon, greylag geese, pinkfooted geese and oyster-catchers have been observed in large numbers.

Beauly Of Norman-French origin as *beau lieu*, this no doubt seemed a proper name for the attractive place in the Moray lowland when a party of monks from Burgundy founded a priory here on land given by Sir John Bisset of Aird and Lovat in 1230. Today, the ruins of Beauly Priory lie close beside the A9 at the north end of the town. There is the roofless shell of a late-medieval church of which the north transept was restored as the mausoleum of the Mackenzies of Kintail. The adjacent town did not come into existence until 1840 when the Lord Lovat of that time secured the right to establish a market town, a burgh with the power to hold seven fairs in a year. This was the time when huge droves of cattle made their way on the hoof from northern Scotland to the markets of the south. Beauly, typical of town-planning in the nineteenth century, is laid out in an ordered grid-iron of streets of which the most attractive feature is a wide central square through which sweeps the original route of the A9 on its way to the north.

The Black Isle, a peninsula with many of the isolated qualities of an island, reaches out towards the North Sea between the firths of Moray and Cromarty. If the term 'isle' is a misnomer for this peninsula, so also the adjective 'black' seems inappropriate to describe a landscape whose highest ridges at 245m (800ft) above the sea are clothed in thousands of acres of forest. One explanation of this regional name is that the Black Isles once consisted of thousands of acres of dark moorland and peat bog. The name, too, has been put down to the climate of this sea-girt peninsula that may remain free of winter snow when the high hills to the west are blanketed in white. But again the true explanation may lie in an old Gaelic name for this district where the language is no longer heard. The Black Isle was known as Eilean Dhubhaich, St Duthac's Isle, the shortened version of which is Eilean Dubh, meaning the black island.

From Muir of Ord to North Kessock a minor road hugs the coast closely for several miles to provide a succession of enticing prospects of woodland, well-kept farms and glimpses of mud-flats and the shining waters of the firth. Tarradale House was the birth-place of Sir Roderick Murchison, a pioneer of geology. This red-sandstone eighteenth-century residence is now a field-centre of Aberdeen University.

Kilmuir occupies a raised beach on an unfrequented piece of the coast between North Kessock and the mouth of Munlochy Bay. It is reached either by footpath along the steep, lower forested slope of Ord Hill or by a tangle of minor roads from the B9161 that end in a rough, gated, unmade track by the ruin of Kilmuir Church (the name Kilmuir means St Mary's chapel). Above Kilmuir is Loch Lundie – a rare inland fresh-water loch in the Black Isle. The narrow wooded ridge that looks down on the loch from the east is the site of a prehistoric dun.

A steep fossil cliff-line backed by wooded whale-back shaped hills dominates the coastal scenery between North Kessock and the Sutors of Cromarty. The only gap in this relentlessly straight coastline, Munlochy Bay, a sea loch, reaches inland between two wooded headlands for a distance of 3.2km (2 miles). Along the coast road to North Kessock one passes through Redcastle and Coulmore. The former, a dilapidated sixteenth-century castle, stands on the brink of a wooded ravine; the latter, with a fine prospect on to the firth and across to the forested hills of Aird, has a restaurant, caravan site and the Black Isle Boating Centre. At Craigton Point, the site of the lately built Kessock Bridge, the coastline of the Black Isle turns abruptly towards the north-east. This long, straight coastline coincides with the eastward prolongation of the Great Glen Fault. It is known that this line of weakness in the Earth's crust, separating the north-west Highlands from the Grampians, has been in existence for over 300 million years. It is still a line of crustal instability as the fifty-six minor earthquakes recorded at Inverness between 1768 and 1906 show. The movements along the Great Glen Fault have acted horizontally; and the sum total involves a change of 133km (83 miles) in relative position between the Northern Highlands block and the Grampian block.

Munlochy, at the head of the bay, has a hotel and guest-house accommodation. The hill-slope of the guarding headland, Craigiehowe, is flanked by a magnificent raised beach and relict cliff. Munlochy and its bay-head salt-marsh form an over-wintering and breeding place for countless birds. The surrounding hills, steeply rounded heights of up to 122m (400ft) above sea-level, bear evidence of a remote prehistoric past. Amid the old Scots pine woods that cap Craigiehowe are an enclosure and hut circles of a Pictish settlement, and across the valley on the wooded ridge of Drumderfit is the site of a Pictish dun. On the northern headland at the mouth of Munlochy Bay are the remains of the twelfth-century Castle of Ormond. Now overgrown with planted forest, this former stronghold of the Earls of Ormond is known only by the name of a farm, Castleton, on the lane encircling the headland of Lady Hill.

Avoch, a fishing village, straddles the Killen burn where it empties into the Moray Firth. The fishermen's cottages in the oldest quarter, gable-end to the street, are reminiscent of the villages of the Banffshire coast and Buchan.

Fortrose At the heart of the town, but removed from the traffic of the High Street, stands the rich red sandstone ruin of a great medieval cathedral. Its only remains – the undercroft of the Chapter House and the south aisle of the nave – date from the thirteenth and fourteenth centuries. This cathedral capital of the Black Isle became a royal burgh in 1592. Steep hills provide a sheltering wall to the north so that the town basks in a southern aspect across the Moray Firth and on many days the sun shines here while rain clouds are banked against the mountains of the Highlands.

Rosemarkie Once a burgh in its own right, Rosemarkie is centuries older than its cathedral neighbour and with ancient ecclesiastical roots that must have given the town as strong a claim to provide a seat for bishops. St Moluag, one of Columba's missioners to the Picts, established a cell here before the end of the sixth century; and in 716 St Boniface established a monastery. By 1124 David I, one of the great makers of medieval Scotland, created the first bishopric of Ross out of the Celtic church's monastic community at Rosemarkie, but he chose to have the cathedral of the newly sketched diocese located at Fortrose. Little visual evidence remains of Rosemarkie's long history, but outside the parish church, built in the 1820s, stands an elaborately decorated Pictish cross-slab that is believed to date from the time of St Boniface's community in the eighth century.

Rosemarkie Glen is classified as a site of outstanding scientific interest. This deep wooded ravine through which the A832 makes its way inland from the coast coincides with a fault-line between two of the main rock series of northern Scotland – the Devonian Old Red Sandstone and the ancient Moine rocks. The glen owes its precipitous slopes of bared clay above the stream bed and strange pinnacles, earth pillars, to the passage across the Black Isle of glaciers bred in the north-west Highland's mountains. The valley along the fault-line was plugged with boulder clay; the burn that dashes towards the sea has quickly re-excavated a course through the boulder clays over the past few thousand years. Pillars of clay protected from destruction under the weather by a capping stone are rare features in the British landscape, hence the interest aroused by Rosemarkie Glen.

North-eastwards from Rosemarkie the outline of the coast is determined by the Great Glen Fault. For the motorist there is no direct access to this uninhabited stretch of shore, although a secondary road breaks away from the main A832 in the upper part of Rosemarkie Glen to run parallel to the coastline at about 1km (½ mile) inland. Lanes branch off to cliff-top farms from where footpaths zigzag shorewards down the steep face of the fossil cliffs. The gorge of the Ethie Burn makes a deep gash in the front of the fossil cliffs. This is a classic site in the history of the unravelling of the geology of the British Isles. Here Hugh Miller, the Cromarty stone-mason, discovered on the north-east side of the gorge a thin band of rock in the Old Red Sandstone rich with fossil fish. He wrote of the geological wealth of this place in his book *The Old Red Sandstone.* Published in 1841, it became not only a classic piece of geological writing but also as a work of English literature. Since then the fish bed in the Ethie Burn has been visited and hammered by countless geologists so that the site is now largely worked out.

Cromarty, with a population of less than 700, controls the entrance to its natural harbour which is screened by bold headlands. Three centuries ago a large fishing fleet was based here; fairs were held and this one-time royal burgh acted as a centre of administration at the heart of the sheriffdom of the Urquhart family. In 1772 George Ross bought the estate of Cromarty, built the harbour, and founded new industries – a cloth mill, brewery, lace industry and workshop for the manufacture of nails and spades. Hugh Miller, the stone-mason who put the Black Isle on the geological map, was born here in 1802. His cottage, now the property of the National Trust for Scotland, serves as a museum of his life and work. Also of interest are the eighteenth-century Town House, white-washed with clock-tower and mercat cross in front, the fisher town gathered around the harbour with its brightly painted cottages and, standing on a raised beach above the sea-shore, Cromarty House and the roofless shell of the Gaelic church that was opened in 1783 for the immigrant workers from the Highlands. Today, Cromarty is mainly a tourist resort. Craft industries – pottery, silver and knitwear – have moved into its restored cottages and tourism has helped in the town's revival.

The most attractive section of the dull north shore of Black Isle is Udale Bay, an important resort of wild fowl. **Jemimaville** grew up during the period of the Improving Movement. George Munro, laird of Ardoch, married a wealthy Dutch lady, Jemima Poyntz. Her capital provided the means to improve the farming of Ardoch through the technique of the new agriculture. His efforts are written on the landscape in a scattering of large isolated farms, the reclamation of wasteland and the founding of a new coastal settlement, on the now B9163 coastal road, for his displaced tenants. Gordon's Mills, a sandstone building close to the shore of Udale Bay, was first a snuff mill and later used its water power for carding wool. Nearby is the ruined church and graveyard of St Michael's. Under a grey sky this is a melancholy place with its crumbling tombs of Munroes and Mackenzies as the grey tide spills over the mud-flats of Udale Bay to the edge of the salt marsh.

At the head of Cromarty Firth where the river Conon empties into the sea are situated the two great arteries of the north-east that took over from the sea as the chief means of communication after the middle of the last century – first the railway to Wick and Thurso and now the A9 trunk road. **Conan Bridge** and **Maryburgh** face each other across the river. Each has its rash of twentieth-century housing. Conan Bridge, astride the A9 where it curves sharply up from the river crossing, came into existence only with the construction of Telford's

The ruined parish church of St Michael beside Udale Bay

bridge. The first houses were built there for workers on the new bridge, but by 1840 it had become a roadside settlement of 300.

Dingwall is an administrative centre with few industries. In the Viking colonisation of eastern Scotland in the years about AD 1000, this must have been a focusing point, a place of central government, for its name, Scandinavian by origin, means 'the meeting place of parliament'. The oldest building on the High Street, the east-west axis of this county town of Ross, is the eighteenth-century Old Tolbooth Tower of the Town House. High Street and Tulloch Street, the heart of the town, are composed of shops and banks, Victorian solidity face-lifted into the latter half of the twentieth century with chrome and plastic. At the east end of High Street, towards the railway station, stands the clock steeple of the Free Church built in 1869. Here, too, are the County Council offices and the northern area headquarters of the Hydro Board – the industry that produces and distributes electricity over much of the Highlands. The parish church, in Tulloch Street at the approach to the bridge over the river Peffery, dates from 1801, but a weathered Pictish symbol stone at the entrance to the kirkyard testifies to man's earliest presence here.

The north coast of Cromarty Firth from Dingwall to the Sutors channel displays a greater variety of landscape and economic development than the dull facing shore of the Black Isle. Hills rise steeply from the sea through broad belts of plantation woodland on their lower slopes to bare heather moorland. The intrusion of large-scale industries – aluminium smelting and the building of oil-rigs – has introduced changes and environmental and planning problems of a kind scarcely known elsewhere in the Northern Highlands.

Evanton, planted at the head of the delta formed by the converging rivers, Sgitheach and Glass, grew up as a result of the Improving Movement. A Mr Evan Fraser, the new owner of the estate of Balconie, decided, in 1810, to replace the old village or 'ferm toun' of Drummond on the right bank of the Sgitheach with a regularly laid-out estate village. All along this northern shore of Cromarty Firth the lairds have left their mark on the landscape in Georgian houses, patches of planted woodland, churchyard mausoleums and monuments.

The Munro family have lived in these parts since the twelfth century. At the earliest parish church – an abandoned site on the shore where the Sgitheach enters the firth – the Munroes of Foulis have been buried here from 1588 to the present day. The summit of one of the hills above Evanton, Cnoc Fyrish at 452m (1,483ft), is crowned by a huge replica of the gateway of Negapatam, an Indian city captured by General Sir Hector Munro in 1782. The Munroes held the Novar Estate, lands between Evanton and Alness where Novar House, a handsome early Georgian mansion, lies among woodland above the A9. Evanton belongs to the fringe of industrial development centred on Alness and Invergordon, but here the change has been in new housing and the founding of an industrial estate on the abandoned airfield on the raised beach to the east of the delta.

Alness, laid out at the head of the Averon's delta, began as a planned estate village in the hands of the Munroes. Until the early 1960s Alness was a quiet holiday resort with a population of about 1,000; ten years later its population had trebled. Alness found itself part of a plan for industrial and urban expansion along the north shore of Cromarty Firth; workers for the aluminium smelter at Invergordon and projected petro-chemical and North Sea oil-related industries were to be housed around the village. Alness was to be enveloped in five new housing schemes, each a planner's self-contained unit of 3,000–4,000 people. Today, the planners' dream of a 'girdle city' on the shores of Cromarty Firth begins to fade with the closure of the smelter at Invergordon.

Invergordon North of the Great Glen the only centre of large-scale industry has appeared at Invergordon, by origin an estate village. Sir John Gordon, Secretary of State for Scotland, planned the layout of a new town at this important narrowing of the Cromarty Firth in the 1750s. Invergordon was to be a fishing and ferry settlement; Sir John also planned to develop a holiday resort. Invergordon's economic future was not to depend on tourism, however, for a deep-water anchorage close inshore and the natural defences of the Sutors make Cromarty Firth the finest harbour and refuge on the east coast of Scotland. During World War I a naval dockyard was established and in World War II RAF flying-boats were centred here. The dockyard was closed in 1956, although the Royal Navy and ships of NATO still use Invergordon for refuelling. Following the closure of the naval base, the British Aluminium Company took over the jetties. One of these reaches out for 1.2km (¾ mile) into the firth where the largest ore carriers, bringing bauxite from the Caribbean, can tie up. One of the striking features of the deep-water berth is the gleaming conveyor system that moves the alumina ore from ships' holds to the smelter. The smelter with its tall chimneys, aluminium silos, workshops and fuel tanks covers a site of 160ha (400 acres) – the biggest industrial undertaking in the north. It can turn out 100,000 tons of aluminium a year and uses as much electricity as would a city of 200,000. Power comes from the Hydro Board's grid, fed partly from the atomic power station on the north coast at Dounreay. Today, the smelter at Invergordon has been closed and the fast-breed reactor at Dounreay is threatened with closure.

At Invergordon the coastline turns northwards into Nigg Bay – at low tide a wet sandy desert whose treacherous mud- and sandbanks are marked off from the deep channel of the firth by a line of beacons.

Barbaraville, a pleasant string of cottages by the shore, was founded in the early years of the nineteenth century and close by, at **Portlich**, stands a deserted pier and warehouse that once imported coal and where cargoes of grain and timber were loaded.

Milton, where the river Balnagown has built up a delta at the head of Nigg Bay, is another estate village, planted amid the woodlands of the Tarbat House Estate and as English-looking as the sound of its name. This is a burgh of barony, a place with a mercat-cross that once held four cattle-markets a year. In 1786 Milton was replanned by James Maclaren, the architect of Newtarbat House, as a 'green village'. Tarbat House, in a secret place by the Balnagown amid clumps of woodland, was built in the 1780s – large and in the style of Robert Adam.

The south-eastern corner of Nigg Bay at Dunskeath Ness was suddenly drawn into the North Sea's oil boom with the decision of Highland Fabricators to locate an oil-rig construction yard here. The chief factor in that decision is the presence of deep water – 10 fathoms only a few yards from the beach of Dunskeath Ness – that allows massive structures to be towed out to sea as well as providing mooring for a passenger liner as accommodation for the huge sudden influx of workers. The construction yard at Nigg has changed the shape of the coastline itself. Dunskeath Ness has disappeared beneath the clutter of sheds, workshops and huge cranes and the former fishing hamlet of Balnapaling has been engulfed in the rig-construction yard. Dunskeath Castle, a green mound of a fort built by William the Lion in 1179, has also disappeared. Evidence of Scotland's past may still be found at the head of the bay, however. The parish church, surrounded by trees above a shallow ravine not far from the shore, has been a place of worship for many centuries. The present building, a simple long low rectangle, dates from the seventeenth century, but its main object of interest, an elaborately carved Pictish cross, tells of the importance of the north-eastern lowlands and the deeply penetrating firths from the time before AD 1000.

From the North Sutor to Shandwick and Balintore the North Sea coast pursues the line determined by the Great Glen Fault. This is a lonely, cliff-bound stretch of coast lacking access by road or even well-marked footpaths. Streams from the lochs on the Hill of Nigg find their way to the sea through twisting gorges that here and there break the front of the 122m (400ft) high cliffs. North-east from the Hill of Nigg a low-lying narrow peninsula reaches to Tarbat Ness where a lighthouse, said to be the second tallest in Britain, crowns a hillock some 15m (50ft) above the shore. On the exposed eastern coast three settlements, **Shandwick, Balintore** and **Hilton of Cadboll**, form the only notable cluster of population. Balintore used to export grain and potatoes, but the sea trade has long been extinguished. Salmon fishing survives on a commercial scale, but now these places are known to the few as quiet, attractive holiday resorts remote from the cloudy, rain-drenched mainland mountains. In the last few years that quiet has been broken by the non-stop activity of the construction yard at Nigg and the intrusion of a large number of richly paid workers into the peninsula. The coastal plain at Balintore bears clear evidence that this was a nucleus of Pictish settlement. A weather-scarred Pictish cross, believed to be of late ninth century date, stands in a field outside Shandwick. On the site of a medieval chapel at Hilton of Cadboll an elaborately sculptured Pictish cross-slab depicting chieftains hunting deer with hounds was removed to the British Museum. Now it can be seen in the Museum of Antiquities at Edinburgh.

Portmahomack, situated on a shallow, gently curving bay, enjoys a fine prospect across the wide entrance of Dornoch Firth to the distant, grey-blue mountains of Sutherland. Portmahomack has survived mainly as a small holiday resort. Its harbour was improved in the early years of the nineteenth century when a pier, more than 122m (400ft) long, was built to provide shelter from destructive northerly gales. Two warehouses, one of seventeenth-century date, survive from Portmahomack's years as a prosperous port. Its harbour was known and used for centuries before this time; the name, Port na Colmac, means the harbour of St Colmac. Its early history is proved by the discovery of numerous fragments of Pictish crosses in the churchyard of the Tarbat old parish church on a knoll outside the village, itself the site of a seventh-century chapel.

The Tarbat peninsula, which has a sense of remoteness from the rest of the northern Highlands, contains several fishing hamlets that have long since lost their main purpose. At **Wilkhaven**, close to Tarbat Ness, a steep lane leads down from a farm to the empty harbour. **Rockfield** is a string of cottages and an abandoned jetty under a steep cliff. On the western shore, **Inver** with its low-built cottages in parallel lanes is a typical fishing settlement that has lost its economic meaning.

Dornoch Firth is the last of the great arms of the sea that determine the character of this part of Scotland's eastern coastline. All three firths – Moray, Cromarty and Dornoch – are the drowned lower courses of rivers that formerly flowed eastward into the North Sea basin. The complex topography of the present shore-line of Dornoch Firth is the result of occupation by a huge slow-moving glacier during the Ice Age and the consequent deposition of morainic clays and sands, which deposits have been shaped and reworked by wave action during the 15,000 years that have elapsed since the waning of the ice, a period of changing sea-levels. The wide entrance to the firth between Tain and Dornoch contains some fine examples of depositional, wave-worked features – Morrich Mhor, a sandy foreland covering 235km^2 (9 square miles), and Ferry Point, a 1.6km (1 mile) long finger of shingle that was once so important in the communications of the north-east coast and the Links at Dornoch. Scenically, too, Dornoch Firth is the finest of the three estuaries. Hills of mountainous proportions come close to the sea, their lower slopes richly clothed in woodland. And in the narrow winding channel of the Kyle of Sutherland, above Bonar Bridge, one feels as if the Highlands have stretched over to the east coast. Here, by the miles of endless sandy bays that reach towards the North Sea, the disturbing presence of the twentieth century's heavy industries is lacking.

Tain, with a population of 2,000, focuses on two parallel main streets on ground that falls steeply towards the shore. Its name may relate to the Scandinavian word *thing*, given to the meeting places and centres of administration in those Viking colonies scattered along the coasts of northern and western Scotland in the years about AD 1000. Otherwise, the name has evolved from the Gaelic *Baile Dhubhaich*, meaning St Duthac's town. St Duthac, one of the last of the great saints of the Celtic church, was born here about the year 1000. He died at Armagh, in Ireland, in 1065 and his remains were brought back to Tain in 1253. Until the Reformation St Duthac's shrine became an important place of pilgrimage. Between 1493 and 1514 James IV made seven pilgrim journeys to the collegiate church of St Duthac at Tain. This is one of those rare places in Scotland, such as Iona or St Andrews, where the medieval centuries have left some impression, however faint, in the present landscape. Near the sea and the eighteen-hole golf course is the ruin of a medieval chapel dedicated to the saint. St Duthac's collegiate church, up in the town, was founded in 1371 and was used as the parish church until the early nineteenth century. It is a rare example of a medieval church in a country where the Calvinist Reformation obliterated so much of the past. Tain's townscape is composed of the expected objects of the small Scottish town. There is a mercat-cross, a Victorian monument of 1879, restored in 1895, to provost Murray of Geanies, and in Queen Street the Town Hall dating from 1875 and a huge battlemented nineteenth-century parish church. The tolbooth, typical of so many built in Scottish towns during the seventeenth and eighteenth centuries, is so complete and well preserved that it must rank as one of the finest examples of this kind of native architecture.

Tain received its charter as a royal burgh from Malcolm Canmore in 1066. To celebrate its ninth centenary in 1966, the Ross and Cromarty Heritage Society founded a museum in Castle Street. It contains manuscripts and photographs illustrative of local history and objects such as the town-crier's bell and the key of the tolbooth. The prehistoric item that causes one to pause is a neolithic stone axe from Great Langdale in the English Lake District. What extent of trade, 4,000 years ago, does this suggest?

Between Tain and Inver, over a distance of 8km (5 miles), a vast wilderness of sand and salt marsh stretches out into the firth towards Dornoch Point. Unfortunately, this nature reserve, also an aerial bombing range, is inaccessible to the public. Morrich Mhòr grew northward into the mouth of Dornoch Firth as sea-level fell during the post-glacial centuries. The highest part, in the south-west, is related to the level of the 8m (25ft) sea and much of the rest of the foreland developed when the sea stood at 4.5m (15ft) above its present height. The feature seems to have grown forward with the formation of a succession of sand-bars on the Whiteness Sands; the latest of these, all but submerged with high tides, is Innis Mhòr. On Morrich Mhòr itself a succession of marshy depressions and elongated lochans, orientated from NW to SE, marks stages in the development of this feature – a piece of the Scottish coastline that in its entirety is little more than 8,000 years old.

A journey along the A9 trunk road between Tain and Dornoch provides a snapshot view of the attractively varied scenery of this part of north-east Scotland. Glen Morangie Distillery, founded in 1843 and the home of 'Highland Queen', is situated 1.6km (1 mile) north of Tain. Ardjachie Farm, beside the main road, was the site of the Pictish stone now on display at the Tain Museum. Here the long narrow spit of Ferry Point reaches out to within 1.6km (1 mile) of the Sutherland shore. The higher features of the spit were built in the 8m (25ft) sea; for the rest, most of it accords with the 4.5m (15ft) level. Until 1812 this crossing of Dornoch Firth, Meikle Ferry, was the major link with the north-east. In 1809, an accident at the ferry with the loss of 100 lives, prompted the bridging of the firth at the narrows of the Kyle of Sutherland. Telford completed the original bridge at Bonar Bridge in 1812; even so, although Tain and Dornoch lie only 8km (5 miles) apart across the sea and sands, the journey along the A9 covers 51km (32 miles). The shore at Ferry Point spit, Tarlogie Scalps, is famous for its mussels.

Ardmore Point, another wave-built feature of recurved shingle ridges, reaches northward into the firth. **Ardmore** is a forgotten harbour, a place that used to unload coal. Beyond **Edderton**, road and railway hug the shore beneath the slopes of Struie Hill. Here, where Dornoch Firth becomes constricted by the delta of the Easter Fearn Burn, the huge wooded hump of Dun Creich rises up across the narrow belt of sea and sand. The Picts must have appreciated the strategic value of this place for, close beside the A9, stands the ruin of Dun Alascaig, a Pictish broch, and the summit of Dun Creich, 113m (370ft) above the sea, is crowned by a double ramparted hill-fort of the late Iron Age centuries. Today, this magnificent prehistoric site is hard to find and impossible to appreciate in its overwhelming blanket of forest.

Ardgay and **Bonar Bridge**, service settlements created by the road and railway, face each other across the complex delta built into the head of Dornoch Firth by the river Carron. Three centuries ago there were ambitions for Ardgay that failed in their fulfilment when an act of the Scottish Parliament in 1686 created a burgh of barony here, to be called Bonarness. The tolbooth and mercat-cross, those outward signs of a town's privileges, were never built, although annual November fairs were held. The failed burgh of Ardgay provides a suitable approach to the empty mountains and deer forests that close in upon the Kyle of Sutherland. Here in the Carron and its tributary glens some of the severest clearances of Highland peasant communities took place in the first part of the nineteenth century.

Spinningdale is the chief place of interest on the A9 between Bonar Bridge and Dornoch. Its ruined cotton mill, built in 1790, and cluster of cottages represent an attempt to bring the early water-powered technology of the Industrial Revolution into northern Scotland. George Dempster, laird of Skibo, inspired by the work of Richard Arkwright in the English Midlands, built a four-storeyed cotton mill and twenty houses for his workers. The experiment was short-lived because in 1808 the mill caught fire and was never rebuilt. Skibo Castle at the head of an attractive estate with planted woodland and artificial lakes belonged to the medieval bishops of Caithness. The present castle was built by Andrew Carnegie in 1898 after he acquired the estate for a Scottish residence. On the shore, Cuthill Links, another foreland of recent evolution, reaches out towards the narrow spit of Ferry Point. This, too, has evolved through the several

The tower of the medieval castle of the Bishops of Caithness in Dornoch has served in its time as tolbooth, court house and prison; now it is part of a hotel

thousand years of falling sea-level since the Ice Age and the 8m (25ft) and 4.5m (15ft) episodes may be traced in its present topography.

Dornoch At first sight St Andrews is called to mind; here is an airy site close beside the sea with fine sandy beaches and a golf course that claims to be the third oldest in the world. The resemblance to St Andrews does not stop there because Dornoch was closely associated in its development with the medieval church. In 1224, Gilbert de Moravia, Bishop of Caithness, began the building of his cathedral here, a church whose stormy history is not exclusively explained by the doctrinal ravages of the Reformation. A fire in 1570 left only a tower standing. Rebuilding followed in the early seventeenth century, but the cathedral, now a parish church, that we see today is the work of a major restoration sponsored by the Duchess of Sutherland in the 1830s. The nave was completely rebuilt. At the 700th anniversary, celebrated in 1924, plaster was stripped from the crossing to reveal stonework of the original thirteenth-century building. Gilbert de Moravia, Norman prelate and founder of the cathedral, also built a castle close by. Its tower still stands as part of the Dornoch Castle Hotel. In a quiet undeveloped way the coast from Dornoch to the mouth of Loch Fleet is a holiday shore. To the south of Dornoch and at **Embo** there are camp and caravan sites; there is water-skiing at Embo and miles of good sand beach.

Loch Fleet is not be compared with the great firths to the south, but what it lacks in grandeur and extent is made up by the unspoilt beauty of its shores and the sentinel Mound Rock, crag-rimmed, at the head. Loch Fleet's exit to the North Sea is by a constricted channel, deep and scoured by strongly flowing tides, between two spits that have grown from the northern and southern shores. Most of the shingle ridges of these features are associated with the 8m (25ft) sea-level, so it may be assumed that the entrance to Loch Fleet has not changed markedly over the past 8,000 years. Earlier, when sea-level stood still higher, this loch was a bay, wide open to the North Sea. At

A broch on a raised beach below the A9 north of Dunrobin Castle

the head of Loch Fleet the A9 is carried across the sandy bay by an embankment 1.2km (¾ mile) in length. Known as The Mound, the causeway was built in 1815 as part of the improved road communications of the north-east designed by Telford. When the Highland Railway extended into Sutherland and Caithness in the 1870s Telford's causeway was used to carry a branch line across Loch Fleet to Dornoch.

In a northward progress by the A9 towards Wick and Thurso the traveller will find that Loch Fleet is the last of the barriers formed by the westward reaching arms of the sea. Henceforward the coast pursues a relentlessly straight line such as we have met over so much of eastern Scotland. The wide horizon of the North Sea is an ever-present element in the scenery from the A9.

Golspie, administrative centre of Sutherland District, is overlooked by the huge statue of the 1st Duke of Sutherland from the summit of Beinn a' Bhragaidh at 366m (1,200ft) above the sea. Golspie was founded in the late-eighteenth century, another of the many planned fishing settlements that came into being with the clearance of the interior glens for large-scale sheep farming. Golspie has prospered as the capital of the estates of the Dukes of Sutherland – estates of many thousand acres that reach across to the Atlantic coast. Dunrobin Castle, former seat of the Earls and Dukes of Sutherland, lies deeply hidden in its wooded policies below the A9 1.6km (1 mile) beyond Golspie. Its building history goes back to the thirteenth century and its several architectural styles reflect not only the changing tastes of the owners of Dunrobin but also the continuing wealth of its owners. Hubert Fenwick in his essay on 'Scotland's Historic Buildings' claims that Dunrobin is 'the oldest inhabited house in Scotland'. The massive inner keep survives from the thirteenth century, but this is enveloped by later additions from the seventeenth and nineteenth centuries. The latter, built by Charles Barry between 1835 and 1850, enclosed the old castle on the north and east to give it the shape we know today, with high pointed roofs and pepper-pot turrets. In 1915 Dunrobin was severely damaged by fire, but the restoration in the

1920s by one of Scotland's most eminent architects, Robert Lorimer, ensured the survival of Barry's architecture. During the 1960s the building was used as an independent boys' school. In the park is a museum of local history of objects from the life and past of the former county of Sutherland, among which the collection of Pictish stones is the most valuable.

Golspie, because of its place at the heart of the properties of the Duke of Sutherland and its position on the economic life-lines of northern Scotland, the A9 and the railway north from Inverness, has functioned as the capital of a vast empty territory in a former county of 5,000km^2 (2,000 square miles) where less than 2 per cent is cultivated. Secondary and technical education is focused here and part of the town's livelihood depends on the provision of boarding accommodation for scholars and students from distant places. Golspie is a pleasant small resort, a good stopping place on the road to the north, with a sandy beach, golf course and a pleasing landscape that climbs to heather moorland through a wide belt of planted woods.

From Golspie to Helmsdale a marked change occurs in the geology of the north-east coast. The mountainous front composed of conglomerates and breccias of Old Red Sandstone age retreats for some distance inland. A narrow belt of lowland composed of rocks of much younger age reaches out towards the shore. In this down-faulted strip lie sedimentary rocks of Triassic and Jurassic age – limestones, clays and sandstones.

Brora The presence of a seam of good quality coal, 1m (1yd) in thickness where the lowland reaches its greatest width near the mouth of the Brora river, largely explains the history of Brora and the development of the landscape since the sixteenth century. A settlement was in existence at the mouth of the Brora as early as 1345 when David II granted the privileges of a burgh of barony here. The earliest record of coal-mining goes back to 1529, but the chief phase in Brora's industrial history belongs to the 1870s when the Duke of Sutherland saw the possibility of a remote outlier of the Industrial Revolution on his estates. Between 1870 and 1871 he built a railway from Golspie to Helmsdale, now part of the main line from Inverness to Wick. In 1872 he invested in the sinking of a fresh shaft for coal-mining close to the sea-shore at Strathsteven, and a brick and tile works was opened to exploit the blue-grey clays among the Jurassic rocks. Perhaps the height of this aristocratic industrial entrepreneur's ambition is shown by the locomotive works built in Brora. Only one engine was completed and the premises soon became a woollen mill. The economic history of Brora provides a fascinating example of the problems of industrial development in the far north of Scotland. Several million tons of good coal are still left here and a century ago an ambitious Duke of Sutherland made a determined effort to develop all the resources of this tiny plain. Today, the coal mine is closed, the result of the migration of its workers to better paid jobs in the oil-rig yards of Scotland's latest industry.

The A9 trunk road and railway run close to each other between Golspie and Helmsdale, and nowhere do they lie more than 1.6km (1 mile) from the shore. A fine series of raised beaches form the chief feature of the physical landscape – evidence of the changing sea-levels that have played such an important role in the evolution of the coast over the past few thousand years. Helmsdale is largely built over the 30m (100ft) beach. Crackaig, below the crofting village of Lothmore, also occupies the beach, while Kilmote stands at a lower level of the 8m (25ft) beach. The attractiveness of the Brora lowland is also exhibited in its wealth of prehistoric sites, particularly from the epoch of the Picts. A few hundred yards from the shore, north and south of Brora, are the remains of two brochs. The former site, at Kintradwell between the road and railway, is one of the more rewarding examples of these usually heavily ruined structures of Scotland's Iron Age. In parts the wall enclosing the circular interior courtyard of the broch is still standing to a height of some 4.5m (15ft).

Helmsdale, with a population of about 800, crouches at the mouth of the Helmsdale river, noted for its trout and salmon fishing.

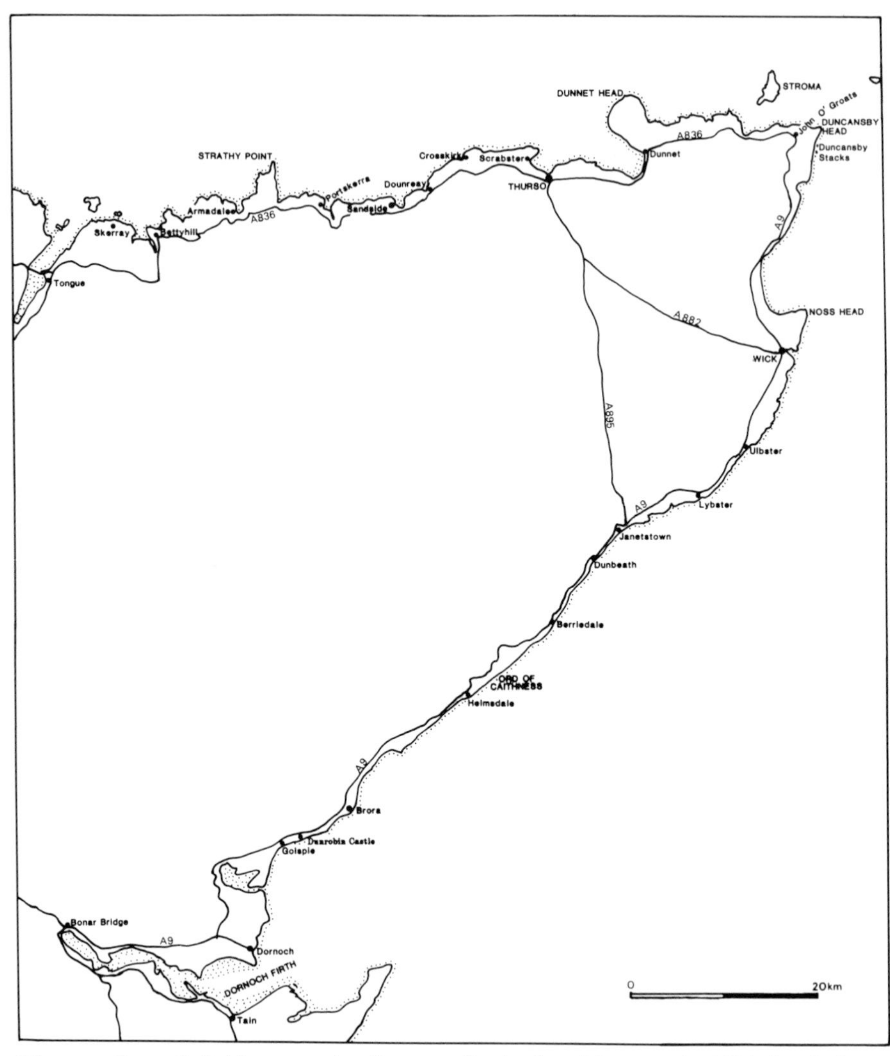

The coastline of Caithness and adjacent stretches to the south and west

The bare hills to north and west recall the sheep-farming boom of the early nineteenth century when the extensive clearances left an emptiness and desolation that still inhabits this landscape. Helmsdale itself, although a fragment of a fifteenth-century castle overlooks the harbour, is a product of those clearances. Much of the population from the inland hamlets was resettled on the coast at Portgower and West and East Helmsdale; and the author of Murray's *Handbook to Scotland* could report in 1894 that 'a busy fishing village with a small harbour' had been successfully established here. The railway, built in the 1870s and largely financed by the Duke of Sutherland, helped to strengthen the life of Helmsdale and now it is a busy place on the A9 before the road starts the long climb across the back of the Ord of Caithness.

Caithness is still another of the lost counties of Britain, administratively speaking, because it was absorbed into the immense Highland Region by the reorganisation of local government in the

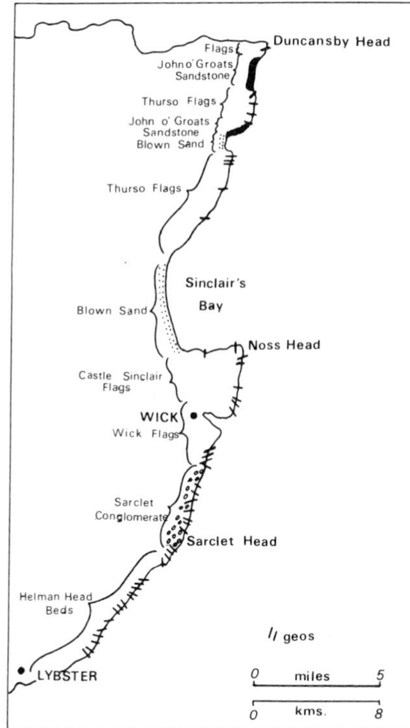

The geos of the Caithness coast and their relationship to the geology of the cliffline

1970s. Over the centuries history has affirmed on many occasions the individuality and remoteness of this north-eastern corner of Britain. The place-names of the coastal fringe tell of the Viking settlements between the tenth and twelfth centuries, and until the eighteenth century the contacts of Caithness with Scandinavia were at times closer than with Scotland. The coastline of Caithness – more than 161km (100 miles) of it – ranks among the finest in Britain. Suddenly, as one comes to the North Sea, the county's interior landscapes of dull peat bogs, slate-fenced pastures and unexciting single-storied cottages squatting beside long, straight treeless roads give way to a visually dramatic cliff-bound coastline. For the greater part the coast cuts a harsh section across the thick series of rocks of Old Red Sandstone age that underlie the low Caithness plateau. Because of the nature of the Old Red Sandstone, clearly bedded in horizontal planes, riven by joints and crossed by faults, the cliffs of Caithness, shaped by the North Sea's storms, possess an architectural quality. So many features of cliffed coasts are here displayed at their best. The stacks at Duncansby Head are the highest in the land, rising to more than 61m (200ft) and exceeding slightly the height of the adjacent mainland cliffs. This seascape abounds in caves that reach several hundred yards under the cliffs whose tops are scarred with ominous hollows that tell of subsidence. Subsequent collapse of cave roofs has led to the formation of the many *geos*, narrow, rock-bound inlets where the sea groans continuously. Where two caves, bored out along a line of weakness from opposite sides of a headland, have united a natural arch is formed.

Between Helmsdale and Berriedale the Highlands seem to reach right across to Scotland's eastern coastline. Here, too, the economic and social problems of Highland communities have left their marks on the landscape. The valley of the Langwell Water that empties into the sea at Berriedale was cleared in 1792 by Sir John Sinclair to make way for a large-scale experiment in sheep farming. Eighty-six families were moved to a new village at **Badbea** 152m (500ft) above the sea on a steep hillside that falls away to a sheer cliff's edge. Sir John Sinclair hoped that Badbea would grow into a viable community through its herring fishing and the draining and ditching of its steep hillsides. Today, the place is marked only by a monument, reached from the A9 by a 0.4km (¼ mile) long footpath, for after two generations at this exposed place the whole community of crofters migrated to New Zealand.

Berriedale ranks among the most spectacular sites of the Caithness coast. The Langwell and Berriedale Waters, flowing through deep, winding wooded glens, meet here to break through a narrow rocky chasm to the sea. From a magnificent cliffed coastline the eye turns inland to the vast empty moors of Langwell Forest and the rocky summits of Morven and Scaraben that reach to more than 610m (2,000ft). Viking settlers 1,000 years ago recognised the character of this landscape when they gave it the name

Berriedale, ie the valley of rocks. On the headland, beneath high cliffs, where the Berriedale Water makes its final twist into the North Sea, stands the fragmentary ruin of a medieval castle. Landscape history here belongs to two widely separate periods of time – the mysterious centuries of the Picts and the eighteenth and nineteenth centuries when the 'improvers' were largely responsible for the creation of the band of coastal settlements in Caithness. Sir John Sinclair emptied of their population the valleys that lead inland from Berriedale. Sheep farming, in its turn, had failed by the middle of the nineteenth century and the country of the Langwell Water became a vast deer forest. In 1857 Langwell House, in a delightful site amid the woodland at the junction of the two rivers, was bought by the Duke of Portland as a shooting lodge and with it 32,640ha (81,600 acres) of deer forest. Situated in this wilderness are overgrown hillocks that mark the cleared villages and the relic of a remoter time in the brochs and burial cairns of the Pictish Iron Age. But the best of the brochs in Caithness is to be found close to the sea above the deep gully of Ousdale. Here the double line of wall stands to a sufficient height to show the circular plan of the central courtyard, 8.5m (28ft) in diameter, and a ledge of projecting stones, the scarcement, that is a common feature in the design of Pictish brochs.

Dunbeath is the first of a string of fishing villages along the cliffed coast to Wick. With a suddenness of other glens in this part of the Caithness coast the Dunbeath Water exchanges a deep, sheltered wooded valley for the wild North Sea. Dunbeath and its river have been given a reputation far beyond the limits of the north-east through the work of a local writer who has found the themes and characters of his novels in his native region. The titles of *The Grey Coast, Morning Tide* and *Highland River* among several of Neil M. Gunn's works arouse a vision of this North Sea coast that in his writing becomes an element as important as any individual character. Most famous perhaps is *The Siver Darlings*, a story of Dunbeath's herring fishermen that was made into a film. Herring fishing began at Dunbeath in the first decade of the last century; by the 1860s it reached its peak when seventy-six boats worked from this exposed inlet. About 1.6km (1 mile) to the south, Dunbeath Castle, which is still inhabited, has escaped the fate of all other castles of the Caithness coast. Records show that a castle was here in 1428 and the core of this medieval keep may be seen in the present building. Extended in the early seventeenth century and enlarged again in 1870, Dunbeath Castle is a Victorian mansion in a magnificent seaward-facing site beneath a line of cliffs.

Along the cliffed coast from Dunbeath to Wick safe harbours are lacking; even so, a succession of fishing villages cling to tiny inlets made more secure by the building of breakwaters during the last century when the North Sea herring fisheries reached a peak of prosperity. **Latheron**, from a Gaelic phrase meaning the place of the seals, lies 1km (½ mile) inland clasped in a hollow of the coastal plateau. **Latheronwheel**, first known as Janetstown, is a planned settlement from the period of the Improving Movement – a single street that leads steeply down to a narrow sheltered inlet. When the many small fishing ports of eastern Scotland were at their best between 1860 and 1880 36 fishing boats worked from Latheronwheel and from the parish of Latheron 1,300 people were employed in the fisheries. At **Forse** 3.2km (2 miles) along the coast the links of Caithness with Viking times are clearly shown. The name comes from Old Norse, meaning 'waterfall', and above the reef-bound shore part of the walling still stands of a castle founded by the Vikings.

Lybster, a name of Scandinavian origin meaning 'the homestead on the slope', is a notable example of a fishing village created to provide a livelihood for the victims of the evictions. The wide, mile-long street that leads from the A9 to the cliff top above Lybster Bay was planned by Temple Sinclair. Lybster has survived as one of the more successful fishing settlements of Caithness. A century ago the harbour provided a base for 100 fishing boats. Lybster successfully adopted the new techniques of the seine net at the beginning of this century and, along with Wick and Scrabster, it has remained one of the three fishing ports of Caithness. Lybster's success may be partly explained by the physical features of the coast hereabouts. The bay, deeper than most of its neighbours, lies along a fault at the mouth of the Reisgill Burn. Even so, the harbour entrance is dangerous at a time of onshore gales from the south-east and under such conditions this coastline provides no safe refuge. Then fishing boats have been known to run to Cromarty for shelter. At the head of Lybster's wide main street, beside the A9, stands the Portland Arms Hotel, once a staging inn, built after the completion of the coast road from the south in 1816.

Sarclet, a street of forbidding stone cottages, above a tiny, cliff-ringed cove, began as a newly planned fishing village in 1788. The name, from the Old Norse meaning the sheep's slope, suggests the presence of an older farm and sheep pasture. The new settlement arose from the stimulus given to herring fishing by the British Fishery Society founded in 1750 with the aim of counteracting the overwhelming role of the Dutch on the North Sea's fishing banks in the eighteenth century. At first the society subsidised the herring catch brought into British ports, but in 1786 its powers were extended to include 'the building of towns, villages, harbours, quays, piers and fishing stations in the Highlands and Islands of North Britain'. Sarclet was laid out by a Captain Brodie and for a time was known as Brodie's Town.

Wick The origins of Wick reach back beyond the time of this sixteenth-century burgh; the name, from the Old Norse *vik*, means a creek or bay. There is little doubt that the Viking longships sailed into this Caithness inlet and that the Castle of Old Wick or Castle Oliphant, a windowless square keep still standing to three storeys height, began as a Viking stronghold. The older settlement is situated on the northern shore of Wick Bay, while the new town was built in the early nineteenth century on the south shore. Pulteneytown, as this quarter of Wick is called, was named after Sir William Pulteney, president of the British Fisheries Association. Thomas Telford made the plan for the new settlement, designed a harbour to replace the former natural fishing haven at Staxigoe, and built the three-arched bridge across the river Wick into the royal burgh.

Wick established its place as the county town of Caithness during the herring boom of the nineteenth century when more than 1,000 vessels were based there. Wick has weathered the revolutions in the fishing industry that have destroyed many of the small ports. This grey stone-built burgh is a product of those Victorian decades. The parish church, built in 1830, at the west end of the High Street, remembers not only the engineers of the Improving Movement in the north-east but also the remoter past of the Earls of Caithness and Orkney.

Today, Wick serves as a shopping centre for miles around. Its port has suffered a severe decline with the gradual collapse of the herring fisheries and, since World War II, the ending of regular passenger shipping routes to Orkney, Shetland, Aberdeen and Leith, although there is some compensation in the growing traffic of its airport. Industry has not stagnated, however. The Pulteneytown Distillery founded in 1826, closed in 1926 and reopened in 1951 by a Canadian company, has bonded-warehouse storage for 90,000 hectolitres (2 million gal) of whisky. There is a modern cheese factory as well as some marine engineering by the harbour. The most exciting industry was the foundation of Caithness Glass in Pulteneytown in 1960, the enterprise of a local laird. Glass technologists from the continent were brought in to establish a skilled industry. The factory uses fifteenth-century methods of glass engraving and its beautiful products have found a market all over Britain. Sand, the raw material of glass-making is imported from Loch Aline on the Sound of Mull. Another unexpected development of recent years has been the opening of a recording studio that specialises in folk music and in particular the Wick Scottish Dance Band. Wick does not rank high among the tourist places of Britain, although the Caithness Glass factory sees several thousand visitors a year. The delights of Caithness lie in the beauty of its coastline

Castles Girnigoe and Sinclair, perched on a finger of rock above the North Sea

and it is between Wick and John o'Groats that this scenery is displayed at its most magnificent.

A notable change comes over the character of the coastline with the appearance of two wide embayments – Sinclair's Bay and Freswick Bay – to break the long line of Caithness cliffs. Scenically, Sinclair's Bay is the finer of the two for a long sand beach is here backed by a spectacular complex of dunes. On the low cliffs that flank the southern rim of the bay stands one of Scotland's most exciting castle ruins. Two castles, Girnigoe and Sinclair, stand perched on a finger of grey-green rock. Girnigoe Castle was built towards the end of the fifteenth century by William, 2nd Sinclair Earl. A ruined keep towers above an artificial ditch that guards the approach to the castle from the landward side of this knife-edged peninsula. In front of the keep and guarded by another ditch stands the outer ward and gatehouse of Girnigoe. It was here that Castle Sinclair was erected in 1606, built partly over and around the entrance buildings of the medieval castle. Besieged in 1690 in a dispute over its rightful ownership, Castle Sinclair was partly destroyed by artillery; abandonment and North Sea gales have since done the rest. About 1.6km (1 mile) away stands Ackergill Tower on a low shore, close by the sea. This medieval tower, much restored in the nineteenth century, rises to five storeys and contains a great hall and minstrels' gallery. For four years it was the main stronghold of Cromwell's troops in their occupation of northern Scotland in the 1650s.

Keiss, another name that commemorates the presence of the Vikings here 1,000 years ago, at first appearance is as dull as any of the coastal villages that came into being at the time of the clearances. Crouching among the formal pattern of fields and scattered cottages are the sites of two brochs. Keiss Castle, down by the shore below its Victorian successor, is a sixteenth-century L-shaped fortress with two diagonally opposite towers, so designed to parry attack from any direction.

A low cliffed coastline with rocky

intertidal reefs separates Keiss and Freswick Bay. A shallow depression in the coastal plateau, a geologically ancient valley, is marked by this coastal embayment containing a sandy beach and inland a stretch of low dunes. Freswick Bay faces into the eye of gales and heavy seas from the south-east and the beach suffers considerable change from year to year. Winter gales remove large quantities of shell sand from the steeply sloping beach, but it is redeposited in the weeks of quiet weather that belong to much of spring and summer. Freswick Bay's rim of dunes lacks the spectacular qualities of Sinclair's Bay. Severe wind erosion has occurred, erosion that has been accelerated by the quarrying of sand from pits along the seaward face. One consequence of the shifting sandhills has been the exposure of a Viking settlement beneath the dunes.

North from Freswick by Skirza Head and its broch is situated one of the finest sections of coastal scenery to be found anywhere in Britain. Caithness faces the sea in sheer cliffs of over 61m (200ft) in height. *Geos*, dark, sunless rock-bound inlets, succeed each other northwards to that critical turning point of the British coastline, Duncansby Head. The highlight in this magnificent seascape occurs in the Stacks of Duncansby, 61m (200ft) high pillars carved out of the John o'Groats sandstone. The pity is that this piece of coast lacks a marked cliff-top path. Access at most points is not easy and entails the crossing of fields and the climbing of fences that reach right to the cliff's edge. For the motorist the easiest way to this fine scenery is by the road to Duncansby Head lighthouse. Long Geo, a 30m (100yd) long inlet with vertical walls of almost 61m (200ft), lies west of the lighthouse. The prospect across Pentland Firth reaches out to the distant cliffs of Orkney while below one's feet the air is alive with the noise and swirl of sea birds.

18 North-west Scotland

Scotland's Northern Coast

The character of Scotland's northern coastline is determined by the ancient rocks that form its many miles of cliffs and also by its outlook upon the stormy North Atlantic. As most topographical writers upon this region never fail to remark, there is no more land between Cape Wrath and the North Pole. In the east, reaching as far as Melvich Bay, the coastal scenery has been shaped out of the slaty flagstones and coarse sandstones of the immensely thick Old Red Sandstone deposits - rocks laid down between 360 million and 400 million years ago. The little visited central section of the northern coastline belongs to the much older Moinian rocks, formed between 600 million and 1,000 million years ago. On the shores of Loch Eriboll the Moinian rocks come to a sudden end along the line of a geologically famous feature, the Moine Thrust - the western limit of the rocks that were involved in the Caledonian mountain building some 400 million years ago. Westward from Loch Eriboll by Durness to Cape Wrath the coastline and the landscape of its hinterland have been shaped from rocks formed before the time of the complex earth movements that made the Caledonian structures. Here we find the Durness limestone, out of which sea and river have carved the Smoo Cave. Torridonian sandstones form the remote and inaccessible sea cliffs of Clò Mór and at Cape Wrath itself we meet the Lewisian Gneiss, the rock of the resistant foreland against which the sediments of the Caledonian mountains were compressed, folded and transposed westward along the plane of the Moine Thrust. The Lewisian Gneiss ranks among the oldest rocks of the Earth's surface. It has been found to bear traces of earth movements that happened between 2,000 million and 2,900 million years ago.

John o'Groats, the goal of all coach tours that take the A9 north from Inverness, has an undeserved reputation as the most northerly point of the British mainland. That honour must go to Dunnet Head whose 91m (300ft) sandstone cliffs provide a far more fitting conclusion to mainland Britain. The name and the reputation of John o'Groats as the last and most northerly place in Scotland seems to date back to the end of the fifteenth century when a Dutchman, Jan de Grot, obtained a grant of land in Caithness and established a ferry between Huna and Orkney. He is reputed to have charged one groat for the crossing of the Pentland Firth, so some confusion surrounds the origin of the place-name. Does it derive from the man or his scale of fares? Tourism has done its best to advertise this bleak, windswept place, but fortunately it has escaped the despoliation of Land's End. There is the last house in Scotland, a white-washed fisherman's cottage, the inevitable traffic in souvenirs, a flagpole near the John o'Groat's Hotel that marks the site of Jan de Grot's house, and a caravan and camping site. John o'Groats offers a fine prospect across the Pentland Firth to the red cliffs of Orkney. During the 1960s, the prospect was held out to John o'Groats of development as a ferry-port for Orkney, but the idea was rejected in favour of Scrabster's sheltered harbour. The site is too exposed, a long jetty would be needed to serve a modern vehicle ferry here, and the

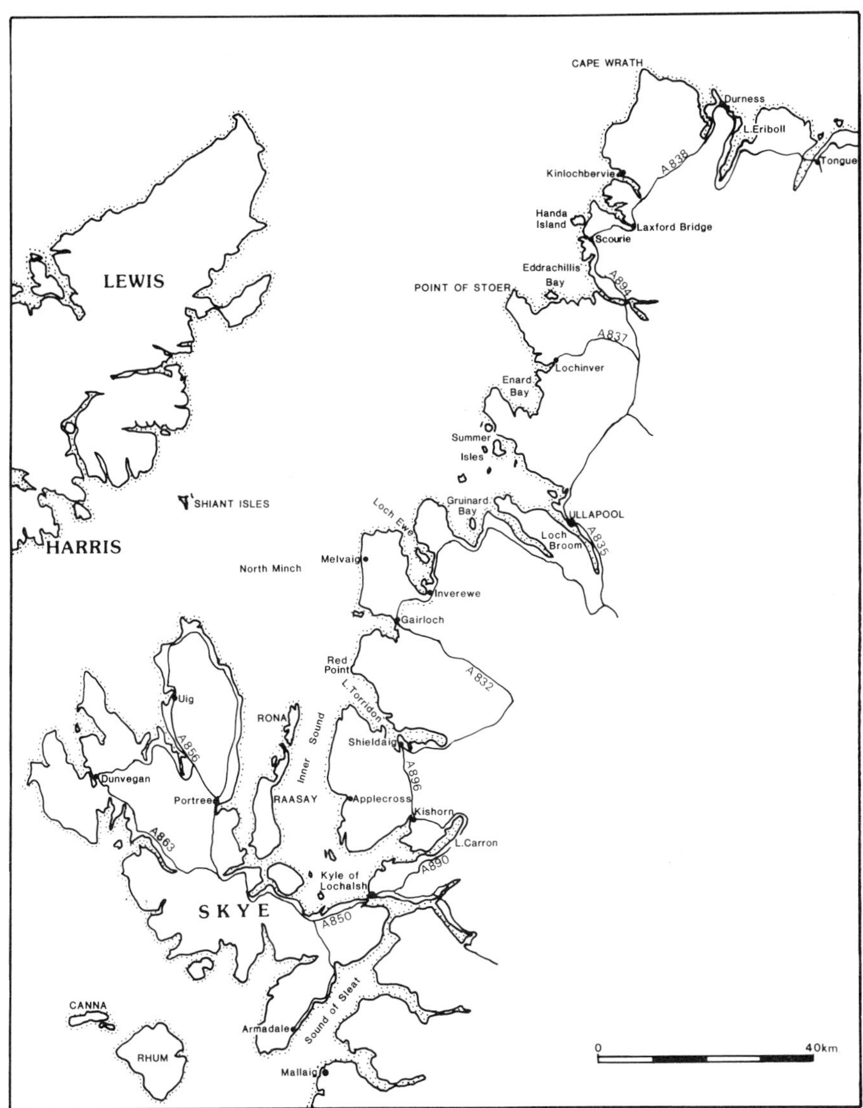

The fjord coastline of North-west Scotland including the Isles of Skye and Lewis

fast tidal currents, the Boars of Duncansby, that roar between Stroma and the mainland, provided another objection to the development of John o'Groats.

Close at hand is the island of Stroma, once famous for its fishermen and its boatbuilders, some of whose yawls have seen service for more than 100 years. Stroma is now deserted. The arctic tern increases its numbers there and grey seals breed in the caves and *geos* of the eastern coast.

The Old Red Sandstone coastline between the two great headlands of Duncansby and Dunnet offers little of scenic interest. For the most part a low, unexciting cliff-line gives way to extensive rocky reefs. The shallow bays are notable for their beaches composed largely of lime-rich shell sand, shells that originate on the offshore reefs. The Bay of Sannick, accessible from the road from John o'Groats to Duncansby Head, has a shell-sand beach piled against the cliff foot to the east of the stream that empties into the sea. Between the Ness of Huna and the Ness of Duncansby a succession of tiny beaches tucked in among the reefs are composed of shell sand, and at one of these many of the shells are still intact. During World War II much of the sand from the John o'Groats beach was quarried for building purposes and agriculture.

Westward from John o'Groats to Dunnet Head a number of sandy bays interrupt this generally low-lying and unattractive reef-bound shoreline. Scotland's Haven, a narrow inlet hemmed in by steep cliffs of boulder clay, is probably the most interesting. The present boulder clay cliffs, carved out of clays that in places are over 30m (100ft) thick, suggests that the inlet was in existence either before the Ice Age or, at least, before the main period of glaciation when Caithness was buried beneath far-spreading glaciers from the mainland hills. Marine erosion over the past 12,000 years of post-glacial time has been engaged in the re-excavation of this ancient coastal feature.

The Castle of Mey is the chief object of interest in this windy landscape of long straight roads with an occasional string of widely-spaced cottages as at Rattar and Scarfskerry. Now well known as a royal residence since its purchase by the Queen Mother in 1952, a castle has stood at this site, less than 1km (½ mile) from the shore, for about 1,000 years. What we see today is a sixteenth-century castle of jutting towers and corbelled turrets to which sham battlements were added in the Victorian years. The Bishops of Caithness owned a grange here in the Middle Ages. In 1566 the episcopal grange was acquired by George, 4th Earl of Caithness and it was converted into a fortified mansion typical of the sixteenth century in Scotland with its Z-shaped plan, defensive towers and numerous gunholes on the ground and first floors. But the original name of the Castle of Mey, *Barrogil*, a Norse name meaning 'the castle by the ravine', suggests that a Viking stronghold once stood here.

Dunnet Head and Dunnet Bay complement each other as major features of the northern coastline. The headland, a high cliffed promontory of Upper Old Red Sandstone is the true northernmost point of mainland Britain. Scenically, it lives up to this particular dignity. If the traveller follows the B855 from the main road at Dunnet village he winds and climbs across the back of the peninsula, a treeless loch-strewn moorland with the ever-growing presence of the sea. Abruptly this narrow single-tracked road finds itself above the sheer 91m (300ft) cliffs at the threshold of the lighthouse. Late on a clear evening of high summer this truly feels like the end of mainland Britain. Sandstone cliffs glow in the sunset light from the north-west and across the cold, dark shield of Pentland Firth – *pettaland fjörthr* of the Vikings, 'the firth of the country of the Picts' – we descry the long rose-red line of the cliffs of Hoy. Sea birds inhabit these wild cliffs. Below the lighthouse is a colony of kittiwakes, their nests of grass and seaweed, cemented with mud, seem perilously perched on the narrowest ledges. Over the past year local ornithologists have noted some striking changes in the bird population of these cliffs. For instance, the Fulmar Petrel first nested at Dunnet Head in 1905. Now it is found everywhere on the cliffs from which it has ousted the Herring Gull.

Dunnet Bay contains the greatest extent of sandy beach on the whole northern coastline. Inland the tide-washed sand gives way to dunes of mountainous proportions reaching to over 15m (50ft) above the sea. Inland from the dune belt with its spectacular wind-shaped hollows, blow-outs, sand has drifted in to form a succession of links. These links with their light, well-drained soils of lime-rich sand support a fine turf as well as a rich variety of flowering plants. The landscape and geography of the dunes is very different from that of the sandy machair of the links. The Dunnet dune barrier is actively moving inland, its progress determined by the vast reserves of sand exposed at low tide on the bay's gently sloping beach. Gales from the north-west

The most northerly stretch of sand on the west coast of Scotland: Sandwood Bay between Kinlochbervie and Cape Wrath

and south-east are largely responsible for the sand dunes' instability but man, too, has intervened, at times to promote erosion and mobility of the dunes and at others to take measures to stabilise the shifting sand-hills. During the eighteenth century considerable erosion took place when the shore and its hinterland stood in common ownership for the grazing of sheep and cattle. During the early nineteenth century the dunes were lotted to adjacent farms and as overgrazing declined stability increased. The most vital change in the landscape came in the 1950s when the Forestry Commission acquired some 360ha (900 acres) of land at the head of Dunnet Bay. The work of the Forestry Commission reduced erosion and stabilised the moving sand in the northern part of Dunnet's dunes. Brushwood hedges were built across blow-outs to prevent sand drifting across the A836, Dunnet–Castletown road. Loose sand in the lee of hedges was planted with Mountain pine from the Pyrenees and Corsican pine. In the space of twenty years the Forestry Commission have transformed the landscape at the northern end of Dunnet's dunes, but there, perhaps fortunately, the process has stopped. The plantations have been a commercial failure. Maintenance costs have been too high, while growth rates on this gale-ridden northern shore have proved too slow. A dark-green blanket of conifers will not destroy this beautiful wild 'dunescape'; the aesthetic and ecological tragedy of the Culbin Sands will not be replayed at Dunnet. At the northern end of the beach there is a car park as well as caravan and camping sites. This fine stretch of sands has become a venue for sand-yachting and there is a club-house for the sport near the car-park at the northern end of the dunes.

Castletown This industrial village with a formal gridiron plan focused on a mile-long straight of the A836 was founded in 1824 when the Castlehill quarries begin the large-scale production and export of paving flags. The quarries, now a long disused, overgrown, man-made cliff face in the Caithness Flags at the west end of Castletown, were opened in 1824 and at the same time Sheriff James Traill saw to the founding of the town to house his workers and the construction of a pier close to his mansion, now a ruin, on the shore at Castlehill. At their height, in the latter years of the nineteenth century, the quarries employed 1,000 hands and Caithness flags, impervious to moisture and resistant even to severe frost, were known as a paving material far beyond the British Isles.

Ullapool was begun as a planned fishing community, established in 1788 by the British Fisheries Society and laid out by Thomas Telford. It has become the major fishing port of the west coast (*G. R. C. Lomax*)

Thurso dates at least to the time of the Viking earldoms in the north. By 1633 Thurso had been made a free burgh of barony by Charles I. The narrow streets by the harbour belong to the late seventeenth and early eighteenth centuries. Here among the fishermen's cottages lies the ruin of St Peter's, last used in 1862 with the tracery of a window strikingly intact. Inland from the shore one passes into the wide formal streets of a Georgian planned town, the work of Sir John Sinclair who is remembered by a statue in Sinclair Square. Here, so unexpectedly in the remote north, one finds a reflection of that greatest piece of Scottish urban planning, the New Town of Edinburgh.

Thurso was not drawn into the railway age until August 1873, when the Sutherland and Caithness Railway opened and the last mail coach ran from Thurso to Inverness. The little terminus was built on open ground on the fringe of the formal chequerboard pattern of streets of Sir John Sinclair's new town. Towards the end of the last century a handful of Victorian villas took up plots of land close to the station, but the latest phase of urban development belongs to the 1950s and 60s in response to the needs of the new population of scientists and technicians employed in the building and running of the Dounreay reactor and power station.

In scarcely a decade Thurso's population trebled; in the landscape this development is reflected in a great swathe of local authority housing, harled and whitewashed, around the austere grey stone core of Sinclair's town.

A glance at Thurso's history shows that it has always been a busy place. As long ago as the fourteenth century the harbour in the narrow sheltered estuary of the Thurso river engaged in the export of grain to Scandinavia and the Baltic lands. By the eighteenth century the salting of meat and the curing of hides was an important occupation for export to Bergen, Göteborg and Hamburg. At the end of the eighteenth century weaving was an industry of some note. By the early years of the nineteenth century the Industrial Revolution lightly cast its influence over Thurso, far as it lay from those coalfields that formed the seat of Victorian enterprise. For almost a century the Thurso Foundry, importing its raw materials by sea, manufactured equipment for water mills. Thurso also played its part in the exploitation and export of the Caithness flagstones. Quarrying of the Caithness flagstones is extinct, but Thurso is deeply involved in the most advanced experiments in energy production. The building of Dounreay employed 3,000 men and since the completion of the reactor in 1958 the plant with its power station, materials-testing reactor and fuel-element fabrication and chemical-processing plants finds work for 2,000.

Scrabster shelters from north-westerly gales in the lee of Holborn Head. To the east, across the wide mouth of the bay, Dunnet's blunt headland reduces the built-up force of storm waves from that direction. This is the safest haven of the Caithness coastline and of late it has developed into the chief ferry port of northern Scotland. The roll-on roll-off vehicle ferry to Stromness in Orkney plies from here with several crossings daily in the height of summer. Now, in the summer months, the ancient seaways of the North Atlantic, the vital communications of the Vikings 1,000 years ago, have been revived in the form of a car ferry that leaves Scrabster once a week, on Mondays, for the Faeroes and Iceland. A modern fishing fleet, diesel-powered and employing seine nets, echo-sounders and radio navigators, is based on Scrabster. Its emergence as a major fishing port and auction market is largely due to the energy of another John Sinclair, Lord Lieutenant of Caithness, in the years after World War II when he was the moving spirit in founding the Thurso Fish-selling Company that brought the boats to Scrabster. Here, too, a lobster pond has been established to keep this valuable commodity alive before its despatch to distant markets.

A fragmentary ruin of a castle lies on the low rocky shore of Thurso Bay. Formerly a seat of the Bishops of Caithness, it certainly pre-dates the earliest recorded reference of 1328. The cliffs, down which the road sidles to the harbour, are composed of boulder clay. The contorted rumpled ground here is the result of land-slipping and slumping, and the road itself has not escaped the effect of such earth movements. During the last twenty years there has been a dramatic increase in land-slipping here from changes in sub-surface drainage, the result of house-building on the Braes of Scrabster as part of the recent growth of Thurso.

Between Thurso and Melvich Bay the scenery of Scotland's northern coastline is largely controlled by the continuing presence of rocks of Old Red Sandstone age. For the motorist following the main road westward towards Tongue and Durness this is dull windswept country with its flagstone walls and fences, bent scrawny trees and widely scattered roadside cottages. The coastline, much of it low and reef-bound, is not easily accessible except by narrow, unmade tracks that lead northward for over 1.6km (1 mile) from the main road. At Holborn Head, the land rises steeply towards a sudden summit and a line of precipitous cliffs riddled with caves and blow-holes that the sea has carved along lines of weakness in the Caithness flagstones. Chasms seem to split the headland from top to bottom and offshore a huge stack, the Clett, stands 46m (150ft) high.

It is worthwhile leaving the main road at **Bridge of Forss** in its grove of close-growing wiry trees to reach **Crosskirk** and its little bay at the mouth of the Forss Water. Here the roofless St Mary's Chapel is the oldest ecclesiastical building in Caithness. This simple rectangular shaped chapel, typical of medieval churches in Highland Britain, seems to be built over an older foundation at its eastern end, suggesting that here was an older Dark Age settlement of the

Picts. The presence of the Picts at Crosskirk is borne out by a symbol stone found in the ruins of a broch, now completely demolished that once stood on the cliff-edge nearby. A rough, cross-country walk from St Mary's Chapel brings one to Brims Ness where a rocky bench, 0.4km (1/4 mile) wide, in the Caithness Flags forms the foreshore. The place-name derives from the Old Norse *brim*, surf, so Brims Ness is 'surf point'. Here, close by the shore and a tiny unused harbour, stands Brims Castle – a rectangular keep, three storeys in height, that belonged to the Sinclairs. Back at Crosskirk and the mouth of the Forss Water are the ruins of a snuff mill that worked intermittently for more than a century using water power to grind the tobacco. It is said that this lonely isolated site provided the commercial advantage of raw tobacco smuggled from Dutch ships passing through the Pentland Firth between the Americas and European ports.

Dounreay The atomic research establishment and power station of Dounreay, situated 4.8km (3 miles) beyond Crosskirk, dominates the landscape. The several buildings occupy the site of an abandoned wartime airfield. For the traveller along the A836 Dounreay is a compelling sight with the gleaming white ball of the huge steel sphere, 41m (135ft) in diameter, that houses the fast reactor, the heat from which raises steam to generate electricity for half of northern Scotland. The control tower of the former airfield contains an exhibition, now an outstanding tourist attraction, that outlines the principles of the harnessing of atomic energy.

Reay The village is strung out along the road, which runs near the shore by the head of Sandside Bay, and the present focus, if it has any at all, is about the early eighteenth-century church. There is evidence of an earlier settlement in the remains of a church, dedicated to St Colman, of which the ruins stand in the north-east corner of the present churchyard. Earlier in history, the Vikings settled at Reay at a site closer to the sea where a village, the forerunner of the present roadside community, was overwhelmed by moving sand in the eighteenth century. Sandside Bay shelters between two headlands of the Caithness Flags whose shaggy faces end abruptly above wide rock platforms. In contrast, the head of the bay is filled with a tumultuous range of high sand dunes. The present landscape of Sandside's dunes has been affected by severe erosion in recent years. The shell-rich sand has long been quarried for agriculture and building purposes and the construction of Dounreay made particularly heavy demands. As a result, high winds have carved deep blow-outs from the inroads into the main dune complex made by sand extraction. Along the west shore of Sandside Bay a little used track leads down to **Fresgoe** where there is an abandoned stone-built harbour, a relic of a once thriving community.

Between Reay and Melvich lies the boundary between the former counties of Caithness and Sutherland. A few miles further west runs a boundary of geological significance.

The rocks of Old Red Sandstone age give way at Melvich to the much older metamorphic rocks of the Moine Series. From Melvich Bay to the Kyle of Tongue the coast is immensely varied, little visited and very beautiful. Rocky peninsulas project northwards into the Atlantic. For the most part it is not easily accessible; for many miles the main A836 runs out of sight of the sea across featureless, loch-bespattered moorland.

The coastline west of Melvich Bay owes some of its topographical variety to its complex geology. Although Moinian rocks form the foundations of this landscape, here and there patches of Old Red Sandstone have been preserved with the caves and deep *geos* that the sea has carved along lines of weakness in these rocks. Again, intrusions of granite, never great in extent, add distinct shapes and colours to parts of this coastline. Melvich Bay has a good beach and at its head the Halladale river winds round a dune-crowned spit into the sea. **Portskerra**, typical of the many fishing settlements planted on the Scottish coastline early in the nineteenth century at the time of the vast inland clearances for sheep farming, is a place of scattered cottages and red corrugated iron roofs. Strathy Bay coincides with an outlier of Old Red Sandstone, preserved among the Moinian rocks, but the peninsula that ends in Strathy Point is a complex of granite and other intruded igneous rocks. The lane that leaves the A836 for Strathy Point dips and twists by red-roofed croft-houses on its way to the lighthouse at the end of the peninsula, built in 1958 and perhaps the last to be raised on the British coastline.

From Strathy Point to Bettyhill this rocky coast shelters a succession of tiny bays with attractive beaches which can be reached with some persistence by the motorist who is prepared to follow narrow, tortuous lanes, sometimes through heather-filled gorges, and, at the end, to make his way on foot to the shore. Armadale Bay's beach is backed by dunes. Kirtomy Bay is screened by a long rocky skerry on its western flank and Farr Bay – easiest of all to reach from the main road – has an attractive beach of sand with dunes and a stretch of machair. At Kirtomy Point and the narrow inlet of the Geodh' Ghamhainn a patch of the Old Red Sandstone makes itself felt in the kind of scenery that is the hallmark of more than 161km (100 miles) of the Caithness coastline. The promontory, the Aird of Kirtomy, is pierced by a long tunnel through which boats may pass. Pennant, the indefatigable eighteenth-century topographer, visited this place that now seems so much off the beaten track and described it as 'the most curious cavern in the world'.

Bettyhill, at the mouth of the river Naver, arose out of the Highland clearances, among which the decimation of Strathnaver is one of the most notorious. Before 1820 the clachans of Strathnaver supported a population of 1,200. By 1834 a traveller through this long Highland glen reported that 'for 24 miles not a house is to be seen except shepherds' dwellings at measured distances'. Bettyhill, founded as a fishing port, was part of the effort to re-establish this disrupted population. It is named after Elizabeth, Countess of Sutherland, wife of George Granville Leverson-Gower who was responsible for the Sutherland clearances between 1810 and 1820. Bettyhill grew up in the ancient parish of Farr and it is the old parish church, lying between the main road and the sea on the right bank of the Clachan Burn, that is the place of greatest interest. The graveyard contains a superb Celtic cross of early Christian date and still in its original position. It is elaborately decorated with spirals and interlaced patterns and stands nearly 2.4m (8ft) in height. Dating from the mid-ninth century the cross was raised after the extinction of Pictland as an independent kingdom and when Strathnaver had already passed under the domination of the Vikings. Farr Church is now a museum in which the history of the Strathnaver clearances of 1812–19 is documented.

Bettyhill looks westward across the wide mouth of Torrisdale Bay into which empty the rivers Nave and Borgie. At low water a wide sand beach stretches between the river mouths; inland, the lower slopes of an intervening ridge, Druim Chuibhe, are ringed with dunes and plastered with blown sand carried from the beach by strong north winds. Here, on a sandy terrace to the east of the ridge, one of the richest prehistoric sites of the northern coast has been discovered. A broch from the Pictish Iron Age, hut circles marking the sites of former dwellings and burial cists from an earlier time have all been located.

From Torrisdale Bay to the Kyle of Tongue main road and coastline lie far apart, but at **Borgie Bridge** a most rewarding diversion to the sea may be made by following a lane to the right through the crofting settlement of **Torrisdale** to Skerray Bay. The approach to the cliff-encircled bay is made along the flat floor of a former sea strait, shaped at a time when sea-levels stood higher than at present. There are patches of oakwood and the high hedge-banks of this single-track road are adorned with wild rose and honeysuckle. Skerray Bay has a harsh boulder beach and an abandoned stone pier. Two islands, Coomb Island and Eilean nan Ròn, act as natural breakwaters to protect the approaches to Skerray Bay from north-west and north-east. At the foot of the ragged line of cliffs is the perfectly developed platform of a raised beach. Abandoned and forgotten, Skerray Bay is a place of sea caves and seals.

Skerray Bay, one of the many deserted harbours of northern Scotland

The Kyle of Tongue introduces a fresh element into the scenery of the northern coast as the first of three deeply penetrating sea lochs. The A836 winds along the foot of Ben Tongue between **Coldbackie** and the important road junction at Tongue where a long lonely traverse across the north-west Highlands to Lairg begins. From Tongue the A838 branches off around the head of the sea loch towards Durness. The Kyle of Tongue, unlike its neighbour Loch Eriboll, is extremely shallow. Extensive sandbanks are exposed at low tide when the Rabbit Islands, a low outcrop of the Moine schists in the entrance to Tongue Bay, are joined by a sand bar to the western shore of the sea loch. Midway along the Kyle at Tongue Lodge a spit, now a raised feature that was originally constructed in the time of post-glacial higher sea-levels, has been employed in the recent road improvements in northern Scotland. A causeway now cuts out the 16km (10 mile) detour by the A838 around the head of the Kyle of Tongue.

Tongue marks the beginning of some of the most impressive scenery in the whole of Britain's coastlands where sea and mountain are together joined in a single prospect. Here the view inland towards the head of the kyle is dominated by the four serrated peaks of Ben Loyal at 762m (2,500ft) above the shore. Tongue House, its policies and gardens an island of luxury in this austere landscape, was the home of the chiefs of Clan Mackay, the Lords Reay. In 1829 the 7th Lord Reay sold his estates to George Granville Leverson-Gower, who was to become the Duke of Sutherland four years later. With the purchase of the Reay estates the Duke of Sutherland invested in the improvement of communications in this north-west corner of Scotland. Roads were laid down that still serve the modern motorist. It is along a route first engineered by the Duke of Sutherland that the motorist follows the A838 from the Kyle of Tongue to Loch Eriboll. The Gaelic place-name, Mhòine, describes a peat bog. Across this desolation the Duke of Sutherland's road was laid – floated may be a better word – on a foundation of coppice wood, turf and gravel. Moin House, now a ruin, was built as a travellers' refuge in the midst of this wilderness.

To the north of the A838 a trackless landscape stretches towards the high cliffed coast which is accessible only by a minor road that branches from the A' Mhòine road where it turns westward from the shore of the Kyle of Tongue up the steep shoulder of the Achuvoldrach Burn. Along this lane a string of crofting settlements, **Melness, Midtown** and **Talmine**, follow each other to the end of the road at **Achininver** where there is a deep inlet with a sandy beach.

A tombolo joins the island of Ard Neackie to the eastern shore of Loch Eriboll

Beyond, a line of lofty cliffs carved out of the mica schists of the Moinian rocks point westward to Whiten Head at the entrance to Loch Eriboll. Like so many of the finest places on the coastline of western Scotland Whiten Head can be reached only with the greatest difficulty. Some 10km (6 miles) of wet trackless moorland broken by the winding gorges of streams draining to the cliff-edge above Loch Eriboll divide the headland from the nearest road. Stout boots and compass are essential for this journey, which should be eschewed when sea mists blot out the landscape.

Loch Eriboll reaches inland for 16km (10 miles). Unlike the shallow, sand-choked Kyle of Tongue, this is a deep fjord of depths of 15–60 fathoms. Used as a naval anchorage in World War II, it was chosen as the assembly place for surrendered German submarines from the Atlantic in 1945. On the eastern shore of Loch Eriboll Cambrian rocks, largely limestones, produce a succession of terraced escarpments; there are patches of woodland and splashes of bright green pasture that indicate the benign influence of limestone among the dominantly acid soils of the north-west Highlands. The western shore of the loch is predominantly composed of the Lewisian Gneiss; wet moorlands reach down to the shore. Along the eastern flank are half a dozen places which reveal evidence of prehistoric man. There was a settlement, as shown by hut circles, beside the river Hope and the presence of hut circles and a ruined broch between two freshwater lochans – Loch Ach'an Lochaidh and Loch Cragaidh – shows another occupied site of the Iron Age.

At the mouth of Loch Eriboll the A838 turns westward towards Durness. Here a track winds down to the shore at **Rispond**. A fishing station was established at this inlet towards the end of the eighteenth century when the systematic exploitation of the herring around the coast of Scotland was encouraged by the British Fisheries Society.

Along the last 6.4km (4 miles) into Durness the A838 closely hugs the coast. For the motorist a succession of fine bays and beaches comes into view. **Sangobeg** has a good sand beach enclosed by headlands of Cambrian Quarzite and Durness Limestone. Below the scattered untidy village of

Durness is Sango Bay with a long white-sand beach divided into compartments by miniature rocky headlands. The finest piece of this north-western shore is Balnakeil Bay, a long curve of white sand sheltered by the peninsula of Faraid Head. The most dramatic sight in this limestone landscape is the Smoo Cave, whose place-name derives from the Old Norse, *smuga*, a cleft. The cave consists of three chambers of which the outermost, beneath the high arch, is the only part accessible to the tourist. The Allt Smoo must be forded inside the cave to reach a point to view above the dark inner chamber into which the river thunders down a 9m (30ft) shaft. The innermost cave ends in a deep cleft 36.5m (120ft) in length and only 2.4m (8ft) wide. Despite its remoteness from Britain's tourist routes the Smoo Cave has become a considerable attraction.

Balnakeil means the village with the chapel. The roofless church, Durness Old Church as it is called, was built in 1619 on the site of a medieval chapel. Balnakeil was the summer residence of the Bishops of Caithness in the Middle Ages and, earlier still, there was a cell here of the monastery at Dornoch. In the graveyard stands a granite obelisk to Rob Donn, a drover who has been described as the northern Robbie Burns, a writer of satirical poems in the Sutherland dialect. A footpath from Balnakeil leads across the neck of the An Fharaid peninsula to Seanachaisteal Dun, 'the old castle', a scanty relic of a Dark Age fortress at the tip of a lofty promontory. A Viking saga records the storming of this fortress in the thirteenth century by a fleet from Bergen. The blunt promontory between Balnakeil and the Kyle of Durness, a rock platform of Durness limestone 17–30m (50–100ft) above sea-level shrouded in blown sand, provides a uniquely favourable environment that was seized by early man. Here dry-stone dykes, burial cairns, the evidence of settlement and cultivation ranging for over 1,000 years have been discovered. Also of interest is the craft village with pottery, art gallery, coffee shop and hotel in the concrete blocks of a World War II radar station.

The climax of any tour of the north coast ought to be Cape Wrath, but the very difficulty of getting there means that only the most determined see its 91m (300ft)

The huge arched entrance to the Smoo Cave in the Durness Limestone

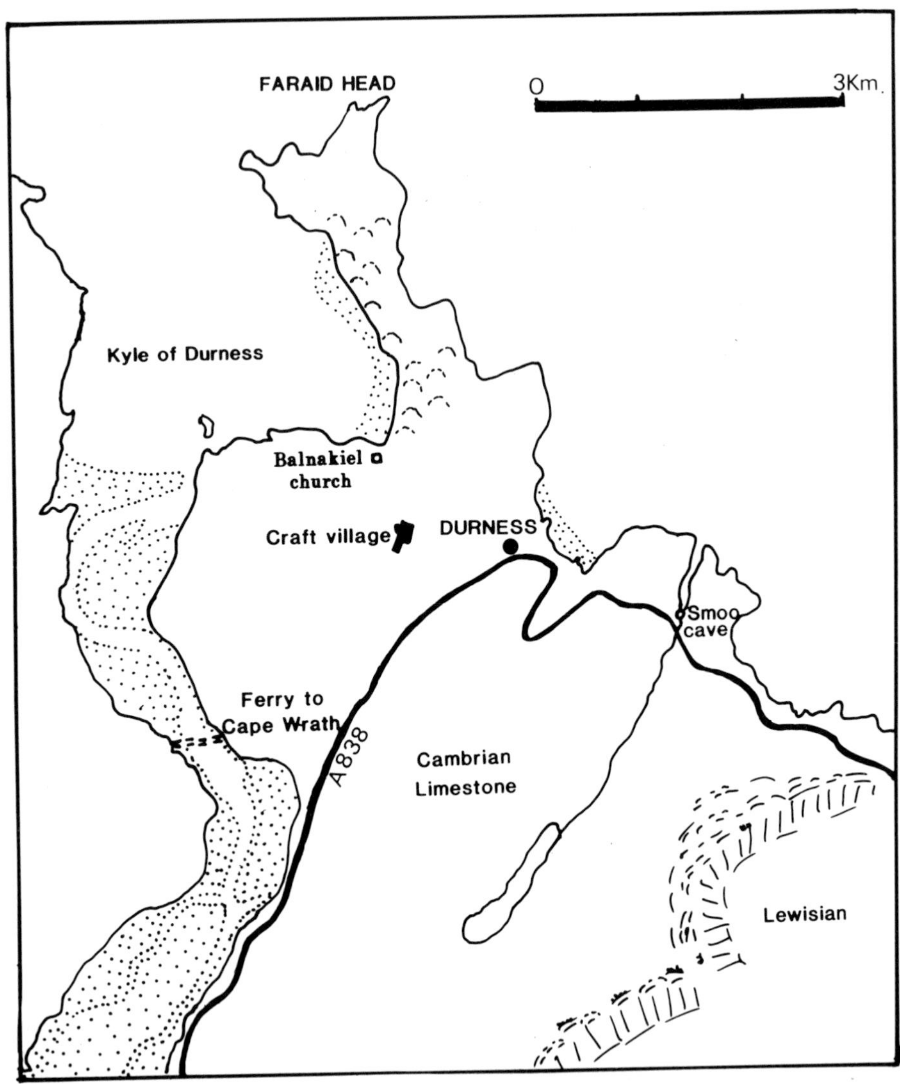

Around Durness: an outcrop of limestone gives a distinctive setting

precipices carved out of the contorted banded Lewisian Gneiss and cut through in all directions with intrusive veins of granite. A steep, winding, single-track road runs for 16km (10 miles) to the lighthouse at Cape Wrath across one of Britain's most desolate landscapes from the ferry across the Kyle of Durness, a ferry that conveys only passengers. In summer, a minibus service runs along this road. The coastline between Cape Wrath and Balnakeil Bay displays some of the finest cliff scenery in the British Isles, but for the average tourist this wilderness with the 183m (600ft) cliffs of Clò Mòr and Cleit Dubh, the 'Black Cliff', a precipice of 259m (850ft) lies out of reach.

The North-west Coast from Cape Wrath to Kyle of Lochalsh

South from Cape Wrath to the great sea lochs of the Clyde the tourist enters upon one of the world's finest coasts. Mountains,

Balnakeil Bay has one of Scotland's finest beaches. In the distance are the dunes and blown sand of An Fharaid

far-reaching fjords and the offshore islands of the Hebrides combine in seascapes whose colours and variety are hard to match anywhere else on Earth's surface. Two rocks of markedly different characteristics, the Lewisian gneiss and the Torridonian sandstone, underlie the topography of the north-west coast. Lewisian gneiss, which belongs to the oldest known rocks in the world, dominates as far south as Enard Bay. A recent dating of rocks around Scourie suggests that some of the grey striped outcrops of the gneiss may be as much as 2,900 million years old. The Lewisian gneiss rarely forms sea cliffs of any grandeur; rounded, ice-scraped knolls and crags fall steeply to green translucent water along an intricately detailed coastline of sandy bays, innumerable low islands and skerries.

Much of the coast between Cape Wrath and the entrance to Loch Inchard is inaccessible for all but the most determined, and those who attempt this wilderness are advised to go fully prepared with stout boots, map and compass, warm clothing and reserves of food. This bare moorland of lonely mountains and scattered lochs may be lost without warning in sea mists that drift inland from the Atlantic. The nearest road, the A838, runs far inland between **Durness** and **Rhiconich**. From Rhiconich a minor road reaches out to the coast along the northern shore of Loch Inchard following a steeply twisting up and down course through a succession of crofting settlements. **Kinlochbervie**, the only place of commercial importance on Loch Inchard, has grown since 1947 into the chief fishing port of the north-west Highlands. It occupies a low-lying neck of land that separates by only a few hundred yards two sheltered bays. Crews of the fishing boats that go out for the herring and white fish of the North Minch may come from as far away as Buckie and Banff on the east coast of Scotland. Rhiconich, at the head of Loch Inchard, and Kinlochbervie – both have hotels – make good places for exploring the remoter parts of this coastline. Seaward from Kinlochbervie stretches a fine succession of sandy bays. **Oldshoremore**, a 1km (½ mile) long arc of sand backed by a machair aflame with wild flowers in high summer, is one of the finest bays of the whole Sutherland coastline. Harder of access is Sandwood Bay, reached only on foot by a 6.4km (4 mile) long peat track that leaves the motor road between Blairmore and Sheigra. After twisting across the open moorland by half a dozen lochs the track drops steeply to the shore at **Sandwood** where a beach stretches for almost 3.2km (2 miles) exposed to the heavy swell that rolls into the North Minch from the Atlantic between the Butt of Lewis and Cape Wrath. Inland from the sandy shore a belt of dunes, covered with marram grass, separates a freshwater loch from the sea. Sandwood Bay is a lonely, beautiful place, but the traveller who may be attracted to this part of the coast on one of those rare, though matchless, summer days of the north-west Highlands is warned that bathing there is notoriously unsafe.

At Sandwood Bay it is possible to appreciate the contrasting coastal forms created by the Lewisian gneiss and the Torridonian sandstone. At the bay itself the gneiss reaches the coast, but on either hand, to the north and south-west, the Torridonian sandstone forms a bold line of cliffs. Am Buachaille, the herdsman, is a huge sandstone stack on the western flank of the bay and the location of two former stacks, now destroyed by the sea, may be traced from nearby rocks that are now awash.

Loch Laxford, whose name means 'salmon fjord', lies at the heart of the landscapes of the Lewisian gneiss. Between the A838 and the coast, a distance of 4.8–6.4km (3–4 miles), lies a confused topography of ice-shorn hummocks, bare rock surfaces, miniature crags and countless lochans where water-lilies open to the bright sun of summer days. In Loch Laxford the submergence, since the Ice Age, of this hummocky, tortuous landscape has produced a bay with many branching embayments and many islands, large and small. Again, the tourist will not find this piece of Scotland's coastline at all accessible. Glimpses of the inner parts of Loch Laxford may be gained from the A838 around **Laxford Bridge**, but they are few and far between as the road winds in and out of the narrow, steep-sided gutters amid this tumbled wilderness of the Lewisian gneiss. The northern shore of the loch is utterly devoid of settlement. Two crofting communities, **Foindle** and **Fanagmore**, eke out a living on narrow bays, screened by a chain of deserted islands, on the south shore of Loch Laxford. They may be reached by a twisting, steeply graded single-track road from the A894 that branches off by Loch a' Bhagh Ghainmhich. But the main object of anyone who diverges along this lane should be **Tarbet** where, in summer, a motor-boat plies regularly to Handa Island, since 1962 a nature reserve in the charge of the Royal Society for the Protection of Birds. The island, 306ha (766 acres) in extent, rises gently from the sandy beaches and reefs of its south coast to the northern sandstone cliffs that fall sheer to the sea through 122m (400ft).

Handa Island is composed entirely of the Torridonian sandstone. Its warm red rocks contrast with the cold grey gneiss of the mainland coast, and the division between the two rock types is marked by a fault that is followed by the Sound of Handa. The ferry boat from Tarbet lands visitors at the south-east corner of the island, a sandy beach known as Port an Eilean where the ruins of croft houses and an old graveyard are situated. Now the only sign of habitation is a bothy used by ornithologists. Handa was deserted in the middle of the last century when the potato famine drove its inhabitants overseas to America. The Statistical Account records twelve families on the island in 1845, a community whose way of life was like that of St Kilda, a lonely Atlantic island abandoned only in the 1930s. They grew potatoes, fished and gathered sea-birds' eggs. Today, Handa's population of more than 100,000 is made up of guillemots, kittiwakes, puffins, fulmars, shags and herring gulls. For the tourist there is a well-marked trail, about 3.2km (2 miles) in length, that leads inland to the high cliffs of the north-west coast, skirts the western shore where the cliff-line becomes ever lower, returning to the ferry landing across the low ground, the former fields and pastures of the crofters at the south end of the island. This excursion is highly recommended; almost every yard of the trail is full of interest, even when the

Loch Laxford: the intricate topography of the Lewisian gneiss coast at Fanagmore

cliffs are deserted of their packed colonies of sea birds in late summer. A green sea washes against the warm red walls of caves cut in the Torridonian sandstone. There is a view 91m (300ft) down the vertical walls of a *geo* and the Great Stack, a huge sandstone pillar whose summit, if records are complete, has been trodden by man on only two occasions. Apart from the immense variety of Handa's coastal features and its noisy colonies of sea birds, the tour of the island is worthwhile if only for the splendid, expansive views of the mainland. Across the desert of the gneiss platform rise the great mountains of the north-west Highlands. To the south, when the weather is right, the complex shore of Eddrachillis Bay forms a crinkled line against the sunlit sea and the eye is led on to the Old Man of Stoer, a distant pinnacle of Torridonian sandstone like the Great Stack of Handa.

Scourie is the only place in the emptiness of the gneiss landscape of south-west Sutherland that has more to offer the tourist than the crofting settlements of Tarbet and Loch Laxford. Here is an hotel, well known to the discriminating tourist, a shop that can supply the needs of campers and caravaners, and a post office. At Scourie one may enjoy the scenery of this gneissic coastline, most of which lies out of reach even if one is prepared to abandon the car and walk. Scourie Bay shelters behind a hummocky dome of Lewisian gneiss. Of no great height, reaching only 61m (200ft) above the sea at most, its contours are dauntingly mountainous. There is a sandy, sheltered, inner bay and at the head of Scourie Bay a bar impounds a tiny lagoon. Apart from the main-road service settlement Scourie and Scourie More consist of a handful of crofts in the shelter of the enveloping gneiss hillocks. Badcall Bay, well seen from the A894 to the south of Scourie, presents a model of the seascapes of this submerged coastline of Lewisian gneiss. A scattering of reefs and islands – almost thirty all told – reaches into Edrachillis Bay.

The coastlands of north-west Scotland bear little evidence of prehistoric man's presence, none of the archaeological riches of western Argyll. It prompts the question of whether the settlers of the Neolithic and

Bronze Age found the gneiss landscape as ungrateful as their successors between 4,000 and 5,000 years later. But at Cnoc an Daimh, close beside the main road 2km (1¼ miles) to the south of Scourie, a chambered cairn – a stony mound from which slabs and boulders protrude – advertises the presence of a prehistoric community.

At Loch A'Chàirn Bhàin (Loch Cairnbawn) the sea bites deeply into the land, branching beyond **Kylesku** and its ferry into two arms, Loch Glendhu and Loch Glencoul, that are hemmed in by some of Sutherland's bleakest mountains. The narrows at Kylesku make a break in the line of the A894 that is filled by a vehicle ferry whose passage takes only five minutes. The long lines of summer tourist traffic have given rise to a demand for a bridge at Kylesku, but the number of vehicles over some ten months of the year does not seem to justify such a capital investment. About 1km (½ mile) inland from the head of Loch Glencoul a waterfall, Eas Coul Aulin, leaps through 200m (658ft) into this gloomy glaciated trough over the precipitous crags that form its southern wall. Like so many of the sights of the Highlands the way of the tourist has not been made easy. An approach from **Unapool** along the trackless south shore of the loch is not to be tried; as one reaches the inner loch, Loch Beag, precipitous rocky noses – deep with heather – plunge to the water's edge making progress extremely difficult. The best route to Eas Coul Aulin follows a deer-stalkers' track that leaves the main road, the A894, a little over 3.2km (2 miles) south of the Kylesku ferry. It branches off along the head of Loch na Gainmhich. After 4.8km (3 miles) and the steep descent from Loch Bealach a'Bhùirich the track must be left at the second burn whose course is followed to the precipice over which the stream tumbles; map and compass are essential for this excursion which otherwise proposes no great difficulty.

About 1.6km (1 mile) beyond Unapool a secondary single-track road loops around the Stoer Peninsula to Lochinver. This route provides an ever-changing prospect of the Lewisian gneiss country at its best. It is a seemingly endless succession of sharp bends and short steep hills as the road dips and climbs through narrow gorges and across bare, ice-scarred crags. Loch follows lochan; there are so many in this coastal plateau where water seems to take up as much space as peat bog and bare rock that most go without a name. But always the views are rewarding. Inland lie the huge shapes of mountains: Quinag, a bastion of Torridonian sandstone, surveys the countless lochans of the coastal plateau, and further afield the whale-backed Suilven and the more distant peaks of Assynt dominate the landscape.

As far as Clahnessie this road, the B869 follows the deeply indented southern shore of Eddrachillis Bay. **Drumbeg** is the only place of any note with a hotel famous for the fishing in nearby lochs. Oldany Island and its cluster of skerries provides good fishing for lobster. At **Clashnessie** with its bay of red sands the B869 turns southwards across the neck of the Stoer Peninsula. Seawards to the Point of Stoer the peninsula is composed of Torridonian sandstone, a striking and visible contrast to its hinterland of Lewisian gneiss. A lane branches off into the peninsula and its several crofting villages to reach the north coast at **Culkein** and the Stoer lighthouse on its 30m (100ft) cliff in the west. There is some fine cliff scenery in the Stoer Peninsula where the red and purple sandstones fall to the sea from heights of 61–122m (200–400ft). The most accessible viewpoints are near the lighthouse, but the most spectacular feature is the Old Man of Stoer, a sea stack 61m (200ft) in height carved out along two systems of vertical joints in the Torridonian rocks. In the search for ever more difficult climbs on Britain's mountains – and more rarely her sea cliffs – the Old Man of Stoer was first climbed in the 1960s. A view of this fine stack may be obtained by following the track that runs inland from Culkein along the shore of Loch Cùl Fradich. After about 1.6km (1 mile) it ends among peat cuttings on the slopes of Sithean Mòr from whence another 1.6km (1 mile) northward of rough cross-country walking, with the aid of an Ordnance Survey

---

The Old Man of Stoer, a sea stack of Torridonian Sandstone, 61m (200ft) high and first climbed in 1966

map, will bring one within sight of the Old Man of Stoer. There are several crofting townships on the peninsula and everywhere are signs of the desertions that have taken place since the end of the eighteenth century. **Balchladich**, on the south-west coast, has a wide sandy bay that is not much sought after by tourists.

At **Stoer** the B869 runs within easy reach of the shore where a beach of reddish sand is clasped between two headlands of Torridonian sandstone. Inland the rocks change abruptly to the Lewisian gneiss. On the machair and close beside the road stand the remains of a Pictish broch and on the southern arm of the Bay of Stoer another broch site and burial cairns bear witness to a settlement here over 2,000 years ago.

Between Stoer and Lochinver this switchback of a road, the B869, twists and turns through the tortured gneiss landscape at some distance from the coast, but a succession of attractive beaches may be reached along footpaths and narrow winding lanes. **Clachtoll** has three sandy coves divided by bold rock ribs. Best known is Achmelvich Bay with a small sand beach at its southern end. Cars and caravans can reach the shore easily here by a lane that skirts the attractive wooded shore of Loch Roe, but a price has been paid for its tourist popularity which has resulted in the erosion of the rich machair turf by vehicles.

Lochinver, the only settlement of any size in Assynt occupies the head of a sheltered sea loch into which empty two large rivers from the wilderness of unnumbered lochs that lies in its hinterland. For the tourist, if he takes the lane past the church at the north end of the village, the most striking feature of Lochinver is the prospect inland across the broken landscape of the gneiss plateau to the huge pillar of Suilven, visually the most spectacular mountain, some would claim, in Britain. Lochinver itself, Suilven hidden behind the immediately rising ground, is a long busy street of shops and guest houses by the rocky foreshore. Useful tourist services are to be found here – accommodation, though insufficient in the busiest weeks of summer, banking, post office, garage. In the tourist season, after the great emptiness of Assynt, Lochinver's main street, cluttered with cars and caravans, has all the bustle of a metropolis. But the serious occupation of Lochinver is with fishing in which it ranks with Ullapool and Kinlochbervie among the fishing ports of the north-west. Boats from Lossiemouth and Buckie, on the east coast of Scotland, use its harbour as a base for the Minch fisheries.

For 9.6km (6 miles) south from Lochinver, as the crow flies, the present coastline has been shaped out of the submerged Lewisian gneiss platform. With a succession of tiny bays and offshore reefs and islands it ranks among the most attractive parts of the whole coast of Scotland. The scale of its topography is small, the detail intricate. For the tourist the enjoyment of this scenery, seen at its best under the bright sunlit skies of early summer, depends very much upon the weather. From Lochinver a winding single-track road takes the traveller out of Assynt, from the Norse word for 'rocky', into Coigach, from the grey terrain of the Lewisian gneiss into the red sea cliffs and mountains of the Torridonian. The shore is touched at only one or two places, for the rest it must be reached on foot across much boggy intractable ground. For 1km (½ mile) the road runs close by the sea along the shore of Loch Kirkaig where there is a good sandy beach at **Inverkirkaig**. Just 1.6km (1 mile) on, after crossing a contorted piece of the gneiss landscape, a brief prospect across Enard Bay opens up on the descent to Loch an Eisg-brachaidh. The road turns inland from the sea along the wooded trough of the Allt Gleann an Strathain, a straight valley whose course has been determined by a fault line in the gneiss platform. Offshore is one of the many islands of Enard Bay, Rubh' a'Bhrocaire which is joined to the mainland shore by a sandy tombolo that is submerged at high water. The road now runs out of sight of the sea with compensating prospects inland towards the great Torridonian mountains, Suilven ringed by the precipice of Caisteal Liath, 'the grey castle', Cùl Mòr – with the finest of views from these remote summits – and Stac Pollaidh, to be reached with comparative ease by the track from the shore of Loch Lurgainn. The little visited coastline has attractions of a different order,

At Lochinver the fishing harbour and service centre nestle beneath hillocks of Lewisian gneiss

best of all perhaps the tiny Lochan Sal, looking seaward from a wooded basin and almost enclosed by a tiny spit.

Lag na Saille marks an important frontier in the geology of the north-west coast. Here the Lewisian gneiss comes to an end and as far as Kyle of Lochalsh the coastline has been shaped almost entirely from the coarse Torridonian sandstones. The Còigeach Peninsula, the shores of Loch Broom and the Summer Isles illustrate all the coastal features that the sea has shaped out of these coarse, jointed, clearly bedded rocks – *geos*, sea caves, stacks and the deep reds and purples of sediments that accumulated in deserts between 600 million and 1,000 million years ago. Achnahaird Bay, a deep indentation on the northern coast of Rubha Mòr, occupies a depression along a fault in the Torridonian Sandstone, a depression that extends across the neck of the peninsula to Badentarbat Bay which in earlier times of high post-glacial sea levels was occupied by a sea strait.

Achiltibuie, a crofting settlement that stretches for almost 4.8km (3 miles) above the shore of Badentarbat Bay, is the starting point for several attractive excursions into the seaward end of the Coigach Peninsula and around the Summer Isles, a tangle of Torridonian islets and skerries that block the entrance to Loch Broom. The beach of Badentarbat Bay is composed of shingle and cobbles, but despite the absence of sand it attracts tourists because of its easy access – cars can pull up on the grassy sward between the road and the shingle beach. A pier in the sheltered northern corner of the bay is the starting point for motor-boat excursions to the Summer Isles and from here, too, trips set off for sea angling in the wide mouth of Loch Broom. A poor but scenically most attractive road runs from Achiltibuie along the west coast of the Coigach Peninsula as far as Reiff. Roadside lochans bright with patches of water-lily, the mingling of sea and islands out in Loch Broom and the distant backcloth of the peaks of Wester Ross make this a constantly enjoyable journey. At low water one may walk across to Isle Ristol by a natural causeway of an exposed sandy tombolo. At **Alltan Duibh** the road passes through the most attractive crofting village

The Summer Isles, with a prospect towards the mainland of Assynt's Torridonian mountains

on the shores of Loch Broom. The lane ends at **Reiff**, a deserted and ruined crofting township with a small sand beach composed largely of comminuted marine shells. Northward from Reiff a freshwater loch stretches for 1km (½ mile) almost to the next bay; beyond lies the spectacular trackless coast of the seaward end of the peninsula with its sandstone cliffs and caves.

The Summer Isles, a name that conjures up in the memory those all too rare Highland summer days of cloudless brilliance. Composed of eighteen islands and numerous skerries, they form a Torridonian archipelago that stretches westward from Tanera More to Priest Island. All are now deserted, but at the beginning of this century there were thriving communities on the larger islands. In 1900 Tanera More had a population of seventy who lived by sheep rearing, fishing and the product of their crofts. The prosperous years for the Summer Isles came with the close of the eighteenth century and the establishment of Ullapool as a fishing port. Tanera More was established as curing station for the herring fisheries. Of late the islands have become known through the writing of the naturalist F. Fraser Darling in his book *Island Years*, an evocative account of an experiment in living solely from the resources of Tanera More. In summer excursions run regularly to the islands from Achiltibuie and Ullapool where basking seals may be seen and a picnic on Tanera Beg enjoyed. Tanera More, richest in bird life and plants, was where Fraser Darling recorded forty-three species of breeding birds and on Glas Leac Beag the winter sees hundreds of barnacle geese.

Ullapool, with a population of little over 1,000, is the largest place on the north-west coast of Scotland. Despite the fact that it never became a railhead, prospects for growth in the future have been strengthened with the establishment of the chief Caledonian MacBrayne link with the Outer Hebrides here. A roll-on roll-off vehicle ferry to Stornoway has taken the place of the daily mail boat that sailed from Mallaig, calling at the other West Highland rail terminal, Kyle of Lochalsh, on the seven-hour journey to Lewis. Recently, Ullapool has emerged as the chief fishing port of the west with the appearance of huge factory ships, mainly from East European states, to purchase and process the catch of herring and mackerel from the Minch.

The town occupies a blunt peninsula on the north shore of a narrow fjord, inner Loch Broom, the head of which lies 38km (21 miles) from the open sea – the longest sea loch of the north-west Highlands. Founded by the British Fisheries Society in 1788 as part of their programme for exploitation of the rich seas around northern Britain, Ullapool's layout – a simple gridiron pattern – was planned by Thomas Telford. The settlement spreads across two raised beaches shaped by the transitory changing sea levels of post-glacial times. The northern part of the town occupies the higher surface of an uplifted delta of the Ullapool river; the seashore quarter with shops, hotel and guest houses is built along the terrace of a raised beach at 12m (40ft) above present sea level. Its harled and white-washed sea-front terraces gleam white across the still waters of Loch Broom from miles away as one drives westward along the main approach road, the A835. Tourism, fishing and now the constant heavy traffic for the Hebrides ferry means that there is life in Ullapool the year round. Its hotels, boarding houses, caravan and camp sites make it the main tourist centre for many miles of the north-west coast, but in the few weeks of the high tourist season – July and August – it is often hard to find accommodation here.

Inland from Ullapool, Loch Broom reaches deeply into the north-west Highlands. It is of geological importance because the Moine Thrust, that great dividing plane marking the edge of transposed rock masses in the folding of the Caledonian mountains, crosses this inner part of the sea loch. The country at the head of Loch Broom lies in the Moine schists, the metamorphic rocks that underlie much of the high land of the interior of northern Scotland. For the traveller on the A835 – the trunk road along the northern shore of Loch Broom – it is worthwhile to drive on for 8km (5 miles) from the head of the sea loch to view the mile-long Gorge of Corrieshalloch into which the river Droma plunges over a fall that is 61m (200ft) in height. The gorge now belongs to the National Trust for Scotland and an excellent footpath and viewing platform give access to its most exciting features.

Little Loch Broom, the southern prong of this extensive fjord that reaches far inland beyond the barrier of the Summer Isles, lies entirely within the territory of the Torridonian sandstones. A peninsula of rough Torridonian hills, their summits reaching 520-610m (1,700-2,000ft), divides it from Ullapool and Inner Loch Broom. There is nothing to attract the explorer of coastal scenery in Little Loch Broom apart from its general setting on the edge of some of the finest mountains of Britain. An Teallach is the mountain that broods over the waters of Little Loch Broom. Its deep ice-scoured corrie of Loch Toll an Lochain and the precipitous summit ridge of eleven peaks are reached by tracks that lead from **Dundonnell**, 3.2km (2 miles) from the head of the Little Loch Broom in Strath Beag. For the motorist only the southern shore of Little Loch Broom is accessible by the A832, a road that records in its making one of the grim events in the more recent history of Scotland. Known as Destitution Road, it was built in 1851 to relieve the severe poverty that followed the potato famine. Food was the only payment made to the starving crofters in return for their labour on the road that was engineered along the shore of Little Loch Broom and Gruinard Bay as far as Aultbea. Later, it was continued as far as Gairloch. Destitution Road is still the only line of communication through one of the most intractable landscapes of Highland Britain.

The shore of Gruinard Bay displays beautifully the two contrasting rocks that compose most of the coastlands of north-west Scotland. Grey, hummocky Lewisian gneiss outcrops in the south-eastern corner of this wide embayment. The peninsulas that form the bay's eastern and western shores belong to the Torridonian Sandstone. Here are rocky coves, sandy beaches and a clear green sea, all easily accessible where the A832 loops along the southern shore through patches of rich woodland and over the tumbled hummocks of gneiss. **Mungasdale**, a beach of reddish-brown sand derived from the Torridonian rocks, occupies an inlet on the east side of Gruinard Bay. This inlet is carved out along the junction between the Lewisian rocks and the Torridonian. The most popular beaches lie close to the main road at **Gruinard**. Gruinard North Beach, Camas Gaineamhaich, has a wide exposure of sand at low tide. The South Beach, lying only a few yards from the A832 and most frequented by tourists, is backed by a narrow sand dune that suffers continual trampling from visitors making their way to the shore.

The most attractive prospects across Gruinard Bay are found by leaving the main road at **Laide**, taking the lane along the west shore to **Mellon Udrigle**. In the brightness of a Hebridean summer's day Mellon Udrigle displays all the picture-postcard qualities of the ideal crofting township – a cove ringed with short green turf, sands that slide into a translucent green sea and cottage gardens coloured with flowers. Mellon Udrigle's other asset is the fine prospect inland across Gruinard Bay towards the great mountains of the north-west Highlands, a panorama that in clear weather extends from An Teallach to the peaks of Assynt. But a recent survey of the beaches of Wester Ross and their future development for tourism has shown that the machair at Mellon Udrigle suffers from considerable erosion. As common land of the crofters, it has suffered from over-grazing by sheep, but damage has been aggravated by caravans, campers and their motor vehicles. Since World War II the name of Gruinard Island has gained a somewhat ghoulish ring because of the experiments into germ warfare conducted there by the Ministry of Defence during the 1940s. Notice boards warn any prospective visitor by boat of contamination by anthrax that prohibits access to the island's fine beaches and pastures.

Between Aultbea and Poolewe the A832 skirts the south-eastern shore of Loch Ewe. Three contrasting elements make up the geology of this extensive sea loch. A narrow belt of young Triassic and Liassic sediments occupies the corridor followed by the main road between Gruinard Bay and Aultbea. The same rocks occur at the southern end of the Isle of Ewe and make their richer presence felt in the present landscape in a patchwork of bright green fields. For the most part Loch Ewe lies within the Torridonian rocks, but the straight shoreline to the south-west, followed by the road from Poolewe to Midtown is marked by a fault that brings to the surface the ancient underlying basement of the Lewisian gneiss.

Poolewe is a service village with two hotels and a camping and caravan site. In a tourist region where the few weeks of high summer traffic overwhelm the accommodation in hotels and guest houses, the Stage House, a caravan park equipped with showers, drying room and washing machines and built by the National Trust for Scotland, collaborating with Shell, has proved a valuable asset. Poolewe once flourished as a port. In the eighteenth century iron ore was shipped here from Cumberland to be taken to the furnace at Letterewe on the northern bank of Loch Maree. An ironworks was located at this remote place because of Loch Maree's rich stands of untouched natural woodland. Timber felling for the iron smelter, the largest in northern Scotland at that time, and the subsequent takeover of these wet northern mountains by large-scale sheep farming destroyed acres of woodland. Today, we can see the last remnant of the original Caledonian forest in the stands of Scots pine of the Beinn Eighe Nature Reserve on the south shore of Loch Maree, a place that not only conserves a fragment of the ancient forest but is also a haven for the vanishing wildlife of the Highlands – the wild cat, pine marten, golden eagle and ptarmigan.

Inverewe The gardens here, the property of the National Trust for Scotland since 1952, are the chief tourist attraction of the Wester Ross coastline. The gardens, rich with exotic shrubs from China, Chile, South Africa, the Pacific Islands, Tasmania and the Himalaya, were established by Osgood Mackenzie on a rocky, exposed promontory at the head of Loch Ewe in 1862. Soil was carried in creels to enrich the rocky hollows and shelter belts of Corsican pine and Scotch fir were planted; thick hedges of rhododendron screen the tender subtropical plants from salt-laden westerly gales. At Inverewe eucalyptus trees

Gruinard Bay: an ice-shorn landscape of gneiss, with a raised-beach platform in the foreground

reach almost 30m (100ft) in height and a *Magnolia stellata* has achieved a circumference of more than 21m (70ft); it is claimed as the largest in the world. Inverewe Gardens are open all the year round from 10am until dusk, but the time of late May and June is recommended for the full blaze of rhododendron and azalea. There is an information centre and restaurant and the gardens receive 100,000 visitors each year.

The northern shore of Loch Ewe is served by a lane that runs from the A832 at **Aultbea** as far as **Mellon Charles**; its route lies through a succession of thriving crofting townships whose long fields, strips of green and gold, reach down to the sea across a raised-beach platform. The Royal Navy has long had an interest in Loch Ewe and its northern shore. This was an anchorage for the home fleet in both World Wars I and II. Mellon Charles with its pier and slipway still serves as a naval ordnance depot and on the hillside at Aultbea a NATO oil-fuel base has been established. The extensive machair above the small sandy beach at Mellon Charles has facilities for camping and caravans. But the most attractive beach, Slaggan Bay, lies at the entrance to Loch Ewe. It can only be reached by a rough gated road that runs across the Rubha Mòr peninsula from the Laide-Mellon Udrigle road. At the approach to the beach is the ruined township of **Slaggan**. Founded in the middle of the nineteenth century, at the time of the clearances when people were resettled at inhospitable coastal sites, Slaggan had a population of forty by the census of 1891. The township was abandoned completely in 1945. The beach has a large permanent tidal pool and it makes a good place for picnics.

The western shore of Loch Ewe may be explored by a road that runs out from Poolewe, through a succession of crofting townships to Cove. At **Inverasdale**, 0.8km (½ mile) beyond **Midtown**, there is a shingle foreland, a favoured habitat of terns, but the only large sandy beach is at **Mellangaun** as one approaches **Cove**.

From Poolewe the main road crosses the base of a broad peninsula that separates Loch Ewe from Loch Gairloch. There are some excellent glimpses inland towards Loch Maree and its panoply of Torridonian mountains. Loch Gairloch, like Gruinard Bay, is clasped within the two main rock types that compose the greater part of the coastlands of north-west Scotland. The north and south shores belong to the Torridonian sandstones while the inner arc of this sea loch, closely followed by the A832, is carved out of the grey hummocky Lewisian gneiss.

Gairloch, the main road settlement, is the most important place between Kyle of Lochalsh and Ullapool. It acts as a service village with its garage, shops, church and school, for a dozen crofting townships strung along the shores of the bay. There is excellent provision for the tourist with bed and breakfast accommodation, the largest hotel on the Wester Ross coastline, a nine-hole golf course and a succession of clean sand beaches tucked in among the rocky promontories of gneiss at the head of the bay. Gairloch's beaches are easily accessible from the main road and they are among the most frequented by tourists of all the beaches in north-west Scotland. Caisteal na Cloinne, a rocky promontory above the south beach, has an indicator point with a fine inland prospect of the backcloth of Torridonian mountains.

From Gairloch the crofting townships of the north coast are served by a narrow, single-track road that ends after 14.5km (9 miles) at **Melvaig**. Thence a private road continues to the lighthouse at the tip of Rudhe Reidhe, a peninsula reaching 16km (10 miles) out into the Minch. **Strath**, the first settlement along the road, is really part of Gairloch with hotel and boarding-house accommodation. **Big Sand** has the largest caravan and camping site of the north-west coast. At the height of the season a hundred and more cars will be parked here and scores of caravans. On the south side of the river Sand there is a fine sandy beach, a place used by aqualung divers. Between **North Erradale** and **Aultgrishan**, the Melvaig road (the B8021) runs high above a narrow sand beach, Seana Chamas, fringed by steep Torridonian cliffs. It has an attractive prospect across the Minch to the Outer Hebrides and south-westward to Skye, but the beach is little visited on account of difficulties of access, either down a steep, unstable cliff face or along the foreshore from Aultgrishan, an approach that can be made only at low tide.

Another minor road, the B8056, leaves the A832 where that main road turns inland to follow the wooded gorge of the Kerry river towards Loch Maree. For 14.5km (9 miles) this road winds through the crofting townships on the southern shore of Loch Gairloch. **Shieldaig**, **Port Henderson**, **Opinan** and **South Erradale** follow each other until the road comes to an end at Red Point. There are clean beaches and safe bathing and when the proposed link road from Red Point to **Diabaig**, on Loch Torridon, is built, one of the finest scenic routes in Highland Scotland will be open to the tourist, to the lasting detriment of the hill-walker who can now follow the lonely footpath around this section of unspoilt coast, making an overnight stop at **Craig** with its isolated youth hostel. At Opinan the wide beach stretches between rocky headlands of Torridonian sandstone. From the present terminus of the road at Red Point two beaches are accessible. One, facing north, and reached from the Red Point car park in 0.8km (½ mile), has a large tract of sand-dunes that rise steeply from the beach backed by a machair that serves as common grazing for the township of Mealveldearg. Red Point south beach is reached after a walk of 2.4km (1½ miles) from the car park. Clean sands are reached across a band of boulders on the upper beach, but one of the greatest attractions is the wide panorama of mountains, sea and Hebridean islands. Eastward lie the Torridonian mountains – some would say the finest in Britain – and southward one looks down the Inner Sound to Raasay and the distant peaks of the Cuillin in Skye.

Loch Torridon calls up superlatives from all those who have written about the north-west Highlands – 'most beautiful of west coast lochs', 'superb sea-loch of the north-west', 'a coast where loveliness is met at every turn'. But the attractions of Loch Torridon do not lie in the details of its shoreline. There are no sand beaches to recommend nor is there any cliff scenery on a dramatic scale. Torridon's landscape quality rests in the juxtaposition of mountains and sea loch.

The Gardens of Inverewe

Towards the head of the loch the eye is led towards a vast arc of bare mountains, Beinn Alligin, an outpost of the northern shore; Liathach, a ridge of white Cambrian quartzite capping the vast bulky shoulders of red-brown Torridonian, and the peaks of the Ben-Damph Forest to the south. This is mountaineers' country *par excellence* and outside the context of a book that deals with the British coast. But if the tourist takes time off from the shoreline on a clear day to make the ascent of Beinn Alligin he will enjoy a prospect of the north-west that reaches from Cape Wrath to Ardnamurchan.

Variety is given to the topography of Loch Torridon by an exposure of Lewisian gneiss between Diabaig and the entrance to Loch Shieldaig. Four other outcrops of gneiss among the Torridonian rocks contribute to the landscape of the deeply indented southern shore; here the picturesque bays to the east of Shieldaig owe their forms to the alternation of sandstone and gneiss. Until the improvement in Highland roads that has taken place since World War II Loch Torridon was hard of access. Only two places on the shores of the loch were touched by motor roads: Fasag at the head of the sea loch by a narrow single-track road from Kinlochewe and Shieldaig by a road from Lochcarron. In 1963 a wide double-tracked road was completed along the southern shore joining Shieldaig and the existing road through Glen Torridon to Kinlochewe. Now the motorist can include this wild mountainous landscape in a grand circuit of the north-west Highlands, but he often does so at the cost of missing the delights of Loch Torridon. Not only does this scenery demand exploration on foot but the new road encourages speeds that would be offences on an English motorway. The whole of Loch Torridon's coastline may become accessible to the motorist. In 1976 a new coast road from Shieldaig to Applecross was opened and a further proposal for a road link along the north shore from Diabaig to Red Point has been made. The narrow winding lane that runs for 14.5km (9 miles) along the north coast of Loch Torridon to Lower Diabaig is one of the delights of the north-west, at least for the scenery if not for the nerves of the motorist as it twists and turns, climbs and falls often high above the placid sea loch. En route one passes through the pine woods of Torridon House, above the crofting settlement of **Inver Alligin**, crouching beneath the steep shoulders of the Torridon mountains like some village in the Norwegian fjords and on to the road's end at Loch Diabaig among a turmoil of ice-sheared hummocks of Lewisian gneiss.

Shieldaig, now well served by roads, is one of the most attractive villages of the north-west, rivalled only by Plockton in the estimation of most summer tourists. By the road from the south, from Lochcarron and Kishorn, you come across it through a screen of pine trees on the steep slopes above Loch Shieldaig. A long row of white harled cottages looks out to Shieldaig Island, a dark green hummock of pines on the face of the sea loch. Generations of soft Gaelic speech have transformed the original Norse name of the place, Sildvik – Herring Bay – into Shieldaig. A fine view of Upper Loch Torridon and its mountains may be gained by leaving the road at the north end of the village and walking out to Camas-ruadh, a distance of about 1.6km (1 mile), part of the bar of gneiss that here crosses Loch Torridon.

Between Loch Torridon and Loch Carron a Torridonian landscape of mountains and dull moorlands fills the Applecross peninsula. Its coastline, looking westward across the Inner Sound to Raasay and Skye, although now completely accessible by a good single-track road, is among the least interesting shores of north-west Scotland. Bare moorland reaches down to a boulder-strewn shore broken here and there by tiny beaches of reddish sand. The road that loops round this coastline from Shieldaig to Applecross was built by the crofters with government aid. It strings together a succession of crofting settlements whose former communications were by sea or else by a steeply climbing, winding footpath above the shores of Loch Shieldaig and Loch a' Chracaich. **Ardheslaig** occupies the head of a narrow inlet. **Kenmore** has a cluster of white-washed cottages huddled together on a green slope above the sea. **Fearnbeg** and **Fearnmore**, crofting townships at the mouth of Loch Torridon, are largely abandoned places with ruins and holiday cottages in a bare landscape of scattered lochans. At **Cuaig**, where a red sand-beach has been piled against the low cliffs, are the remains of several ruined crofts on a raised-beach platform. The new road has come too late to resuscitate communities killed by extreme isolation.

Applecross lies within a deep indentation of this dull coastline coinciding with an embayment of rocks of Triassic and Liassic Age, 1,000 million years younger than the Torridonian sandstone that composes the rest of the peninsula. And the presence of these younger limestones, shales and clays is reflected in the landscape: a featureless rim of drab moorland gives way to lush pastures and woodlands where the river Applecross comes down to the sea. The oasis of Applecross occupies an important place in the history of north-west Scotland. A monastery was founded here in AD 673 by St Maelrubha, an Irish monk from the great monastery at Bangor. The site of Maelrubha's monastery with its little chapel and crude huts is not known with certainty, but it most likely stood on the north bank of the river where we now find the church and manse. There is a ruined chapel in the churchyard of whose history nothing is known, and in the church are two fragments of an ancient sandstone cross believed to date from the time of Maelrubha. Applecross, consisting of a string of white painted cottages along a raised beach, once enjoyed a regular steamer service with the outside world. Today, there is an infrequent ferry from Toscaig, 4.8km (3 miles) to the south, to Kyle of Lochalsh, but the chief link is the road that climbs across the back of the peninsula to Kishorn and Lochcarron. From Applecross to the summit of the Bealach na Bà, the Pass of the Cattle, at 626m (2,053ft) above the sea, the journey is a steady winding climb across the dull moorland of a deer forest, but beyond the summit the road plunges steeply to the shores of Loch Kishorn as it clings to the precipitous wall of a corrie carved in the Torridonian sandstone. This has the reputation of the worst road in the Highlands. Certainly a driver has not much chance to enjoy the view and it is a dangerous road in the gales and snowstorms of the long months of winter and spring. But the prospect westward across Raasay to the mountains of Skye must be reckoned among the prime rewards of Highland travel.

South from Applecross a road runs on for another 4.8km (3 miles) to **Toscaig** passing by crofting villages sited on tiny bays. **Camusterrach**, sheltered by Eilean nan-Naomh, the Holy Isle, is a good natural harbour with shelter for fishing boats. The name Holy Isle suggests that this is the place where St Maelrubha landed in the seventh century. Offshore from Toscaig lie the Crowlin Islands composed of Torridonian sandstone and crossed by basalt dykes. They have been used as a base by the Kishorn oil-platform construction yard.

The southern coast of the Applecross peninsula looks out across the wide entrance of Loch Carron. The geology of this sea loch – a fjord in every sense of the word – displays a pattern similar to that of Loch Torridon. Torridonian rocks form the shores of the wide outer loch and its northern branch, Loch Kishorn, but beyond the narrows at Strome Ferry a ridge of Lewisian gneiss makes a dominant feature. The long, narrow, innermost arm of Loch Carron reaches beyond the Moine Thrust into the territory of the Moine schists. Loch Kishorn, a lovely place of deep summer meadows and sunlit woodland presided over by the huge shapes of Torridonian mountains, Beinn Bhàn and Sgùrr a' Chaorachain, has been dragged roughly into the high technology of the late twentieth century by a sudden ministerial decision that transferred, after much public protest, the site of a projected oil-rig construction industry from National Trust property at Drumbuie to Kishorn.

Lochcarron, a mile-long crofting township, occupies an attractive, south-facing site on a raised beach of the inner loch. Here the traveller will find hotel and bed and breakfast accommodation as well as shops and a garage. With the new industry at Kishorn, Lochcarron has endured far too much heavy traffic on its inadequate coastal road as well as the social disruption of the sudden intrusion of an alien, high-earning labour force. Close neighbour to Lochcarron along the road to **Stromemore** is the strung-out township of **Slumbay**. It has a good harbour and fishing was the former mainstay of its economy.

Strome Ferry occupies the narrow strait where the Lewisian gneiss outcrops. To the north stands the fragmentary ruin of Strome Castle, one of the chief strongholds of the west coast in medieval times, belonging to the MacDonnells of Glengarry. Clan warfare saw its destruction early in the seventeenth century by Kenneth Mackenzie. Strome Ferry enjoyed a brief period of prosperity between 1870 and 1897 when it was the terminus of the railway from Dingwall. The promoters of the Dingwall-Skye Railway, as it was called, could not find the capital for the building of the line over the last difficult 16km (10 miles) to Kyle of Lochalsh, so Strome Ferry emerges as a port for sailings to Portree, in Skye, and to the Outer Hebrides. Until the 1970s a ferry connected the two shores of Loch Carron here, a ferry that became woefully inadequate in the face of the growing tourist traffic of the 1960s. When a new road was opened along the south-east shore of Loch Carron in 1970 between Strome Ferry and Strathcarron, the six-vehicle ferry ceased. In the late 1970s activity returned briefly to Strome Ferry when it became a base on the railway for the Kishorn oil-platform industry.

Plockton, facing east towards Strome Ferry and inner Loch Carron, has been reckoned among the most beautiful of the Highland's villages with its prospect of mountains and woodlands across the calm surface of the sea loch. Before the coming of the railway and the concentration of traffic at Kyle of Lochalsh, Plockton was a port for the Minch fisheries and was visited by schooners trading with the Baltic countries. Now it is a place of summer yachts and sailing dinghies; its neat sandstone cottages are in demand as holiday homes.

Kyle of Lochalsh to Fort William

From the narrow strait of Kyle Akin to the head of Loch Linnhe the coast of mainland

Loch Kishorn: Sgùrr a' Chaorachain, a mountain of layered Torridonian Sandstone

Scotland is one of the least accessible parts of Britain. Sea lochs, fringed by forbidding mountains, reach far into the interior of the north-west Highlands. The total length of coastline is not far short of 644km (400 miles). Railways touch it in only three places – at Fort William, Mallaig and Kyle of Lochalsh. Main roads give access to the same areas and the only settlements of any size came into being in the early years of the twentieth century with the completion of the railways.

If much of the mainland is an empty, depopulated mountain wilderness, one must look westward to the islands of the Inner Hebrides to complete the geographical picture of this part of western Scotland. Two large islands, Skye and Mull, are merely extensions of the mainland isolated by rising sea-levels at the close of the Ice Age – the Sound of Sleat and the Sound of Mull are valleys drowned by the rising post-glacial sea. And it is in these islands, made accessible by easy water communications, that most of the important, though tiny, nodes of settlement are found.

Two narrow straits, Kyle Akin and Kyle Rhea, separate the south-eastern wing of Skye from the mainland. Between these tide-ripped channels Loch Alsh spreads widely like a sheltered inland sea, and at its head two narrow sea lochs, fjords in every sense of the word, Loch Long and Loch Duich, reach inland among the clustered peaks of Kintail.

Kyle Rhea, despite its swirling fast-running waters at some states of the tide, was the crossing by which cattle from Skye and the Outer Hebrides were driven to the mainland on their way to the great fairs of Falkirk and Crieff. Today, an independently owned car ferry runs from the end of May until the middle of September. The single-track road that climbs steeply from the ferry slipway opens up a fine backward prospect towards the mainland mountains and there is an even more exciting panorama of the Cuillins on the descent towards Broadford.

Among the sea lochs of this sector of western Scotland Loch Alsh and Loch Duich are among the most accessible because of the trunk road, the A87, that follows their northern shore to end at Kyle of Lochalsh on the Skye ferry's slipway. The 24km (15 miles) of main road between Shiel Bridge and Kyle offer several places and panoramas of great interest. At the head of Loch Duich the road skirts a vast tract of mountain wilderness, once restricted deer forest, that now belongs to the National Trust for Scotland. Here the motorist will find the beginnings of long and arduous trails leading into some of the loneliest landscapes of northern Britain. To the north-east are the Falls of Glomach, plunging into a chasm some 152m (500ft) in depth. Between Inverinate and Dornie the main object of tourist interest is the castle of Eilean Donan. The site is an ancient one: the earliest surviving evidence of man lies in the fragment of a vitrified fort, proof of a settlement in the Iron Age some 2,000 years ago. Early in the thirteenth century a castle was raised on this tiny island by Alexander II of Scotland, probably as a defensive outpost against the Viking colony in Skye. Like other strongholds of the north-west, Eilean Donan became a pawn in the Jacobite struggle for power in the eighteenth century. It was a focus for the 1719 rebellion and was reduced to a ruin by bombardment from three English frigates that sailed into Loch Alsh. The restoration of the castle began in 1912 and was completed only in 1932.

Beyond Dornie, Balmacara is the most winning of a number of roadside settlements. The road follows the edge of a wide bay where the regular steamers to Portree and the Outer Hebrides once called before the railway brought a new and rival port into existence at Kyle of Lochalsh. Between Balmacara and Kyle the recently engineered road presents a dramatic, albeit brief, foretaste of the mountains and seascapes of Skye.

Kyle of Lochalsh cannot be considered without reference to **Kyleakin**, its near neighbour a little more than 1km (½ mile) away over on Skye. They are joined by large car-carrying ferries that run almost continuously from 6am until 11pm. Both places bear the scars of their function as transit ports, with large parking places and a busy stream of tourist cars and heavy lorries on the way to the ferry slipways. Each has a scattering of shops and cafés, and Kyle of Lochalsh also provides banking facilities. Of

Loch Duich: the Five Sisters, veiled in early-morning cloud. Kintail Forest now belongs to the National Trust for Scotland

late, Kyle's dock has been busy with the ferrying of supplies to the oil-rig construction base at Kishorn. Kyle of Lochalsh is a settlement of the railway age, largely displacing earlier embarkation points on this part of the mainland coast at Kylerhea, Balmacara and Stromeferry. The rising volume of road traffic since World War II and the improvement of the A87 has further emphasised its importance. Apart from the incessant journeyings of its car ferries across the narrow strait, Kyle has almost ceased to function as a passenger port for the Hebrides, and at the time of writing the last link by sea of any length, the thrice-weekly sailing to Mallaig, is threatened with extinction.

Despite their prime importance as communications centres, Kyle of Lochalsh and Kyleakin have something to attract the tourist. The rocky knolls above the untidy scatter of buildings at Kyle of Lochalsh offer a fine prospect of the Cuillins in Skye – a good place for picture-postcard sunsets when the weather is right. Of the two settlements Kyleakin is the older and the more attractive. The now ruined Caisteal Maol, built by the daughter of a Norse king in the thirteenth century to exact tolls from traffic through the strait, is an impressive sight against the mist-drenched slopes of Sgurr na Coinnich as the ferry approaches the Kyleakin slipway. But Kyleakin was also the object of a town planner's dreams that came to nothing. Early in the nineteenth century Lord MacDonald proposed to found a new town around the shores of the tiny inlet, An t-Ob, that lies secluded from the swirling tidal currents and reefs of the sea strait. The place was to be called New Liverpool. If one leaves the main road and walks across to the lane with its white-washed cottages along the south shore of the harbour, an impression of the quieter, less hurried Kyleakin of the previous century can be gained.

Southward from Loch Alsh stretches one of the remotest sections of Scotland's mainland coast. Two valleys, Glen More and Gleann Beag, empty into Glenelg Bay at the head of the Sound of Sleat. Here there is a stretch of coast that roads have made accessible to the motorist. Approaching from Shiel Bridge, the Old Military Road contours gently down the northern flank of Glen More to reach the sea at Glenelg Bay. This road was built in the troubled decades of the eighteenth century to speed the movement of troops and supplies after Jacobite uprisings had threatened Hanoverian power in northern Britain. The rising of 1719, aided by Spanish mercenaries who fought in the losing battle of Glen Shiel, prompted the building of the Bernera Barracks a few hundred yards from the shore at Glenelg in 1722.

Gleann Beag contains two important ruins from the prehistory of Scotland. Dun Telve and Dun Troddan, an impressive pair of Iron Age brochs, lie scarcely more than 0.4km (¼ mile) apart in the middle glen. They must belong to the Late Iron Age, a period in Scottish prehistory that extends from the first century BC to the fifth century AD. Nevertheless, even in their present ruinous state, they rank among the finest examples of brochs in northern Britain, and there are scores of such sites in the Northern Isles of Shetland and Orkney. The ruined tower of Dun Telve, a ragged semicircle of drystone walling still rises to some 10m (32ft) at its highest, displaying to perfection the characteristic hollow walled construction with an interior spiralling passage-way that was part of the broch's design.

From the mouth of Gleann Beag, at Eilanreach, a narrow though well-made single-track road leads southwards to Loch Hourn, ending at Corran. Beyond that another 16km (10 miles) is needed to reach the head of the loch at Kinloch Hourn – a journey that can be traversed with difficulty by a footpath along the southern shore of this sunless chasm. Alternatively, the motorist can reach the head of Loch Hourn, across the mountain divide of the north-west Highlands, heading westward from Loch Garry along the desolate shores of Loch Quoich to make the final descent to the loch through a succession of hairpin bends in a gorge that is loud with the noise of waterfalls. In recent years the scene of Gavin Maxwell's *Ring of Bright Water* at Sandaig has become an object of curiosity if not of pilgrimage.

Arnisdale and **Corran**, two settlements of neat white cottages, illustrate some of the unhappier events in the history of the Highlands over the past century and a half. The middle decades of the nineteenth century saw the rise of large-scale sheep farming and the destruction of practically all the crofting settlements of the interior glens. Arnisdale and Corran were founded to settle those evicted from Glen Arnisdale, who were given 0.4ha (1 acre) of land and expected to supplement their living from fishing. By 1890 the economics of sheep farming in the Highlands had plunged into a steep decline and the mountain land to the north of Loch Hourn passed into fresh ownership with the purchase of the Arnisdale Estate by Robert Birkbeck who determined upon its conversion to deer forest. Kinloch Hourn was chosen as the site for the Lodge where stalking parties gathered, and the 'insanitary hovels on the edge of the loch' at Arnisdale were rebuilt as an estate village, resulting in the pleasant cottages that are seen today.

The Knoydart peninsula, between Loch Hourn and Loch Nevis, has been ignored in all the phases of road building that have improved the communications of the Highlands since the surveying of the military roads at the beginning of the eighteenth century. Some 6.4km (4 miles) of poor, single-track road connect the tiny harbour of **Airor**, a one-time ferry point for Skye, on the Sound of Sleat, with **Inverie**, the only inhabited settlement on the peninsula. The landscape of Knoydart still bears the scars of clearances made over a century ago. A series of deserted settlements fringes the western coast – Inverguseran, Samadalan, Doune and Sandaig.

For the motorist Loch Nevis is even less accessible than Loch Hourn. No road reaches the long-deserted hamlets at the head of the loch across the desolate mountain divide from the east. The only way to enjoy Loch Nevis is by sea and, lacking one's own boat, that means the infrequent ferry service that connects Mallaig with the only inhabited places, Inverie, Stoul, Tarbet and Camusrory. The rewards of the journey are many. Under a bright summer sky there is a feeling of space and light; even at the head of the loch the sea expands widely in two branching arms, the mountains seem to hold their distance and there is none of the oppressiveness of the gloomy inner reach of Loch Hourn. The silent shores of Knoydart tell the same story of the destruction of settlements and the eviction of their inhabitants that we find in so many other parts of the Highland west. The northern shore of Loch Nevis nourished a population of about 1,000 in the 1790s. By 1841 the wholesale clearance of the interior of Knoydart for sheep rearing had concentrated the people into a string of coastal townships between Inverguseran and Inverie. By 1846 the population of Knoydart had been reduced to 600, but worse lay in store. The sale of the estate in 1852 to James Baird, an ironmaster from the lowlands, led to the complete clearance of the coastal townships of Loch Nevis. The inhabitants of Samadalen, Doune and Sandaig were forced to emigrate to Australia.

Between the mouth of Loch Nevis and Loch Sunart some subtle differences become apparent in the character of west Scotland's coastline. The highest mountains lie far back from the sea and the deeply penetrating fjords are replaced by two fresh-water lochs, Morar and Shiel, draining seawards by short turbulent rivers across rocky bars. The greater part of this coastline is easily accessible by the main road that joins Mallaig to Fort William. Ease of access is not gained, however, without a loss of what many would consider the most precious aspects of the Highland scene. In high summer the meadows of the Back of Keppoch break out in a rash of caravans.

Morar presents one of the most attractive stretches of coastline in western Scotland. One sandy bay succeeds another, and they are of dazzling whiteness in those days of late May and early June when the Hebrides so frequently record the highest sunshine figures of the British Isles. Offshore, a barrier of dark reefs breaks the glistening surface of the sea. In places, at Glenancross, for instance, high sand dunes make a background of rippled hills behind the shore. The Road to the Isles, today the A830 trunk road, curves around the edge of sandy bays and elsewhere, at Bunacaimb, tracks fringed with clumps of wild iris lead down to shore.

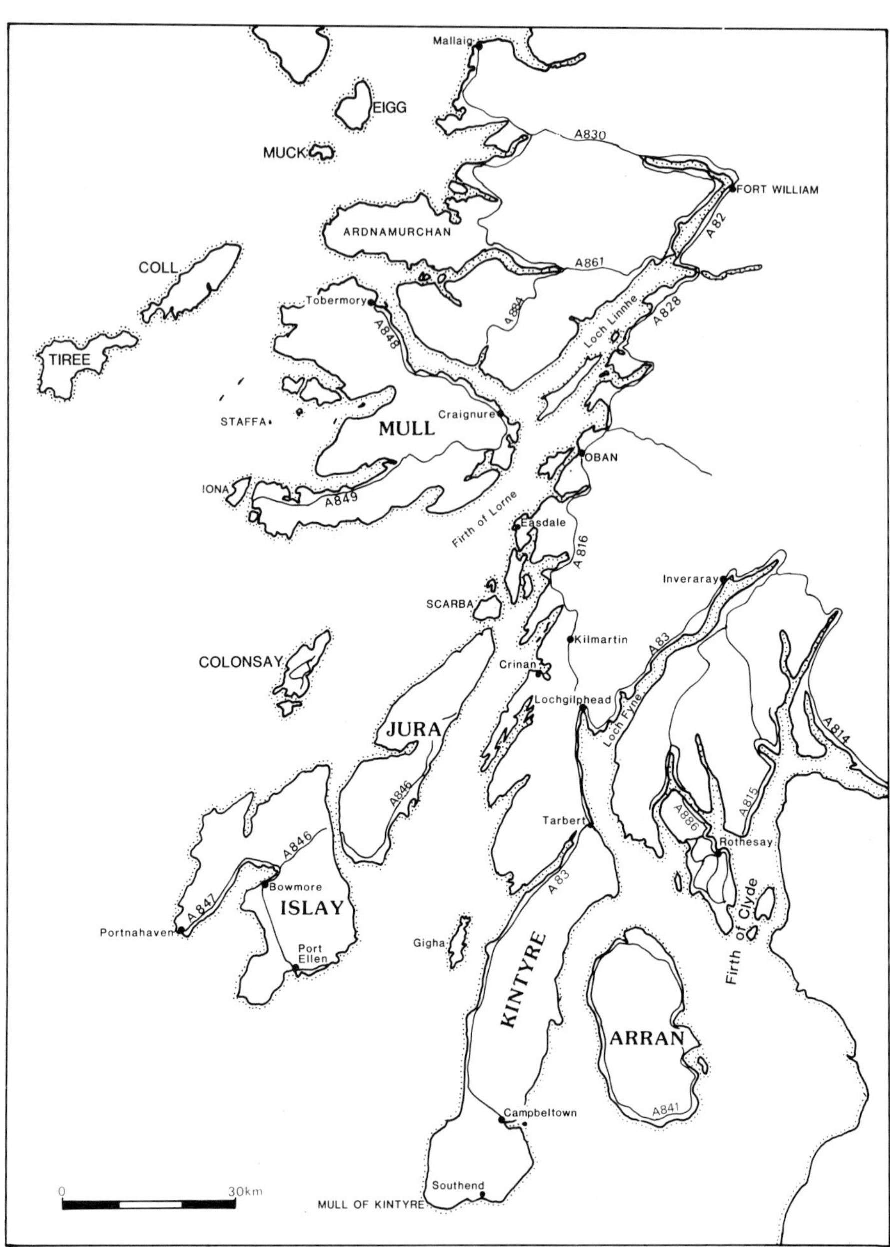

West Scotland from Mallaig to the Mull of Kintyre

Loch Morar is Britain's deepest lake, plunging to 310m (1,017ft) off South Tarbet Bay. Loch Morar's physical history is no different from that of the other sea lochs of the West Coast. It was occupied by a westward flowing glacier of immense thickness during the Ice Age. Subsequently, during the past 12,000 years, the sea flooded the deep trenches lately occupied by ice. Towards the mouth of the sea loch where the glacier was able to spread laterally, released

Caledonian MacBrayne's vehicle ferry on its summer service between Mallaig and Skye

from the narrow, rock-walled valley, it is believed that the downward erosive powers of the moving ice weakened. Here a rock-bar was left and in most of the sea lochs this feature is now submerged. But at Loch Morar a temporary marine incursion has been followed by an uplift of the land that raised the rock-bar above sea-level. Today, the river Morar flows across a low rocky neck of land for a distance of 91m (300yd) into the sea. This short but powerful river provides the site for a hydro-electric station; unfortunately, its construction has destroyed what was one of the finest waterfalls of this part of Scotland. Loch Morar, too, possesses one of those inevitable objects of Scotland's tourist industry – the story of a monster in its depths. Morag, the loch's legendary monster appears, it is said, only to foretell the death of a MacDonald of Clanranald.

Mallaig, with a population of about 1,000, is the largest and busiest place on this part of the west Highland coast. Two phases of the township's history are recorded in its streets and buildings. The foundation of Mallaig goes back to the beginning of the nineteenth century when Lord Lovat set about the replanning of his extensive estate of North Morar. He settled sixteen crofters, each with something less than 1.5ha (4 acres) of land, on this rock-bound peninsula at the mouth of Loch Nevis. The extension of the West Highland Railway to Mallaig in 1901 was to transform a poor crofting settlement into one of the busiest fishing ports of the west coast. By 1903 boats from the east coast of Scotland fishing the waters of the Inner Hebrides began to land their catches at Mallaig. The 1920s saw the migration of fishermen and their families from places on the east coast to make their homes in Mallaig. Today, Mallaig is the most important herring fishing port of western Britain, and even more valuable is the harvest of shellfish. The lobster fleet from Mallaig fishes along 3,000km (1,900 miles) of coastline and as many as 4,500kg (10,000lb) of lobster may be seen in the Saturday morning auctions on the quay.

With the coming of the railway Mallaig also emerged as a passenger and cargo port for regular steamship services to the Inner and Outer Hebrides. This was the mainland terminus of the Stornoway Mail, a daily boat that connected with the overnight train from King's Cross, and that made it possible to travel from London to the Outer Hebrides within the space of twenty-four hours. Since the early 1960s radical changes have come over the sea communications of the Hebrides with the introduction of car ferries. The Stornoway Mail no longer sails and the main route to the Outer Isles is now by means of the roll-on roll-off car ferry from Ullapool. Mallaig as a passenger port is left with a remnant of local services to the Small Isles and Skye. A car ferry runs less than half a dozen times a day between Mallaig and Armadale, in Skye, from the middle of May until the end of September. On four days a week mail, supplies and passengers can reach the Small Isles of Eigg, Muck, Rhum and Canna. In summer the seven-hour round trip to these islands makes one of the finest excursions that can be had around the coasts of Britain.

Arisaig, before the opening of the West Highland Railway, lay on the regular shipping routes through the Sea of the Hebrides. Steamships called at the pier at Rhue before all traffic became concentrated on Mallaig.

Eastward of Arisaig the shores of Loch nan Uamh are rich with woodlands, wild flowers and lochs richly carpeted with water lilies. The peninsulas and tiny islands that reach out into Loch nan Uamh preserve the remains of a number of vitrified forts, inhabited sites of the Iron Age. The Prince's Cairn stands at the head of Loch nan Uamh, 'the loch of the caves'. For more than two months in the final episode of the '45 Prince Charles must have spent much of his time hiding in the numerous caves along the rocky shore of the Sound of Arisaig. None can be firmly established as the princely lair, although Prince Charlie's Cave, close by the Borrodale burn, is usually accorded that honour.

South from Loch Ailort one enters Moidart. The dominant feature of this landscape is the 32km (20 mile) long fresh-water lake, Loch Shiel. It lies only 6m (20ft) above sea-level; the uplift of the land in the post-glacial centuries, over the last 10,000 years, has excluded the sea from this narrow, ice-shorn trough. In 1966 it saw the start of an experiment in fish farming that may have important repercussions on the economy of north-west Scotland, an experiment that perhaps becomes even more urgent with the depletion of fish stocks in the British seas. Here, using large anchored pens in the middle of the loch, sea trout and salmon are bred.

The ambitious road-building programmes in the Highlands in the 1960s have broken down the isolation of many places, among which is the Moidart peninsula. Until 1966 the only approach for vehicles was along the single-track road from Strontian that ended near the post office and deserted pier at the head of Loch Moidart. From there a foot-track led over the hills to Glenuig Bay, thence for 10km (6 miles) along the southern shore of Loch Ailort to meet the Road to the Isles and give access to the railway at Lochailort. Now a double-track motor road sweeps through this landscape revealing some entrancing views across the sea to the Small Isles and the trackless unspoilt coast of Arisaig. Nevertheless, the quiet of the Highlands as it used to be can still be discovered along the lanes and footpaths that lead into the seaward end of the Moidart peninsula beyond Glenuig. Samalaman Bay, sheltered by a low island and fringed by woodland, possesses one of the best sand beaches of the peninsula. The particular qualities of Loch Moidart rest in the abundance and maturity of its woodland, and in the large islands, Eilean Shona and Shona Beag, that close the passage between the inner loch and the open sea. But the most fascinating piece of this landscape is the fourteenth-century stronghold of the MacDonalds of Clanranald. The shell of Castle Tioram stands on a tiny island close to the southern shore of the loch that is joined to the mainland by a shingle ridge exposed at low tides. This ruined, five-sided stronghold with its high curtain wall and turreted keep seems to be in a good state of preservation when you approach its green island refuge across the sands, but the silence of its confined and ruined courtyard reminds one that the age of clan warfare is as remote from the present as the prehistoric centuries that left their mark on the landscape in scores of ruined duns and brochs. In summer, one can see Loch Moidart and its islands by the occasional motor boat cruises that start from Arisaig.

The dull lower reach of Loch Shiel may be seen well from the road between Acharacle and Kinlochmoidart. The head of the loch presents a picture-postcard prospect at Glenfinnan both from the road and the railway, and of late a recently constructed Forestry Commission road has opened up many miles of the eastern shore between Polloch and Glen Finnan.

The peninsula of Ardnamurchan reaches out into the Atlantic more than 32km (20 miles) beyond the longitude of Lands End; this is the furthest point west of mainland Britain. But here we find no empty ocean's horizon. There lie the islands of Atlantic Britain – the long level backbone of Coll, the Sgurr of Eigg, a pillar of volcanic rock, and further still the shapely peaks of Rhum. And when clear polar air blows from the north-west, we espy on the far horizon the final rampart of western Europe, Barra and South Uist. A winding single-track road wanders down the Ardnamurchan peninsula. For several miles this lane hugs the northern shore of Loch Sunart. Entrancing views along the sea loch, glimpsed through clumps of pines, surprise one at certain turns of the road.

Glenborrodale, after Kilchoan the only settlement of any size on the peninsula, occupies one of those lush, sheltered sites that always provide a pleasant shock for the traveller in the austere landscapes of northern Britain. Much of Glenborrodale's richness results from the lavish planting of exotics by Victorian landowners. Here the road winds through banks of rhododendron ablaze with colour in early summer. The name means the 'valley of the fort', and on a spur above the present village one finds the site of an Iron Age dun.

Beyond the scattered hamlet of **Glenbeg** the road begins to climb steeply above the coast. This is one of the fine viewpoints in Ardnamurchan. Below lies a pattern of rich green pastures stretching almost to the water's edge of the deep inlet of Camas nan Geall. Beyond, the long slopes of Ben Hiant, the 'holy mountain', fall steeply to the sea. The seaward end of Ardnamurchan has been shaped from the deep roots of an old volcano, active between 50 million and 70 million years ago. Ben Hiant has been carved out of a complex of rocks that formed in one of the volcanic vents. Camas nan Geall also preserves one of those rare associations with history that can be so welcome in the great wilderness of the north-west Highlands. A tall stone pillar, Cladh Chiarain, stands at the centre of a field a few yards from the shore. With a large cross carved on one face it marks an early Christian site.

Kilchoan is a scattering of white-washed crofts along a raised beach. Here the tiny strip-like fields with their different crops stand out along the sea-shore; inland, the cultivated ground gives way to wilder land coloured yellow with patches of gorse and cleft with the dark chocolate-brown slits of peat cuttings. Mingary Castle was the stronghold of the MacIains of Ardnamurchan over a period of almost four centuries. During the summer months a ferry runs four times a day from Kilchoan to Tobermory. With the reorganisation and reduction of ferries that Caledonian MacBrayne has carried out over recent years it seems unlikely that this route will survive, and Ardnamurchan's only link with the outside world will then be along the tortuous road to Strontian and Fort William.

Sanna, with its mountainous sand dunes clothed in coarse grey-green streamers of marram grass, sums up this piece of the west Highland coast. A substantial stream, its banks rich with wild flowers and the tall flags of the yellow iris, wanders through the dunes to the foreshore where an unspoilt beach of white sands spreads between jutting reefs of black rock; the seas are crystal green and the air is filled with the noise of the Atlantic. But even at this far end of the peninsula the baleful threats of tourism begin to loom. Provision has had to be made for the parking of cars. But a more serious threat to the landscape, however, emerges from trampling over the dunes where the loosened sand begins to move inland, burying the rich pastures of the machair.

Sanna came into existence in the middle of the last century. It was founded by settlers from Swordle, on the north coast of Ardnamurchan, after the evictions of 1853. Sanna is enclosed by a ring of wild hills, broken by crags and precipices. Despite their insignificant heights, never reaching more than 244m (800ft) above sea-level, they nevertheless display the contours and topography of mountains. These hills are part of the volcanic complex, and the hardness of their rock, in an arc-shaped outcrop, has produced this upstanding ring of miniature mountains. In fact, the circular layout of the volcanic complex of Ardnamurchan has imprinted itself on so many of the landscape features at the western end of the peninsula.

The northern coast of Ardnamurchan is hard to reach, except for those who are prepared to abandon cars and explore the 10km (6 miles) of footpath that connect Ockle and Kentra Bay. A motorable road comes within reach of the coast only between Kilmory and Ockle. The north-western section of the coast between Sanna and Kilmory is even more difficult of access, lacking any clear footpaths. The sea cliffs along many miles of northern Ardnamurchan contain numerous caves. The most important, in the shallow bay to the north-east of Kilmory, was, according to tradition, used by St Columba on his visit to Ardnamurchan in the sixth century. Until recent times it was a place of pilgrimage where the sick sought out a shallow pool at the cave's entrance for the healing property of its water. Kentra Bay, at the neck of the peninsula, bites deeply into the land and a wide expanse of sand lies exposed at low tide.

Ardtoe has been the scene for experiments in fish farming over the past fifteen years where 2ha (5 acres) have been enclosed at the head of a sheltered creek for the rearing of plaice.

Loch Sunart reaches far inland, a distance of more than 48km (30 miles) from its opening into the Sound of Mull. The inmost part of the loch between Salen and Strontian lies cradled between scented woodlands and meadows rich with wild flowers. This is granite country and with the massive intrusion of the Strontian granite, an event that dates far back in Scotland's geological history, the enrichment of the surrounding rim of rocks with minerals took place. From the early eighteenth century lead mining was active in the hills above Strontian. The straggling settlements of Anaheilt and Scotstown on the flanks of Strontian Glen date from this time. Abandoned shafts close to the summits of the grey wet hills above Loch Sunart mark the once busy mines that yielded some 400 tons of lead concentrate per annum in the years about 1800. Here, too, in 1764 the distinctive mineral that came to be called strontianite was discovered, and some years later the radio-active element strontium was recognised.

Strontian is now the focus of a social experiment to inject fresh life into stagnant rural communities in the remote parts of the Highlands. The first phase of a government project was completed in 1969 with the opening of a village centre, a building that houses a shop, tea-room and an information bureau. Since then, the new Strontian has grown considerably with a village hall and library, the building of a primary school and old people's home, as well as a considerable amount of housing. A new nucleated settlement has emerged around a central 'green' – one whose appearance and functions are completely foreign to the lonely, scattered crofting communities of the western Highlands.

To the south of Loch Sunart lies the extensive territory of Morvern. Its western coastline faces the long sheltered passage of the Sound of Mull; no part is exposed to the open Atlantic. Consequently, one of the primary attractions for the tourist, extensive sandy beaches, is lacking. Western Morvern belongs to the same geological province as Mull. Here we find the black basalt rocks, lavas that flowed from a huge volcanic

The largely deserted fishing village of Smearisary on the Sound of Arisaig; only the odd holiday cottage survives (*Anthony J. Lambert*)

complex of the Tertiary period located in the south of Mull, where Ben More and its neighbouring mountains have been carved out of an immense accumulation of volcanic rocks. In Morvern the basalt lavas end abruptly in a precipitous eastward-facing escarpment that rises out of the forest above Loch Arienas. The greater part of eastern Morvern is composed of the vastly older Strontian granite whose rounded mountains with aprons of greyish-pink scree overlook Loch Linnhe.

Isolation has affected severely the economic development of Morvern over the past century. Although part of mainland Scotland, the deeply penetrating sea lochs – Linnhe, Eil and Sunart – make almost an island of Morvern. The total population of the peninsula is now less than 500. The clearances of the nineteenth century saw the desertion of several large townships at the north-western end of the peninsula; now the greater part of this land is in the possession of the Forestry Commission.

Lochaline The life of Morvern centres on Lochaline – a pier and ferry slipway lying midway along the Sound of Mull. Lochaline is an industrial village of considerable importance. World War II promoted the mining of a layer of white sandstone, some 5m (18ft) in thickness, that lies beneath basalt lavas forming the hills around Loch Aline. The sands, used for the manufacture of optical glass and abrasives, are screened, washed and loaded by conveyor-belt into ships. By the 1960s an output of 1 million tons per year had been reached. The changing character of West Highland ferry services since the early 1960s, especially the growing importance of car ferries, has affected Lochaline. The daily service between Oban and Tobermory that used to put in at Lochaline has disappeared. Now the main link is a six-vehicle car ferry across the Sound of Mull to Fishnish. The churchyard, above the village, contains the ruin of a pre-Reformation chapel and a fifteenth-century Celtic cross. On the shores of the loch are two medieval castles. The fifteenth-century keep of Kinlochaline Castle is lost among the rich woodland while Ardtornish Castle, a stony ruin, occupies the tip of a peninsula extending into the Sound of Mull. Lochaline, too, played an important part in one of the most recent events in the history of the depopulation of the north since the end of the eighteenth century. The crofters of St Kilda were given land here, at Larachbeg, when their island was depopulated in 1930.

The Firth of Lorn and Loch Linnhe form the greatest of Scotland's sea lochs. Fort William, standing at the head of this mountain-girt fjord, is more than 96km (60 miles) from the open sea. The grandeur of Loch Linnhe lies not only in its location among some of the highest and wildest mountains of Britain, but also in the eastward continuation of this deep trench across the Scottish land-mass as the Great Glen. Here is one of the major features of the geology of Great Britain. Several earth tremors a year are still recorded along this line of faulting whose origins lie in the remote Old Red Sandstone times, almost 400 million years ago. A narrow, single-track road skirts the northern shore of Loch Linnhe. For miles it follows a raised beach, representing a former higher sea-level, at some 6m (20ft) above the present shore-line. Scenically, this road presents the motorist with a most attractive drive. Ben Nevis, a foreshortened shapeless hump when seen from Fort William, can be enjoyed in its true proportions in the prospect across the sea where the A861 rounds the headland between Achaphubuil and Trislaig. In other sections this little used road into Morvern passes through sunlit woodland planted with masses of rhododendron. It twists into bays where brown rivers foam down from the hills of Ardgour. Corran Narrows provide the main link between Fort William and the northern shore of Loch Linnhe. A five-minute journey by car ferry brings most of the traffic into Morvern by this route, although at some states of the tide a fierce current runs through the strait, delaying the ferry. Road widenings and improvements in the past twenty years have confirmed this as the main artery into the peninsula between Loch Sunart and Loch Linnhe. Beyond

Tarbert, on Loch Fyne, south-west Scotland

Inversanda, where the A861 sweeps into Glen Tarbert to climb away from the coast beneath the grey corries of the granite hills, the shore becomes less accessible. A winding single-track road hugs the coast as far as the strung-out settlement of Kingairloch, there turning inland by grey lochs and empty moorland to Lochaline. To the west of Kingairloch no road gives access to a mountainous landscape whose main use is for deer forest. Only a deer-stalkers' track runs for some miles along the coast through a number of completely deserted settlements. Farming, even on the flat land where the glens come down to the sea is not easy, for the hungry granite sands are combined with excessively high rainfall. But even this harsh country has one worthwhile resource in the granitic sand deposited on the floor of the shallow bays. It has been in demand for use in filter beds at the sewage plants of the towns and cities of central Scotland; 'puffers' used to sail regularly from the Clyde in summer to extract it from the sea bed by mechanical grab.

Fort William is the largest and busiest town on the west Highland coast north of the Clyde. Its heavy industries, aluminium smelting and pulp and paper production, tend to dominate the Inverlochy plain at the foot of the crouching mass of Ben Nevis. One cannot deny that the enjoyment of the prospect of Britain's highest mountain is lessened by all that the recent industrial development around Fort William has done to the scene.

Fort William's narrow drab main street, made pleasanter of late with the removal of through traffic by a wide bypass along the foreshore of Loch Linnhe, provides the best shopping centre for miles around. For the tourist there is good hotel accommodation and the number of motels that have sprung up around the 'Fort' indicate the volume of tourist traffic that passes this way. The West Highland Museum displays aspects of the region's prehistory, its associations with the Jacobite risings, and evidence of the Highland's extinct modes of farming. The fort that finally gave its name to the place, built by General Monck in 1654 and reconstructed in stone in William III's reign, was demolished to make way for the railway in the 1860s. An older fortress from the medieval period still stands at Torlundy near the A82 close behind the aluminium works. Inverlochy Castle dates from about 1260. It is a square rough-hewn building with towers at each angle and the curtain wall much reduced by subsequent robbing for stone. Fort William is an excellent centre for the tourist who relies on public transport, and for the rock climber and fell walker the mountains and glens in the immediate neighbourhood are without rival in Britain.

19 West Scotland

South-westward from the wide mouth of the Firth of Lorne stretches one of the lesser known parts of Britain's coastline, one that has much to offer the tourist. Offshore lies a cluster of islands that culminate in the shapely summits of Jura. Long, deeply sheltered sea lochs run inland between wooded hills and meadows riotously alive with wild flowers. Further south still two topographical features are dominant – the seemingly endless peninsula of Kintyre with a succession of wide Atlantic sand beaches on its western coast and Loch Fyne's many miles of sheltered water. The building of railways in the second half of the nineteenth century only strengthened the individuality of this part of Scotland. Its landscape of mountains and far branching fjords discouraged the railway engineer, and a scattered population with low industrial prospects offered no incentive to the Victorian investor. Argyll remained one of the most extensive regions of Britain without railways. Sea communications remained supreme until the making of good roads allowed the successful competition of motor transport after the middle of this century.

The southern shore of Loch Linnhe is well served by communications. Two major trunk roads form part of the national network – the A82 approaches through the Pass of Glencoe and the A85 reaches the shores of Loch Etive and Oban through the Pass of Brander. The main obstacle to travel through the country between Fort William and Oban has been the long arms of three tributary sea lochs – Loch Leven, Loch Crerran and Loch Etive. Until recent years the road between Fort William and Oban was interrupted by two ferries across the mouths of lochs at Ballachulish and Connel. In summer, long queues of traffic would build up delays of several hours at the Ballachulish ferry, an impediment that has been removed with the construction of a suspension bridge. At Connel the closing of the branch line to Ballachulish has allowed the conversion of the railway bridge above the Falls of Lora at the mouth of Loch Etive for road traffic.

Loch Leven is set among some of the most austere mountain scenery of western Scotland. At its head, from Kinlochleven, mountain trails lead into the wilderness of Mamore Forest where several summits rise above 914m (3,000ft).

Onich Its southern aspect and screening forests and mountains have given Onich some reputation as a resort, reputedly milder and sunnier than most other places in this wettest part of the British Isles. Of late it has benefited by the industrial growth around Fort William and has been favoured by managers of the new industries as a place to live, hence its newly acquired nickname of 'the gold coast'.

Ballachulish hums with the ceaseless traffic that flows along the Glencoe trunk road and bears the deep scars, in mountains of grey waste rock, of the slate-quarrying industry that began towards the end of the seventeenth century and closed down in 1955.

Kinlochleven, whose problems of development have been hindered both by its claustrophic barrier of mountain and its location on the boundary of Argyll and

Inverness-shire, lies at the sunless head of the loch. This is a company town founded in 1909 when the British Aluminium Company built what was then one of the world's largest smelters fuelled by hydro-electricity from the Blackwater Reservoir in the headwaters of the Leven. Until the 1920s Kinlochleven lived in great isolation without access by road. Bauxite, the raw clay from which aluminium is extracted, had to be shipped up the loch from the railway terminus at Ballachulish. Only in 1922 was the present road along the south side of Loch Leven completed and another five years passed before the opening of the single-track road along the north shore.

As the A828 road leads southwards towards Oban, the severe mountain scenery of Loch Leven gives way to a smiling, almost pastoral countryside in Benderloch. When the road climbs around the headland at Portnacroish a brief view opens across a much wider Loch Linnhe, now almost an inland sea with a scatter of reefs and islands.

Appin, a clutch of wooded peninsulas thrust into Loch Creran, possesses in Castle Stalker a medieval clan stronghold as attractive as Eilean Donan. Castle Stalker, a corruption down the centuries of its Gaelic name *Caisteal Stalcair* meaning the castle of the hunter, was built in the thirteenth century by the clan MacDougall. This romantic medieval stronghold, a keep four storeys in height, has been reroofed and renovated since 1966. Its tiny island site, in the entrance to Loch Laich, can be reached only by boat from either Port Appin or Portnacroish.

Benderloch The main Oban road clings to the southern shore of Loch Creran as it leaves Appin for Benderloch. At the seaward end of Loch Creran an extensive low peninsula, indented with several tiny bays, projects into the Lynn of Lorn – the sea channel between the mainland and the long, narrow limestone island of Lismore. The qualities of such a lowland tract in this mountainous sea-girt landscape were realised in prehistoric times. Clusters of burial cairns and standing stones from the Bronze Age, and an earlier Neolithic chambered tomb, all suggest the attractions of the light soils of the raised beaches composed largely of glacial outwash material of the Ice Age. On a grassy hillock close to the shore at Benderloch survives the faintest trace of what, according to tradition, was the chief centre of this region some 2,000 years ago. Dun Mhic Uisneachan, meaning the Fort of the Sons of Uisneach, was most likely a stronghold of the Picts. Several defensive works have occupied this hill and the latest was a vitrified fort characteristic of the Late Iron Age in Scotland – a time that coincides with the Roman occupation of southern Britain.

Loch Etive reaches far inland to the mountains that are massed around the head of Glen Coe. Its long upper section above the grey granite quarries of Bonawe is completely roadless and inaccessible to the motorist. The head of the loch may be reached by a road that follows Glen Etive from the A82 near Kingshouse Inn on Rannoch Moor. The uniqueness of Loch Etive lies in the shallow, narrow exit to Loch Linnhe. Here, just beneath the Connel Bridge, a rock bar interrupts the flow of water at the change of tides. At ebb tide the water-level of Loch Linnhe falls faster than that of Loch Etive and a cataract of several feet in height pours across the bar. On the rising flood-tide the Falls of Lora are reversed as Atlantic salt water thunders into the loch.

The rich lowland that extends from Oban to the lower reach of Loch Etive, a smiling sunlit corner of the Highland west after the overpowering mountains and gloomy glens of the inner recesses of Loch Linnhe, has several visible links with Scotland's medieval history. Dunstaffnage Castle is the most important, a thirteenth-century fort whose curtain walls rise to a height of (18.2m) 60ft between its circular angle towers. The castle was raised on the site of an earlier Dark Age fort, reputed to be one of the early seats of the kings of Dalriada. In the eighteenth century, Dunstaffnage, then part of the numerous Campbell estates, was held as a Hanoverian base in the risings of 1715 and 1745. The interior of the castle was burnt out in 1810, but in recent years the Ministry of Works has undertaken its restoration.

Close by lies a ruined medieval chapel, scene of a vicious murder during the wedding ceremony of Sir John Stewart in 1463. Loch Etive also boasts a monastic site. Ardchattan, on the northern shore, was established in 1230 by a branch of the Benedictines. A private house has occupied the greater part of the site since the Reformation, but enough remains to justify its preservation as an ancient monument that is open to the public.

Bonawe, the furthest accessible place for the motorist on Loch Etive, is one of the rare settlements in the Highland west to be touched by the industrial developments of the eighteenth century. A Lancashire iron-master, Richard Ford, agreed with the local landowner, Campbell of Lochnell, to establish furnaces and a forge for the smelting of iron ore on the south side of the loch. The ore was imported by sea from Furness, on the edge of the English Lake District. The motive for the establishment of a blast furnace at this remote place was the abundance of timber for making charcoal in western Scotland at a time when the woodland resources of England had already become severely depleted. Bonawe's furnace finally ceased in 1873. On the northern shore of the loch, where a drab settlement has grown up, granite quarrying that has now worked for more than a century was already active. However, the product has changed over the years for granite-paving setts that went to the streets of Edinburgh and many lowland towns have given way to the crushed rock for road making.

In recent years Loch Etive has become an increasing barrier to movement. The ferry that linked Taynuilt and Bonawe quarries no longer runs, and others that once joined places on the northern and southern shores of the loch have long been forgotten. However, a mail service still runs the year round between Taynuilt pier and Lochetivehead and there are tourist excursions on the loch between May and October.

Lismore The 16km (10 mile) long island of Lismore, a rib of limestone never more than 3.2km (2 miles) wide, presents several rare features in the Highland landscape. Limestone is extremely rare in the geological make-up of western Scotland. Here in Lismore the Dalradian Limestone provides light, well-drained soils of an unmatched fertility in this landscape of harsh granites, schists and ancient volcanic rocks. The road that follows the backbone of the island southwards from Port Ramsay knows scarcely any traffic; in the last miles by the shores of Loch Fiart it peters out into a grassy unmade track. The island is a place abounding in wild flowers and in high summer the salt air is scented with honey-suckle, wild rose and meadow-sweet. A scattering of duns and brochs shows that the island was a centre of settlement in late prehistoric times. The ruin of a tall galleried broch stands on the east coast and another occupies the low ground beside the outflowing stream from Loch Fiart. A line of Iron Age earthworks straddles the middle of the island - Dùn Cuilein, Dùn Mor and Sean Dùn.

A contemporary of St Columba in the Celtic church, St Moluag, founded a monastery on the island. The name Lismore possibly recalls this Dark Age monastery, for in western Britain the monastic communities of the early Christian centuries occupied a cluster of beehive-shaped huts within a circular banked enclosure. The original Gaelic name, *leis mor*, means the 'great enclosure'. For a brief period in the thirteenth century Lismore became the focus of the diocese of Argyll. A cathedral, perhaps the smallest in Scotland, was raised at Kilmoluaig and Achadun Castle was built on the west coast of Lismore as a bishop's palace. Lismore's medieval cathedral was burnt to the ground at the Reformation and the present simple parish church has been restored from the ruined choir of its predecessor.

From Oban Caledonian MacBrayne run a vehicle ferry to the pier at Achnacroish, a service that has benefited the 200 inhabitants of the island whose economy depends mainly upon the fattening of livestock for the Oban markets. The former important occupation of quarrying and burning lime for fertiliser has been dead for more than fifty years. Evidence of this industry may still be seen in the abandoned quarries at Salen. There, too, in a tiny inlet on the west coast is the deserted quay from which schooners exported lime to places as distant as Stornoway in the Outer Hebrides.

Oban ranks among the main holiday resorts of Scotland; there are some forty hotels in the town and much of its income derives from tourism. For more than a century the two piers have been the terminus of shipping routes to Mull, Tiree, Coll, Colonsay and the Outer Hebrides. In addition, the seas off Oban are blessed with what became three of the greatest tourist attractions of Victorian Britain - Staffa and Fingal's Cave, Iona and, closer at hand, the dreaded tidal whirlpool of the Gulf of Corryvreckan. Tourism combined with trade to make Oban one of the busiest ports of Scotland's western seaboard.

With a total population of a little more than 6,000, Oban has a varied and comparatively healthy economic structure. As a fishing harbour it competes closely with Mallaig. In recent years there has been an increasingly prosperous trade in shell-fish, particularly in lobsters that are stored in ponds on the off-lying island of Kerrera before export by air to markets on the Continent. A distillery, a tweed mill, and a now widely known but recently founded glass factory are among the other occupations of Oban, but the town's chief function is to act as a service centre for a very extensive part of Argyll. Shopping facilities are the best for miles around and the town can boast two cathedrals. The town also possesses in the Corran Hall one of the few places among the small and scattered towns of Highland Scotland where theatrical performances and large conferences can satisfactorily take place. At the beginning of August one of Scotland's most famous regattas takes place and during the last week of that month Mossfield Park on the higher outskirts of the town is the scene of the Highland Games. Oban has left its mark on the cultural life of the Highlands because it was here that the National Mod, a Gaelic gathering with competitions in poetry and song, originated and was first held.

There is a busyness and liveliness about Oban that is missing from most Highland towns. For the tourist the lasting impression is one of warm sandstone buildings neatly gathered around the curve of the bay, of a harbour bustling with ferries, fishing boats and yachts, and the whole dominated by one of Scotland's most impressive 'follies', MacCaig's Tower (built in 1897 by a local banker on the summit of a wooded hill above the town centre). John McCaig built the tower, in the shape of the Colosseum in Rome, as a means of relieving unemployment in Oban, but the work was abandoned and the look-out tower, designed to be 100ft (30m) in height, and its museum were never completed. Today, the interior shell of McCaig's Tower has been laid out as a garden after remaining a tangled wilderness for more than seventy years.

By following the coast road past Corran Hall and St Columba's Cathedral 1.6km (1 mile) north, one comes to Dunollie Castle, an ivy-grown keep that crowns a rocky crag at the northern approach to Oban Bay. Its exact date is unknown, but it seems most likely that the keep was raised by the lords of Lorne in the twelfth century. The name reveals that this was a fortified site long before the Middle Ages. Dunollie was a Dark Age strong-point. Along with Dunadd, that historic site in the isthmus of Crinan, Dunollie was one of the original cores from which evolved the kingdom of Dalriada.

Oban first appears in the documentary record at the beginning of the eighteenth century as 'a creek in the Renfrew customs area'. In 1811 the first step towards the making of a town was taken with the granting of a charter to the Duke of Argyll. Between 1869 and 1894 the Oban that we know today was laid out on the edge of its raised beach. It was in the making of the Victorian town that the earliest presence of man at Oban came to light. No less than seven caves were discovered in the ancient cliff line behind the raised beach containing remains of prehistoric, Mesolithic cultures. The bone harpoons, flints, stone hammers and kitchen middens - the remains of shell-fish and the bones of sea-birds - from the Oban caves dates back 8,000 years. Two incentives towards the expansion of Oban came after the middle of the nineteenth century. First, in the 1850s, the use of steamboats led to improvements in shipping services. Even more important in the

Oban, a Victorian town and holiday resort developed on the 25ft (7.5m) raised beach. MacCaig's Tower is in the background

growth of Oban's role as a communications centre was the coming of the railway in 1880.

Nether Lorn, lying to the south and west of Oban, must rank among the most attractive and distinctive regions of Scotland. An extensive coastal plateau, scarcely higher than 152m (500ft), projects long rocky fingers into the Atlantic. Among the ancient highly contorted rocks of Nether Lorn a wide band of black slates extends through the offshore islands of Seil, Easdale and Luing to form the eastern flanks of Scarba and Jura. On exposed stretches of coast the slates form dark jagged cliffs that have been the source of roofing slates, quarried over a period of 200 years. The last slate quarry closed at Balvicar in 1965. The individuality of Nether Lorn belongs also to the complex archipelago of some 30 islands and 200 skerries. Between the islands and the mainland coast Atlantic tides flow through an intricate pattern of sounds and channels. Here run the most notorious tide races of the British seas. Between Scarba and the desolate northern shore of Jura lies the Gulf of Corryvreckan where a tidal whirlpool roars around a submerged rock pyramid. The whirlpool of Corryvreckan is stilled only for one hour at both high and low water and, under certain conditions of tide and wind, waves of 6m (20ft) in height are formed and the roar of its turbulent waters may be heard for miles along the coast of Lorn. Corryvreckan is the most famous of the tidal whirlpools with its legend of a swallowed Viking fleet of fifty ships and the constant danger that it presents to small holiday craft. The Dorus Mór, the Great Gate, lies off Craignish Point. The tide that moves northward up the Sound of Jura pours through the Fladda Narrows off the island of Luing. The Grey Dog, another tidal race, fills the channel between Scarba and Lunga – a passage only a few hundred yards wide.

For the motorist the only accessible islands of the slate archipelago are Seil and Luing. Seil is separated from the mainland by a sound whose narrowest part is only 21m (70ft) in width. Here the handsome single-arched bridge, built by Telford in 1792, rising 12m (40ft) above the Sound of Seil, is a great tourist attraction. **Easdale** confronts the unwitting motorist with a great surprise for, amid one of the finest seascapes in Britain, he finds a huge parking ground for the accommodation of tour buses, souvenir shops, 'take-away chips' and Aladdin's Cave – an emporium complete with muzak that would not be lost in Blackpool. Even so, Easdale is not to be missed, for it was one of the main centres of the slate industry and the relics of two centuries of quarrying are still the most obvious features of the landscape. By the middle of the nineteenth century the output of the quarries scattered among the Slate Islands had risen to 7 million slates a year. The most striking remains of this extinct industry are the flooded slate pits, excavated at sites perilously close to the shore, for easy access to the sea for export. Remoteness from markets and the competition of newer synthetic roofing materials contributed to the decline of the slate industry, but the Atlantic also played a part in its demise. A heavy storm on 22 November 1881 broke through the sea wall at Ellanbeich flooding the quarry to a depth of 75m (250ft). Both at **Ellanbeich** and on the nearby island of Easdale many of the single-storeyed white-washed cottages that housed the quarrymen have been turned into holiday homes.

For the motorist Easdale is the most accessible of the slate-quarry settlements. It is worth climbing by a steep, though easy track, to the summit of the hill, Dun Mor, for an exciting prospect of the Slate Islands. Southward lies the barren conical mass of Scarba. Out on the Atlantic the Garvellachs, holy islands of the earliest years of the Celtic church, lie darkly on the silver surface of the sea in the afternoon sun. Easdale is spread at one's feet with its cottage rows, the abandoned heaps of waste and the still, expressionless eyes of flooded slate-pits.

The name of the four rocky islands lying about 10km (6 miles) seaward – Garvellachs – was derived from that of the largest, Garbh Eileach, meaning the large rocky mound. The islands are completely deserted and in the settled days of the early Hebridean summer their rich pastures beneath the rocky outcrops are ablaze with wild flowers. But the place-names and landscape of Garvellachs bear evidence of the islands' former inhabitants. The *Old Statistical Account* of the 1790s records a population of 200. At its north-eastern tip the tiny island of Dùn Chonnuill carries the remains of a Dark Age fort that had been rebuilt in the thirteenth century by the MacDougalls. The most exciting evidence of man in Garvellachs appears in the remains of a Dark Age monastery on Eileach an Naoimh, the Rock of the Saints. The monastic site, including two beehive-shaped cells, one of which has been rebuilt by the Ministry of Works, lies in a secluded hollow sheltered to the west by the steep slopes of Dun Bhreanain, a hill rising some 61m (200ft) from the sea whose name recalls St Brendan. St Brendan, it is believed, established a monastic community in the Isles of the Sea in AD 542, two decades before St Columba reached Iona. At present the Garvellach islands may be reached – when the weather and state of the sea allow – by motor-boat excursions run by private operators from Cuan Ferry on Luing. A frequent car-ferry service connects Seil and Luing throughout the day between 8am and 6pm in the summer months.

For the motorist there is only one way southwards from Nether Lorn into the Kintyre peninsula and that is by following the A816 that connects Oban and Lochgilphead. Along many miles of the route access to the coast is not easy. The road skirts the southern shore of Loch Melfort and for scarcely 1.6km (1 mile) at Asknish Bay bursts out to the sea's margin with magnificent westward views to the Slate Islands. Loch Craignish presents an even more fleeting prospect as the main road crosses its head, but at least there is a rewarding view down the full length of this sea loch as the road climbs steeply into the Bealach Mór, the pass that leads over to Kilmartin. Topographically, Loch Craignish sums up the scenery of the deeply indented coastline of mid-Argyll. Thickly wooded low hills come down to the water's edge and the surface of the loch is broken with a pattern of long, narrow islands rising steeply to almost 61m (200ft). These are partially submerged ridges, green with lush pastures and patches of woodland, unlike the bare rocks and reefs that occasionally break the wide surface of

Dunadd, a rocky hummock that was the Dark Age capital of Dalriada

the huge sea lochs, the fjords, of the north-west Highlands.

Inland from the low uninteresting shore-line of Loch Crinan a true coastal plain has developed. A line of hills, never more than 152m (500ft) in height, lies at a distance of 4.8–6.4km (3–4 miles) from the sea. The flat land that extends to the shore of Loch Crinan from the foot of the hills, themselves an ancient cliff-line, is the Moine Mhór. Across this largely reclaimed landscape of marsh and peat bog the river Add meanders lazily into the head of Loch Crinan. Here and there the prosperous farmland of the Mòine Mhór is broken by stark rocky out-crops. One such rocky island, rising to a height of 46m (150ft) above the plain, Dunadd, ranks among the places of greatest historic importance in the whole of Scotland. Here, about the year AD 500 colonists from Ireland founded the kingdom of Dalriada. At Dunadd the colonising Scotti took over an already existing Iron Age fort on the summit of the crag. Twelve hundred years and more have not erased every evidence of Dunadd's Dark Age glory, for rock carvings close to the summit ridge depict a wild boar as well as two or three lines of indecipherable Ogham script – a symbolic alphabet used widely in the post-Roman centuries in western Britain.

The importance of Dunadd, its encom-passing lowland and fringe of hills, in the prehistoric and Dark Age centuries is emphasised when we remember that within a 16km (10 mile) radius of this capital of Dalriada more than seventy structures, forts or duns, from the years between 200 BC and AD 500 are to be found. In addition, the valley of the Kilmartin Burn has a rich scattering of objects – standing stones, burial chambers, stone circles and cairns – that reach back across the Bronze Age to the Neolithic settlers in the third millennium BC. Kilmartin has been compared with that focus of the prehistoric communities of lowland England at Avebury in Wiltshire.

Kilmartin is situated on a steep, flat-topped bluff, a fragment of a raised beach from higher late-glacial sea-levels. The place-name itself, the chapel of St Martin, takes the mind back to the earliest days of

A 'puffer' passes through the Crinan Canal

Christianity in western Europe if the dedication indeed remembers Martin of Tours who lived in the fourth century. Kilmartin's importance as a church site is undoubted when one examines the collection of crosses and sculptured stones, fine examples of a regional art form that flourished in western Scotland in the Middle Ages.

At the head of the Kintyre peninsula the stormy seas of the Hebrides are divided from the sheltered waters of Loch Fyne by a neck of land scarcely 10km (6 miles) across. The cutting of the Crinan Canal across the isthmus in the 1790s revolutionised the sea passage from the Clyde to Scotland's north-western coasts for the rounding of the stormy Mull of Kintyre – a sea passage of 129km (80 miles) – was no longer necessary. The canal came into its own in the latter half of the nineteenth century when the Clyde 'puffers', flat-bottomed steam-ships, were grounded on Hebridean beaches to unload their cargo of coal between high tides which was then carted away by crofters. The highest point of the canal is reached at 27m (88ft) above sea-level and the journey of the coal-laden puffers is made more sedate by their passage through fifteen locks. Along its course the lock keepers' cottages, bridges, harbour basins and the canal settlement of Cairnbaan survive as memorials to the beginning of an age that was to transform the communications and the very face of Britain. Only here in mid-Argyll the Industrial Revolution was to go no further. The Crinan Canal became a fashionable tourist attraction for the wealthy after Queen Victoria sailed through it on a tour of western Scotland in 1847. Later, the leisured businessmen who bought up Highland deer forests were to follow the 'royal route', as it was called, through the Crinan Canal. Today, it is more important as a short-cut for hundreds of summer yachts and motor cruisers between the Clyde and the many islands of the north-west.

Knapdale occupies the head of the Kintyre peninsula, extending from the thickly forested hills above the Crinan Canal to the long re-entrant of West Loch Tarbert that comes within 1.6km (1 mile) of converting Kintyre into the island that it used to be in former post-glacial times of temporarily higher sea-levels. The name Knapdale literally means the land of hills and valleys, and the most distinctive feature of this landscape is the regular pattern of narrow hummocky ridges and parallel sea lochs, all trending from north-east to south-west.

Around the shores of Knapdale's two major sea lochs, Loch Sween and Loch Caolsport, the historical associations of the region with Dark Age Dalriada and the even remoter centuries of prehistory are clearly evident in the stone circles and the tumbled ruins of duns. Loch Sween is served by only two winding single-track roads and the mainland coast that faces the Sound of Jura is accessible at only one point, Carsaig Bay, between Crinan and Keillmore. At its head, beyond Tayvallich's sheltered bay, the loch divides into four narrow fingers. Dark green forests, planted by the Forestry Commission in the thirties, come down to the water's edge, clothing completely the intervening ridges. There is an enfolding stillness in this small-scale landscape that is rarely encountered elsewhere in Scotland. One stumbles across the forgotten relics of prehistory in twentieth-century woodland. In a forest clearing close to the road to Tayvallich stands the Barnluasgan stone circle, a relic of the Bronze Age that for more than 2,000 years stood on a rock-strewn open moorland.

Tayvallich Its neat cottages and villas encircle the edge of the completely sheltered Loch a' Bhealaich. The very richness of this place with its patches of lush woodland, roadside verges ablaze with wild flowers and colourful gardens is foreign to one's everyday conceptions of the western Highlands. In summer the glassy waters of Tayvallich's bay provide sheltered moorings for scores of yachts. The low ground, scarcely 1km (½ mile) across, that separates Tayvallich from Carsaig Bay on the inaccessible west coast of Knapdale, formed a sea strait at the time of higher sea-levels. **Carsaig**, reached by a lane from Tayvallich, has a caravan and camping site, but there is no sand at the beach, only an attractive prospect of Jura across the Sound.

A journey to the end of the peninsula at **Keillmore** takes the traveller into a rougher, more windswept landscape. Where the narrow lane twists along the shore of Loch na Cille towards its end in the deserted farmyard at Keillmore there is an increasing sense of desolation. A jetty, built strong against Atlantic gales in close-keyed mortarless slate slabs, is reminiscent of the cattle traffic that once came this way across the Sound from Jura. And on the gentle slope above Loch na Cille, the loch of the chapel, stands the shell of a medieval chapel, a vivid reminder of those distant centuries when Celtic saints and, later, Viking war bands and traders sailed these seas. Keills chapel, dedicated to St Columba, and dating from the eleventh century, is a place not to be missed. Of late the building has been restored to the extent of a new roof and inside there are gathered together some of the elaborately worked coffin lids that are characteristic of the coastal fringe of south-west Scotland in the fourteenth and fifteenth centuries. A lost world is glimpsed in the sculptured shapes of wild cats, wolves, otters and foxes intermingled with swords and leaf decorations. One scarcely decipherable inscription on a coffin lid reads 'MacNeil caused me to be made'. The greatest treasure of the Keills chapel is the twelfth-century cross, hewn out of blue slate and elaborately decorated on one side. It is one of the oldest of the free-standing crosses of Argyll and used to stand on the open hillside a few yards from the church.

Many students of scenery in the twentieth century have had hard things to say about the work of the Forestry Commission. Certainly, distant prospects have been obliterated, stone circles and other prehistoric monuments have lost their meaning in relation to the whole landscape, and 'regimented lines of conifers' has become a common description of the dullness of some of our forest landscapes. But in Knapdale the foresters have created a landscape of great attractiveness. The wooded shores of Caol Scotnish and the secret embayment of the Fairy Isles – seven islands in all – present a type of scenery not to be found elsewhere in the Western Highlands. The Forestry Commission in Knapdale also invite the visitor to explore their territory through forest walks and to seek further information at a log-cabin centre close to the road junction for Tayvallich and Kilmory.

The coastal hills of the peninsula that separates Loch Sween and Loch Caolisport are clothed in extensive woodlands; inland, the country rises into bare moorlands with many scattered lochs and hills, trackless and unvisited by tourists, that rise to just over 305m (1,000ft) above the sea. Castle Sween, built in the twelfth century, on the eastern shore of Loch Sween, represents the earliest penetration of the architectural ideas of the Norman castle-builders into Celtic western Scotland. Its rectangular stone tower, strengthened with large buttresses, was elaborated in the thirteenth century with the building of a rectangular keep at the north-east corner and later still, in the fourteenth century, with the construction of a round tower at the north-west angle.

The history of the early Christian church is also strongly written into the landscape of this peninsula. The medieval chapel ruin at Kilmory has been reroofed to protect a collection of thirty engraved stones. But the most exciting reminder of the church in the Dark Ages is found in a cave traditionally associated with St Columba on the northern shore of Loch Caolisport. St Columba's Cave is reached by a winding single-track road from Achahoish, the little scattered settlement at the head of Loch Caolisport. The cave lies at the head of a fragment of raised beach in a little embayment, a bay blocked by a rocky reef, Eilean na h-Uamhaidh or the 'island of the cave'. Inside the cave, a place of worship 1,300 years ago, lies a rock platform with a rough, drystone altar. An outline of the cross is cut in the rock wall, and a basin, in the floor of the cave, it has been argued, was for the washing of feet before the celebration of mass. A few yards from the mouth of the cave stands the gable of a ruined medieval chapel, and all around in this sheltered, sunny place on the raised beach beneath an abandoned sea cliff is a tangle of wild flowers, roses, honeysuckle, tall yellow iris and forget-me-not.

Beyond St Columba's Cave another 1km (½ mile) of road is open to the motorist as far as **Ellery**. After that the northern shore of Loch Caolisport is inaccessible to those who cannot leave their cars behind. As in so many of the less accessible parts of western Scotland, we enter a world that scarcely knows the twentieth century. Woods reach down to the sea and forgotten Iron Age duns crown a craggy ridge. **Stronefield**, in a south-facing sheltered embayment above the valley of the Abhainn Mhor, was deserted in the widespread Highland clearances of the last century. And where that valley enters the sea the rich meadows of its floor give way to what has been described as 'the most beautiful of Argyll's mainland beaches', Muileann Eiteag Bagh.

For the traveller from the north the low isthmus, scarcely 15m (50ft) above sea-level at its highest point, between East Loch Tarbert and West Loch Tarbert, forms the gateway into Kintyre. This long narrow peninsula reaches almost 80km (50 miles) from **Tarbert** – one of the half-dozen busy little towns that make up the sum total of the urban geography of Argyll – to the Mull, and the name Kintyre itself means 'land's end'. At the Mull of Kintyre lighthouse, perched on the brink of a 91m (300ft) cliff, the land ends within sight of and only 19km (12 miles) from the coast of Ireland.

A journey down the west coast of Kintyre from Tarbert to the Mull soon makes clear its individuality among the regions of western Scotland. Once you have left behind the entrance to West Loch Tarbert at Clachan, coastline and road run beside each other for many miles, pointing south-westward, without the interference of any deep bays or barriers of sea lochs. A succession of sand beaches culminates in the 6.4km (4 mile) long strand between Westport and Machrihanish, a beach of Atlantic breakers, surf and sand, hemmed in by a high rim of dunes. The closed inaccessible world of the north-western fjords has given way in Kintyre to an open, smiling seascape. The individuality of Kintyre expresses itself through the rocks that make up its landscape. In the south, where the lowland known as the Laggan reaches from the mountainous dunes of Machrihanish across to Campbeltown Bay, rocks of an age and kind that dominate lowland Scotland appear. Limestone and sandstone with beds of shale and coal seams of Carboniferous age have been preserved in a down-faulted rift valley structure. At Machrihanish colliery, close beside the famous golf links, coal was mined until the late 1960s. In the early years of this century a dozen collieries mined coal, and in 1906 a light railway was opened to Campbeltown to carry fuel to the several distilleries, and to the harbour for export to Ireland. This was Kintyre's only brush with 'the railway age' and an episode in its economic history that is now completely closed, although it is known that a great thickness of coal measures still exists.

For the motorist following the A83 down the western flank of Kintyre to Campbeltown there is a succession of ever-widening prospects across the sea. Many miles of the route are confined to a level raised-beach platform - one of the finest raised beaches in the British Isles - frequently hundreds of yards in breadth, that is abruptly limited by cliffs between 46 and 61m (150 and 200ft) in height. This is an ancient sea cliff shaped by storm waves when mean sea-level stood between 8 and 11m (25 and 35ft) higher than at present. In some places this steep grassy slope above the level bench of the raised beach betrays its origins more clearly. There are vertical rock faces with the dark entrances of former sea caves and chasms cut out by the sea along lines of weakness. In front of the former sea cliffs the remnants of stacks, no longer standing out of an effervescent sea, rise as rock pinnacles out of the fields of potatoes and corn. At Muasdale there is a fine cluster of former sea stacks, the cottages of the settlement crouched among them. At the south end of Bellochantuy Bay the road winds among a jumbled gathering of rocky pinnacles that were awash in the few thousand years of higher sea-level as the Ice Age waned.

Kintyre's prehistory spans some 6,000 years. The first site of importance along the road south from Tarbert is reached at the mouth of West Loch Tarbert where an isolated hill, Dun Skeig, is crowned by a group of earthworks from the Iron Age. Superimposed upon the earthwork defences of a hill-fort are two duns, enclosures of close-set drystone masonry of a slightly later date. These complex works of man hint at the occupation of this strategic look-out over a period of several centuries some 2,000 years ago. Further south along the A83 the crest of the former sea cliff, 30m (100ft) above the raised beach platform and the road, is the site of the standing stones of Ballochroy. It has been argued that the standing stones of Ballachroy were raised on certain important astronomical alignments. One, through the Megalithic burial chamber that was formerly covered by a cairn, leads the eye across the west end of the little island of Cara on a line that pointed to the setting of the sun at midwinter's day in late Neolithic times about 1800 BC. Above the old cliff-line, on gentle slopes 61–91m (200–300ft) above the sea at Beacharr, lies another Neolithic site, a standing stone and a chambered cairn. The standing stone, the tallest in Kintyre, reaches 5m (16½ft). There is abundant evidence of man's presence here in the Iron Age. The ancient cliff-line is crowned in several places with duns, rough-walled enclosures. Above Bellochantuy Bay are the sites of no less than five duns, many of which stand close beside present-day farms, hinting that the location of settlements on Kintyre's Atlantic coast has not changed greatly since late prehistoric times.

Campbeltown provides the main approach to the blunt southern end of the peninsula. Here, close to the west coast, are the highest mountains of the peninsula, a landscape of Dalradian schists. Most of the Mull of Kintyre is inaccessible by road. The motorist can follow the heavily graded, winding, but well-surfaced road to the Mull lighthouse, but even here journey's end cannot be made on four wheels. Cars must be left behind at the Gap, over 305m (1,000ft) above the sea, and the steep descent to the lighthouse completed on foot. The Mull lighthouse on its 91m (300ft) sheer cliff was built in 1788. If you leave the lighthouse road and make your way across the trackless moorland on the south-western flank of the Borgadel Water, you come to a ruined dun, circular in shape and enclosed by a wall 4m (12ft) in thickness, on a rocky bluff overlooking the sea. Further west, a hard 1.2km (¾ mile) walk along the cliff top, lies the relic of the late Iron Age, Sròn Uamha, an enclosure composed of three drystone walls on the edge of a precipitous cliff.

Southend Situated on the south-eastern tip of the Kintyre peninsula, the landscape is coloured by rocks of the Old Red Sandstone series. Southend has sandy beaches, and further to the east Macharioch Bay has been described as 'the finest bay of the south coast' with its sandy beach and quiet coves sheltered by sandstone crags. Inland, prosperous farms, solidly built in dark sandstone, inhabit the wide glens that open to the sea at Southend. The chambered cairn at Blasthill, standing on the shoulder of a green hill scarcely 1.6km (1 mile) from the sea, suggests that the tiny lowland was already a core of settlement in Neolithic times. Just 1.6km (1 mile) from Blasthill stands the largest hill-fort in Kintyre, the triple-banked Cnoc Araich, probably the tribal stronghold of the Epidii in Roman times. For prehistoric man the beaches of Southend must have provided an early landfall, and the finds preserved in the museum at Campbeltown prove the links with Ireland. And the saints of the Celtic church came this way too; Keil Point at Southend is said to be the place where St Columba first set foot in Dalriada in the sixth century.

Campbeltown, with a population of over 6,000, serves as a regional centre for the greater part of Kintyre. On wet days, when the Atlantic rain swirls in horizontal sheets through Campbeltown's streets, it is an uninviting place, grey but achieving some kind of character in the very lack of attractive individual characteristics in its urban make-up. The name of this compact little borough at the sheltered head of Campbeltown Loch recalls the dominance of Argyll's most famous clan in the peninsula since the seventeenth century.

Campbeltown belongs to Britain's deliberately planted towns. It was brought into being by an Act of Parliament, passed in 1597, for the planting of burghs in Kintyre, Lochaber and Lewis. The new urban parish, at first known as Lochhead, came into existence in 1617. The growth of the new town came only with the rising prosperity of Kintyre after the final victory of the Campbells and the resettlement of some of the best lands in the peninsula by 'lowlanders'.

Fishing, shipbuilding and whisky distilling have been the main occupations of Campbeltown through the past three centuries. The fishing fleet has declined greatly in numbers, but has also become mechanised and more efficient. Shipbuilding died in the early 1920s and the whisky distilleries are now reduced to two firms. A hundred years ago Campbeltown possessed thirty-four distilleries, and it was said that her fishermen could navigate their way to harbour through the stillness of a sea-fog by the bouquet of the town's distilleries. Since World War II regular steamer services to the mainland ports of the Clyde have ceased. The only public transport to Glasgow is the twice-daily bus that takes 5 hours over the 225km (140 mile) journey by the head of Loch Fyne and the shores of Loch Lomond.

The chief attractions of Campbeltown are the museum in Hall Street, the ruined fragment of the fifteenth-century Castle Kilkerran, by the shore on the southern outskirts of the town, and **Davaar Island**. A shingle spit, the Dhorlin, almost 1.6km (1 mile) in length, connects the island with the shore just east of Campbeltown. The island can be reached on foot along the Dhorlin at low tide, but it is wiser to use the ferry service that runs daily in the summer from Campbeltown. The green back of Davaar Island gives way to sandstone cliffs, riddled with caves, along its southern shore. Here the main attraction is a wall-painting of the crucifixion, executed secretly in 1887 by Alexander MacKinnon.

The B842, between Campbeltown and Claonaig, runs between open pastures with fine views across the sea to Arran's western mountains. In places it finds the shade of deep woodland thickly banked with the blaze of rhododendron in the weeks of early summer. The distant views of Arran and the ever-changing variety of the local scene make the exploration of Kintyre's east-coast road worthwhile.

Saddell The ruins of Saddell Abbey lie 1km (½ mile) inland from the shore. Its

Part of the fine collection of late medieval tomb slabs at Saddell Abbey

foundation, attributed to one of the sons of Somerled, Reginald, King of the Isles, belonged to the Cistercian order. As a visual piece of architecture Saddell is not exciting, but the place is worth visiting for the impressive collection of sculptured medieval tomb-slabs that have been gathered together and beautifully displayed. Saddell also has a castle, built at the beginning of the sixteenth century by a bishop of Argyll.

Carradale Here Kintyre's longest river empties into a bay with a 1.6km (1 mile) long sandy beach. After Campbeltown, this is the main settlement of the east coast. Its rich woodlands with lime and beech and brightly

The Firth of Clyde and adjacent coastlands, including the Isle of Arran

coloured rhododendron bear witness to the activity and enterprise of private planters at Carradale House, a sharp contrast with commercial planting of conifers by the Forestry Commission that has taken over so many hundred of acres in Kintyre since the 1930s. There is a liveliness about Carradale that is expressed in the little fishing settlement gathered around the new harbour and its breakwater, constructed in 1959. The Forestry Commission, now the largest landowner in the district, have helped in the modernisation of farms on their estates. Carradale has much to offer the tourist – the best beach of the east coast of Kintyre fringed by a pleasant strip of machair, the gardens of Carradale House that are open to the public, and a vitrified fort on a rocky island at the end of the peninsula that can be reached only at low tide.

Claonaig is now the terminal for a vehicle ferry that sails to Loch Ranza in Arran between the beginning of May and mid-October, providing eight daily crossings in each direction through the weeks of high summer.

Skipness, the last settlement of east Kintyre. Both crofting and herring fishing have died at Skipness and the last steamer made a regular call there in 1935. The remains exist of a medieval castle with a square keep built of the local grey mica-schists offset by red sandstone dressings from Arran. Close to the shingle beach stands the ruin of a thirteenth-century chapel, dedicated to St Brendan.

The estuary of the Clyde and its several branching sea lochs form the largest system of sheltered sea-ways in the British Isles. To the east of Loch Fyne a complex group of fjords – Loch Riddon, Loch Striven, Loch Goil and Loch Long – project into the Highlands from the Firth of Clyde, a wide waterway busy with merchant ships, oil tankers, car ferries and the shapes of submarines slipping out from bases at Holy Loch and Faslane to the Atlantic. The peninsulas, long fingers of mountain and forest that stretch out between the sea lochs, make up the region of Cowal.

From Tarbert northwards the western shore of Loch Fyne is followed closely by the A83, the lifeline of the entire peninsula of Kintyre now that the regular shipping services to Inveraray, Ardrishaig, Tarbert and Campbeltown have ceased. For several miles between Tarbert and Ardrishaig the road hugs the shore closely. Thickly wooded slopes hide the ancient cliffs that were shaped when the sea-level of Loch Fyne stood some 9m (30ft) higher than at present. Loch Gilp has two settlements on its shores.

Ardrishaig, a 1.6km (1 mile) long string of cottages, came into being with the cutting of the Crinan Canal. A century ago when Loch Fyne was flush with herring it owned a fishing fleet and was the terminus of the 'Lord of the Isles Route' from Glasgow. But all that has passed. Now the buses stop on their way to Campbeltown and the summer yachts and motor launches besiege the lock gates at the entrance to the Crinan Canal on their way to the Atlantic coast.

Lochgilphead is one of Argyll's six burghs and the last to receive a charter in 1859. Its sheep and cattle markets serve a wide district. It provides secondary education for children from many distant settlements and it is the administrative centre of mid-Argyll.

Crarae Crarae Forest Garden merits more than a brief stop. Since the early years of this century the steep slopes of Glen Crarae, some 12ha (30 acres) in all, have been planted with rare conifers and massed banks of azaleas and rhododendrons. In 1955 the creator of Crarae, Sir George Campbell, gave his forest garden to the nation and it is now maintained by the Forestry Commission. At Crarae and Furnace granite has been quarried since the 1840s. It was exported by sea to pave the streets of Glasgow and the towns of the Clyde valley; now the rock is crushed for road metal.

Furnace The settlement arose with the building of an iron smelter in 1754. The attraction of this remote site far from markets and economic sources of iron ore lay in the rich natural woodlands of Loch Fyne – at that time, woods of oak, ash, beech, birch and holly that provided an abundant source of charcoal. Iron ore from the district of Furness in Cumbria was brought by sea for smelting in Furnace. The intrusion of the iron-smelting industry at Loch Fyne contributed to the decimation of the natural woodlands of this part of Scotland, a process that was hastened in the early years of the nineteenth century by the rise of sheep farming.

Auchindrain, a late-eighteenth-century township that had been largely deserted; in 1963 a local trust was set up to restore the site as a folk museum. Some twenty buildings have been refurbished and Highland life and crafts of two centuries ago can be enjoyed in this life-size open-air museum.

Inveraray was built, all of a piece, between 1744 and 1794, and so little has happened since that we are presented with a 'fossil' of eighteenth-century town planning. The castle, one of the earliest examples of the Gothic revival, was rebuilt close to its old site. The town was subjected to much severer treatment in that it was removed to a completely fresh site, 1km (½ mile) to the south, on the edge of Loch Fyne at Gallows Foreland. The architects who indulged the wishes of the Third, Fourth and Fifth Dukes of Argyll in this replanning of a fragment of the Scottish landscape were Roger Morris, William Adam, who was the father of the more famous Robert Adam, and Robert Mylne. Inveraray is a supreme example of an 'estate settlement' – a place where the wishes and whims of a manorial lord are written into every detail of the landscape. Here we can attach a name of one of the architects, Robert Mylne, to almost every detail of the townscape. The high-backed double-arched bridge by which you enter the burgh from the north across the river Aray was his work. The white-washed triple arch that forms such an imposing and unique feature of the new Inveraray was his idea. And the core of the burgh, the wide Main Street, severely plain with its white harled shop fronts, that leads into the little square filled by the plain, white-washed church was also designed by Mylne. Even the design of the church is hardly to be matched elsewhere in Britain, for its interior has a dividing wall that left one half for services in English and the other for those who worshipped in Gaelic.

Inveraray is an immensely attractive place, a fact recognised by the Historic Buildings Council in 1958 when its preservation as 'a good example of eighteenth-century town planning' was made possible by a large grant for the restoration of 100 houses. Its white harled walls reflect the light that comes from summer skies and the great mirror of the placid sea loch.

Strachur, a long straggling village, is the biggest settlement on the eastern shore of Loch Fyne, though the population of the whole parish of almost 104sq km (40 square miles) is less than 600. It is an important road junction where the A815 branches away south-eastwards to Dunoon. This is the motorist's long way round from Glasgow to that resort if he wants to avoid the tolls of the vehicle ferries from Gourock. The face of the landscape has reacted to the demands of man down the centuries. Around Strachur the transformation of sheep pastures into forests is evident. Since 1930 the Forestry Commissioners have acquired six of the largest farms in the parish, and of late a wood-working industry has been established to make garden furniture and quickly assembled 'Argyll' bungalows.

Strathlachan, situated on the B8000, a single-track road, has been in the ownership of the MacLachlans for 700 years. A ruined castle stands on a promontory by a sandy bay of Loch Fyne. The MacLachlan estate also has a model village, Newton, planned at the end of the eighteenth century to house crofters turned off their inland holdings to make way for sheep. The census of 1801 shows a well-established settlement with a population of 433. A century and a half later the population of Newton had fallen to little more than 200. Croft-houses were in ruins and some had been used as quarries for wall-building materials.

Southward, the B8000 leads to the seaward end of the peninsula where the huge parish of Kilfinan occupies 130sq km (50 square miles) of moorland and forested hills between Loch Fyne and the Kyles of Bute. Between Otter Ferry and Ardlamont the woodlands become ever more extensive as the Forestry Commission acquires estates. The seaward end of the peninsula towards Ardlamont Point presents a succession of little known sandy beaches at Glenan, Asgog and Kilbride Bays. The latter, with 1.2km (¾ mile) of sandy shore, is reached from Kilbride Farm, where there is parking for cars, along a bridle road and footpath that leads down to the sea. But if Ardlamont and the remoter seaward ends of Kilfinan parish seem beyond the reaches of mass tourism and twentieth-century industrialism that is only an illusion created by this quiet landscape of wooded glens, heather-stained hills and bright sand beaches.

Portavadie The rush to develop the oil resources of the North Sea in the 1970s saw the establishment of a base for the building of oil-construction platforms at Portavadie, a place of some dozen houses mainly occupied as holiday cottages. The choice of this place, so remote from the oil resources of the northern North Sea, was determined by the deep waters of Loch Fyne and the 24ha (60 acre) site was complete in 1975. Not one order came to Portavadie, however, and now the Argyll and Bute Council planning committee is attempting to enforce the restoration of the site that includes a workers' village and a huge dock basin.

Tighnabruaich occupies a sheltered site on the western arm of the Kyles of Bute. Backed by low green hills, and patches of woodland, and enriched with gardens planted with subtropical species, Tighnabruaich has been described as the most beautiful village of the Clyde. More than 3.2km (2 miles) of its shore-line from Port Driseach to Kames have been taken up by villas, hotels and the homes of Clydeside's retired businessmen. A quiet, restful place, Tighnabruiach's main occupation as a resort is with sailing.

Until after World War II the Kyles of Bute enjoyed regular steamer services to the Clyde ports serving Glasgow. Now, the last remaining Clyde paddle-steamer, the *Waverley*, plies the Kyles of Bute on summer excursions. In 1969 an 11km (7 mile) long trunk road was opened into Tighnabruaich following a course along Loch Riddon and high above the shores of the Kyles of Bute. It has established much more direct communications with Dunoon and regular service buses reach Glasgow in three hours. Now that the approach by one of the most beautiful sea routes in Britain is no longer possible, small compensations for the motorist are the excellent viewpoints over the Kyles of Bute from the new road and the wildlife centre with nature trails to be visited on Loch Riddon.

Eastward of the Kyles of Bute, Loch Striven reaches far inland. Untouched by any road-making plans of recent years this is one of the loneliest and most isolated parts of Cowal. Many miles of its shores are completely lacking in communications. The large parish of Inverchaolain embraces this long sea loch and its enveloping hills. Until World War II the community life of its small and scattered population centred upon the landed estates. The only settlement of any importance in Inverchaolain parish lies remote from Loch Striven on the western boundary along the shore of the Kyles of Bute. Here, **Colintraive** has grown along a 3.2km (2 mile) stretch of coastal road. It is a place of twenty houses, two shops and a hotel whose chief importance lies in the vehicle ferry that makes a five-minute crossing of the narrow sea loch to the island of Bute. Loch Striven itself, quiet and unfrequented, is the resort of seals. Recently, these sheltered deep waters have provided a mooring for unwanted oil tankers.

From Toward Point and beyond Dunoon we reach the inner estuary of the Clyde. In almost every sense this is one of the most complex stretches of the British coastline. Four great sea lochs reach far inland among the gloomy forested mountains of Argyll from its northern shore – Holy Loch, Loch Long, Loch Goil and Gare Loch. Inland, a little more than 4.8km (3 miles) from the Clyde, lies the island-studded foot of Loch Lomond whose waters are only 6m (20ft) above sea-level. But for the uplift of northern Britain since the Ice Age – a recovery from the immense weight of ice – Loch Lomond would still form another sea loch in this cluster of fjords. The complexity of this region of closely interlocked mountains and fjords is emphasised by its proximity to the Glasgow conurbation. The long fingers of land stretching southward between the sea lochs have been taken over by those who could afford to buy themselves out of the desolation of the Clyde's industrial landscapes. In the Victorian era rich Glasgow merchants built up estates. Holiday cottages and the bungalows of the retired, strung out along miles of coastline, represent the properties of the less well-to-do in the twentieth century. At the head of Loch Long we find the finest group of mountains in the south-west Highlands. Beinn Ime, Beinn Narnain and the Cobbler, their precipice-bound summits rising to 914m (3,000ft) above the head of the loch, are known as the Arrochar Alps. This is day-tripper country, easily accessible by railway and trunk road from suburban Glasgow. It is a wilderness with all the finest qualities of the remoter Highlands on the very threshold of Scotland's largest node of population. The sea lochs of the Clyde harbour one of the largest military bases in Britain. Holy Loch, with its floating pier and dry dock, is a supply base for nuclear-powered submarines. A naval torpedo range has been established on Loch Long since the early years of this century and Coulport, on the Rosneath peninsula, is an armament depot for Polaris missiles.

Ardgartan, at the exit to Glen Croe, where the main A83 road to Inveraray and Campbeltown begins the long climb to the Rest and be Thankful, is the only settlement on the western shore of upper Loch Long. It is the chief point of entry for the Argyll National Forest Park where there is access to 40km (25 miles) of forest roads for pony trekkers and hikers. Here are camping and caravan sites run by the Forestry Commission, and Ardgartan House, one of the several mansions on former Victorian estates, is now a youth hostel.

Lochgoilhead The only approach to Lochgoilhead, where Glasgow businessmen built their homes in the nineteenth century, is by Arrochar, the pass of Rest and be Thankful, and the still higher col at almost 305m (1,000ft) above sea-level between Beinn an Lochain and Beinn Donich. Lochgoilhead's white-washed late-medieval church is first mentioned in a document of 1405.

Carrick The minor road that follows the western shore of Loch Goil comes to an end at Carrick. Here, on a rock by the sea, stands the shell of Carrick Castle, first raised in the fifteenth century as a hunting lodge for Stewart kings and destroyed in 1685 when John Murray, Marquis of Atholl, brought devastation to the country of the Campbells. Since World War II only summer cruises from the Clyde put in at Carrick.

The eastern shores of Loch Goil and the forested slopes that rise to moorlands about Beinn Donich at 854m (2,774ft) all belong to another extensive Victorian estate, the Ardgoil Estate. In 1904 this land was bought by Lord Rowallan and presented to Glasgow Corporation as a place of recreation for its citizens. The maintenance of this wilderness park, not of easiest access from much of the conurbation, led the city authority into large financial losses, and in 1965 the estate was transferred to the Forestry Commission at a time when Clyde steamers ceased to serve Loch Goil.

Between Toward Point and Ardentinny is the most populated and developed section of all the intricate coastline of Argyll. Dunoon, with a population of 9,000, lies at the heart of the string of settlements.

Ardentinny, the end of the road from Dunoon, is a quiet resort for holiday-makers and escapees from Glasgow who have made their homes here. It lies within the Argyll National Forest Park and close by is Glenfinart House, a forest nursery that supplies forest plantings all over the British Isles. Taking the road south from Ardentinny one passes through an almost unbroken ribbon of summer holiday homes. Kilmun – the chapel of St Munnu – on the edge of Holy Loch, has a much longer history of settlement, for a monastery was established in the Dark Ages. No trace remains of Kilmun's monastery, and the collegiate church, founded there in 1442, is known only by a ruined tower.

Dunoon During the nineteenth century Dunoon became a terminus and port of call in the dense ferry traffic of the Clyde estuary. Its accessibility and isolation from industrial Clydeside determined Dunoon's role as a holiday resort and a place for retirement. On a low headland between the East and West

Bays stood a castle whose origins are said to date back to the kingdom of Dalriada. The medieval fortress, now visible only as a few stones, was a target in the intermittent warfare between England and Scotland. From the end of the seventeenth century, after the castle had been destroyed by Murray of Atholl in 1685, Dunoon's role as the capital of the Lordship of Cowal declined. The town was to revive only in the ninteenth century as Glasgow's leading holiday resort.

The construction of the Caledonian Railway's station and pier at Gourock in 1889 opened up Dunoon to a large day-tripper traffic. Its rising tourism was soon reflected in the changing topography of the town. In 1893 the castle grounds were opened as a public park. Ten years later, to meet the growing demand for entertainment, a pavilion was built in the Castle Gardens. The first years of this century saw the making of a formal promenade, the esplanade in East Bay. In 1937 Dunoon's attractions as a popular resort were enhanced with the opening of the Lido. Changes in the Clyde ferry services since World War II have served only to benefit Dunoon, while many places around the Argyll coast have lost all their regular sea communications. Dunoon's communications were strengthened with the introduction in 1954 of roll-on roll-off vehicle ships in a frequent all-the-year-round service to Gourock. With the improvement of roads in its mountainous hinterland Dunoon has also grown as a service centre for a large area of southern Argyll.

Southward from Dunoon the 10km (6 miles) of coast road, the A815, to Innellan and Port Lamont sum up so many aspects of the Clyde estuary. The link with Glasgow and its business world is evident in the succession of large and varied villas. The subtropical palms that decorate the gardens of these holiday homes bear testimony to the mildness of the climate on this sheltered south-east facing coastline, a climate whose mildness is unrivalled anywhere else in the world at these latitudes. At the end of the Dunoon peninsula stands Castle Toward, shrouded in mature woodland. Built in 1832 as a residence for the Lord Provosts of Glasgow, today it is the Castle Toward School, a school for the children of Glasgow who are in need of special care. At Ardyne Point, at the blunt south-west corner of the Dunoon peninsula, a construction yard for oil platforms was established in the early 1970s; the failure to attract any orders led to its closure in 1979, since when there have been plans to convert the site to fish farming. And in the hills that rise up from the coast, providing much of the shelter for this Clyde riviera, thousands of acres have been given over to forestry – apart from tourism this is the major growth industry and the mainstay of the economy of Cowal.

The innermost part of the Clyde estuary and its tributary fjord of Gare Loch lies at the very threshold of the Clyde conurbation. It also straddles the geological frontier of the Highlands, the great boundary fault known as the Highland Line, that crosses the foot of Loch Lomond to reach the Clyde near Helensburgh. The north-eastern shore of the Clyde between Dumbarton and Garelochhead displays several aspects of Scotland's history in its buildings and settlements, and if one follows the busy A814 road northwards the rapid transition from the scenery of the Central Lowlands to the Highlands is inescapable.

Dumbarton This striking industrial town with its dead-white tower blocks, grey streets of tenements, moribund shipyards and glaring red-brick distillery, crouches around a volcanic hill that rises sheer above the clutter of the Industrial Revolution. This volcanic hill, one of the greatest landmarks of the Clyde, ranks among the longest defended sites in Britain. The Dark Age earthworks on the summit of this hump-backed hill were in existence by the fifth century AD, if not much earlier. They were the capital of the kingdom of Strathclyde until the early years of the eleventh century a kingdom that embraced the Clyde and the greater part of south-west Scotland. By 1222 Dumbarton had become a royal burgh and a medieval fortress crowned the rock above the Clyde. The fortifications were rebuilt in the eighteenth century when Dumbarton acted as an important garrison on the road to the Highlands. The barracks were occupied until the early years of this century; now the austere eighteenth-century buildings of Dumbarton Castle house a museum. All visible evidence of the royal strongholds of medieval Scotland and Dark Age Strathclyde have been swept away in the long centuries of occupation on Dumbarton Rock.

Railway and road hug each other closely along the shore of the Clyde and Gare Loch. The views westward down the widening estuary towards the mountainous peninsulas of Cowal present a foretaste of Highland landscapes. The Ardmore peninsula, planed by the waves of a former higher sea-level, is a fragment of raised beach, now a wildlife sanctuary.

Craigendoran, a century ago one of the busy ferry ports of the Clyde, now presents a rash of bungalows, recent building by escapees from the Glasgow conurbation.

Helensburgh is a planned town of the eighteenth century founded by Sir James Colquhoun of Luss on an estate that occupied the hills between the Clyde and Loch Lomond. Its mile-long façade of shops and lodging houses facing the sea across a grassy promenade still retains a pleasant early-Victorian atmosphere. Helensburgh's history as a planned town is evident in its grid-iron pattern of streets laid out across the lower hill-slopes behind the sea front and garnished with Victorian villas. This is among the most accessible of all the Clyde's resorts from Glasgow. It is a place for retirement, day-trippers and commuters.

Rhu has changed little in character since Murray's Guide to Scotland was published in the last decade of the nineteenth century when it was described as 'one of the most select of the Clyde watering places' with its 'large villas, permanent residences and beautifully kept gardens'.

From Rhu onwards through Shandon to the head of Gare Loch palatial houses with sea views have colonised the wooded hill-slopes. Faslane contains the vastly extended British Navy's submarine servicing base – a jungle of cranes, block-like buildings of glass and concrete, and a scatter of tennis courts.

Islands of the Clyde

Before the reorganisation of local government in 1972 that swallowed up so many small counties into larger units of administration, Bute was an independent entity composed of the islands in the Clyde estuary. From its county town, Rothesay, it encompassed the island of Bute, Arran and the islands of Great and Little Cumbrae. Now it is part of that geographically meaningless territory, the Strathclyde Region.

The position of **Bute** astride the Highland Boundary Fault leads to considerable landscape contrasts between the north and south of the island. The fault crosses Bute in a north-east to south-west direction from Rothesay by Loch Fad to Scalpsie Bay. The northern two-thirds of the island consists of Dalradian rocks – schists, grits and slatey rocks changed in ancient mountain-building movements. South of Loch Fad are red sandstones typical of Lowland Scotland, and at the southern tip of the island volcanic lavas, poured out in Carboniferous times 300 million years ago, give rise to an angular and scarped landscape.

The contrasts between the east and west coasts of Bute arise from the closeness of the former to mainland Scotland. The bulk of the island's 10,000 population lives close to the east coast.

Rothesay, with a population of almost 8,000, is the chief settlement of Bute. Its rapid growth into a flourishing resort occurred during the nineteenth century with the growth of ferry services in the Clyde estuary. By the 1890s Murray's *Guide to Scotland* claimed that Rothesay could boast the 'busiest pier of the Clyde after Greenock'. Rothesay contains more than its present hotels, boarding houses and holiday amusements might suggest. Towards the end of the eighteenth century, when James Kenyon built his first cotton mill there in 1779, Rothesay became one of the pioneers of the Industrial Revolution in Scotland. By the early 1800s there were 5 cotton mills and the water power from Loch Fad turned 50,000 spindles and provided energy for a 1,000 looms. By 1813 William Kelly and

Robert Thorn had taken over Rothesay's mills. They introduced the kind of industrial community to Rothesay that is better remembered in the annals of economic history at New Lanark. Workers' houses were built and a confined local economy operated through the issue of tokens and the setting up of a company shop. Two of the mills remain as well as the cuts that took the water from Loch Fad.

In the very heart of the town is one of the best preserved of Scotland's medieval castles. On this moated site four drum towers project from the huge circular curtain wall of pink and grey sandstone. The ringed enclosure of the castle now contains only the roofless ruin of a chapel and the foundations of other medieval buildings. Like other castles around the Clyde it was sacked and burnt in the closing years of the seventeenth century, never to be occupied again. During the Middle Ages the Clyde was an essential link between the central lowlands, the core of the Scottish kingdom, and the isles of the west with their inheritance from the Viking settlements. It is believed that Rothesay castle was raised during the twelfth century when Somerled defeated the Vikings at sea and gave the Lordship of Bute and Arran to his son, Angus. In 1263 the Norsemen occupied Rothesay when King Haakon sailed with his longships into the Clyde. During the reigns of James IV and James V, Rothesay and its fortress formed a valuable base in their attempt to subdue the Hebrides.

Rothesay's history reaches back much further, however. At Townhead, post-holes that formed the timber foundations of dwellings built in 2000 BC or earlier have been unearthed.

Port Bannatyne, on Kames Bay, was founded in the early years of the nineteenth century by the Bannatyne family. The Bannatynes held lands in Bute since the Middle Ages and were the builders of Kames Castle in the fourteenth century. In 1863 their estates and castle were acquired by the Marquess of Bute who added, in 1910, a modern house to the original medieval tower. Kames Castle, lying amidst the woods and pastures at the head of Kames Bay, ranks among the oldest of Scotland's inhabited castles. Since 1965 the castle and park have been used as a home for spastic children.

Montstuart is the estate of the Marquess of Bute. An avenue of beech and lime trees 1.6km (1 mile) long forms the main approach to the house built towards the end of the last century after the original mansion had been burnt in 1877. The lawns and woodland of Mount Stuart House come down to the sea and the coastal road is diverted inland for a distance of some 4.8km (3 miles). Kerrycroy, an arc of estate cottages beside the pale pink sands of Kerrycroy Bay, is a model village built by the Bute family.

Kilchattan is a small resort remote from the noise and bustle of Rothesay. The name implies that a sixth-century saint established a cell on the shore of this bay. Further south, St Blane's Chapel, a twelfth-century ruin, of which two broken gables and a Norman arch still stand, marks the site of a much older monastic community. Nearby lie the remains of a round stone hut, a monk's cell, and the whole place is enclosed by a low, oval-shaped, flat-topped wall or *cashel* – the boundary of a monastery of the Celtic church. Only 1km (½ mile) from St Blane's Chapel stands Dunagoil, an Iron Age fort straddling a narrow, steep-sided ridge close to the sea. The many tools and ornaments discovered at Dunagoil, show that men were here from the eighth century BC until after AD 400. Nearby are the relics of another Iron Age enclosure and beside its ramparts are the foundations of two Viking long houses.

The west coast of Bute lacks towns or hamlets. A journey along the coast road, the A844, reveals a succession of large and prosperous farms. There is visible evidence of remains from all the major phases of prehistory over a time span of almost 4,000 years. Duns – stone-walled enclosures – located on seaward-jutting promontories or on low cliffs that fringe a raised beach suggest the settlement patterns of the Iron Age and Dark Age centuries. Clusters of burial cairns and standing stones date from the Bronze Age, from 1000 BC and earlier. And older still are the long cairns, the communal burial places of Neolithic farmers, of which there are four important sites in the north-west of the island alone.

The only attempt at tourist development on western Bute, at Ettrick Bay, failed. Ettrick Bay with a curving sand beach, over 1.6km (1 mile) in length, is one of the most attractive places on the whole coastline of Bute. Westward the prospect across the sea is to the jagged outline of Arran's granite mountains. An electric tramway used to run from Rothesay to Ettrick's sand beach and a resort was planned but came to nought.

Between Bute and the mainland coast the passage of the Clyde is severely narrowed by two islands, Great Cumbrae and Little Cumbrae. The chief route for shipping approaching Glasgow and its outlying ports passes between the low volcanic headlands of south Bute and Little Cumbrae, an island which would be deserted except for the population of the lighthouse station.

Great Cumbrae covers little more than 13sq km (5 square miles). The main features of its landscape are a pronounced raised beach that forms a rim to the whole island and an interior whose dull Old Red Sandstone plateau is broken by outcrops of volcanic rock that stand out as ridges bright with the yellow of gorse in flower through the weeks of late spring. The original main settlement of Great Cumbrae was at Kirkton, but since the establishment of regular steamer services in 1833 the chief focus of population has migrated to Millport. Now the main approach to Great Cumbrae is by the car ferry that crosses from Largs to the north-eastern tip of the island in ten minutes.

Millport belongs to the quiet resorts of the Clyde and is a favourite place for retirement. Among its tourist attractions is the Museum of the Cumbraes where various items of island life and history are displayed and the Scottish Marine Biological Station whose aquarium is open to the public. A curiosity of Millport is the Episcopal church, on the outskirts of the town, built by the Earl of Glasgow and designed by Butterfield in 1851. For a brief time in 1876 the church was raised to the rank of cathedral as the heart of the diocese of Argyll and the Islands.

Arran is the most dramatic of the island landscapes of the Clyde. No British island can match the complexity of its geology, and this is reflected in its scenery and coastal features. The Highland Boundary Fault follows an arcuate course around the huge mass of granite mountains that dominate the north of the island. The rocks of the east and south are mainly of Carboniferous and New Red Sandstone age and are immensely varied in type – the thick Corrie Limestone, brilliant red sandstones washed clean by the sea on foreshore rocks, and even coal seams that have been mined in years past at the Cock of Arran.

The landscape of central and southern Arran has been complicated by volcanic activity in the Tertiary period 50 million years ago. The outpouring of lavas from a volcanic centre with several vents in the heart of the island, focused on the present inconspicuous mountain of Ard Bheinn, has given rise to several of the landscape features among the New Red Sandstone rocks of south Arran. Sills of volcanic rock give rise to waterfalls in wooded glens or stand out prominently on the coast in cliffs and headlands. Brown Head and Bennan Head in the south-west owe their precipitous cliffs to the presence of these harder rocks and the vertical, rocky cliff-line at Drumadoon Point is formed of a quartz-porphyry sill. The most striking section of Arran's coastline, Lamlash Bay and Holy Island, owes its main outline to the presence of igneous rocks among the New Red Sandstone. Here a steeply dipping sheet of igneous rocks, known as crinanite, forms a broken arc in the hills around the bay. The two headlands that enclose the bay, Clauchlands Point and Kingscross Point, occur where this sheet of hard volcanic rock cuts the coastline. The curving channel of Lamlash Bay has been eroded out of the softer sedimentary rocks within the ring of crinanite, while Holy Island, rising to just over 305m (1,000ft) from the sea is composed of another mass of igneous rock that invaded the sediments within the circle of the crinanite cone-sheet.

A succession of pleasant holiday resorts arose on the east coast of the island after the establishment of regular Clyde steamer services before the middle of the last century.

The Isle of Arran: Goat Fell seen across Brodick Bay, with the policies of Brodick Castle on the further shore

Until the introduction of large vehicle ferries in the past twenty years, calls were made daily at the chief settlements of the east coast – Corrie, Brodick, Lamlash and Whiting Bay. Now there remains only the roll-on roll-off ferry disgorging its long lines of vehicles at Brodick six times a day through the summer months, with only a slightly less frequent service in the rest of the year.

Brodick Brodick Bay and its background of granite mountains culminating in Goat Fell ranks among the most famous prospects of the Scottish landscape. Its woods and curving beach of warm red sand provide an attractive setting for Brodick's straggling street of hotels and shops. Brodick, because of its busy ferry terminus, is the chief service centre of the island. Its expansion was discouraged by the Dukes of Hamilton, landlords of Brodick Castle and even by the end of the nineteenth century Brodick had only one hotel, at the pier-head. The castle, a baronial mansion from the Victorian years, now belongs to the National Trust for Scotland, and its gardens, with their rich collection of rhododendrons and semi-tropical plants and shrubs, beautifully sited beside the sea and beneath the crouching granite shoulders of Goat Fell, are the chief attraction for visitors.

Corrie, a string of picturesque white cottages oppressively overshadowed by the spurs of Goat Fell. On fine days – and there are many of them in the weeks of late spring and early summer in Arran – Corrie is remembered for its contrasts of brilliant colour – the fresh greens of the lower hillsides and the intense reds of the foreshore rocks set against a sparkling translucent sea.

Lamlash extends for more than 1.6km (1 mile) along the northern edge of the arc-shaped channel that is protected from the wide estuary of the Clyde by Holy Island. This is the oldest of Arran's holiday resorts whose expansion took place before the end of the nineteenth century. It is one of the most strikingly beautiful bays in the whole of Scotland and enjoys an unusually mild climate that is emphasised by a southern aspect and the sheltering hills to north and west that reach over 305m (1,000ft) above the sea. The only drawback of Lamlash for the holiday-maker is its beach, which lacks sand and at low tide is a desolation of huge black boulders. Lamlash Bay and the lower slopes of its encircling hills have provided a focus for settlement for over 3,000 years. A cluster of standing stones and cairns on the Clauchland Hills is evidence of the presence of prehistoric man.

Holy Island, situated within the curve of Lamlash Bay, was one of the many 'island' monasteries of the Celtic church. A cave in the narrow belt of red sandstone that forms the north-western tip of the island was used as a hermit's retreat. Lamlash Bay, too, lay at the centre of one of the two huge medieval parishes that served the whole of Arran before the expansion of population in the nineteenth century. On the lower hill-slopes above the present resort the site of Kilbride Chapel still remains, and Kilbride was the name of this older parish.

Whiting Bay is a child of the nineteenth-century Clyde ferries. Its growth was unrestricted and with more than thirty hotels and boarding houses strung out along the raised beach as well as twice as many holiday lettings, Whiting Bay is still a favoured resort. This south-eastern corner of Arran still bears abundant evidence of settlement in prehistoric times, especially on the spurs of coastal hills at 91–152m (300–500ft) above the sea. Giants Graves, a Neolithic chambered cairn above the wooded gorge of Glenashdale Burn, is one of several such burial places of the first farming communities around the Clyde.

Lochranza, on the north-west coast of Arran, is situated on a stony northward-looking bay hemmed in by gloomy grey mountains. A half-ruined medieval castle occupies an arm of shingle that stretches into the sea. Lochranza was once a daily port of call for the Campbeltown steamer. All sea traffic ceased with the abandonment of that route from Glasgow and the Clyde ports, but of late Lochranza has revived as a ferry port in summer with the running of a car ferry eight times daily across Kilbrannan Sound to Claonaig in Kintyre. In connection with the Ardrossan ferries Arran has now become an important stepping-stone in the communications of Scotland, providing a short direct route between south-west Argyll and roads to the English border across the Southern Uplands.

Blackwaterfoot is the only resort of any importance on Arran's west coast. With its golf course and sand beach, Blackwaterfoot caters for those who prefer a quiet holiday. On Machrie Moor, 3.2km (2 miles) inland, are the remains of a complex of stone circles and standing stones from the Early Bronze Age. Fifteen sites occupy an extent of about 1.6km (1 mile). The most striking relic is Fingal's Cauldron Seat, a double stone circle of granite boulders half-buried in the peat. Another circle of stones has been completely covered by peat, and has been traced only by probing. This, one of the most important prehistoric sites of Scotland, still needs a systematic exploration.

Beyond Blackwaterfoot the coast road winds round the south of Arran to Whiting Bay. It climbs above the cliffs of Brown Head and drops steeply into densely wooded glens of the several rivers that drain the inland moors. No resorts have grown up here; prosperous farms run down to a shore where the wave-worn slabs of sandstone are interrupted by narrow outcrops of volcanic rock, dykes, that stand up as black parallel walls at low tide.

20 South-west Scotland

The Clyde to the Mull of Galloway

The coastline of south-western Scotland between Cloch Point and the Mull of Galloway looks out to the ever-widening Firth of Clyde and the North Channel, the sea passage that separates Scotland from Northern Ireland. For many miles this section of coast presents a profile of the geology and topography of the Central Lowlands of Scotland. Just as the Highland Boundary Fault that abuts on the northern shore of the Clyde at Helensburgh marks the geological frontier between Lowland and Highland Scotland so the Southern Uplands Fault, crossing the country from the mouth of Loch Ryan to the North Sea coast at Dunbar, signals the southern limit of the central lowland. Between the two fault lines, along some 96km (60 miles) of coast from Gourock to Girvan, the coastal scenery is carved out of a great variety of sandstones, limestones, shales and coal-bearing rocks – all belonging to a period of formation between 400 million and 300 million years ago. In addition, the outpouring of volcanic rocks during the same period of time has left many striking features in the landscape.

From the inner estuary of the Clyde to Farland Head, where the Cumbrae Islands and Bute form a natural portal into the 16km (10 mile) wide firth, the dour moorlands of the Renfrew Hills closely hug the coast. Industrial towns, busy outports of Glasgow and seaside resorts have evolved as strung-out linear settlements confined to narrow belts of shore-line.

Port Glasgow, with a population of 23,000, was founded by the merchants of Glasgow in 1668. The motives that lay behind the creation of this new town in green fields beside the Clyde were physical – the difficulties of navigating the shallow river-channel to the wharves at Glasgow – and financial – the charges for landing and trans-shipment imposed at the neighbouring burgh of Greenock. Little more than a century later, in 1775, Port Glasgow itself became a chartered burgh. Its claim to fame in the industrial history of Scotland is the construction of the first graving dock, designed by James Watt, in 1762 and the launching in 1812 of the *Comet*, one of the earliest steam-driven ships. Port Glasgow, along with the other towns of this Clydeside conurbation, presents in its local history and topography most of the major phases and problems of Lowland Scotland's growth and decline over the past century and a half. Today, little survives of the engineering shops of the boom years in the 1880s and 90s. Since World War II there has been a considerable migration of its working population to England and overseas to North America. For the tourist Port Glasgow has one great surprise: Newark Castle, hemmed in by the sites of shipyards, is a turreted late-medieval mansion that belonged to the Maxwells and was given to the nation in 1909.

Greenock, with a population of 66,000, is the main focus of the conurbation that crouches between the volcanic Renfrew Heights and the western shore of the Clyde. Its overseas trade was already important by the end of the seventeenth century, partly a result of Greenock's acquisition of a burghal charter that gave the town the privilege of engaging in foreign trade. Nature, too, had endowed Greenock with one of the best anchorages in the Clyde estuary. The succession of dock basins that line the waterfront record its evolution as a port. In 1805 John Rennie designed the East India Harbour. The Victoria Harbour and the Albert Harbour were opened to traffic in 1850 and 1862 when cotton, sugar and tobacco were among the main imports of Greenock. More dock basins were excavated in the 1870s and 80s – the Garvel Graving Dock in 1871 and the James Watt Dock in 1881. Unlike so many ports, Greenock and its trade have been strong enough to keep up with the changes of the twentieth century. In 1964 one of the world's biggest dry docks was opened, capable of serving huge tankers and bulk carriers, and early in the 1970s the Clydeport container terminal enabled Greenock to participate in the new, more economical means of trans-shipment for its North American trade.

Greenock is essentially a town of the nineteenth century. James Watt was born here in 1736 and its urban topography reflects the demands of the Industrial Revolution. Behind the 80ha (200 acres) of wharves, warehouses and dock basins a dense pattern of streets in the heart of the industrial town is laid out. To the west, beyond the Clydeport container terminal, is the West End which grew up as a planned residential quarter, a place of churches, stone-built villas and neatly organised streets. Even the hills behind the town were drawn into Greenock's industrial expansion to supply water for its sugar refineries and rum distilling. In the 1820s Robert Thom designed one of Britain's earliest water-supply schemes with a 8km (5 mile) long aqueduct along the face of the hills to the slopes above the town.

Gourock A place mainly concerned with Clyde ferries and tourism. The holiday resort clusters around Tower Hill, the site of a castle that was demolished in the early years of the nineteenth century. Gourock acts as one of the main centres of the Clyde's ferry traffic and pleasure cruises, a role that developed from the opening of the station and pier by the Caledonian Railway in 1889. Today, it is the busy car traffic of the A8 that streams into Gourock for the half-hourly service of vehicle ferries to Dunoon.

Beyond Gourock the industrial conurbation of the Clyde's south bank comes to an abrupt end. At Cloch Point and its major lighthouse that guides shipping into the inner estuary the coastline turns southwards, hugged closely by the moorlands of the Renfrew hills.

The opening of the Caledonian Railway to Wemyss Bay in 1865 did much to break down the inaccessibility of this piece of coast. It was an essential part of the opening up of the main ferry route to Rothesay in Bute. Today, the passage is still worked by a modern vehicle ferry that maintains an hourly service for most of the day. The railway station itself has now entered the lists of industrial archaeology as an object of historic interest and worthy of sightseers' attention.

Skelmorie The first of its wealthy residents built their mansions here in the middle years of the last century. The settlement developed its residential streets, lined with substantial houses and terraces of red sandstone, on the gentle hill-slopes parallel to the coastline. In 1868 a hotel and hydro in flamboyant Scottish baronial style was added to the topography of Skelmorie. Now its buildings and their present uses bear witness to the social changes of the latter half of the twentieth century. Several of the mansions in their spacious grounds have been converted into hotels or convalescent homes, and since World War I there has been much building of bungalows for the retired.

Largs, sheltered by the island of great Cumbrae, is the most important place on this part of the north Ayrshire coast. Its shingly foreshore was the scene of one of the most famous battles in the history of medieval Scotland when a Viking army was defeated by the Scots in 1263. The destruction of the Vikings and their fleet at the Battle of Largs secured the command of the Firth of Clyde to the Scots and opened the way to their ultimate overlordship of the Hebrides. Largs remembers its role in the history of northern Britain with a Viking festival held in the first week of September. The museum in Kirkgate House mounts a display of the Viking period in Scotland and its effect on Scottish life. There is a Scottish-Scandinavian folk festival, a conducted walking tour to view the traditional battle site - itself commemorated by a memorial pillar, the Pencil - and one of the evenings sees a Viking funeral, a traditional sunset burial of the Viking chief in his burning longship, followed by a 'Thor' fireworks display.

Largs is a place of red sandstone Prebyterian churches, golf is played, day-trippers congregate and the ceaseless car ferry plies to Great Cumbrae. Its sheltered waters are frequented by yachtsmen and in the summer the resort makes an excellent centre for trips around the Clyde on the excursion boats of Caledonian MacBrayne - cruises that reach out to Arran, Campbeltown, the ports of Loch Fyne and the Kyles of Bute.

The chief feature of the coastal scenery between Largs and Ardrossan is Farland Head. Not only are the sites of an Iron Age hill-fort and Dark Age dun at Portencross to be found here but also, in striking contrast, a nuclear power station at Hunterston. The first nuclear power station was opened here in 1964, producing enough electricity to supply any one of Scotland's major cities. In the late 1960s Hunterston B, using an advanced gas-cooled reactor and producing four times as much power as its predecessor, rose beside the earlier plant.

Ardrossan, Saltcoats and **Stevenston**, joined together into a miniature conurbation of some 30,000 people, form the main nucleus of settlement on the northern fringe of the Ayrshire plain. The original natural beauty of this piece of coastline cannot be denied. Gently curving sandy beaches between low headlands of volcanic rock look out across the wide firth to the serene blue outline of Arran's mountains. Between the long estuary of the Garnock and the miles of sandy foreshore lay a wilderness of dunes. But it requires an act of the imagination to see an unspoilt coastline beyond the grimy tenements, the dull wastelands of local authority housing, the coal bings and dereliction of nineteenth-century mining and the clutter of the vast chemical industry that has now covered the dunes with almost 2,000 separate buildings and 161km (100 miles) of railway track. Ardrossan and Stevenston both possess medieval castle sites that recall the part played by powerful landlords in the development of this segment of Ayrshire's coast. The castle at Ardrossan, on its low-lying volcanic crag between the North and South Bays, represented the territorial interests of the Montgomeries of Eglinton. The castle at Kerilaw, the medieval core of Stevenston, belonged to an equally important family, the Cunninghames of Glencairn. Where the territories of the two medieval baronies marched beside each other arose the coastal settlement of Saltcoats, a fishing harbour and a place where the locally outcropping coal was used in the extraction of salt from sea water. The old pier-head at Saltcoats includes part of the seventeenth-century harbour works that were associated with the salt pans and coal-mining developed by the Cunninghame family. The Cunninghames pioneered the mining of coal at Saltcoats and Stevenston while their neighbouring landowners, the Earls of Eglinton, were responsible for the making of the port and burgh of Ardrossan during the early years of the nineteenth century. The new town of Ardrossan, designed by Peter Nicholson in 1806, is evident in its pattern of wide regularly planned streets.

Ardrossan succeeded as a port, but its close neighbour, Saltcoats, was eclipsed and Irvine, much troubled by the navigation of its shallow estuary, was to feel the effects of this rival a few miles to the north. Coal from the Ayrshire pits became the dominant export of the nineteenth century; today that traffic has declined sharply. Ardrossan has maintained its role as a passenger port, however. A large vehicle ferry provides the chief link with Arran through half a dozen daily sailings; there is a service to Belfast, and in the summer holiday season to the Isle of Man.

Heavy industries and tourism provide an uneasy contrast in the economic life of Ardrossan. In 1927 the southern shore of

North Bay was taken over by Shell as the site of an oil refinery. Today, it is used for the bulk storage of oil products and the ground is taken up with scores of storage tanks. Marine engineering – the making of engine castings, gaskets and valves – is one of Ardrossan's occupations. Tourism took over the South Bay early in the nineteenth century with the building of a crescent of villas along the margin of the sandy arc of beach to join Ardrossan and Saltcoats.

The fine sand beach that extends between Saltcoats and Stevenston is a chief attraction for day-trippers. A recent investigation of the problems of the beaches of Scotland has described this foreshore as 'suffering a greater measure of dereliction' than almost any other beach in the country. At its eastern end there is a man-made headland of slag from a former ironworks. In the last century there was a coal mine close to the shore and today active sand dunes creep across the coal bing, the dumped waste of those former workings. The backcloth to this fine expanse of sand, unmarred by rock outcrops, is a large holiday estate of caravans, railway tracks, industrial plant and the derelict land of Victorian coal-mining and iron-making. And there is the unattractive townscape of Saltcoats and Stevenston. Of the latter it has been said: 'there is no more depressing half mile in all Scotland'. The beaches of Ardrossan and Saltcoats, it has been claimed, are the most visited in the whole of Scotland. A recent survey found that 400,000–500,000 day-trippers make for these shores each year.

Southward from Stevenston to the tip of the flat low peninsula overlooking the estuary of the Irvine is the finest landscape of sand dunes in the whole of south-west Scotland. The dunes reach inland for a distance of more than 3.2km (2 miles) and in places they achieve heights of up to 18m (60ft). But what might have been an attractive wilderness has been severely changed by the intrusion of industry on a grand scale. In 1873 Alfred Nobel established an explosives factory among the dunes. Natural hollows enfolded in steep sandy ridges provided some security for this dangerous industry that was scattered through forty separate wooden buildings. Today, Ardeer, covering almost 800ha (2,000 acres), is one of the main factories of ICI, producing gunpowder, fuses and detonators and a host of derivative cellulose products. The landscape of the Ardeer peninsula has been deeply modified. Dunes have been levelled, others have been planted with conifers in order to stabilise the moving sand, and elsewhere storage bunkers have been cut into the dune slopes. At the south end of the peninsula there is a tip of industrial refuse. This is a little visited stretch of the Ayrshire coast, although access to the beach is allowed from the northern end at Stevenston Point where cars can be parked. Until lately the beach has suffered from heavy industrial pollution by acidic waste, a problem that has now been overcome by the building of a pipeline into the deep water of Irvine Bay.

Irvine, the most important settlement of the north Ayrshire coastline, lies at the heart of a flat, uninteresting plain where three rivers – the Garnock, Annick Water and Irvine – join together to empty into the Firth of Clyde across Irvine Bar. Irvine was a chartered town by the beginning of the thirteenth century. By the latter half of the eighteenth century it ranked as the third port of Scotland, largely because the shallow course of the Clyde below the wharves of Glasgow made it the main outlet for the rising traffic of that city. The decline of Irvine's link with Glasgow followed the deepening of the Clyde's channel in the latter years of the eighteenth century along with the growth of outports at Greenock and Port Glasgow. Traffic was maintained by the expanding exports of the Ayrshire coalfield. Irvine as a port has suffered in the twentieth century because constant deposition at the bar hinders entrance to the harbour, which itself has become too shallow for much modern shipping. Since World War II the harbour has been acquired by ICI and its modest trade consists of the import of raw materials for the Ardeer chemical and explosives plant.

Over the past century Irvine's industrial structure has undergone radical changes. Its Victorian industries were focused on engineering in shipyards, railway workshops, brass and iron foundries. Until the early 1920s 10,000 ton ships for the Clan

Line were built here; the deep economic depression of that decade brought these activities to an end and Irvine limped through the thirties as a repair yard of Lithgows for small vessels of up to 2,000 tons. Since then, shipbuilding has been dead. Likewise, coal-mining, the railway workshops of the former Glasgow and South-Western, and of late the Royal Ordnance Factory have all ceased to exist.

The economic and visual transformation of Irvine has been achieved since 1966 when it acquired the status of Scotland's fifth new town. The new Irvine covers 52sq km (20 square miles) and its administrative boundary encompasses several surrounding villages and Kilwinning to the north. The new town aimed to achieve a population of more than 100,000 by 1985. In the early 50s the burgh with its declining Victorian industries stood at 16,000; by 1980 the population had risen to 55,000, partly by the incorporation of existing communities and also through migration from the over-crowded streets of Glasgow. New industries have appeared – light engineering, the manufacture of fork-lift trucks, synthetic textiles, sports equipment and pharmaceutical products.

On the coast, south of the Irvine estuary, the new town development has brought about the renewal of several acres of land devastated by the dumping of chemical waste and the extraction of sand. Here the Beach Park has been planted with trees and shrubs and there is a massive place of entertainment, the Magnum Leisure Centre. Of all the places along the lowland coast of Ayrshire, Irvine displays the greatest energy in coping with a legacy of Victorian industry.

From Irvine southwards to Ayr the lowland plain of Ayrshire and its rich coalfield abuts on to a coastline composed of long sandy beaches, clusters of sand dunes where some of Scotland's most famous golf courses have been laid out, and low headlands and tidal reefs of dark volcanic rocks.

Troon The Troon or *Trin*, meaning 'a nose', is the name given to the rocky headland of dolerite that provides a natural safe anchorage for this port with a population of 12,000. At the end of the eighteenth century Troon consisted of an inn and a scatter of cottages, but already its dune-fringed beaches were attracting sea-bathers from Kilmarnock. Its development as a town belongs to the railway age. The building of the railway between Kilmarnock and Ayr began its career both as a port and a holiday resort. Along with Ayr and Ardrossan, Troon became one of the chief exporters of house coal to the West Highlands and the Hebrides. Shipbuilding began there in the 1860s and in 1886 the Ailsa Shipbuilding Company, designers of luxury yachts and paddle-steamers, was founded. In the twentieth century ship-breaking and repairing has become the main industry.

Troon has developed two distinct quarters – an industrial core focused on the harbour and North Bay, and a residential quarter facing the South Bay. The town grew through the closing decades of the Victorian era under the direction of the Duke of Portland; by 1896 it achieved the status of a burgh. The town is hemmed in by golf courses – five in all – of which Troon Old and Troon Portland are of championship standard. The two beaches – North and South Sands – express the contrasting characteristics of Troon as a resort and industrial centre. North Bay, flanked on the south by the harbour, has been condemned in a recent report on the beaches of Scotland for its three outfalls of untreated sewage and a level of pollution that far exceeds the limits suggested by the EEC for the pollution of sea water. The South Sands are backed by dunes and laid out with lawns, putting greens and paddling pools.

Beyond a reef of igneous rocks, Meikle Craigs, the South Sands of Troon give way to the long sandy foreshore of Prestwick Bay. Much of the beach, flanked by the land of the Royal Troon Golf Club, is difficult of access, at least as far as the mouth of the Pow Burn, a place where bathing is dangerous. This section of the Ayrshire coast lies within a green-belt zone that has been established in relation to the runways of Prestwick Airport. South of the Pow Burn's outfall the character and problems of coastal development are noticeably to the fore with regard to Prestwick Bay and its beach. The town of Prestwick has grown up on part of the dunes and tipping and removal of sand has further modified the coastline. This, the most polluted of Ayrshire's beaches, is among the most visited. It is a place that displays all those uninviting aspects of the man-made landscapes of our British coasts – huge car parks, cafés, amusements.

Prestwick, placed over some of the richest seams of the Ayrshire coalfield, exhibits the contrasts and conflicts between industrial and tourist activities. The founding of the Prestwick Golf Club in 1851 set this former medieval burgh on a course of development as a resort. Its golf course, one of the world's finest, occupies the links to the north-west of the town. The Pow burn meanders through this landscape of miniature sand-hills. Altogether, Prestwick has four golf courses, but the dominating feature of its twentieth-century development has been the growth of Scotland's only international airport. A seaward location, for the most part free of fog, and the initiative of a small company, Scottish Aviation, led to the establishment of a small airfield here in 1935. It was World War II that confirmed Prestwick's priority among Scottish airfields, and in 1940 it became the main European air terminal for the ferrying of aircraft across the Atlantic.

Ayr, the major settlement of the Ayrshire plain, is the county town at the outfall of the river Ayr into the Firth of Clyde. Created a royal burgh by William the Lion in the thirteenth century, Ayr can still display in its townscape some evidence of its long history. The Tower of St John's, close to the foreshore and on the south bank of the river, belonged to Ayr's medieval parish church – a place it is believed where the Scots Parliament met in 1315. Nothing else of this medieval church remains because of a later brutal event in British history. Cromwell built the Citadel, now known as the Fort, on this site, for his occupying English army in 1655. The medieval church of St John the Baptist was converted into a storehouse in Cromwell's fortress, and as a recompense the present Auld Kirk of Ayr was built in 1655.

The town of Ayr that we see today has largely evolved since the end of the eighteenth century. A fashion for sea-bathing began Ayr's career as a resort. It also became a social centre and watering place for the Scottish gentry. As well as sea-bathing there was golf and a race meeting that has now been held for more than 250 years. The terraces of Wellington Square and Barns Park show that Ayr was an attractive place for the rich countryman to own a town house.

The opening of the Glasgow–Ayr Railway in 1840 and the coal that lay beneath Ayr's surrounding countryside helped make the town one of the chief centres of the Industrial Revolution on the west coast of Scotland. Most of the new industries – drop-stamping and forging, foundries, the manufacture of mining machinery, ship-building, chemicals and textiles – were planted to the north of the river, in Newton upon Ayr, and close by the harbour. During the medieval centuries its port was the most important on the west coast of Scotland. By the 1700s Ayr was deeply engaged in the Atlantic traffic as an importer of tobacco, sugar and rum. The expansion of the coalfield and the coming of the railway in the nineteenth century saw the bulk of Ayr's trade engaged with the export of coal to Ireland, and the docks and wharves of the north bank of the river are equipped mainly for the handling of coal.

Ayr is one of Scotland's major holiday resorts. In July and August the resident population of almost 50,000 is more than doubled. The villas and town houses of the Victorian gentry in the southern quarter have now been turned into hotels and boarding houses. The fine sand beach, broken here and there by dark reefs of volcanic rock, is backed by a rim of urban development that has completely obliterated the former sand dunes. But there is a spaciousness and a feeling of maturity about Ayr's sea-shore owing to the wide grassy space of Low Green, at one time the town's common where sheep and cattle grazed, and the solid background of Georgian and Regency building. It has been claimed that Ayr's beach is the most heavily used in the whole of Scotland. On a fine day at the end of July as many as four thousand people may be bathing, paddling and castle building on this sandy playground.

Between Ayr and Girvan the character of this part of the Clyde coast can be appreciated from the A719, but the detailed features of the coastline, its several secluded bays and bold cliffs of volcanic rock, are frequently hard of access. The whole coastline from the mouth of the river Doon to Turnberry has been listed as an area of special scientific interest owing to its volcanic rocks intruded among the bedded Calciferous Sandstones. Greenan Castle stands on a volcanic plug 18m (60ft) above the sea. Today, the castle ruin is perched on the very edge of the sea cliff; it is said that at the end of the eighteenth century a carriage could be driven right round it. The most prominent feature of this coast, the Heads of Ayr rising to 61m (200ft), consists of an ancient volcanic vent in the bedded Calciferous Sandstone rocks that form the shore platform. Dykes, too, are a prominent feature of the seascape where they stand out as reefs and walls of dark rock in the intertidal zone. On the foreshore between Greenan Castle and the Heads of Ayr are the Deil's Dyke and Long Rue. Bracken Bay, to the west of the volcanic headland, is divided by a north-westward trending dyke in the middle of the rock platform.

The chief development of this coast was the opening of a holiday camp in 1947 on the site of a World War II naval station, HMS Scotia. The camp has accommodation for more than 2,000 and has direct access to the beach eastward of the Heads of Ayr – a beach that has suffered from an increase of litter and pollution.

Dunure, with its bright, colour-washed cottages around the tiny harbour, flourished in the last century as a fishing settlement, an occupation that is still not completely extinct there. In the first years of the nineteenth century Dunure's landowner had ambitions to build a busy seaport that would form the chief outlet of the Ayrshire coalfield. Evidence of Dunure's early history is found in the ruin of the coastal castle of the Kennedys occupying a blunt promontory above the harbour. Now the castle has been turned into a public park.

Maidens In the 1940s the Scottish Office recommended the reconstruction of the harbour at Maidens to make it the chief landing place on the Ayrshire coast for vessels engaged in seine fishing. A pier and breakwater were built using materials from abandoned RAF camps after World War II. Now the tourist trade has largely displaced fishing as the main occupation of Maidens. A small twentieth-century resort is evolving with caravan sites, chalets, cafés and a handful of shops. It is evident that the building of the breakwater has produced minor changes in the physical character of the beach. The accumulation of sand has quickened at the south end of the beach, while erosion continues at the north end.

Turnberry Here an exposed westward-facing beach is backed by a massive line of dunes that in places reach almost 15m (50ft) in height. The tract of blown sand to the rear of the high seaward foredune ridge is occupied by Turnberry Golf Courses, a venue for international championships. Turnberry owes its development as a highly specialised resort to the opening in 1906 of the light railway connecting Ayr and Girvan. The Glasgow and South-Western Railway, wanting to rival the Caledonian Railway's luxury hotel and golf course at Gleneagles, decided to build an expensive hotel at Turnberry on an attractive site near the sea and in one of the sunniest parts of western Scotland. The railway, formerly the chief means of approach to the hotel, has long since closed, but Turnberry's fame and its fine golf courses have ensured its success. Prestwick Airport lies not many miles away and the hotel boasts a landing strip of its own for light aircraft.

The most impressive and exciting feature of the coastline between Ayr and Girvan is Culzean Castle and its 224ha (560 acres) of woods, gardens and cliffed coast that formed Scotland's first Country Park in 1969. One of the dozen or so coastal castles of the Kennedys stood on the cliffs at Culzean in the late Middle Ages. A medieval tower, perched 30m (100ft) above the sea, was protected from the landward side by a deep natural gully. During the reign of James IV of Scotland the head of the Kennedy family had been created Earl of Cassilis and it was his descendant, the 10th Earl, who set about

Culzean Castle, on the Ayrshire coast, rebuilt by Robert Adam for the 10th Earl of Cassilis around the core of a medieval tower

the transformation of Culzean. He employed Robert Adam to rebuild the castle between 1777 and 1792. Culzean ranks among Scotland's most spectacular buildings.

Culzean now belongs to the National Trust for Scotland, and since the establishment of the Country Park, it has become one of the 'show-places' of the south-west. At the Home Farm, built by Robert Adam at a discreet distance from the castle, the Park Centre has a lecture theatre. There is a model of the park as well as taped talks and slide shows about the development of the estate. The park itself contains picnic places and nature trails. The castle too, under the care of the National Trust for Scotland, is more than a hollow show place of the vanished world of an eighteenth century aristocracy. A suite of rooms has been set aside as a guest-house for eminent people distinguished by service to Scotland or the British Commonwealth.

Southwards from Turnberry to Girvan the A77 and the track of the former light railway lie close to each other. Much of the land, composed of light sandy soils of extensive raised beaches, is given over to early potatoes – the most important crop along Ayrshire's coastline. **Dipple** has a plant that processes seaweed imported from the Hebrides and Northern Ireland. Grant's whisky distillery is situated north of Girvan as are the many scattered buildings of an explosives and sulphuric acid plant belonging to ICI.

Girvan The core of the town occupies the south bank of the Water of Girvan where the river swings through a final meandering curve to empty into the Firth of Clyde. Two centuries ago Girvan lived by its herring fisheries and a small textile industry. The *First Statistical Account of Scotland*, published in the 1790s, records the expansion of Girvan as a result of rich catches of herring and it mentions a cotton-weaving industry that employed a hundred looms. The textile industry vanished long ago and although still a harbour of some importance, Girvan since the end of the nineteenth century has become a holiday resort. The resort developed on the bare stretch of shore to the south of the harbour. A concrete sea wall and promenade protects a piece of coastline subject to severe erosion. Behind the promenade are putting greens, boating ponds, ice-cream kiosks and a park.

Dow Hill, a moorland spur, less than 1.6km (1 mile) to the south-east of Girvan, is crowned by an impressive prehistoric site.

The summit is ringed by a stone wall, 9m (30ft) in thickness and severely ruined in places. This is a *dun*, a Dark Age settlement, built over the site of an Iron Age fort. Five successive ramparts across the eastern slopes of Dow Hill are all the visible remains of the earlier Iron Age structure.

Girvan lies closer than any other Ayrshire resort to Ailsa Craig, the huge granite sea-mark in the wide mouth of the Firth of Clyde. In the holiday season and with favourable weather, excursion boats regularly make the 16km (10 mile) crossing. Only 1.6km (1 mile) in diameter, Ailsa Craig's summit reaches to over 335m (1,100ft) above the sea and its ring of sheer cliffs soars for 152m (500ft) above a marked raised beach. The rock, a basal remnant of an ancient volcano, is mainly composed of a fine-grained granite, speckled and bluish-grey in colour. Ailsa Craig's granite, its origin unmistakable wherever it is found, has helped to trace the movement of ice in the Ice Age – ice that moved from Highland Scotland southwards into the basin of the Irish Sea. Pieces of this granite, erratics, are found among the coastal boulder clays on the fringe of the Lake District and further south in Wales. Dykes of dolerite provide lines of weakness along which the sea has gnawed caves deep into the rock. The Swine Cave, at the northern tip of the island, penetrates a dyke that is almost 15m (50ft) in thickness. Ailsa Craig's granite was once quarried for curling stones.

A striking feature of the coastline between Girvan and Ballantrae are the clusters of ancient sea stacks that stand up from the smooth platforms of the raised beach. The main road threads its way through such a rocky wilderness at Kennedy's Pass and elsewhere, towards Lendalfoot, rocky needles, the last remnants of former battering seas, stand starkly amid the pale brown ploughlands of the potato fields.

Lendalfoot A shallow embayment of the coastline between Kennedy's Pass and Bennane Head contains Lendalfoot, the only settlement for several miles of the A77. The clean sands of Carleton Bay make it one of the most attractive beaches of the Clyde coast. The permanent population of Lendalfoot numbers little more than 100. The fisheries of Carleton Port are defunct; today, it caters mainly for the few brief weeks of the summer holiday industry. The lane that curves and climbs steeply out of Lendalfoot across the moors to the Stinchar valley and Colmonell passes between medieval defensive sites – a mound of unknown date and a ruined watch-tower of the Kennedy country, Carleton Castle.

Ballantrae, at the mouth of the river Stinchar, is the focus of a vast area of

Relict sea stack on a raised beach on the Ayrshire coast

trackless moorland that stretches south to the border of Galloway. A group of standing stones, the Seven Grey Stanes o' Garleffin, less than 1km (½ mile) to the south of the town where gentle wooded hill-slopes abut on the valley floor, suggests the occupation of this tract by prehistoric man some 3,000 years ago. Ardstinchar Castle, today a ruined tower by the river on the outskirts of Ballantrae, gave hospitality to Mary Queen of Scots in 1563 and inland along the attractive valley of the Stinchar one finds the ruins of several medieval strongholds of the Kennedys.

Ballantrae was once a busy centre of the fishing industry, but today its main link with the sea is as a holiday resort; otherwise, its economic interests are turned to the land. Early potatoes, particularly from the wide raised beach platform that stretches towards Bennane Head, are the most valuable element in the local economy. Forestry in the surrounding glens has become a subsidiary source of employment. The red sandstone breakwater of Ballantrae, sheltering a little used harbour, forms the boundary between two different kinds of shore-line. Northwards for almost 4.8km (3 miles) towards Bennane Head stretches a long, narrow exposed beach. The land between the beach and the A77 is still given over to the traditional use of wintering cattle.

To the south of Ballantrae the river Stinchar empties into the Firth of Clyde, making its passage to the sea through a complex bar of shingle. Research has revealed several striking changes in the shape of this pebbly bar and the outlet of the river over the past century, and there is some evidence that in the early years of the last century the mouth of the river was in the form of an estuary and that it was only by the 1850s that a bar had developed. Today the mouth of the Stinchar, a seascape that changes with every phase of the tides, is a nature reserve, notable for its bird life and especially as a refuge for terns. The seaward face of the pebble bar at Ballantrae is very steep; it is a place unsafe for bathing.

Towards Stranraer several miles of the coastline are difficult of access and sand beaches altogether lacking. The A77 turns inland only to reach the sea again above Finnarts Bay, at the mouth of Loch Ryan. **Currarie Port**, a deeply indented cove at the seaward end of a secret glen, forms the only break in this exposed coast. The landscape elements are typical of much of south-west Scotland. Steeply rounded cliffs, brilliant with gorse in the clear light of early summer, fall to a narrow raised beach platform that isolates them from wave attack at the present time. Old volcanic rocks, lavas of Silurian age, compose some of the stronger topographical features of this lonely and unvisited piece of coast, as at Downan Point and in Currarie Cliff.

Finnarts Bay and inland the long straight trench of Glen App mark one of the primary geological features in the landscape of Scotland. Here the main fault-line, dividing the Southern Uplands from the Central Lowlands, reaches the west coast. The linear shape of Glen App has been eroded along this line of weakness in the Earth's crust. Finnarts Bay has an attractive and unspoilt setting – woods clothe the valley slopes of Glen App and rounded richly coloured moorland hills reach up towards the 305m (1,000ft) contour. The beach composed of cobbles and shingle is no place for buckets and spades. The present shingle ridges grade upward into higher overgrown ridges that were formed when the sea-level stood higher some 10,000 years ago.

Cairnryan was developed as a harbour for the import of weapons and war materials from the USA during World War II. The derelict railway that follows the main road for several miles into Stranraer was built to serve the military port. At a peak of activity, early in 1944, much of the equipment for Mulberry Harbour – the floating landing stages of the Normandy beach-heads – was built here. For a decade and more after the end of the war Cairnryan had its uses. Surrendered German submarines were gathered here. It was the assembly place for old ships and useless ammunition that was to be sunk deep in the Atlantic and until its closure in 1959 shipbreaking of battleships was an active operation. A mile to the south of the military port at Cairnryan is the terminus of the vehicle ferry that runs to Larne in Northern Ireland.

Stranraer, with a population of about 10,000, spreads across the flat land of a raised beach at the head of Loch Ryan. The old town with its narrow twisting streets is ringed around by extensive estates of twentieth-century municipal housing. Although a holiday resort, Stranraer lacks the fine beaches and aspects of open sea that are among the assets of so many places on the Galloway coast. The wet grey beaches at the head of Loch Ryan are unattractive and plagued with debris. Such natural deficiencies have in part been made good for the tourist industry. An enclosed pool has been constructed with sluices that allow the regular exchange of water with Loch Ryan. The greater part of the pool is used for boating, but part is set aside for bathing and there is an artificial sand beach. Other holiday facilities include two parks at the western and eastern ends of the town with paddling pools, putting greens, tennis courts and a bandstand.

For over a century Stranraer has been one of the main links with Northern Ireland. Now that the main railway line to Carlisle has been closed for several years the container lorries thunder incessantly along the A75 to the east. The Irish traffic dominates the topography of the central parts of the town where the long railway pier stretches out to the deeper waters of Loch Ryan. Stranraer is also the chief market for the rich farmlands of Galloway. Its wholesale market is usually first with the early potatoes from the Rhinns of Galloway at the end of May.

A fine view over the town and harbour is obtained from the parapet walk of the sixteenth-century castle that served as a town gaol over a period of two centuries. A little more than 3.2km (2 miles) from the burgh, along the A75, is the magnificent estate of Lochinch Castle. A Victorian mansion in the full romantic Scottish baronial style, Lochinch was built in 1867 as a successor to Castle Kennedy that had been burnt and never rebuilt at the beginning of the century. The gardens occupy a spectacular site on a narrow neck of land between the White Loch and the Black Loch. There is a pinetum, the first to be planted in Scotland, with some 200 species of conifer. One of the main attractions is a spectacular avenue of monkey

The railway pier at Stranraer, a busy ferry port for Northern Ireland

puzzle trees, planted 100 years ago. Rich in rhododendron and azalea, the best time of the year to see Castle Kennedy is in the early summer.

Galloway and The Solway Firth

One of the most attractive regions of Britain extends between the savage cliffs of the Mull of Galloway and the trackless mud-flats at the head of the Solway Firth where the river Sark marks the frontier of England and Scotland. Deep bays reach inland between quiet unspoilt pastoral peninsulas. Bold rounded granite mountains raise their vast hummocks above this intricate attractive coastline in Cairnsmore of Fleet and Criffel. Further away, to the north and east, one glimpses the distant shapes of the high hills of the Southern Uplands, Merrick in Glentrool Forest reaching almost 914m (3,000ft). The individuality of Scotland's southern coastline lies not only in its long sandy estuaries and pastoral landscapes that are reminiscent of parts of Devon and southern Ireland, but also in the seaward prospects on clear days to the mountains of Cumbria, the Isle of Man and distant Ulster across the North Channel. Sheltered by its encircling mountains and facing south across the sea, the Solway coastline is indeed a riviera.

Westward of Stranraer two long hummocky peninsulas, known as The Rhinns, stretch out to north and south.

From Milleur Point, at the entrance to Loch Ryan, to Portpatrick the northern and western coast of The Rhinns is not easy of access. Rough high-banked lanes lead to farms on the rolling plateau that lies inland from the cliff's edge; thence the way to the sea may be along a steep and treacherous footpath. The most accessible piece of this long cliffed coastline is at Killantringan Bay. It is approached by the tarred single-track road that leads to the lighthouse on Black Head. Killantringan continues northwards into Broadsea Bay to form the largest beach on the west coast of The Rhinns. A raised beach, shaped by a higher sea-level in prehistoric times, lies close above the present shore and inland the steep face of a relict cliff rises to a richly farmed plateau. North of Portpatrick there are a number of small attractive bays and inlets.

Portamaggie, a narrow cliff-bound inlet with clean, attractive sands lies beneath Black Head. At Salt Pans Bay we find the site of an industry – the extraction of salt from

The shores of Galloway from the Mull of Galloway to the Solway Firth

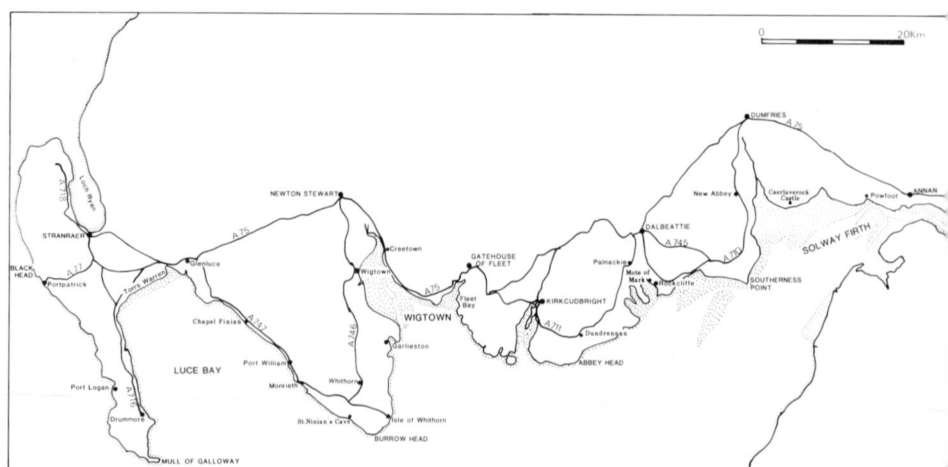

Portpatrick once aspired to become the chief port for traffic to Northern Ireland

sea water – that persisted in Galloway into the nineteenth century. The salt pans, cut into the rocks at the cliff foot, can still be seen at this lonely place reached only by a 1.6km (1 mile) long footpath from Galdenoch Castle, a sixteenth-century ruin.

Portpatrick has a resident population of about 1,000. Its most striking feature is a shelterless harbour, mercilessly exposed to gales and heavy seas from every westerly quarter. The sad history of this natural defect is inscribed on its townscape in the jumbled masses of stone and concrete that form the storm-battered pier built in the early years of the nineteenth century when Portpatrick aspired to become Galloway's chief port for traffic with Northern Ireland.

A royal charter in 1620 established a burgh on this tiny exposed inlet of the west coast. The building of the Military Road across south-west Scotland between Dumfries and Portpatrick in 1766 gave this harbour an advantage over any rivals in the growing Irish traffic. Not only was Portpatrick the terminus of an engineered road across much difficult and trackless country, but the 34km (21 miles) of the North Channel that separated it from Ireland provided the shortest sea crossing from Britain. The gales of the 1890s demolished the South Pier, and the inner harbour became a base for a small fishing fleet.

Portpatrick's decline as a port was partly offset by its growth as a resort in the early twentieth century. Its exposed site on Scotland's most south-westerly peninsula has given Portpatrick a renewed importance in communications in this century. Submarine cables to Northern Ireland leave the coast here. There is a radio station with a range of 483km (300 miles) that maintains contact with shipping in the north-west approaches and the Irish Sea and here, too, has been established a microwave television link with Northern Ireland.

South from Portpatrick the peninsula narrows, in places to scarcely 3.2km (2 miles). The scenery gains in magnificence as one approaches the Mull of Galloway. A small intrusion of granite forms the steep, castellated cliffs of Laggantalluch Head and Crammag Head. From Crammag Head to the Mull of Galloway a fine series of cliffs

The cliffed coast of the Mull of Galloway

and tiny inaccessible bays looks out to the south-west. It is a deserted, unvisited place, out of reach of the motorist for the most part. At Dunman, where the cliffs fall to the sea through 122m (400ft), a massive, ruinous wall runs acrosss the cliff top, probably an Iron Age fort.

Port Logan The beach, backed by low cliffs plastered with blown sand and shapeless dunes, is a favourite day-tripper resort. The settlement of Port Logan consists of two parallel rows of cottages – the lower, on the sea-shore, protected by a high embankment. A storm-wrecked quay, a forlorn jumble of red sandstone blocks, juts out into the sea – the only memorial of a plan to make a harbour here that aimed to wrest the Irish traffic from Portpatrick. The quay was the investment of the laird of the Logan estate, Col Andrew McDouall, in 1820. In the controversy, lasting for almost a century from the 1760s, over the short sea passage to Ireland, it is known that Telford, aware of the physical disadvantages of Portpatrick, favoured the development of Port Logan.

Logan Fish Pond, at the north end of the beach, was built in 1788 by the laird of the Logan estate – a sheltered, walled-in rock-pool, refreshed by every tide, from which the fish are unable to escape. The original aim of its construction was to supply fresh fish to the laird's table. Now the cod that cavort in its dark translucent water, so tame that they feed from the hand of a keeper, attract some 10,000 tourists a year. Inland from the beach are the gardens of the Logan Estate, rich in sub-tropical plants that are able to survive in the mild sea-climate of Galloway.

Drummore Much of the raised beach here on the unattractive east coast of The Rhinns has been removed by erosion in recent times and the protective sea wall at the north end of the bay was undercut and collapsed. Local residents at Drummore can remember cultivation strips at the beginning of the century on this now vanished beach. The cause of these changes in the physique of Drummore Bay lies in the building of the quay early in the nineteenth century, when Drummore's little harbour was the main link between much of the southern part of the peninsula and the world outside.

At the head of Luce Bay lies one of the largest sand beaches and collection of dunes in the whole of Scotland. Luce Sands extend over a distance of 10km (6 miles) from Sandhead to the Water of Luce; at the northern end 2.4km (1½ miles) of sand is exposed at low tide. Inland, one enters a chaotic landscape of dunes, sand hills, and winding depressions or 'slacks' – wet places rich with bog myrtle and willow scrub. Further inland, where the A715 trunk road skirts this directionless wilderness of sand, the dunes give way to a sandy plateau clothed in heather. The dunes, accumulating and eroding over the past 8,000 years, lie on top of the deposits of a raised beach.

Luce Sands and the dune complex of Torrs Warren have been listed as a place of high scientific importance by the Nature Conservancy Council, not only for their vegetation, wildlife and the problems inherent in the understanding of their physical evolution, but as an archaeological site with evidence of occupation from several different periods of prehistory. Proof of man's early occupation goes back at least 6,000 years with the discovery in abundance of Mesolithic flint tools. Later still in time, a buried soil surface with indication of ploughing suggests the presence of Neolithic farmers in the second or third millennium BC.

Today the Forestry Commission has planted a long strip by the Piltanton Burn in the north; the greater part of Torrs Warren is a bombing range and weapon-testing station for the Royal Aircraft Establishment. Consequently, public access to much of Luce Sands and their hinterland is prohibited. Only on the southern margin at **Sandhead**, where there are camping and caravan sites, can one take in this unique tract of south-west Scotland's coastline. On the northern edge, a long rough forest road leads for 3.2km (2 miles) to a picnic site set up by the Forestry Commission at Ringdoo Point.

The Wigtown peninsula stretches southwards to the rocky promontory of Burrow Head. Its interior landscapes – low, undulating and lacking in any exciting topographical features – are forgotten by most of Scotland's tourist writers. Nevertheless, there is a quiet attractiveness about the peninsula's interior region, known as The Machars. For the most part the western coast presents many miles of boulders, sea-worn cobbles and shingle. Sand beaches are scarce apart from **Auchenmalg**, below **Glenluce**, at **Craignarget** with its two small sandy beaches amid the wilderness of boulders that make up the residue of eroded glacial deposits, and in **Monreith Bay**, considered the most attractive part of this coastline.

The historic sites of the Wigtown peninsula give immense importance to this

The storm-wrecked breakwater of Port Logan, a harbour planned in the 1820s to play a part in the Irish trade

The approach to St Ninians's Cave at Whithorn

part of south-west Scotland. Chapel Finnian, sited on the edge of the relict cliff above the raised beach and the main A747 road, was probably used by medieval pilgrims who had come ashore here on their way to St Ninian's holy place and monastery at Whithorn. Here proof has been obtained of the presence of early man, hunters and fishermen, in Scotland long before the first farmers tilled the soils of western Britain. A Mesolithic site on the top of the fossil cliffs above Clone Point has revealed the hearths of migrating hunters who camped here some 6,000 years ago. **Monreith** has numerous standing stones, rock surfaces pecked with abstract patterns, as well as a stone circle that seems to be aligned on the midwinter sunset of Bronze Age times over the rocky islet of Big Scare to the south west in the mouth of Luce Bay. The Iron Age and the Early Christian centuries are represented by earthworks and cliff-top enclosures. The parish of Mochrum alone contains twenty forts. At **Kirkmaiden**, in one of the most attractive parts of this long, unexciting eastern shore of Luce Bay, we find the ruins of a medieval church on the foreshore.

Isle of Whithorn This little rock-bound harbour situated east and north of Burrow Head leads the traveller who approaches south-west Scotland by sea into a countryside that is as rich as any part of northern Britain in its associations with history. **Whithorn** lies 5km (3 miles) inland. It is associated with St Ninian, a Christian missionary saint of the late fourth century who, it is believed, founded the first Christian church and monastery here in about 397. The beautifully arranged sculptured stones in the museum at Whithorn carry the mind back to the age of St Ninian. There, the Latinus stone dates from the fifth century, and it has been argued that this may have been in existence even when Ninian founded the first church at Whithorn.

Until pilgrimages ceased with the Reformation at the end of the sixteenth century the Isle of Whithorn was the chief landing place for pilgrims. On the island, long connected to the mainland by an artificial causeway, there is the ruin of a medieval chapel and at the seaward end the outline of an Iron Age earthwork. St

Ninian's Cave is concealed in the high cliffed coast to the west of Burrow Head. The cave is reached from the main A747 road by the lane that leads to Physgill House and Kidsdale Farm. Close by the farm a widening of the road provides a car park. Thence on foot for less than 1.6km (1 mile) through a sheltered wooded valley that leads direct to the sea-shore. About 0.4km (¼ mile) westward along the steeply banked shingle one comes to the cave, a narrow slit in the cliff-face. The cave floor is now almost 8m (25ft) above present sea-level. An excavation at the end of the last century revealed stone pavements and numerous boulders marked with crosses in the pecked technique of Early Christian memorial stones. This was a retreat, a hermitage, in a wild and lonely place that is so typical of the organisation of the Celtic Church.

Cruggleton Bay has one of the most attractive sand beaches on the east coast of Wigtown's peninsula. To its general attractions are added the woodlands in the park of Galloway House, built in 1740, that here form the background to sea and sands.

Garlieston has great charm. It is a perfect example of so many of the small ports founded on the Scottish coastline in the eighteenth century. Its formal pattern of streets and terraced cottages was established in 1760 by John, Lord Garlies, 7th Earl of Galloway. Here we can see the ideas of an improving landlord of the eighteenth century written on the landscape of our own times. Garlieston prospered as a port through the nineteenth century and even in the 1950s the writer of the *Third Statistical Account* of Wigtownshire could report the import of Norwegian timber, fertilisers, cement and lime, and the occasional sailing of an excursion steamer to the Isle of Man in summer.

Wigtown A quiet place of grey Victorian building gathered around a wide market square atop the steep cliff that looks across the salt-marsh and sands where the rivers Cree and Bladnoch empty into the sea. The site of Wigtown Castle is known only by a grassy mound between the marshy shore and the line of the disused railway. On the cliff above the castle stood a Dominican monastery. That, too, disappeared beneath the expanding town. Its stones have been used for house-building and a few place-names alone recall the days of the monastery – Friarland, Monk Hill and Friars Well. Only in 'the old churchyard' can one trace the remains of Wigtown's pre-Reformation church. Wigtown had a population of almost 3,000 in the middle years of the nineteenth century; now this medieval royal burgh numbers little more than 1,000. Its harbour was defunct by the early years of this century. The once busy market and business life have been taken over by Newton Stewart, a new town of Charles II's reign that is advantageously placed at the main bridge-point of the Cree.

Creetown was founded in 1791 as a burgh of barony by James McCulloch of Barholm. The earliest factor in its development was the ferry traffic across the head of Wigtown Bay, hence the old and forgotten name of Ferrytown of Cree. But Creetown was to acquire industrial interests after the 1830s when granite quarries were opened up in the steep hill-slopes to the south of the town. A pale, silvery-grey granite with fine qualities as a building material is still quarried along a narrow band in the hills, an outcrop of less than 183m (200yd) in width. During the high Victorian decades Creetown granite went to the building of bridges, dock basins, banks and town halls; today, it is crushed for road making.

The eastern shore of Wigtown Bay between the estuaries of Cree and Dee displays some of the finest coastal scenery in the whole of Britain. In particular, Fleet Bay has been listed as a national scenic area because of its arc-shaped beaches of white sand held between reefs and spurs of dark rock.

At Cairnholy, reached by a steeply winding lane from the A75 at Kirkdale, two Neolithic burial places, chambered tombs, lie near each other. The finer of the two, Cairnholy I, where six tall stones form a concave arc at the entrance to the burial chamber, was excavated in 1949. Flint arrow-heads and pottery showed the

Cairnholy I, a semi-circle of standing stones forms the forecourt of this Neolithic chambered tomb

affinities of the folk who lived here almost 5,000 years ago with New Stone Age settlements in the Isle of Man and Ulster. Fragments of pitchstone that could come from nowhere else but Arran suggest trade in those remote times with the Clyde. Barholm Castle, a stronghold of the McCullochs, dates from the sixteenth century. Even finer examples of late-medieval tower-houses that express the exposure of Galloway to the ravaging English are found close beside the main road in Carsluith Castle and Cardoness Castle. The roofless sixteenth-century tower at Carsluith rises from a cluster of farm buildings on a raised beach overlooking Wigtown Bay. Cardoness Castle is situated at a bend of the road approaching Gatehouse of Fleet. This fifteenth-century tower-house, standing four storeys in height, occupies a high rocky knoll at the head of Fleet Bay.

Situated between Creetown and Gatehouse of Fleet, Kirkdale House was built in the 1780s by Sir Samuel Hannay, a Galloway laird who held shipping interests, was a London drug merchant and sat as Member of Parliament for Camelford in Cornwall. This grey granite mansion, designed by Robert Adam, has been described as 'the finest house in Galloway'. Here the plantations on the steep flanks of Kirkdale burn were threaded with walks and stone causeways. Down on the shore, below the A75 trunk road, Dirk Hatteraick's Cave is perhaps the most famous folly of Sir Samuel Hannay's estate. Scarcely two centuries have gathered an encrustation of legend that conceals its origin as a fanciful piece of Georgian landscaping.

Gatehouse of Fleet survives as one of the most perfect examples of the Industrial Revolution. James Murray built his mansion at Cally in the 1760s and in 1795 obtained a charter for the foundation of Gatehouse as a burgh of barony. This new town, at the head of the estuary of the Water of Fleet, based its future on water power and the cotton industry. Yorkshire businessmen, the Birtwhistles, who had been engaged in the cattle trade of Galloway, built two mills before 1800 on the bank of the Water of Fleet. By the 1850s the cotton mills had closed; the high ambition to establish a tannery, brewery, soap-works and brass foundry had failed. The straightened course of the Fleet below Gatehouse, a canal cut by Irish labour from Alexander Murray's Donegal estates in lieu of unpaid rents, ceased to guide any ships to the moribund quay of Port Macadam after 1900. Gatehouse of Fleet is now a tourist town, plagued by the constant rumble of heavy traffic along the Stranraer road.

Cally House and its grounds occupy much of the eastern shore of the Fleet estuary. Robert Mylne drew the plans for James Murray in 1763. With its stables, home farms, dairy, laundry, chapel, ice-house, dovecotes, follies, temples and fashionable ruins, Cally represents a total replanning of the landscape. And all was shaped into a harmonious pattern by the planting of woodland. A traveller of the time, overwhelmed by the elegance of Cally, could write 'every deformity within these grounds is concealed or converted into a beauty by wood'. It is now a luxurious country hotel and the grounds of the estate belong to the Forestry Commission as a nursery for the development of the Fleet Forest.

Between the Water of Fleet and the Dee estuary the coastline is accessible to the motorist at only half a dozen places, reached by narrow, high-banked winding lanes. A succession of earthworks, banked and ditched enclosures from the centuries between 100 BC and AD 500, crown the low cliffs of Silurian rocks between Carrick Point and Meikle Ross.

The western shore of Fleet Bay has been listed as a national scenic area. **Cardoness** with its clean sands, jagged rocks and woods has been rated among the most attractive beaches in the whole of Scotland. **Sandgreen**, at the mouth of Fleet Bay, has an extensive sand beach, open to the south-west. There are holiday bungalows and huts, a caravan site, and zones have been set aside on the beach for bathing, sailing and power boating. Between Carrick and Kirkandrews the low rocky shore conceals several tiny embayments with short arcs of beach sand. The islands of Fleet make an attractive offshore prospect. **Ardwall** and **Barlocco** may be reached on foot across the sands at low tide. The former island is the site of a chapel and cemetery dating from the sixth century AD. Carved memorial stones from this important centre of early Christianity on Ardwall Island are to be seen in Dumfries museum. The most popular beach of this part of the Solway coast is **Brighouse Bay**, a deep embayment flanked by woodland on its western shore. A motorable road leads to the water's edge and cars can be driven unhindered on to the beach. Behind the woods, at Pennymuir, is a caravan and camp site, and there is water-skiing in the bay. Along the shores of Kirkcudbright Bay one enters a lush landscape of woods and green fields that reach down to the sea.

The peninsula of St Mary's Isle, below Kirkcudbright, is the site of a twelfth-century nunnery.

Kirkcudbright, at the head of the Dee Estuary, ranks among the most attractive of Scotland's coastal towns. This medieval royal burgh stands on the last great bend of the Dee before the river becomes lost among the wide sands of Kirkcudbright Bay. The outward impression is of a bright Georgian town of wide streets and handsome houses. Only four objects in this townscape are older than the eighteenth century. The High Street, its western end dominated by the seventeenth-century tolbooth, marks the line of a gravel ridge that was the earliest settlement at Kirkcudbright. MacLellan's Castle, a dark keep out of tune with its prim Georgian surroundings, dates from the close of the sixteenth century. Greyfriars Church, on the site of a monastery, faces MacLellan's Castle.

In its heyday Kirkcudbright was a major port with ships trading to the Baltic and the West Indies, and until the beginning of this century regular services ran to Whitehaven and Liverpool. Now there are only fishing boats, pleasure craft and the occasional coaster making its way up the long sandy estuary on a high tide. Kirkcudbright's industries are unobtrusive. A Shell Oil depot was established here in 1952 and there is a knitwear factory. Its chief fame in the world outside attached to the artists who were inspired by the work of E. A. Hornel to paint the local landscapes. Hornel died in 1933 and bequeathed his home, Broughton House in the High Street, to the town. There one may see some of the impressionist child paintings that made him famous. Further along the street is the Harbour Art Gallery where exhibitions of the Kirkcudbright School are displayed occasionally.

A blunt peninsula of Silurian rocks divides Kirkcudbright Bay from the deep embayments of Auchencairn Bay and Rough Firth, although for a considerable distance along the coast the scenery is shaped out of rocks of a younger age, the Calciferous Sandstones laid down in Carboniferous times. The gentle rounded hills that rise behind the low lines of cliff reach more than 91m (300ft) above sea level. This is a rich well-farmed countryside specialising in dairy cattle. The greater part of this coast is difficult of access. The main road, the A711 from Kirkcudbright to Dalbeattie, lies 3-4km (2-3 miles) distant from the coast. Narrow twisting lanes end abruptly in farm-yards before they reach the sea. Since the beginning of World War II access to several miles of coast westward of Port Mary is precluded by the presence of a military tank training-ground whose creation in the 1940s resulted in the evacuation of fifty households from farms and cottages.

Dundrennan Dundrennan Abbey, a Cistercian foundation in 1142, of which the remains still stand, was colonised by monks from Rievaulx in Yorkshire. The abbey escaped suppression until 1606. Mary Queen of Scots spent her last night in Scotland at Dundrennan after the failure of her attempt to regain the throne in 1568. Thence she sailed to England from the little creek of Port Mary below Dundrennan.

Around the shores of Auchencairn Bay and Rough Firth, little, rounded, ice-scarred granite hills rise suddenly from the shore to heights of over 30m (100ft). Patches of planted woodland abound and sunny, sheltered south-facing coves look out across the sand-choked embayments of Rough Firth and Auchencairn Bay.

White Port, at the south-eastern tip of the knobby peninsula dividing Orchardton Bay from Rough Firth, is perhaps the most attractive of sand beaches in this granite landscape. Approach by land is difficult because no road reaches down to the coast; visitors get here mainly by sail and motor boat across Rough Firth. With a landward northern aspect into Rough Firth, White Bay has extensive spreads of soft mud that inhibit bathing. Balcray Bay, likewise, is disfigured by coastal defences of tipped rock and rubble against a beach of cobbles, sand and mud.

Palnackie, a little clustered settlement sheltered within the lowest meanders of the Urr, was a thriving port until the first quarter of this century. Timber from the many acres of surrounding forest is the other industrial preoccupation of Palnackie with its three sawmills.

Dalbeattie owes its existence as a town to the granite industry. Less than 200 years ago there was only a farm of that name. In about 1800 Andrew Newall began the quarrying of granite as a monumental stone. By the 1840s his works had become the show-place of Dalbeattie and in the Victorian century the grey granite of Dalbeattie went to public buildings, banks, town halls and law courts, all over Britain. Today, Dalbeattie's founding industry is remembered only in this little town's pale grey buildings and shining steeples and in abandoned quarries lost in the enveloping forests.

Kippford and **Rockliffe** Tourism now forms the main occupation of the shores of Rough Firth where Kippford and Rockliffe emerged as small resorts towards the end of the last century. Kippford, once a small port, traded with harbours along the Cumbrian coast on the south side of the Solway Firth, but the building of the railway into Galloway ended its career. Both places, facing south and west across the sheltered waters of Rough Firth and screened by tumbled granite hills, acquired a local reputation as a Scottish riviera. The two small resorts and the rocky shore-line that separates them present a unique element in Scotland's coastal scenery. Luxuriant gardens come down to the sea with its small beaches of clean granitic sand.

The hummocky eastern shore of Rough Firth now belongs to the National Trust for

Rockliffe: the seaward prospect from the Mote of Mark towards Rough Island, a National Trust property and bird sanctuary

Scotland. **Rough Island**, reached across the sands at low tide by a stony causeway, is a National Trust property and a bird sanctuary – a place of terns, gulls, oyster catchers and, in the winter season, thousands of migrant geese. On one of the rocky knolls above Rough Firth lies an outstanding prehistoric site, the Mote of Mark. This settlement, a vitrified fort of the Iron Age, has revealed occupation across many centuries. Its main rampart, once a massive stone wall with an internal framework of timber beams, is now much denuded, but excavation has revealed animal bones, the clay floors of hearths, and evidence of metal-working and iron smelting. There were also fragments of Roman pottery dating from the second century AD and clay moulds as well as pieces of glass from the ninth century. The Mote of Mark makes a short exhilarating walk with, at the end, a prospect of this uncommonly lush and varied piece of the Solway coast.

Sandyhills Bay, a favourite day-tripper beach, is easily accessible from the A710 that rounds the peninsula between Dumfries and Dalbeattie. The approach to Sandyhills along the main road is immediately attractive to the motorist. A narrow upper beach of fine sand is flanked by wooded slopes and a scrubby vegetation composed of wild rose, blackthorn and bramble. The muddy channel of the Southwick Water, however, runs parallel to the narrow sand beach, making bathing dangerous except during high water. The western end of the beach has a small caravan and camping site and there are some holiday huts and shacks.

Southerness sprawls untidily among the sand dunes at the end of a long lane from the A710. Apart from its golf course, Southerness is primarily a place for day-trippers and holiday-makers in caravans. It is a desolate, unfriendly place when an unbroken lid of cloud oppresses the Solway shores, but under the clear skies of an early summer anticyclone Southerness and its featureless far horizons create a great sense of space. On the reef of Carboniferous rocks that form the foreshore of the ness stands one of Scotland's oldest lighthouses, built in 1747 by the merchants of Dumfries to mark the entrance to the Nith Estuary. At the close of the eighteenth century and for long after, this was one of the important shipping routes of western Britain when 500 ships a year brought their imports to Dumfries.

The lighthouse built at Southerness in 1747, by the merchants of Dumfries, to mark the entrance to the Nith estuary

Carsethorn One of the several lost ports of the Solway, Carsethorn once imported coal from Whitehaven and traded with Liverpool, the Baltic lands and with North America.

The estate at Arbigland appears in all the tourist guides to Galloway as the birth-place of Paul Jones – instigator of the raid on St Mary's Isle, Kirkcudbright, at the time of the American War of Independence and known as the founder of the United States' Navy. Along this road the place of outstanding attraction is New Abbey. This Cistercian monastery, of which an impressive amount of the red sandstone buildings still remain, was founded in the thirteenth century. The name New Abbey is meant to distinguish this monastic settlement from Dundrennan where a community had already been in existence for more than a century. Today's upstanding remains are those of the abbey church. The medieval masons of New Abbey quarried their building stone from Locharbriggs, quarries on the outskirts of Dumfries. Apart from the abbey church with its tall central tower and arches of the nave open to the sky, the only surviving relic of the monastic landscape at New Abbey is the precinct wall composed of rough shapeless boulders garnered perhaps in the original land clearance there.

Dumfries, with a population of almost 30,000, is the largest town in Solway's Scottish hinterland. Dumfries already held the status of a royal burgh before the end of the twelfth century, and it can claim an active part in the making of Scotland. The war of independence that preceded Bannockburn started here by Robert Bruce when the representative of the English king, Sir John Comyn, was murdered at the high altar of the Greyfriars monastery.

Before the middle of the last century and the coming of railways, brewing, hat-making, tanning and the manufacture of leather goods were the chief industrial occupations. The latter half of the nineteenth century saw the transformation of Dumfries into a busy textile town. It became for a brief time the largest producer of tweed in Scotland. Until the depression of the 1930s, an important member of the Scottish car industry, Arrol-Johnston, was located here. During World War II ICI set up a nitro-cellulose plant at Cargenbridge; now it produces plastics and paint. There was a revival of the hosiery industry and the rubber industry was established.

For the tourist this attractive, warmly coloured town built of the freestones from Locharbriggs quarries offers the sight of its broad-flowing river with a late medieval bridge, the Devorgilla Bridge, and below the Caul, a weir that provided power to the eighteenth-century grain mills. Much eighteenth- and early nineteenth-century building in stone gives character to the town, chief among them the Midsteeple, erected in 1707 to provide municipal offices, a court-house and prison. The Burgh Museum in Maxwelltown was opened in 1836 in the shell of an old windmill that was used as a *camera obscura*. This regional museum, extended in the 1930s, makes a valuable introduction to a study of the archaeology and history of Scotland's south-west with its collection of Roman altars and early Christian inscribed stones.

Robert Burns' tomb lies in St Michael's Church and at his house, now a museum, in Burns Street, manuscripts and relics are on display. Among the dull streets of the big municipal housing scheme in the north of Maxwelltown one finds the ruin of a twelfth-century religious foundation, Lincluden College.

During the eighteenth century wharves were built at two places down-river from Dumfries. **Glencaple** was opened to shipping in 1747 and **Kingholm Quay** provided another landing stage much closer to the royal burgh. As late as the 1930s 100 ships navigated the narrow twisting channel between the mud-banks of the Nith Estuary to reach the two quays. Today, Glencaple, a picturesque place of white-washed cottages, caters only for the tourist trade. The maintenance of the passage of the Nith has always presented a problem and despite the works of the Nith Navigation Company to straighten and control the channel in the nineteenth century, the difficulties of reaching the wharves from the sea were scarcely eased. By the early years of this century the Nith was navigable to Glencaple on only three days in a month and then only for vessels of less than 500 tons.

At the foot of the low hills that mark the eastern entrance of the Nith stands Caerlaverock, a grim triangular-shaped ruin of a castle flanked on all sides by the water of a broad moat. This stronghold of the Maxwells was raised during the thirteenth century. In 1570 much of the castle's fabric was ravaged, but was rebuilt in 1638 by Lord Maxwell in the form of a range of guest-houses with the courtyard contained by the earlier ragged walls of the medieval ruin. As one explores the ruins of Caerlaverock, there is no greater surprise

New Abbey, some of the most impressive monastic remains in Scotland, built by the Cistercians in the thirteenth century

than the sudden transition from its sullen medieval exterior to the warmth of the Renaissance architecture in the sheltered concealed courtyard. The contrasts of two periods of Scotland's history, before and after the Union of the Crowns, are expressed in one building. However, Caerlaverock was ravaged by the Covenanters in 1640 and the site was abandoned.

The Merse, an extensive salt-marsh, extends for almost 10km (6 miles) between the Nith Estuary and the Lochar Water. Research has shown that the sudden extension of Caerlaverock Merse is probably related to the efforts of the Nith Navigation Company to improve the river's channel for shipping. Today, this Solway salt-marsh is a National Nature Reserve, part of which has been handed over to the Wildfowl Trust. During the winter months birds gather here in large numbers. Barnacle Geese, Pink-footed geese and Golden Plover seek out the refuge in flocks of thousands. The Wildfowl Trust has established observation towers and hides in the marshland refuge and at certain times of day escorted visits take place.

Powfoot, at the outflow of the Pow Water into Solway, has seen several unsuccessful efforts to develop a holiday resort. Its wide expanse of sands at low tide were much visited at the end of the eighteenth century when the hamlet of fishermen here was known as Queensberry. In the years before World War I some development of a summer resort took place but all that survives of this project is a terrace of fifteen houses. Since the 1920s Powfoot has become a place for retirement. Its amenities, apart from a salubrious climate, are a hotel, golf course, bowling green and tennis.

Seafield, where the river Annan empties into the Solway Firth, is the site of one of the more spectacular achievements of the railway age. Here the Solway Junction Railway joined the shores of Scotland and England in the 1860s with a viaduct 2km (1¼ miles) in length and composed of 193 piers. The main purpose of this railway was to carry iron ore from Cumberland to the furnaces of Lanarkshire. The railway was never a commercial success. In 1881 the viaduct was severely damaged by floating ice and the line, to the south of Annan, was out of use until 1884. All traffic between Annan and the English shore was ended in 1921. The viaduct was finally dismantled and removed in 1933–5. Today, only the embankment at Seafield, ending abruptly by the Solway Sands, reminds one of the engineering achievements of those Victorian pioneers.

East of Seafield stands the Lochmaben Stone: 2m (7ft) in height, this prehistoric monument is situated on the low ground where the Kirtle Water mingles with the Solway. Long before the drawing of the frontier between Scotland and England, Lochmaben Stone played an important part in the relations between the two nations. In 1398 a truce between England and Scotland was arranged here, and throughout the Middle Ages this was a trysting place and a venue for markets and fairs.

Annan, with a population of little more than 6,000, dates its urban origins to the twelfth century when it was the head of the lordship of Annandale, although its earliest surviving charter as a royal burgh is dated 1538. Medieval in origin, the burgh is largely Victorian in appearance. The near extinction of sea traffic in the Solway Firth has seen the demise of Annan as a port. In the 1950s only ten ships a year tied up at its quay; a century earlier its chief industry was shipbuilding, among them the clippers from Nicholson's yard that made record trips to China and Chile. Shipbuilding died here in 1901 and Annan's chief occupations have since been with explosives and, in 1955, the building of an atomic power station on a disused aerodrome at Chapelcross.

Eastriggs An isolated farm, Eastriggs was transformed into a township of 1,000 by the building of a munitions factory during World War I. Although Eastriggs became a ghost town after that war, the terraces of single-storyed houses that sheltered the munition workers have gradually become permanent homes for retired people. During World Ward II Eastriggs became the chief storage depot for explosives and war material in the south of Scotland.

Gretna The chief claim to fame of Gretna is for the marriages of runaway couples from England, two centuries ago, under a Scots law that required no banns or licences. The town was largely created by the munitions industry of World War I. A settlement, housing at its peak a population of 20,000, grew up in 1915 on both sides of the Carlisle to Annan road. To the east of Gretna runs the river Sark and the frontier between Scotland and England, established in 1552 across the peat mosses, marsh and mud-flats of Solway, where the fast-running tide rises 7.5m (25ft) at high springs in the wasteland of winding channels.

21 The Islands of Scotland

No survey of Scotland's coastline is complete without some consideration of the girdle of islands, almost 800 in all, that encircles its western and northern shores from Islay to Shetland. Only 136 of these islands are reported as inhabited. If we consider the coastal features of these islands – and the total coastline is immensely long – we find that they contain some of the most important elements of the British landscape. The desolate uninhabited shores of western Jura possess the spectacular raised-beach platforms shaped by the changing sea-levels of the last 12,000 years. Mull and its attendant islands contain Fingal's Cave, basalt cliffs with the fossil impression of a tree buried in the lavas of a volcanic eruption some 60 million years ago, and on Iona, a tiny island of grey gneiss set in a crystal-green sea, Columba's monastery – the potent centre of Christianity in Dark Age Scotland. In the Outer Hebrides the western Atlantic coast has miles of empty sand-beaches, unmatched elsewhere in the British Isles and unexploited by the tourist industry. The northernmost island clusters, Orkney and Shetland, have an immensely rich and visible legacy from prehistoric times. Skara Brae, in Orkney, a Neolithic village which lay buried beneath sand dunes until revealed by a violent storm in 1850, ranks among Europe's most important archaeological sites. And there is so much else remaining from the earliest periods of human history in the northern isles – scores of brochs, and at Jarlshof in Shetland a place where settlements have succeeded each other on the same patch of land close by the sea from the Bronze Age until the early years of the seventeenth century. In the following pages it is possible only to hint at the variety of riches, both scenic and historic, that may be encountered in an exploration of the islands off western and northern Scotland.

Shetland

The archipelago of Shetland is made up of 117 islands, but of these fewer than 20 are inhabited. The islands of Mainland, Yell and Unst, with a cluster of lesser islands and skerries, form the core of Shetland. Foula and Fair Isle lie remote from the main group, entailing journeys of between two and three hours when the sea permits. There are two means of getting to Shetland for the tourist. P&O Ferries operate a direct link between Aberdeen and Lerwick on alternate days through the summer months, with a roll-on roll-off vehicle ferry. The overnight journey takes fourteen hours. There are also regular air services, much increased in the years of the oil boom, to the islands' airport at Sumburgh on the southern tip of Mainland. A car is essential for the enjoyment of the widely scattered delights of Shetland's coastline because the sketchy public transport of the islands is not geared to the needs of the tourist in its timetables or its destinations. The visitor should therefore weigh up the considerable cost of the car ferry, together with the inconvenience of a service that does not run every day, against the flight to Sumburgh and the hiring of a car.

Shetland has the most intricate coastline of any part of the British Isles. Everywhere long sea channels reach inland; 'voe' is the Shetland term to describe these drowned valleys that the geographer would know as 'rias' in Cornwall. The sea is ever present in the Shetland landscape, so much so that nowhere is more than 5km (3 miles) from salt water. The complex pattern of voes results from the submergence over several thousand years since the Ice Age of a landscape of hills and valleys rising up from the plains of the North Sea's floor at some 120m (400ft) below present sea-level.

Geologists noting the absence of raised beaches in Shetland have concluded that the archipelago has not been subject to the recovery from the weight of the Quaternary Ice sheets that is visible in the landscape of so many parts of mainland Scotland. Only the rising sea-levels from the water returned to the world's oceans by the melting of the ice caps are recorded in the drowned landscape of Shetland. The geology of the islands is as complicated as in many parts of the Highlands. The north-south orientation of the main islands is reflected in a backbone of severely folded and faulted Dalradian rocks of an age and character similar to those of the Grampian Highlands. This ancient geological backbone stretches from the cliffs of the south-west corner of Mainland to Britain's northernmost point at Herma Ness in Unst. To the west the Dalradian rocks are abruptly cut off by the Walls Boundary Fault, a structural break in the earth's crust that is believed to be a continuation of that important Highland feature, the Great Glen fault. Apart from the Dalradian rocks – schists, crystalline limestones, gneiss, gabbro and serpentine – considerable parts of the islands lying to east and west of this ancient geological backbone are composed of the younger Old Red Sandstones. Much of the Walls peninsula, the magnificent 300m (1,000ft) cliffs of Foula, the cliffed bird sanctuary of Noss, and south-east Mainland and Mousa are all of Old Red Sandstone.

Mainland, with its tangle of voes and retinue of islands and skerries, extends for more than 80km (50 miles). Here the life of the county of Shetland – a county that has almost the independence of a nation – is largely focussed. Lerwick, Britain's most northern town, is the capital of Shetland with a population of 7,000. Sheltered by the island of Bressay, its harbour has provided an important base for North Sea fishermen ever since Dutch herring fleets exploited these waters in the seventeenth century. In recent years Lerwick's economic life has switched to the wealth of oil lying beneath its surrounding sea, and it has become a servicing base for the rigs that lie to east and north-east.

The old town, stone built in the eighteenth and nineteenth centuries, is huddled around the harbour. Its chief attraction for the tourist is Commercial Street, a long curving shopping street above the harbour that looks like a late-twentieth-century planner's shopping precinct because of the absence of pavements. It was designed for a community that went everywhere in boats; now the unsuspecting shop-gazing tourist will find himself nudged by cars and vans in Commercial Street. For the rest Lerwick reveals itself as a boom town. Down by the quays where the Aberdeen car ferry ties up, there are acres of the clutter of a busy expanding industry. Inland spread faceless streets of local authority housing.

For the tourist Lerwick, apart from providing an excellent centre for exploring the rest of Shetland, has two important offerings. Clickhimin, a Pictish broch on the site of an earlier Iron Age fort, lies on the outskirts of the town. Later, about AD 200, a large wheelhouse was constructed inside the broch, and it is believed that the site was occupied until the coming of the Vikings in the ninth century. Clickhimin, with its evidence of occupation over a span of 2,000 years, ranks among the most important prehistoric sites in Britain. An excursion of a very different kind from Lerwick takes one across the ferry to Bressay and thence across the sea strait to the Isle of Noss where the countless ledges in the Old Red Sandstone cliffs provide nesting places for vast numbers of sea birds. Noss became a bird sanctuary in 1955.

The axial road of Mainland, the A970, follows the east coast southward to Sumburgh. Three places of outstanding interest lie close to this route. A diversion to the shore at Sandwick gives access to the now deserted island of Mousa, where the finest broch of northern Britain stands near the shore. The tower of thinly layered sandstone is still standing to almost 15m (50ft) in height. Inside the walls of the broch, galleries and stairs lead to a walkway circling the top of the tower. A diversion from the A970 to the west coast by the B9122 brings one within sight of St Ninian's Isle, beautifully joined to Mainland by the sandy curving beaches of a tombolo. Here, between 1955 and 1958, the foundations of a medieval chapel were excavated to reveal the walls of an earlier, pre-Norse church, beneath the twelfth-century building. Within the area of the medieval nave, the archaeologists from Aberdeen University uncovered a collection of silver objects – the only known collection of plate of the Celtic church – which must have been hurriedly buried, perhaps under the threat of a Viking invasion at some time early in the ninth century. But the greatest of Shetland's prehistoric sites is Jarlshof on the sea-shore in the lee of Sumburgh Head. The name is of recent origin, having been given by Sir Walter Scott, in his novel *The Pirate*, to the laird's house, built in the sixteenth century, on top of this complex of prehistoric dwellings. A great storm of 1897 exposed the foundations of prehistoric buildings. Since then excavation has revealed seven major phases of occupation at Jarlshof – Bronze Age and Iron Age villages, a broch, a wheelhouse settlement, a Viking village, a medieval farmstead and the sixteenth-century laird's mansion that sparked Scott's imagination.

North from Lerwick the A970 and A968 lead by two vehicle ferries across Yell Sound and Bluemull Sound to Unst. Apart from the knowledge that one has reached the very limits of Britain, where the Arctic Circle lies only half as many miles away as London, the chief attraction of **Unst** is the Herma Ness Nature Reserve. A walk of about 2.5km (1½ miles) from the shore of Burra Firth, the only inlet in Shetland with some of the grandeur of a Norwegian fjord, brings one across a bare windy moorland within sight of the grey sea stacks of Muckle Flugga, with its thousands of guillemots, kittiwakes and gannets. But the most startling inhabitants of this gale-swept peninsula are the huge skuas that dive and swoop within inches of those who walk the beaten track to the end of the peninsula.

At Hillside, in north Mainland, where the A970 and A968 diverge, another 10km (6 miles) or so along the A970 and thence by the B9076 bring one to Sullom Voe, the nexus of Shetland's oil industry. Here oil is brought ashore by pipelines from the Ninian and Brent fields for loading into tankers. Figures of a thousand tankers per year at the oil jetties have been published, but for the casual visitor Sullom Voe and its huge storage tanks can appear strangely inactive and one can truly say that only here, in Lerwick and in the incessant clatter of helicopters at Sumburgh airport, has Britain's most important industrial development of the twentieth century made any impact on the landscape and coastline of Shetland.

Orkney

Scotland's islands seem to be countless; certainly no two people reach the same conclusion when enumerating the islands of the northern archipelagos. In their accounts of Orkney three different writers quote widely varying figures. One says that there are 90 islands and skerries; another claims that of the 70 islands one third are inhabited; and a third source believes that Orkney is composed of 67 islands of which 21 are inhabited. What is evident is that the shape and number of these islands are a transitory stage in the process of changing sea-levels which has gone on during the few thousand years since the waning of the Ice Age. If the present mean sea-level fell by only 36m (120ft) Orkney would be transformed into a single island. As in Shetland the rising sea-level of post glacial times has created an intricate pattern of deeply penetrating firths and out-reaching peninsulas. The islands of Orkney fall into four groups aligned from north-west to south-east. Sea channels – former river valleys – separate the island groups. Hoy, from the Norse meaning 'high island', lies westward of Mainland across that veritable inland sea, Scapa Flow. Mainland and its pendent islands, Burray and South Ronaldsay, form the core of Orkney and in their prosperous countryside and two towns – Kirkwall and Stromness –

house most of the archipelago's population. Adjacent to Mainland, but separated by Wide Firth and Eynhallow Sound with its foaming tide rip, are Rousay, Wyre and Shapinsay. Further out to the north-east, across Westray Firth and Stronsay Firth, lies a lonely group of islands scarcely disturbed by the changes of the twentieth century – Westray, Eday and Stronsay with remoter outliers in Papa Westray and North Ronaldsay.

For the motorist a comprehensive exploration of Orkney is perhaps more complicated than a journey to the main islands of Shetland. Getting to the islands is much easier and cheaper because a modern roll-on roll-off vehicle ferry plies daily – several times during the summer months – between Scrabster and Stromness. But once on Mainland the tourist will discover that the vehicle ferries that make it possible to drive from Sumburgh to the northern coast of Unst in Shetland provide no such service between the islands of Orkney. The motorist and his car are confined to Mainland and South Ronaldsay. Without a vehicle Hoy may be reached easily by the regular ferry from Stromness, but the northern islands and their archaeological riches can only be seen after an intricate juggling of ferry timetables and with an ample allowance of time. For instance, North Ronaldsay has one return service weekly from Kirkwall.

Hoy, for those who reach Orkney by the Scrabster – Stromness ferry, and that means almost everyone who visits the islands, presents some of the most exciting coastal features of the archipelago. But in most ways Hoy is the least representative of Orkney and it landscapes. Ward Hill, 477m (1,565ft), is the highest point in the subdued topography of these low fertile islands formed of rocks of Old Red Sandstone age. The hills of Hoy end abruptly in the line of towering red cliffs that form the whole of the island's western coast. At St John's Head the cliffs rise sheer from the sea to a height of 348m (1,140ft), one of the highest vertical sea cliffs in the British Isles. Beneath the cliff face of Western Hoy, the Old Man of Hoy – a stack 137m (450ft) in height – stands on a platform of volcanic rock which is awash at high tide. A fine view of the stack, a premier object in Britain's seascapes, may be obtained from the deck of the Stromness ferry as it steers towards the entrance of Hoy Sound.

Mainland has seen, on its western and eastern coasts, the growth of Orkney's only urban communities. Stromness, now the busy ferry port for the mainland, only emerged in the seventeenth century after Orkney became administratively part of Scotland. For more than two centuries, from 1670 to 1891, it was an important base of the Hudson Bay Company and in the heyday of the North Atlantic's whalers the Stromness fleet exploited the seas off Greenland and Labrador. The chief attraction of Stromness is the long, twisting street beside the harbour where each house, gable end to the street, faces the sea from its own quay.

Kirkwall, with a population of 6,000 and three times as big as Stromness, is the capital of Orkney. Unlike most towns in Scotland's islands, Kirkwall greets the visitor with a long and visible history. It was the capital from the ninth to the fifteenth century when Orkney, ruled by Viking earls, belonged to the political world of Scandinavia. At the heart of the town a cluster of great medieval buildings takes the mind back to this period in Scotland's history. The cathedral of St Magnus in glowing Eday Sandstone ranks among the finest and most complete medieval buildings in Scotland. Founded in 1137 by Earl Rognvald and dedicated to his kinsman Magnus, who had been murdered on Egilsay, this great Romanesque church was designed, it is believed, by the Durham school of masons. Like all great churches St Magnus's cathedral encompasses the work of several generations, and in the course of its building architectural fashions changed from the Romanesque through the Transitional to the Gothic. The oldest part of the building, at the crossing and part of the choir, was completed between 1137 and 1200. Beside the cathedral stands the Bishop's Palace, a sixteenth-century re-building of a twelfth-century hall. The Earl's Palace, a tree-shaded castellated ruin, lies across the road from the cathedral. It was built in the first years of the seventeenth century by Earl Patrick, Steward of Orkney

Skara Brae, Orkney. Because of its remarkable state of preservation, buried beneath sand dunes for more than 2,000 years, this is one of the most notable prehistoric sites in Europe

and Shetland, in the last decade before the island's administration was absorbed into that of Scotland. Not only has Kirkwall the buildings of a capital, but its shops, schools, hospital and nearby airport make it the major service centre of Orkney. There is a strong cultural life, cathedral concerts and art exhibitions from time to time, as well as a most attractive museum in Tankerness House, an eighteenth-century merchant's house with courtyard and garden that displays aspects of Orkney life over the past 4,000 years.

From either Stromness or Kirkwall good roads provide access to the main coastal features of Mainland. The A967 reaches to the north-western corner of the island. Much of this Atlantic-facing coast is composed of cliffs in the grey flagstones that lack the height and grandeur of western Hoy. Marwick Head, among the most accessible and impressive places of this cliff-line, falls vertically for 60m (200ft) to the sea. Here a grim stone tower on the cliff top commemorates the mysterious disappearance in these grey waters of HMS *Hampshire* in 1916 with Lord Kitchener, on a war-time mission to Russia, on board. The most important feature of the west coast of Mainland is Skara Brae, a Neolithic village on the very edge of the curving sandy beach of the Bay of Skail. It is reached by following a minor road, the B9056, which branches from the A967 some 10km (6 miles) north of Stromness. For archaeologists this is one of the most important sites of western Europe. The life of a whole village community of early farmers – now dated, by radio-carbon analysis of animal bones found there, to a period between 3100 BC and 2450 BC – has been preserved for more than 4,000 years beneath sand dunes. A great storm in the 1850s revealed the presence of one-room houses, with carefully built flagstone walls 2m (6½ft) in thickness, clustered together and joined by connecting passages. Since its discovery more than a hundred years ago Skara Brae has been excavated no less than six times. With the ever present sound of the sea, and provided that a tour bus has not just disgorged its cargo of passengers, Skara Brae under the clear light of an Orcadian summer sky is a place of haunting beauty.

The joining of the west and east coast roads through northern Mainland brings the traveller to a piece of Orkney's coastline that contains evidence of many aspects of the islands' history. Earl's Palace, an extensive and unexpected ruin in this quiet well-farmed countryside, was built by Lord Robert Stewart, an illegitimate son of King James V. He had obtained a grant of the earldom of Orkney and the office of sheriff from Mary Queen of Scots in 1564. He and his son, Earl Patrick – builder of the Earl's Palace in Kirkwall – were responsible for one of the darkest epochs of Orkney's history – a time only recalled now by these two great architectural landmarks. Beyond Earl's Palace a footpath leads above the shore to the Brough of Birsay, an island accessible at low tide across a cobbled causeway. Here, on a gentle slope that climbs to a cliff-bound Atlantic front, are the visible remains of more than 1,000 years of Dark Age and medieval history. The centrepiece of Birsay is a church, variously described as a minster and a cathedral, built in the middle of the eleventh century at the time of Earl Thorfinn the Mighty, who is on record in the Orkneyinga Saga as resident on Birsay after the year 1050. Beside Earl Thorfinn's church a bishop's palace was built in the early years of the twelfth century, a palace laid out with four halls around three sides of a square of which the church forms the fourth. On the hillside above the ecclesiastical enclosure are the foundations of a Norse settlement with the rectangular shapes of Viking long-houses. Beneath the church the remains of a much earlier place of worship have been discovered, suggesting that Birsay was the site of a Celtic monastery before the Norse invasions of the eighth century.

The east coast road through northern Mainland, the A966, skirts the low shoreline of Eynhallow Sound. Here is one relic of outstanding importance in the prehistory of Britain. The Broch of Gurness, an impressive ruined Iron Age tower from the Pictish centuries, is reached by an attractive coastal footpath that runs for almost a mile from the last place for parking cars. The confused appearance of Gurness broch results from the long use of the site and the different styles of architecture that have been employed there. Apart from the ruined stump of the Pictish broch, later structures were thrown up in its interior courtyard and a secondary settlement grew up around the outside of the tower. Later still, a courtyard house similar to that at Jarlshof in Shetland was built over the ruins of these outbuildings and more building, a long-house, belongs to Viking times. Gurness speaks of the long occupation, over many centuries and through different cultures, of favoured places in Orkney.

Southwards from Kirkwall two roads give access to southern Mainland and South Ronaldsay. The A960 skirts the boundary of the airport to reach Upper Sanday and the Deerness peninsula, whose slender link with Mainland is a narrow spit of shingle and sand, an 'ayre', that is now used as a causeway by the main road. On a 30m (100ft) high cliff at the north-eastern tip of Deerness is the site of an early Christian monastery established by Irish missionaries in the eighth century. Around the ruins of a chapel are the foundations of nineteen rectangular-shaped buildings. Deerness also has The Gloup, one of the fearsome chasms characteristic of the Old Red Sandstone coastlines, where the sea groans incessantly in the depths of a sea cave whose inner part opens to the sky.

South Ronaldsay is reached by the A961 across the Churchill Barrier, a causeway built during World War II to exclude entry into Scapa Flow through its eastern channels, after the sinking of HMS *Royal Oak* by a German submarine in October 1939. Today, as one drives across the causeways of the Churchill Barrier, which connects the islets of Lamb Holm, Glimps Holm and Burray, the rusty wrecks of boom ships, placed there before the completion of the causeway to block these channels, may still be seen. On Lamb Holm is the Italian Chapel, a Nissen hut converted into a place of worship in 1943 by Italian prisoners of war, who were kept here in Camp 60 to provide labour for the Churchill Barrier.

Orkney: a 'gloup'

From the A961 there are fine prospects westward across Scapa Flow to the mountainous outline of Hoy. On the island of Flotta an oil pipeline makes its landfall, and there is a tanker terminal and a servicing and supply base for the oil industry.

Access to Orkney's northern islands is not easy and they offer little scope to the motorist, but here is a world immensely rich in archaeological remains. **Eynhallow** – Holy Island – is a bird sanctuary and has a ruined twelfth-century church. Down by the western shore of **Rousay** is Midhowe Cairn, almost 25m (80ft) in length, of Neolithic date and containing twenty-four burial chambers. Close by is Midhowe Broch with massive outworks and a cluster of later domestic structures – a site whose architectural history closely follows that of the Broch of Gurness. **Wyre Island** has, in Cobbie Row's Castle, one of the oldest stone castles in Scotland, a square keep with massive outer defences that dates from the Viking period. On **Egilsay**, St Magnus's church with its round tower ranks among the most impressive medieval buildings of northern Britain. The outermost islands have their little visited places that are of great importance. **Westray** has two early churches as well as the grim sixteenth-century ruin of Noltland Castle. **Papa Westray**, the priests' island, the site of a Dark Age monastery, has two prehistoric houses on its west shore. Excavation and radio-carbon dating of refuse from the midden in 1973 showed them to date from between 3500 and 3100 BC. They are the oldest known standing stone houses in Western Europe and on this lonely Atlantic shore they make one pause to think of man's long acquaintance with this archipelago of Northern Britain.

The Outer Hebrides

This chain of islands, extending over 210km (130 miles), from Barra Head in the south to the Butt of Lewis, forms a natural bastion of Europe's Atlantic frontier. The wide passage of the Minch means that the islands lie 80km (50 miles) from the Scottish mainland; only if the traveller approaches by the car ferry that plies from Uig in north-west Skye can he reduce the sea passage to less than 50km (30 miles). Apart from a patch of younger sandstones that occupy the low ground about Stornoway, the islands are composed entirely of Lewisian gneiss or volcanic rocks – granites and gabbrodiorites – that have been intruded among these most ancient rocks. Although grey- and pale-pink-banded gneiss abounds everywhere in the landscape of the Outer Hebrides, an important feature of these rocks is a thrust plane – a very ancient line of earth movement – that extends along the whole of the eastern coastline. Earth movements have severely crushed the rocks resting on this thrust plane, and their nature contributes to the distinctive character of the scenery of the eastern coastlands of the islands. For instance, the cliff-girt shore of the Eye peninsula, to the east of Stornoway, is formed of crush gneisses; and in the south, in Barra, Kisimul Castle stands on an islet in

Castle Bay composed of the same flinty-crush rock.

The most vital events in the shaping of the coastlines of the Outer Hebrides have been the Ice Age and the 12,000 or so years that have elapsed since the glaciation of northern Britain. At the maximum of glaciation, mainland ice spread in a vast sheet towards the Atlantic, overrunning most of this long low gneissic ridge. But it has been contended that the ice front stagnated westward of the Hebrides, perhaps even short of St Kilda where it is believed that flora survived from warmer inter-glacial or pre-glacial times. Ice scoured and shaped the hard gneiss outcrops of the islands, shaping the rounded, steep-sided hummocks that characterise much of the eastern coastline. The westward-moving ice sheet also modified the shapes of the valleys, now drowned, that form the eastern sea lochs, Lochs Seaforth and Erisort among several others. On the shallow submerged bench that flanks the Atlantic coast, there were deposited boulder clays that have contributed in post-glacial times the material that now, along with vast quantities of comminuted shells, forms the beaches and sandy machairs of the western parts of the islands. Since the waning of the ice sheets, the shape of the islands has been determined by a rising sea-level, as water previously locked up in the masses of ice over the northern hemisphere returned to the oceans. With continuing submergence, one island – the gneissic ridge – has been split into five main islands and countless islets and skerries. The drowning of the Outer Hebrides is evident in the intricacies of their coastline, and in the patches of submerged forest and deposits of peat that are exposed in some sandy bays at the time of lowest spring tides.

Lewis and **Harris** are one island, but clearly separated as communities by a line of bare hills and lochan-bespattered moorland, an empty wilderness of deer forest and lonely places where peat is cut in the drier weeks of early summer. Before the local government reorganisation of 1974, the division between Lewis and Harris was emphasised by the county boundaries. Harris was part of Inverness-shire and Lewis formed the Atlantic outpost of Ross and Cromarty. Now they, with the rest of the Outer Hebrides, belong to the Western Isles Area.

Stornoway, with a population of 8,660, is the chief point of entry to Lewis, one that has been strengthened by the reorganisation in recent years of the ferry services. The once daily mail-boat to Mallaig – a ten-hour crossing – has been replaced by a more frequent roll-on roll-off ferry doing a three-hour journey to Ullapool. Stornoway, like other island towns, Tobermory and Kirkwall for example, comes as a pleasant surprise amid the grand and wild landscapes of the islands. Its shops and streets are busy and alive with people, except on the Sabbath, which Lewis keeps very strictly. The town was founded by James VI in the early years of the seventeenth century, but it only emerged as a port and urban centre in the closing years of the eighteenth century, with the expanding market for the Minch fisheries and the growth of the cattle trade with the mainland. Fishing – for herring, white fish prawns and lobster – is still important, and there is a modern deep-freezing plant and cold storage depot, but no longer can Stornoway boast a fleet of a thousand fishing boats, all under sail, as in the early years of this century. Lews Castle, whose policies and groves of rhododendron are another oddity in the austere landscapes of the Hebrides, was built in the 1850s by Sir James Matheson after he had purchased the whole of Lewis as a single estate. When Lewis was bought by Lord Leverhulme in the 1920s, the castle was presented to the town, and since 1953 it has housed the island's technical college, which is already well known for its school of navigation.

The east coast of Lewis and Harris, facing the Minch, is rocky, with deep inlets whose shapes have been modified by the passage of the mainland ice sheet across the Hebrides. Sand beaches are scarce; the best, Tràigh Mhor, a 3km (2 mile) stretch of sand nestling in the curve of Tolsta Head, is reached by following the B895 along the shore of Broad Bay from Stornoway to North Tolsta. On the way, one finds good sand beaches in the bays of the crofting townships at Coll and Grest.

Roads allow the motorist access to the north-west coast of Lewis. The A858 reaches the head of East Loch Roag at Garynahine. From there one may drive southwards to Uig and for a few miles further along a rough deteriorating single-track road to Brenish. From there one looks southward along the trackless mountainous coastline of west Harris across the mouth of Loch Resort to the island of Scarp and the grey mountainous cone of Strone Romul rising 300m (1,000ft) from the sea. To make the passage on foot along this rough coastline to the next road south at Husinish presents an immense challenge to the explorer of the remoter parts of the British coastline. Nevertheless the road to Uig and Brenish opens up much of great interest and attraction. The cliffs and bays of this section of the coast between Valtos and Mangersta make this the finest piece of the whole coastline of Lewis. On clear days, and there are many when clean polar air sweeps out of the north-west, the ragged spine of St Kilda raises itself westward, above the Atlantic horizon, at a distance of almost 80km (50 miles). Northward from Garynahine a good road takes the motorist through a succession of crofting townships – dull places, busy with the clatter of tweed-making when times are good – to the Butt of Lewis. This is also dull country where the peat moors of the interior reach close to the sea, but there are compensations in glimpses of fine sandy beaches ringed by cliffs, and two of the most impressive prehistoric sites in the Hebrides. Callanish, a stone circle of late Neolithic/Bronze Age date, rivals Stonehenge among the monuments of Britain's prehistory. But the ring of grey gneiss monoliths is not all; at the centre of the circle of standing stones lies a Neolithic burial cairn, and lines of standing stones reach out to the main points of the compass from the perimeter of the circle. Running north from the circle is a double line of stones, an avenue, which stretches over 83m (272ft). Callanish seems to have formed a vital nucleus in the settlement of the Hebrides some 4,000 years ago, for two other stone circles lie close by, visible from the first, and there are four others near the head of Loch Roag. Taking the A858 north from Callanish, a short distance along a minor road to the left stands Dun Carloway, a ruined broch whose galleried double wall still reaches a height of 9m (30ft).

South Harris is all but an island for the isthmus between the East and West Lochs Tarbert extends for only just under 1km (½ mile). At the head of the island-studded East Loch are the white-washed cottages of the little township of Tarbert, chief service centre and capital of Harris whose business has vastly increased with the coming of large vehicle ferries to the Scottish seas in the 1960s. It is now a key point in a triangular car-ferry route in the Minch based on Uig in Skye and Lochmaddy in North Uist.

The coastlines of South Harris illustrate beautifully the contrasts that belong to the coastal scenery of the whole of the Outer Hebrides. The south-east coast is rocky, visibly shaped by ice and the submergence of post-glacial times. On this deeply indented coastline there are thirty bays in the 20km or so (12 miles), as the crow flies, between Tarbert and Renish Point. Despite the hungry, barren soil-less character of this south-eastern coastline, the Bays district is one of the most populated parts of Harris – a population that on tiny patches of land at the head of an inlet may reach densities of 500 per .4km^2 (1 square mile). This desert of steeply sloping gneiss hillocks was settled in the middle years of the nineteenth century as people were cleared from more fertile land in the west of the peninsula. The settlers of the new clachans at Stockinish, Cluer, Geocrab and Beocravik lived from the prolific fisheries of the Minch and by the creation of soils from peat and seaweed amid the bare ribs of the gneiss for potato plantings. The north-west coast of South Harris is a succession of fine sandy beaches backed by grassy dunes and flower-scented machair. In the wide embayment between Toe Head and Luskentyre there are eight sandy bays. At Tràigh Luskentyre the beach stretches for 3km (2 miles). Toe Head is joined to mainland Harris by a long stretch of machair at sea-level. Beyond the neck of shingle, dune and machair-pasture the land rises to mountainous heights – Chaipaval is 366m (1,201ft) above the encircling sea. Given a day of high visibility this is one of the finest viewpoints in Scotland; the eye ranges from the blue-green island-splashed Sound of Harris to the distant Cuillins in Skye, across the Minch, and westward to the far rocky outline of St Kilda.

The main road into South Harris, the A859, leads from Tarbert by the western beaches to Leverburgh and Rodel. Leverburgh, on the deep indentation of Loch Obbe and Loch Steiseval, was planned to develop into a major British fishing port after the purchase of Lewis and Harris by Lord Leverhulme in 1923. Jetties, kippering sheds and a fleet of trawlers were established there, but the death of Lord Leverhulme in 1925 and the only lukewarm acceptance by the islanders of the industrialised modes of twentieth-century fishing spelt the end of the experiment. Beyond Leverburgh the traveller reaches Rodel where the late-medieval church dating from about 1500 provides a pleasant surprise in islands notably devoid of any architectural interest. Inside is the sixteenth-century tomb of the 7th Chief of the MacLeods; dating from 1528 it ranks alongside Callanish as one of man's finest works in the Outer Hebrides.

The Sound of Harris separates the biggest island of the Outer Hebrides, Lewis and Harris, from the Uists and Benbecula. The Sound, with its indiscriminate scattering of islands, has no great depth. Much is less than ten fathoms deep, and when the summer sun shines out of an indescribably blue Hebridean sky the sea above its shallow sandbanks glistens in translucent colours of green and turquoise. Berneray, the only inhabited island in the Sound of Harris, has a population of little more than a hundred scattered through three villages on the bays of its eastern coast. The west coast has one long sandy strand, as fine a beach as one will find anywhere in the Hebrides. Pabbay too, once known as the granary of Harris and now deserted, has a 6km (4 mile) long beach of white sand on its western coast.

A contrast between the east and west coastlines, a characteristic of the outer isles, is even stronger in the Uists than in Lewis and Harris. The eastern shore of **North Uist** and **Benbecula** is a labyrinth of islands, skerries and sea channels. Apart from the ferry port of Lochmaddy, with a population of less than 500, the greater part of this coast lacks any kind of settlement, and unless one travels by boat is largely inaccessible. The main road, the A865, connecting North Uist, Benbecula and South Uist, runs at no great distance from the west coast and its 80km (50 mile) long rim of rich machair, where all the townships are concentrated.

Vast sand-flats are the dominant feature of the north coast of North Uist. On Vallay Strand at low tide the sea runs out for about 3km (2 miles). A scheme for the reclamation of 3,700ha (1,500 acres) of Vallay sands for horticulture was rejected in 1972. Only the north-west corner of North Uist displays a cliffed rocky coast, with geos and natural arches between Griminish Point and Balranald. Griminish Point, approached by the track to Scalpaig Farm, is cut through by a natural arch whose tunnel runs for 140m (150yd) beneath the headland. South from Griminish Point we find a succession of semicircular sandy bays locked between rocky outcrops. Here are the crofting townships of Tigharry, Hougharry and Paible, set in one of the most attractive environments to be found among Scotland's islands – a blue-green sea, white sand beaches and the summer-scented machair.

Benbecula, the stepping-stone between the Uists, formerly linked by treacherous routes across the tidal sands of the North and South Fords, is now firmly joined by the causeways carrying the A865 between the islands. The airfield on the north-western flats at Bailivanich provides a daily service to Glasgow and Stornoway. Sand beaches and machair prevail all along the west coast of the island, and Culla Bay is one of the best of the former.

The topographical division between west and east becomes even more pronounced in **South Uist**. Soggy desolate moorland rises in Beinn Mhór to a height of more than 600m (2,000ft) above the sea; the still, dark surfaces of sea lochs reach far inland in Loch Skiport and Loch Eynort. The western shore of South Uist is completely different, with its vast beaches of shell sand, and a 30km (20 mile) strip of flower-rich machair broken by countless pools and freshwater lochs carpeted with water lilies and abundant in wild life. To reach this unique landscape on the edge of the Atlantic one must leave the

A865 by any of the two dozen tracks leading to the townships in the machair. Then a walk across springy turf and a mountainous ridge of dunes will bring one to the exposed foreshore where the Atlantic pounds incessantly. Points of interest in South Uist are the rocket range by Loch Bee, the birthplace of Flora Macdonald at Milton marked by a cairn on a ruined wall where a cottage once stood, and the Roman Catholic church at Bornish – a modern building as gaunt in its bare gneiss interior walls as much of the Hebridean landscape.

Lochboisdale, at the southern end of South Uist, is at the centre of the most populous part of the island. It is the terminus of a Caledonian MacBrayne vehicle ferry that sails from Oban to call at Castlebay in Barra. Passenger ferry services to Eriskay and Barra, landing at Eoligarry on Barra's northern peninsula, sail from Ludag and are infrequent.

Barra is the chief focus of tourism in the southern islands of the Outer Hebrides, largely because of its links with the mainland. A daily air service operates to the natural air-strip on the sand beach of Tràigh Mhor, and a vehicle ferry makes the long crossing, between 5 and 6 hours, four times a week from Oban. Tourism in Barra has been encouraged by the building by the Highlands and Islands Development Board of a luxury hotel at Tangusdale, on the west coast of the island where there are five delectable beaches. The population of Barra, a little more than 1,000, is largely concentrated around Castlebay, a busy port and service centre whose only historic object is Kisimul Castle, a square keep with blank windowless outer walls. It was raised in the fifteenth century and restored as a residence between 1938 and 1959. Castlebay reached its peak as a port at the end of the nineteenth century when, for a brief period, the herring fisheries brought it prosperity. Its population climbed towards 3,000 and there were a score of fish-curing stations scattered around the harbour – all now disused and ruined. Today the island lives from its crofts, lobster fishing, tourists and the employment that its young people have found in the merchant navy.

Of the twenty islands that make up the southern end of the Outer Hebrides only two, Barra and Vatersay, remain inhabited – and the future of Vatersay is much in doubt. South of Barra these lonely islands include some of the finest seascapes in Britain. Mingulay, only 1½km (1 mile) by 3km (2 miles) in extent, had a population of 140 at the beginning of this century. One may still see on the east coast of the island the township deserted in 1908, when the people of Mingulay squatted on the land owned by Lady Gordon Cathcart in the island of Vatersay, which forms the western flank of Castle Bay. Mingulay is now the domain of guillemots, kittiwakes and puffins, which populate the magnificent 250m (800ft) high sea cliffs and stacks of the south-west coast.

Tourism thrives on legend and history's romantic moments. With these the southern Hebrides are richly endowed. In 1745 the Young Pretender first set foot in Scotland at Coilleag a Phrionnsa, the Prince's Strand, in Eriskay, and in February 1941 another historic event gave birth to a tale of legendary quality when a cargo steamer, *The Politician*, ran aground with 20,000 cases of whisky aboard.

The Inner Hebrides

The island of Skye and its close neighbours, the Small Isles, form the northern members of the Inner Hebrides. The low islands of Tiree and Coll lie out in the Sea of the Hebrides beyond the most westerly part of Scotland's mainland, the Point of Ardnamurchan. Both in their scenery and economy, Coll and Tiree belong to the Outer Hebrides rather than to their mountainous neighbours of the inner islands. Geologically the Inner Hebrides form one of the most complex elements of the British landscape. Tiree and Coll, like the Outer Hebrides, are formed of the Lewisian Gneiss – one of the world's oldest rocks. The empty wastelands of northern Raasay and South Rona, islands lying off the eastern shores of Skye, have also been shaped out of the ancient Lewisian rocks, but close by, across the narrow Sound of Raasay, the basalt hills of Skye, are built of rocks that were poured on to the earth's crust in a long phase of volcanic activity along the margins of western Britain in

Tertiary times, some 62 million years ago according to the latest isotopic measurements. Even younger are the rocks that make up the Black Cuillins in western Skye. The intrusion of the plutonic complex that now forms the Black Cuillins took place 50 million years ago. Since then a long period of erosion and the work of the Ice Age has unroofed this volcano to its very depths.

Skye is an island of peninsulas and each peninsula displays an individual topographical personality. There are three points of approach from the mainland unless the traveller chooses to use the recently established air service from Glasgow to the airstrip at Broadford. The largest and most frequent ferries operate a service for almost eighteen hours of each day between Kyle of Lochalsh and Kyleakin. A more restricted link runs through the summer months by a small six-vehicle ferry at Kylerhea, a crossing that may be interrupted at some states of the tide. Caledonian MacBrayne provide a commodious vehicle ferry during the summer months between Mallaig and Armadale in the Sleat peninsula of South Skye, but through the winter only a skeleton service continues for passengers. For the motorist the greater expense of the longer crossing of the Sound of Sleat from Mallaig is perhaps compensated by the many miles of fine scenery from Fort William along the A830, the Road to the Isles.

The east coast of Skye is easily accessible along a good main road, the A850. Between Kyleakin and Broadford the A850 provides excellent prospects of the mountainous heart of Skye with the islands of Scalpay – mostly wet moorland and Torridonian Sandstone – and Raasay off the eastern shoreline. Broadford, Skye's second service centre after Portree, crouches beneath the granite slopes of Beinn na Caillich, the sentinel mountain of the Red Hills. Broadford is a disorderly string of townships, Breakish, Skulamus, Harrapool and Broadford itself – an untidy succession of garages, shops and bed-and-breakfast accommodation. It also has banking facilities, a hospital, a junior secondary school and, since the completion of an airstrip in 1972, a daily service to Glasgow.

For much of the 40km (25 miles) between Broadford and Portree the road hugs the coastline closely, with some fine views into the Cuillins where it follows the gloomy shores of Loch Ainort and Loch Sligachan. Sand beaches are largely lacking along Skye's eastern coast, but there are some tourist attractions along this busy road – a marina and pony-trekking facilities at Strollamus, a cottage museum at Luib that recalls the days of the black houses in the Hebrides and, at Sligachan, an hotel and a much-used camp site that gives easy access to some of the finest mountaineering in Britain. Sconser, at the mouth of Loch Sligachan, is the ferry terminal for Raasay – a journey of twenty minutes operating thrice daily on weekdays by a vehicle ferry with accommodation for half a dozen cars. An improved single-track road straggles along half the length of Raasay to end at Brochel with its dangerously crumbling ruin of a medieval castle perched atop a relict sea stack on a raised beach of the island's deserted eastern coast.

Portree, the administrative centre of Skye, has a population of 1,500. In the early years of the nineteenth century, the Macdonalds, owners of the land here, laid out a town on the bluff above the harbour and its street names recall their family history. Portree provides essential services for the whole of Skye and Raasay. The harbour, physically one of the most impressive in the Hebrides, ceased to have a regular passenger service with the mainland in 1975. It has a small oil depot.

Trotternish is the most frequented of Skye's peninsulas because good roads allow a circuit of its eastern and western coasts. For much of its course along the eastern shore above the Sound of Raasay the A855 runs high above the cliffs of Jurassic limestones, clays and sandstones, crowned in the spine of high hills that forms the backbone of the peninsula by thick outpourings of Tertiary lavas. The Storr Lochs – Loch Leathan and Loch Fada – are the site of a hydro-electric power station opened in 1952. The power house stands on the beach at the exit to the gorge which drains Loch Leathan. The Kilt Rock is the main tourist attraction of the road between Portree and Staffin. There is a parking place a short distance from the edge

The Cuillin Hills, Skye, seen across the Sound of Raasay

of this 120m (400ft) vertical sea cliff, so called because the black columns of an olivine-dolerite sill resemble the folds of a kilt. On the north-western tip of Trotternish the ruins of Duntulm – a fifteenth-century castle and ancient seat of the MacDonalds of the Isles – look across the Minch to the hills of Harris. Uig Bay, a deep inlet of Loch Snizort hemmed in by basalt cliffs, was awakened to a much busier life when a roll-on roll-off car ferry to the Outer Hebrides was based here in 1964.

Westward Skye reaches into the Minch in the peninsulas of Duirinish and Vaternish. Apart from Dunvegan, reached by the A863, much of this fine coastline is inaccessible to all but the most determined tourist who is prepared to take to long, arduous, little-used footpaths. Dunvegan Castle, the stronghold of the MacLeods and now the main object of tourism, has been continuously occupied for 700 years. The house, as we see it today, is largely the result of restoration and rebuilding in the nineteenth century. A small settlement with hotels and bed-and-breakfast accommodation has grown up at the approach to the castle.

The drive along the A863 between Sligachan and Dunvegan presents some of the finest views of mountains, sea lochs and coastal cliffs in the whole of the Hebrides. From the head of Loch Harport the motorist may follow the B8009 and its branch roads to Talisker Bay, Loch Eynhort and Glen Brittle on the largely inaccessible west coast of Skye. It is a forbidding uninhabited coastline where waterfalls tumble over precipitous basalt cliffs and there is not even a coastal footpath. The most extensive settlement in this region of Skye consists of a string of townships along the western shore of Loch Harport.

The coastline of south-west Skye is reached by two roads that branch from Broadford. The A881 ends at Elgol, at the mouth of Loch Scavaig. En route the prospects of mountain, sea and the Small Isles are superb. Across Loch Slapin one sees in full profile the rocky mass of Blà Bheinn – visually the finest mountain in the whole of Britain. Elgol, served by a post-bus from Broadford, has its own classic postcard view of the Cuillins across Loch Scavaig. This is the stepping off point for Loch Coruisk, an ice-carved basin in the heart of the Cuillins that is gloomy on the brightest of summer days because of its overwhelming ring of rock. The easiest way to reach Loch Coruisk is by the motor-boat excursions that run from Elgol in the summer season, but one can go by foot, though it is not an easy route.

From Broadford the A851, the road to the Armadale–Mallaig ferry, serves Skye's south-eastern peninsula, Sleat. The eastern shore, boulder-strewn and lacking sand beaches, gives fine views across the Sound of Sleat to Loch Hourn and Loch Nevis and a back-cloth of some of the greatest mountains in the north-west Highlands. The west coast, particularly from Tarskavaig and Ord, has a more distant comprehensive prospect of the Cuillins across a wide belt of sea and the Strathaird peninsula. Among the places of Sleat's east coast, reached by the A851, is Isle Ornsay – once a flourishing port. Knock Castle is a crumbling sixteenth-century ruin close by the road, seat of the MacDonald clan that was abandoned for Armadale Castle, a pseudo-gothic redesigning of Armadale House by James Gillespie Graham in 1815. Since 1950 it has fallen into decay. Funds raised by MacDonalds in distant parts of the world have led to the creation of the MacDonald Centre, a display of clan history in the oldest part of the castle.

The Small Isles, Canna, Sanday, Rhum, Eigg and Muck form a notable cluster in the Sea of the Hebrides off south-west Skye. They are reached by a mail boat from Mallaig, and in the summer months Caledonian MacBrayne offer an excursion fare for the round trip to the islands.

Rhum, the largest of the Small Isles, has been described as 'the most mountainous island in Britain'. The superlatives continue for it is 'the wettest, most barren and most deserted' of the islands that make up this group in the Inner Hebrides. The mountainous core of Rhum consists of the deep roots of a volcano that was active, like the Cuillin volcanic focus in Skye, in Tertiary times. The second main constituent of the landscape of Rhum is the immensely older Torridonian Sandstone that forms the greater part of the north of the island. During the last million and a half years of geological time ice has played an important part in the shaping of Rhum and its coastline. At times the island was largely overrun by massive ice-sheets from the mainland; at others its mountains were the centre of a local glaciation. Ice was probably responsible for considerable deepening in the constricted channels between the islands of the Inner Hebrides.

Rhum has gained notoriety because of the wilderness created there by the Clearances, the first of which took place in 1826 and 1827 after a Dr Lachlan Maclean of Coll had obtained the lease of the island as a sheep-walk. In 1888 the island was sold to a rich industrialist, John Bullough, who converted the sheep pastures to deer forest. Under John Bullough and his son George an incongruous red sandstone mansion, Kinloch Castle, was built on Loch Scresort. Since 1957 Rhum has belong to the Nature Conservancy.

Canna and **Sanday** are virtually one island, joined together at low tide – and the connection has been made good for all times by a footbridge. Both islands are made up of lava flows of Tertiary age which are revealed to perfection in the cliffs of northern Canna composed of a thick layer of volcanic agglomerates, beds of volcanic ash and sheets of dolerite that present a columnar structure in the cliff-face. Elsewhere the Tertiary basalts form extensive platforms along the coast of Canna with reefs barely awash and upstanding dark needles of more resistant rock. Canna, through the good and sympathetic management of its landlord in the twentieth century, has escaped the extinction of its life and economy that has been the fate of so many parts of northern Britain.

Eigg and **Muck** Even among the group of islands with the collective name of the Small Isles, Eigg and Muck are indeed small. Eigg covers 4.5km^2 (12sq miles) and rises in the spectacular profile of An Sgurr to a height of more than 400m (1,300ft) above the sea. Muck, a low island, covers only 1km^2 (2½sq miles). Eigg is composed of two basalt plateaux in which the lava flows rise from a platform of Jurassic limestones and shales. The mixing of volcanic rocks and lime-

Wreck north of Port Ascaig, Sound of Islay

stones, especially in the big landslips that characterise the island, has produced some of the richest soils in the Hebrides.

Both Eigg and Muck have evidence of Dark Age and prehistoric settlement. The most important relic of those long lost centuries is the Iron Age fort at Rubha na Crannaig, the headland at the entrance to Kildonan's bay. Over the past century Eigg has had many owners. Most notable among them was Sir Walter Runciman and his sons who owned the estate from 1925 until 1966. In the 1930s, cottages and farms were modernised, tractors introduced and large-scale forestry began. The improvements have continued under the island's most recent owner.

The most distinctive feature of the physical landscape of Muck is the swarm of dykes, intruded igneous rocks of resistant olivine-gabbro, that now stand up as dark seaweed-covered walls on the foreshore, etched out by the action of the sea. The dykes have a general trend from north-west to south-east and occur in such abundance as to give a peculiar fretted appearance to the coastline and its off-shore reefs. Muck enjoyed a brief period of prosperity at the turn of the eighteenth century when the kelp industry rose to unequalled heights.

Tiree lies remote from the mountainous large islands, Rhum, Mull and Skye, that have been built around the Tertiary volcanic centres. The foundations of the island's geology are completely foreign to most of the rocks of the Inner Hebrides. Tiree is composed entirely of Lewisian Gneiss, the oldest material in the fabric of Britain. Much of the island lies below the 50ft (15m) contour. Tiree's individuality is also expressed in its climate. Far removed from the mainland mountains and lying low on the sea, the island enjoys a much reduced rainfall and far higher sunshine figures than its scenically more spectacular neighbours.

Tiree enjoys an historic reputation as a fertile island. Two thousand years ago, in the Iron Age, Tiree was a well-populated island the evidence for which may be seen in the remains of earthworks, duns and brochs, sited on rocky promontories overlooking the sea. There are also several church sites and monasteries of the early Christian centuries. Kilkenneth was the site of a monastery of the Celtic church among the extensive belt of dunes that occupies the whole of Tiree's western coastline.

Today Tiree's population numbers about 1,000. A Caledonian MacBrayne vehicle-carrying ferry provides a link with the mainland at Oban on three days a week. Loganair run a regular service to Glasgow. For the tourist the chief attraction of Tiree lies in the extensive sand beaches that fringe practically the whole coastline, but one should remember that the high sunshine figures belong particularly to the early summer and that Tiree is known also for its frequency of gales. Scarinish, the ferry port, the island's only township, has hotel and bed-and-breakfast accommodation.

Coll, close neighbour to Tiree, closely resembles that island except that its present population amounts to little more than a tenth of its richer neighbour. Both islands are about the same size, 20km (12 miles) in length and 5km (3 miles) in breadth. They share the same mild, remarkably sunny, extremely windy oceanic climate. Coll too is a low lying island shaped out of the Lewisian Gneiss, but here this hungry profitless rock is exposed over more than three-quarters of the island's surface. Tracts of blown sand and machair play a minor role in the scenery of Coll when compared with its more populated neighbour. The greatest extent of blown sand occupies the south-western tip of the island between Feall Bay and Crossapol Bay. Lesser tracts of sand dunes and, in their lee, machair occur at places along the north-west facing coastline – at Hogh Bay, where an airstrip has been constructed across the level machair, and at Cliad Bay and inland from Bàgh an Traillеich. The eastern coast, a rock-bound shore of grey gneiss, lacks the lime-rich machair which would have encouraged settlement.

For the tourist Coll has one attraction – Breachacha Castle. It is one of the four intact and inhabited castles of the Hebrides and a splendid example of medieval military architecture.

Coll suffered severe depopulation in the Clearances of the nineteenth century. Today most of the population is concentrated around Arinagour, the ferry port on the Oban–Tiree passage.

Mull Even more than in Skye, past igneous activity, involving active volcanoes outpouring vast spreads of lava, has had a profound effect on the landscape of Mull. The highest mountain, Ben More, 966m (3,170ft), is built up of a succession of lava flows which in parts of the island are estimated to be more than 2,000m (650ft) thick. In the south-east corner, where the collapsed remains (*caldera*) of the vent of the volcano are still discernible, there are several peaks rising to over 750m (2,500ft) so giving this southern part a very mountainous appearance. In contrast the north and west is more plateau-like and at a lower elevation with a succession of lava flows giving the countryside a stepped appearance. The final element of the landscape of Mull is provided by the pink granite and schists of the western end of the long, low peninsula of the Ross of Mull.

Most visitors to Mull arrive at Craignure on the car ferry from Oban though there is an alternative entry by the Lochaline–Fishnish ferry. Many parts of the island are served by reasonable roads though, particularly in the Ross of Mull and in the Ardmeanach Peninsula, the more exciting stretches of coastline have to be approached on foot, often entailing walks across difficult terrain. On a short visit a car is essential to make a complete circuit of the island. Starting at Craignure with its inn and cottages overlooking the Sound of Mull the road leads along the coast to Salen, a nineteenth-century planned village. From Salen the road still hugs the shore of the Sound of Mull but now across wooded country formed of lava beds, with numerous waterfalls tumbling over the shelf edge into the sea. Tobermory, the 'capital' of the island, has one of the best and most sheltered harbours. With its promenade of brightly coloured cottages, guest houses and hotels arranged in a gentle curve around the harbour, it is the major tourist centre of the whole island.

The north coast of Mull facing the Ardnamurchan Peninsula across Loch Sunart is composed entirely of lava cliffs with extensive conifer plantations running down to the sea at Ardmore Bay. The only real access point is near Glengorm Castle which is reached by a minor road. For the main circuit of Mull it is necessary to follow the B8073 road to Dervaig at the head of Loch à Chumhainn, often looked upon as the most beautiful village of the whole island. Calgary, the next settlement, lies facing a fine west-coast bay. South of Calgary the road strikes southwards across the shoulder of the peninsula and then runs for several kilometres close to the northern shore of Loch Tuath. This part of the island was largely depopulated in the last century when two hundred people in the villages of Crackaig and Clac Gugairidh were evicted. Offshore the islands of Gometra, Ulva and Little Colonsay, with their distinctive stepped outlines formed of successive lava flows, suffered a similar depopulation.

After rounding Loch na Keal, the road past the Gribun comes closest to some of the wildest coastal scenery of Mull. Offshore lies Inch Kenneth. Although its chapel is now in ruins there are still sculptured stones and Celtic crosses which date back to the period when the island was a place of burial of the Lords of the Isles and a centre of pilgrimage. As the road from Gribun now turns inland it is necessary to explore the wild coast forming the head of the Ardmeanach Peninsula on foot and this only with difficulty. A short distance to the south lies Mackinnon's Cave, 200m (650ft) deep with stalactites in its inner recesses. Progress further south can be painfully slow but the reward at Rubha na h-Uamha, 8km (5 miles) from Gribun, is the cast of a fossil tree set in the columnar basalt of the cliff face and engulfed by molten lava perhaps 50 million years ago.

The longest of the island's peninsulas, the Ross of Mull, can be crossed by following the road which runs along the low shore of Loch Scridain and then on through Bunessan to Fionnphort, the ferry crossing point for Iona. It is the south, less accessible coastline of the Ross of Mull peninsula which is more varied and attractive but unfortunately it can only be approached down two minor roads. In the extreme east there is a route to Carsaig Bay with its substantial house set in wooded grounds. From the abandoned stone quarries here it is a 6km (4 mile) walk to Malcolm Point to view the famous Carsaig Arches formed as columnar basalt cliffs have been pierced by the sea at some time in the past. East from Carsaig the coastline is seldom visited though it does offer rewarding views of basalt cliffs with numerous caves. Beyond Loch Buie the gentle curve of the coastline as far as the entrance to the Sound of Mull is believed to coincide with a geological boundary as the lavas of the cliffs give way to Mesozoic rocks lying on the bed of the Firth of Lorn. On the projecting promontory at the northern end of Duart Bay stands the thirteenth-century Duart Castle.

Iona Though the island is quite small, measuring only 5km by 3km (3 miles by 2 miles), it has an importance out of all proportion to its size. Scenically it is not very different from many other islands of the Inner Hebrides, with a low rugged coastline carved out of gneiss with flagstones near its northern end. For the thousands who make the short crossing in an open boat across the narrow Sound of Iona from Fionnphort or make a brief stop on a sea trip around the Island of Mull it is the abbey site and its antiquities which are the attraction. The religious association began after St Columba landed in AD 563 and founded a monastery from which he could convert the mainland Picts. What we see today is the most recent of several restorations, carried out in the present century.

Staffa Unlike Iona, the tiny island of Staffa is geologically part of Mull for it is entirely composed of lava which cooled slowly to give hexagonal tension cracks that form the prominent columns seen in cliff sections. A succession of caves penetrate the cliff wall with names like Goat Cave, Clamshell Cave and Boat Cave but the most renowned is Fingal's Cave. It was Sir Joseph Banks, the naturalist and President of the Royal Society, who first visited it in 1779 and soon a whole succession of eminent people came to this isolated spot off the coast of Mull. The uniqueness of Staffa still attracts and fascinates, though most of today's visitors have to be satisfied with a view from the boat making the circuit of Mull from Oban in the summer months.

The Southern Hebrides

Islay Though relatively small, Islay has a surprisingly long coastline, largely because of two major indentations, Loch Gruinart in the north and Loch Indaal in the south. At periods during the Ice Age the heads of the two lochs were joined, thus splitting Islay into two separate halves. The presence of the lochs and some large bays has meant that the island is made up of a number of peninsulas, each of which has its own rock type and different coastal scenery. In the south west the Rinns of Islay are formed of rocks of Pre-Cambrian age with tough, uncompromising gneiss in the south and almost equally resistant grits in the north. The most southerly of the peninsulas, The Oa, is made up of an assemblage of different rock types ranging from quartzites which form the spectacular cliff scenery at the Mull of Oa while the centre consists of softer slates and phyllites giving somewhat tame inland scenery. Quartzite is also the dominant rock type in the northern part of Islay where, with some conglomerates, it forms the rugged cliff line bordering on the Sound of Islay. In the south-east corner from Port Ellen to Claggain Bay the most diverse scenery occurs and led John Ramsay to build his Kildalton 'Castle' here.

After passing through the wooded Kildalton Estate the road turns inland until at Tallant there is a lane leading to Kildalton Chapel, with the famous Celtic cross carved about AD 800 from local stone and in a remarkable state of preservation. Though not on the coast the Celtic associations of the chapel are very much related to the sea. North of Claggain Bay the road ends so that further exploration of the rugged coastline to the north must be on foot. Access by car to this lonely coastline overlooking the Sound of Islay is only possible at Port Askaig, the crossing point for Jura and the port of call for the MacBrayne boat from the mainland twice a week.

A short walk over the cliff top from the jetty at Port Askaig leads to one of Islay's distilleries, the recently rebuilt Caol Ila, and there is another 4km (6 miles) further north at Bunnahabhainn. The minor road which leads to Bunnahabhainn distillery gives excellent views across the Sound of Islay to the raised beaches which fringe most of the south and west coasts of the neighbouring island of Jura. Dominating the whole coastal setting are the grey-topped Paps of Jura, a succession of quartzite, rounded peaks which rise much higher than any of the Islay hills.

Further west and best approached from Bridgend is the major inlet of Loch Gruinart, but it is very shallow and therefore of little commercial value. The most striking of the coastal scenery of the north-west coast occurs close to Sanaigmore, reached by the B8018, and this whole stretch of coastline as far south as Saligo Bay is worth exploring on foot. The remainder of the west coast of the Rinns of Islay consists of intricate cliffs with geos and natural arches which in turn give way to wide sandy bays. There is very little habitation on the coast, though at Kilchoman and Kilchiaran the church and chapel suggest an early Celtic foundation. Only in the extreme south at Portnahaven, with its colour-washed cottages set around an inlet in the lee of Orsay Island is there any concentration of settlement.

At the head of Loch Indaal the coastal road crosses a fine raised beach backed by a degraded cliff line cut in soft glacial deposits. Islay House lies hidden in the trees at the eastern end. It was from here that the Campbell family in 1768 founded the first of Islay's planned villages, Bowmore. South of Bowmore the main road runs some distance from the coast but there is access to the fine sandy shore of Laggan Bay at a number of places where tracks lead through the extensive dune belt. Islay airport uses some of the flatter land behind the dune belt while at the southern end the Machrie golf course takes full advantage of the natural dune setting. From the southern end of the bay there is marked through-valley running across the neck of the Oa Peninsula which came into being as a glacial overflow channel during the Ice Age. Apart from one road, much of the coastline of the peninsula is difficult to approach and the walk often means crossing ill-drained peat hags or boggy valleys. The monument at the Mull of Oa, dedicated to those lost when SS *Otranto* was sunk in 1917, forms a prominent land-mark. The circuit of the island is completed at Port Ellen, yet another of the new villages which the Campbell family created in the 1820s.

(See M. Storrie, *Islay: Biography of an Island*, 1982.)

Jura At the present time the neighbouring island of Jura is closely linked with Islay, for its only contact with the Scottish mainland is by using the Islay ferry either from Port Askaig or Port Ellen. This puts Jura at a great economic disadvantage compared with other offshore islands and could well lead to a further drop in the population, which now numbers just over 200. For an island which is 45km (28 miles) long and 13km (8 miles) broad at its widest point, the extremely low population means that vast areas are completely uninhabited. It is only the south eastern coastal fringe, running from the ferry at Feolin to Inverlussa and joined by the only road in the island, which offers any real possibilities for settlement. Shales and phyllites with occasional bands of epidiorite, give rise to low-lying land with some pastoral farming while along the coast the shelter afforded by the string of offshore epidiorite islands has led to a small inshore fishing industry. Much of the island, with its quartzite backbone forming the famous Paps of Jura, is barren and inhospitable and largely given over to deer forests.

Exploration of the coast is made difficult because so much of the island is trackless waste, especially the boggy interior. It is for this reason that the raised beaches of the west coast, undoubtedly the finest in Scotland, are virtually unknown. Those in the south are best approached by taking the coastal path from Feolin ferry which leads past Inver cottage. The best raised beaches occur north of Loch Tarbert, which runs in from the west to almost completely sever the island. Many occur in distinct embayments backed by a cliff. Rising out of the raised beach are numerous rocky columns of former sea stacks while the old cliff line behind has many caves, now fossilised as part of the raised beach complexes.

The north coast of the island is just as isolated, for once the metalled road has ended just beyond Inverlussa there is only a track leading towards Kinuachdrach harbour. The difficult journey is worthwhile on two counts. Bagh Gleam nam Muc is a large cave 60m (200ft) deep, and it overlooks the Gulf of Corryvreckan with its spectacular whirlpool, seen at its best when a westerly wind opposes a spring flood tide running through the narrow strait.

Colonsay and Oronsay

Lying about 12km (7 miles) west of Jura is the more compact and completely different island of Colonsay and its near neighbour, Oronsay, to which it is joined at low water. Just over a hundred people now live on Colonsay and perhaps it is this feeling of emptiness which contributes to what Professor Steers claims to be the most interesting island, from a coastal standpoint, along the west coast of Scotland. Most of the island consists of a varied sequence of rocks belonging to the Torridonian formation including mudstones, grits, flags and conglomerates, each of which makes its mark on the varied coastal setting. While the east coast is rugged and uninhabited save for the few cottages at Scalasaig, the ferry port with connections to Oban, the west coast is more deeply embayed and has some fine bay-head beaches. The biggest is Kiloran Bay where the sea has etched out the softer strata in the lap of a downfold. Behind lies a fine strip of machair while further to the west is the highest raised beach, 40m (130ft), at Uragaig, probably of pre-glacial age. There are also lower beaches and, as on Jura, many are formed of great banks of pebbles. When sea level was at its highest Colonsay must have been split up into three parts by sea straits now represented by the valleys of Loch Fada and Abhainn a Ghlinne. To the north of Loch Fada, spectacular cliff scenery occurs below Beinn Bhrene.

Oronsay, a much smaller island lying to the south and approached across the Strand at low water, is formed almost entirely of Torridonian mudstones which give rise to much softer scenery. The chief glory of the island is the ruined Augustinian priory dating from 1380. Close by is a collection of slab-shaped tombstones with intricate carving.

Scotland: A Select Bibliography

The following titles contain general works from which further information may be gleaned on most parts of Scotland's coastline, but a number of references are to research papers and more detailed works on places and themes that are only lightly touched on in this gazetteer.

Caird, J. B., 'The Outer Hebrides', in Steers, J. A. (ed), *Field Studies in the British Isles* (Nelson, 1964)

Childe, V. G., *Scotland before the Scots* (Methuen, 1946)

—— *Ancient dwellings at Skara Brae, Orkney* (HMSO, 1950)

Craig, G. Y. (ed), *The Geology of Scotland* (Oliver & Boyd, 1965)

Crofts, R., and Mather, A., *The Beaches of Wester Ross* (Department of Geography, Aberdeen University, 1972)

Darling, F. F. (ed), *West Highland Survey* (Oxford University Press, 1955)

Darling, F. F., and Boyd, J. M., *The Highlands and Islands* (Fontana, 1969)

Donnachie, I., *The Industrial Archaeology of Galloway* (David & Charles, 1971)

Donnachie, I., and Macleod, I., *Old Galloway* (David & Charles, 1974)

Feachem, R., *A Guide to Prehistoric Scotland* (Batsford, 1963)

Fenwick, H., *Scotland's Historic Buildings* (Hale, 1974)

Flinn, D., 'Continuation of the Great Glen Fault beyond the Moray Firth', *Nature*, 191(1961), 589

—— 'Coastal and submarine features around the Shetland Isles', Proceedings of the Geological Association 75(1964), 321

Haldane, A. R. B., *The Drove Roads of Scotland* (Edinburgh University Press, 1952)

Hamilton, J. R. C., *The Brochs of Mousa and Clickhimin* (HMSO, 1970)

Henderson, I., *The Picts* (Thames & Hudson, 1967)

Jones, S. J. (ed), *Dundee and District* (The British Association, Dundee, 1968)

Kennedy, W. Q., 'The Great Glen Fault', *Quarterly Journal of the Geological Society*, 102(1946), 41

Kirk, W., 'Prehistoric site at the Sands of Forvie, Aberdeenshire' *Aberdeen University Review* 35(1953), 150

MacKie, E. W., 'The Vitrified Forts of Scotland' in Harding, D. W., (ed), *Hillforts* (Seminar Press, 1975)

—— *Scotland: an archaeological guide* (Faber & Faber, 1975)

Mackie, R. L., and Cruden, S., *Arbroath Abbey* (HMSO, 1954)

Marwick, H., *Ancient Monuments in Orkney* (HMSO, 1952)

Mather, A. S., *Beaches of Southwest Scotland*, vols I and II, (Department of Geography, Aberdeen University, 1979)

McCann, S. B., 'The raised beaches of north-east Islay and western Jura, Argyll', *Transcript of the Institute of British Geographers* 35(1964), 1

McLaren, M., *The Shell Guide to Scotland* (Ebury Press, 1973)

McWilliam, C., *Lothian* (Series: *The Buildings of Scotland*, ed N. Pevsner) (Penguin, 1978)

Miller, R., 'Orkney: a land of increment' in Miller, R., and Watson, J. W., (eds), *Geographical Essays in memory of A. G. Ogilvie* (Edinburgh University Press, 1959)

Moray Firth Development Ecological Survey, 1969–74 (Department of Geography, University of Aberdeen, 1971)

Mowat, I. R. M., *Easter Ross, 1750–1850: The double frontier* (John Donald, 1981)

Murray, W. H., *The Hebrides* (Heinemann, 1966)

—— *The Companion Guide to the West Highlands of Scotland* (Collins, 1968)

—— *The Islands of Western Scotland* (Eyre Methuen, 1973)

O'Dell, A. C., *The Historical Geography of the Shetland Islands* (1939)

—— 'Excavations of St Ninian's Isle', *Scottish Geographical Magazine* 75(1959), 41

O'Dell, A. C., and Walton, K., *The Highlands and Islands of Scotland* (Nelson, 1962)

O'Dell, A. C., and Mackintosh, J., *The North-east of Scotland* (British Association, Aberdeen, 1963)
Omand, D., *The Caithness Book* (Highland Printers, Inverness, 1973)
—— *The Moray Book* (Highland Printers, Inverness, 1976)
Peck, J., *North-East Scotland* (Bartholomew, 1981)
Piggott, S. (ed), *The Prehistoric Peoples of Scotland* (Routledge & Kegan Paul, 1962)
Prentice, R., *The National Trust Guide for Scotland* (Cape, 1976)
Radford, C. A. R., *The Early Christian and Norse Settlements at Birsay, Orkney* (HMSO, 1959)
Richey, J. E., *The Tertiary Volcanic Districts*, British Regional Geology, Scotland (HMSO, 1961)
Ritchie, Graham and Anna, *South-East Scotland* (Heinemann, 1972)
—— *Scotland: Archaeology and Early History* (Thames & Hudson, 1981)
Ritchie, W., and Mather, A., *The Beaches of Sutherland* (Department of Geography, Aberdeen University, for the Countryside Commission of Scotland, 1970)
—— *The Beaches of Lewis and Harris* (Department of Geography, Aberdeen University, for the Countryside Commission of Scotland, 1970)
—— *The Beaches of Caithness* (Department of Geography, Aberdeen University, for the Countryside Commission of Scotland, 1970)
Scott, J. G., *South-west Scotland* (Heinemann, 1967)
Shaw, J. E., *Ayrshire 1745–1950: a social and industrial history* (Oliver & Boyd, 1953)
Simpson, W. D., *Scottish Castles* (HMSO, 1959)
—— *Ancient Stones of Scotland* (Hale, 1965)
Sissons, J. B., *The Evolution of Scotland's Scenery* (Nelson, 1967)
Steers, J. A., *The Coastline of Scotland* (Cambridge University Press, 1973)
—— 'The Culbin Sands and Burghead Bay', *Geographical Journal* 90(1937), 498
Storrie, M. C., 'Islay: A Hebridean Exception' *Geographical Review*, 51(1961), 87
—— *Islay: bibilography of an island* (The Oa Press, Port Ellen, Islay, 1981)
The Hub of the Highlands: The Book of Inverness and District (Albyn Press, Edinburgh, 1975)
Thom, A., *Megalithic Sites in Britain* (Oxford University Press, 1967)
Thomas, C., *The Early Christian Archaeology of North Britain* (Oxford University Press, 1971)
Tranter, N., *The fortified house in Scotland* vols 1–5 (Chambers, 1963–70)
—— *The Eastern Counties* (Series: *The Queen's Scotland*) (Hodder & Stoughton, 1972)
—— *The North-East* (Series: *The Queen's Scotland*) (Hodder & Stoughton, 1974)
Turnock, D., 'Hebridean Car Ferries', *Geography* 50(1965), 375
—— 'Fort William: problems of urban expansion in a Highland area' *Tijdschrift voor Economische en Sociale Geografie*, 59(1968), 260
Turnock, D., *Patterns of Highland Development* (Macmillan, 1970)
Wainwright, F. T., (ed) *The Problem of the Picts* (Nelson, 1955)
—— *The Northern Isles* (Nelson, 1962)
Walton, K., 'Rattray: a study in coastal evolution' *Scottish Geographical Magazine*, 72(1956), 85
—— 'Ancient elements in the coastline of north-eastern Scotland' in Miller, R., and Watson, J. W., (eds) *Geographical Essays in Memory of A. G. Ogilvie* (Edinburgh, 1959)
—— 'The site of Aberdeen', *Scottish Geographical Magazine*, 79(1963), 69

Volumes of the Third Statistical Account of Scotland consulted include those on Aberdeen City (ed Mackenzie, H., Oliver & Boyd, 1953); Aberdeen County (ed Hamilton, H., Collins, 1960); Angus (ed Illsley, W. A., Herald Press, Arbroath, 1977); Argyll (ed MacDonald, C. M., Collins, 1961); Ayrshire (ed Strawhorn, J., and Boyd, W., Oliver & Boyd, 1951); Banff (ed Hamilton, H., Collins, 1961); Bute (ed Somerville, A. C., and Stevenson, W., Collins, 1962); Dunbarton (ed Dilke, M. S., and Templeton, A. A., Collins, 1959); East Lothian (ed Snodgrass, C. P., Oliver & Boyd, 1953); Edinburgh (ed Keir, D., Collins, 1966); Kircudbright (ed Laird, J., and Ramsay, D. G., Collins, 1965); Moray and Nairn (ed Hamilton, H., Collins, 1965); Renfrew (ed Moisley, H. A., and Thain, A. G., Collins, 1962); Wrighton (ed Arnott, M. C., Collins, 1963).

Index